P9-DEO-859

TAKING SIDES

Clashing Views on Controversial
Issues in Western Civilization

Selected, Edited, and with Introductions by

Joseph R. Mitchell
Howard Community College

and

Helen Buss Mitchell
Howard Community College

Dushkin/McGraw-Hill
A Division of The McGraw-Hill Companies

For Jason, our first successful collaboration

Photo Acknowledgement
Cover image: © 2000 by PhotoDisc, Inc.

Cover Art Acknowledgment
Charles Vitelli

Library of Congress Cataloging-in-Publication Data
Main entry under title:
Taking sides: clashing views on controversial issues in western civilization/selected, edited, and
with introductions by Joseph R. Mitchell and Helen Buss Mitchell.—1st ed.
Includes bibliographical references and index.
1. Civilization, Occidental. I. Mitchell, Joseph R., *comp.* II. Mitchell, Helen Buss, *comp.*
909
ISBN-13: 978-0-07-237155-0
ISBN-10: 0-07-237155-2
ISSN: 1527-6058

Printed on Recycled Paper

Preface

In *Taking Sides: Clashing Views on Controversial Issues in Western Civilization,* we identify the issues that need to be covered in the teaching of Western civilization and the scholarly and readable sources that argue these issues. We have taken care to choose issues that will make this volume multicultural, gender-friendly, and current with historical scholarship, and we frame these issues in a manner that makes them user-friendly for both teachers and students. Students who use this volume should come away with a greater understanding and appreciation of the value of studying history.

Plan of the book This book is made up of 23 issues that argue pertinent topics in the study of Western civilization. Each issue has an issue *introduction,* which sets the stage for the debate as it is argued in the pro and con selections. Each issue concludes with a *postscript* that makes some final observations and points the way to other questions related to the issue. In reading the issue and forming your own opinions, you should not feel confined to adopt one or the other of the positions presented. There are positions in between the given views or totally outside them, and the *suggestions for further reading* that appear in each issue postscript should help you to find resources to continue your study of the subject. We have also provided Internet site addresses (URLs) in the *On the Internet* page that accompanies each part opener. At the back of the book is a listing of all the *contributors to this volume,* which will give you information on the historians and commentators whose views are debated here.

A word to the instructor An *Instructor's Manual With Test Questions* (multiple-choice and essay) is available through the publisher for the instructor using *Taking Sides* in the classroom. A general guidebook, *Using Taking Sides in the Classroom,* which discusses methods and techniques for integrating the pro-con approach into any classroom setting, is also available. An online version of *Using Taking Sides in the Classroom* and a correspondence service for *Taking Sides* adopters can be found at http://www.dushkin.com/usingts/.

Taking Sides: Clashing Views on Controversial Issues in Western Civilization is only one title in the Taking Sides series. If you are interested in seeing the table of contents for any of the other titles, please visit the Taking Sides Web site at http://www.dushkin.com/takingsides/.

Acknowledgments We would like to thank Larry Madaras of Howard Community College—fellow teacher, good friend, and coeditor of *Taking Sides: Clashing Views on Controversial Issues in American History*—for encouraging us in the production of this volume, introducing us to the editorial team at Dushkin/McGraw-Hill, and suggesting issues for us to pursue. Special thanks also go to David Stebenne of Ohio State University—friend, scholar, teacher, and author

i

of *Arthur J. Goldberg: New Deal Liberal* (Oxford University Press, 1996). We are grateful to Jean Soto, Susan Myers, and the entire staff of the Howard Community College Library for their assistance with this volume. A special debt of gratitude goes to Shan Tenney, our good friend, who read every word, caught many errors, assisted in our research, and offered sage advice on presentation. Thanks also go to Ted Knight, list manager for the *Taking Sides* series, and Juliana Poggio, developmental editor, who guided us through the publishing side of the book and gave encouraging words and positive feedback.

Joseph R. Mitchell
Howard Community College

Helen Buss Mitchell
Howard Community College

Contents In Brief

PART 1 The Classical World   1

Issue 1. Was a Slave Society Essential to the Development of Athenian Democracy? 2

Issue 2. Does Alexander the Great Merit His Exalted Historical Reputation? 22

Issue 3. Did Christianity Liberate Women? 40

Issue 4. Did the Roman Empire Collapse Due to Its Own Weight? 60

Issue 5. Did Same-Sex Unions Exist in the Early Middle Ages? 80

PART 2 The Medieval/Renaissance Worlds   99

Issue 6. Were the Crusades Motivated Primarily by Religious Factors? 100

Issue 7. Did Women and Men Benefit Equally from the Renaissance? 120

Issue 8. Did Martin Luther's Reforms Improve the Lives of European Christians? 136

Issue 9. Did Convents Expand Opportunities for European Women? 156

PART 3 The Premodern World   175

Issue 10. Was the West African Slave Trade a Precondition for the Rise of British Capitalism? 176

Issue 11. Were the Witch-Hunts in Premodern Europe Misogynistic? 196

Issue 12. Was the Scientific Revolution Revolutionary? 218

Issue 13. Was the French Revolution Worth Its Human Costs? 234

Issue 14. Did British Policy Decisions Cause the Mass Emigration and Land Reforms That Followed the Irish Potato Famine? 256

PART 4 The Modern World   277

Issue 15. Were Economic Factors Primarily Responsible for Nineteenth-Century British Imperialism? 278

Issue 16. Were German Militarism and Diplomacy Responsible for World War I? 300

Issue 17. Did the Bolshevik Revolution Improve the Lives of Soviet Women? 322

Issue 18. Was World War II the Result of Hitler's Master Plan? 342

PART 5 The Contemporary World   365

Issue 19. Was Stalin Responsible for the Cold War? 366

iv

Issue 20. Were Ethnic Leaders Responsible for the Disintegration of Yugoslavia? 386

Issue 21. Will the European Monetary Union Increase the Potential for Transatlantic Conflict? 406

Issue 22. Should Contemporary Feminism Ally Itself With Individualism? 428

Issue 23. Is Western Civilization in a State of Decline? 448

Contents

Preface   i

Introduction: Western Civilization and the Study of History   xiv

PART 1   THE CLASSICAL WORLD   1

Issue 1.   Was a Slave Society Essential to the Development of Athenian Democracy?   2

YES: **Orlando Patterson,** from *Freedom, vol. 1: Freedom in the Making of Western Culture* (BasicBooks, 1991)   4

NO: **Donald Kagan,** from *Pericles of Athens and the Birth of Democracy* (Free Press, 1991)   12

Sociology professor Orlando Patterson states that the presence of a large slave population was a necessary ingredient in the development of Athenian democracy. History professor Donald Kagan maintains that Athenian democracy developed gradually over three centuries and the leadership of Pericles was crucial to its success.

Issue 2.   Does Alexander the Great Merit His Exalted Historical Reputation?   22

YES: **N. G. L. Hammond,** from *The Genius of Alexander the Great* (University of North Carolina Press, 1997)   *24*

NO: **E. E. Rice,** from *Alexander the Great* (Sutton Publishing, 1997)   *30*

Professor emeritus of Greek N. G. L. Hammond states that research has proven that Alexander the Great is deserving of his esteemed historical reputation. Senior research fellow and lecturer E. E. Rice maintains that, other than his conquests, Alexander the Great left few tangible legacies to merit his exalted historical reputation.

Issue 3.   Did Christianity Liberate Women?   40

YES: **Karen Jo Torjesen,** from *When Women Were Priests* (HarperSanFrancisco, 1995)   *42*

NO: **Karen Armstrong,** from *The Gospel According to Woman: Christianity's Creation of the Sex War in the West* (Anchor Press, 1987)   *51*

Professor of religion and associate of the Institute for Antiquity and Christianity, Karen Jo Torjesen, presents evidence of women deacons, priests, prophets, and bishops during the first millennium of Christianity—all roles that suggest both equality and liberation for women. Professor of religious studies Karen Armstrong finds in the early Christian Church examples of hostility toward women and fear of their sexual power which she contends led to the exclusion of women from full participation in a male-dominated church.

Issue 4.   Did the Roman Empire Collapse Due to Its Own Weight?   60

YES: **Averil Cameron,** from *The Later Roman Empire: A.D. 284–430* (Harvard University Press, 1993)   *62*

NO: **Derek Williams,** from *Romans and Barbarians: Four Views from the Empire's Edge, First Century A.D.* (St. Martin's Press, 1998)   *70*

Historian Averil Cameron states that, although the barbarian invasions played a role in the demise of the Roman Empire, internal political, social, and economic problems were primarily responsible for its fall. Writer Derek Williams counters that the barbarian tribes, once Rome's allies, were principally liable for the empire's fall.

Issue 5.   Did Same-Sex Unions Exist in the Early Middle Ages?   80

YES: **John Boswell,** from *Same-Sex Unions in Premodern Europe* (Villard Books, 1994)   *82*

NO: **Philip Lyndon Reynolds,** from "Same-Sex Unions: What Boswell Didn't Find," *The Christian Century* (January 18, 1995)   *89*

Yale University history professor John Boswell states that same-sex unions, which date back to pagan times, existed in medieval Europe until they were gradually done away with by the Christian Church. Reviewer Philip Lyndon Reynolds, while admitting that "brotherhood" ceremonies took place in medieval Europe, asserts that these ceremonies did not have the same authority as sacred unions and therefore cannot be equated with marriage rites.

PART 2   THE MEDIEVAL/RENAISSANCE WORLDS   99

Issue 6.   Were the Crusades Motivated Primarily by Religious Factors?   100

YES: **Hans Eberhard Mayer,** from *The Crusades,* 2d ed., trans. John Gillingham (Oxford University Press, 1988)   *102*

NO: **Ronald C. Finucane,** from *Soldiers of the Faith: Crusaders and Moslems at War* (St. Martin's Press, 1983)   *110*

German historian Hans Eberhard Mayer states that although there were other factors important to the development of the Crusades, the strongest motivation was a religious one. British historian Ronald C. Finucane counters that although the religious influence on the Crusades was significant, political, social, economic, and military factors in medieval Europe also played a role in their origin, development, and outcome.

Issue 7.   Did Women and Men Benefit Equally from the Renaissance?   120

YES: **Mary R. Beard,** from *Woman as Force in History: A Study in Traditions and Realities* (Collier Books, 1946)   *122*

NO: **Joan Kelly-Gadol,** from "Did Women Have a Renaissance?" in Renate Bridenthal, Claudia Koonz, and Susan Stuard, eds., *Becoming Visible: Women in European History,* 2d ed. (Houghton Mifflin, 1987)   *128*

Historian Mary R. Beard contends that during the Renaissance, Italian women of the higher classes turned to the study of Greek and Roman literature and committed themselves alongside men to developing well-rounded personalities. Historian Joan Kelly-Gadol argues that women enjoyed greater advantages during the Middle Ages and experienced a relative loss of position and power during the Renaissance.

Issue 8.   Did Martin Luther's Reforms Improve the Lives of European Christians?   136

YES: **Bernard M. G. Reardon,** from *Religious Thought in the Reformation,* 2d ed. (Longman, 1995)   *138*

NO: **Richard Marius,** from *Martin Luther: The Christian Between God and Death* (Belknap Press, 1999)   *146*

Bernard M. G. Reardon, retired head of the Department of Religious Studies at the University of Newcastle upon Tyne, contends that Martin Luther was neither a political nor a social reformer. Instead, he was a spiritual genius who created a new religion within Christianity that remained true to its traditional orthodoxy. Professor emeritus Richard Marius views the Reformation as a catastrophe in the history of Western civilization. He sees Martin Luther's challenge as inaugurating more than a century of religious bloodshed that could have been averted if Luther had remained silent.

Issue 9.   Did Convents Expand Opportunities for European Women?   156

YES: **Olwen Hufton,** from *The Prospect Before Her: A History of Women in Western Europe* (Alfred A. Knopf, 1996)   *158*

NO: **Elisja Schulte van Kessel,** from "Virgins and Mothers Between Heaven and Earth," in Natalie Zemon Davis and Arlette Farge, eds., *A History of Women in the West, vol. 3: Renaissance and Enlightenment Paradoxes* (Belknap Press, 1993)   *165*

Professor of history Olwen Hufton finds that, despite the harsh reforms instituted by the Council of Trent (beginning in 1563), convents remained a viable alternative for European women—a place where they could write, think, and live more independent lives than they could in the secular world. Professor of early modern cultural history Elisja Schulte van Kessel emphasizes the harshness of the Tridentine reforms, which took away the homey atmosphere of convents and restricted affectionate relationships between women, thus making convents a much less attractive alternative for European women.

PART 3   THE PREMODERN WORLD   **175**

Issue 10.   Was the West African Slave Trade a Precondition for the Rise of British Capitalism?   176

YES: William Darity, Jr., from "British Industry and the West Indies Plantations," in Joseph E. Inikori and Stanley L. Engerman, eds., *The Atlantic Slave Trade: Effects on Economies, Societies, and Peoples in Africa, the Americas, and Europe* (Duke University Press, 1994)   *178*

NO: James A. Rawley, from *The Transatlantic Slave Trade: A History* (W. W. Norton, 1981)   *187*

Economics professor William Darity, Jr., argues that the profits derived from the West African slave trade and its concomitant economic ventures played a crucial role in the development of British capitalism. History professor James A. Rawley states that the economic effects of the West African slave trade on the development of British capitalism have been exaggerated due to the faulty use of data and statistics.

Issue 11.   Were the Witch-Hunts in Premodern Europe Misogynistic?   196

YES: Anne Llewellyn Barstow, from *Witchcraze: A New History of the European Witch Hunts* (HarperCollins, 1994)   *198*

NO: Robin Briggs, from *Witches and Neighbors: The Social and Cultural Context of European Witchcraft* (Penguin Books, 1998)   *207*

History professor Anne Llewellyn Barstow asserts that the European witch-hunt movement made women its primary victims and was used as an attempt to control their lives and behavior. History professor Robin Briggs states that although women were the European witch-hunts' main victims, gender was not the only determining factor in this sociocultural movement.

Issue 12.   Was the Scientific Revolution Revolutionary?   218

YES: Herbert Butterfield, from *The Origins of Modern Science, 1300–1800,* rev. ed. (Free Press, 1965)   *220*

NO: Steven Shapin, from *The Scientific Revolution* (University of Chicago Press, 1996)   *226*

Historian of ideas Herbert Butterfield argues that the late sixteenth and early seventeenth centuries witnessed a radical break with the past and the emergence of dramatically new ways of understanding both knowledge and the world—in short, a Scientific Revolution. Professor of sociology and historian of science Steven Shapin questions the idea of a Scientific Revolution, suggesting that there was no philosophical break with the past and rejecting the existence of a single event that might be called a Scientific Revolution.

Issue 13.   Was the French Revolution Worth Its Human Costs?   234

YES: Peter Kropotkin, from *The Great French Revolution, 1789–1793,* trans. N. F. Dryhurst (Schocken Books, 1971)   *236*

NO: Simon Schama, from *Citizens: A Chronicle of the French Revolution* (Alfred A. Knopf, 1989)   *243*

Peter Kropotkin (1842–1921), a Russian prince, revolutionary, and anarchist, argues that the French Revolution eradicated both serfdom and absolutism and paved the way for France's future democratic growth. History professor Simon Schama counters that not only did the French Revolution betray its own goals, but it produced few of the results that it promised.

Issue 14.   Did British Policy Decisions Cause the Mass Emigration and Land Reforms That Followed the Irish Potato Famine?   256

YES: **Christine Kinealy,** from *This Great Calamity: The Irish Famine 1845–52* (Roberts Rinehart, 1995)   *258*

NO: **Hasia R. Diner,** from *Erin's Daughters In America: Irish Immigrant Women in the Nineteenth Century* (Johns Hopkins University Press, 1983)   *267*

Christine Kinealy, fellow of the University of Liverpool, argues that the British government's response to the Irish potato famine was deliberately inadequate. The British government's "hidden agenda" of long-term economic, social, and agrarian reform was accelerated by the famine, and mass emigration was a consequence of these changes. Historian Hasia R. Diner documents large-scale emigration both before and after the Irish potato famine. Diner credits the Irish people with learning from their famine experiences that the reliance of the poor on the potato and the excessive subdivision of land within families were no longer in their own best interests.

PART 4   THE MODERN WORLD   277

Issue 15.   Were Economic Factors Primarily Responsible for Nineteenth-Century British Imperialism?   278

YES: **Lance E. Davis and Robert A. Huttenback,** from *Mammon and the Pursuit of Empire: The Economics of British Imperialism,* abridged ed. (Cambridge University Press, 1988)   *280*

NO: **John M. MacKenzie,** from *The Partition of Africa, 1880–1900: And European Imperialism in the Nineteenth Century* (Methuen & Co., 1983)   *289*

Lance E. Davis and Robert A. Huttenback state that, although statistics prove that British imperialism was not a profitable venture, it was supported by an economic elite that was able to promote and derive profits from it. John M. MacKenzie argues that the motivation for British imperialism was multicausal and that most of the causes can be found in the general anxiety crisis permeating British society in the late nineteenth century.

Issue 16.   Were German Militarism and Diplomacy Responsible for World War I?   300

YES: **V. R. Berghahn,** from *Imperial Germany, 1871–1914: Economy, Society, Culture, and Politics* (Berghahn Books, 1994)   *302*

NO: **Samuel R. Williamson, Jr.**, from "The Origins of the War," in Hew Strachan, ed., *The Oxford Illustrated History of the First World War* (Oxford University Press, 1998)   *311*

History professor V. R. Berghahn states that, although all of Europe's major powers played a part in the onset of World War I, recent evidence still indicates that Germany's role in the process was the main factor responsible for the conflict. History professor Samuel R. Williamson, Jr., argues that the factors and conditions that led to the First World War were a shared responsibility and that no one nation can be blamed for its genesis.

Issue 17.   Did the Bolshevik Revolution Improve the Lives of Soviet Women?   322

YES: **Richard Stites**, from *The Women's Liberation Movement in Russia: Feminism, Nihilism, and Bolshevism, 1860–1930* (Princeton University Press, 1978)   *324*

NO: **Françoise Navailh**, from "The Soviet Model," in Françoise Thébaud, ed., *A History of Women in the West, vol. 5: Toward a Cultural Identity in the Twentieth Century* (Belknap Press, 1994)   *333*

History professor Richard Stites argues that in the early years of the Bolshevik Revolution, the Zhenotdel, or Women's Department, helped many working women take the first steps toward emancipation. Film historian Françoise Navailh contends that the Zhenotdel had limited political influence and could do little to improve the lives of Soviet women in the unstable period following the revolution.

Issue 18.   Was World War II the Result of Hitler's Master Plan?   342

YES: **Andreas Hillgruber**, from *Germany and the Two World Wars,* trans. William C. Kirby (Harvard University Press, 1981)   *344*

NO: **Ian Kershaw**, from *The Nazi Dictatorship: Problems and Perspectives of Interpretation,* 3rd ed. (Edward Arnold, 1993)   *353*

German scholar and history professor Andreas Hillgruber states that Hitler systematically pursued his foreign policy goals once he came to power in Germany and that World War II was the inevitable result. Ian Kershaw, a professor of history at the University of Sheffield, argues that Hitler was responsible for the execution of German foreign policy that led to World War II but was not free from forces both within and outside Germany that influenced his decisions.

PART 5   THE CONTEMPORARY WORLD   365

Issue 19.   Was Stalin Responsible for the Cold War?   366

YES: **John Lewis Gaddis**, from *We Now Know: Rethinking Cold War History* (Clarendon Press, 1997)   *368*

NO: **Martin J. Sherwin**, from "The Atomic Bomb and the Origins of the Cold War," in Melvyn P. Leffler and David S. Painter, eds., *Origins of the Cold War: An International History* (Routledge, 1994)   *375*

Historian John Lewis Gaddis states that after more than a half a century of cold war scholarship, Joseph Stalin still deserves most of the responsibility for the onset of the cold war. Historian Martin J. Sherwin counters that the origins of the cold war can be found in the World War II diplomacy involving the use of the atomic bomb, and he places much of the blame for the cold war on the shoulders of Franklin D. Roosevelt, Harry S. Truman, and Winston Churchill.

Issue 20.   Were Ethnic Leaders Responsible for the Disintegration of Yugoslavia?   386

YES: **Warren Zimmermann,** from *Origins of a Catastrophe* (Times Books, 1996)   *388*

NO: **Steven Majstorovic,** from "Ancient Hatreds or Elite Manipulation? Memory and Politics in the Former Yugoslavia," *World Affairs* (Spring 1997)   *395*

Career diplomat Warren Zimmermann, the United States' last ambassador to Yugoslavia, argues that the republic's ethnic leaders, especially Slobodan Milosovic, bear primary responsibility for the nation's demise. Political science professor Steven Majstorovic contends that while manipulation by elite ethnic leaders played a role in the disintegration of Yugoslavia, the fragile ethnic divisions within the country also played an important role in the country's demise.

Issue 21.   Will the European Monetary Union Increase the Potential for Transatlantic Conflict?   406

YES: **Martin Feldstein,** from "EMU and International Conflict," *Foreign Affairs* (November/December, 1997)   *408*

NO: **Werner Weidenfeld,** from "The Euro and the New Face of the European Union," *The Washington Quarterly* (Winter 1999)   *418*

Harvard economics professor Martin Feldstein states that the real rationale for the European Monetary Union is political rather than economic. He predicts that a united Europe, free of threats from the Soviet Union, may seek alliances and pursue policies contrary to the interests of the United States. Werner Weidenfeld, director of the Munich Center for Applied Policy Research, sees the European Union as a vehicle for restructuring the transatlantic relationship between Europe and the United States. If they develop a partnership between equals, they will be positioned for international crisis management and other global challenges.

Issue 22.   Should Contemporary Feminism Ally Itself With Individualism?   428

YES: **Françoise Thébaud,** from "Explorations of Gender," in Françoise Thébaud, ed., *A History of Women in the West, vol. 5: Toward a Cultural Identity in the Twentieth Century* (The Belknap Press, 1994)   *430*

NO: **Elizabeth Fox-Genovese,** from *Feminism Without Illusions: A Critique of Individualism* (The University of North Carolina Press, 1991)   *438*

A lecturer in women's history at the Université Lumière Lyon, Françoise Thébaud states that the pursuit of individualism and the acquisition of full citizenship rights have permitted women to escape from the confines of the family and achieve independence in the modern world. Elizabeth Fox-Genovese, Emory University professor of history and director of women's studies, argues that individualism, which refuses to place any limits on the tyranny of the individual will, is a dead end for feminists, who must insist that the rights of individuals derive from society and not from their innate nature.

Issue 23.   Is Western Civilization in a State of Decline?   448

YES: **Samuel P. Huntington,** from *The Clash of Civilizations and the Remaking of World Order* (Simon & Schuster, 1996)   *450*

NO: **Francis Fukuyama,** from *The End of History and the Last Man* (Free Press, 1992)   *458*

Samuel P. Huntington, a professor of the science of government, maintains that due to internal weaknesses and threats from potential rivals organized along civilizational lines, the West is in danger of losing its status as the world's preeminent power base in the twenty-first century. Francis Fukuyama, a former deputy director with the U.S. State Department, argues that with the end of the cold war and the absence of alternatives to liberal democracy, the West is in a position to maintain and expand its role as the world's primary power base.

Contributers   470
Index   475

Introduction

Western Civilization and the Study of History

Helen Buss Mitchell

What Is a Civilization?

What do we mean by the term *civilization?* Usually it designates a large group of people, spread out over a vast geographical area. In the modern world, we typically think in terms of nations or states, but these are a relatively recent development, traceable to sixteenth-century Europe. Before the rise of national states, what we call Europe belonged to a civilization known as Christendom —the unity of people ruled by the spiritual and temporal power of the Christian church. At that time, other great civilizations of the world included China, Africa, India, Mesoamerica, and the Islamic empire.

Civilization began about 5,000 years ago, when humans reached high levels of organization and achievement. When we look at world civilizations, we are considering the ancient and the contemporary versions of human alliances. Even in this age of national states, perhaps it makes sense to think of the West (Europe and North America) as a civilization. And the movement for European unity, which includes the creation of a common currency, suggests that Europe may be thought of as a civilization despite its division into many separate nations. Postcolonial Africa is a continent of separate countries, and yet, in some ways, it remains a unified civilization. China, once a vast and far-flung group of kingdoms, has kept its unity as a civilization under communism. And Islam, which united the warring tribes of the Arabian Peninsula in the seventh century, is again defining itself as a civilization. What would be gained and what would be lost by shifting our focus from the national state to the much larger entity of Western civilization?

Civilizations are systems for structuring human lives and generally include the following components: (1) an economic system by which people produce, distribute, and exchange goods; (2) a social system that defines relationships between and among individuals and groups; (3) a political system that determines who governs, who makes the laws, and who provides services for the common good; (4) a religious and/or intellectual orientation by which people make sense of the ordinary and extraordinary events of life and history —this may appear as a formal religious system, such as Judaism, Christianity, Islam, Buddhism, or Hinduism, or as an intellectual/values system, such as communism, Confucianism, or democracy; and (5) a cultural system, including the arts and symbol systems that give expression and meaning to human experience. Some of these components will appear more clearly than others in the selections in this volume, but all are present to one degree or another in every civilization.

What Is History?

History is a dialogue between the past and the present. As we respond to events in our own world, we bring the concerns of the present to our study of the past. What seems important to us, where we turn our attention, how we approach a study of the past—all are rooted in the present. It has been said that where you stand determines what you see. This is especially true with history. If we stand only within the Western tradition, we may be tempted to see its story as the only story, or at least the only one worth telling. And whose perspective we take is also critical. From the point of view of the rich and powerful, the events of history take one shape; through the lens of the poor and powerless, the same events can appear quite different. If we take women, non-Western cultures, or the ordinary person as our starting point, the story of the past may present us with a series of new surprises.

Revisionism

History is not a once-and-for-all enterprise. Each generation will have its own questions and will bring new tools to the study of the past, resulting in a process called *revisionism*. Much of what you will read in this book is a product of revisionism as historians reinterpret the past in the light of the present. One generation values revolutions; the next focuses on their terrible costs. One generation assumes that great men shape the events of history; the next looks to the lives of ordinary people to illuminate the past. There is no final answer, but where we stand will determine which interpretation seems more compelling to us.

As new tools of analysis become available, our ability to understand the past improves. Bringing events into clearer focus can change the meaning that we assign to them. Many of the selections in this book reflect new attitudes and new insights made possible by the tools that historians have recently borrowed from the social sciences.

Presentism

Standing in the present, we must be wary of what historians call *presentism*, that is, reading the values of the present back into the past. If we live in a culture that values individualism and prizes competition, we may be tempted to see these values as good even in a culture that preferred communalism and cooperation. And we may miss a key component of a past civilization because it does not match what we currently consider worthwhile. We cannot and should not avoid our own questions and struggles. They will inform our study of the past, yet they must not warp our vision. Ideally, historians engage in a continual dialogue in which the concerns but not the values of the present are explored through a study of the past.

Historiographical Focuses

All cultures are vulnerable to the narrow-mindedness created by *ethnocentrism* —the belief that one culture is superior to all others. From inside a particular culture, certain practices may seem normative—that is, we may assume that all humans or all rational humans must behave the way we do or hold the same attitudes that we hold. When we meet a culture that sees the world differently than we do, we may be tempted to write it off as inferior or primitive. An alternative to ethnocentrism is to enter the worldview of another and see what we can learn from expanding our perspective. The issues in this book will offer you many opportunities to try this thought experiment.

Stepping outside the Western tradition has allowed historians to take a more global view of world events. And, within the Western tradition, women have challenged the male-dominated perspective that studied war but ignored the family. Including additional perspectives complicates our interpretation of past events but permits a fuller picture to emerge. We must be wary of *universalism*—for example, the assumption that patriarchy has always existed or that being a woman was the same for every woman no matter what her historical circumstances. If patriarchy or the nuclear family has a historical beginning, then there must have been a time when some other pattern existed. If cultures other than the West have been dominant or influential in the past, what was the world like under those circumstances?

The New Social History

Proponents of the new social history reject what they call "history from the top down." Instead of studying the "great man" whose influence shaped his age, they study the lives of ordinary people, doing history from the "bottom up." Social history assumes that all people are capable of acting as historical agents rather than being passive victims to whom history happens. With this shift in attitude, the lives of slaves, workers, all women, and children become worthy of historical investigation.

Because the poor and powerless seldom leave written records, other sources of information must be analyzed to understand their lives. Applying the methods of social scientists to their own discipline, historians have broadened and deepened their field of study. Archaeological evidence, DNA analysis, the tools of paleoanthropology, and computer analysis of demographic data have allowed the voiceless to speak across centuries.

What historians call "material culture" (the objects that the people discarded as well as the monuments and other material objects they intended to leave as markers of their civilizations), for example, reveals to historians the everyday lives of people. At certain points in human history, to own a plow made the difference between merely surviving and having some surplus food to barter or sell. What people left to their heirs can tell us how much or how little they had while they lived.

The high-speed comparative functions of computers have allowed historians to analyze vast quantities of data and to look at demographic trends. How old are people when they marry for the first time, have a child, or die? Looking at the time between marriage and the birth of a first child can help us to calculate the percentage of pregnant brides and to gain some insight into how acceptable or unacceptable premarital sex may have been to a certain population at a certain time in the context of an expected future marriage. If we study weather patterns and learn that certain years were marked by periods of drought or that a glacier receded during a particular time period, we will know a little more about whether the lives of the people who lived during these times were relatively easier or more difficult than those of their historical neighbors in earlier or later periods.

Race, Class, and Gender

The experience of being a historical subject is never monolithic. That is, each of us has a gender, a race, a social class, an ethnic identity, a religion (even if it is atheism or agnosticism), an age, and a variety of other markers that color our experiences. At times, the most important factor may be one's gender, and what happens may be more or less the same for all members of a particular gender. Under other circumstances, however, race may be predominant. Being a member of a racial minority or of a powerful racial majority may lead to very different experiences of the same event. At other times social class may determine how an event is experienced; the rich may have one story to tell, the poor another. And other factors, such as religion, ethnic identity, or even age, can become the most significant pieces of a person's identity, especially if prejudice or favoritism is involved. Historians generally try to take into account how race, class, and gender (as well as a host of other factors) intersect in the life of a historical subject.

Issues Involved in Historical Interpretation

Often historians will agree on what happened but disagree about why or how something occurred. Sometimes the question is whether internal or external factors were more responsible for a happening. Both may have contributed to an event but one or the other may have played the more significant role. Looking at differing evidence may lead historians to varying interpretations. A related question considers whether it was the circumstances that changed or the attitudes of those who experienced them. If we find less protest about an issue, can we conclude that things have gotten better or that people have found a way to accommodate themselves to a situation that is beyond their control?

Periodization

The student of the past must wonder whether or not the turning points that shape the chapters in history books are the same for all historical subjects. The process of marking turning points is known as *periodization*. This is the more or less artificial creation of periods that chunk history into manageable segments by identifying forks in the road that took people and events in new directions. Using an expanded perspective, we may find that the traditional turning points hold for men but not for women or reflect the experiences of one ethnic group but not another. And when periodization schemes conflict, which one should we use?

It is also important to keep in mind that people living at a particular moment in history are not aware of the labels that later historians will attach to their experiences. People who lived during the Middle Ages, for example, were surely not aware of living in the middle of something. Only long after the fact were we able to call a later age the Renaissance. To those who lived during what we call the Middle Ages or the Renaissance, marriage, childbirth, work, weather, sickness, and death were the primary concerns, just as they are for us today. Our own age will be characterized by future historians in ways that might surprise and even shock us. As we study the past, it is helpful to keep in mind that some of our assumptions are rooted in a traditional periodization that is now being challenged.

Continuity or Discontinuity?

A related question concerns the connection or lack of connection between one event or set of events and another. When we look at the historical past, we must ask ourselves whether we are seeing continuity or discontinuity. In other words, is the event we are studying part of a normal process of evolution, or does it represent a break from a traditional pattern? Questions of continuity versus discontinuity are the fundamental ones on which the larger issue of periodization rests. Did the Industrial Revolution take the lives of workers in wholly new directions, or did traditional behaviors continue, albeit in a radically different context?

Sometimes events appear continuous from the point of view of one group and discontinuous from the point of view of another. Suppose that factory owners found their world and worldview shifting dramatically, whereas the lives and perspectives of workers went on more or less as they had before. When this is the case, whose experience should we privilege? Is one group's experience more historically significant than another's? How should we decide?

Public or Private?

Another consideration for historians is whether we can draw firm lines between public and private worlds. For instance, if a person is highly respected in private but discriminated against in public, which is the more significant experience? Is it even possible to separate the two? In the postindustrial world, women were able to exercise some degree of autonomy within the sphere of home and family. This might have compensated for their exclusion from events in the wider world. On the other hand, can success in the public sphere make up for an emotionally impoverished or even painful personal life? Every person has both a public and a private life; historians are interested in the balance between the two.

Nature or Nurture?

It seems plausible that our experiences within the private sphere, especially those we have as children, may affect how we behave when we move outside the home into a more public world. However, some of what we are in both worlds may be present at birth—that is, programmed into our genes. When historians look at the past, they sometimes encounter one of the puzzles of psychology and sociology: Are we seeing evidence of nature or nurture? That is, does biology or culture offer the more credible explanation for people's behavior through history? Do women and men behave in particular ways because their genetic makeup predisposes them to certain ways of acting? Or is behavior the result of an elaborate system of socialization that permits or rewards some actions while forbidding or punishing others? If people in the past behaved differently than those in the present do, what conclusions may we draw about the relative influence of nature and nurture?

The Power of Ideas

Can ideas change the course of history? People have sometimes been willing to die for what they believe in, and revolutions have certainly been fought, at least in part, over ideas. Some historians believe that studying the clash of ideas or the predominance of one idea or set of ideas offers the key to understanding the past. What do you think? Would devotion to a political or religious cause lead you to challenge the status quo? Or would poor economic conditions be more likely to send you into the streets? Historians differ in ranking the importance of various factors in influencing the past. Do people challenge the power structure because they feel politically powerless, or because they are hungry, or because of the power of ideas?

A related question might be, What makes a person feel free? Is it more significant to have legal and political rights, or is the everyday experience of personal autonomy more important? If laws restrict your options but you are able to live basically as you choose, are you freer than someone who has guaranteed rights but feels personally restricted? Does it matter to us whether we are regarded as equals, or does the ability to accomplish our personal goals override the impact of our legal status as well as how people may think of us? And, again, does the public sphere or the private sphere exert the greater influence? Suppose that you belong to a favored class but experience gender discrimination. Which aspect of your experience has a greater impact? On the other hand, suppose you are told that you have full political and economic rights and you are treated with great respect but are prevented from doing what you like. Will you feel freer or less free than the person who is denied formal status but acts freely? In the quest to understand the past, these questions are interconnected, and they are becoming increasingly difficult to answer.

The Timeliness of Historical Issues

If you read the newspaper or listen to the news, you will find that there are a confusing number of present-day political, economic, religious, and military clashes that can be understood only by looking at their historical contexts. The disintegration of the Soviet empire; the future of NATO, especially in Yugoslavia-type conflicts; new possibilities in U.S.-European relations; the question of whether revolutions are ever worth their costs—these concerns of the global village all have roots in the past. Understanding the origins of conflicts increases the possibility of envisioning their solutions. The issues in this book will help you to think through the problems that are facing our world and give you the tools to make an informed decision about what you think might be the best courses of action.

In a democracy, an informed citizenry is the bedrock on which a government stands. If we do not understand the past, the present will be a puzzle to us and the future may seem to be out of our control. Seeing how and why historians disagree can help us to determine what the critical issues are and where informed interpreters part company. This, at least, is the basis for forming our own judgments and acting upon them. Looking critically at clashing views also hones our analytic skills and makes us thoughtful readers of textbooks as well as magazines and newspapers.

Western Civilization in a World Context

Often the West has felt its power and dominance in the world make only its own story worth studying. History, we are sometimes told, is written by the winners. For the Chinese, the Greeks, the Ottoman Turks, and many other victors of the past, the stories of other civilizations seemed irrelevant. The Chinese considered their Middle Kingdom the center of the world, the Greeks labeled all other people barbarians, and the Ottoman Turks expected never to lose their position of dominance. From our perspective, however, these stories form a tapestry. No one thread or pattern tells the tale, and all seem equally necessary for a complete picture of the past to emerge.

Any single story—even that of a military and economic superpower—is insufficient to explain the scope of human history at a given moment in time. Your story is especially interesting to you. However, as we are learning, any one story achieves its fullest meaning only when it is told in concert with those of other civilizations, all of which share an increasingly interconnected planet. As communications systems shrink the Earth into a global village, we may be ignoring the rest of the world at our own peril. As we are beginning to learn, no story happens in isolation. The history of the West can perhaps be accurately told only within a global context that takes into account the actions and reactions of other civilizations as they share the world stage with the West.

The readings in this book will enrich your understanding of how the peoples of the Western world have understood themselves and their relationships with others. As we become a more clearly multicultural society, we have an additional reason for studying Western civilization in the context of other civilizations that have blended with our own through colonization and immigration. Perhaps the biggest challenge for an increasingly diverse America is to understand its own role in world affairs and its relationship with other civilizations that may have different histories, value systems, and goals.

The Perseus Project

The Perseus Project Web site is a library of study materials on ancient Greece that was created and edited by classics professor Gregory Crane of Tufts University.

http://medusa.perseus.tufts.edu

CivWeb Home Page from Providence College

The CivWeb home page is a guide to Internet sources related to the development of Western civilization. Information is available on Mesopotamia, ancient Egypt, ancient Palestine, ancient Greece, ancient Rome, the Middle Ages, and the Renaissance.

http://www.providence.edu/dwc/index.html

Alexander the Great

This site contains an excellent bibliography and a synopsis that explores Alexander's life, military campaigns, and death. This site also includes a summary of the Hellenistic era that he introduced.

http://www.1stmuse.com/frames/index.html

The Roman Empire Web site

The Roman Empire Web site offers information on the Roman Empire: the time of Augustus, the Julio-Claudian dynasty, the Flavian dynasty, the *Pax Romana*, and Constantine and the decline of Rome.

http://tqd.advanced.org/12654/roman.html

People With a History: An Online Guide to Lesbian, Gay, Bisexual, and Transgendered History

This site offers original texts, discussions, and images addressing lesbian, gay, bisexual, and transgendered history in all historical eras and all regions of the world. It includes both a guide to online bibliographies and an onsite bibliography.

http://www.fordham.edu/halsall/pwh/index.html

PART 1

The Classical World

*O*ur journey begins with the Greco-Roman classical era, the cornerstone of Western civilization. Much of what is significant in the Western
world today emanates from this historical period. This section also covers the rise of Christianity and includes a discussion of the early Middle
Ages. It is inconceivable to present an analysis of Western civilization
without including an account of the influence of these forces.

- Was a Slave Society Essential to the Development of Athenian Democracy?

- Does Alexander the Great Merit His Exalted Historical Reputation?

- Did Christianity Liberate Women?

- Did the Roman Empire Collapse Due to Its Own Weight?

- Did Same-Sex Unions Exist in the Early Middle Ages?

ISSUE 1

Was a Slave Society Essential to the Development of Athenian Democracy?

YES: Orlando Patterson, from *Freedom, vol. 1: Freedom in the Making of Western Culture* (BasicBooks, 1991)

NO: Donald Kagan, from *Pericles of Athens and the Birth of Democracy* (Free Press, 1991)

ISSUE SUMMARY

YES: Sociology professor Orlando Patterson states that the presence of a large slave population was a necessary ingredient in the development of Athenian democracy.

NO: History professor Donald Kagan maintains that Athenian democracy developed gradually over three centuries and the leadership of Pericles was crucial to its success.

U ntil recently Periclean Athens was considered to be the birthplace of Western democracy, home of the culture—with its philosophy, drama, poetry, history, sculpture, architecture, science, and mathematics—that built the intellectual foundations of the West. While most people still give Athens credit for these accomplishments, recent scholarship has raised interesting questions regarding the role of Greece in the development of Western civilization. In *Black Athena: The Afroasiatic Roots of Greek Civilization*, 2 vols. (Rutgers University Press, 1987–1991), Martin Bernal has questioned the Greek role, stating that much of Athens's cultural and intellectual accomplishments had African and Asian roots. There are also those scholars who challenge Athens's claim as the creator of democratic government since only a small percentage of Athenians (free, native-born, male citizens) were allowed to participate in governmental activities such as voting and holding political office. With a large percentage of Athenians shut out from participation, how democratic could the government have been?

The Athenian move toward a democratic form of government was an evolutionary process encompassing more than three centuries. Many leaders —Solon, Peisistratus, Cleisthenes, Ephialtes, and Pericles—contributed to a direct democracy in which citizens gathered to debate and vote on the issues of the day, including budgets and taxation, war and peace, and the conduct of inhabitants and citizens. Furthermore, the practice of paying citizens a salary for public service became a guiding principle of Athenian democracy and a prerequisite for its success.

Nevertheless, Athenian democracy was far from perfect, as the lives and works of Socrates, Plato, Aristotle, Sophocles, and Aristophanes remind us. One of the most significant flaws was the limitation of the rights of citizenship to free, native-born males. Such restrictions led to a situation in which less than 15 percent of Athens's population participated in the city-state's governance. The presence of a large slave population (almost 40 percent) was not a new phenomenon. The situation had existed in past times and would continue to exist for the next two thousand years. Neither was it an anomaly for slavery to exist within a democratic society—witness the antebellum United States, where in many areas of the South slaves outnumbered free people by large margins.

In the past 50 years, we have seen a revolution in history reporting, with its new emphasis on content gleaned from bottom-up sources rather than top-down ones. Along with looking at slavery from the slave's perspective, historians have begun to investigate the institution itself and the dilemma it has presented to the development of Western democracy. David Brion Davis's *The Problem of Slavery in Western Culture* (Cornell University Press, 1966) examines the coexistence of slavery and democracy, reporting how Western societies have reconciled this contradiction and its contemporary and future consequences.

Scholars of the ancient world have also examined slavery in light of historical changes. Sir Moses I. Finley (1912–1986) spent his academic career surveying ancient history, with a special emphasis on Greece. In "Was Greek Civilization Based on Slavery?" *Historia 8* (1959), he concluded: "The pre-Greek world... was... a world without free men in the sense in which the West has come to understand that concept. It was equally a world in which chattel slavery played no role of any consequence. That, too, was a Greek discovery. One aspect of Greek history, in short, is the advance, hand in hand, of freedom *and* slavery."

A generation later Orlando Patterson expanded on Finley's work. He stated that not only did Greek freedom and slavery exist hand in hand but there was a definite symbiotic relationship between the two; without slavery, Greek freedom could not have existed! In *Freedom in the Making of Western Culture* (Basic Books, 1991), he stated: "The origins of Western culture and its most cherished ideal, freedom, were founded... not upon a rock of human virtue, but upon the degraded time full of man's vilest inhumanity to man."

Donald Kagan has also written extensively on Greek civilization. While not openly disputing Patterson's thesis, Kagan prefers to credit three factors for the successful development of Greek democracy: "a good set of institutions,... a body of citizens who possess a good understanding of the principles of democracy,... [and] a high quality of leadership, at least at critical moments," *Pericles of Athens and the Birth of Democracy* (The Free Press, 1991). He sees the role of Pericles as a crucial factor in the development of Greek democracy.

Freedom

The Greek Origins of Freedom

The Significance of Greece in the History of Freedom

Between the end of the seventh and the early fourth century B.C., five great revolutions took place in ancient Athens that were to transform the history of the West and, by extension, that of the world.

One was economic: the creation of a complex preindustrial economy of independent family farms and large peri-urban estates, centered on an export-oriented mining and urban craft economy, occupationally dominated by slave and ex-slave labor.

The second was social and of a twofold nature. On the one side, there emerged for the first time in human history a relatively large slave population which sustained the aristocratic, and a good part of the nonfarm, population of a society. On the other side, we find, also for the first time, the majority of a population entirely emancipated from ties of economic and social dependency on its ruling class.

The third revolution was political: quite simply, the invention of the democratic state in Athens engaging the full participation of all adult male members of the political community.

A profound change in human thought marked the fourth revolution: the discovery of rationality as an end in itself and, by this means, the generation of secular philosophy and the social and moral sciences.

The fifth of these revolutions was the social construction of freedom as a central value, in the course of which we find the creation of personal freedom and its unique configuration with the other two forms of freedom in a triadic value that was to remain preeminent in the Western system of values.

All five revolutions were intimately related. They were so much of a piece that it is impossible to imagine the emergence of one without the others. Yet, though all were inextricably linked, one of these developments formed the base for the other four: that foundation being large-scale slavery. The origins of Western culture and its most cherished ideal, freedom, were founded, we will see, not upon a rock of human virtue but upon the degraded time fill of man's vilest inhumanity to man. . . .

The Emergence of Slave Society and Civic Freedom

… [T]he sectoralization of the economy led increasingly to the growth of a "modern" urban sector concentrating on the production of craft goods by slaves, freedmen, and resident aliens as well as citizens and, especially from the early fifth century, to a greatly expanded mining sector almost wholly dominated by slaves. The modern sector made possible the urban civilization and all its manifold cultural achievements. It supported both the aristocratic elite, which continued to gain its wealth mainly from their slave-farmed land and which had dual residence in both city and country, and an urban-based middle class of metics and citizens. The slave-based sector, it must be emphasized, also included the freedman class, which was directly generated by the institution of slavery; [one] reason why simply relying on counts of slaves is likely to be misleading. Even so, the generally accepted proportion of slaves in the population of Athens during the late fifth century is in no way out of line, in terms of the comparative data on large-scale slave societies. Indeed, the consensus estimate that one in three adults was a slave is almost identical with the estimates of the American South, at the height of the antebellum slave system. Furthermore, as [Carl] Degler cogently observed, less than a quarter of all southerners owned any slaves and less than 3 percent of all slaveholders owned lots of more than fifty, yet no one ever questions whether the antebellum south was a large-scale slave society.

However, this economic configuration had societywide social and cultural implications for all Athenians (in much the same way that antebellum southern slave society had major consequences for the 75 percent of all southerners who owned no slaves), which is why we use the term *slave society,* rather than slave economy. The first implication was that the modern sector was not divorced from the traditional rural sector. Athens was simply too small a society for that to happen. There was structural articulation, mainly because the elite used their slave-based wealth to control and transform the society. Second, the mere mass of slaves in such a small society also had direct effects on the class of smallholders whether or not they owned slaves. The smallholders not only used slaves as an optional supplementary force when they could afford it but, as I will argue shortly, had strong views about the intrusion of these aliens into their midst, as they did about the extraordinary structural changes taking place in what we have called the modern sector. And third, there were the vital cultural and psychological effects, the most important of which was the promotion of freedom consciousness. This whole process was fraught with conflict, especially between the independent small farmers in the traditional economic sector (whether or not they used slaves) and the slaveholding elite and middle classes in the modern rural and urban sector. It was out of this conflict that democracy emerged.

The sixth century saw a continual struggle on the part of the Attic lower classes to expand the limited gains achieved through the Solonan reforms. Their repeated demand was for a redistribution of land. They did not succeed in achieving any significant economic redistribution. However, the Peisistratids [followers of Peisistratus, tyrant of Athens] responded to their claims with certain social and legal reforms which emphasized the collective solidarity of all free persons, but met the economic crisis only in a stopgap way. This tradition began with Solon himself, who did not redistribute wealth, but in addition to... legal reforms... introduced certain jural and religious reforms which have led many to view him as the initiator of the jural-political process which culminated in the fully developed democracy instituted in the reforms of Ephialtes [a leader who represented the common people]. Accompanying these jural reforms were religious ones. Indeed, it is the main argument of James H. Oliver that the Greek invention and promotion of the value of freedom always had a religious basis. In a felicitous passage, Oliver sums up the achievements of Solon as follows:

> What did Solon do to the Athenian assemblies? Solon re-established the union of all citizens by rejecting the theory that only men of property were entitled to sit in the Assembly.... As he guaranteed to the *thetes* [new class] their place in the Assembly, he gave his action a religious basis by founding a sanctuary of Aphrodite Pandemos. With this dedication Solon called for mutual affection, a union of hearts within the community, a love for each other and for the city, and thereby he created a social ideal not only for Athens but for all Greece and eventually for the whole Mediterranean.

I can accept all of this, even the ringing Grecophilic rhetoric. What Oliver never attempts to answer, however, is the question immediately posed by his encomium: Why did the Athenian ruling class end up inviting its formerly semi-enslaved masses to such a communal love fest? I said earlier that the threat of revolt brought on by the reduction of native Greek farmers to domestic and foreign slavery is what initiated the process. What consolidated and intensified it was the enslavement of non-Greeks in the Attic homeland, within the context of the continued struggle of the Athenian small farmers for greater economic equality.

Plutarch, citing Theophrastus, tells us that Peisistratus "devised the law against unemployment, which made the city more peaceful and the countryside more productive." This sounds for all the world like the make-work, special employment projects of modern Third World governments, desperately staving off lower-class rebellion. The Greek tyrants, however, were smarter, in that they actively pursued programs aimed at enhancing social solidarity. The building program of the Peisistratids, by increasing the social capital of the state, was also a form of indirect redistribution, although the emphasis was clearly on social solidarity and the centralization of the state. This is most clearly seen in the religious reforms of Peisistratus. His glorification of the cult of Athena reinforced the role of the state cult. At the same time, the more primitive aspects of Athena's divine attributes were removed, and replaced by an emphasis on the three dimensions of her divinity which would appeal directly to the three major classes of men in Athens: Athena the armed goddess and champion of the aristocratic warrior ethic; Athena the goddess of handicrafts, protector of the new commercial groups; and Athena the goddess to whom the olive tree was sacred, with immediate appeal to the agricultural sector, but especially that segment involved with the most modern and progressive area of Greek farming. As Walter Burkert has pointed out, "what unites these divergent spheres of competence is not an elemental force, but the force of civilization."

This appeal to collective solidarity would have been facilitated by slavery in several ways. First, the wealth of the Peisistratids and other tyrants was based on mining and trade, two activities heavily dependent on slave labor. Second, the intrusion of slaves into the Athenian body politic would have created resentment on the part of the average Athenian. The religious reforms then attempted to kill two birds with one stone. On the one hand, they muted resentment over the growing number of slaves by emphasizing the value of being a freeborn Athenian. On the other, they displaced resentment over the refusal of the upper classes to grant meaningful redistribution by offering a sharing of collective goods.

These reforms, however, did not remove the desire for greater equality on the part of the mass of freeborn Greeks. If anything, they stimulated the need for more such reforms. "The *tyrannis*," as Victor Ehrenberg has observed, "was the necessary and creative antecedent of democracy." If political equality was the price the elite was going to pay for its growing wealth and increase in the size of the slave population, much more than collective religious participation and the juridical reforms introduced by Solon would be demanded. Those demands came to a head during the last decades of the sixth century and culminated in the reforms of Cleisthenes.

... Empathy was not the prevailing response of men in the face of the large-scale introduction of slavery. Rather, it was envy, envy of the master for his good fortune. And the entrenched nature of envy and competition in Athenian culture is now sufficiently established among scholars for me not to have to belabor this point. What impressed the average Greek male about slavery was not the plight of the slave but the power and honor enhancement of the master. In the zero-sum approach to life which typified these men, rich and poor alike, the recognition of the master's gain would immediately have induced a sense of outrage about what was being lost to those who were not benefiting from the large-scale introduction of slavery. The answer came easily: what was being lost, or rather being threatened, was the integrity of the homeland. The slave's, and later the metic's, alienness was emphasized because it was precisely on this basis that the class of large-scale masters was most vulnerable and that concessions could be wrung from it. Such concessions, I am saying, took the form of growing civic freedom. The slave's alienness enhanced the value of the freeman's nativeness. And the master class, in turn, paid for its desecration of the community with the intrusion of slaves and other foreigners by making a special value of what it shared with all who were neither slaves nor aliens. Citizenship, then, had its crucible in the contradistinction with the non-native, the most extreme case of which was the slave. The mass of Greek men never lost sight of this valuable contradistinction. As we will see, nothing is more fully supported by the available evidence on Athenian democracy than the close causal link between the value of citizenship and the exclusion of the non-native. The slave, as the quintessential non-native, was the focus of this culturally creative contradistinction. But it was extended to all foreign elements which the slave system encouraged—indeed, in the case of freedmen, generated. As David Whitehead, writing more of the end result of this process in the late fifth century, pointed out,

> Their preoccupation was with a single, all-embracing demarcation between citizen and metics, which reserved for themselves alone not only all political decisions but the eligibility (if not always the ability) to be permanent and honored shareholders in the social, economic and religious focus of the community, the soil of Attica.

What is more, this emphasis remained wholly male. Athenian democracy, it cannot be too often stressed, was an exclusively male club. Indeed, as Pierre Vidal-Naquet has pointed out, the exclusion of the alien slave was conflated with that of women: "The Greek city in its classical form was marked by a double exclusion: the exclusion of women, which made it a 'men's club'; and the exclusion of slaves, which made it a 'citizens club.'"

It is possible to trace the emergence of this process in the development of the Greek language, more particularly in the terms used for freedom, slavery, and citizenship, and to relate this to contemporary events. Two scholars have undertaken this task: Max Pohlenz, the first modern scholar to expose the central role of slavery in the development and nature of freedom, and, more recently, Kurt Raaflaub, in a brilliant and painstaking study that is as culturally sensitive as it is philologically informed. Both show how freedom began as a term confined to the private-individual realm, in other words, describing what I have called, simply, personal freedom. . . . The first significant change . . . came with Solon in his writings on debt bondage. That he was dealing with fellow members of the community, struggling for a recognized place within it, made this the ideal situation for the stimulation of freedom consciousness, and this is faithfully reflected in his language. Men, for the first time, began to take freedom seriously. In doing so, however, they transferred it from the individual personal domain of language to the public realm. There is clear philological evidence of a growth in the appreciation of the free status of the citizen with the growth of slavery and the resident alien population during the sixth century. Raaflaub finds a strong correlation between the development of the polis and the concept of citizenship, on the one hand, and a sharpened polarization between free and unfree, on the other.

However, it was not only among the mass of Athenian citizens that freedom consciousness developed. Slavery had rendered the independence of the mass of native Greeks possible, not by making them a leisure or idle class, as was once naively thought, but by making their independence tolerable to their former masters by providing them with an alternative, more flexible labor force. But in doing so, slavery had also made the ruling class independent of native free labor, a point that is rarely emphasized. In gaining their labor independence, the small Greek farmers had lost the leverage power of threatening to withdraw their labor in their struggle for greater equality. This is why they turned to renegade members of the aristocracy to help them in their continued struggle for a greater share of the expanding Athenian economic pie. As I argued earlier, what the tyrants gained for them was a greater share of the expanding civic and cultural-religious pie. They offered solidarity with the ruling class on the basis of a common ancestry in the soil of Attica, over against all non-natives, especially slaves. Apart from being a brilliant strategy for maintaining peace with the disgruntled and envious free natives, this strategy would certainly have had a second, equally important function, which no one has ever mentioned with respect to Athens but which is immediately apparent to any student of comparative slavery: it was a powerful means of controlling the growing slave population. Encouragement of hostility to the slave, and identification with the slaveholder class in a unified civic community—given powerful symbolic expression in the promotion of Athena—made not only good political but good economic sense, since it greatly reduced the supervisory costs of slavery. The proud, free citizen-farmer, jealous of any alien intruding on the civic community, would happily do that for the slaveholders.

Nonetheless, the encouragement of civic participation and a sense of contradistinctive identity with the elite alarmed the more traditional aristocrats, who now, for the first time, ceased to take their freedom for granted. A point to note here is one emphasized some time ago by Anthony Andrews: that during the course of the sixth century there was a permanent expansion of the Athenian elite. Many of the tyrants he persuasively argued, were supported by the richer section of the hoplite class in its conflict with the more traditional elements of the nobility.

The philological and related cultural data examined by Pohlenz and by Raaflaub reveal how the internal threat of tyrannies, combined with the external threat of invasion—ever real throughout the late sixth and early fifth centuries—and the need to avoid both, led to what Raaflaub calls a "breakthrough" toward their own notion of freedom among the aristocrats. For the aristocrats, freedom meant power and political equality, *among their class equals.* As Pohlenz neatly stated it, "The concept was transferred from the private sphere when in the class struggles the victory of the other party was described as slavery, so that freedom came to be appreciated from the point of view of home politics," and not just external defeat. For the masses, of course, it also meant equality, but *among class unequals.* The final resolution of intra-elite and interclass conflicts came with the extraordinary reforms of Cleisthenes, reforms made possible, according to Herodotus, only because Cleisthenes, who had been on the losing side in an intra-elite squabble, "took the people into his party," people whom he had "previously held in contempt."

This is where the situation stood at the turn of the fifth century B.C. It was a tense moment in the history of freedom, in consciousness of it, and in the very language used to convey it. But it was a tension pregnant with enormous possibilities....

Slavery, Empire, and the Periclean Fusion

... The Athenian system of civic freedom proved to be astonishingly stable. Between the reforms of 508-7 and the destruction of the democracy by the Macedonians in 322, there were only two brief periods of oligarchic rule—in 411 for four months and in 404-3—led by men from the wealthiest classes.[G. E. M. De] Ste. Croix has rightly described the Athenian demos' resistance to the second of these as "one of the most remarkable and fascinating episodes in Greek history." It should be further noted that so strong was the commitment to democratic rule that when its conqueror Macedon fell to the Dardani in 230, Athens seceded and reestablished a democratic republic, an event celebrated by the creation of a new cult dedicated, significantly, not to Zeus any longer but to the Demos and the Graces. The days of war and imperialism were over. Freedom was now identified with love and graciousness, a development James Oliver finds "full of meaning for a student of the history of freedom." This clearly implies that imperialism, as such, was not a prerequisite for the continuation of the democracy, even though it played a vital role in ensuring its survival during the critical period following its fruition in the reforms of Cleisthenes and Ephialtes. The distinction between those factors that bring a process into being and ensure its early institutionalization and those that account for its perpetuation is one of the most fundamental in historical sociology. It is a distinction, unfortunately, which is too often neglected.

Slavery, unlike the empire, remained with Athens throughout the period of its independence, and beyond, supporting the elite and thereby obviating any need on its part to exploit the demos. What slavery continued to do for the mass of Athenian citizens—to repeat one of my main points—was less to provide them with an economic base... than to keep their elite off their backs and to grudgingly reconcile it to the juridical system that was the foundation of the democracy. Nor should one overlook the wisdom of the reforms themselves, in explaining the longevity of the system. As Martin Ostwald has made clear, Ephialtes and his successors "built sufficient safeguards into the system to prevent it from getting out of hand."

Perhaps one of the most effective of these safeguards, however, is something none of the reformers could have built into the constitution: the fact that the most important offices of the state remained in the hands of the rich and the aristocratic. And this remained so, astonishingly, even though they were filled by direct election. How do we explain the extraordinary willingness of the Athenian masses to let the ruling class rule, even though it was in their powers so easily to undo it? As [M. I.] Finley observed, "The people claims *isegoria* [equal freedom of speech and the right to be heard in the Assembly, Council, and jury courts] but left its exercise to a few." The reason for this, he argues, is that the people were more interested in the decisions arrived at and "were content with their power to direct those decisions through their power to select, dismiss and punish their political leaders." The insufficiency of the governmental machinery, the system of pay for holding political office, and the state pensions for war veterans all added to this willingness to let the rulers rule, Finley goes on, for it supported a conception of democratic freedom as a bundle of "claims on the state, not merely the right not to be interfered with in the private sphere."

This is all correct and important, but it still does not get to the heart of the problem. Assuming that the mass of Athenians shared the strong competitive ethos of the culture, the love of glory, and the chance to rule, it is hard to understand why some elements of the ordinary people did not force the issue and offer themselves for leadership. For me there is one obvious answer: the strong sense of civic solidarity that existed between the masses and their rulers, which had been nurtured during the sixth century by the deliberate fostering of the idea of their common Greek freedom, vis-à-vis all slaves, freedmen and other aliens, was given renewed vigor by the Persian Wars, and following it, by the even greater growth of the servile, alien population. Finley once remarked, in a much-cited passage, that Greek slavery and freedom developed "hand in hand." However, he meant this only in the preconditional sense. The relation between slavery and freedom, however, ran much deeper than that, as we have already emphasized. The demos accepted the rulership of the traditional ruling class because they saw its members as kinsmen, kith and kin against a world of unfree barbarians. It was slavery that created this conception of the world, one shared by rulers and demos alike. . . .

In the funeral oration, most notably that of Pericles, a subtle ideological struggle is going on, a struggle in which the distinction between style and substance becomes critical. The substance of civic and personal freedom is expressed in terms of the aristocratic style of sovereignal freedom, and [Nicole] Loraux argues that style may well have triumphed over substance. The central paradox of political thought in classical Athens, she notes along with many others, is that, in the absence of a democratic way of speaking about democracy, the funeral oration became "an aristocratic eulogy" and discourse on democracy. Perhaps.

It seems to me important, however, that another critical new dimension was being added to the discourse. This was the final renaming and reconception of *arete* [glory] as a form of freedom, one intimately related to the other three, but the one that should be dominant. Pericles leaves this abundantly clear: "Make up your minds," he says, "that happiness depends on being free, and freedom depends on being courageous." Thus, at this most critical moment in the social construction of freedom, we find a mutual intellectual appropriation rather than a hegemonic triumph through mode of discourse: the masses have finally appropriated the aristocratic ethos; *arete,* the manly Greek virtue which alone is free, has been democratized and is accessible to all. Or so it seems. But the aristocratic ethos has also appropriated, in the process, the most valued ideal of the masses. From now on it is not only the common man who can sing of freedom in all its three meanings. The chordal triad of freedom has now become the common cultural property of all classes. From this point onward, and throughout the agonistic course of Western history, the struggle was no longer over whether there should be freedom or not, or even over whether one or other of the three notes in the chord should exist, but which note, which conception, should dominate the chord and which class should control its meaning.

Donald Kagan

 **NO**

Democrat

After Ephialtes' death, Pericles rose from being a secondary member of a dissident political faction to a position as the uniquely powerful leader of a great democratic city ruling over a rich naval empire. He achieved this, first, through a series of constitutional reforms that gave a greater political role to the lower classes, and then by creating a powerful coalition with the great majority of Athenian farmers who fought in the heavy infantry. His rhetorical talent, political sense and organization, and the success he achieved allowed him to meet challenges from all directions. He also gained important support because of the power of his ennobling, carefully conceived, and forcefully communicated vision of a great city that gave meaning to the lives of all its citizens.

In the 450s, under Pericles' leadership, the Athenian assembly passed a series of laws that went far toward establishing a constitution as thoroughly democratic as the world has ever seen. It gave direct and ultimate power to its citizens in the assembly and the popular law courts, where they made all decisions by a simple majority vote, and it provided for the selection of most public offices by lot, for the direct election of a special few, and for short terms of office and close control over all public officials. This constitution reflected Pericles' vision of government, and within its confines he was able to achieve and maintain a position as leader and foremost citizen.

In 458, members of the class of small farmers... who fought as hoplites became eligible for the archonship [similar to a modern-day presidency], previously limited to rich men in the top two economic classes. Therefore, they would join the Areopagus [a council made up of wealthy land owners] and put an end to its domination by the rich and well-born. This step further reduced the influence of the archons and Areopagus to the advantage of the randomly chosen Council of 500, of the assembly, and of the popular law courts....

In 451/450, Pericles himself introduced a law imposing a stricter definition of Athenian citizenship. Up to then, children of an Athenian father and a foreign mother were legitimate Athenian citizens; the new law required that both parents be Athenian. The purposes of the new definition are far from clear, but whatever its other consequences, the new law meant that henceforth political membership in the community would be determined not by traditionally aristocratic religious bodies, or even by individual local townships, but by the people as a whole. It was an assertion of the sovereign power of the Athenian assembly as the seat of the democracy.

Another important change arose from the new burden carried by the popular courts. The growth of the Athenian population, the burgeoning commercial economy, the increased number of disputes arising from contact with foreigners, and the growth of the litigious spirit common to democracies put great pressure on the existing judicial system. Later in the century, Aristophanes plausibly estimated that the six thousand jurors... empaneled annually heard cases on three hundred days each year....

The democratic ideal required that the majority of citizens take part in public decisions, but the poor could not do so without pay. To meet the problem, Pericles introduced a law authorizing such payments. It was not long before the democratic policy of payments for service extended beyond jurors to the five hundred men who served on the council, to the archons, to all public officials chosen by lot, and to soldiers and sailors on duty. Aristotle calculated the number of citizens receiving pay at the same time for public services, military and civilian, domestic and imperial, at over twenty thousand. Pericles' introduction of payment for public service made many Athenians full citizens for the first time, and the life of the full Athenian democracy begins with his reforms.

It is important to have a clear understanding of the kind of regime Pericles' reforms produced, for it is not easy even for citizens of what are called democracies in the twentieth century to comprehend its nature. To a degree hard for us to grasp, politics was primary in the ancient Greek city, and the form of the constitution was understood and expected to shape the character of its citizens. The art, the literature, the philosophy, and all the great achievements of Periclean Athens cannot be fully understood apart from their political and constitutional context in the democracy established by Cleisthenes about 508 and extended by Pericles a half-century later.

The place to start a description of the Athenian democracy is with a definition of the term. Developments in the modern world, however, make that a difficult task, for the word has become debased and almost meaningless. Few modern states will admit to being anything but democratic. States as different as the United States, the Soviet Union, Great Britain, China, Switzerland, Cuba, South Africa and Nigeria all assert that they are democracies. That is confusing enough, but there are further complications. Many people today would insist that to qualify as a democracy a state must offer full constitutional and political protections and opportunities to all who have legal permanent residence within its borders and desire citizenship. But the Athenians limited the right to vote, hold office, and serve on juries to adult males who were citizens. Slaves, resident aliens, women, and male citizens under the age of twenty were denied these privileges. Modern critics question the democratic character of the Periclean regime because of the presence of slavery and the exclusion of women from political life. In excluding such groups, the Athenians were like every other society since the invention of civilization about 3000 B.C. until just recently. What sets Athenians apart are not these exclusions but the unusually large degree of inclusion, as well as the extraordinarily significant and rewarding participation of those included. It is useful to remember that what has been called the Jacksonian democracy in America co-existed with slavery, that women were everywhere denied the right to vote until this century, and that we continue to limit political participation to those of a specified age. To deny the title of democracy to Periclean Athens because of those excluded would be to employ a parochial and anachronistic set of criteria that produce paradoxical results. Certainly, no contemporary Greek doubted that Athens was a democracy; the only argument was whether democracy was good or bad, an argument almost unthinkable in our time.

The Athenians, on the other hand, would have been astonished at the claims of modern states to that title, even such states as the United States and Great Britain, for to them an essential feature of democracy was the direct and full sovereignty of the majority of citizens. Government by elected representatives, checks and balances, separation of powers, appointment to important offices, unelected bureaucracies, judicial life tenure, terms for elective office of more than one year—all these would have seemed clear and deadly enemies of what reasonable people might understand as democracy. These differences require a brief examination of how the Athenian democracy worked if we are to shed our modern prejudices and grasp its true character.

To use a helpful if anachronistic device, let us consider the three familiar branches of government: legislative, executive, and judiciary. At the heart of what we would call the legislative branch of the Athenian democracy was the assembly.... It was open to all adult male citizens of Athens, during Pericles' lifetime perhaps as many as forty thousand men. Most Athenians lived many miles from the city and few owned horses, so attendance required a long walk to town. As a result, the number taking part was probably from five to six thousand, although some actions required a quorum of six thousand. The meetings took place on a hill called the Pnyx, not far from the Acropolis and overlooking the Agora. The citizens sat on the earth of the sharply sloping hill, and the speakers stood on a low platform. It was not easy for them to make themselves heard; Demosthenes, the great fourth-century orator, is said to have practiced speaking by the seashore over the crashing surf to make his voice strong enough for his work on the Pnyx....

An assembly of thousands, of course, could not do its business without help. For that it relied on the Council of 500, chosen by lot from all the Athenian citizens. Although it performed many public functions that the larger body could not handle efficiently, its main responsibility was to prepare legislation for consideration by the people. In this respect, as in all others, the council was the servant of the assembly. The assembly could vote down a bill drafted by the council, change it on the floor, send it back with instructions for redrafting, or replace it with an entirely different bill. Full sovereignty and the real exercise of public authority rested directly with these great mass meetings. Almost no constitutional barrier prevented a majority of the citizens assembled on the Pnyx on a particular day from doing anything they liked.

In Athens, the executive was severely limited in extent, discretion, and power, and the distinction between legislative and judicial authority was far less clear than in our own society. To begin with, there was no president or prime minister, no cabinet or any elected official responsible for the management of the state in general, for formulating or proposing a general policy. There was nothing that Americans would call an "administration" or that the British would call a "government." The chief elected officials were the ten generals all serving one-year terms. As their title indicates, they were basically military officials who commanded the army and navy. They could be reelected without limit, and extraordinary men like Cimon and Pericles were elected almost every year. But they were most exceptional. The political power such men exercised was limited by their personal ability to persuade their fellow-citizens in the assembly to follow their advice. They had no special political or civil authority, and, except on military and naval campaigns, they could give no orders.

Even in military matters, the powers of the generals were severely limited. Leaders of expeditions were selected by vote of the full Athenian assembly, which also determined the size of the force and its goals. Before the generals took office they were subjected to a scrutiny of their qualifications by the Council of 500. After completing their year of service, their performance on the job, and especially their financial accounts, were subject to audit in a process called *euthyna*. Aristotle describes how the process could continue, even after that hearing:

> Officials called Examiners sit during the regular market hours at the statue of the eponymous hero of each tribe. If any citizen wishes to prefer a charge, either of a private or public nature, against any of the officials who have rendered their accounts at an *euthyna*, within three days he must write on a whitened board his own name, and the name of the man he accuses, the offense with which he charges him, and the fine he considers appropriate.

If the examiner decides the charge has any merit, he passes it on to the appropriate popular law court for final judgment. This was not the only control the people had over the few officials chosen by election. Ten times a year the popular assembly voted "to determine whether [the generals'] conduct of military affairs appears satisfactory; and if the people vote against someone's confirmation in office he is tried in a law court. If he is found guilty they assess his punishment or fine; if he is acquitted he resumes office." Since elected office conferred prestige, elected officials were carefully watched lest they undermine the rule of the people.

Even with these severe controls, the Athenians filled only a few public offices by election, choosing their military officials, naval architects, some of their treasurers, and the superintendents of the water supply in that manner. All other officials were chosen by lot, in accordance with the democratic principle that any citizen was capable of performing civic responsibilities well enough, and its corollary that feared the fall of executive or administrative power into the hands of a few men, even those with experience or special abilities....

For all its flaws, the Athenian system was simple, speedy, open, and easily understood by its citizens. It contained provisions aimed at producing moderate penalties and at deterring unreasonable lawsuits. It placed no barriers of legal technicalities or expertise between the citizens and their laws, counting as always on the common sense of the ordinary Athenian.

The Athenian democratic system, brought to its height in the time of Pericles, has been harshly criticized through the ages. Ancient writers directed most of their attacks against the idea of government by mass meeting and the selection of public officials by lot. The Athenian renegade Alcibiades told a Spartan audience: "As for democracy... nothing new can be said about an acknowledged foolishness." Plato has Socrates make the same point more fully and seriously. He observes that when it is a matter of building a house or a ship the Athenian assembly listens only to experts. If someone without expert qualifications tries to give advice in such matters, "even if he is very handsome and rich and noble," they refuse to listen to him. Instead, "they laugh and hoot at him until either he is shouted down and withdraws of his own accord or the sergeants-at-arms drag him off or he is expelled by order of the presidents." But when the discussion is about affairs of state, "anyone can get up to speak—carpenter, tinker, cobbler, passenger and ship-owner, rich and poor, noble and commoner—and nobody rebukes him, as they did in the earlier case, for trying to give advice when he has no knowledge and has not been taught."

The Athenians did, in fact, appreciate the importance of knowledge, skill, talent, and experience where they thought these things existed and could be used in the public interest. Thus they elected military officers, treasurers, naval architects, and managers of the water supply. If they did not elect professors of political science or philosophers or lawyers to govern and judge them, it was because they were skeptical that there was a useful expertise in these areas, and that if it did exist, it could safely and profitably be employed for the public good. It is not clear that the experience of the last twenty-five hundred years has shown them to be wrong.

Second, it is most unlikely that many fools or incompetents played a significant role in public affairs, perhaps no more so than today. The assembly itself was a far less unwieldy or incompetent body than is generally assumed. If a citizen attended no more than half the minimum number of yearly sessions, he would still hear twenty sets of debates by the ablest people in the state, chiefly elected officials or those formerly holding elective office, the leading politicians in all factions, and a considerable number of experts on a variety of subjects. Moreover, these were true debates in which it was not possible to hold to prepared remarks; speakers had to respond extemporaneously to hard questions and arguments from the opposition; nor were they irresponsible displays but serious controversies leading immediately to votes that had important consequences for the orators and their audience. If each attendant at the assembly had been listening to such discussions for an average of only ten years, such experiences alone must have fashioned a remarkable body of voters, probably more enlightened and sophisticated than any comparable group in history. Furthermore, each year five hundred Athenians served on the council, where every day they gained experience in the management of Athens' affairs, from the most trivial to the most serious, producing bills that served as the basis for the debates and votes of the assembly. In any assembly, therefore, thousands of those attending, perhaps a majority of them, would have had that kind of training on the council. In light of such experience, the notion that decisions were made by an ignorant multitude is not persuasive.

But were debates in the assembly carried on by ordinary Athenians, citizens without the necessary special knowledge and capacity for informed advice? The evidence suggests not, for there were impressive deterrents that would make an inexperienced, ill-informed, poorly educated man reluctant to speak up....

Meetings of the Athenian assembly... were not always quiet, seemly occasions. We should not forget Dicaeopolis' threat "to shout, to interrupt and abuse the speakers" or Plato's report of how the Athenians laughed and hooted or shouted down speakers who lacked what they thought was the necessary expertise. These informal deterrents alone sharply limited the number of speakers in the assembly. But there was also a formal device that encouraged them to take thought before speaking. At some time, perhaps during the career of Pericles but certainly not more than fifteen years after his death, the Athenians introduced a procedure called the *graphe paranomon* that had the effect of making the citizens in the assembly guardians of the constitution. Any citizen could object to a proposal made in the council or the assembly by asserting that it contradicted an existing law. This stopped action on the proposal or suspended its enactment if it had already been passed. The proposer was then taken before a popular court. If the jury decided against him, his proposal was disallowed and he was fined. Three findings of this kind deprived the proposer of his rights as a citizen. The expectations of the assembly and its procedures, therefore, make it most unlikely that ignorant incompetents played a significant role in its deliberations.

An even graver charge has been leveled through the ages against the kind of democracy promoted by Pericles. It is said to be inherently unstable, inviting faction and class warfare, to be careless of the rights of property, and to result in the rule of the poor, who are the majority, over the rich minority. The "Old Oligarch," the name given to the unknown author of an antidemocratic pamphlet written a few years after the death of Pericles, simply assumes that democracy promotes the interests of the poor at the expense of the rich. According to this writer, the Athenians chose democracy because "they preferred that the masses should do better than the regular citizens."

Plato says that "democracy originates when the poor win, kill or exile their opponents, and give the rest an equal share in the citizenship and in opportunities of office, and most of the magistrates are chosen by lot." He goes on to describe how democracy, after a time, degenerates into tyranny: The group that is most numerous and powerful is "the mass of the people, who work with their own hands, take little interest in politics, and possess very little." They come to the assembly only to get their share of the loot: "their leaders deprive the rich of their property, give some to the masses, keeping most of it for themselves." The attacks on the propertied lead them to defect from the democracy, which, in turn, causes the people to become a bloodthirsty mob. They rally to a leader and support him as he carries out "exiles and executions, hinting all the while at cancellations of debts and redistributions of lands until he reaches the point where he must either be killed by his enemies or become a wolf instead of a man—that is, a tyrant."

... [T]here is no ... excuse for Plato's misrepresentation of the Athenian democracy. Starting with the fuller democracy instituted by Ephialtes and Pericles from 461, we discover an almost unbroken, orderly regime that lasted 140 years. Twice it was interrupted by oligarchic episodes. The first resulted from a coup in the midst of a long and difficult war and lasted four months. The second was imposed by the Spartans after the Peloponnesian War and lasted less than a year. On each occasion the full democracy was restored without turmoil —without class warfare, revenge, or confiscation of property. Through many years of hard warfare, military defeat, foreign occupation, and oligarchic agitation, the Athenian democracy persisted and showed a restraint and moderation rarely equaled by any regime.

This behavior is all the more remarkable in light of the political and constitutional conditions that prevailed in the Periclean democracy and thereafter. The mass of Athenians were not faced with the power of what has been called a military-industrial complex, thwarted by the complexities of representative government, checks and balances, and machinations of unscrupulous lobbyists, or manipulated by the irresistible deceptions of mass media. They had only to walk up to the Pnyx on assembly day, make speeches, and vote in order to bring about the most radical social and economic changes: the abolition of debt, confiscatory taxation of the rich, the simple expropriation of the wealthy few. But this they never did. Although political equality was a fundamental principle of democracy, economic equality had no place in the Athens of Pericles. On the contrary, the democracy he led defended the right of private property and made no effort to change its unequal distribution. The oath taken by jurors included the following clause: "I will not allow private debts to be cancelled, nor lands or houses belonging to Athenian citizens to be redistributed." In addition, the chief magistrate each year swore that "whatever anyone owns before I enter this office he will have and hold the same until I leave it."

The last thirty years of the century were terrible times of war, plague, impoverishment, and defeat. Yet neither during or after the war did the Athenian masses interfere with private property or seek economic leveling. In the Periclean democracy, the Athenian citizen demanded only equality before the law, full political rights, and the kind of even chance these provided. By these rules he was willing to abide in the face of the greatest disasters and the greatest temptations. It was this politically equal, individualistic, law-abiding, and tolerant understanding of democracy that Pericles had done much to create and to which he could appeal and point with pride, confident that his fellow-citizens shared it....

What of the charge of insincerity—that Pericles used the democracy to achieve his own ends without believing in its principles? Pericles' political behavior is a sufficient refutation. He remained active for more than thirty years after acquiring the leadership of the dominant faction in Athens, and his prestige and influence grew with the years. At times his policies were rejected. On occasion he was compelled to stand by while his friends and loved ones came under attack by political enemies. In the year before his death, the assembly rejected his policy, removed him from office, and punished him with a heavy fine. They could have done the same at any time in the previous three decades, but of course they did not. Nor did Pericles ever try to protect himself against this democratic constitution or to place himself above it by changing its rules.

But why should such a man, who could live as a lord in an aristocracy or as the master in a despotism, prefer a democracy? In the case of Pericles several answers suggest themselves. First, support of popular government was part of a family tradition. His maternal grandfather, Cleisthenes, was the founder of democracy, and it was natural that his descendants should be imbued with respect for it. Second was the teaching of Anaxagoras. If we have understood it correctly, it provided a philosophical support for the democratic system of government as against the more hierarchical traditional beliefs, and Pericles was a man much influenced by rational, philosophic analysis.

Finally, we may speculate that Pericles was devoted to democracy because he saw better than any contemporary its capacity for greatness. Pericles . . . wanted to move his city toward a vision of unmatched quality. Athens' safety, wealth, and power depended on control of the sea and the men of the lower classes who were its oarsmen. It was their enthusiastic allegiance that the democracy had won. Other regimes, which excluded great numbers from active citizenship, thereby wasted a considerable portion of their potential strength. The need for oppressive regimes to keep watch on the excluded masses further sapped their potential power. Only democracy held the prospect of releasing the full energy of all the people, thereby creating a polis of unprecedented potential. Perhaps that prospect, more than anything else, made Pericles the convinced democrat that he always was.

POSTSCRIPT

Was a Slave Society Essential to the Development of Athenian Democracy?

When we examine the two sides of this issue, we see several differences. First, we have Kagan's traditional account of the development of Greek democracy contrasted with Patterson's contemporary multidisciplinary account. Second, we have a historian versed in the political aspects of history contrasted with a sociologist interested in the interaction of various groups within society. Finally, Kagan returns to the "great person" approach to history (which stresses the impact of privileged individuals on the course of history), while Patterson believes that the forces of history are more significant than the leaders who shaped them.

This issue also raises the question of presentism. Is it fair for us to hold the Greeks accountable to standards and practices that have only become commonplace only in the past two hundred years? But if we don't, aren't we overlooking the origins of one of humanity's greatest crimes against itself—chattel slavery? Therefore, does Greek civilization deserve credit for the birth and development of democratic government? Interesting question!

For further information, students are encouraged to consult the work of the late Sir Moses I. Finley: *Ancient Slavery and Modern Ideology* (Viking Press, 1980) and *Economy and Society in Ancient Greece* (Viking Press, 1981), a compilation of his journal articles edited by Brent D. Shaw and Richard P. Saller. Another recommended source is Yvon Garlan's *Slavery in Ancient Greece* (Cornell University Press, 1988), which attempts to examine Greek slavery within its own context. Our two contributors to this issue have also written extensively on the ancient Greek world and slavery. Please consult Kagan's *A New History of the Peloponnesian War*, 4 vols. (Cornell University Press, 1974–1987) and Patterson's *Slavery and Social Death* (Harvard University Press, 1982). The second volume in his two-part *Freedom in the Making of Western Civilization* (Basic Books) should be available soon.

ISSUE 2

Does Alexander the Great Merit His Exalted Historical Reputation?

YES: N. G. L. Hammond, from *The Genius of Alexander the Great* (University of North Carolina Press, 1997)

NO: E. E. Rice, from *Alexander the Great* (Sutton Publishing, 1997)

ISSUE SUMMARY

YES: Professor emeritus of Greek N. G. L. Hammond states that research has proven that Alexander the Great is deserving of his esteemed historical reputation.

NO: Senior research fellow and lecturer E. E. Rice maintains that, other than his conquests, Alexander the Great left few tangible legacies to merit his exalted historical reputation.

In the fourth century B.C.E. Greek city-states (poleis) were destroying themselves in a series of wars that have become known as the Peloponnesian Wars. Chronicled by Thucydides (460–400 B.C.), an eyewitness and participant, these wars showed the Greek polei at their worst—selfish, contentious, avaricious, and power-hungry. The result was a series of conflicts in which one side, Sparta and its allies, was able to defeat its enemy, Athens and the Delian League. Both sides suffered heavy losses and learned no lessons from the conflict. In their weakened, unenlightened state, they were easy prey to a strong, united Greek kingdom from the north—the Macedonians and their powerful king Philip.

The Macedonians were considered by the Greek city-states of the south to be barbaric. However, they had unification and military prowess on their side, and soon all of Greece was under their control. Philip was deprived of his chance for a more exalted place in history when he was assassinated by a bodyguard while participating in a festival in 336 B.C.E. He was succeeded by his son Alexander, then a young man of 19 years.

Alexander seemed to be destined for greatness. At an early age he displayed strong leadership and military skills. His father hired Aristotle as a tutor to help develop his intellectual side. Aristotle exerted a strong influence on the young man. Given the devious nature of Macedonian politics, Alexander's accession to his father's crown was not guaranteed. But he succeeded and within 14 years he conquered most of the then-known world. This earned him a place in history with the sobriquet—Alexander the Great.

Alexander's place in history was created immediately after his death. There were some who spoke of him as a divinity, even while he was alive, and the process continued through the next few centuries. The Romans, who featured likenesses of him in many of their art works, saw themselves in him as they began to follow in his footsteps, conquering much of the known world. The apex of his Roman reputation occurred when Plutarch (42–102 C.E.) wrote glowingly of him in his book *Lives,* claiming that Alexander was descended from Hercules. A few of the historical figures who engaged in Alexandrine worship included Julius Caesar and Napoleon Bonaparte. Alexander has been featured in countless literary works from ancient to modern times.

What is the basis of Alexander's glowing historical reputation? Obviously, his conquests form its essence—but it is based on more than territorial accumulation. It is the story of the "philosopher-king," the cultured leader who attempted to create a cultural synthesis by fusing the best of the East and the West. It is the saga of an attempt by a man to create a "one world" ideal, a man trying to achieve the "impossible dream" and coming close to it.

For most of recorded history, humankind's story has been told through the words and deeds of its great men, and occasionally, great women. This is the "heroic" approach to the study of history. In the first part of the twentieth century, this version of history dominated. Historical figures such as Alexander still received favorable press. But with new tools of the trade, recently discovered materials and manuscripts, and perhaps a need to interpret history in a different vein, books about historically famous people have tended to be more critically inclined. How will Alexander fare in this new era? We will have to wait and see.

N. G. L. Hammond, who has written three books about Alexander, still finds much to admire in him, and deems him worthy of his historical appellation. On the other hand, E. E. Rice counters that Alexander's historical reputation may be undeserved due to the death and suffering caused by his military campaigns, and because he left little of permanent value as his legacy to the world.

The Plans and Personality of Alexander

Arrangements Affecting the Macedonians and Macedonia

After the reconciliation in late summer 324 Alexander [the Great] offered his terms for any Macedonians who might volunteer to go home. They would be paid the normal wage up to their arrival in Macedonia, and each man would receive a gratuity of one talent. They were ordered to leave their Asian wives and children in Asia, where Alexander undertook to bring up the boys 'in the Macedonian manner in other respects and in military training'; and he said he would send them thereafter to their fathers in Macedonia. He made provision also for orphans of Macedonian soldiers in Asia. Some 10,000 Macedonians accepted these terms. 'He embraced them all, with tears in his eyes and tears in theirs, and they parted company.' They were being released from the campaign in Asia, not from military service. In summer 323 they reached Cilicia, where Alexander intended that they should winter. In spring 322 they were to be transported to Macedonia by his newly built fleet. By then Alexander expected to have completed his Arabian campaign and to be in Egypt or Cilicia. He was to be joined there by 10,000 Macedonians 'in their prime', who would be replaced in Macedonia by the returning veterans. . . .

Arrangements Affecting the City-States

Alexander respected the sovereignty of the Greek Community in the settlement of affairs after the defeat of Agis and his allies, and he continued to do so, for instance by sending captured works of art to the states in the Greek Community. His conduct in these years indicates that the allegations of exceeding his powers as *Hegemon*, which were made in a speech 'On the Treaty with Alexander' in 331, were groundless. Within the Greek Community only one breach of the charter was reported in our sources, the expulsion of the people of Oeniadae from their city by the Aetolians. It happened perhaps in 325; for Alexander said that he himself would punish the Aetolians, presumably on his return to the West. In the years of peace a large number of Greek allies went east to serve in Alexander's army, and no doubt others emigrated to trade or settle in Asia. At

Athens Phocion was re-elected general repeatedly as the advocate of compliance with the Charter, and Lycurgus used the prosperity which Athens enjoyed under the peace to complete the construction in stone of the auditorium of the theatre of Dionysus and to improve the naval shipyards.

In June 324, when Alexander was at Susa, one of his financial officers, Harpalus, fled to Greece in order to escape punishment for misconduct. He came to Cape Sunium with 5,000 talents, 6,000 mercenaries and 30 ships, and as an Athenian citizen (for he had been honoured earlier by a grant of citizenship) he proceeded to Athens and asked for asylum and in effect alliance against Alexander. The Assembly rejected his request. He and his forces went on to Taenarum in the Peloponnese, but he returned as a suppliant with a single ship and a large amount of money. The Assembly then granted him asylum as an Athenian citizen. Although he gave bribes freely in Athens, he did not win over the leading politicians. Meanwhile Antipater [general "with full powers"] and Olympias [handler of religious and financial affairs] made the demand that Athens as Macedonia's ally should extradite Harpalus; and envoys from Alexander came from Asia with a similar demand. On the proposal of Demosthenes the Assembly voted to arrest Harpalus, confiscate his money, and hold him and his money 'for Alexander'....

When his forces were assembled at Susa, Alexander announced to them that all exiles, except those under a curse and those exiled from Thebes, were to be recalled and reinstated.... The wording was as follows: 'Alexander to the exiles from the Greek cities... we shall be responsible for your return... we have written to Antipater about this, in order that he may compel any states which are unwilling to restore you.'... The purpose of Alexander was twofold: to resettle the floating population of exiles (we may call them refugees today), which caused instability and often led to mercenary service; and to reconcile the parties which had fought one another and caused the vicious circle of revolutionary faction.

Such an act of statesmanship was and is unparalleled. It affected almost all Greek city-states to varying degrees, and it hit Athens and Aetolia hardest. For Athens had expelled the population of Samos in 365 and occupied the island herself; and now, forty years later, she would have to restore the island to its proper owners. And Aetolia had to hand back Oeniadae to the Acarnanians she had expelled. At the time Alexander could not be accused of restoring his own partisans; for the bulk of the exiles had been opponents of the pro-Macedonian regimes in power. According to Hieronymus, an objective historian born around 364, 'people in general accepted the restoration of the exiles as being made for a good purpose'. In many states the restoration had taken place at the time of Alexander's death, but Athens and Aetolia were still making objections....

Alexander's Beliefs and Personal Qualities

Alexander grew up in a kingdom which was continually at war, and he saw it as his duty to lead the Macedonians in war not from a distance but in the forefront of the fighting. He saw the destiny of Macedonia as victory in war, and he and his men made military glory the object of their ambitions. Thus he spoke of the victorious career of Philip [king of Macedonia (359–336 B.C.) and father of Alexander] as conferring 'glory' both on him and on 'the community of Macedonians'. His own pursuit of glory was boundless. As he declared to his Commanders at the Hyphasis, 'I myself consider that there is no limit for a man of spirit to his labours, except that those labours should lead to fine achievements.' He made the same demand on his Commanders and his men. They had committed themselves to following him when they had sworn the oath of allegiance (*sacramentum pietatis*), to be loyal and have the same friend and enemy as their king. If a man should be killed in his service, Alexander assured them that his death would bring him glory for ever and his place of burial would be famous.

Life was competitive for boys in the School of Pages and for boys being trained for the militia in the cities, and thereafter in civilian affairs and in the services. No Macedonian festival was complete without contests in such arts as dramatic performance, recitation of poetry, proclamation as a herald, and musicianship, and in athletic events which on occasion included armed combat. Alexander was intensely competitive throughout his life. He would be the first to tame Bucephalus [a wild horse], to attack the Theban Sacred Band [an army of the boldest Theban warriors, organized to fight the Spartans in 371 B.C.], to mount a city wall or climb an impregnable rock. He was the inspirer and often the judge of competition in others. He alone promoted soldiers and officers, awarded gifts for acts of courage, bestowed gold crowns on successful Commanders, and decided the order in the hierarchy of military rank up to the position of Senior Friend and Leading Bodyguard. Competitions between military units and between naval crews were a part of training and of battle. Alexander himself believed that he must compete with Philip, Cyrus the Great, Heracles and Dionysus and surpass them all, and as Arrian remarked, 'if he had added Europe to Asia, he would have competed with himself in default of any rival.'

His belief in the superiority of Greek civilisation was absolute. His most treasured possession was the *Iliad* of Homer, and he had the plays of the three great tragedians sent to him in Asia, together with dithyrambic poems and the history of Philistus. They were his favourite reading. He admired Aristotle as the leading exponent of Greek intellectual enquiry, and he had a natural yearning (*pothos*) for philosophical discussion and understanding. His mind was to some extent cast in the Aristotelian mould; for he too combined a wide-ranging curiosity with close observation and acute reasoning. His belief in the validity of the Greek outlook of his time was not modified by his acquaintance with Egyptian, Babylonian and Indian ideas. One mark of Greek civilisation was the vitality of the city, both in Europe and in Asia, and Alexander believed that the best way to spread Greek culture and civilisation was by founding cities throughout Asia. At the outset the leaders in these cities were the Macedonians and the Greek mercenary soldiers, who conducted the democratic form of self-government to which they were accustomed. At the same time the future leaders were being educated 'in Greek letters and in Macedonian weaponry' in the schools which Alexander established. The process was already well under way before Alexander died, as we see from a passage in Plutarch's *Moralia:* 'When Alexander was civilising Asia, the reading was Homer and the boys (*paides*) of the Persians, Susianians and Gedrosians used to chant the tragedies of Euripides and Sophocles . . . and thanks to him Bactria and Caucasus revered the Greek gods'. Egypt has yielded a teaching manual of the late third century, which was designed to teach Greek as a foreign language and included selections from Homer and the tragedians. The excavations at Ai Khanoum in Afghanistan have revealed Greek temples, theatre and odeum (for music) alongside a very large Asian temple in the late fourth century. Alexander was the standard-bearer of Greek civilisation. His influence in education and so in civilisation has been profound, extending even into our own age.

Faith in the orthodox religion of Macedonia was deeply implanted in Alexander's mind. He sacrificed daily, even in his last illness, on behalf of himself and the Macedonians and on innumerable other occasions. He organised traditional festivals in honour of the gods in the most lavish fashion. He believed as literally as Pindar had done in the presence in our world of the Olympian gods, in the labours of heroes such as Heracles and the exploits of Achilles, both being his ancestors. The deities made their wishes or their warnings manifest to men through natural phenomena and through omens and oracles, which were interpreted and delivered by inspired men and women. It was an advantage of polytheism that the number of gods was not limited, and Alexander could see Zeus in the Libyan Ammon and in the Babylonian Belus, and Heracles in the Tyrian Melkart or the Indian Krishna. His special regard for Ammon was probably due to the prophetic oracles which he received at Siwah and which were evidently fulfilled *in toto* when Alexander reached the outer Ocean. He gave thanks time and again to 'the usual gods' (the twelve Olympians) for the salvation of himself and his army, and he must have thought that he owed his charmed life to them. Even in his last illness he believed that his prayers in the course of sacrifices would be heard and that he would live. For he died without arranging for the transition of power.

Of the personal qualities of Alexander the brilliance, the range and the quickness of his intellect are remarkable, especially in his conduct of warfare. At Gaugamela and at the Hydaspes he foresaw precisely the sequence of moves by his own units and the compulsion they would place on his enemies. As Ptolemy, himself a most able commander, observed of the first campaign, 'the result was as Alexander inferred that it would be', and after the last campaign 'not a one of the operations of war which Alexander undertook was beyond his capability'*(aporon)*. In generalship no one has surpassed him. Arrian wrote that Alexander had 'the most wonderful power of grasping the right course when the situation was still in obscurity'. Thus he knew on his landing in Asia that he must set up his own Kingdom of Asia and obtain the willing cooperation of his subjects. Already at Sardis he began the training of boys who would become soldiers of that kingdom. The orginality of his intellect was apparent in his development of the Indus, the Tigris and the Euphrates as waterways of commerce and his reorganisation of the irrigation of Mesopotamia. The boldness of his calculations was rewarded with success in many engagements and especially in the opening of navigation between the Indus Delta and the Persian Gulf.

His emotions were very strong. His love for his mother was such that one tear of hers would outweigh all the complaints of Antipater. He sent letters and gifts to her constantly, and he said that he would take her alone into his confidence on his return to Macedonia. His loyalty to the friends of his own generation was carried sometimes to a fault, and his passionate grief for Hephaestion [his closest friend from childhood days] was almost beyond reason. He loved his soldiers and they loved him; he and his veterans wept when they parted company; and he and they acknowledged that love in his last moments. When he killed Cleitus [an old-fashioned noble in a drunken brawl], his remorse was desperate. His compassion for the Theban Timoclea and for the family of [Persian ruler] Darius and his love for [wife] Roxane were deeply felt and led to actions which were probably unique in contemporary warfare.

As King of the Macedonians and as King of Asia he had different roles to fill. His way of life was on the same level as that of the Macedonians on campaigns and in leisure. As he said at Opis, his rations were the same as theirs and he shared all their dangers and hardships; and he enjoyed the same festivals and drinking parties as they did. He led them not by fiat but by persuasion, and a crucial element in that persuasion was that he should always tell them the truth, and they should know that he was telling them the truth. Thus he respected the constitutional rights of the Macedonians, and his reward was that he was generally able to convince them in their Assemblies that they should accept his policies. His role as King of Asia was almost the opposite. His court, like that of the Persian King of Kings, was the acme of luxury and extravagance. He gave audience in a huge pavilion which rested on fifty golden columns, and he himself sat on a golden chair, surrounded by so many richly-dressed guardsmen that 'no one dared approach him, such was the majesty associated with his person'. He accepted obeisance, and he ruled by fiat. The wealth at his command was beyond belief; for he had taken over the accumulated treasure of the Persian monarchy, and he received the fixed tribute which was paid by his subjects over a huge area. His expenditure was extraordinary by Greek standards, for instance on memorials commemorating Hephaestion, but it was in proportion to his wealth as King of Asia. The strength of his personality was such that he was able to keep the two roles separate in his mind and in his behaviour, and Ptolemy and Aristobulus were correct in seeing the real Alexander as Alexander the Macedonian.

Alexander combined his extraordinary practicality with a visionary, spiritual dimension which stemmed from his religious beliefs. As a member of the Temenid house he had a special affinity with his ancestors Heracles and Zeus, and he inherited the obligation to rule in a manner worthy of them and to benefit mankind. His vision went beyond Macedonia and the Greek Community. When he landed on Asian soil, his declaration, 'I accept Asia from the gods', and his prayer, that the Asians would accept him willingly as their king, were expressions of a mystical belief that the gods had set him a special task and would enable him to fulfil it. This spiritual dimension in his personality created in him the supreme confidence and the strength of will which overrode the resistance of the Macedonians to his concept of the Kingdom of Asia, and which convinced the Asians of the sincerity of his claim to treat them as equals and partners in the establishment of peace and prosperity. The power of his personality was all-pervading. It engaged the loyalty of Persian commanders and Indian rulers after defeat in battle and the loyalty of Asian troops at all levels in his service. It inspired *The Alexander Romance* in which Asian peoples adopted Alexander as their own king and incorporated his exploits into their own folk-lore. We owe to Plutarch [Greek writer and historian (45 A.D.–125 A.D.)], drawing probably on the words of Aristobulus, an insight into this spiritual dimension in Alexander.

> Believing that he had come from the gods to be a governor and reconciler of the universe, and using force of arms against those whom he did not bring together by the light of reason, he harnessed all resources to one and the same end, mixing as it were in a loving-cup the lives, manners, marriages and customs of men. He ordered them all to regard the inhabited earth (*oikoumene*) as their fatherland and his armed forces as their stronghold and defence.

Alexander the Great

Return and Death

The Departure from India

In the end, Alexander's schemes of further conquest were defeated by his army's refusal to go further, and he was forced to retreat and return to the west. The army retraced its steps back across the tributaries of the Indus to the Hydaspes, where a fleet of transport ships had been readied. The return journey took the troops south down the Indus to the sea. Arrian [a Greek historian] recounts the details of the trip in his *Indika,* based on the account of Nearchus, the admiral of the fleet. The flotilla suffered considerable damage in the fierce currents of the river. A sizeable force accompanied it by land along the banks of the Indus, receiving the submission of the local peoples or subduing them by force.

A particularly fierce campaign was waged in 326/5 BC against the Mallian people, a self-governing Indian tribe living on the east bank of the Indus between the Hydraotes and Hydaspes rivers. Numerous cities of the Malli were captured with great savagery, until their remaining combined forces, numbering some 50,000, converged upon a strongly defended city. Alexander encircled the city and mounted a siege against it. When the Macedonians had penetrated the city as far as the citadel, they mounted an attack scaling the walls by means of ladders. Alexander, leading from the front as always, mounted the wall but was isolated upon it in full view of the enemy when the ladder beneath him broke. Here occurred one of the most foolhardy acts of Alexander's career. So that he would not be such a visible target, the king leapt from the wall down into the city and engaged in hand-to-hand combat with the Indians within. A few Macedonians managed to come to his aid, but Alexander received a severe chest wound and finally became unconscious from loss of blood. The sources paint a vivid picture, with many variations, of his comrades fighting while standing over his body, one allegedly protecting him with the sacred shield from the Temple of Athena at Ilion (Troy).

In the end the attacking Macedonians broke through the wall of the citadel, and massacred every inhabitant they could find, including women and children. Alexander's unconscious body was retrieved and carried off to safety on his shield. This was not the first time that Alexander had been wounded during the course of the campaigns, but he somehow managed to survive this wound, which was by far the most serious he had received. Rumours of the king's death circulated the camp, which caused great lamentation, but in due course he was reunited with the main body of troops. Their joy was unbounded when they saw their king get up from a litter, walk, and mount his horse. Arrian records that Alexander was angry when some of his friends blamed him for taking risks, because he knew it to be true. The Malli surrendered unconditionally, and a Macedonian was appointed satrap over them. This campaign marked a new level in the savagery displayed by Alexander and his troops.

Throughout the remainder of 325 BC, the army proceeded south along the Indus river. Some of the forces travelled by ship, and others marched along the banks. More new cities and ship-stations were fortified, and Alexander received the surrender of several more Indian kings. Finally they reached Patala in the Indus delta, fortifying its citadel and constructing shipyards and docks to make it into a permanent port. The journey through this complex delta was not all smooth: on occasions the ships were damaged by storms, stranded by tides, and the captains were totally reliant on native pilots. Time was spent exploring the various mouths of the delta to find the most navigable branches for the fleet.

Alexander planned to send his fleet back west along the coast and up into the Persian Gulf to the mouths of the Tigris and Euphrates rivers. Some troops were sent back along a northern route through Afghanistan, but Alexander himself led a large detachment of troops overland in order to dig wells and stockpile provisions for the fleet as they put into land. They advanced through the Makran, ancient Gedrosia, attacking the Oritai and Gedrosian peoples and receiving their surrender as they went on.

The sixty-day march through this Gedrosian desert nearly spelled disaster for the expedition. The terrain is inhospitable in the extreme. The sources present a vivid picture of the suffering of the troops, who had little food and hardly any water. In order to stay alive they were forced to take a more inland route and send supplies to the coast for the fleet. The troops were reduced to pilfering sealed rations destined for the coast. It is reported that they feared imminent death from starvation more than punishment from their king. They endured unbearable heat and ceaseless thirst, and killed and ate their pack animals, pretending that the beasts had already died or had collapsed from fatigue. Many men were left behind to die since the wheeled vehicles could not traverse the terrain and had, in any case, few animals left to draw them. A disastrous flash flood in a dry gulley killed most of the women and children and the surviving animals. Alexander reputedly underwent the same torments as his men and was seen to pour on to the ground a helmet full of water since not all of his men could drink from it.

Many have argued that this ill-fated journey across the desert was one of Alexander's few major tactical mistakes, although others hold that the conditions were not really as dire as the sources paint them. The opinions of the ancient writers on Alexander's motives are intriguing. Nearchus the admiral alone claimed that Alexander decided on this route through ignorance of its difficulty, but most writers claim that Alexander had heard that this desert had been crossed with an army only by Cyrus the Great (the founder of the Persian Empire) and the Assyrian Queen Semiramis, and that he aspired to emulate the achievements of these legendary figures. I would argue that either ignorance of conditions or a romantic whim points to a serious lapse of judgement. In any event, Alexander was lucky that some of his troops survived.

The army rested at the end of their desert crossing, and went on through the region of Carmania (between Gedrosia and Iran). Most sources record a celebratory revel of colossal scale, with musical and athletic events witnessed by drunken troops drawn along on carts adorned as Dionysiac bowers. Arrian states clearly that he does not believe such reports, but the comparisons between Alexander's expedition to India and that of Dionysus have already been noted (elsewhere). Nor should we underestimate the relief expressed by men who had nearly died in the desert and who were given the chance to celebrate freely after months of deprivation.

Alexander and his troops returned to the heartland of Persia during 324. This journey is described briefly in the sources, but it is marked by Alexander's harsh punishment of both Macedonian and Persian satraps who were accused of disobedience or corruption as he passed through. Many no doubt had never expected Alexander to return, and had taken upon themselves extreme powers amounting to royal prerogatives. Alexander could not tolerate this, and executed several officials in what has been likened to a 'reign of terror' (the phrase used by the eminent historian Ernst Badian). Regardless of what these actions reveal about Alexander's increasingly autocratic behaviour and deteriorating temperament, they clearly demonstrate the fragility of the administrative arrangements he had put into place on his outward journey.

Alexander reached the royal Persian city of Pasargadae, where he was enraged to see the defilement of the tomb of Cyrus the Great. He appointed Aristoboulos, one of Arrian's two main historical sources, as overseer of its restoration. This is a further indication of the regard in which he held King Cyrus, who was exempt from the stigma of the later Persian Wars in Greece. He returned to Persepolis, which his troops had already looted and burnt, hanging the acting satrap and punishing others on his way.

In 324 BC they reached the royal city of Susa, and here Alexander staged a mass wedding of his highest-ranking officers to native ladies of noble birth. Alexander (who was already married to the Bactrian Rhoxane) also married Statira, the eldest daughter of Darius, and another Persian lady as well. We are told specifically that the ceremonies were in the Persian style. In addition, some 10,000 Macedonians who had already 'married' Asian women registered them and were given generous wedding gifts. It would appear that Alexander was urging a policy of racial fusion between Persians and Macedonians and the creation of a mixed-race ruling class to govern his empire. It is noteworthy that after Alexander's death we only hear of one of the noblewomen still married to a Macedonian general. This was Apama, daughter of the Sogdian Spitamenes, who married a general named Seleucus and became his queen when he declared himself king of the Syrian (Seleucid) Empire. Alexander continued his beneficence by discharging the debts of all his soldiers and by presenting honours and decorations to officers and men distinguished for their bravery and deeds.

At this point the 30,000 Epigoni from the Upper Satrapies joined Alexander, dressed in Macedonian fashion and trained in the Macedonian art of war.

The Macedonian rank and file disapproved very much of Alexander's policy of fusion between Macedonians and Persians. It is recorded that even the bridegrooms did not like the Persian-style weddings, and that no one liked to see Alexander in Persian dress or promoting those who espoused Persian customs. They thought that the arrival of the Epigoni and the incorporation of native units into the infantry and cavalry signalled the end of his reliance upon the Macedonian troops who had endured so many adventures and hardships with their king.

These grievances exploded into mutiny again at the city of Opis on the Tigris, after Alexander had explored the delta of the Tigris which flows into the Persian Gulf. When the king proposed to discharge the time-expired and unfit veterans and send them home, keeping only those who wished to stay, the troops interpreted this as an insult to them and reacted in fury. The ringleaders said that they would all go home and leave him to fight along with his father—by whom they meant Ammon. Alexander was incandescent with rage, had the ringleaders arrested, and delivered a long speech justifying his career and the campaign (much of the preserved speech in Arrian is probably his own rhetorical elaboration of what he thought Alexander said). Again the king withdrew to his tent for three days, but, when he began to install Persians in military commands, the Macedonians flocked to his tent and begged forgiveness. At a banquet of reconciliation, Alexander proclaimed both Persians and Macedonians as his kinsmen.

Alexander's special friend Hephaistion died at Ecbatana in 324 BC, after an illness lasting a week. Alexander was prostrate with grief, and the sources vie with each other in detailing the extravagant things he did in his despair (ordering the manes and tails of all the cavalry animals to be shorn in mourning, to give but one example). Diodorus describes in detail the elaborate funeral monument he planned for Hephaistion in Babylon, and Alexander sent to the oracle at Ammon enquiring what honours it would be appropriate to pay his friend. Yet the king was not to survive Hephaistion for long. The army proceeded to Babylon, and he entered the city in 323 BC despite dire warnings from seers, and several other portents that danger would befall him there.

The account of Alexander's last days are derived in part from a source called the 'Royal Journals' by Arrian and Plutarch. The form and content of these journals have been widely debated without universal agreement, since they do not seem to be official documents such as might have been compiled by Alexander's secretariat, but an account mainly of the excesses of Alexander's last days on earth. They are generally regarded as a bogus document forged at some stage for some reason by some unknown person to cast a gloss on the events of that turbulent period, but there is no consensus of scholarly opinion beyond that. However we are to interpret these journals, they record serious drinking sessions between Alexander and a man called Medius, after which the king contracted a fever. The fever did not abate even though Alexander rested and was carried several times to bathe in the river, offering sacrifices each time. For days he ate little, became extremely ill, and finally was unable to talk although he could still recognize his officers. We are told that the army insisted on filing past his bed, and his last actions were to greet each one by raising his head and making a sign with his eyes. He died shortly afterwards.

Many have tried to make posthumous diagnoses of Alexander's illness, but we will never know for certain what it was. Clearly the years of hardship and the various wounds he sustained took their toll and probably made his system less able to resist the fever. Perhaps the final drinking bouts exacerbated his condition. Poison was of course alleged, and the sources tell us various stories about possible motives and culprits, but, on the whole, dismiss these tales as malicious rumours. In the end, Alexander was only a mortal like all men.

It adds to the mystery of Alexander the Great that so much uncertainty still surrounds his last days and death, but with his passing the dream was shattered, and it was left to lesser men to pick up the pieces.

Alexander's Personality

I do not believe that it is possible to attempt a reconstruction of Alexander's personality without attributing to him motives which are not found in the ancient sources—our best, but ultimately unsatisfactory, evidence about him. I have therefore tried... to stay close to our sources, although it is a problem that the recorded opinions of Arrian, Diodorus and Plutarch (all of whom lived hundreds of years after Alexander) on the king's behaviour may not be preferable to those of any modern scholar who thinks that he understands Alexander and what motivated him to act as he did in any given instance. The historiography of Alexander the Great (by which I mean the study of the histories written about him) is in itself a fascinating overview of trends in historical writing and the personalities of their authors. I hope that I have not 'identified' myself with Alexander and written an account based on what would have led me to act as he did, but perhaps this is what all biographers do despite their protestations to the contrary. What follows is not a full assessment of the man, but a short discussion of aspects of his character which I think are illuminated in the sources.

There is no doubt that Alexander was a brilliant military tactician. His battle plans are still studied in military colleges in Europe and America. Elements of his genuis were speed of movement, an appreciation of terrain, the use of his troops in the most advantageous way, and a charismatic and inspiring quality of leadership. Obviously, he was lucky to have the highly trained and experienced Macedonian army and skilled officers behind him, and he must have had a superb intelligence corps and commissariat. Because our sources focus on the king himself, these unsung heroes tend to be ignored, but without a highly developed infrastructure the huge army would have starved to death before getting far into Asia. His notions of invincibility were reinforced by spectacular military successes in set battles, siege warfare, and guerrilla tactics. Alexander led from the front and, although this was undoubtedly an inspiration to his troops, he took foolhardly risks. On more than one occasion he was lucky not to have been killed. The successive wounds which he endured must have contributed to his demise by increasing his susceptibility to the fever which killed him.

What about Alexander the man? We have no reason to suppose that he did not love his wife Rhoxane, nor that he did not take his pleasures with other women when he wished. His close friendship with Hephaistion may indicate that he was bisexual, but this was a common trait among men in ancient Greece. He rewarded loyalty, punished suspected treachery, and became increasingly autocratic in his treatment of people. Many scholars have claimed that he became a virtual tyrant by the end of his life. He had a court sculptor, portrait painter, and gem engraver to ensure that he was depicted in the correct image. Clearly it was important that an identifiable likeness of him was recognisable by the many peoples of his far-flung empire, but such a conscious manipulation of his image indicates considerable vanity. It is not a coincidence that the extant ancient portraits of Alexander are easily recognisable. They all feature an upturned gaze with consequent wrinkled forehead, eyes deep-set apparently to show fixed determination, and thick leonine locks falling from a peak in the centre of his forehead.

Much has been made of Alexander's drinking habits. Certainly the consumption of wine played a large role at court banquets, festivals, victory celebrations, and around the campfire, and it must have been a considerable consolation during long winters spent in unspeakable conditions far from home. Drinking was an accepted part of Macedonian aristocratic society and army life, and we should not see it as something out of the ordinary. It appears that Alexander drank more as he got older, and that his personality deteriorated during the years of the campaign, whatever may be the reason for this. Nor do we have any reason to doubt the various monumental drinking binges which are recorded in the sources, most famously the one which exacerbated his final illness. Clearly the influence of alcohol had occasional catastrophically detrimental effects on Alexander—his inebriated murder of Cleitus is the most striking example—but I find it hard to believe that he was an alcoholic by the modern clinical definition of the term. His military achievements alone argue that he was in control of his faculties, and more, when he needed to be.

Finally, what were Alexander's views about a divine ancestry, rivalry of the exploits of the gods, and deification? Yet again, these are impossible questions to answer because of our complete lack of evidence about what Alexander himself thought. We have seen that he repeatedly compared himself with the gods Heracles and Dionysus and with Persian heroes such as Cyrus the Great and the legendary Queen Semiramis. He also evidently saw himself in a special relationship with Zeus Ammon after his visit to the oracle at Siwah. His unsuccessful attempt to introduce proskynesis [respect or awe] among his Macedonians, and his unclear motives for so doing, have already been discussed. It is certain that Alexander was worshipped as a god after his death (he was worshipped as the 'Founder' god in Egyptian Alexandria, for example), but what is still disputed is whether Alexander demanded divine honours during his lifetime, and, if so, whether he was the first living mortal in the Greek world to do so. We cannot know whether he was intentionally deluding others to increase his stature in their eyes, or whether, in a spectacular case of *folie de grandeur*, he was ultimately deluding himself.

Epilogue: Alexander's Legacy

On 10 June 323 BC, Alexander the Great died of fever in Babylon at the age of thirty-three. According to some accounts, he is alleged to have said on his deathbed, when asked to whom he was leaving his kingdom, 'to the best man'. Some sources add that he gave his signet ring to the general Perdiccas, who was virtually his second-in-command at the time. Most sources relate the further story that Alexander said that there would be a great 'funeral game' over him. This comment—whether real or invented—drips with considerable irony. Equestrian and athletic funeral games (in Greek 'epitaphia') were indeed staged as a way of commemorating the dead in ancient Greece, but here of course Alexander is referring proleptically to the bloody contest over his succession. (Diodorus describes the elaborate funeral carriage constructed for Alexander's body.)

This prophecy proved all too true. A vast conquered empire, the focus of which had been the personality of Alexander himself, and which was governed only by interim, *ad hoc* administrative arrangements, was unexpectedly left leaderless. The generals in Babylon—self-made men who had become powerful by virtue of their connection with Alexander and who by now were hardly going to be satisfied by the thought of a quiet life back in Macedonia—immediately fell out over the succession. The main party declared Alexander's posthumous half-Bactrian son by Rhoxane as King Alexander IV, while the rank and file of the army proclaimed Alexander's half-witted half-brother Philip Arrhidaeus as King Philip III (Arrhidaeus was the son of Philip II by one of his minor wives). The infant and the simpleton were placed under the control of a regent. The turmoil which followed in the next two decades presents difficulties of nightmarish complexity, with continually shifting alliances among the leading protagonists who struggled for power even as they pretended to protect the rights of the two kings. The fight was between those who thought that they could take Alexander's place and keep his empire intact, and those who were content with control of self-contained segments of that empire. Constant warfare and the violent deaths of various contenders ensued before three separate kingdoms emerged which form the focus of the history of the next three centuries. Ultimately, the impact of Rome's increasing domination of the Greek East by the first century BC put an end to the independent existence of these empires and what is known as the 'Hellenistic' period of Greek history. Alexander's empire, by which I mean the personal empire he created in these years and not the Macedonian state, did not survive his death. In terms of the attempt to control the whole of Greece and Asia, and to create an empire based on his personality alone, Alexander's achievement was ephemeral.

Nor did he leave the legacy of a bloodline. Within thirty years of his death every member of his immediate family had been brutally murdered: his mother, his wife, his child (the teenage Alexander IV is probably the occupant of Tomb III at Vergina), an alleged illegitimate son, his half-brother Arrhidaeus, his two half-sisters and the daughter of one of them, and his full sister. This is comment enough upon those troubled years which saw the extinction of the royal

Argead family to which Alexander belonged. Most of the surviving generals (the so-called 'Diadochi' or 'Successors') were killed in battles against each other, so no Macedonian dynasty of kings over the whole of Asia was created. It was only after fifty years of chaos that Antigonus Gonatas, the grandson of one of Alexander's generals, securely established himself upon the throne of Macedonia itself, thereby beginning what is known as the Antigonid dynasty in that kingdom. No descendant of Alexander had previously lived to occupy this throne for more than a few years.

Finally, what was the significance of Alexander's expedition in the history of the ancient world? On the one hand, it is undeniable that his exploits brought him everlasting fame and made him a yardstick against which many later conquerors measured themselves—Julius Caesar, the Roman emperor Trajan, and even Napoleon, to name but three. Alexander died at the pinnacle of his fame, and thereby became the quintessential romantic figure. Legend has immortalised him as the consummate young, brave, swashbuckling, invincible hero, but his early death means that we can never know what might have happened later. Could he have held his empire together? How would he have ruled it? Did he really intend the megalomaniac so-called 'Last Plans' recorded in some of our sources, which even included the circumnavigation of Africa? (The authenticity of these plans, which were read out to the army and rejected after Alexander's death, is still hotly debated.) Might he have gone on to conquer the whole inhabited world? Could he really have crossed China and reached the Pacific Ocean? What would Alexander have been like at the age of sixty? We will never know.

There are two legacies which Alexander the Great did bequeath to us, the value of both being dubious. The first was the subsequent condition of Macedonia, which he left as a youth of twenty and to which he never returned. This kingdom had to endure for eleven years with an absent king, far away and in only sporadic contact. It has been estimated that up to 40,000 men in their prime were taken out of Macedonia between 334 and 331 BC. Most of these never returned; many of those who had not succumbed to their wounds lived and died in Asia, populating the new cities founded by Alexander's successors in their new kingdoms. The consequences of this upon the Macedonian families—parents, wives, children—of these soldiers can hardly be imagined. Macedonia was supreme and invincible at the end of the reign of Philip II in 336 BC, but Alexander died leaving behind him bitter memories of brothers, husbands and sons who went with him, and the consequences of severe depopulation. One might argue that Alexander the Great, the greatest conqueror of the ancient Greek world, set his country on a path of decline that proved irreversible. In terms of the Macedonian heartland, the period of Macedonian greatness was the reign of King Philip II, not that of his overambitious heir.

John Keegan, the eminent military historian, has examined various styles of generalship in his magisterial book *The Mask of Command*. His definition of the 'mask of command' is the facade or persona which any general must wear, or the stage upon which any leader must act, to ensure that his troops follow him to the end. His discussion of Alexander the Great concludes that his style of leadership combined the ideals of heroism and nobility with that of the 'conquering urge', a savagery which all those who opposed him faced. Keegan's conclusion, with which I wholly concur, is that Alexander's 'dreadful legacy was to ennoble savagery in the name of glory and to leave a model of command that far too many men of ambition sought to act out in the centuries to come'. It is that legacy which we have inherited.

POSTSCRIPT

Does Alexander the Great Merit His Exalted Historical Reputation?

Someone once stated, "Pity the nation that has no heroes!" Someone else wryly replied, "Pity the nation that needs them!" To what extent have national desires created the aura of Alexander the Great? How many historical figures were so inspired by his story that they sought to emulate it? And what were the results of such actions? Military historian John Keegan, in *The Mask of Command* (Jonathan Cape, 1987), contends that the Alexandrine conquest model inspired others to emulate him, with the same disastrous results. Barbara Ehrenreich shares this assertion in *Blood Rites: Origins and History of the Passions of War* (Henry Holt, 1997). We may want to ask the question, Should Alexander the Great's historical reputation suffer due to the actions of those who followed and attempted to emulate him?

As one can imagine, the number of books about Alexander are numerous. The late Ulrich Wilcken's classic biography, *Alexander the Great,* first published in 1931, has been reissued in 1997 (W. W. Norton). It contains an insightful chapter entitled, "Introduction to Alexander Studies" by Eugene N. Borza of Pennsylvania State University. Robin M. Fox's *The Search for Alexander* (Little, Brown & Company, 1980) was written for an accompanying television series and contains some wonderful visual images, along with a highly readable and interesting text.

Other Alexander biographies that are worth reading are A.B. Bosworth, *Conquest and Empire: The Reign of Alexander The Great* (Cambridge University Press, 1993) and Peter Green, *Alexander of Macedon: A Historical Biography* (University of California Press, 1991). Michael Wood's *In The Footsteps of Alexander the Great* (University of California Press, 1997) is a book/television series that is worth recommending. Since the book contains the program narration, rent the videos and get the visual images along with the words.

ISSUE 3

Did Christianity Liberate Women?

YES: Karen Jo Torjesen, from *When Women Were Priests* (Harper-SanFrancisco, 1995)

NO: Karen Armstrong, from *The Gospel According to Woman: Christianity's Creation of the Sex War in the West* (Anchor Press, 1987)

ISSUE SUMMARY

YES: Professor of religion and associate of the Institute for Antiquity and Christianity, Karen Jo Torjesen, presents evidence of women deacons, priests, prophets, and bishops during the first millennium of Christianity—all roles that suggest both equality and liberation for women.

NO: Professor of religious studies Karen Armstrong finds in the early Christian Church examples of hostility toward women and fear of their sexual power which she contends led to the exclusion of women from full participation in a male-dominated church.

Have women been excluded from leadership roles in the Christian Church from the beginning? The ordination of women as ministers and priests during the twentieth century gives the impression that new ground is being broken by women who seek to lead congregations. Some believe that these women are carrying the movement for women's liberation in civil society inappropriately into churches and defying a nearly two-thousand-year tradition that has properly excluded them.

It is deeply challenging to our modern notions of progress to think that, even by present standards, women may have been more "liberated" two thousand years ago than they are today. Our greatest challenge might come from trying to imagine how early Christian women regarded their own status in the newly formed religion. Did they feel liberated from the more patriarchal world of first-century Palestinian Judaism and Hellenistic paganism? And, regardless of how they felt, does our assessment of their status merit claiming that Christianity liberated them?

Before the Christian Church became institutionalized and before a theology was clearly defined, early converts acted out of intense personal conviction and met informally to share their faith. Most churches were based in people's homes and some state that it was this private dimension that made women's leadership possible. Gender conventions of the time identified the male's sphere of influence as being in the public arena and confined the women's sphere of influence to the home. Christianity remained an underground religion until the early fourth century when Constantine, the Roman emperor, forbade government persecution and made Christianity a legal religion.

Missionaries converted many Greeks to Christianity, resulting in more Gentile, or non-Jewish, Christians than Jewish Christians by the third century. The Greek-speaking world was the first to accept Christianity in large numbers. If Christian women in both Jewish and Gentile environments during the early centuries enjoyed equality with men, what happened to create the climate of misogyny, or hatred of women, during later centuries?

In the sixth century a Christian Church Council actually debated whether or not women had souls. The question seemed to be whether women were made in the image and likeness of God, as men were, or merely in the image and not in the likeness. Women are still barred from the Roman Catholic priesthood, primarily using a theological argument introduced by Saint Thomas Aquinas in the thirteenth century. He stated that women are inferior by nature and incapable of assuming leadership positions.

Karen Jo Torjesen uses ancient texts, funerary epitaphs, papal letters and inscriptions, as well as mosaic art as evidence to support her thesis that women were accepted as equals and honored as leaders in the early Christian Church. However, this was only as long as Christianity remained a private phenomenon. Once it achieved official status during the fourth century, worship became more formalized and moved into public temples, called basilicas. Eager for credibility and legitimacy, church leaders bowed to prevailing gender conventions and restricted women's contributions.

Karen Armstrong focuses on negative cultural attitudes toward women. She begins the chapter from which the following selection is taken by quoting modern feminist Germaine Greer, "Women have very little idea of how much men hate them." She finds our modern culture uncomfortable with sex and traces the roots of hostility between men and women to the early days of Western Christianity. The Eastern (primarily Russian and Greek Orthodox) Christian Church, which split with the Western Church in an act of mutual excommunication in 1054, is judged by Armstrong as less misogynistic.

When Women Were Priests

Introduction...

The complexity of the issue of women clergy, given its larger context of gender, can best be treated by first analyzing the connections among women's roles, female character, and sexuality in the culture of Christ's day. Women's leadership in Christianity is a dramatic and complex story, one in which the radical preaching of Jesus and deeply held beliefs about gender sometimes melded and sometimes clashed. Jesus challenged the social conventions of his day: He addressed women as equals, gave honor and recognition to children, championed the poor and the outcast, ate and mingled with people across all class and gender lines, and with bold rhetoric attacked the social bonds that held together the patriarchal family. When Jesus gathered disciples around him to carry his message to the world, women were prominent in the group. Mary Magdalene, Mary of Bethany, and Mary his mother are women whose names survived the retelling of the Christian story in the language and literary conventions of Roman patriarchal society. Paul's letters reflect an early Christian world in which women were well-known evangelists, apostles, leaders of congregations, and bearers of prophetic authority.

Because Christians distanced themselves from the polytheism of Greek and Roman religions, they avoided using the pagan term "priest" (*hieros*) for their clergy. Instead they used a variety of terms taken from secular life: *diakonos* (minister), *apostolos* (missionary), *presbyteros* (elder), *episcopos* (overseer), prophet, and teacher. Eventually the titles of bishop (*episcopos*), priest (*presbyteros*), and deacon (*diakonos*) came to be identified with the principal offices of the Christian church. Throughout this period of development, women held each of these offices. The Christian title presbyter (elder), meaning an older person entitled to respect, was borrowed from the Jewish synagogue, which was governed by a group of presbyters. After the emergence of the office of bishop as the head of the congregation, the presbyters governed under his or her guidance. Catholic historians translate *presbyter* as "priest." Protestant scholars simply retain the word *presbyter*. In either case, a fully ordained clergyperson is meant. When a woman's name is associated with a title, both

Catholic and Protestant translators tend to minimize the office. Instead of translating *diakonos* as "minister" as they do for male office holders, they translate it as "deaconess."

During the first and second centuries, when Christian congregations met in homes, women were prominent as leaders. In early Christian communities women came to clerical offices by the same routes that brought their secular counterparts to public offices in Roman and Greek society. Preliminary training was provided by their assigned social roles as household managers. Women's authority in this domain was well established. Their administrative, economic, and disciplinary tasks in that role were excellent preparation for church (and public) office. In addition, women with relatively more wealth or higher status assumed the role of patron of a group. These patrons were often elected to public office, sometimes as a way of honoring them, and sometimes as a strategy for ensuring the patrons' continued generosity.

By the third century the processes of institutionalization gradually transformed the house churches, with their diversity of leadership functions, into a political body presided over by a monarchical bishop. Over the next two centuries, the legitimacy of women's leadership roles was fiercely contested. In the polemical writings of this period we encounter for the first time the arguments that Jesus appointed only male disciples and therefore women cannot be ordained; that Paul instructed women to keep silent during public discussions and thus women cannot teach; that if Jesus had wanted women to baptize, he would have been baptized by his mother, Mary. Although these arguments were rather weak in themselves, they were buttressed by the Greco-Roman world's beliefs about gender.

Opponents of women clergy appealed to a gender ideology that divided society into two domains, the *polis* (city), a male domain, and the *oikos* (household), a female domain. This system gave a great deal of power to women in the household while attempting to segregate them from public, political life. Christian polemicists insisted that public offices and public honors were a masculine affair and that women exercising such authority in the churches were usurping male prerogatives. During the first three centuries these voices represented a minority of the church's intellectuals, but as the church became increasingly institutionalized during the third and fourth centuries, these arguments carried greater weight.

The public-versus-private convention was in turn supported by a system of cultural values that associated men with honor and women with shame. The quest for honor and precedence associated with public office was viewed as an exclusively masculine enterprise. In contrast, a woman's honor was her shame, that is, her reputation for chastity. A woman exercising public authority could be accused of projecting a masculine personality; but, even worse, she could be called unchaste.

Although these notions about female shame and women's sexuality have their roots in the social order of ancient Greece, they have had a profound effect on Christian understandings of women, sexuality, and sin throughout the history of the church; they are foundational to the Western doctrine of sin, the church's theology of sexuality, and the Christian concepts of the self and even of God.

Understanding why and how women, once leaders in the Jesus movement and in the early church, were marginalized and scapegoated as Christianity became the state religion is crucial if women are to reclaim their rightful, equal place in the church today. Jesus' message and practice were radically egalitarian in their day and constituted a social revolution that likely provoked his crucifixion. It is high time that the church, which claims to embody his good news to the world, stop betraying its own essential heritage of absolute equality.

Preachers, Pastors, Prophets, and Patrons

The Evidence for Women's Leadership

Under a high arch in a Roman basilica dedicated to two women saints, Prudentiana and Praxedis, is a mosaic portraying four female figures: the two saints, Mary, and a fourth woman whose hair is veiled and whose head is surrounded by a square halo—an artistic technique indicating that the person was still living at the time the mosaic was made. The four faces gaze out serenely from a glistening gold background. The faces of Mary and the two saints are easily recognizable. But the identity of the fourth is less apparent. A carefully lettered inscription identifies the face on the far left as Theodora Episcopa, which means Bishop Theodora. The masculine form for bishop in Latin is *episcopus;* the feminine form is *episcopa.* The mosaic's visual evidence and the inscription's grammatical evidence point out unmistakably that Bishop Theodora was a woman. But the *a* on Theodora has been partially effaced by scratches across the glass tiles of the mosaic, leading to the disturbing conclusion that attempts were made to deface the feminine ending, perhaps even in antiquity.

At a burial site on the Greek island Thera there is an epitaph for an Epiktas named as priest or presbyter (*presbytis*). Epiktas is a woman's name; she was a woman priest sometime in the third or fourth century.

In the opening scene of the *Gospel of Mary,* a second-century gnostic Gospel, Mary Magdalene rallies the despondent disciples after the ascension of their Lord. By exhortation, encouragement, and finally a rousing sermon on the teachings of Jesus, she revives their flagging spirits and sends them off on their mission. Because of her strong leadership role, she appears in some texts with the title Apostle to the Apostles.

Historical evidence like this, from art, inscriptions, and literature, belongs to the hidden history of women's leadership, a history that has been suppressed by the selective memory of succeeding generations of male historians.

In his book *The Ministry of Women in the Early Church,* Roger Gryson exemplifies this consensus of his and preceding generations of scholars:

> From the beginnings of Christianity, women assumed an important role and enjoyed a place of choice in the Christian community. Paul praised several women who assisted him in his apostolic works. Women also possessed

the charism of prophecy. There is no evidence, however, that they exercised leadership roles in the community. Even though several women followed Jesus from the onset of his ministry in Galilee and figured among the privileged witnesses of his resurrection, no women appeared among the Twelve or even among the other apostles. As Epiphanius of Salamis pointed out, there have never been women presbyters.

Most Christians today, including clergy and scholars, presume that women played little or no role in the Jesus movement or in the early church as it spread throughout the Mediterranean. But women did in fact play crucial roles in the Jesus movement and were prominent leaders along with men in a wide variety of roles in the early church. The Christian church, of course, did not spring up suddenly into a well-defined organization with buildings, officials, and large congregations. In its earliest stages it is best understood as a social movement like any other. It was informal, often countercultural in tone, and was marked by a fluidity and flexibility that allowed women, slaves, and artisans to assume leadership roles.

Why, then, are we so unaware of the prominence of women in the birth of Christianity? Why does this powerful misperception continue to marginalize women in even the more enlightened branches of contemporary Christianity? The answers to these questions are complex, but they begin and end in cultural views about gender.

The societies to which early Christians belonged (like our society) held definite ideas about male and female roles. According to the gender stereotypes of the ancient Mediterranean, public speaking and public places were the sole prerogatives of males; private spaces, like the household, were the proper sphere for women's activities. Furthermore, society insisted that a respectable woman be concerned about her reputation for chastity and her seclusion in the household; modesty and reticence were accepted as testimony to her sexual restraint. Public activities and public roles seemed incompatible with modesty.

But the real women of that time led lives that were not as circumscribed as we might think. As householders they directed the men and women who lived and worked under their authority and supervised the production and distribution of the wealth. As businesswomen they traveled, bought, sold, and negotiated contracts. Women with sufficient wealth and social status acted as patrons of individuals and groups of lower social standing by providing financial assistance, recommendations to officials, and political protection.

In order to understand the role of women in the early church, it is necessary to understand what functions secular leaders performed and what kind of people they were. We know that leaders arbitrated disputes between members of communities, collected and distributed money, represented the interests of their community to city and imperial governments, financed communal feasts, made gifts of places of worship, taught, and arranged marriages. We also know that social status was the most important factor in the makeup of potential leaders.

For its part the church took its cue from society's leadership models. Mindful of their precarious status in Roman society, Christian communities looked to members with social status and wealth to be patrons and to function as their protectors. On a smaller scale, heads of households, who were accustomed to wielding authority and who had the stores of the household at their disposal, often became leaders of house churches.

In the ancient world, both men and women were patrons and householders. The social authority, economic power, and political influence associated with these roles were not restricted by gender. Even religious authority in Greek and Roman worship was not limited by gender. Women as well as men functioned as prophets and priests. Each of these social positions in Roman society—patron, householder, prophet, and priest—provided an individual with the kind of status, authority, and experience that could be translated into similar leadership roles in the Christian community.

Among ancient mosaics, paintings, statuary, dedicatory inscriptions, and funerary epitaphs, scholars have found numerous pieces of evidence for women's leadership. In literary sources such as the writings of the New Testament, letters, sermons, and the theological treatises of the early church, women's leadership is also well attested. In the literary sources, however, we can see shadows cast by the conflict over women's leadership and the prevailing social conventions about gender roles. The New Testament writers generally mentioned women leaders only as a passing fact while hurrying on to address more pressing concerns. When they paused for a longer discussion of women's leadership, as Paul did in his first letter to the Corinthian church, one catches tones of ambivalence and anxiety. In New Testament passages where women leaders played prominent roles, the male authors muted their contributions by the way they wrote their stories....

Women Patrons in the Gospels and Epistles

Phoebe, the minister (*diakonos*) of the congregation at Cenchreae, carried Paul's letter to the Romans. She was a woman of some wealth and social status and traveled to Rome in connection with her business and social life and the affairs of the Christian church. She had agreed to carry Paul's letter to the Romans, which he hoped would provide him entry into the Roman Christian community on his upcoming visit. In his letter Paul also introduced Phoebe to the Roman Christians, identifying her as his patron (*prostatis*). With this title Paul acknowledged her generosity and her support of him, then he urged the Roman Christians to help her in whatever way she required in repayment of his own debt of gratitude to her.

Joanna, the wife of Chuza, a steward in Herod's household, was a woman in a position to be a patron (Luke 8:1–3). It is intriguing to find her traveling with the group of evangelists that accompanied Jesus from village to village. Certainly her connections to the ruling Herodian family would have eased the way in any conflicts with minor local officials. It seems that she was a member of a group of women—Mary of Magdala and Susanna are also mentioned—whose patronage protected and supported the Jesus movement. Women as well positioned socially and economically as these often established patron-client relationships.

Paul concluded his letter to the Roman Christians with personal greetings to the leaders of the community there; some he knew by reputation, and others he had met in the course of his ministry. Among the leadership of the Roman Christian community were many women. Prisca, Junia, Mary, Tryphaena, Tryphosa, and Persis were women whom Paul addressed as co-workers; they had established the faith of the Christian community through their work of teaching and exhortation. Other prominent women greeted by Paul were Julia, Olympas, the mother of Rufus, who Paul says was a mother to him also, and the sister of Nereus. Of the twenty-eight prominent people whom Paul considered it politic to greet, ten were women.

Among these women leaders of the Roman congregation was a woman apostle, Junia, whom Paul hailed as "foremost among the apostles" (Rom. 16:7). She and her husband, Andronicus, traveled teaching and preaching from city to city. The turmoil and riots occasionally provoked by Christian preaching landed her and her husband in prison, where they encountered Paul. She was a heroine of the fourth-century Christian church, and John Chrysostom's elegant sermons invoked the image of Junia, the apostle, for the Christian women of Constantinople to emulate.

Wherever Christianity spread, women were leaders of house churches. Mary, the mother of John Mark, presided over a house church of Hellenistic Jews in Jerusalem. It was on her door that the astonished Peter knocked to announce to the Christians assembled there that he been liberated from prison by an angel (Acts 12:12–17). Apphia presided with two others as leaders of a house church in Colossae (Philem. 2). Nympha in Laodicea, Lydia in Thyatira, and Phoebe at Cenchreae supervised the congregations that met in their homes (Col. 4:15; Acts 16:15; Rom. 16:1).

In John's Gospel Mary Magdalene, not Peter, is presented as the model for discipleship. At a time when Peter and the other male disciples had fled, Mary stood loyally at the foot of the cross. She was not only the first witness to the resurrection but was directly commissioned to carry the message that Jesus had risen from the dead. The original version of the Gospel of John ends with the resurrection appearance to Mary Magdalene and her witness to the Twelve in chapter 20. The story of the appearance to "doubting Thomas" at the end of chapter 20 teaches early Christians to believe without seeing. "Now Jesus did many other signs in the presence of the disciples, which are not written in this book; but these are written that you may believe that Jesus is the Christ, the Son of God, and that believing you may have life" (John 20:30–31). A later copyist added another ending to the Book of John, chapter 21. In this chapter Peter was made the key witness of the resurrection when Jesus appeared to Peter and the disciples while they were on a fishing expedition in Galilee and commissioned Peter to be the shepherd of the flock. New Testament scholars have long puzzled about the reasons for this Gospel's two endings, chapter 20 highlighting the role of Mary Magdalene as witness to the resurrection and chapter 21 highlighting Peter. A recent proposal suggests that chapter 21 was appended at a time when the Johannine community was seeking to integrate with the Christian community that saw Peter as its head. Thus chapter 21 was added to bring the Johannine community within the pale of Petrine orthodoxy by emphasizing Peter's leadership.

Ambivalence and Conflict Over Women's Leadership

When Paul wanted to claim that he too was an apostle because he had seen the risen Lord, he listed the appearances of Jesus: "He was raised on the third day in accordance with the scriptures.... He appeared to Cephas [Peter], then to the twelve. Then he appeared to more than five hundred brethren at one time.... Last of all... he appeared to me" (1 Cor. 15:4–8). Paul omitted the announcement of the resurrected Christ to Mary even though it is attested in all four Gospels. Even some of the Gospel writers themselves betray signs of ambivalence over women's leadership. Matthew and Mark recount the women's witness to the resurrection, but the women's witness plays no role in the faith of the rest of the disciples. Luke reports that the women delivered their message to the rest of the disciples, "but these words seemed to them an idle tale, and they did not believe them" (Luke 24:12).

Women's leadership was a widespread phenomenon in the early Christian churches. Tensions were nevertheless generated by the disparity between the socially established fact of women's leadership and the strict Greco-Roman demarcation of gender roles. The mixed messages about Mary Magdalene's significance reflects the ambivalence about women's leadership as the Gospels were taking their final canonical form.

The second-century *Gospel of Mary,* discovered in 1945 among a collection of manuscripts at Nag Hammadi in upper Egypt, reveals a lost tradition about the leadership of Mary Magdalene and portrays Peter as her opponent. The scene described in the fragments of this Gospel took place on the Mount of Ascension after Jesus had departed into heaven. The disciples were disconsolate, depressed, and afraid until Mary stood up and addressed them all. She exhorted them to stop grieving, assured them that the grace of the Savior would be with them, and urged them to prepare for the work of preaching to which they had been called. Finally the disciples took heart and began to discuss the teachings of the Savior. After a while, at Peter's prompting, Mary began a long teaching discourse. When she had finished, she was quiet. Andrew was the first disciple to break the silence. He said, " 'Say what you [wish to] say about what she has said. I at least do not believe that the Savior said this. For certainly these teachings are strange ideas.' " Peter then broke in with a resentful challenge: " 'Did he really speak with a woman without our knowledge (and) not openly? Are we to turn about and all listen to her? Did he prefer her to us?' " Mary, hurt, turned to Peter and said, " 'My brother Peter, what do you think? Do you think I thought this up myself in my heart or that I am lying about the Savior?' " Finally Levi rebuked Peter:

> "Peter, you have always been hot-tempered. Now I see you are contending against the women like the adversaries. But if the Savior made her worthy, who are you indeed to reject her? Surely the Savior knows her very well. That is why he loved her more than us. Rather let us be ashamed and put on the perfect man and acquire him for ourselves as he commanded us, and

preach the gospel, not laying down any other rule or other law beyond what the Savior said."

When Levi finished his speech, the disciples set out on their teaching mission.

The ambivalence about women's role, implied in Peter's comment "Did he prefer her [*a woman*] to us?" indicates tensions between the existing fact of women's leadership in Christian communities and traditional Greco-Roman views about gender roles. The discomfort of the writer/editor of John with Mary Magdalene's prominence as a witness to the resurrection, and the other Gospel's similar ambivalence about the importance of the women at the empty tomb, betray the deep conflict over women's place that developed as Christianity was becoming established and the canon was being set.

There seems to be no doubt that women figured prominently in Jesus' life and ministry, both during his lifetime and after his resurrection when the first communities were formed and his message began to spread. If these accounts of women's important participation hadn't been grounded in intractable fact, they would not have survived in such a male-dominated culture. But because such independence and prominence on the part of women conflicted directly with the view of women's roles that pervaded Greco-Roman society, these traditions were ignored and submerged as much as possible in order to conform Christian teaching and practice to social convention.

Yet up until the mid-third century, only occasional sparks were generated by this clash between the social strictures on women's roles and the freedom women found in Christianity. For more than two hundred years Christianity was essentially a religion of the private sphere, practiced in the private space of the household rather than the public space of a temple. Its concerns were the domestic life of its community rather than the political life of the city. But during the third century Christianity began evolving toward its eventual form as a public religion. The burgeoning numbers of adherents and the new formality and dignity of the Christian liturgies meant that Christian participation was increasingly a public event. By the fourth century Christians were worshiping in their own public temples, called basilicas. During this period the friction between the social conventions about women's place and women's actual long-standing roles as house church leaders, prophets, evangelists, and even bishops precipitated virulent controversies. As Christianity entered the public sphere, male leaders began to demand the same subjugation of women in the churches as prevailed in Greco-Roman society at large. Their detractors reproached women leaders, often in strident rhetoric, for operating outside the domestic sphere and thus violating their nature and society's vital moral codes. How could they remain virtuous women, the critics demanded, while being active in public life?

With their survival instincts honed, Christian communities had gradually begun to assimilate themselves into Hellenistic culture. Jewish communities had done the same. In their increasing desire for credibility and legitimacy, the church leaders no longer resisted the tide of culture. Gradually they adopted Greco-Roman conventions regarding women's proper place and behavior. Both

Jewish and Christian writers, like their pagan counterparts, argued that it was inappropriate for women to hold positions of authority in the public sphere. For both Jewish and Christian theologians, as for pagan philosophers, the good woman was a chaste woman. In their view, female sexual promiscuity posed the greatest threat to women's character. Every aspect of female deportment should evince a concern for shame, expressed through reticence, deference toward men, and sexual restraint.

NO

Karen Armstrong

The Result: Eve

From almost the earliest days of Western Christianity, men started to see women as sexually dangerous and threatening, and in the grip of this fear they started a process which would eventually push women away from the male world into a separate world of their own. This might at first seem an odd development: neither Jesus nor Paul had pushed women away, but had worked closely with them and granted them full equality with men. However, later books of the New Testament, particularly the First Epistle to Timothy, which was probably written at the beginning of the 2nd century some sixty years after Paul's death, have a very different message. By this time Christianity is coping with the Gentile world of the late Empire and its terrors of sexual excess. A fear of sexuality had changed official Church policy toward women:

> I direct that women are to wear suitable clothes and to be dressed quietly and modestly without braided hair or gold and jewellery or expensive clothes; their adornment is to do the sort of good works that are proper for women who profess to be religious. During instruction, a woman should be quiet and respectful. I am not giving permission for a woman to teach or to tell a man what to do. A woman ought not to speak, because Adam was formed first and Eve afterwards, and it was not Adam who was led astray but the woman who was led astray and fell into sin. Nevertheless, she will be saved by childbearing, provided she lives a modest life and is constant in faith and love and holiness.

> — (1 Timothy 2:9–15)

When Paul had told the women in Corinth to keep quiet in Church, there was no hint of sexual disgust, nor was there any idea that women were potentially wicked (they just have to remember their place!). In 1 Timothy we have something different and sinister. Woman is not just inferior, she is wicked also, because of Eve. Eve fell into sin first and led Adam into sin. This is a theme which will recur again and again in the writings of the Early Fathers, and is also a deeply sexual idea.

The author of 1 Timothy begins his remarks about women with directions about the sort of clothes they should wear. Glancing through the works of the Fathers, it is extraordinary how much time they devoted to writing about women's dress—a concern that should have been beneath them. Diatribes about the way women load themselves with jewelry, cake their faces with makeup and douse themselves with perfume crop up with extreme frequency. One of the first was written by Tertullian in the 3rd century. In a treatise written to his "best beloved sisters" in the faith, Tertullian glides from affection and respect to an astonishing attack:

> If there dwelt upon earth a faith as great as we expect to enjoy in heaven, there wouldn't be a single one of you, best beloved sisters, who, from the time when she had first "known the Lord" and learned the truth about her own condition, would have desired too festive (not to say ostentatious) a style of dress. Rather she would have preferred to go about in humble garb, and go out of her way to affect a meanness of appearance, walking about as Eve, mourning and repentant, so that by her penitential clothes she might fully expiate what she has inherited from Eve: the shame, I mean, of the first sin, and the odium of human perdition. *In pains and anxieties dost thou bear children, woman; and toward thine husband is thy inclination and he lords it over thee.* And do you not know that you are each an Eve? The sentence of God on this sex of yours lives in this age: the guilt must of necessity live too. *You* are the devil's gateway: *you* are the unsealer of that forbidden tree: *you* are the first deserter of the divine law: *you* are she who persuaded him whom the devil was not valiant enough to attack. *You* destroyed so easily God's image, man. On account of *your* desert—that is death—even the Son of God had to die. And do you think about adorning yourself over and above your tunics of skins.

> — (*On Female Dress*, I:i)

It is exactly the same complex of ideas that we find, less clearly articulated, in 1 Timothy: female appearance, Eve, childbirth. It seems at first sight strange that this enormous attack—each woman is completely responsible for destroying men and crucifying Christ—should start and finish with something as apparently unimportant as women's clothes. What prompts Tertullian's virulent attack is pure irrational fear. As the treatise goes on, we see that it is wholly about sex. Woman is as much of a temptation to man as Eve was to Adam, not because she is offering him an apple but because she is offering the forbidden fruit of sex. She can cause a man to lust after her just by walking around looking beautiful. "You must know," Tertullian insists, "that in the eye of perfect Christian modesty, having people lusting after you with carnal desire is not a desirable state of affairs but is something execrable" (II, ii). He is thinking of Jesus' words when he said that a man who looks at a woman lustfully has already committed adultery in his heart. Jesus was not making a particular issue of lust here, but was illustrating his admirable religious insight that mere external conformity to a set of rules is not enough for the truly religious man. It is the attitude in his heart that counts, not a meticulous performance of burdensome commandments. Tertullian twists this potentially liberating idea into a truly frightening view of the moral world. "For as soon as a man has lusted after your beauty, he has in his mind already committed the sin which his lust was imagining and he perished because of this, and you [women] have been made the sword that destroys him" (II, ii). A man's lustful glance may be entirely involuntary, but he still perishes. The woman is guilty of destroying him just as Eve was guilty of destroying Adam. She may have had absolutely no intention of tempting him—she may not even realize that she has caused any lustful thoughts at all, but she is still guilty. Both the man and the woman have sinned even though what happened was quite beyond their control.

Tertullian is quite clear that women are to blame: "even though you may be free of the actual crime, you are not free of the odium attaching to it" (II, ii). This means that, far from dressing up and making herself look pretty and desirable, a woman has a duty to look as unattractive as she possibly can:

> ... it is time for you to know that you must not merely reject the pageantry of fictitious and elaborate beauty, but even the grace and beauty you enjoy naturally must be obliterated by concealment and negligence, because this is just as dangerous to the people who glance at you. For even though comeliness is not to be censured exactly, because it is certainly a physical felicity and a kind of goodly garment of the soul, but it is to be feared, because of the injury and violence it inflicts on the men who admire you.
>
> — (II, ii)

This is an oft-repeated theme for Tertullian. In his treatise *On the Veiling of Virgins*, it surfaces in a particularly disturbed form. St. Paul had said that women had to wear veils in Church "because of the angels." Here he was referring to the legend of the "Sons of God," the "angels" who lusted after earthly women and came down from heaven to mate with them.

> For if it is "because of the angels"—those beings of whom we read as having fallen from God and from heaven because of lusting after women—who can presume that it was bodies already defiled and relics of human lust which the angels yearned after, but that rather that they were inflamed for virgins, whose bloom pleads an excuse for human lust? ... So perilous a face, then, ought to be kept shaded, when it has cast stumbling stones even so far as heaven. This face, when it stands in the presence of God, at whose bar it already stands accused of driving the angels from their heavenly home, may blush before the other angels who didn't fall as well.
>
> — (*On the Veiling of Virgins*, VII)

There is something extremely unpleasant here. It is not simply the view that sex always defiles a woman, so that afterward she is merely a "relic of human lust," a memory of a shameful act. There is also a horrible leering prurience about unsullied virgins being especially lustworthy, and there is a real terror in the idea that a woman's beauty is so dangerous and powerful that it can even cause angels to abandon heaven and fall irretrievably into sin. If even angels are not safe from a woman's beauty, then what hope is there for mere men? A woman must keep her "perilous" face hidden. She must disguise her beauty, or she will destroy men just as surely as Eve destroyed Adam. Already, years before Augustine would finally formulate for the West the doctrine of Original Sin, the emotional trinity which exists at the heart of that doctrine has been formed in the Christian neurosis of Tertullian: woman, sex and sin are fused together in his mind indissolubly. The only hope for man is that women hide themselves away—veil their faces from man's lustful eyes, hide their beauty by disfiguring themselves and make themselves ugly and sexless in the penitential garb that befits each woman as an Eve.

Christian men were told to inhabit a separate world from women. When Jerome wants to defend his friendship with the noble Roman lady St. Paula, who became one of his staunchest disciples, he stresses the fact that he was scrupulous about keeping away from women:

> Before I became acquainted with the household of the saintly Paula all Rome was enthusiastic about me. Almost everyone concurred in judging me worthy of the highest office in the Church. My words were always on the lips of Damasus of blessed memory. Men called me saintly: men called me humble and eloquent. Did I ever enter a house of any woman who was included to wantonness? Was I ever attracted by silk dresses, flashing jewels, painted faces, display of gold? No other matron in Rome could dominate my mind but one who mourned and fasted, who was squalid with dirt, almost blind with weeping. All night long she would beg the Lord for mercy, and often the sun found her still praying. The psalms were her music, the Gospels her conversation: continence was her luxury, her life a fast. No other could give me pleasure, but one whom I never saw munching food.

> — (Letter xiv: To Asella)

For Jerome the only good woman is a sexually repulsive one. Paula has made herself "repellent." When Jerome went to visit her, he felt disgusted by her and his virtue was quite safe. He was in no sexual danger. Paula herself would have been delighted by this appalling description; she was only one of the new breed of Roman ladies who were taking up the ascetic life and mutilating themselves physically and spiritually in this way. This pattern of mutilation is one that recurs in all sorts of psychological and physical ways among the women of Western Christianity. By telling a woman that she should not be physically attractive if she wanted to consort with men and still be virtuous, Jerome and his like were deeply damaging the women who obeyed them.

If a woman is not repulsive then she must be isolated and ostracized. In his letter to Nepotian, a young priest, Jerome tells him that he must be careful to keep himself away from women, even the most innocent and virtuous women, unless they are sexually repellent:

> A woman's foot should seldom or never cross the threshold of your humble lodging. To all maidens and to all Christ's virgins show the same disregard or the same affection. Do not remain under the same roof with them; do not trust your chastity. You cannot be a man more saintly than David, or more wise than Solomon. Remember always that a woman drove the tiller of Paradise from the garden that had been given him. If you are ill let one of the brethren attend you, or else your sister or your mother or some woman of universally approved faith. If there are no persons marked out by ties of kinship or reputation for chastity, the Church maintains many elderly women who by their services can both help you and benefit themselves, so that even your sickness may bear fruit in almsgiving.... There is a danger for you in the ministrations of one whose face you are continually watching. If in the course of your clerical duties you have to visit a widow or a virgin,

never enter the house alone.... Never sit alone without witnesses with a woman in a quiet place. If there is anything intimate she wants to say, she has a nurse or some elderly virgin at home, some widow or married woman. She cannot be so cut off from human society as to have no one but yourself to whom she can trust her secret.

— (Letter lii)

Merely sitting with a woman or letting her nurse you is to put yourself in grave danger. Women, therefore, have to be shunned, even if they are in trouble and need help. A woman is to be avoided and left alone in a world which is quite apart from men.

It becomes part of the advice that is given to your aspirants of both sexes who want to lead virtuous Christian lives. Men are to shun women, and women are urged to withdraw from the world and take themselves off into a separate and totally female existence. Inevitably that will be maiming, even without the fasting and the deliberate physical mutilation that the woman is urged to undertake in the name of physical penance. Simply by being deprived of the realities of the male world, by being deprived of education and normal activity, women were only being able to function in half the world. However, the most destructive thing of all was the sexual disgust which drove women into their separate worlds. There is a continual process of repulsion which we have already seen in Tertullian, a process which is neurotic and probably not even conscious. You begin speaking lovingly to your "best beloved sisters" and you end up castigating "Eve." Jerome has exactly the same reaction. Here he is writing to a young girl who has written asking for his advice about the Christian life. Jerome urges her to lock herself away from the world. Simply by walking around she will inspire male lust, however virtuous she is. In fact, virtue itself can turn a man on:

What will you do, a healthy young girl, dainty, plump, rosy, all afire amid the fleshpots, amid the wines and baths, side by side with married women and with young men. Even if you refuse to give what they ask for, you may think that the asking is evidence of your beauty. A libertine is all the more ardent when he is pursuing virtue and thinks that the unlawful is especially delightful. Your very robe, coarse and sombre though it be, betrays your unexpressed desires if it be without crease, if it be trailed upon the ground to make you seem taller, if your vest be slit on purpose to let something be seen within, hiding that which is unsightly and disclosing that which is fair. As you walk along your shiny black shoes by their creaking give an invitation to young men. Your breasts are confined in strips of linen, and your chest in imprisoned by a tight girdle. Your hair comes down over your forehead or over your ears. Your shawl sometimes drops, so as to leave your white shoulders bare, and then, as though unwilling to be seen, it hastily hides what it unintentionally revealed. And when in public it hides the face in a pretence of modesty, with a harlot's skill it shows only those features which give men when shown more pleasure.

— (Letter cxvii)

It is not surprising that Jerome doesn't let himself near women, because this letter shows him to be sexually obsessed and one of the great voyeurs of all time. He has obviously studied women minutely, and is pruriently eager to pick up each and every movement, every mannerism. He is even excited by the creaking of a woman's shoe. Watching a woman walk down the street, he immediately imagines her underwear; his eyes are skinned to catch a glimpse of her white shoulders. It is taken for granted that she is teeming with lust. Every movement, intentional or unintentional, is a sign of her "unexpressed" sexual desire. What Jerome is doing is over-sexualizing women because of his own sexual repression. *He* is rampantly frustrated so he tells women that *they* are sexually insatiable. He has forgotten here that he is writing to a good little girl, who has asked him for advice. He is so lost in his fantasy that by the end of the paragraph he is comparing her to a harlot. In just the same way Tertullian begins by calling his readers "best beloved" and ends by calling them "Eve." Christian love for women easily modulates into sexual hatred.

Woman then is man's deepest enemy. She is the harlot who will lure a man to his doom because she is Eve, the eternal temptress. Just as Original Sin comes to be linked with sex, so woman is Eve because she is sexual. Jerome's pathological disgust with sex is shown in his letter to Furia, who had written to seek his advice about getting married again:

> The trials of marriage you have learned in the married state: you have been surfeited to nausea as though with the flesh of quails. Your mouth has tasted the bitterest of gall, you have voided the sour unwholesome food, you have relieved a heaving stomach. Why would you put into it again something which has already proved harmful to you. *The dog is turned to his own vomit again and the sow that was washed to her wallowing in the mire.*
>
> — (2 Peter 2:22)

What must Furia have felt like when she received this letter? Again she seems to have been a virtuous woman, a genuine and enthusiastic Christian, but because of her sexuality she would have been made to feel foul and sinful. Jerome is clear that she is sexually obsessed and voracious. As a widow she must be inflamed by the "pleasures of the past." The widow "knows the delights that she has lost and she must quench the fire of the devil's shafts with the cold streams of fast and vigil." Jerome sees a woman as having such strong sexual cravings that if she dresses attractively she is crying out for sex, her "whole body reveals incontinence." Again he sees her as luring poor unsuspecting men into sex and sin. Woman is Antichrist:

> What have rouge and white lead to do on a Christian woman's face? The one simulates the natural red of cheeks and lips, the other the whiteness of the face and neck. They are fires to inflame young men, stimulants of lustful desire, plain evidence of an unchaste mind. How can a woman weep for her sins when tears lay her skin bare and make furrows on her face? Such adorning is not of the Lord, it is the mask of Antichrist.
>
> — (Letter liv)

Reading this one might assume that Jerome is writing about prostitutes whose garish makeup advertises their availability. In fact here, as elsewhere, he was writing about ordinary Roman matrons who used frequently to wear cosmetics at this time.

This hostility and fear of women's sexual powers we see again and again. Augustine sees danger even in the virtuous women of the Old Testament, sometimes with ludicrous results. Trying to come to terms with the sex lives of the Patriarchs, he presents Abraham and Isaac copulating with their wives dutifully but with enormous distaste, in order to obey God's command to found the Chosen Race. They would far rather have abstained. Abraham, Augustine says, had to go on copulating with his wife Sarah for years before he managed with God's help to conceive his son Isaac. Abraham, who seems to have been a highly sexed man, would have read all this with considerable bewilderment. Isaac, Augustine continues, was more fortunate. The Bible only mentions his having sex once, and he was lucky enough to produce the twins,' Esau and Jacob, straight off so he never had to do it again. When he came to Jacob, however, who had twelve sons, Augustine is in a bit of a quandary. This looks like zeal in excess of duty. However, he decides that Jacob would gladly have followed the example of Isaac and only had sex once in his life, but his two wives, Leah and Rachel, kept pestering him because of their excessive lust and sexual greed, forcing the holy Patriarch to abandon his high ideals. Yet Rachel and Leah are good women. For Augustine, as for his predecessors Jerome and Tertullian, all women, however virtuous, are men's enemies. "What is the difference," he wrote to a friend, "whether it is in a wife or a mother, it is still Eve the temptress that we must beware of in any woman" (Letter 243, 10).

There is no room for this enemy in the male world. Indeed, there is no room for her at all in God's plan. Augustine seems puzzled about why God made women at all. It is not possible that she was a friend and helpmate to man. After all, "if it was good company and conversation that Adam needed, it would have been much better arranged to have two men together, as friends, not a man and a woman" (*De Genesis ad Litteram* IX, v, 9). The only reason he made women was for the purposes of childbearing. Luther shared this view. The only vocation he could see for a woman was to have as many children as possible, so that all the more people could be led to the Gospel. It didn't matter what effect this might have on women: "If they become tired or even die, that does not matter. Let them die in childbirth—that is why they are there." There was no other way that a woman could help man. Her place was "in the home" (the famous phrase was actually coined by Luther). There was no place for her in the male world of affairs. Similarly Calvin, who is virtually the first Christian theologian to speak favorably of women, might insist that woman *was* created to be a companion to man and that marriage was instituted by God precisely for that companionship, but his Geneva was entirely male dominated, and women's role as a companion was confined to the domestic female world of the home. Protestantism shared fully the misogyny that the Fathers had bequeathed to the Catholic Church. When Lutherans at Wittenberg discussed the question whether women were really human beings at all, they were not discussing anything new. Theologians had always been perplexed about women's place in God's plan. Thomas Aquinas was as puzzled as Augustine had been about why God had made her at all and decided that woman was a freak in nature:

> As regards the individual nature, woman is defective and misbegotten, for the active force in the male seed tends to the production of a perfect likeness in the masculine sex; while the production of woman comes from a defect in the active force or from some material indisposition, or even from some external influence.

— (Summa Theologica, IV, Part I. Quaest. XCII, art 1, 2)

It does not help that Aquinas decides that womankind in *general* is human. The "individual nature" of women is a defect, an idea he picked up from Aristotle's biology. The norm is the male. Every woman is a failed man.

Women are therefore emotionally excluded from the male world, for all that Paul had originally insisted upon sexual equality. Even now that we are breaking into the male preserves we still tend to feel ill at ease in it. Recent surveys show that college women are even more afraid of success today than they were when Betty Friedan did her original survey in the early 1960s. Dons at Oxford and Cambridge have complained about the quality of women who are gaining admission to the colleges that used to be all-male. They have asked schools to stop sending them girls who are polite, efficient and well-behaved, and instead send them students who will argue with them as aggressively as the boys do. Breaking into the male world is not simply a matter of opportunity. It is a question of attitude on the part of both men and women. Women are still ambiguous and fearful in these new male worlds that have recently been opened to them. They are still maintaining their guilty apologetic stance. For centuries they have been excluded not simply because they were supposed to be inferior but because they inspired sexual fear and disgust in men. Marilyn French's novel *The Women's Room* puts this humorously when she imagines the male world of Harvard terrified to admit women in case they drip menstrual blood all over this pure male preserve. Where Moslems have traditionally locked their women into harems inside their homes because they owned and valued them, men in the Christian West have locked their women outside their lives because they hate them, exiling women to a lonely, separate world.

POSTSCRIPT

Did Christianity Liberate Women?

The Bible and many other sources provide evidence of women's active roles during the early years of what would later be called Christianity. Eusebius (263–339 C.E.), a Greek Christian and an intimate friend of Emperor Constantine, wrote the only surviving account of the first 300 years of Christian Church history. Sometimes called the Christian Herodotus, he certainly earned the title Father of Ecclesiastical (church) History. A translation of his work by G. A. Williamson, *The History of the Church* (Dorset Press, 1984), is easy to obtain.

In the early years of Christianity, different schools of what would later become theology existed side by side. One of these was Gnosticism, a mystical worldview that predominated in Greece and Rome. Remarkable for its androgynous view of God as father and mother, Gnosticism was condemned as the first heresy primarily because of its insistence that God only appeared to suffer and die in the person of Jesus. Four Gnostic gospels, part of what scholars call the Nag Hammadi library, found in Egypt in the 1940s, are available in Marvin W. Meyer's translation in *The Secret Teachings of Jesus* (Vintage Books, 1986).

A documentary sampling of women in history from the ancient Greeks to the modern Victorians may be found in *Not in God's Image* edited by Julia O'Faolain and Lauro Martines (Harper & Row, 1973). Including both religious and nonreligious writings, this book places Western attitudes toward women in a broader context.

Feminist theory points to an Eve/Mary split within Christianity. According to this thesis, women are offered only two roles—Eve, the temptress whose disobedience brought about the loss of Eden, or Mary, the mother of Jesus whose obedience to the will of God made possible human salvation. The two extremes represented by these roles seem to exclude all living women. If Mary is held up as an ideal—as she clearly has been during certain periods of Christian history—then women, if they remain pure and demure, may share in the honor accorded Mary. However, to slip even slightly from the perfection embodied by Mary is to fall all the way to the disdain accorded Eve. There is no middle ground. Film historians call this the virgin/whore split and cite numerous examples of film heroines who play out one of these two roles. Students may be interested in reading Molly Haskell's *From Reverence to Rape: The Treatment of Women in the Movies* (Penguin Books, 1974) and Marjorie Rosen's *Popcorn Venus* (Avon Books, 1973), which explore this theme.

Did the Roman Empire Collapse Due to Its Own Weight?

YES: Averil Cameron, from *The Later Roman Empire: A.D. 284–430* (Harvard University Press, 1993)

NO: Derek Williams, from *Romans and Barbarians: Four Views from the Empire's Edge, First Century A.D.* (St. Martin's Press, 1998)

ISSUE SUMMARY

YES: Historian Averil Cameron states that, although the barbarian invasions played a role in the demise of the Roman Empire, internal political, social, and economic problems were primarily responsible for its fall.

NO: Writer Derek Williams counters that the barbarian tribes, once Rome's allies, were principally liable for the empire's fall.

Using periodization, historians can illuminate the past and note significant changes in humanity's progress from one time to another. The European Renaissance, which marks the transition from the medieval to the modern world, is one such example. The decline and fall of the Roman Empire is another, because it notes the end of the Greco-Roman classical era and the beginning of the Middle Ages. Greek and the Roman cultures provided Western civilization with some of its greatest historical and cultural endowments. Thus, the demise of these cultures continues to interest Western historians.

Not until the Italian Renaissance, with its renewed interest in classical antiquity, did the fall of the Roman Empire earn an official place in the world of scholarship, which opened the debate on what was responsible for the empire's demise. Humanist scholar Francesco Petrarca (Petrarch) (1304–1374) blamed internal problems for the empire's fall. In the next century, however, Niccolò Machiavelli (1469–1527), perhaps Europe's first modern political scientist, blamed the constant attacks of neighboring barbarians, which eventually wore down the empire and caused its collapse.

Modern historical scholarship on the fall of Rome began with Edward Gibbon (1737–1794), who injected another variable into the mix. In his multivolume work, *The Decline and Fall of the Roman Empire* (first published between 1776 and 1782), Gibbon stated that the rise of Christianity may have played a significant role in Rome's collapse. Because he was a product of Europe's Enlightenment era and shared its skepticism regarding the effects of organized religion on a civilization's progress, his focus on Christianity has since been overemphasized. In general, he took a fatalistic approach to the empire's demise, stating that "the decline of Rome was the natural and inevitable effect of immoderate greatness."

More recently, countless reasons have been given for Rome's fall: the disintegration of the imperial economy, agricultural problems caused by climatic changes, manpower shortages due to lead poisoning from the empire's water pipes, destruction of the leadership class through imperial executions and civil wars, racial mixing that diluted the old Roman stock, the drain of gold and silver, widespread slavery that made the rich richer and the poor poorer, and a class war waged by peasant soldiers against the ruling class. This list is not complete, but it does testify to the interest historians have taken in the fall of Rome.

While recognizing the probability of multiple causation in most historical events, twentieth-century historians continue to debate the reasons for Rome's demise by analyzing and evaluating the role of internal and external forces. By applying the Roman experience to the rise and fall of other civilizations—past and present—contemporary historians continue to revitalize the debate.

In this issue, we have an opportunity to test that hypothesis. While acknowledging the role of the barbarian tribes in Rome's demise, Averil Cameron argues that Rome generally collapsed due to forces of its own making. Derek Williams counters by emphasizing the role that the barbarians played in the process.

The Later Roman Empire: A.D. 284–430

The Late Roman State

... Entry into the imperial service was extremely attractive for men of mid-dling status from the municipal class, since these positions now carried military ranks and entitlement to provisions..., and, still more important, the oppor-tunity in most cases for substantial fees... on the side. Emperors therefore legislated to stem the flow of recruits from the cities, where they were needed in order to perform their municipal responsibilities: 'all those who have aspired to imperial service... which is not their due are to be released from that service and returned to their own orders and offices.' The trend was already apparent in Constantine's day. However, the general approach of the emperors was prag-matic: success was rewarded or at least recognized, and if a man had managed to stay away from his city for long enough the situation was *de facto* accepted.

The government responded in the same way to the fact that many peo-ple were prepared to pay large amounts in order to secure themselves such advantageous positions: by the fifth century, payment for office had become the norm, and so in AD 444 Theodosius II regularized it by law. Some sections of the imperial service were far more desirable than others. The corps of im-perial couriers... were for instance in a position to exact substantial fees for their services; these posts were accordingly so desirable by the end of the fourth century that the right of nomination to appointment had to be controlled by legislation. The eunuchs of the bedchamber... also had great opportunities for enrichment by receiving bribes and exploiting inside information, and by the early fifth century the highest of them had acquired top senatorial rank. Court eunuchs were of course in a special category; in general, access to office was ob-tained by a combination of influence, recommendation, and the expenditure of cash, practices which the lucky candidate then continued in other spheres or practised in reverse once he was appointed.

An army of officials—the late Roman system looks at first sight like cor-ruption run riot. Everything was for sale, including government.... Much of the apparatus of a modern state was simply non-existent: there was for instance no police force to seek out criminals or enforce the law and no organized sys-tem of legal advice or representation (though there were innumerable laws to be obeyed). There was no banking system as such, and health was a matter for whichever agencies were available, from doctors for the few to sorcerers and holy men for the many; though education received more attention from the state, the benefits were reserved for an elite. There were many state employees in the later Roman empire, but when compared with the proportion of citizens directly employed by the state in modern developed societies their number pales into insignificance. A large majority of the population was not directly 'employed' (working for wages) at all, but belonged either to the class of patrons, especially as wealthy landowners, or dependants (slaves, tenants, *coloni*, [tenant farmers]); the latter class also included the urban poor, sustained by public grants and religious charity. ...

Late Roman Economy and Society

Inflation continued to rise precipitously during the reign of Constantine, irrespective of Diocletian's attempts to control prices and to reform the coinage. The main base of the economy still lay in agriculture, and while Constantine imposed new taxes on senators and traders, little could be done to bring about a general turn-round. Neither general considerations nor such indicators as there are would suggest that the actual shrinkage of the economic base which probably took place during the mid-third century had been significantly reversed. Even if we are sceptical about the very large figures for the size of the late Roman army in the literary sources, the state would still be hard pressed to finance it. It seems unlikely, moreover, that the level of taxation could really have been raised on a significant scale, simply because most of those paying taxes had no effective way of increasing their surplus. Nor—though the reverse is often claimed—could seizure of temple treasures by Constantine really have accounted for wide-scale economic recovery...

There are many complaints in late Roman sources about the impoverishment of *curiales* [townsmen], and about rapacious tax-collectors. Motivated by political advantage or traditional expectations, emperors still resorted to *en bloc* remission of tax arrears, as Constantine did in Gaul; whatever the actual reason, this indicates a system not under full control. Yet to set against these negative indicators there are also contrary signs. The first stages of a return to collection and delivery in gold of the main taxes, the poll-tax and the *iugatio*, can be seen in the late fourth century, though it took several generations to complete the process. Many landowners, especially the senatorial class in the west, amassed enormous quantities of wealth and land. . . .

The church also became wealthy from a variety of sources, which now included inheritance. Many Christians gave large sums to the church and a good deal of expenditure went on church building and works of Christian charity, while the growing fashion for pilgrimage to the Holy Land stimulated local trade and settlement. Some sectors of society were very rich, and [Roman historian] Ammianus's many scathing remarks about the contemporary love of display and extravagance are not wholly confined to the senatorial class. . . .

One striking feature of the fourth century is the tendency of landowners to amass estates and wealth on an enormous scale. This manifests itself particularly in relation to senatorial estates in the late fourth and early fifth centuries, on which we are well informed. Most impressive is the wealth of the younger Melania and her husband Pinianus, whose estates were spread throughout the western provinces, from Italy to Britain, Gaul and North Africa. No one in Rome could afford to buy their palace on the Caelian when they put it up for sale, and they were able to send 45,000 pieces of gold to the poor at one time, 100,000 coins at another, and to distribute funds to Mesopotamia, Syria, Palestine and Egypt. Even so, their wealth may not have put them in the richest category, although their property at Thagaste in North Africa had silver and bronze workshops, was larger than the town itself and included two bishoprics. The fifth-century Greek historian Olympiodorus says that the richest senators had annual incomes of 4,000 pounds of gold, and middling ones 1,000 to 1,500 pounds.... Petronius Probus ... was another wealthy senator with estates all over the Roman world, and Symmachus, though not one of the richest by any means, had nineteen houses and estates scattered through Italy, Sicily and North Africa, and spent 2,000 pounds of gold on the games given during his son's praetorship. Though by no means all senators were as rich as these, the general phenomenon of large estates had both economic and political implications. It revealed a dangerous concentration of wealth in the west in private hands, especially in the fifth century, while the government itself became increasingly weak. In the east, by contrast, senatorial fortunes were smaller, partly in view of the very recent development of the Senate of Constantinople and the prominence in it of men of much more ordinary origins.

How and when did their owners acquire these large estates? One answer must be that they did so in the troubled conditions in the western provinces in the later third century and after. The families of the late Roman senatorial aristocracy were not all as old as they liked to pretend, and much land was either deserted or ravaged by warfare, making it easy and cheap to acquire. Another question involves the impact of such conglomerations on neighbouring settlement, their use of local labour and their effects on the local economy. Finally, the question of how they were themselves managed affects our understanding of late Roman trade and commerce generally, as well as that of slavery *vis-à-vis* free labour in the late empire.

Slavery as an institution (we are here talking mainly about the use of slaves in agricultural production) has assumed a major place in all discussions of the late Roman economy. In particular, the role of slavery in the economic systems of the ancient world has been a major theme of Marxist historiography, which has always seen a connection between the existence of classical slavery and the fact that classical antiquity eventually came to an end. Recent discussion has moved the issue onto a more sophisticated level. Thus the notion of a typical 'slave mode of production' has come under heavy criticism, and it has been pointed out that chattel slavery on large estates was never the norm outside Italy, and even there only for a short period and in limited ways. At the same time, it is now clear that contrary to what had been claimed, slaves were not replaced by free labour in the late empire but continued to exist in large numbers. But since there has also been a persistent assumption among historians (despite comparative evidence from other historical periods) that slave-run estates must inevitably have been more productive, it is necessary to ask not just whether slaves were still used on the large estates, but also how they were used and how their condition differed from that of free men.

Late Roman agricultural slavery does not seem to have been organized along the lines familiar from the American Deep South. Nevertheless, the younger Melania had many slaves on her estates; while she freed eight thousand of them, this was perhaps more as part of the process of liquidation of property than from Christian conviction, and many were also sold with the land. Melania had the problems of a landowner as well as the convictions of an ascetic, and she was worried when the slaves on certain estates rebelled as to whether the unrest would spread; moreover, freeing eight thousand slaves would have created considerable local problems in itself. Slaves could themselves be tenants, but how often they occupied this role is unfortunately very difficult to establish; we must allow for a good deal of variation, both between estates and between regions. Rural slavery had never in fact been a general phenomenon in the empire, and while it is attested in late Roman Italy, Spain and Asia Minor, and the islands, it does not appear in the Egyptian papyri. We very rarely have direct information about individual estates, still less generalizations or of course figures for larger areas, and Palladius, the author of a fourth-century manual on agriculture, makes no mention of slave labour in the fields. However, his descriptions of a typical complex and diversified estate, with villa, vineyards, gardens, cattle and fields, suggest central organization of the work rather than a simple parcelling out of the land into tenant-farmed plots; so do the mosaics depicting the busy life of North African villas like that of a certain Julius from Carthage, now in the Bardo Museum at Tunis. This does not however in itself imply the use of slaves. One of many such villas in the west was at Mungersdorf near Cologne, while in Britain, where there was considerable expenditure on villas in the fourth century, there was also local variation in their economy, combined with interdependence on local towns, as is also attested for villas in the area round Trier in Germany. By the end of the fourth century, however, in Britain as in Gaul, there is evidence of a degree of destruction and decline which must be connected with the barbarian invasions, even if this is not certain in an individual case.

In any case, the degree to which ancient agricultural writers are a reliable guide to real economic activity at any period is itself problematic. Symmachus writes as though slaves are the norm, and Augustine describes the practice of slave-traders who kidnapped unsuspecting villagers to sell; poor parents often sold the children they could not rear. But hired labour had been used alongside slaves for centuries, especially at peak times like harvest, and even the Italian *latifundia* in the main period of so-called slave production seem to have been engaged in mixed farming rather than specialization for cash crops.

Much remains obscure about slaves in the late empire, and their importance should neither be overestimated nor minimized. We need to remember that they now became plentiful at certain times through conquest (though barbarian prisoners of war could also be treated as *coloni*), and that following Roman precedent, slavery continued as a well-established institution in the medieval west. Yet, ... the status of agricultural slaves and free *coloni* gradually came closer and closer together. As for estate management in the late empire, it no doubt varied greatly. While we should not think in lurid terms of slave chain gangs, we should also not give up the idea that central management ('domanial farming') continued to exist.

It is nevertheless risky to attempt to argue from the presence or absence of slavery to the level of production. But another feature of the existence of large estates had a more direct impact on the general economy. This is the fact that many dealings will have taken place between one estate and another of the same landowner, or through arrangements with his friends and relations, and so will have by-passed the open market altogether. The nobles needed money and reckoned their income in gold; but much of their production went to maintain their estates and their labour forces, while other goods were given as gifts, in accordance with the social expectations of their class. Rich landowners did not need to pay others for transport either—they owned their own ships, just as when they needed anything, they called upon all kinds of skilled craftsmen from their own estates. The evidence for market exchange as such, as it affected this class, is elusive: there was much arranging to be done by *negotiatores*, and we hear something about that in the sources, but the *negotiatores* themselves might be middle men rather than traders in their own right. Furthermore, as the lands of the great landowners increased in number and extent, the place left for markets in general will have been correspondingly reduced. As the church acquired estates it inevitably took over the same system and the same habits— after all, most bishops came from exactly this class of rich landowners themselves. We see the Alexandrian church engaging in trading ventures, just as we read of landowners profiteering from agricultural sales. Finally, the pattern of non-market exchange was also built into the state system of supply and distribution in kind. The state had even taken the initiative in setting up its own means of manufacturing necessary items such as arms, and even if these were far from being factories in any modern sense, but rather conglomerations of craftsmen, they nevertheless circumvented the very limited processes of market exchange which did exist.

Patronage, dependence, 'tied labour', all these are characteristic of the late Roman economic system, and all are factors which tell against growth on any real scale. A further deep-rooted feature of late Roman exchange and distribution which points in the same direction needs to be noted, namely the provision of free food supplies to the population of Rome and on the same model to Constantinople. This was a long-established practice which entailed that much of the grain production of North Africa and Egypt was in practice commandeered for the purpose as part of the land tax. In Rome, the distribution went back to the late Republic. In the fourth century AD, as before, the ration was given out on the strength of tickets, by now both hereditary and saleable. Following precedent, Constantine extended the distribution to Constantinople, with eighty thousand destined recipients, and by the later fourth century these tickets too ... had become hereditary and saleable; thus it is by no means clear that those properly entitled to the ration actually received it. However, those who built houses in Constantinople were automatically entitled to be among the recipients. Not just corn, or bread, but also oil and pork were distributed free in Rome, the latter being levied from other towns in Italy. A similar system operated in Alexandria in the third century, and may have been taken over later by the church. . . .

Many factors therefore combined to depress the level of large-scale market exchange, in addition to general considerations based on the agrarian society of the Roman empire and the nature of ancient towns. Trade has recently been receiving more attention from economic historians of the ancient world, as is clear for instance from the second edition of [M. I.] Finley's *The Ancient Economy,* published in 1985; this allows a larger place to trade than was the case in the very influential first edition. At the end of our period, the evidence of late Roman pottery, a relatively recent subject of serious study for archaeologists, seems to suggest that long-distance exchange, for example between Vandal Africa, Italy and Constantinople in the fifth century, took place on a greater scale than had been previously imagined on the basis of the literary evidence. This is extremely important in relation to the highly contentious issue of the decline of the west and the transition to the medieval world, though it is not at all clear for instance how much of that exchange was accounted for by trade as such; furthermore, the debate has focused mainly on the period after the substantial barbarian settlements in Gaul and the Vandal conquest of North Africa in AD 430. But it is now clear that the cities of North Africa were in a surprisingly flourishing condition in the fourth century, while the later fourth century in Palestine and Syria represented a time of clear population growth and increasing prosperity. Local conditions were extremely important here as elsewhere: the limestone *massif* of northern Syria was particularly suited to olive cultivation on a large scale, and was exploited in this way, though not apparently as exclusively as formerly argued, while in the desert of the Negev in southern Palestine irrigation systems which had been in existence since the Nabataean period, permitting mixed farming and working monasteries with market gardens, contributed to support a larger population than at any time until the present day. At Antioch, one of the few cities for which we have detailed information from the sources, it is clear that the population included many different sorts of craftsmen and traders, though on what scale or for whom they worked is less clear. Scholarship is moving fast in this area, and generalizations about the late Roman economy are as yet necessarily crude; nevertheless, we can at least now begin to set real archaeological evidence with more confidence against the copious and potentially misleading evidence of the law codes, and thus to reach a more rounded picture than was possible only a generation or so ago. . . .

Modern writers often give the impression that life in the late empire had degenerated into a state of crisis. The following statement, taken from a recent book, is by no means untypical:

> In all periods of Roman history, poverty, lack of freedom and oppression were the normal facts of life for broad strata of society. But in the Late Empire the sufferings of the population were worse than ever before in some respects.

The key factors singled out are the increased element of compulsion and the alleged alienation of the mass of the population, which is said, among other things, to have led to mass desertion to the barbarians and the inability of the state to deal with the military problem: 'men preferred to live under barbarian rule as the lesser evil, compared to the system of the Roman state'.... As for the general issues, such historical judgements depend not only on one's own perspective, but also on where one looks....

Conclusion

The fall of the Roman empire is conventionally dated to AD 476; thereafter there were no more Roman emperors in the west. Equally conventionally, it is usually pointed out that the line continued in the east, based at Constantinople, until the conquest of the city by the Turks under Mehmet the Conqueror in AD 1453. The year AD 476 itself is more of a convenience for historians than anything else for, as we have already seen, the fifth-century emperors had been weak even before that, in many cases not much more than tools in the hands of the generals who held the powerful position of Master of the Soldiers. It was the last of these, Odoacer, who deposed the young Romulus Augustulus, emperor for less than a year, and declared himself *rex* ('king'), a title traditionally hated at Rome since the overthrow of the kings and the establishment of the Roman republic in 510 BC. By the early sixth century several barbarian kingdoms had come into existence and were in some cases the eventual forerunners of the western medieval states. Among them the most important were the Ostrogoths in Italy, under their king Theodoric (AD 493–526), the Franks (also called the Merovingians), whose kingdom came into being with the victory of Clovis at the battle of Vouillé in AD 507, and the Visigoths, who, despite their defeat in that battle and later reverses at the hands of the Franks, established a unified kingdom in Spain in the mid-sixth century.

Even after these kingdoms were in place, so many Roman traditions and institutions continued that they are sometimes referred to as 'sub-Roman' societies. In particular, Roman landowning families, with their strong cultural traditions, provided many of the powerful bishops in the period, and Latin continued to be used as the language of administration and culture....

This brings us back to the inescapable question of why the Roman empire in the west 'declined' or 'fell' in the fifth century. Old-fashioned moralizing explanations are no longer acceptable (though they still abound), and it is too simplistic to lay all the blame on the barbarian invasions (though what might have happened had there been no barbarian invasions is an interesting hypothetical question). A more recent theory juxtaposes the fall of the Roman empire with that of other major cultures in world history and provides an explanation in terms of the collapse of complex societies. Roughly, on this view, as a society grows, it becomes more and more socially differentiated and more complex and simply in order to maintain itself its needs correspondingly increase. There comes a point however when the 'marginal return' from strategies of maximization such as conquest or taxation diminishes, under pressure of 'continued stresses, unanticipated challenges and the costliness of sociopolitical integration'. A period of difficulty (economic stagnation, political decline, territorial shrinkage) typically follows, which will be followed by effective collapse unless new factors intervene. In the case of the Roman empire, the unexpected challenges included long-term pressure from real and potential invaders, a problem which the empire did not succeed in managing or containing. There is much that is familiar in this analysis, even though it rests on the questionable assumption that the historical development of societies is itself in some sense historically determined. At least it allows Roman historians to look more objectively at their own field, and to see that the problems which the late Roman government faced were not unique, any more than were its often ineffective attempts to find solutions. We should add to the equation in this particular case the relative lack both of economic understanding and of economic structures, and the inability of the centre even after Diocletian to ensure the economic well-being of the empire as a whole. The Roman empire had always been in precarious balance between centre and periphery, and its survival had depended not only on external peace but also on a high degree of internal goodwill. In the late fourth and fifth centuries all these factors were endangered.

Barbarians and Romans

It was 800 years since Romulus had given his name to the Eternal City; and she was tiring. Trajan's wars had been especially strenuous. Despite Hadrian's tours of inspection, his pep-talks, his efforts to keep the soldiers on their toes with drills, manoeuvres and the building of defensive works, the army began to relax. The 2nd century would be among military history's most complacent; almost without improvements in defensive works, weaponry or tactics. Though still largely dormant, the *Barbaricum's* size and the profusion of its people meant that any policy which did not guarantee military superiority must eventually lead to ruin.

Central to this self-deception was the imperial frontier, with its supposition that the army's proximity would suffice to make the outside world behave. It had taken strength and watchfulness to make and maintain clear borders, without grey areas or debatable lands; to create a world which was either Roman or not Roman, a division so distinct and so zealously guarded that it would be as safe to plough the first field behind the front line as any in Latium. None the less, for all its majesty and authority, the peace imposed by Rome will not long outlive the 2nd century. Time reveals it as an extended truce, a respite from the gruesome norms of human conduct. Though two predominantly peaceful centuries were a formidable achievement, the effect would be to pond up external pressures which must one day overflow. In any case it had been optimistic to believe that Mediterranean standards of stability could indefinitely be imposed north of the Alps and in—or beyond—the Balkans. Iron Age man had little taste for order. Indeed it remains questionable whether even his post-atomic counterpart has the skill or the will to do better.

Human nature is slow to change; as may be seen in our language. A glance at that indispensable work of reference, Roget's *Thesaurus of English Words and Phrases,* shows how unequal are the vocabularies of peace and war; from which we may deduce which of those pursuits has most exercised minds and bodies. The vocabulary of peace occupies five lines of synonyms on the printed page, that of war twenty-eight. Searching further: under 'harmony', 'concord', 'mediation', 'passivity' and related meanings there are forty-five lines; while 'discord', 'disunity', 'combat', 'armament', 'retaliation' and so on, yield no less than 287! So, in one major language at least, there are five-to-six times more words available to hawks than doves; a telling comment on our dedication to violent solutions during the millennia in which English and its parent tongues evolved, not to mention the ample additions from the warlike, cold-warlike and terrorist jargons of recent years. Returning from words to facts: though Rome's emperors tried their best to do so, no age or country can insulate itself from eternal verities. It is one of the strangest developments in military history that a state, summoned from mid-Italian obscurity by the trumpet of Mars, should have ended by devising a strategy dedicated to passivity and a tactic based on sitting and waiting; though the techniques of war wait for no one.

In short, a single defensive line, without secondary or in-depth support, would prove progressively vulnerable as the empire weakened. Subdividing the army and posting it in penny packets along a 4,000-mile perimeter not only promoted the habit of dispersal but also blinded the high command to the importance of centrally held reserves. Rome had spun a web round western Europe, the Near East and Mediterranean Africa, yet neglected to put a spider in the middle. The empire's geography, the moral importance of Italy at its heart, the middle Danube and upper Rhine as the likeliest and deadliest points of entry: all indicated a need for counterstrike provisions based on northern Italy. There the Alps would perhaps have dictated a twofold grouping, with a powerful army at each end: one in north-western Italy or at Basle and another in north-eastern Italy or at Ljubljana. However, the implementation of anything resembling a centralized strategy would be postponed until the western empire's dotage, when it was too late to be decisive. The truth is that large clusters of legions were unwelcome to a regime founded in suspicion and obsessed with fear of usurpation and conspiracy. The caesars slept more soundly in the knowledge that their regiments were scattered.

It will not be till the 3rd or 4th centuries that meaningful improvement occurs; albeit erratically, with each autocrat imposing an often contradictory view. Positive developments will include enlargement of the imperial bodyguard into a rapid-response force and conversion to heavy cavalry, with mounted regiments deployed behind each major front. Rome will cease to be the empire's military headquarters and subsequent capitals will be more realistically positioned in relation to external dangers. Finally there will be division of command within a partitioned empire: first, experimentally, into four; then, more permanently, into two. But despite modernization and increased flexibility, Rome will never assemble a united force. More typically, she will continue to improvise and compromise, mustering armies in reaction to news of attack and punching with fingers rather than fist.

However, till the late 2nd century, perimetric defence continued to seem valid simply because no crisis arose to prove it otherwise. Unlike the Maginot Line, which was tested within a decade, the imperial frontier was not placed in serious question for a century-and-a-half. Prior to the Marcomannic War of AD 167–75, the absence of deep fortification or strategic reserves was disguised and seemingly made unnecessary by developmental factors: Rome's forwardness and unity contrasted with barbarian backwardness and bickering. As Tacitus had put it:

> Nor have we weapon stronger against the strong than this: that they share no common purpose. Long may it last this—if not love for us—at least detestation of each other. Fortune grants us nothing greater than our enemies' disunity.

Rome's strength lay in diplomacy, breadth of experience and staying power; barbarian weakness in divisiveness, myopia and transience, as well as ignorance of organization, logistics and siege techniques. Yet all was changing and the long span of peace, supposedly braced by the girders of Roman vigilance and readiness, would sag surprisingly soon.

First, however, with the resplendent reign of Hadrian's successor, Antoninus Pius (139–61) the empire reached the watershed of its well-being and stability. The Augustan dream of a benign balance between emperor, senate and army; the Hadrianic hope of a creative correspondence between provinces and centre, city and country, Roman and barbarian, seemed at last to be working. Economic penetration of the outside world and the outward spread of Romanization were proceeding. Three questions nevertheless persisted. Had the Romans matured sufficiently to value peaceful objectives? Could the office of emperor, so subject to the quirks and swings of each incumbent, provide continuity for the achievement of such goals? And would the European *Barbaricum*, with its dark currents of disturbance, allow time for the improved relationships to root? The answer to all three questions will be in the negative and would soon be given. Under Antoninus' successor, Marcus Aurelius (161–80), the European theatre erupted. The Marcomannic War had its epicentre in today's Czech and Slovak lands, anciently part of Germany, postulated by archaeology as the least hostile of all frontier stretches. Here was a region rich in cross-frontier activity; a sector most penetrated by mercantile and diplomatic effort; with nearly forty known Roman or part-Roman sites reaching up to a hundred miles beyond the Danube. They are thought to have included commercial depots and military or diplomatic missions, whose mixture of south Germanic and Roman-style buildings points strongly to coexistence. These findings confirm what Tacitus had written (in the context of Marcomannia) of 'divers Roman businessmen, coaxed abroad by the hope of some franchise; seduced into staying first by the money to be made and finally by oblivion of their own homeland'. In short, here were the beginnings of a Romano-Germanic co-operation which might in time have reduced economic and cultural differences to the point of peaceful merger.

This possibility was exploded for ever by the Marcomannic conflict. Not only was north-eastern Italy invaded but, more ominously, the attacks spread along the entire front between Black Sea and North Sea. Though Marcus eventually won the war, it revealed two unfavourable developments. First, the tribes had learned to sense Roman adversity and act together. Curiously, the disturbances were in some cases discontinuous, with one warlike tribe apparently responding to another across gaps of several hundred miles.

The second fact was that the frontier failed: its thin membrane punctured in a dozen places, wherever strong force had been applied. Events revealed it as overstretched and undermanned. Its forts were outdated; with *castella* in no way matching what the Middle Ages would call castles. The entire system had been evolved against weak, divided and demoralized enemies during the 1st century and never upgraded during the 2nd.

Neither defensive works nor strategic thinking would find remedy in Marcus' son and heir, the idle and dissolute Commodus (180–92) of whose accession Cassius Dio lamented: 'My history now descends from realms of gold to those of iron and rust, as did Rome's fortunes on that day.' Henceforward, despite noble exceptions and striking recoveries, the state will begin to stumble in the face of its own weaknesses: the absence of a reliable rule of succession, excessive power in unworthy hands and inability to control the army. The milestones on this descending path would include assassination, *coup* and counter-*coup*, civil war, appeasement of the barbarians with gold and employment of barbarians to fight barbarians, culminating in the eventual loss of Roman control.

Returning, however, to the War: its abiding question is why Marcomannia (Czechoslovakia), so propitious for cross-border friendship, should have detonated with such abruptness and violence. Did it signify a backfiring of the slave trade and a breakdown of the three-tier model of Roman control through 'prestige goods dependency'? An explanation better matched to outcomes is perturbation, caused by disturbances in the Eurasian living space, outside the Roman view. The deep *Barbaricum* of Eastern Europe and beyond, was a seismic zone of unpredictable tendency. Age-old impulses to flee from hunger or danger by migrating, usually in a westward or southward direction, had been long frustrated by the Roman empire's presence.

More specifically, responsibility for transforming the middle Danubian tribes from friends to foes may lie with the Goths. This Germanic confederacy originated in southern Sweden, where names like Gothenburg and Gotland survive. They crossed the Baltic, and Claudius Ptolemy, writing around AD 150, locates them on the lower Vistula. A hundred years after the events of Marcus' reign they would arrive on the north Pontic coast; and though their route between is guesswork, it probably lay through today's southern Poland, passing close outside the Sudeten Mountains, adjacent to today's Czech and Slovak Republics. It is therefore probable that the transit of this powerful nation displaced east-German groups like the Vandals and Langobards, who in turn drove the Marcomans and neighbouring Quadans hard against the Danube; overwhelming Rome's intelligence network, brushing aside her diplomatic screen, fording the river and putting her extended army to the test of all-out conflict. Without reserve regiments, reinforcement of the middle Danube could only be made by transfers from other frontier sectors, weakening them and inciting yet more tribes to attack. If there is substance in these surmises, the Marcomannic War was a remarkable preview of 4th and 5th-century calamities.

Before moving on to the late period we must attempt to answer a crucial and difficult question: how did the transformation from Roman to barbarian dominance come about? From the Augustan to the Antonine Age we have seen a majestic Rome facing divided, bewildered and largely passive tribes. The Celts were still reeling from Caesar, the Germans dazed by Drusus and Germanicus. On the rare and probably minor occasions when Roman territory was infringed, it was on a raid-and-return basis, like boys daring an orchard wall; though from Marcus onwards, the view is of growing menace and ever more damaging raids. In the 4th century, however, the character of incursion changes from raids to migrations, and the barbarian goal from loot to land: a wish to be part of the empire and partake of its wealth and security.

In fact the emergence of barbarian power has never been satisfactorily explained; and the absence of a clear answer has clouded the long-standing conundrum of why the western empire succumbed. Our two impressions—of the earlier and later barbarian—are bewilderingly disconnected, for we have little knowledge of the outside peoples during the period of change which might explain their dramatic gain in strength. Indeed we are seldom sure of the extent to which we are witnessing gains in barbarian or losses in Roman strength. One of the blackouts in the written sources most crippling to ancient history occurs during the 3rd century. It is especially irksome for the fifty years from 235 to 285, though never so total that the gravity of events cannot be guessed. Indeed, these were sufficiently serious to merit history's description: the 'Third Century Crisis'. Its characteristics were a seething army, provinces defecting and emperors or pretenders averaging one a year. Though these weaknesses—and the raids upon imperial territory which they invited—shocked the Roman command into improvement and drew a heroic response from soldier-emperors like Claudius II, Aurelian and Probus, more meaningful in the long run was the readiness to buy off the barbarian so that Roman could be left in peace to fight Roman. This folly would not end with the 3rd century; for in Kipling's words, 'once you have paid him the Danegeld, you never get rid of the Dane.' On the other hand, the drain on hard currency was less decremental than might appear. Owing to his taste for Roman trade goods, the barbarian and his money were easily parted; and what governments gave, businessmen could sometimes win back. Be this as it may, an even more dangerous change in barbarian military capability was now afoot.

In the 3rd century unfamiliar names begin to appear opposite much of the European frontier: seemingly new tribes, but in fact new names for combinations of the old. They are exemplified by the Alamans of south-western Germany, meaning 'all men' and signifying a fusion of the Suebian tribes into a coalition, so long and vividly remembered that *allemand* will enter the future French language, meaning 'German'. At a time of internal weakness it is improbable that the Roman army was sufficiently aggressive to provoke such alliances. It seems more feasible that interruptions to cross-border trading, caused by the commotions within the empire, upset the tribal equilibrium, promoting unstable conditions in which the formation of one coalition would almost certainly be followed by others. In this event we have the irony that commercial relationships, created to ensure the loyalty of puppet chiefs, should recoil on Rome as soon as her merchants and officials failed to keep their part of the bargain.

More widely, it is arguable that whenever Rome sneezed the *Barbaricum* caught a cold; for stoppages in commercial traffic between large partners and small (as between the empire and individual tribes; or between Rome and China, in which barbarians were middlemen) were so destructive to the smaller economies that trouble was virtually guaranteed. M. G. Raschke has proposed that bolts of Chinese silk became, as it were, the cash of the Asian steppe, on whose existence basic transactions came to depend; and it is likely that interruption to the silk traffic aggravated all problems in the vast space between China's western and Rome's eastern approaches. Similarly a faltering in Roman bribery payments, or hitches in the wine and slave trades, would not only create headaches for Quisling chieftains but also filter-down effects of grave consequence for the tribes as a whole. The seriousness of mercantile matters is born out by the little we know of cross-frontier treaties, in which the granting or withholding of access to markets was evidently a prime diplomatic lever, as in the peace terms of AD 175:

> The Quadans were refused the right to attend markets for fear other tribes might mingle with them and spy out the Roman disposition [and] Marcus restored to the *Marcomanni* half the neutral zone along their frontier, allowing them to settle up to five miles from the Danube. He established places and days for markets and exchanged hostages...

In view of barbarian commercial addiction we may imagine the empire's neighbours under acute stress, with Rome comparable to a drug dealer who becomes so involved in gang feuds that he forgets to supply his customers. The Third Century Crisis must therefore have been critical for the barbarians too: a time of trouble in the empire, but of even more fateful upheaval outside it. These commercial upsets, the scenting of Roman weakness, the impulse toward coalition and finally migration, would be the ingredients of the western empire's destruction. Overextended, with declining wealth and her technical lead over the outside peoples eroding away; an ageing state, whose civilian majority had forgotten how to fight, now faced an unhinged barbarian world in which all had learned to be warriors from childhood.

However, the migratory fluxes, which signalled the destabilization of central and eastern Europe required an outside push to give them irreversible motion. We have already noted their origins, on the extreme wings of the empire's European horizon: in the Scandinavian and Black Sea regions. Jordanes, chronicler of the Gothic nation, would refer (in the late 6th century) to Scandinavia as 'the Scandza Peninsula: a man-manufactury, a womb of nations'. The Goths would be neither the first nor last to emerge from this hungry corner. It is possible that they were responding to even larger folk movements, comparable to those impelling the steppe peoples, a thousand miles to their south-east. The relationship (in the Ural-Altaic language group) between Finnish, Hungarian and Turkish—and all of them with Mongol—demonstrates that there was more than one route for wanderers from Asia. It is therefore possible that the northernmost Germans were already being squeezed by arriving Finns; though a more common explanation is that crop failure promoted the Scandinavian exodus. Migrating south-eastwards and encountering Ukrainian winters even colder than those of their homeland, the Goths pushed on, reaching the Black Sea by the 4th century. There, in the last and greatest misadventure of European prehistory, they would collide with the next arrivals on the inexorable conveyor belt of the Eurasian steppe.

The Huns entered Europe's south-eastern approaches in the 370s. Their arrival was disastrous for the Goths who, disastrously for the Romans, were driven into the Balkans. A catastrophic Roman defeat at Hadrianople (Edirne, western Turkey) in 378, led to a Gothic takeover of the Danubian provinces and attempts on Italy via the eastern Alpine passes. Meanwhile the Huns, who had based themselves in Hungary, conquered northwards into eastern Germany and today's Poland. This displaced further people, notably of the Vandalic coalition, who fled westwards, appearing on the Rhine in 405. Theirs was another portentous name: from the German *wandeln,* to wander. A sweeping left hook, through Gaul, Spain, across the Straits of Gibraltar and along the northern coast of Africa to Carthage (in due course followed by the seaborne invasion of Rome) put the Vandals among military history's immortals and presaged the end for Italy. By the mid 5th century, Ravenna, the western empire's last capital, had become so flooded with barbarian officers, bodyguards, opportunists and refugees that Romanity was quietly drowning in Germanity; to the extent that Goths were able, almost absent-mindedly, to take charge of the governmental machine. Throughout the West, Roman provinces were dissolving into Germanic kingdoms and the hazy outlines of medieval Europe beginning to emerge. The Romans and the outside peoples, who had clashed and mingled during the empire's creation, did so again during its disintegration, producing new aptitudes, releasing new energies and reaping an immediate peace dividend. With the end of the centuries-old Roman-barbarian conflict, the tax burden ceased and a defensive commitment, whose crushing cost was all but destroying town and country, was lifted at last. Land-sharing and other accommodations between Frank and Gaul, Visigoth and Spaniard, Ostrogoth and Italian, appear to have been accomplished amicably. The Church was at once a salve, a cement and an agency for continuity. In any case, because the barbarian brought few institutions or ideas, he would need to draw deeply on those of conquered Rome. Because his confederations embodied mixtures of dialects and customs, they would make no unified impact on classical culture; demonstrated by the survival of Romance language throughout western Europe. Only in Noricum (Austria) is there evidence for an evacuation of the Roman population in the face of Alamanic attack, resulting in a German language gain. Only in post-Roman Britain was there a fight to the death between native and invader, leading to an eradication of Romanity from the entire east and centre of the island; though roads and other infrastructure remained.

It is revealing to think back upon the bad press given to the outside tribes by Roman authors. Naturally this had worsened with the military situation. Barbarians were seen to be gripped by *Schadenfreude* and intent on destruction; as repeatedly stated or implied by Ammian (*c.* 325–95), greatest of late Roman historians:

> It is as if bugles were blowing all round the Roman world [...] the cruellest tribes awoke and burst the nearest frontiers [...] the barriers were down and savagery pouring like lava-streams from Etna [...] the caged beasts had broken their bars and were rampaging over Thrace [...] numberless peoples,

long assembling to put a torch to the Roman world and encompass its destruction [...] this ravening age, as if the Furies had incited the world and madness was spreading into every corner.

Similarly St Jerome (*c.* 340–420), from a different standpoint:

How many mothers, Christian virgins and gentlewomen have become the sport of these wild beasts? Bishops held to ransom, clerics murdered, churches sacked, horses stabled at the altar, holy relics scattered?

This was perhaps true of earlier attacks. The Huns were especially to be feared; and the fourteen-day sack of Rome by the Vandals, which gave birth to the term 'vandalism', darkened the image further. By contrast, the evacuation of Noricum and the trek of its citizens across the eastern Alps shows a kinder barbarian face. The Italy to which they were retreating was already an Ostrogothic kingdom. With the exception of Britain, as successive parts of the empire fell into barbarian hands, the hands became gentler. It was not the conquerors' intention to destroy their new home. By the 5th century the invaders had adopted a 'promised land' view of Rome, more comparable with a Mexican view of America today.

Most early 20th-century historical work on the so-called migrations period was French or German, giving us the equivalent but different expressions, *invasions barbares* and *Völkerwanderungzeit*, each reflecting its own national experience. The French emphasizes the onslaught and horror; the German implies readjustment, as Europe sought to resume the natural patterns of flow and resettlement which the imperial frontier had so long obstructed. With the passing years our century has presented us with a far wider choice of interpretations than was offered by these early labels. After all, we are still not far removed from the migrational storm which followed the New World discoveries; and well placed to understand that our own restless age is largely a product of its disturbances. The making of countries like the United States reminds us how stimulating demographic upheaval can be.

A further, almost comparable human commotion followed the Second World War, prompted by the collapse of colonialism, the fall and rise of ideologies and the burgeoning of aspirations; with the spread of communications tempting aspirants to move and of cheap transportation, bringing temptation within reach. Countries not affected by these 20th-century migrations are rare. To a degree they are fortunate. On the other hand, there are economic miracles related to movement into places like California, West Germany, Hong Kong and Taiwan which confirm yet again that migrations need not be destructive, for it is usually true that incomers work harder than incumbents.

With this complex human tide, released since 1945, has come a new vocabulary of flux: refugees, job-seekers, guest workers, foreign advisers, brain-drainers, expatriates, displaced persons, illegal aliens, unlawful immigrants, gate-crashers, tax exiles, Zionists, pursuers of the American dream and so on. In some cases there is no parallel with late antiquity, in others the resemblance is marginal. However, two of our late 20th-century categories of vagrancy do seem to fit 5th-century circumstances, namely 'economic opportunists' and 'asylum seekers': those seeking a better life and those fearing for life itself. Both imply civilian rather than military impulses and neither suggests destructive intent. A place to settle, land to till, safety from the great churning of tribes which attended the close of the Iron Age: we may guess that food and fear were uppermost in barbarian minds, as they are for the needy and desperate of our own day.

Was this the reality of the barbarian invasions? Is it closer to the truth than the essentially martial 19th-century image of sword-waving hordes, hurling themselves against the empire's defences? Were the Angles and Saxons, with a drowning coast in front and frightened tribes behind, a military conspiracy against Britain; or were they a sort of 'boat people'? Did the Vandals plan their sensational march from the Rhine to Carthage; or were they refugees, set into motion by terror and hunger, who merely stumbled against doors which chanced to be unlocked? Of course, while today's migrants tend to respect the strength of their host countries, the barbarians came armed and ready to fight for their promised lands. And yet our own century is not without its homeland seekers (like the creators of the Boer Republics, Pakistan and Israel), prepared if necessary to go to war. One way and another, we are well placed to understand the migrations period.

Perhaps not surprisingly the view of Rome as a noble flame, quenched by barbarians, is no longer in fashion. The 'Dark Ages' have been replaced by a creative merger in which Roman and barbarian combine with unexpected ease and (except for Britain) proceed with relative calm into the 'post-Roman' or 'sub-Roman' era. On the contrary, we now accept that the 5th century's most destructive event was the Byzantine reconquest of Ostrogothic Italy. Today, more aware of other cultures, accustomed to exotic faces and foreign languages on the street and at school, striving for solutions of togetherness, we are readier to allow the outside nations a hearing. So we should be; for the Romano-barbarian mergers of the 5th century made Europe; Europe made the New World; and all Western peoples are their children.

POSTSCRIPT

Did the Roman Empire Collapse Due to Its Own Weight?

Most historians studying the fall of Rome agree that neither internal nor external forces can be ignored, yet many continue to produce works that emphasize one side of the debate. Arthur Ferrill's *The Fall of Rome: The Military Explanation* (Thames & Hudson, 1986) is the definitive source on the role played by the barbarians in Rome's collapse. In *Warfare in the Classical World* (Salamander Books, 1998), John Warry surveys the role of wars and their effects on Greco-Roman civilization, titling a concluding chapter "The Coming of the Barbarians."

A. H. M. Jones's *The Decline of the Ancient World* (Oxford University Press, 1964) and Peter Brown's *The World of Late Antiquity* (Thames & Hudson, 1971) are classics of the internal factors side of the debate. Geza Alfoldy's *The Social History of Rome* (Johns Hopkins University Press, 1988) is a short but well-packed volume on Rome's social history that sets the stage for the empire's fall. For a more literary flavor, see Thomas Cahill's *How the Irish Saved Civilization: The Untold Story of Ireland's Heroic Role from the Fall of Rome to the Rise of Medieval Europe* (Anchor Books, 1995), which offers a balanced treatment of Rome's demise in the chapter "How Rome Fell—And Why."

Despite its age, one should not ignore Gibbon's classic *The History of the Decline and Fall of the Roman Empire* (Methuen, 1896–1900). Interestingly, the role of Christianity in the late Roman Empire has received much attention from modern historians. For example, see Jaroslav Pelikan's *The Excellent Empire: The Fall of Rome and the Triumph of the Church* (Harper & Row, 1987).

There has been renewed interest in the role of the barbarians in the process. Many historians are now willing to credit them with helping to establish the Middle Ages. In the words of Williams, the author of one of this issue's readings: "Perhaps not surprisingly the view of Rome, as a noble flame quenched by barbarism, is no longer in fashion. The 'Dark Ages' have been replaced by a creative merger in which Roman and barbarian combine with unexpected ease and (except for Britain) proceed with relative calm into the 'post-Roman' or 'sub-Roman' era." Perhaps the barbarians don't deserve the name—and reputation—that history has attached to them.

ISSUE 5

Did Same-Sex Unions Exist
in the Early Middle Ages?

YES: John Boswell, from *Same-Sex Unions in Premodern Europe* (Villard Books, 1994)

NO: Philip Lyndon Reynolds, from "Same-Sex Unions: What Boswell Didn't Find," *The Christian Century* (January 18, 1995)

ISSUE SUMMARY

YES: Yale University history professor John Boswell states that same-sex unions, which date back to pagan times, existed in medieval Europe until they were gradually done away with by the Christian Church.

NO: Reviewer Philip Lyndon Reynolds, while admitting that "brotherhood" ceremonies took place in medieval Europe, asserts that these ceremonies did not have the same authority as sacred unions and therefore cannot be equated with marriage rites.

Few topics are as controversial today as homosexuality. Newspapers are filled with stories involving the discomfort that individuals—and institutions—have in dealing with the subject. In the United States, violence against gay males and lesbians seems commonplace, as are debates within states concerning the extent of gay rights. Even U.S. presidents find it difficult to enact policies under their jurisdiction (e.g., the role of gays in the military). Some accuse governmental leaders of first proposing policies and then reversing their position to gain public approval. The total acceptance of gay males and lesbians in society will likely be a question for debate for years to come.

No segment of society has had more difficulty dealing with this subject than religious communities. All denominations seem to have divisions in their ranks with regard to how homosexuality is to be considered in canons and doctrines and how gay males and lesbians are to be treated as members of congregations. News accounts abound concerning clergy members who challenge their church's stance on homosexuality and are reprimanded or censured for it. Occasionally, the debate reaches the highest orders of the sect, when bishops or other high-ranking officials express doubts about existing church beliefs and concomitant practices. There seems to be no way to satisfy all parties.

Some scholars have attempted to seek out the historical roots of this problem, to discover if there are any historical antecedents that can be useful in creating a consensus of understanding in regard to homosexuality. They have discovered that what some today would refer to as homosexual practices have been in existence throughout recorded history. But what may have been startling to discover was the level of acceptance such practices were afforded in the past; in fact, to many, the status of these practices has been questioned in the Western world only within the last millennium.

What significance do these historical antecedents have for the current debate? For one thing, they are vivid examples that societies can exist and thrive in times of open tolerance. If they could then, why not now? Also, it is important for gay males and lesbians to find reaffirmation for their beliefs and practices in the past, as almost all groups have found some solace in their historical, ethnic, and religious roots. Finally, a study of the past can inspire current interest in seeking solutions to our current problem with understanding and accepting sexual orientation.

If there was a wider acceptance of homosexuality in past religious histories, can that acceptance be recreated today? And can we not discover what factors in the last 1,000 years altered those earlier, more accepting conditions and use them as a catalyst for change? Such hope is at the heart of the late John Boswell's book, from which the following selection has been excerpted. Researching into archives and manuscripts long ignored, he discovered that not only was there a wider acceptance of what some today refer to as homosexual practices in the past but that there also existed in classical and medieval Europe religious rites and ceremonies he refers to as "same-sex unions." These practices existed for centuries until late medieval Christendom closed the door to such practices.

While Boswell's work was well received, it was not without its critics. Philip Lyndon Reynolds, in a lengthy review in *The Christian Century*, found that Boswell may have assigned a sacramental nature to these same-sex rites that did not exist. Also, Reynolds states that there has been a lack of clarity of purpose to Boswell's work. His review (and others) has inspired rejoinders and counterrejoinders. What will the outcome of this debate be in the hands of future historians and theologians?

John Boswell

 **YES**

Same-Sex Unions in Premodern Europe

The History of Same-Sex Unions in Medieval Europe

The historical setting of the [same-sex union] ceremony is a bit harder to track than its liturgical context and development. It is, for example, impossible to know whether it represents the Christianization of an ancient same-sex rite—and if so, which one—or a Christian innovation. Since most ancient nuptial and same-sex union rites involved sharing of wine and a feast, it is easy to imagine that these ancient customs were simply arrayed in Christian garb to keep up with the prevailing ethos, just as Roman heterosexual marriage customs were reinvested with Christian meaning and persisted throughout the Middle Ages, or pagan statuary (e.g., of Venus and Cupid) was reconsecrated to Christian use (the Virgin Mary and the baby Jesus).

Saint couples—especially military pairs like Serge and Bacchus or the Theodores—continued to fascinate and preoccupy the Christian public (or at least the males who left literary and artistic records), and provided a Christian voice for the same sentiments that had produced the Roman phenomenon of sexual or institutional "brotherhood." Churches continued to be built for and dedicated to Serge and Bacchus throughout the Eastern end of the Mediterranean all during the early Middle Ages. Many Christians may have understood such couplings simply as expressions of devoted friendship, while those whose own romantic interests were chiefly directed to their own gender doubtless understood them in a more personal way. Both views were probably correct: coupled saints like Peter and Paul may have been overinterpreted as romantic pairs, while Serge and Bacchus were probably correctly so understood. The oldest church in Egypt, widely believed to occupy a spot where the Holy Family lived for some time during their exile in Egypt, is dedicated to St. Serge. Justinian himself, the instigator of laws sharply penalizing homosexual behavior, was believed to have added a structure dedicated to SS. Serge and Bacchus to one already consecrated to SS. Peter and Paul.

Nor should the fact that an area became Christian be interpreted to mean that all of its inhabitants suddenly embraced and followed the most ascetic teachings of the new religion. In many areas of Europe ancient practices persisted for centuries among a populace officially Christian. In Egypt, although Christianity was lively and often quite severe (as exemplified in the Didache, the Apostolic Canons, and the writings of Clement of Alexandria), there was also much variety, as appears in the Gnostic writings and the prominence of dissenting movements in the Egyptian church. Centuries after Christian doctrine had penetrated Egypt and long after the Theodosian Code had made the upper reaches of the Roman state a Roman Catholic theocracy, an Egyptian man wrote down a magical incantation seeking supernatural help to obtain the love of another male. The sixth-century African poet Luxorius, also living in a Christian world, nonetheless wrote a poem about a passively homosexual male who gave his property away to the men with whom he had sex.

The Roman custom of forming a union with another male by the legal expedient of declaring him a "brother" appears to have persisted into the early Middle Ages, although it became controversial for a somewhat unexpected reason related to the decline of urban culture and the range of lifestyles around the Mediterranean. Collateral adoption was declared invalid for some outlying provinces in a handbook of Roman law compiled (in Greek) in the fourth or fifth century and translated into Syriac, Armenian, and Arabic for Roman citizens living in regions of the East where Latin and Greek were not understood....

It is, in addition, clear that same-sex unions were commonplace in early medieval Byzantine society, even among the prominent and notable. Strategios, an imperial treasurer, was twice said in the ninth century to have been the same-sex partner... centuries before of the emperor Justinian. No other information about this relationship survives. Procopius in his *History* mentioned Strategios as a trusted patrician, "a man of good sense and ancestry" ..., but said nothing about this relationship, which may be apocryphal, although in Procopius, Strategios does seem to have been close to Justinian. In another text Severus, a patrician, is casually mentioned as the same-sex partner of another emperor, but no further details are given.

By contrast, details survive about some Byzantine cases of the early Middle Ages. St. Theodore of Sykeon, for example, a contemporary of Justinian (d. 613), was born in Galatia. He was the illegitimate son of a prostitute and an imperial messenger, Kosmas, who had been an acrobat and performed in the imperial circus on camels. Theodore became a hermit, lived for two years in a cave, and then for a time inhabited an iron cage. (This sort of flamboyant asceticism was common in the Christian East.) He became bishop of Anastasioupolis, but ultimately resigned to return to monastic life.

Theodore traveled widely (e.g., to Jerusalem and Constantinople), and was always under the special protection of St. George, whose intervention when he was a child appears to have been largely responsible for his holy life. (The Eastern St. George was invoked in the ceremony of same-sex union....) While he was visiting Constantinople the patriarch Thomas became "so attached to him and had such confidence in him that he begged him to enter into ceremonial union with him and to ask God that he would be together with him in the next life."

Although it is hardly credible that such an energetically ascetic man would enter into *any* sort of carnal relationship, it is nonetheless possible that the union was based on passionate feelings, at least on Thomas' part. Indeed, it is difficult to interpret otherwise the latter's desire for them to be together in heaven, since traditionally the chief joy of paradise consisted in the beatific vision of God. This whole incident strongly recalls the story of Serge and Bacchus, one of very few other places in early Christian literature where a personal union in heaven was emphasized. Theodore might have consented to a relationship that ordinarily had sexual possibilities without any intention of partaking in them himself: his near-contemporary St. John the Almsgiver agreed to a heterosexual marriage even though he intended to remain a virgin, and had to be forced by his father-in-law to consummate the relationship.

A few centuries later Basil I (867–886), the founder of the Macedonian dynasty that ruled the Byzantine Empire from 867 to 1156, was reported to have been twice involved in ceremonial unions with other men. Although the most important sources for his life—composed under the rule of his descendants within a century of the events in question—are contradictory on some points and occasionally unreliable, their take on this matter is largely consistent. His biographers (including Western sources . . .) all agreed that when Basil arrived in Constantinople with nothing but a staff and a knapsack—a young man from the provinces with no connections in the capital—he was befriended by a certain Nicholas of the church of St. Diomede, who rescued him from sleeping in the streets, brought him into the church, bathed and clothed him, and supported him for some time, until the ambitious Basil was able to attract the attention of a well-placed courtier related to the imperial family.

In most accounts of their relationship Nicholas and Basil are united in a church ceremony. According to one tradition, on the morning after finding him Nicholas "bathed and dressed Basil and was ceremonially united to him, and kept him as his housemate and companion." Another version is more explicit about the ceremony: "and on the next day he went with him to the baths and changed [his clothes] and going into the church established a formal union with him, and they rejoiced in each other." The odd final phrase would probably recall to a Christian Greek reader the biblical "Rejoice with the wife of thy youth."

Given the wording in the chronicles . . . and the fact that the union is accomplished in a church, there can be little doubt that the writers have in mind some form of the ceremony published and translated in this text. There is no suggestion of any tribal or family aspect to the relationship, nor of the exchange of blood; it has no military or strategic aspect, nor are any circumstances adduced as requiring or occasioning it (e.g., rescue from danger, a serious illness, which would all be occasions in later Slavic relationships modeled on it). It is clearly a personal relation, undertaken for personal reasons. Both Basil and Nicholas had living biological brothers with whom they were in regular and close contact, so it could hardly have been inspired by a need for a sibling. Indeed, it was Nicholas' own natal brother, a physician, who was responsible for Basil's introduction at court, a fact adduced immediately after the union in all versions. Nor does the mention of rejoicing suggest a coldly calculated relationship. Taken with the statement by Hamartolos that the union led to a sharing of home and hearth, it strongly evokes a wedding, followed by jubilation and a shared life.

It is striking that in a tradition about this relationship in which Nicholas is identified as a monastic, the ceremonial union is not mentioned. By contrast, the chroniclers who do discuss the union characterize Nicholas as a parish cleric in minor orders—hence, not prohibited by ecclesiastical law from entering into same-sex union. . . .

From the perspective of Basil, who would otherwise have been sleeping on the streets, formalizing Nicholas' benevolent interest in him could only have been advantageous, at least until he found a means of advancing his career more rapidly with someone more powerful and better connected. It is less clear what Nicholas gained from the impetuous union. Taking the story —including Nicholas' supernatural information about Basil's future greatness— at face value, one could conclude that Nicholas imagined he would ultimately profit from entering into a formal relationship with someone who would one day become emperor. . . .

While Basil was still in the service of Theophilos, they made a trip together to Greece. A wealthy widow in Achaia showered him with gifts of gold and dozens of slaves. In return for her generosity she asked nothing but that Basil should enter into ceremonial union with her son, John. At first he refused, because he thought it would make him look "cheap," but at length she prevailed and he agreed. "I seek and ask nothing from you," she assured him, "except that you love and deal kindly with us." A surviving medieval illustration of this incident shows Basil and John being united before a cleric in church, with the Gospel open before them and John's mother looking on. An accompanying frame depicts Basil, John, and Danelis (John's mother . . .) at a table—doubtless the artist's conception of the feast that would usually follow such a ceremony.

When he subsequently became emperor Basil immediately "sent for the son of the widow Danelis, honored him with the title *protospatarius*, and granted him intimacy with him on account of their earlier shared life in ceremonial union." The widow herself—now too elderly to ride—came to the emperor on a litter, but rather than requesting any munificence from him, she brought more extravagant gifts "than nearly any other foreign ruler had up to that time ever bestowed on a Roman emperor." In addition, she "who was worthy to be called the emperor's mother" made a large gift of her patrimony in the Peloponnese to her son and the emperor *together*. . . .

Were it not for the genders involved, this incident would seem quite a familiar feature of the premodern political landscape: a wealthy widow offers her marriageable child to a powerful young man on the rise, along with a substantial dowry, hoping to ally her fortunes to his. Basil's own father had been married to the daughter of a wealthy widow in a striking parallel. The previous Byzantine dynasty, the Amorian, had been established under similar, though apparently heterosexual circumstances: born of humble parents, uneducated and unconnected, its founder Michael II advanced himself through strength of arms and military skill until he was able to marry Thekla, the daughter of a high-ranking officer, and attracted the attention of the emperor Leo V, who made him *protostratarius*—the same position Basil had held in the service of

Theophilos—and became godfather to one of his sons. When Leo attempted to have Michael executed on charges of treason, he was himself assassinated and Michael was crowned emperor.

The widow Danelis was much richer than Basil and, when he became emperor, realized no material gain from the relationship, so it can hardly be viewed as a mercenary arrangement on her part. On the contrary, every year of Basil's life she sent *him* expensive gifts, and years later, when both Basil and her son had died, the widow came again on a litter to see Basil's son Leo, now emperor, and made him her heir, although she had a grandson and other relatives.

The two stories about Basil are similar: in each there is a divine revelation, to a cleric or monk, about Basil's future greatness; in each the relationship established is to Basil's material advantage. It is possible that in imperial circles it was later known that Basil had profited substantially as a young man from a formal relationship with another male, and different chroniclers simply supplied different details. Each of the biographies written within a century of the events contains *one or the other* of the same-sex unions; none contains both. On the other hand, Nicholas does appear in *all* of the most important accounts of Basil's life as his benefactor, even those that mention the union with John, and the wealth of detail about the widow Danelis (including her subsequent relations with Leo) makes it seem unlikely that she was pure invention. Possibly Basil was united to both men. It is not clear that this would have been improper in Basil's day—or that issues of propriety would have constrained his behavior....

It is ... clear that ceremonial same-sex unions were parallel to heterosexual marriage in the ninth century in a number of ways: they were relationships between individuals of a personal nature (rather than tribal, religious, or political); they entailed consequences for the immediate family (John's mother; Nicholas' brother) comparable to the obligations or rights of in-laws; they were recognized by society, and even respected by descendants.

It was most likely for this reason that monks were always and everywhere prohibited from entering into same-sex unions, just as they were forbidden to contract heterosexual marriage in both East and West, by both civil and ecclesiastical law (although in the East other members of the clergy could marry). Basil the Great (in the fourth century) had argued that no sexual relations ... of persons in orders ... could be regarded as "marriages," and that such unions ... must by all means be dissolved. Around 580, monks were also forbidden to make "leagues" or "associations." This rule was presumably based on a provision aimed at the laity in the same collection. In the case of the laity the prohibition was certainly *not* aimed at same-sex unions, but it is conceivable that in the case of monks the same canon was interpreted as a blanket condemnation of *all* relationships requiring an oath. A more or less contemporary ruling for laypeople makes perfectly evident that same-sex unions were altogether legal.

The real context of the prohibition to monks is evident in a restatement of St. Basil's rule for monks (the equivalent of the Rule of Benedict in the West) by St. Theodore of Studium (759–826), in which the monks were told, "Do not contract same-sex unions with or become spiritual kin [i.e., godparents] to the laity, you who have left behind the world and marriage. For this is not found among the fathers, or if it is, only rarely; it is not legal." This rule was often repeated in later ages (e.g., "It is prohibited for monks to form same-sex unions or be godparents, and the church recommends, by way of admonition, the same [prohibition] for leaders or heads of monasteries. The law does not recognize so-called same-sex unions altogether"). Such blanket condemnations inspire skepticism, both because of the historical evidence treated in this [selection] and because same-sex union is coupled in such texts with godparenting, which was not only legal but a key element of liturgical life for most Christians in the Middle Ages. . . .

The most obvious interpretation of such prohibitions is that they parallel the rule against monks marrying women. It would, however, be possible to understand them as stemming from a more general Christian antipathy to homosexuality of any sort. This ascetic tendency of Christian Rome—unknown before the advent of the new religion—was certainly plain in such Western legal compilations as the Theodosian Code and the Laws of the Visigoths, and in the great legal code of Justinian—all unprecedented efforts to make a Christian theocracy of the traditionally secular Roman state. But in fact sustained and effective oppression of those who engaged in homosexual behavior was not known in Europe until the thirteenth century, and was never common in the Byzantine East. Troianos notes somewhat loosely that in the High and later Middle Ages one finds fewer and fewer penalties for homosexual acts in civil and ecclesiastical sources from Byzantium, although "this circumstance in no way indicates that homosexual relations were not widespread in Byzantium." . . .

Roman law survived only fragmentarily in Europe after the collapse of the Roman state, and was usually replaced by Germanic law codes, which were not likely to take cognizance of same-sex relationships. Nonetheless, in Italy and Spain—comparatively urban societies by the standards of the times—the legal fiction of "brotherhood" was not complicated by questions of wife and children, since remaining a bachelor had long been a part of urban Roman life, and was enhanced by the social and financial rewards offered by the position of the diocesan clergy (i.e., as opposed to monks), who were pressured throughout the first millennium of Christian history to aspire to complete celibacy, but were not actually required to observe it until a bitter fight over the issue in the eleventh and twelfth century. In many communities, even where the ceremony of same-sex union was not known, informal relationships reminiscent of the Roman legal fiction of "brotherhood" between male lovers served many of the same functions as heterosexual unions—either legal marriages or long-term alternatives like concubinage—in their duration and legal ramifications.

The ambiguity of the few surviving texts precludes categorizing them unequivocally as same-sex marital contracts, but it equally rules out pretending that they were simply business contracts, as previous commentators have tried to do. It is, in fact, possible to interpret them as business documents, but it would also be possible (if utterly mistaken) to interpret most premodern heterosexual marriage agreements (especially prenuptial contracts among the wealthy) as business contracts. (Indeed, Roman law specifically spoke of heterosexual marriage as a "lifelong partnership.") Many aspects of the documents and the arrangements they prescribe argue forcefully against a simple partnership. In most of them there is no quid pro quo: it is not that one party provides capital or labor or land and in return the other invests property or expertise or time. In each case it is simply a division of one person's estate with another, apparently for purely voluntary and personal reasons....

Epilogue

Although many questions remain about same-sex unions in premodern Europe, much has also emerged with reasonable clarity. Such unions, in various forms, were widespread in the ancient world, where heterosexual matrimony tended to be viewed as a dynastic or business arrangement, and love in such relationships, where it occurred, arose *following* the coupling. Ordinary men and women were more likely to invest feelings the twentieth century would call "romantic" in same-sex relationships, either passionate friendships or more structured and institutional unions, as exemplified by the recognized couples of Crete or Scythia, the swearing of perpetual love among other Greeks, and the social phenomenon and legal stratagem of "brotherhood" among the Romans.

Since the advent of Christianity only exacerbated doubts about the emotional significance of matrimony, there was little pressure (other than widespread heterosexual desire) to re-evaluate such attitudes. Christianity's main innovation was to privilege and make real widespread voluntary celibacy, implicitly or explicitly suggesting that heterosexual matrimony was a mere compromise with the awful powers of sexual desire, even when it was directed exclusively to the procreation of children, the one rationale Christians found convincing. But passionate friendships, especially among paired saints and holy virgins, continued to exercise a fascination over the early Christians—still residents of the ancient world—and in time were transformed into official relationships of union, performed in churches and blessed by priests.

In many ways from a contemporary point of view, the most pressing question addressed by this work is probably whether the Christian ceremony of same-sex union functioned in the past as a "gay marriage ceremony." It is clear that it did, although, as has been demonstrated at length, the nature and purposes of every sort of marriage have varied widely over time. In almost every age and place the ceremony fulfilled what most people today regard as the essence of marriage: a permanent romantic commitment between two people, witnessed and recognized by the community. Beyond this, it might or might not fulfill specific legal or canonical expectations predicated on the experience of the heterosexual majority (procreative purpose, transfer of property, dowry), but the extent to which particular heterosexual unions matched such niceties did not usually determine whether the neighbors regarded the couple (same-sex or heterosexual) as married. Indeed, in all times and places in its history (including the present) the official teaching of the Roman Catholic church (one of the two bodies in which the ceremony developed) has been that the two parties *marry each other;* the priest merely acts as a witness. If the couple intend to be married, they are. By contrast, in the Eastern Orthodox church the priest *does* perform the ceremony, and in all known cases priests performed the same-sex union.

Philip Lyndon Reynolds

Same-Sex Unions:
What Boswell Didn't Find

Few works of historical scholarship are treated in *Time* and *Newsweek,* much less summarized in a syndicated cartoon strip. According to the digest of [Same-Sex Unions in Premodern Europe] that appeared in Gary Trudeau's *Doonesbury,* John Boswell reveals that the Catholic Church recognized gay marriages for a thousand years. The church even provided liturgies for such marriages, liturgies that included communion and in which kissing signified union, and that were in crucial respects "just like heterosexual marriages." Later in church history, a persecuting and homophobic culture suppressed this tradition of gay marriage.

One can readily understand why a book that seems to be saying something like this would attract attention. The issue of homosexuality is extremely vexed in most Christian denominations in North America. If gay marriage used to be a regular part of Christian tradition, then the official Roman Catholic prohibition of homosexual acts must be unfounded, for the prohibition rests chiefly on the argument from tradition. Tradition still counts for a great deal in the minds of most thoughtful Protestants as well. Because they usually regard homosexual unions as something novel and experimental, Christians tend to regard them as artificial and false. If they were to be convinced that, on the contrary, homosexual union was an ancient tradition within the church that was later suppressed, they should not only have to abandon the former view but should tend to regard homosexual union as something natural and authentic. Its suppression or marginalization in the churches today would appear baseless and contrived. Is this the conclusion toward which Boswell—who died . . . at age 47—directs us?

Boswell's argument consists of pointing to certain liturgical forms, some written in Greek and some in Slavonic, from the tenth to the 16th centuries. These texts record an ecclesiastical ritual for the formation of a "brotherhood" of some kind between two men. The ritual belongs to the churches of the eastern Mediterranean and represents the Christianization of a custom much older than Christianity. The liturgical forms have been unfamiliar until now, although a few classical historians have studied and written about the custom of brotherhoods in Greek society (and have come to conclusions different from Boswell's).

From Philip Lyndon Reynolds, "Same-Sex Unions: What Boswell Didn't Find," *The Christian Century,* vol. 112, no. 2 (January 18, 1995). Copyright © 1995 by The Christian Century Foundation. Reprinted by permission of *The Christian Century.*

Boswell provides the original texts and English translations for several of these liturgical forms. Let us consider the first text in his appendix of English translations, which comes from the manuscript Grottaferrata... VII. This form, which was written in Greek in the tenth century, consists of three prayers. In the first the minister, having invoked God as the one who made humankind in his image and likeness, calls to mind two exemplary male pairs who had God's blessing: the apostles Philip and Bartholomew and the martyrs Serge and Bacchus. The text then asks for God's blessing upon the two men, N. and N., who are the subject of the ritual, asking God to enable them "to love each other and to remain unhated and without scandal all the days of their lives." In the second, briefer prayer, the minister beseeches God to bless N. and N. so that they should know the Holy Spirit and "become united more in the spirit than in the flesh." The third and longest prayer is densely rhetorical and difficult to summarize. Suffice it to say that the minister beseeches God to grant that there should be between N. and N. the brotherly love and peace known to the Apostles.

Other examples indicate (chiefly in the rubrics) what ritual acts and non-verbal symbols were used. For example, Grottaferrata... II (in Greek from the 11th century) begins with the rubric: "The priest shall place the holy Gospel on the Gospel stand and they that are to be joined together place their (right) hands on it, holding lighted candles in their left hands. Then shall the priest cense them and say..." The rubric for the conclusion of this ceremony directs the two men to "kiss the holy Gospel and the priest and one another."

One should emphasize that these ceremonies were peculiar to the liturgical traditions of Greece and the Balkans. Boswell says that the ceremony "disappeared from most of Western (as opposed to Central and Eastern) Europe," and that "no Latin versions of the ceremony survive at all, although it must have been performed in Latin in Ireland, and probably sometimes in Italy." The heterogeneous bits of evidence (some of them colorful and anecdotal) that he presents do not convince me that there was ever anything akin to the Eastern ceremony in the Latin West.

The liturgical texts that Boswell brings to our attention are certainly very interesting, and their similarities to nuptial liturgies (though not as great as Boswell suggests) call for careful consideration and comment. Nevertheless, I have some profound problems with Boswell's treatment....

Boswell does not bring the ceremonies into focus until roughly half-way through the book, by which point a judgment has already been made as to what the ceremonies were. Prior to this, Boswell discusses the vocabulary of love and marriage; "heterosexual matrimony"; various forms of same-sex and homosexual relationships in the Greco-Roman world; the Christian understanding of marriage; and nuptial liturgies. All of this material seems to be provided by way of background, not marshaled on behalf of a thesis. Scholarly opinions on the alliances in question appear piecemeal in the course of the book, so that Boswell does not give us any clear impression of the interpretations that he rejects.

... What is Boswell trying to prove? What does he suppose the ceremonies in question to have been? The texts themselves use names such as *adelphopoiêsis* ("brother-making") to denote the ritual. What kind of "brotherhood" was really involved?

◦◈◦

Boswell recounts discovering in Italy "many versions of the ceremony that were obviously the same-sex *equivalent* of a medieval heterosexual marriage ceremony" (my italics). A stronger form of the thesis would be the claim that the ceremony was a celebration of homosexual marriage. Actually, Boswell himself never claims this much. Indeed, when he at last raises the question, "Was it a marriage?" he replies that the "answer to this question depends to a considerable extent on one's conception of marriage." The discussion that follows is inconclusive. Moreover, Boswell adds that "the concept of someone innately and exclusively 'homosexual' was largely unknown to the postclassical world," and that "relationships of this sort were not understood in a sense comparable to modern 'gay marriage.' "

Nevertheless, Boswell implies in an indirect way that these were gay marriages. For example, he speaks of those (i.e., scholars who do not share his point of view) who are "reluctant to contemplate a *nuptial rite* for same-sex union." But elsewhere he observes: "The ambiguity of the few surviving texts precludes categorizing them unequivocally as *same-sex marital contracts*." (Italics are mine in these two quotations.) This implies that there were same-sex marital contracts in the East. Crucially, Boswell consistently refers to "heterosexual matrimony," which implies that there is a generic matrimony of which there are hetero- and homosexual species. The same implication is present (although less apparent) in the phrase "comparison of same-sex and heterosexual ceremonies of union" (which is the subtitle of chapter six). Thus Boswell declares the stronger form of his thesis only by innuendo.

Much of his argument depends upon ambiguity and equivocation. Perhaps the most serious case of conceptual slipperiness arises in the phrase "same-sex union," which Boswell uses to translate (even in the appendix of translations) terms such as *adelphopoiêsis*. Boswell argues that terms involving the word "brother" would have been confusing to English readers because of what "brother" connotes in our usage. But it is arguable that the term "same-sex union" is just as confusing for similar reasons. To any modern reader (such as Gary Trudeau, apparently), it suggests "gay marriage." Inasmuch as one assumes this, the translation of the term begs the entire question of the book.

Boswell claims that "union" is a neutral term:

> To retain this rich multiplicity of connotations [of the Greek and Slavonic words equivalent to "brother," "brotherhood," etc.]—sexual, asexual; transcending and incorporating sex—I have employed the most neutral terms I could devise in translating the original concepts, such as "union" for *adelphotês* (which could be rendered "brotherhood"), or "be united" instead of "become siblings," which would be overtly and distinctly misleading to most English speakers, since it would evoke notions of adoption.

But "union" is by no means a neutral term; it is a very strong term. Readers will inevitably assume that "union" means "marriage," and in this context the word seems to connote sexual union and the joining of "two in one flesh."

To buttress his case Boswell observes that prejudiced scholars will find the idea that the alliances in question are same-sex unions to be repellent. For example, he says that anthropologists and others are anxious to "explain away the ceremony of same-sex union" as a form of blood brotherhood. But if "same-sex union" is a neutral term, what is there to explain away? Likewise, Boswell speaks of "the native and profound disinclination of most people brought up in modern Christian societies to believe that there could have been a Christian ceremony solemnizing same-sex unions." Again, regarding a curious Irish ceremony recorded by Gerald of Wales (from the late 12th or early 13th century), Boswell writes: "Its nature has long been obscured both by artful mistranslation and a general unwillingness to recognize something *as ostensibly improbable as a same-sex union*" (italics mine). But inasmuch as "same-sex union" is a neutral term, no one can find anything ostensibly improbable in the existence of such a union.

It seems to me, therefore, that "same-sex union" is an ill-chosen and dangerously slippery term. Nevertheless, let us stipulate that it is a neutral expression that means exactly what *adelphotês* or *adelphopoiêsis* means, whatever that may be. The existence of liturgies for same-sex unions is then incontrovertible. The question is: Were these ceremonies the "equivalent" of heterosexual marriages (to use the weaker form of Boswell's thesis)? What kind and what degree of equivalence are we looking for? Equivalence in what respect?

Boswell claims that the relation is evident (to those not blinded by their prejudices and preconceptions) in the liturgies themselves. He notes that the texts for brother-making ceremonies are often contiguous to nuptial liturgies in the manuscripts. When one compares the brother-making liturgies with nuptial liturgies, however, the similarities one finds, while interesting, are not enough to imply equivalence or to suggest that the brother-making ceremonies were in any sense nuptial.

❦

To exemplify the "heterosexual" nuptial liturgy, Boswell provides a translation of a Western rite: that of the Gelasian Sacramentary. (Why this choice? One would have supposed that an Eastern rite would have been more pertinent.) Conspicuous in this rite are references to procreation. Thus the minister invokes God as the one who instituted matrimony "so that in the multiplication of children of adoption the fecund chastity of the holy married may persist" (Boswell's translation). Again, the rite beseeches God that husband and wife "may see the children of their children unto the third and fourth generation." And as in all Western nuptial liturgies (and, indeed, as in the more elaborate early medieval dotal contracts), the rite commemorates how God fashioned Eve from Adam's side so that all humankind should descend from them. Petition for the "fruit of the womb" is equally conspicuous in the Eastern liturgies. Needless to say, there is nothing like this in the rites for "same-sex union."

Boswell notes that there are "interesting differences" in the choice of scriptural texts. These differences are not very surprising. Among the texts commonly used in marriage were Genesis 1:28 (on fecundity), Genesis 2:18 (on the formation of Eve from Adam's side), Matthew 19:1–6 (where Jesus deduces from marriage "in the beginning" and in particular from Genesis 2:23 that divorce is contrary to God's will), and John 2:1–11 (on the marriage at Cana). In same-sex unions, Boswell tells us, the most common texts were John 15:17, 17:1 and 18–26 (on love and harmony), 1 Corinthians 13:4–8 (on love), and Psalm 133 ("Behold, how good and how pleasant it is for brethren to dwell together in unity"). There is nothing to suggest equivalence here, and no hint of anything nuptial.

Boswell writes that "the most striking parallels have to do with visual symbolism," and that the "principal structural similarities between the ceremony of same-sex union and heterosexual nuptial offices were binding with a stole or veil, the imposition of crowns, the holding of a feast after the ceremony for the families and friends, the making of circles around the altar, the use of a cross, occasionally the use of swords, and—virtually always—the joining of right hands."

If it is true that crowning was regularly involved, this would indeed be very remarkable, for the ceremony of crowning was and is central to the Eastern nuptial rite, where it took on immense and specifically nuptial significance. Boswell provides just two pieces of evidence for this. One is an obscure Greek text that prohibits monks from receiving boys from baptism, "laying hold of the crowns of marriage," and forming brotherhoods with them. Since this is a set of things *prohibited* to monks, it is not clear which elements might be permissible to non-monks. Perhaps what is in question is an abuse of the traditional brotherhood.

The other piece of evidence offered seems to me to be a serious error. "An eleventh-century exemplar [for a ceremony of same-sex union] does not mention the *removal* of crowns, which necessarily implies their previous imposition." The exemplar in question is Grottaferrata... II, which is in two parts. The first part, which is explicitly a ceremony for brother-making, appears to end with the rubric: "Then shall they kiss the holy Gospel and the priest and one another, and conclude..." At this point, Boswell notes, a scribe has drawn a line across the manuscript. There follows a prayer beginning with the title "Ecclesiastical canon of marriage of the Patriarch Methodius." This prayer, which is very clearly from a nuptial rite, ends with a rubric that refers to the removal of crowns.

It should be obvious that the second prayer is from a different rite, and that this text mentions only the removal, not the imposition, of crowns because the early part of it is missing. It is likely that a scribe grafted on the second text by mistake, and that he or someone else noticed this and drew the line to alert the reader's attention to the error. In a long and difficult footnote, Boswell tries to show that the line does not have this significance, but the final, manifestly nuptial prayer is different from Boswell's other examples of brother-making prayers in crucial respects: its title refers to marriage; the prayer itself refers to the "bond of marriage" and to making "two into one"; and the concluding rubric refers to the crowns. Even without the scribe's warning line, we should know that this does not belong to the brother-making ceremony.

⁂

The genuine common elements are very interesting, but what may one deduce from them? None of them is specifically nuptial. The kiss, for example, acquired a specifically nuptial meaning in marriage ceremonies (where some regarded it as a kind of premonition of sexual consummation), but in itself it was a universal and asexual symbol of greeting and concord. Similarly, the joining of right hands was a token (then as now) of any kind of agreement. To make much of this evidence, one would need carefully to analyze the history and meaning of each element, which Boswell does not do.

Moreover, the similarities between the brother-making ceremonies and nuptial ceremonies are striking and even a little shocking to us *because* we have a concept of homosexual orientation and gay marriage. A culture that possessed no such notion would not have been struck in this way by the similarities. Lacking surface evidence, one needs to know what same-sex union was and what marriage was, so that one can compare the two or at least make sense of Boswell's claim. But Boswell does not even make clear what *he* takes same-sex union to have been.

Setting out his policies of translation at the outset, Boswell explains that where the Greek and Slavonic texts for the ceremonies use terms that might be literally translated "brother" or "become brothers," it would be misleading to translate them thus. This is because, on the one hand, "the meanings of the nouns to contemporaries were 'lover,' and 'form an erotic union,'" while on the other hand English readers will "relate such concepts more to feelings of goodwill and fraternal concern than to intimacy or romantic attachment."

Should we assume, then, that in Boswell's view same-sex unions were homoerotic? Not necessarily. Later in the book Boswell modestly claims that sexual relations between men "joined in some sort of ecclesiastical union... *probably* did not seem even mildly sinful" (my italics). (This is mere guess-work.) On the next page, he raises the question of whether same-sex unions were homosexual. Obviously (he points out), they were homosexual in the literal sense of the word, since the partners were of the same sex. But was the ceremony erotic? Boswell replies: "This is hard to answer for societies without a comparable nomenclature or taxonomy." Was the relationship intended to become erotic: "Probably, sometimes, but this is obviously a difficult question to answer about the past, since participants cannot be interrogated." Boswell then points out that "a sexual component is not generally what constitutes the definitive test of 'marriage,' particularly in premodern societies, where few people married for erotic fulfillment."

Just as Boswell fails to explain what same-sex unions were, he also fails to provide any clear account of what (heterosexual) marriage was. Statements like the one just quoted, as well as his frequent observation that in premodern societies, romantic love was (ideally) a consequence of marriage rather than its motive and origin, seem intended in part to loosen our sense of what marriage was. But this merely negative approach, while very proper in itself, does not help Boswell's case. If one aims to prove that some new virus is a variety of influenza, one can do so only to the extent that one knows what influenza is.

To grasp the sense of Boswell's claim that the brotherhoods were equivalent to (heterosexual) marriage, one needs to have some account of what the latter was. In Christian Europe during the patristic and medieval periods, numerous exigencies—cultural, legal, theological, ascetic—caused the notion of marriage to be modified, analogically transposed, extended, stretched and delimited. Nevertheless, certain basic ideas remain visible beneath the surface.

First, marriage was by definition "the union of a man and a woman" (as the Roman jurist Ulpian said). If Boswell's implied notion of generic (homo- or heterosexual) matrimony ever existed in premodern European culture, there was never a name for it. Matrimony was a union of opposites (see Colossians 3:18–19). Second, marriage was a stable joining of a man and a woman for the sake of procreating and raising children. Hence the phrase *liberorum procreandorum causa* ("for the sake of procreating children"), which appeared on Roman nuptial documents as a way of distinguishing marriage from other relationships. The difference between marriage and concubinage, in Roman law, was that only a man's children by marriage were his own children: that is, his heirs, members of his family, and (in the case of males) the continuation of his paternal power.

More basic yet in the Judaic and Christian traditions was the notion of marriage as a union of two in one flesh. As it appears in Genesis 2:24, this is probably a complex notion, but 1 Corinthians 6:16 (where Paul, by a curious irony, applies the text to prostitution) suggests that sexual union is part of the idea. Despite the efforts of some medieval theologians, the notion of sexual consummation remained integral to the church's notion of marriage. Sex is integral to marriage in other ways—for example, in the Pauline conjugal debt (see 1 Cor. 7:2–5), which was hugely important in both Eastern and Western thinking about marriage, and in the impediments of relationship (since even an unconsummated marriage is invalid when its sexual consummation would be incestuous).

Subsuming all these elements was the nuptial symbolism that entered the Bible in the Book of Hosea and culminated in Ephesians 5:31–32, a text that compares the union of "two in one flesh" to the union between Christ and the church. This text and its theology did not appear much in the nuptial liturgies, but they were central to the theology of marriage. Moreover, the symbolism was manifest in the quasi-nuptial rite in which a woman took the veil to become a religious (a bride of Christ).

To claim that there were same-sex equivalents of marriage in this historical context is to claim that same-sex unions were supposed in some way to embody this model or something analogous to it. This does not seem possible, and in any case, I see no evidence for it. One should note that Boswell does not claim or offer any evidence to suggest that the brotherhoods were in any sense an alternative to (heterosexual) marriage or exclusive of marriage.

Buried in this very muddled book is an interesting and plausible thesis, which goes like this: On the one hand, premodern Christian culture knew nothing of gay marriage, had no concept of the homosexual person and condemned homosexual acts. On the other hand, institutionalized or otherwise socially recognized same-sex relationships, such as the brotherhoods studied here, provided scope for the expression of what we would now regard as homosexual inclinations—much more scope than was possible, for example, in the cultures of the late Middle Ages and the Reformation. They may even have occasionally provided cover for homosexual acts. (If this is what Boswell had been judged to be saying, however, the book would not have captured the media's attention.)

This book has very little bearing on the issue of gay union and gay marriage in churches today. A Christian proponent of gay marriage or even of tolerated gay unions must face the fact that such acts are a radical departure from traditional norms. One can make this departure either by honestly abandoning some or all of the tradition, or (much more tenuously) by using an historical, relativist hermeneutic to locate some deeper stream within the tradition. Both of these lines of argument have appeared in the discussion of women's ordination, which also represents a radical departure from traditional norms but which is now widely accepted. But one cannot find support either for the licitness of homosexuality or for the validity of gay marriage within the tradition of the premodern church.

POSTSCRIPT

Did Same-Sex Unions Exist
in the Early Middle Ages?

There is little dispute that the same-sex unions that Boswell describes actually existed and were used as ritualistic ceremonies. A crucial factor in this issue is what these ceremonies represented. Were they considered the equivalent of heterosexual marriages? Or, were they merely "brotherhood" agreements, which had little religious sanction? The linguistic and textual difficulties involving the sources of these ceremonies make this a difficult choice for scholars.

Another problem to consider is to what extent have current conditions and exigencies powered this issue? Have present views of same-sex unions influenced the issue's historical construction?

Boswell's *Christianity, Social Tolerance, and Homosexuality: Gay People in Western Europe from the Beginning of the Christian Era to the Fourteenth Century* (University of Chicago Press, 1980) is a useful general introduction to this issue. Volume I and II of the series *A History of Private Life,* Philippe Aries and Georges Duby, eds.; Paul Veyne, ed., *From Pagan Rome to Byzantium* (Harvard University Press, 1987); and Georges Duby, ed., *Revelations of the Medieval World* (Harvard University Press, 1988) provide general information on sexuality and sexual relations during the times covered.

Scholarly journals from the 1994–1996 years might have reviews of Boswell's books and rejoinders to them. There is an interesting review and response to them in *The New Republic.* Brent D. Shaw's review in the July 18, 1994, edition prompted a response from Ralph Hexter and a reply by Shaw in the October 3, 1994, edition of the magazine. A perusal of these pieces provides an interesting view of the workings of the historical profession.

On the Internet ...

HyperHistory Online

The HyperHistory Online site traces 3,000 years of world history via colorful graphics, life lines, time lines, and maps. It enables the user to understand what was happening simultaneously in widely separated parts of the world.

http://www.hyperhistory.com/online_n2/History_n2/a.html

Crusades: A Guide to Online Sources

This site, part of the Online Reference Book for Medieval Studies (ORB) Encyclopedia, features original essays, primary sources, bibliographies, works of art, maps, and links to museums and libraries.

http://orb.rhodes.edu/encyclop/religion/crusades/crusade.html

Medieval and Renaissance History

The medieval and Renaissance history site offers information on art, architecture, music, culture, literature, medicine, science, paleography, religion, and women. It also includes links to primary historical documents, translations of classical texts, and an online reference book for medieval studies.

http://www.nyu.edu/gsas/dept/history/internet/geograph/europe/medieval/

Martin Luther (1483–1586)

This site includes a time line of the Protestant Reformation, and also contains information on Martin Luther's anti-Semitism as well as some of his writings. You may listen to music written by Luther while you browse.

http://www.geocities.com/Vienna/1667/luther.htm

PART 2

The Medieval/Renaissance Worlds

*T*his section begins with Europe's medieval era, a period when Roman, Christian, and barbarian forces combined to create a new Western culture. This change led to another synthesis—when the Renaissance and the Protestant Reformation ushered in the beginnings of premodern Europe.

- Were the Crusades Motivated Primarily by Religious Factors?

- Did Women and Men Benefit Equally from the Renaissance?

- Did Martin Luther's Reforms Improve the Lives of European Christians?

- Did Convents Expand Opportunities for European Women?

ISSUE 6

Were the Crusades Motivated Primarily by Religious Factors?

YES: Hans Eberhard Mayer, from *The Crusades*, 2d ed., trans. John Gillingham (Oxford University Press, 1988)

NO: Ronald C. Finucane, from *Soldiers of the Faith: Crusaders and Moslems at War* (St. Martin's Press, 1983)

ISSUE SUMMARY

YES: German historian Hans Eberhard Mayer states that although there were other factors important to the development of the Crusades, the strongest motivation was a religious one.

NO: British historian Ronald C. Finucane counters that although the religious influence on the Crusades was significant, political, social, economic, and military factors in medieval Europe also played a role in their origin, development, and outcome.

One of western European history's defining moments occurred in Clermont, France, in 1095 C.E. when Pope Urban II delivered an address in which he urged Christian Europe to support a movement to wrest the Holy Land from Moslem forces, which had been in control for almost 500 years. This speech set in motion a series of events, which were to span more than two centuries, and caused results that would dramatically shape the future not only of Western Europe but of the Muslim world as well. The name given to this movement was the Crusades.

From the onset, the Crusades were shrouded in myth and mystery. For example, although there are four known versions of Urban's speech, none of them has a real claim on authenticity. So the exact words Urban used to stir the crowd are not known. It has been up to historians to discern the pope's intentions from the accounts of his speech as well as his subsequent writings and actions. Even 1,000 years later there are more questions about the Crusades than answers. And, as historian Ronald C. Finucane has stated, many of the questions raised are perhaps unanswerable.

There are many important questions about the Crusades for historians to ponder: What was the physical composition of the Crusades? What social classes were represented? To what extent did women participate? How good was the leadership? How organized were those who participated in the Crusades? What immediate and long-range effects did the Crusades have on Western Europe and the Muslim world?

In spite of the significance of these questions, the one that seems to be of paramount importance to historians is the question of motivation. What caused thousands of people from all countries in Europe, representing a cross section of the continent's class structure, to leave their lives behind and make a perilous journey from which they might not return? What did they hope to gain?

At first glance, the answer seemed simple: the Crusaders embarked on their quest for religious reasons, to wrest the Holy Land from the Muslim world, thus allowing Christians to participate in the ultimate pilgrimage. Stories abounded of Muslim desecration of Christian holy sites and Muslim mistreatment of Christians. And with Western Christendom's primary leader urging the Crusaders on—even offering indulgences (full or partial remission of one's sins) as an incentive—the question seemed to have a logical answer.

But historical questions seldom have simple answers, and further study brought several other possibilities. Could the feudal system with its insistence on primogeniture (the inheritance of family lands by the oldest son, leaving younger sons with few opportunities, and possibly encouraging the younger sons to seek fame and fortune elsewhere) have been a factor? Were economic factors involving trade and commerce important? And how much was the militaristic nature of medieval society responsible for the Crusades?

In a millennium of Crusade historiography, motivation seems to revolve around two different interpretations—the religious and the secular. The former seeks the answers to Crusader incentive in sacred dimensions, pilgrimages, indulgences, and participation in a just war against despised infidels. The latter discovers interpretations in the economic, social, political, and military worlds of Western Europe, with impetus coming from potential upward mobility, the possible revival of trade and commerce, the search for new kingdoms in the East, and the martial spirit that characterized the Middle Ages.

From all of this, one certainty can be deduced: it is impossible to separate the two factors—the sacred and the profane—with regard to Crusader motivation. Thus, most historians consider both motivations as important to our understanding of the Crusades. For example, in the following selections, Hans Eberhard Mayer stresses the role of the "other-worldly," while Ronald C. Finucane spotlights the influence of secular motivations.

Hans Eberhard Mayer  **YES**

The Origins of the Crusades

Pope Urban II opened the Council of Clermont on 18 November 1095—the moment that has gone down in history as the starting point of the crusades....

The success of the Clermont appeal has still not been fully explained and probably never can be. Nor will any definitive interpretation be offered here; after all, the reasons for taking the cross varied considerably from one individual to another. All one can do is to examine a whole range of spiritual and worldly motives of different kinds which coalesced not only to produce the spark of that unique and spontaneous success at Clermont but also to light a fire which burned for two hundred years.

Originally the object of the crusade was to help the Christian Churches in the East. However unnecessary such help may, in fact, have been, it was in these terms that Urban is supposed to have spoken at Clermont. But very soon men had a more definite object in mind: to free the Holy Land and, above all, Jerusalem, the Sepulchre of Christ, from the yoke of heathen dominion.... Jerusalem cannot have been used merely as a lure; the name was too potent and would inevitably have pulled the whole enterprise in this one direction. It is rather more likely in view of the evident lack of over-all planning that Urban had not in fact made much of Jerusalem while at Clermont but that during the course of the next year he gave in to public opinion which needed and created a concrete goal....

Even the mere sound of the name Jerusalem must have had a glittering and magical splendour for the men of the eleventh century which we are no longer capable of feeling. It was a keyword which produced particular psychological reactions and conjured up particular eschatological notions. Men thought, of course, of the town in Palestine where Jesus Christ had suffered, died, been buried, and then had risen again. But, more than this, they saw in their minds' eye the heavenly city of Jerusalem with its gates of sapphire, its walls and squares bright with precious stones—as it had been described in the Book of Revelation and Tobias. It was the centre of a spiritual world just as the earthly Jerusalem was, in the words of Ezekiel 'in the midst of the nations and countries'. It was a meeting place for those who had been scattered, the goal of the great pilgrimage of peoples where God resides among his people; the place at the end of time to which the elect ascend; the resting place of the righteous; city of paradise and of the tree of life which heals all men. . . .

Counting for just as much as the images conjured up by a child-like, mystical faith was the long tradition of pilgrimage to Jerusalem. As early as 333 a pilgrim from Bordeaux reached Palestine; and not much later a Gallic noblewoman named Egeria visited the Holy Places leaving to posterity a report which is as important a monument of a Latin changing from ancient to medieval as it is for the topography of the *loca sancta*. In 386 Saint Jerome settled in Bethlehem; half a century later the Empress Eudocia went into retreat at Jerusalem. Monasteries and hospices were built to receive the travellers who, following the new fashion—as it can fairly be called—came to Palestine. The stream of pilgrims never dried up, not even after the Arab conquest of the Holy Land in the seventh century. The growing east-west trade in relics played some part in awakening and sustaining interest in the Holy Places, but more important was the gradual development of the penitential pilgrimage. This was imposed as a canonical punishment and for capital crimes like fratricide it could be for a period of up to seven years and to all the great centres: Rome, San Michele at Monte Gargano, Santiago di Compostella and, above all, Jerusalem and Bethlehem. With the belief that they were effective ways to salvation the popularity of pilgrimages grew rapidly from the tenth century onwards. Saint John of Parma journeyed no less than six times to the Holy Land—given the conditions of travel at the time an astonishing achievement. Men of violent passions like Fulk Nerra, Count of Anjou, or Robert the Devil, Count of Normandy, went on pilgrimages to Jerusalem when their consciences plagued them on account of the crimes they had committed against church and monastery, so sometimes they had to go more than once. Returning from one of these pilgrimages Fulk founded the abbey of Beaulieu near Loches and gave it as its chief relic a piece of stone which he was said to have bitten off the Holy Sepulchre while kneeling before it in ecstatic prayer. The new Cluniac order, gaining all the time in prestige and influence, used its far-flung net of contacts and its genius for organization both to urge men to go on pilgrimages and to improve facilities for those who did. For many pilgrims in the eleventh century the journey to Jerusalem took on a still deeper religious meaning; according to Ralph Glaber, himself a Cluniac monk, it was looked upon as the climax of a man's religious life, as his final journey. Once he had reached the Holy Places he would remain there until he died.

It is clear that in the middle of the eleventh century the difficulties facing pilgrims began to increase. In part this was a result of the Seldjuk invasions which made things harder for travellers on the road through Anatolia—a popular route because it permitted a visit to Constantinople. But it was also a consequence of the growing number of pilgrims, for this worried the Muslim authorities in Asia Minor and Palestine, just as the Greeks in south Italy looked sceptically upon the groups of Norman 'pilgrims' who were all too easily persuaded to settle there for good. It has been suggested that the Muslims may have had a commercial interest in promoting pilgrimages but, except perhaps in Jerusalem itself, the income from this source cannot have been very significant—poverty was, after all, one of the ideals of the pilgrim. So there was little or no incentive for them to make the journey any easier. Conditions were, of course, nothing like as bad as they had been during the persecution of the Christians under the mad caliph, Hakim, who, in 1009, had had the Church of the Holy Sepulchre in Jerusalem destroyed; but neither were they as favourable as they had been during the great days of the Byzantine Empire or in the time of Charlemagne who had himself taken a keen interest in the pilgrimage to Palestine. Yet despite the occasional trouble the number of pilgrims grew steadily. In 1064–5 Bishop Gunther of Bamberg led a party over 7,000 strong into the Holy Land. Near Ramleh in Palestine they were suddenly attacked by Muslims and for several days they had to fight a defensive battle. It is not easy to explain how they managed this since pilgrims were always unarmed.

Here we have reached the critical point of difference between crusader and pilgrim. The crusader carried weapons. A crusade was a pilgrimage, but an armed pilgrimage which was granted special privileges by the Church and which was held to be specially meritorious. The crusade was a logical extension of the pilgrimage. It would never have occurred to anyone to march out to conquer the Holy Land if men had not made pilgrimages there for century after century. The constant stream of pilgrims inevitably nourished the idea that the Sepulchre of Christ ought to be in Christian hands, not in order to solve the practical difficulties which faced pilgrims, but because gradually the knowledge that the Holy Places, the patrimony of Christ, were possessed by heathens became more and more unbearable. If the link between pilgrimage and crusade is obvious, the credit for bringing it about belongs to Urban II. Although historians today are less inclined to argue that the crusades were caused by increasing difficulties in the way of pilgrims, it still remains true that pilgrimages were of decisive importance in the rise of the crusading movement. In Erdmann's words, Urban 'took the popular but, in practical terms, unfruitful idea of pilgrimage and used it to fertilize the war upon the heathen'. It is significant that contemporaries were at first unable to distinguish clearly between the two things. Not until the mid-thirteenth century was there a Latin word for 'crusade' and even then it was seldom used. (The English word crusade, like the German word *Kreuzzug*, was only invented in the eighteenth century.) In the Middle Ages men almost always used circumlocutions like *expeditio, iter in terram sanctam* (journey into the Holy Land) and—especially early in the crusading period—*peregrinatio*, the technical term for pilgrimage. The line between crusade and pilgrimage was obviously a blurred one. . . .

One more motive for taking the cross remains to be considered; and this one was to put all the others in the shade. It was the concept of a reward in the form of the crusading indulgence. In modern Roman Catholic doctrine the indulgence comes at the end of a clear process of remission of sins. First the penitent sinner must confess and receive absolution so that the guilt of the sin is remitted and instead of suffering eternal punishment he will have to suffer only the temporal penalties due to sin. (It is important to note that these penalties may take place either in this world or the next and will include purgatory.) Then in return for indulgence-earning works the Church may grant him remission of all or part of the penalty due to sin, depending on whether the indulgence is a plenary one or not. This is a judicial act of grace based on the authority of the Church's power of the keys and is entirely separate from the sacrament of penance. The indulgence would affect both the canonical punishment imposed by the Church—the penitential punishment—and the temporal punishment imposed by God, since the Church could offer God a substitute penance from the 'Treasury of Merits'—an inexhaustible reservoir of merits accumulated by Christ and added to by the saints on a scale far in excess of what they themselves needed. Undoubtedly then the indulgence has a transcendental effect before God (in foro Dei). Where the theologians disagree with one another is on the question of whether one can absolutely guarantee that this judicial act will have a positive result in foro Dei or whether it runs up against the problem of God's freedom. In this case the positive result is only indirectly and morally assured in as much as the Church guarantees that the offer of a substitute penance is sufficient to discharge the whole of the punishment due, i.e. the sinner could not have achieved any better result even if he had himself done full penance. But when considering early indulgences, especially the first crusading indulgences, it is vital to remember that this logical doctrine was a later construction designed to give theological authority to customs which, in practice, already existed.

Not until after the First Crusade did the theologians of the twelfth century, first among them Hugh of St. Victor, work out—in practical, if not yet in formal terms—the distinction between the guilt of sin and the punishment due to sin which is crucial to the theory of indulgences. And not until c. 1230 was the important doctrine of the 'Treasury of Merits', which provided the equivalent substitute necessary if punishment were to be remitted, formulated by Hugh of St. Cher. The detailed problems of the precise nature of an indulgence and the justification for it were hotly disputed in the twelfth and thirteenth centuries. Even St. Thomas Aquinas was clearly hard put to it to explain the indulgence because he began his proof of it by producing a classic logical fallacy (petitio principii): 'Everyone agrees that indulgences are effective because it would be godless to say that the Church does anything in vain.' Where even theologians found much obscure, there was little chance of popular opinion being well-informed. Any discussion of the crusades must take this point more fully into consideration than has hitherto been customary. In assessing the effect of the crusading indulgence what matters is what people understood or believed they understood by it, not what it actually was. And it is worth noting that the debate about indulgences which started c. 1130 was sparked off by the fact that they were being abused. As long as the abuses were not too blatant, people looked upon the indulgence as an acceptable innovation without bothering too much about the theology of the matter. We must always remember that the publicizing of the first crusading indulgence took place in an atmosphere which was free of the limitations imposed either by an official Church pronouncement or by a proper theological debate. The only way the new elements could be defined was by comparing them with earlier penitential practices.

The indulgence must, in fact, be seen as a development of the Church's earlier penitential discipline. This was originally divided into three stages: confession, satisfaction, and reconciliation (i.e. being readmitted to communion). Satisfaction was looked upon as the element which earned extinction of sins and thus made the reconciliation possible. At this time no distinction would have been made between remission of guilt and remission of punishment. In principle, the penance had to be equivalent to the sin committed. One had to pay, as it were, pound for pound. But obviously it was only a matter of chance whether or not a precisely equivalent penance was found; thus in addition there had to be the temporal penalties due to sin which, being imposed by God, could measure exactly any guilt that was still remaining. Since God's temporal punishment was feared far more than any earthly penance, a penitential system of draconic severity was developed on the theory that the harsher the penance in this world, the smaller would be the settlement in the next. The fact that up until the sixth century only serious offences were subject to the penance of the Church helped to establish the severity of penitential practice. Yet when, for reasons which cannot be gone into here, this changed so that penance had to be done for venial sins as well, the old system at first remained in force. But now harsh tasks and long penances during which the sinner remained excluded from the sacraments were no longer always appropriate, so inevitably there developed a trend towards a milder and a more differentiated system of punishment. At first this was done by the use of commutation and redemption, i.e. one form of punishment was exchanged for another which theoretically was still equivalent to the sin committed. Thus if it were shorter, it was also supposed to be harder; but in practice it tended to be more lenient. Lists of the penalties due to various sins were drawn up tariff-fashion in the 'Penitentials', together with the appropriate redemptions. In these redemptions we have one of the main roots of the crusading indulgence. In the eleventh century the system became still milder when it became customary to allow reconciliation to take place as soon as a man had begun his penance, though of course he still had to complete it. Thus long-term excommunication—one of the most feared consequences of sin—was in effect abolished. This change also meant the end of the old custom of total reconciliation. Its place was taken by an absolution granted immediately after confession. This involved reconciliation with God and the Church, i.e. forgiveness of the guilt of sin, but it did not mean full remission of the punishment due to sin. Nevertheless absolution went further than redemption and thus came closer to the indulgence in that the Church made a powerful plea for pardon; so a transcendental effect was at least intended. This was still not a judicial act, however, nor was it a remission of punishment granted independently of the sacrament of penance. But from here it was only a short step to the indulgence, i.e. to a more clearly defined and more certainly effective remission of the penance imposed by the Church. By an act of grace allowance was made for the transcendental effect *in foro Dei* of the Church's plea. This then made it possible to curtail the penance imposed by the Church. According to Poschmann, one of the leading Catholic experts on the subject, 'the indulgence was no longer just a part-payment on the time after death, it was also a most welcome relief during this earthly life'. The special feature of the indulgence was that the ideal of equivalence was no longer adhered to in practice. Later on the doctrine of the 'Treasury of Merits' was developed in order to justify this practice.

It is revealing that the idea of indulgence only became really effective when it was linked with the pilgrimage to Jerusalem. Papal pronouncements rather similar to indulgences were occasionally made before the crusades, but these were, in fact, usually absolutions. Alexander II, for example, promised a remission of penance to the soldiers who had joined the Barbastro expedition of 1063. In addition he also offered them the *remissio peccatorum,* the remission of the temporal penalties due to sin. It has been argued that the pope's letter is a forgery, but in fact it is a perfectly genuine plenary indulgence. Yet for various reasons it had very little effect. For one thing, it was addressed to a much smaller group than was the crusading indulgence of 1095. Alexander's offer applied only to those who had already decided to take part in the Spanish campaign; and he left it open whether he would extend the terms of the indulgence to include those who joined later. Furthermore normal penitential practice was adhered to in that a penance had first to be imposed, at least formally, before it could be considered as cancelled by the indulgence. Finally a campaign in Spain did not have the same mass-appeal as an expedition to the Holy Land. This example shows clearly why the full effects of the indulgence were felt only when it became linked with the pilgrimage to Jerusalem.

In this context it was important that the penitential journey to Jerusalem was thought to be especially meritorious and salutary. In theory the Church had always taken the view that movement from one place to another did not bring a man any nearer to God; but it was impossible to extinguish the popular belief in the value of a pilgrimage to Jerusalem. Its popularity was assured from the moment when the reconciliation with the Church was moved forward to the beginning of the work of penance, in this case the pilgrimage. This applied, of course, to any penitential pilgrimage; what gave Jerusalem its special significance was the tradition of the Holy Places. There is evidence from as early as the eighth century for the belief that remission of sins could be earned by a visit to the Church of the Holy Sepulchre. But those who shared this belief in the value of pilgrimages were denounced at the Council of Chalons in 813. The Council was relying on the authority of Jerome who had said that it was not seeing Jerusalem that was praiseworthy, but living a good life there. Indeed, in Jerome's eyes, even this had no special purifying value. He wrote that he had gone to Palestine in order to understand the Bible better, not to obtain spiritual advantages. But since the Council quoted only Jerome's first statement and not his commentary on it, it was possible to believe that both Jerome and the Council were prepared to concede an indirect purifying value to the journey to Jerusalem—i.e. when it led to a long period of residence there. Later on the Church quite patently failed to combat the belief that the pilgrimage to Jerusalem was worth an indulgence. Indeed it formally granted partial indulgences for it, like the year's indulgence allowed by Alexander III. This was during the heyday of the crusades, when the crusader was granted an unlimited plenary indulgence; understandably the peaceful pilgrim obtained just a partial indulgence....

It would, of course, be wrong to assert that the crusade propagandists avoided a more spiritual approach and worked only in . . . blatantly commercial terms. Nevertheless a great deal was done by such methods; we should remember that it was an age which witnessed a tremendous boom in long-distance trade. St. Bernard, though he used the vocabulary of merchants, did, of course, also say very different things, but he too did not want to renounce this effective propaganda theme.

It is perhaps better to put aside the question of whether or not the Church gave the impression that a complete remission of sin, both guilt and punishment, was possible through the indulgence and therefore through a procedure outside the Church's sacrament of penance. It is certainly possible that sometimes contemporaries did so interpret the Church's ambiguous terminology. But in any case the difference between remission of penance and remission of the temporal punishment due to sin, a difference which existed in the Church's traditional doctrine of indulgences, was of itself quite enough to explain the success of Clermont. There had been nothing new about being able to obtain remission of penance by going to fight the heathen. But that the penalties due to sin could be remitted simply as a result of taking the cross—as the crusade propagandists suggested—this was an unheard of innovation. Previously both the reconciliation granted at the start of the penance and the redeeming commutation had affected only the penances and had had no transcendental effect upon the penalties due to sin. It was indeed hoped that absolution would have such an effect, but it could certainly not be guaranteed. The indulgence on the other hand availed before God in a certain and in a quantitatively measurable fashion so that both the temporal penalties due to sin and the earthly penances were remitted and, in the case of a plenary indulgence, fully cancelled. Only Alexander II had promised as much as this for the war against the heathen and his promise, being addressed only to a small group, had met with little response. It was when linked with the universally popular idea of pilgrimage to Jerusalem that the explosive force of the crusading indulgence was revealed. Ekkehard of Aura spoke of 'a new way of penance' now being opened up. Here lies the secret of the astonishing success of Urban's summons, a success which astonished the Church as much as anyone else. Imagine a knight in the south of France, living with his kinsmen in the socially and economically unsatisfactory institution of the *frérèche*. His feuds and the 'upper class' form of highway robbery which often enough went with them, were prohibited by the Peace of God. Suddenly he was offered the chance of going on a pilgrimage—in any event the wish of many men. This pilgrimage was supervised by the Church; it was moreover an armed pilgrimage during which he could fulfil his knightly function by taking part in battle. There would be opportunities for winning plunder. Above all there was the entirely new offer of a full remission of all the temporal penalties due to sin, especially of those to be suffered in purgatory. The absolution given in the sacrament of penance took from him the guilt; taking the cross meant the cancellation of all the punishment even before he set out to perform the task imposed. Not to accept such an offer, not—at the very least—to take it seriously, would indeed have been mad. The 'shrewd businessman' seized his chance. And who did not want to be numbered among the shrewd?

Taking the cross in these circumstances was, of course, an act of faith just as much as an act of naive trust in the promises made by Church publicists. Naturally not all crusaders were moved by piety. In the Middle Ages too there were sceptics and the motives for going on crusade were many, various, and tangled, often social and economic in character. But the offer of indulgence must have had an irresistible attraction for those who did not doubt the Church's teaching, who believed in the reality of the penalties due to sin, or at least accepted the possibility of their existence. Such believers must have made up a great part of those who went on the First Crusade—whatever proportion of the total population of Europe they may have been. And, of course, the crusaders of 1095 could not have guessed that the offer which they were accepting was in reality much more limited than the one promised them by the 'fishers of men'.

Ronald C. Finucane

Soldiers of the Faith:
Crusaders and Moslems at War

The Crusades: An Overview

'He who fights so the word of God may prevail is on the path of God.' The sentiments embodied in this saying attributed to Mohammad do much to explain the amazing success of Islam, which, through the zeal for *jihad* or holy war, extended from the borders of France to those of India by the early eighth century. Religious enthusiasm also lies behind the equally amazing accomplishments of the Christian warriors of the First Crusade. In both Moslem expansion and Christian conquest, however, luck was just as important as zeal. The Moslems were able to profit from the weaknesses of early seventh-century Christendom just as the crusaders, when they entered Jerusalem in bloody triumphs four and a half centuries later, were able to attribute their victory in part to dissension and weakness among the Moslems.

Because of assassinations and rivalry which could be traced back to the period following Mohammad's death, by the tenth century the Moslem world had fallen into two major (and several minor) rival camps. One of these, the Shi'ite faction, was supported by the successors of Ali, Mohammad's cousin and son-in-law. By the later tenth century, they had gained control in Egypt as the Fatimids; a fanatical offshoot, the Assassins, would spill the blood both of Christians and other rival Moslem groups. The other faction, the Sunnites, originally supported the succession of Abu Bakr, one of Mohammad's closest allies. On both sides the picture is further confused by the establishment of semi-independent emirates and caliphates of varying political and religious allegiances. Moslem Spain, for example, began to go its own way as early as the eighth century. Not only was there internal rivalry, but also, from the tenth and early eleventh centuries, the Moslem world was shaken by progressive incursions of the Seljuk Turks. These people, having become Sunnites, brought to the Near East a vitality and fervour that were reminiscent of the earliest stages in the rise of Islam. They were proud, warlike, zealous and—more to the point—very successful: in the 1050s, they captured Baghdad; by the 1070s, Asia Minor (with the defeat of the Byzantines at Manzikert in 1071), Palestine and

From Ronald C. Finucane, *Soldiers of the Faith: Crusaders and Moslems at War* (St. Martin's Press, 1983). Copyright © 1983 by Ronald C. Finucane. Notes omitted.

Damascus; and by the 1080s, Antioch and Edessa. After one of their strongest leaders, Sultan Malik Shah, died in 1092, Turkish unity was dissipated by the establishment of several rival emirates, particularly in Asia Minor and Syria. This was why, during the 1090s, even as crusader swarms were moving from western Europe, the Holy Land was the scene of internal conflict and rivalry; why the crusaders often found themselves, from practical considerations, willing to accept or ask for the assistance of one or other of the Moslem parties in the ever-shifting sands of near-eastern politics. The fact that Greek Constantinople was to many westerners suspect as a perfumed den of vice and treachery, only complicated matters....

The crusaders, then, were aided not only by their own religious zeal, cupidity, curiosity and many other motives that pushed them eastwards, but also by the turmoil and rivalries among the Moslems themselves. Though this may help to explain how they succeeded in their extraordinary venture, an even more interesting problem involves timing: why, since Jerusalem had been continuously occupied by Moslems since the seventh century, did the Christian West only attempt recovery at the end of the eleventh century? What had changed in European society and thought? One way to approach this question is through an examination of earlier military relations between the Moslem and Christian worlds, beginning, for convenience, with Spain. Visigothic Spain was attacked in 711 by Tarik and his converted Berbers in a campaign which, according to legend, was brought on when the daughter of Julian, a local lord, was abducted and impregnated by King Rodrigo of Toledo. In revenge, Julian is supposed to have invited the Moslems from North Africa to overthrow Rodrigo. Finding the job so easily accomplished, they went on to take over Spain itself, though there was resistance; by tradition the first important battle launched against the invaders by the Christians occurred in 718. Though they were eventually pushed into a narrow coastal lair behind the northern mountains, by the ninth century the Christians had begun their *Reconquista*. They had also provided themselves with a supernatural champion in St. James, at Compostella, which would become one of Europe's premier pilgrimage centres, as Jerusalem was at the other end of the Mediterranean. By the middle of the eleventh century, determined Christian kings had extended their hegemony southwards, bringing many Moslem princelings under their control. This success at last united the Moors and persuaded them to invite more ruthless co-religionists from north Africa, who reversed many of the Christian conquests. This was the confusing milieu for El Cid's sometimes unchristian adventures. In any case, on the eve of the First Crusade, Spain had already witnessed more than three centuries of warfare with the Moslems.

It was from Spain, about 720, that the Moslems moved on into south-west France. Historians still debate the extent of this threat and its potentialities, though in the short term many cities and towns undoubtedly suffered its harmful effects. Charles Martel, the 'hammer', earned his epithet by turning back in 732 or 733 near Poitiers this Moslem advance, the start of a long tradition of Frankish resistance to the Saracens. By about 770, most of the enemy had been pushed from Gaul, though they continued to harass Charlemagne and his successors. The Frankish *Annals* report that around 799 Moslem insignia captured while defending the Balearics were sent to Charlemagne, and, in 801, at the fall of Barcelona, it is said that many Saracen prisoners were taken. Heroic deeds in the Spanish March or borderlands gave rise to one of the seminal works of medieval literature, the *Chanson de Roland;* though nominally-Christian Basques seem to have attacked the proud Roland, the ultimate enemy was the Moslem. Charlemagne's son, Pepin, King of Italy (d. 810), sent a fleet against Moslems pillaging Corsica in 806, but this did not stop their overrunning both Sardinia and Corsica in 810. Even before Charlemagne's death, the *Annals* compiler mentions the ravaging of Nice—a hint of unpleasant things to come, for later in the ninth century enterprising Moslems set up a bandits' nest some fifty miles along the coast from Nice, near Fréjus, from which they terrorized the neighbourhood, the Alpine passes and the north Italian seaports. There were other robbers' dens, but Fréjus was particularly troublesome. The stronghold was destroyed in the later tenth century when a league of aggrieved parties finally captured it.

It is not surprising that Moslem pirates should show an interest in Italian ports, since the peninsula and Sicily jutted out so invitingly into what the Moslems could call, with almost as much justification as the Romans, *Mare Nostrum.* Mohammad had been dead a mere twenty years, for example, when the first (recorded) attack on Sicily occurred. Things became serious during the ninth century, and, by 902, Sicily belonged to the Moslems. Southern Italian cities also suffered during the ninth century, and Naples often found it more expedient to ally itself with the Moslems than to fight them. Even the Eternal City itself was lusted after by the infidel, though they had to content themselves with a rampage through the suburbs, including St Peter's basilica. Pope Leo IV, in consequence, threw a wall around the saint's church and thereby laid the foundations—in the figurative sense only, considering the extensive resisting and rebuilding of later centuries—of the Vatican mini-city. Another casualty of ninth-century Moslem activities in Italy was Monte Cassino, the venerable home of Benedictine monasticism. At last the Italians began to organize resistance, and by the early tenth century managed to expel the Moslems from Italy proper. Pope John X himself took the field in 915, successfully adding spiritual to martial forces. From this point on, Italian cities turned to offensive tactics: Pisa and Genoa in particular began launching aggressive raids against Moslem ports and, by the early eleventh century, were attacking the enemy in north Africa itself. These two cities were interested in protecting their western Mediterranean trade. On the other side of the peninsula, Venice was equally concerned about maintaining commercial ties with rich Byzantium to the east.

The Byzantines were just as anxious about the Moslem threat; when Pope John X defeated the Moslems at the Garigliano in 915, it was with the help of Byzantine military power, whose encounters with the Moslems stretched back to the seventh century, with Emperor Heraclius. In fact, Roman emperors were sending troops out to skewer Saracens long before Mohammad's birth....

Among the more successful of mercenary troops hired by the Byzantines were the Varangian Guard of Scandinavians, who were established in service in Constantinople about AD 1000. After the conquest of England in 1066, many displaced or dispossessed Anglo-Saxon warriors joined them. One of the key figures and victims of that 1066 conflict, Harald Hardradi, had taken service with the Varangians for a short time in the 1030s. According to his *Saga*, on this tour he attacked the lands of the Saracens and captured eighty towns, some of which surrendered, the rest being taken by assault. Even as Harald was spilling Moslem blood, however, the Seljuk Turks were moving westward, thus creating a new, formidable enemy whose incursions would compel Emperor Alexius Comnenus to call upon the West for help and set the scene for the First Crusade.

Long before this, western Christians had acquired centuries of experience battling Moslems in Spain, France and Italy. This aggression had been encouraged by the Church in its articulation of a doctrine of holy war. Warfare presented early Christians with yet another problem through the continuous process of accommodating their ideals to the 'real' world.... By the early fifth century, that giant who helped to shape medieval thought, St Augustine, had formulated a doctrine of just war in Christian terms. Provided that a war were declared by legitimate authority, for a just cause, and fought with the right intention, Christians should have no qualms about participating. In addition to this, even during Augustine's lifetime Europe was being transformed by incoming peoples whose leaders held prowess and *virtus* in battle of great importance and needed no excuses for rushing into battle. These Germanic tribes were eventually converted, thereby bringing to Christianity their own sublimation of the warlike virtues. With the rise of the Moslems, these new Europeans, and especially the Franks, stood out as defenders not only of their kingdoms, but also of Christianity itself. And yet, this was not holy war—though it may have been just—for the rewards of victory or valour were not yet envisaged as essentially spiritual....

The Church helped to prepare the ground for... holy wars in yet another way,... through the application of a sacramental mystique to knighthood. By the early eleventh century, religious ceremonial sometimes accompanied bestowal of the sword. At the same time, knights were encouraged to observe the growing Peace and Truce of God movements. The Church, and papacy, thereby (in theory) turned this potentially dangerous lynchpin of feudalism into an ally, a knight of St Peter. Before the First Crusade, these free-ranging fighters, trained to battle but exposed (at least) to religious exhortation, formed a corps which the Church was on occasion able to direct against her enemies....

Besides these spiritual and theoretical predispositions, eleventh-century men and women were also being 'prepared' for the first great crusading outburst of 1095–99 by changing conditions within their society and economy. Decades ago Henri Pirenne used words like 'optimism', 'native strength', 'fecundity' and 'revival' to describe eleventh-century Europe, while another equally famous medievalist (Marc Bloch) spoke of a new feudal age beginning about 1050. In general, this is still the fashion among most historians, who date the inception of the 'High Middle Ages'—the flowering of medieval society—to the eleventh century. Obviously the crusades cannot be understood without reference to this general awakening of western Europe, any more than they can be 'explained' only by the factors mentioned above. Perhaps the most important and correlated developments, in a strictly material sense, were the economic as well as the demographic expansion that affected all social levels. After the external invasions of western Europe had come to an end by about AD 1000, life was less precarious, food production rose, families increased in size, new arable fields were created in forest and waste land, and more and more merchants plied their trades in and between the growing towns. About 1080, the monks of St Aubin of Angers issued the following regulation, among others, for their peasants at Meron:

> If several men have loaded an ass with different kinds of merchandise, they shall owe toll for the ass, save if it is foreign or costly merchandise.
> For [these] other things, the toll shall be paid according to its value...

The good monks were not about to ignore possible profits from these small-time business ventures by their villeins. Something similar was happening to more and villagers throughout western Europe. An obvious motive was the desire for immediate personal gain from new and growing markets; another, especially for peasants, was the wish to escape the sometimes crushing obligations of manorial regimes. Many others would take up the generous offers of their lords—medieval land developers—and, especially in the twelfth century, pack up their families and rude furnishings and move off as colonists to take advantage of the lighter rents and work-loads. In the eleventh century, then, social and geographical mobility were distinct possibilities.

But larger families, especially among the middle-range nobility (of feudal Normandy for instance), created problems. As the medieval tradition of primogeniture spread, hunger for land and lordship drove many frustrated younger sons far from their home territories. Even where primogeniture was not the rule, many sought escape from the limitations of too many siblings and too little land by venturing into Spain, Italy and the Balkans. The enthusiastic knights of the First Crusade were aware of the practical opportunities, as well as spiritual advantages, awaiting them in the Holy Land. These conditions may also have complicated relations between neighbouring aristocratic families, who now would have to guard constantly against trespass (while, of course, encroaching against neighbours whenever possible). Often, the Church and peasantry suffered more than anyone else in these petty feudal wrangles. It was in the interests of both that the middling nobility should curb their appetites for contention, or at least satisfy them elsewhere. This was the background to another set of conditions, which led to the crusades—the part played by the Church not only in controlling the behaviour of the laity, but in imposing its own ideals upon ordinary men and women of high and low estate....

As the foregoing suggests, the crusading movement developed out of different sets of conditions laid down before and during the eleventh century. At least this seems to be the consensus today, when the political-colonial motives and immediate papal stimulus tend to be played down, while the sociopsychological background to the movement is emphasized. [Pope] Urban II is no longer thought of as the 'founder' of the crusading surge, but as a catalyst acting upon preformed sentiments and social circumstances. Yet there is no doubt that his sermon of 1095 was crucial. Also, in the decades leading up to 1095, military conflicts with the Moslems accelerated and thereby intensified pre-existing attitudes. In Spain, for example, the army of King Alfonso VI suffered overwhelming defeat in 1086 at the hands of the north African Murabits (or Almoravids, the Veiled Ones). Christian knights from France and elsewhere in western Europe were encouraged to attempt to regain lost Spanish territory. 'My Cid plies his lance until it breaks and then takes his sword and slays Moors without number, blood dripping from his elbow down.' In Italy at about the same time—1087—several cities collaborated in launching attacks against a north African Moslem base; the successful foray was led by a papal legate. In southern Italy, the ambitious Roger and his brother Robert Guiscard—products of a large, ambitious Norman family—were active as early as mid-century. By 1072, the two had successfully blockaded, besieged and conquered Sicily's Moslem capital, Palermo. The job was completed by Roger in 1091, when the island, as well as Malta and southern Italy, came under Norman control, a southern pendant to the Norman conquest of England a generation earlier....

By [October 1097] rivalries had split the crusader armies. Some of the leaders detached their contingents and went off on their own, like Baldwin of Boulogne, who travelled east to establish himself as ruler of the Armenian Christians at Edessa by March 1098. Meanwhile, the bulk of the crusader army besieged Antioch, captured in June 1098. Bohemond of Taranto (southern Italy) took over as Prince of Antioch, with the backing of Genoese merchant-shippers who gained concessions in the city. Raymond, Count of Toulouse and *soi-disant* leader of the crusade, after bickering with Bohemond about Antioch, finally gave in to pressure from the rank-and-file and pushed on in January 1099. Jerusalem was reached and taken in mid-July 1099; Godfrey, Duke of Lower Lorraine, became 'advocate' of the Holy Sepulchre, claiming to be unworthy of any higher honour in Christ's city. On his death in 1100, his less fastidious brother, Baldwin of Edessa, took the title King of Jerusalem. Thus, on the eve of the twelfth century, the crusaders had taken the Holy Land and had established the Kingdom of Jerusalem, Principality of Antioch, County of Edessa and (by 1109) County of Tripoli, held by Bertrand, son of Raymond, Count of Toulouse. These were the so-called Crusader States. The capture of Jerusalem renewed interest in the West and resulted in three crusades in 1101, which ended in victories for the Turks and worsening Western-Byzantine relations. In fact, by 1105, Bohemond of Antioch, fearing Byzantine pressure, convinced Pope Paschal II to preach a crusade against Byzantium itself. Nothing came of this, but it was an ominous foretaste of things to come. Meanwhile, King Baldwin of Jerusalem managed to extend crusader control by taking Acre in 1103 with Genoese help and Sidon in 1110 with Norwegian and Venetian assistance. But his attack on Tyre failed, and a raid into Egypt accomplished little. Yet by 1118 when he died, most of Palestine and much of Syria were under Christian control, the crusaders now assisted by the sometimes mutually antagonistic military orders, the Templars and Hospitallers....

Conclusion

Though it is difficult to summarize and draw conclusions about such a varied and long-lasting movement as the crusades, certain generalizations are unavoidable. For instance, it is apparent that the expression 'the crusades' must be qualified, for the First Crusade differed in many ways from those which followed. Thousands of Europeans, affected by the emotional and social upheavals of the eleventh century, undertook a long, dangerous trek towards a mystical goal which was, for them, both a place and a state of salvation. During the next two centuries, crusades became increasingly structured, moving from general to specific aims and means; the idealism of the First Crusade was superseded by sometimes incompatible ideologies imposed from above by the papacy, by the noble and royal leaders of later expeditions, and by the secular rulers of *Outremer.*

Concurrently, Christendom itself was changing: the crusades exemplified these changes, revealing much about the dynamics of religious, economic and political realignments and alterations in western Europe. To take the religious aspect as an example, the crusades encouraged a growing concern about gaining indulgences, first by service abroad, then eventually by purchase of exemption from such service; the papacy attracted more and more criticism—from thirteenth-century poets who castigated Roman greed, for instance—because of what appeared to be diversions from the crusading impulse. By the sixteenth century, such matters would become important issues in the breakdown of European religious unity. Certainly this is not to suggest that the crusades led to the Reformation, but merely that the later crusades disclosed ominous stresses within a Europe that would ultimately undergo a Reformation. In the same way, conflict between French and English crusaders during the Third Crusade was a harbinger of that later confrontation known as the Hundred Years' War. Crusader activities and interrelationships in the Holy Land, then, as well as European responses to calls for crusades, provide models of wider, more deeply rooted attitudes, ambiguities and animosities within western Europe; in this sense, each crusade was a microcosm, a diminished image of Christendom.

Another inevitable conclusion to any general study of the crusades is the fact that many questions remain unanswered, perhaps unanswerable. The sorting out of motivations, for instance, still engages the interest of scholars, as does the very composition of the groups called 'crusaders': for each knightly or noble participant, for each foot-soldier or archer, how many unarmed pilgrims, women, clergymen, went along as 'crusaders'? Did the lower classes, as [Benjamin] Kedar suggested, continue to participate as avidly in the thirteenth century as they did in the twelfth century? How many women were actively, and how many passively, 'crusaders'? Such problems, considered individually, may seem to be mere froth that floats on the surface, puzzles propounded for the delectation of scholars. Yet every clue that can be found is meaningful, every attempt to answer such questions is worth considering because, as suggested above, each crusader band that detached itself from Europe reveals to the historian varying aspects of contemporary society.

Another conclusion to be drawn from a study of the crusades is that Moslem reactions to and interactions with the crusaders, who were intrusive elements, is a topic that is usually relegated to secondary status by western historians. Yet the Islamic viewpoint is as deserving of study as the Christian; fortunately, some western scholars (who are not primarily Orientalists) are forcefully and convincingly presenting the crusades in an Islamic context, pushing us away from the Christian-centered world into a wider universe, instigating a long-overdue Copernican revolution in Christian-Moslem studies. There is a practical side to this as well: the need to understand Islam and the various peoples who call themselves Moslems is as pressing today as it ever was; and yet modern western European Christians seem in general to be as ignorant of the fundamentals of Islam as their twelfth-century predecessors. The words of a thirteenth-century Jew, Ibn Kammūna of Baghdad, concerning the lack of comprehension between Jews and Moslems of his day, apply equally well to modern Christians and Moslems:

> (D)espite numerous contacts of the bulk of the Jews with the Muslims, many Jews still do not know the basic Islamic tenets known by the rank and file Muslims, let alone the elite. It is even more natural that a similar situation should obtain on the Muslim side ...

The question of Christian-Moslem interaction naturally includes the problem of the Christian attitude towards war. An examination of the course of the crusades has led some historians to suggest that Church doctrine was deliberately manipulated to suit specific ends: though committed to condemning bloodshed, the Church itself promoted it. Keith Haines even goes so far as to remark that in Europe

> It is impossible to discern a totally pacifist ideology amongst virtually any of the leading moral, theological or political philosophers of the twelfth and thirteenth centuries ...

Another leading crusade historian has also recently emphasized how the fundamental message of Christian charity was reinterpreted to suit crusade exigencies. Crusade preachers, for instance, must have deliberately presented Christian *caritas* to their audiences in such a way as to play upon the xenophobia of the masses.

One final conclusion to be drawn from the crusading experience is the futility—in practical terms—of the Christian attempt to co-exist with Moslems peacefully in the Holy Land, while trying to maintain political control of the area. Permanent peace between Moslems and Christians, in Moslem territory, was not feasible: caught between an Islam newly dedicated to *jihad* (from Saladin's time) on the one side, and mistrusting, uncomprehending westerners on the other, the Christian Europeans of *Outremer* were, as [Jonathan] Riley-Smith points out, in an untenable position. Christian residents in the Holy Land, then, were surrounded by hostile forces, harassed by problems of logistics and military support and by divisions of opinion in Europe about crusader policy; difficulties of a similar nature would confront many modern European states in their own colonial enterprises. Eventually expelled from positions of political and military power in the Levant, Christians were allowed to return to the Holy City only as pilgrims and suppliants at the Tomb of Christ, as they had been for centuries before that fateful sermon preached by Urban II in 1095.

POSTSCRIPT

Were the Crusades Motivated Primarily by Religious Factors?

With the emergence of Islamic revivalism in the modern world, the historical relationships between the West and the Muslim world have attained a renewed level of interest. The relevance of the Crusades to this contemporary situation provides some interesting food for thought. The Islamic world has always viewed the Crusades as an invasion of its territory by a foreign power; it appears the West has not viewed them in the same light. An interesting question with contemporary applicability is to what extent can the Crusades be viewed as a Christian jihad (holy war)? As the West responds to Islamic-inspired terrorism today with shock and outrage, is it not possible that a millennium ago, Middle Eastern Muslims responded in the same manner to the European Crusaders?

Another example of the ties between past and present is the religious motivation found in both the Crusades and current Islamic revivalism. The former were at least partially motivated by several religious factors: fighting a just war in the service of God; gaining indulgences for services rendered; and the ultimate prize, gaining the right to eternal salvation. The latter is motivated by fighting a war against the infidels in the name of Allah; participating in a fierce struggle between the forces of good and evil; and ultimately acquiring a special place in heaven as martyrs of the faith. Is this an example of repeating the past without learning any lessons from it?

As far as sources on the Crusades are concerned, start with Steven Runciman's three-volume work *A History of the Crusades,* 4th ed. (Cambridge University Press, 1954). Karen Armstrong's *Holy War* (Macmillan, 1988) is a Western source, which speaks of the Crusades in an objective and critical manner, especially as they relate to contemporary problems between Muslims, Christians, and Jews in the Middle East. Jonathan Riley-Smith's *The First Crusaders, 1095–1131* (Cambridge University Press, 1997) represents current scholarship. Smith states that the Crusades "drew on the tradition of Pilgrimage to Jerusalem," and pious violence was a motivating force. He also points out that many of the Crusaders from the times he researched came from the same families and clans and concludes that the sustenance they received from these ties helped make the Crusades possible. For an Arab perspective on the Crusades, see Amin Maalouf, *The Crusades Through Arab Eyes* (Schocken Books, 1985), which finds them partially responsible for the beginning of the disintegration of the Islamic world.

ISSUE 7

Did Women and Men Benefit Equally from the Renaissance?

YES: Mary R. Beard, from *Woman as Force in History: A Study in Traditions and Realities* (Collier Books, 1946)

NO: Joan Kelly-Gadol, from "Did Women Have a Renaissance?" in Renate Bridenthal, Claudia Koonz, and Susan Stuard, eds., *Becoming Visible: Women in European History*, 2d ed. (Houghton Mifflin, 1987)

ISSUE SUMMARY

YES: Historian Mary R. Beard contends that during the Renaissance, Italian women of the higher classes turned to the study of Greek and Roman literature and committed themselves alongside men to developing well-rounded personalities.

NO: Historian Joan Kelly-Gadol argues that women enjoyed greater advantages during the Middle Ages and experienced a relative loss of position and power during the Renaissance.

In 1974 Joan Kelly-Gadol published a pathbreaking essay that challenged traditional periodization. Before that, virtually every publication on the Renaissance proclaimed it to be a great leap forward for everyone, a time when new ideas were everywhere discussed and the old strictures of the Middle Ages were thrown off. The difficulty for Kelly-Gadol was that her own work on women during the medieval and Renaissance periods told a different story. She was one of the first to raise this troubling question: Are the turning points in history the same for women as they are for men? Kelly-Gadol found that well-born women lived in a relatively free environment during the Middle Ages. The courtly love tradition allowed powerful, property-owning women to satisfy their own sexual and emotional needs. With the arrival of the Renaissance, however, the courtly love tradition was defined by powerful male princes who found it desirable for women to be passive and chaste in order to serve the needs of the rising bourgeoisie.

Mary R. Beard is considered the original pathfinder. Her stunning 1946 book *Woman as Force in History* was written, she said, to "destroy the myth

120

that women have done and are suited for little else than bearing and rearing children." Beard, like Kelly-Gadol, studied women of the upper classes. She was eager to find a place for women in history to counter the prevailing view of male historians that by studying the "great man" we could understand the age he created. Beard began looking for the "great woman" and found traces of her throughout human history. After Beard's book was published, it became much more difficult for historians to treat women as passive victims of history.

The field of women's history has a history of its own. Beginning with the pioneering work of historians such as Beard, scholars first engaged in what Gerda Lerner has called "compensatory history"—compensating for past omissions by researching and writing about the great women of history. In a second phase, women's history moved to "contributory history." Looking past the great women, historians took all the traditional categories of standard male history and found women who filled them—women who spent their lives as intellectuals, soldiers, politicians, and scientists. The current phase of women's history parallels more general trends in social history, concentrating on the ordinary people who lived during historical epochs. In this more fully mature phase, the emphasis is on women's culture—how women saw the world from within their own systems and ways of doing things. If Beard was doing compensatory history, Kelly-Gadol might be said to be engaging in contributory history. The women she writes about led lives similar to those of men in their class during the Middle Ages, but Kelly-Gadol contends that they had a different experience during the Renaissance.

One caution to keep in mind is that people are not aware of the times in which they live in terms of the historical periods that scholars later use for identification. People of the past, like people today, are more concerned with their personal lives and fortunes than with historical trends. Periodization, or the marking of turning points in the past, can be useful. It can help to identify broad trends and forks in the road as we explore the past. What women's history has taught us, however, is that looking at the experiences of men may or may not tell us what the experiences of women were like during the same time periods.

Beard collaborated with her husband Charles Beard on many widely read history books. When she wrote *Woman as Force in History*, which is excerpted in the following selection, her aim was to demonstrate that women "have been a force in making all the history that has been made." Her book and the field of women's history that it inspired made possible the work of later scholars such as Kelly-Gadol. Beard challenged traditional notions about the role of women in history; Kelly-Gadol challenged history itself. If what has been said about certain turning points in human history is true only for men or much more true for men than for women, then the whole field of history must be reconceptualized. Although both of the selections that follow were written some time ago, the questions they raise remain lively today.

Mary R. Beard

 **YES**

Evidences in Mediaeval Educational and Intellectual Interests

Humanizing Education—Individual, Civic, and Philosophic

Many things conspired to give leadership and acclaim in education and letters to the women of Italy, earlier than to women of other countries. Italy was the original home of the revival of the Latin classics and it was to Italy that the choicest of Greek classics were brought from Byzantium, before and after the fall of Constantinople to the Turks in 1453. To Italy came able scholars and tutors straight from the Near East; and at their hands, or under their influence, Greek and Latin grammars and texts of the classics were issued in profusion.

With the revival of classical learning came the humanizing of intellectual interest, knowledge, and public measures; that is, thought and action were directed by this learning to human concerns, as distinguished from the divine, and to the human race in general, as distinguished from individual salvation and particular peoples. Now educated men and women in Italy had at their command, for example, the great histories written by Greek and Roman authorities in antiquity and were attracted by the difference between these human and secular works and the monkish chronicles which, besides being fragmentary, twisted the story of the past to fit theological conceptions of the universe. Now Italian men and women were in possession of literary and philosophic works dealing entirely with the great human and nature subjects, without regard for those "ultimate causes" with which theologians occupied themselves on the basis of theories and convictions respecting the nature and designs of God. Moreover, instead of the degraded Latin so often employed by monkish chroniclers, Italian men and women now had models of writing by Greek and Roman thinkers and stylists, inviting them to lofty aspirations and lucid expressions whether in poetry, letters, the arts, history, philosophy, or politics.

In the promotion of the new learning, two tasks had to be carried out. The first included the recovery of additional classical works, the preparation of critical editions, the reissue of the best in manuscript form and, after the

From Mary R. Beard, *Woman as Force in History: A Study in Traditions and Realities* (Collier Books, 1946). Copyright © 1946 by Mary R. Beard; renewed 1974 by William Beard and Miriam Vagts. Reprinted by permission of Scribner, a division of Simon & Schuster, Inc.

invention of printing, in book form, and critical study of the new texts. The second was the dissemination of the knowledge derived from the critical study.

The number of women who devoted themselves to scholarship was by no means as large as the number of men, for reasons other than the lack of talents; but in the fifteenth century and early sixteenth century many Italian women displayed the highest technical competence in the study, interpretation, and exposition of the revived humanist learning. Some of them, for example Isotta Nogarola, we are told by Dr. G. R. Potter in *The Cambridge Mediaeval History* (Volume VIII, Chapter XXIII), "could hold their own in matters of scholarship with the best of their male contemporaries and... were accepted and even acclaimed everywhere."

According to Dr. H. J. Mozans' *Women in Science,* women took "an active part in the great educational movement inaugurated by the revival of learning" and won "the highest honors for their sex in every department of science, art, and learning.... The universities, which had been opened to them at the close of the middle ages, gladly conferred upon them the doctorate, and eagerly welcomed them to the chairs of some of their most important faculties.... Cecelia Gonzaga, pupil of the celebrated humanist, Vittorino da Feltre, read the gospels in Greek when she was only seven years old. Isotta and Ginevra Nogarola, pupils of the humanist, Guarino Verronese, likewise distinguished themselves at an early age by their rare knowledge of Latin and Greek.... Livia Chiavello, of Fabriano, was celebrated as one of the most brilliant representatives of the Petrarchian school.... Cassandra Fidele, of Venice, deserved, according to Poliziano, the noted Florentine humanist to be ranked with that famous universal genius, Pico de la Mirandola. So extensive were her attainments that in addition to being a thorough mistress of Latin and Greek, she was likewise distinguished in music, eloquence, philosophy, and even theology.... But for the extent and variety of her attainments, Tarquinia Molza seems to have eclipsed all her contemporaries. Not only did she excel in poetry and the fine arts, she also had a rare knowledge of astronomy and mathematics, Latin, Greek and Hebrew. So great was the esteem in which she was held that the senate of Rome conferred upon her the singular honor of Roman citizenship, transmissible in perpetuity to her descendants."

In nearly every great intellectual center of Italy women were lecturing on literature and philosophy, and religious faith could not escape impacts of the new knowledge. They were studying medicine and natural science in the light of pagan learning in these subjects. Great Italian women teachers of the awakening "sent forth such students as Moritz von Spiegelberg and Rudolph Agricola to reform the instruction of Deventer and Zwoll and prepare the way for Erasmus and Reuchlin."

Some of the women crossed the Alps themselves, as the ancient learning was said to do when Erasmus and other returning students bore back to outlying countries the knowledge gleaned in Italy. One of the most distinguished classical scholars of the age, Olympia Morata, for example, meeting difficulties as Renée's court where the duchess and all her friends were persecuted by the Duke for their religious independence, fled to Germany, with a young Bavarian student of medicine and philosophy, and was planning to continue her teaching of the classics in Heidelberg, to which she had been invited, when an untimely death closed her career.

In the dissemination of the new learning among the Italian people, especially among the rich but including some not as well off in this world's goods, five methods were widely and intensively employed: tutoring and self-directed study in families, education in schools, humanist lecturing, conversations in small private groups and larger coteries, and correspondence.

As soon as the Renaissance had got under way, Italian women in the rich commercial cities and at ducal or princely courts, such as Ferrara and Urbino, turned with avidity to the study and discussion of Greek and Roman literature.

While men of the governing class were away from their castles fighting in wars, women and girls of their families thus "improved their minds" and displayed their accomplishments to the warriors when they came home on furloughs. French officers and Spanish ambassadors who were guests in the great houses from time to time were so impressed that they let their own women relatives and friends know how backward they were and how advisable it would be for them to catch up with Italian women. When Erasmus, Grocyn, and Colet joined in the student pilgrimage to Italy early in the sixteenth century, they found women immersed in the ancient languages and lore, surrounded by poets, artists, scholars, and writers from near and distant places as companions in the new intellectual movement.

This linguistic and literary development was not confined to the ruling circles, however. Classical schools for girls and boys were opened in Italian cities, giving to the business and professional circles, as well as to patricians, opportunities to acquire knowledge of the ancient languages and the natural, or secular, philosophies embodied in Greek and Latin literature. Here entered the insurgent bourgeois influence which Henry Adams, looking back from the twentieth century and his vantage point within it, concluded was an invincible menace to the throne of Mary, Queen of Heaven.

Among the outstanding Italians of the fifteenth century who promoted education, letters, and arts were Gian Francesco Gonzaga II and his wife, Paola Malatesta, who brought to Mantua in 1425 the exceptional humanist, Vittorino da Feltre, and established him there as the teacher of their sons and daughters. The Gonzagas took it as a matter of course that their daughters should have the same kind of instruction as their sons—in an age when women, according to a tradition of our time, were supposed to have no education at all. It was with the full support of both patrons that Vittorino was to devise and execute a program of education that made his school one of the most creative in the Italy of the Renaissance.

In Chapter XVI, Volume I, of *The Cambridge Modern History,* Sir R. C. Jebb describes the new type of civic education created by Vittorino at his school in Mantua under the patronage of Gian and Paola Gonzaga in 1425 and carried on until his death in 1446: "His aim was to develop the whole nature of his pupils, intellectual, moral, and physical; not with a view to any special calling, but so as to form good citizens and useful members of society, capable of bearing their part with credit in public and private life. For intellectual training he took the Latin classics as a basis; teaching them, however, not in the dry and meagre fashion generally prevalent in the mediaeval schools... but in the large and generous spirit of Renaissance humanism. Poetry, oratory, Roman history, and the ethics of Roman Stoicism, were studied in the best Latin writers.... By degrees Vittorino introduced some Greek also.... He provided for some teaching of mathematics, including geometry... arithmetic, and the elements of astronomy. Nor did he neglect the rudiments of such knowledge as then passed for natural philosophy and natural history. Music and singing also found a place.... With great insight and tact, Vittorino saw how far social education could be given in a school with advantage to morals and without loss to manliness; he inculcated a good tone of manners, and encouraged the acquirement of such social accomplishments as the age demanded in well-educated men."

It was not only as scholars, tutors, lecturers, members of coteries, participants in the work of academies, and patrons of schools that Italian women led and cooperated in the dissemination of the humanist learning. They carried on extensive correspondence with men and other women engaged in spreading humanist knowledge and doctrines in Italy and throughout Western Europe. Of Olympia Morata, we are told that she "corresponded on equal terms with the most learned men of the day."

All these free, wide-reaching, and influential activities of Italian women in the promotion of humanist learning were in keeping with the very spirit of the Renaissance. In the third chapter of *Die Kultur der Renaissance*, Jacob Burckhardt, a renowned authority, says: "In order to understand the higher forms of social intercourse during the Renaissance, it is necessary to know that woman was regarded as in a position of perfect equality with man. One should not allow one's self to be deceived by the cunning and in part malicious researches respecting the presumptive inferiority of the beautiful sex.... Above all, the education of the woman among the higher classes is essentially the same as that of the man. There was not the slightest hesitation among the Italians of the Renaissance in according the same literary and even philological instruction to sons and daughters; for as they saw in this new classical culture the highest possession of life, so they assumed gladly that girls were welcome to it.... There was no question of a conscious 'emancipation' of woman or anything so out of the ordinary, for the situation was understood to be a matter of course. The education of the woman of rank, just as well as that of the man, sought the development of a well-rounded personality in every respect. The same development of mind and heart that perfected the man was necessary for perfecting woman."

Men of the Renaissance not only accepted as a matter of course this free and easy association with women in the advancement of learning and the civic spirit. Many writers of the period made a point of paying special tributes to women, if frequently in exaggerated form. Take, for example, Boccaccio (1313–1375), the fervent humanist, poet, story-teller, and friend of Petrarch. Besides writing *De Casibus Virorum Illustrium*, dealing with the troubles and vanities of illustrious men from the time of Adam to the fourteenth century, he wrote illustrious women, *De Claris Mulieribus*, starting with Eve and coming down to Giovanna, queen of Naples; included were Cleopatra, Lucretia, Portia, Semiramis, and Sappho. This work passed through many editions and is esteemed as among the important texts of the Renaissance. It was translated into Italian by Joseph Betussi who "in the ardor of his zeal enriched it by fifty new articles."

About a hundred years later, Henry C. Agrippa (1486–1525), German writer, soldier, physician, architect, historiographer, doctor of law, and traveler in many lands, outdid Boccaccio. In 1509 Agrippa published a work on the nobility and superexcellence of women (*De nobilitate et praecellentia feminei sexus*), dedicated to Margaret of Burgundy. In this volume of thirty chapters, Agrippa employed the writings of fable-makers, poets, historians, and the canon law in efforts to prove the case, and resorted to theological, physical, historical, moral, and even magical evidences to support his argument. He declared that he was moved to write the book by his sense of duty and obligations to duty.

Many men wrote paeans to women, as Lucian the Roman had done and as men were to continue to do in the mood of the Renaissance, in many countries, for centuries. Finally, in 1774, just two years before the Declaration of Independence at Philadelphia, an account of such hymning of women was published at Philadelphia. This was a work in two volumes: *Essay on the Character, Manners, and Genius of Women in Different Ages*—enlarged from a French work of M. Thomas by Mr. Russell, an Englishman. It included a section on the "Revival of Letters and the Learning of Women, Of the Books written in Honour of Women, and on the Superiority of the Sexes, and the subject continued."

After giving an account of the work by Boccaccio and Betussi, the author of the *Essay* continued: "Philip de Bergamo, an Augustine monk, published a volume in Latin OF ILLUSTRIOUS WOMEN. Another performance on the same subject was published by Julius Caesar Capacio, secretary to the city of Naples; one by Charles Pinto, in Latin, and in verse; one by Ludovico Domenichi; one by James Philip Tomassini, bishop of Venice; and one by Bernard Scardioni, a canon by Padua, OF THE ILLUSTRIOUS WOMEN OF PADUA.

"Francis Augustine della Chiesa, bishop of Saluca, wrote a treatise on THE WOMEN FAMOUS IN LITERATURE; Lewis Jacob de St. Charles, a Carmelite, wrote another on THE WOMEN ILLUSTRIOUS BY THEIR WRITINGS; and Alexander Van Denbushce, of the Low Countries, wrote one on THE LEARNED WOMEN.

"The celebrated Father le Moine published a volume under the title of GALERIE DE FEMMES FORTES; and Brantome wrote THE LIVES OF ILLUSTRIOUS WOMEN. But it is to be observed that Brantome, a French knight and a courtier, speaks only of queens and princesses. . . .

"After Brantome, Hilario da Costa, a Minim, published two volumes in quarto, each volume consisting of eight hundred pages, containing, as he tells us, the panegyrics of ALL the women of the fifteenth and sixteenth centuries, distinguished by their valour, their talents, or their virtues. But the pious ecclesiastic has, in fact, only given us the panegyrics of the CATHOLIC women of that period. He does not say a word, for example, of queen Elizabeth. . . .

"But all must yield to the indefatigable Italian, Peter Paul de Ribera, who published in his own language, a work entitled 'The Immortal Triumphs and heroic Enterprises of Eight hundred and forty-five women.' . . .

"Besides these large compilations dedicated to the honour of the whole sex, many of the writers of those times, men of taste and gallantry, addressed panegyrics to individuals, to women who were the living ornaments of their age. This practice was most common in Italy, where every thing conspired to favour it.... The courts of Naples, of Milan, of Mantua, of Parma, of Florence, and several others, formed so many schools of taste, between which reigned an emulation of glory and of talents. The men distinguished themselves by their address in war, or in love; the women, by their knowledge and accomplishments."

From Italy zeal for classical learning fanned out like rays from a sun. Queen Isabella of Spain became interested in it through her acquaintance with Vittoria Colonna and brought Italian men and women to Spain to instruct her courtiers and students in the universities. She studied the classics herself. She established a school of the classics in her palace. She attended examinations of students and watched with eagle eyes and sharp ears the progress of this education among her retinue. She collected texts for the courtiers to read and for students to use in the universities. One woman was commissioned to lecture on the classics at Salamanca; another on rhetoric at Alcalá. Later Philip II enriched this Spanish Renaissance by his patronage of Italian artists. He encouraged Spanish women to paint portraits as well as write letters, by inviting the Italian women portrait painter, Sophonisba Anguisciola, to his court. Of this portrait painter Van Dyck long afterward was to say that he learned more from her, even in her blind old age, than he had learned from many seeing men.

In France enthusiasm for classical learning was stimulated by Christine de Pisan—Italian in background—who grew up at the court of Charles V, in the late fourteenth century, where her father was installed as an astrologer. After the visit of Petrarch to France in quest of Greek and Latin texts possibly among the monastic treasures, monarchs began to accumulate a library for the French court. But Christine de Pisan did more than read texts there. She studied Plato and also Arab scientific learning in some books in the library. She shared Dante's interest in the State and urged the French to come to grips with their problem of national survival so seriously menaced by the invading armies of the English King. By coming to grips she meant more than war; she meant coming to realize the necessity of granting privileges to the middle class without which, she contended, France could not get up on its feet. Before Christine died, Jeanne d'Arc took the field as commander of French troops—her actual leadership financed by the great capitalist, Jacques Coeur, her will to lead inspired by her "voices," her acceptance as leader facilitated by French adoration of the Virgin.

Christine de Pisan tried to offset the influence of Jean de Meung's stereotype of the perfect lady in his *Roman de la Rose* by her *Le Livre des trois Vertus (The Book of the Three Virtues)* addressed especially to women. She hoped to arouse and develop political consciousness among French women. To this end she defended the spirit of the freer-thinking Italian women of her day in her *Cité des Dames* and awakened such interest that she was invited to the English court. She did not accept the invitation on the ground that her supreme duty lay in France, but this book was translated into English as *The City of Women*.

 **NO**

Did Women Have a Renaissance?

One of the tasks of women's history is to call into question accepted schemes of periodization. To take the emancipation of women as a vantage point is to discover that events that further the historical development of men, liberating them from natural, social, or ideological constraints, have quite different, even opposite, effects upon women. The Renaissance is a good case in point. Italy was well in advance of the rest of Europe from roughly 1350 to 1530 because of its early consolidation of genuine states, the mercantile and manufacturing economy that supported them, and its working out of postfeudal and even postguild social relations. These developments reorganized Italian society along modern lines and opened the possibilities for the social and cultural expression for which the age is known. Yet precisely these developments affected women adversely, so much so that there was no renaissance for women —at least, not during the Renaissance. The state, early capitalism, and the social relations formed by them impinged on the lives of Renaissance women in different ways according to their different positions in society. But the startling fact is that women as a group, especially among the classes that dominated Italian urban life, experienced a contradiction of social and personal options that men of their classes either did not, as was the case with the bourgeoisie, or did not experience as markedly, as was the case with the nobility.

Before demonstrating this point, which contradicts the widely held notion of the equality of Renaissance women with men, we need to consider how to establish, let alone measure, loss or gain with respect to the liberty of women. I found the following criteria most useful for gauging the relative contraction (or expansion) of the powers of Renaissance women and for determining the quality of their historical experience: 1) the regulation of *female sexuality* as compared with male sexuality; 2) women's *economic* and *political roles*, that is, the kind of work they performed as compared with men, and their access to property, political power, and the education or training necessary for work, property, and power; 3) the *cultural roles* of women in shaping the outlook of their society, and access to the education and/or institutions necessary for this; 4) *ideology* about women, in particular the sex-role system displayed or advocated in the symbolic products of the society, its art, literature, and philosophy. Two points should be made about this ideological index. One is its rich inferential value. The literature, art, and philosophy of a society, which give us direct knowledge of the attitudes of the dominant sector of that society toward women, also yield indirect knowledge about our other criteria: namely, the sexual, economic, political, and cultural activities of women. Insofar as images of women relate to what really goes on, we can infer from them something about that social reality. But, second, the relations between the ideology of sex roles and the reality we want to get at are complex and difficult to establish. Such views may be prescriptive rather than descriptive; they may describe a situation that no longer prevails; or they may use the relation of the sexes symbolically and not refer primarily to women and sex roles at all. Hence, to assess the historical significance of changes in sex-role conception, we must bring such changes into connection with all we know about general developments in the society at large.

This essay examines changes in sex-role conception, particularly with respect to sexuality, for what they tell us about Renaissance society and women's place in it. At first glance, Renaissance thought presents a problem in this regard because it cannot be simply categorized. Ideas about the relation of the sexes range from a relatively complementary sense of sex roles in literature dealing with courtly manners, love, and education, to patriarchal conceptions in writings on marriage and the family, to a fairly equal presentation of sex roles in early Utopian social theory. Such diversity need not baffle the attempt to reconstruct a history of sex-role conceptions, however, and to relate its course to the actual situation of women. Toward this end, one needs to sort out this material in terms of the social groups to which it responds: to courtly society in the first case, the nobility of the petty despotic states of Italy; to the patrician bourgeoisie in the second, particularly of republics such as Florence. In the third case, the relatively equal position accorded women in Utopian thought (and in those lower-class movements of the radical Reformation analogous to it) results from a larger critique of early modern society and all the relations of domination that flow from private ownership and control of property. Once distinguished, each of these groups of sources tells the same story. Each discloses in its own way certain new constraints suffered by Renaissance women as the family and political life were restructured in the great transition from medieval feudal society to the early modern state. The sources that represent the interests of the nobility and the bourgeoisie point to this fact by a telling, double index. Almost all such works—with certain notable exceptions, such as Boccaccio and Ariosto—establish chastity as the female norm and restructure the relation of the sexes to one of female dependency and male domination.

The bourgeois writings on education, domestic life, and society constitute the extreme in this denial of women's independence. Suffice it to say that they sharply distinguish an inferior domestic realm of women from the superior public realm of men, achieving a veritable "renaissance" of the outlook and practices of classical Athens, with its domestic imprisonment of citizen wives. The courtly Renaissance literature we will consider was more gracious. But even here, by analyzing a few of the representative works of this genre, we find a new repression of the noblewoman's affective experience, in contrast to the latitude afforded her by medieval literature, and some of the social and cultural reasons for it. Dante and Castiglione, who continued a literary tradition that began with the courtly love literature of eleventh- and twelfth-century Provence, transformed medieval conceptions of love and nobility. In the love ideal they formed, we can discern the inferior position the Renaissance noblewoman held in the relation of the sexes by comparison with her male counterpart and with her medieval predecessor as well.

Love and the Medieval Lady

Medieval courtly love, closely bound to the dominant values of feudalism and the Church, allowed in a special way for the expression of sexual love by women. Of course, only aristocratic women gained their sexual and affective rights thereby. If a knight wanted a peasant girl, the twelfth-century theorist of *The Art of Courtly Love,* Andreas Capellanus, encouraged him "not [to] hesitate to take what you seek and to embrace her by force." Toward the lady, however, "a true lover considers nothing good except what he thinks will please his beloved"; for if courtly love were to define itself as a noble phenomenon, it had to attribute an essential freedom to the relation between lovers. Hence, it metaphorically extended the social relation of vassalage to the love relationship, a "conceit" that Maurice Valency rightly called "the shaping principle of the whole design" of courtly love.

Of the two dominant sets of dependent social relations formed by feudalism—*les liens de dépendance,* as Marc Bloch called them—vassalage, the military relation of knight to lord, distinguished itself (in its early days) by being freely entered into. At a time when everyone was somebody's "man," the right to freely enter a relation of service characterized aristocratic bonds, whereas hereditability marked the servile work relation of serf to lord. Thus, in medieval romances, a parley typically followed a declaration of love until love freely proffered was freely returned. A kiss (like the kiss of homage) sealed the pledge, rings were exchanged, and the knight entered the love service of his lady. Representing love along the lines of vassalage had several liberating implications for aristocratic women. Most fundamental, ideas of homage and mutuality entered the notion of heterosexual relations along with the idea of freedom. As symbolized on shields and other illustrations that place the knight in the ritual attitude of commendation, kneeling before his lady with his hands folded between hers, homage signified male service, not domination or subordination of the lady, and it signified fidelity, constancy in that service. "A lady must honor her lover as a friend, not as a master," wrote Marie de Ventadour, a female troubadour or *trobairitz.* At the same time, homage entailed a reciprocity of rights and obligations, a service on the lady's part as well. In one of Marie de France's romances, a knight is about to be judged by the barons of King Arthur's court when his lady rides to the castle to give him "succor" and pleads successfully for him, as any overlord might. Mutuality, or complementarity, marks the relation the lady entered into with her *ami* (the favored name for "lover" and, significantly, a synonym for "vassal").

This relation between knight and lady was very much at variance with the patriarchal family relations obtaining in that same level of society. Aware of its incompatibility with prevailing family and marital relations, the celebrants of courtly love kept love detached from marriage. "We dare not oppose the opinion of the Countess of Champagne who rules that love can exert no power between husband and wife," Andreas Capellanus wrote (p. 175). But in opting for a free and reciprocal heterosexual relation outside marriage, the poets and theorists of courtly love ignored the almost universal demand of patriarchal society for female chastity, in the sense of the woman's strict bondage to the marital bed. The reasons why they did so, and even the fact that they did so, have long been disputed, but the ideas and values that justify this kind of adulterous love are plain. Marriage, as a relation arranged by others, carried the taint of social necessity for the aristocracy. And if the feudality denigrated marriage by disdaining obligatory service, the Church did so by regarding it not as a "religious" state, but an inferior one that responded to natural necessity. Moreover, Christianity positively fostered the ideal of courtly love at a deep level of feeling. The courtly relation between lovers took vassalage as its structural model, but its passion was nourished by Christianity's exaltation of love.

Christianity had accomplished its elevation of love by purging it of sexuality, and in this respect, by recombining the two, courtly love clearly departed from Christian teaching. The toleration of adultery it fostered thereby was in itself not so grievous. The feudality disregarded any number of church rulings that affected their interests, such as prohibitions of tournaments and repudiation of spouses (divorce) and remarriage. Moreover, adultery hardly needed the sanction of courtly love, which, if anything, acted rather as a restraining force by binding sexuality (except in marriage) to love. Lancelot, in Chrétien de Troyes's twelfth-century romance, lies in bed with a lovely woman because of a promise he has made, but "not once does he look at her, nor show her any courtesy. Why not? Because his heart does not go out to her.... The knight has only one heart, and this one is no longer really his, but has been entrusted to someone else, so that he cannot bestow it elsewhere." Actually, Lancelot's chastity represented more of a threat to Christian doctrine than the fact that his passion (for Guinevere) was adulterous, because his attitudes justified sexual love. Sexuality could only be "mere sexuality" for the medieval Church, to be consecrated and directed toward procreation by Christian marriage. Love, on the other hand, defined as passion for the good, perfects the individual; hence love, according to Thomas Aquinas, properly directs itself toward God. Like the churchman, Lancelot spurned mere sexuality—but for the sake of sexual love. He defied Christian *teaching* by reattaching love to sex; and experiencing his love as a devout vocation, as a passion, he found himself in utter accord with Christian *feeling....*

The Renaissance Lady: Politics and Culture

In his handbook for the nobility, Baldassare Castiglione's description of the lady of the court makes [the] difference in sex roles quite clear. On the one hand, the Renaissance lady appears as the equivalent of the courtier. She has the same virtues of mind as he, and her education is symmetrical with his. She learns everything—well, almost everything—he does: "knowledge of letters, of music, of painting, and... how to dance and how to be festive." Culture is an accomplishment for noblewoman and man alike, used to charm others as much as to develop the self. But for the woman, charm had become the primary occupation and aim. Whereas the courtier's chief task is defined as the profession of arms, "in a Lady who lives at court a certain pleasing affability is becoming above all else, whereby she will be able to entertain graciously every kind of man" (p. 207).

... The Renaissance lady is not desired, not loved for herself. Rendered passive and chaste, she merely mediates the courtier's safe transcendence of an otherwise demeaning necessity. On the plane of symbolism, Castiglione thus had the courtier dominate both her and the prince; and on the plane of reality, he indirectly acknowledged the courtier's actual domination of the lady by having him adopt "woman's ways" in his relations to the prince. Castiglione had to defend against effeminacy in the courtier, both the charge of it (p. 92) and the actuality of faces "soft and feminine as many attempt to have who not only curl their hair and pluck their eyebrows, but preen themselves... and appear so tender and languid... and utter their words so limply" (p. 36). Yet the close-fitting costume of the Renaissance nobleman displayed the courtier exactly as Castiglione would have him, "well built and shapely of limb" (p. 36). His clothes set off his grace, as did his nonchalant ease, the new manner of those "who seem in words, laughter, in posture not to care" (p. 44). To be attractive, accomplished, and seem not to care; to charm and do so coolly—how concerned with impression, how masked the true self. And how manipulative: petitioning his lord, the courtier knows to be "discreet in choosing the occasion, and will ask things that are proper and reasonable; and he will so frame his request, omitting those parts that he knows can cause displeasure, and will skillfully make easy the difficult points so that his lord will always grant it" (p. 111). In short, how like a woman—or a dependent, for that is the root of the simile.

The accommodation of the sixteenth- and seventeenth-century courtier to the ways and dress of women in no way bespeaks a greater parity between them. It reflects, rather, that general restructuring of social relations that entailed for the Renaissance noblewoman a greater dependency upon men as feudal independence and reciprocity yielded to the state. In this new situation, the entire nobility suffered a loss. Hence, the courtier's posture of dependency, his concern with the pleasing impression, his resolve "to perceive what his prince likes, and... to bend himself to this" (pp. 110–111). But as the state overrode aristocratic power, the lady suffered a double loss. Deprived of the possibility of independent power that the combined interests of kinship and feudalism guaranteed some women in the Middle Ages, and that the states of early modern Europe would preserve in part, the Italian noblewoman in particular entered a relation of almost universal dependence upon her family and her husband. And she experienced this dependency at the same time as she lost her commanding position with respect to the secular culture of her society.

Hence, the love theory of the Italian courts developed in ways as indifferent to the interests of women as the courtier, in his self-sufficiency, was indifferent as a lover. It accepted, as medieval courtly love did not, the double standard. It bound the lady to chastity, to the merely procreative sex of political marriage, just as her weighty and costly costume came to conceal and constrain her body while it displayed her husband's noble rank. Indeed, the person of the woman became so inconsequential to this love relation that one doubted whether she could love at all. The question that emerges at the end of *The Courtier* as to "whether or not women are as capable of divine love as men" (p. 350) belongs to a love theory structured by mediation rather than mutuality. Woman's beauty inspired love but the lover, the agent, was man. And the question stands unresolved at the end of *The Courtier*—because at heart the spokesmen for Renaissance love were not really concerned about women or love at all.

Where courtly love had used the social relation of vassalage to work out a genuine concern with sexual love, Castiglione's thought moved in exactly the opposite direction. He allegorized love as fully as Dante did, using the relation of the sexes to symbolize the new political order. In this, his love theory reflects the social realities of the Renaissance. The denial of the right and power of women to love, the transformation of women into passive "others" who serve, fits the self-image of the courtier, the one Castiglione sought to remedy. The symbolic relation of the sexes thus mirrors the new social relations of the state, much as courtly love displayed the feudal relations of reciprocal personal dependence. But Renaissance love reflects, as well, the actual condition of dependency suffered by noblewomen as the state arose. If the courtier who charms the prince bears the same relation to him as the lady bears to the courtier, it is because Castiglione understood the relation of the sexes in the same terms that he used to describe the political relation: that is, as a relation between servant and lord. The nobleman suffered this relation in the public domain only. The lady, denied access to a freely chosen, mutually satisfying love relation, suffered it in the personal domain as well. Moreover, Castiglione's theory, unlike the courtly love it superseded, subordinated love itself to the public concerns of the Renaissance nobleman. He set forth the relation of the sexes as one of dependency and domination, but he did so in order to express and deal with the political relation and its problems. The personal values of love, which the entire feudality once prized, were henceforth increasingly left to the lady. The courtier formed his primary bond with the modern prince.

In sum, a new division between personal and public life made itself felt as the state came to organize Renaissance society, and with that division the modern relation of the sexes made its appearance, even among the Renaissance nobility. Noblewomen, too, were increasingly removed from public concerns—economic, political, and cultural—and although they did not disappear into a private realm of family and domestic concerns as fully as their sisters in the patrician bourgeoisie, their loss of public power made itself felt in new constraints placed upon their personal as well as their social lives. Renaissance ideas on love and manners, more classical than medieval, and almost exclusively a male product, expressed this new subordination of women to the interests of husbands and male-dominated kin groups and served to justify the removal of women from an "unladylike" position of power and erotic independence. All the advances of Renaissance Italy, its protocapitalist economy, its states, and its humanistic culture, worked to mold the noblewoman into an aesthetic object: decorous, chaste, and doubly dependent—on her husband as well as the prince.

POSTSCRIPT

Did Women and Men Benefit Equally from the Renaissance?

Once we begin to consider the experiences of women in history as separate from those of men, we meet a new set of challenges. Women are not a universal category, and their experiences throughout history are as varied as their race, social class, ethnicity, religion, sexual orientation, and a host of other categories make them. In recent years historians have begun to consider both the ways in which women's historical experiences are more or less the same and the ways in which one woman's experience differs radically from another's. There are instances in which being a woman is the most important variable (with regard to childbirth, access to birth control or lack of it, and female sexuality, for example), times when race is what matters most and women feel more attuned to men of their own race than to women of different races, and times when social class is the key factor and both racial and gender differences seem less significant than a common class experience or approach to life.

The periodization question remains a fascinating one. Following Kelly-Gadol, other scholars began to look at historical periods with which they were familiar with an eye to using women's experiences as a starting point. For example, in *Becoming Visible* (from which Kelly-Gadol's selection was excerpted), William Monter poses this question: Was there a Reformation for women? Beginning with women's experience, this anthology offers a number of good points of departure for exploring the issue of periodization. For a fuller explanation of the differences among compensatory, contributory, and women's culture approaches, see Gerda Lerner's essay "Placing Women in History," in *Major Problems in Women's History*, 2d ed., edited by Mary Beth Norton and Ruth Alexander (D. C. Heath, 1996). This book also contains Gisela Bock's "Challenging Dichotomies in Women's History"—which explores nature versus culture, work versus family, public versus private, sex versus gender, equality versus difference, and integration versus autonomy—and "Afro-American Women in History," by Evelyn Brooks Higginbotham, which questions the concept of a universal womanhood by exploring the varying experiences of African American women.

For a Marxist analysis of women in history, see the chapter entitled "Four Structures in a Complex Unity" in Juliet Mitchell's *Woman's Estate* (Pantheon Books, 1972). In it, Mitchell argues that production, reproduction, sexuality, and the socialization of children must all be transformed together if the liberation of women is to be achieved; otherwise, progress in one area can be offset by reinforcement in another. This links the question of women's roles in history to economic forces such as production and social forces such as sexuality and childrearing.

Another good way to start is to explore our understanding of gender—what it has meant to be a woman (or a man) at a specific time in human history. Historian Joan W. Scott considers how gender and power designators construct one another in "Gender: A Useful Category of Historical Analysis," *American Historical Review* (December 1986). She sees in the categories "man" and "woman" a primary way in which social relationships are defined and power is signified. Linda Nicholson, in "Interpreting Gender," *Signs: Journal of Women in Culture and Society* (Autumn 1994), explores the question of biological foundationalism —the extent to which physicality influences gender construction. In this analysis, the body becomes a historically specific variable whose meaning changes or is capable of changing over time.

ISSUE 8

Did Martin Luther's Reforms Improve the Lives of European Christians?

YES: Bernard M. G. Reardon, from *Religious Thought in the Reformation*, 2d ed. (Longman, 1995)

NO: Richard Marius, from *Martin Luther: The Christian Between God and Death* (Belknap Press, 1999)

ISSUE SUMMARY

YES: Bernard M. G. Reardon, retired head of the Department of Religious Studies at the University of Newcastle upon Tyne, contends that Martin Luther was neither a political nor a social reformer. Instead, he was a spiritual genius who created a new religion within Christianity that remained true to its traditional orthodoxy.

NO: Professor emeritus Richard Marius views the Reformation as a catastrophe in the history of Western civilization. He sees Martin Luther's challenge as inaugurating more than a century of religious bloodshed that could have been averted if Luther had remained silent.

When Martin Luther was born in 1483, his father, Hans, hoped the boy would become a lawyer. Instead, a mystical experience during a thunderstorm led young Martin to enter religious life as an Augustinian monk. Scrupulous in observing his religious duties, Luther became increasingly aware of his own sinfulness and his fear of divine justice. He came to believe that fallen humans can never do anything to merit salvation; it is the grace of God alone that "justifies" them.

Sent by his order to teach philosophy at the University of Wittenberg, Luther was appalled at the selling of indulgences (pardons for sins) and denounced the practice, along with other abuses, in 95 theses of protest addressed to the Archbishop of Mainz in 1517. The newly invented printing press spread his ideas throughout the German states and beyond. Summoned to appear before the Imperial Diet at Worms in 1521, Luther clung to his beliefs, displeasing the emperor and earning himself a condemnation. Hidden from danger by his patron, the Elector Frederick of Saxony, Luther translated the Bible into German, unaware that he had launched a radical religious revolution.

Eager for reform rather than revolution, Luther sought to modify what he regarded as abuses within the Christian church. His intention was to strip the modern church of power and corruption and return it to its roots—the pristine days of early Christianity. Certainly he had no intention of founding a new religion. This theological conservatism was matched by his opposition to the Peasants' Revolt of 1524–1525. Siding emphatically with the forces of law and order, Luther urged the princes to put down the rebellion and safeguard the God-given social order. In many ways, he was a reluctant revolutionary.

Lutherans (as they called themselves against Luther's wishes) gathered to read the scriptures in their own language, sing, pray, and listen to sermons. Widespread anticlerical feeling inspired many to challenge the wealth and influence of what they saw as an Italian church. Luther's religious alternative was also attractive to those whose feeling of national pride in the semi-autonomous German states made them resent pronouncements from Rome. Violent conflict between Protestant princes and imperial Catholic forces broke out during Luther's lifetime, and people were instructed to follow the religion of their local prince—Lutheran or Catholic.

Luther had married a former nun, Katherine von Bora, and fathered a number of children. Living a family life, like those in his congregation, rather than observing the Catholic requirement for celibacy, Luther may have seemed more approachable than the Catholic priests. Insisting on "the priesthood of all believers," he urged his followers to read the scriptures for themselves and find the truth within them. But as the Reformation spread to Switzerland, England, and beyond, thousands died in religious conflicts, and Christianity became increasingly fragmented. At the time of Luther's death in 1546, much of Western Europe was dissolving centuries-old ties that had bound people and nations into a spiritual and temporal unity called Christendom.

If we admit that reform was needed, the next question becomes, "Was the reform movement initiated by Luther worth the theological, political, and, especially, human cost?" For Bernard M. G. Reardon, Luther was a man completely in tune with his time. Although he remained medieval and unmodern—untouched by the new humanism of people such as the Dutch thinker Erasmus of Rotterdam—Luther was filled with the dynamism that sprang from his spiritual conviction. Believing himself divinely called to a holy mission, he was able to inspire others to an intense, personal relationship with the God of history and the redeemer of human frailty and despair.

Richard Marius is willing to grant that Luther brought a simplicity and clarity to religious practice that was and is a comfort and a welcome spiritual discipline for many people. But he wonders whether the challenges introduced by Erasmus might have brought about a less traumatic, if slower, path to reform that would have left Christianity intact and avoided much suffering and death. Many would have lived more normal lives if Luther had followed a different life journey, with less hatred and bloodshed and perhaps a more serene history for all of us.

Bernard M. G. Reardon

 **YES**

Religious Thought in the Reformation

Martin Luther: The Religious Revolutionary

The Age and the Man

It has been said that 'they who do not rightly estimate the Reformation cannot rightly understand Luther, since Luther apart from the Reformation would cease to be Luther'. This certainly is true, but no less true is it that apart from Luther the Reformation itself cannot be understood. He is its key figure, protagonist and spokesman alike, upon whom all others zealous for change were more or less dependent. Indeed, whether but for Luther the Reform movement of the sixteenth century would have swept over Europe in the way it did is highly questionable. What he achieved was rendered possible because the time and the milieu were matched in him by the man also, so that all the necessary elements were present to issue in events such as, in the most authentic sense, were epoch-making. That achievement was not therefore something external to him, but the utterance of the man himself and of his profound personal experience. Over the preceding century voices had repeatedly called for the reform of abuses and corruptions, but there had emerged no guiding principle on which Reformation could successfully be carried through, nor a dominant personality to give it impetus.

As opinions varied so counsels differed, whereas what was needed—the outcome proved it—was the dynamism of a spiritual conviction that struck at the very heart of the evils which men of conscience yearned to see cast out. Luther it was who reached such a conviction and proclaimed it forthrightly and fearlessly. Yet to begin with it was one [of] the full implications of which he himself did not comprehend. Only as opposition mounted did he sense the extent either of the changes that would perforce be necessary or the risks and temptations to which he, a monk and an academic, was to be exposed when thrust upon the state of world politics. But as he was wont afterwards to declare: 'I simply taught, preached, wrote... otherwise I did nothing.... The Word did it all.' That, politically speaking, he could have set Europe alight, he realized, but he knew too that this was no game for him to play. For the remarkable thing is that he did not feel himself to be an autonomous agent, deploying his own resources against however powerful odds—in short, a hero challenging fate—but the instrument rather of an overriding providence and purpose. Quite apart from his talents as a man, which in any case were outstanding, Luther's sense of mission, of doing the work to which he firmly believed, despite every doubt and difficulty that might confront him, God had called him, made him in truth a prophet; for even the soberest historian can scarcely withhold the word. Moreover, his ability to communicate verbally his overwhelming intimations of the reality of God has rarely been equalled in Christian history. In this not even St Augustine surpassed him.

Yet the presentation of Luther's thought, and it is with this aspect alone of his work as a religious leader that we are here concerned, is not altogether easy for an Englishman writing for English readers. As he contemplates his task he will perceive more and more how beset he is with problems. For the great reformer, as his modern compatriots always tell us, is *echt deutsch,* a German to the core, expressing himself (when of course not using the scholar's medium of Latin) very much in the German idiom of his time, an idiom that repeatedly taxes the skill of the translator. Further, Luther's ideas have to be culled from a vast number of diverse writings—polemical treatises, pamphlets, tracts, exegetical commentaries, lectures and sermons in multitudes, not to mention the letters and the famous *Table Talk:* a treatise a fortnight, it has been estimated, sustained over a period of twenty-five years. And the difficulty is enlarged by the fact that although as an author he was so prolific Luther was not, as was Melanchthon or, still more signally, Calvin, a systematic expositor of his own teachings. He wrote as occasion demanded, often impulsively, sometimes violently, never without prejudice, with the result that he does not always appear self-consistent, and views and opinions can readily be cited in support of even sharp differences of interpretation. But this, as he would have said himself, 'is what happens when things were moving.... Now this work has to be done, and now that.'

Again, the leader of the German Reformation has always been a highly controversial figure: to some, as to Adolf Harnack for example, he is a spiritual hero whose authority is only a little below that of the New Testament itself, a Mr Valiant-for-Truth contending manfully against the embattled powers of error embodied in the Roman Anti-Christ; whereas for others he is, not indeed the grotesque caricature drawn by Cochlaeus (or even, in modern times, by Heinrich Denifle), yet still the unhappy disruptor of Christendom and harbinger of the secularizing individualism of the Enlightenment. But perhaps the chief obstacle to a sympathetic understanding of Luther from our standpoint in time is the sheer medievalism of his outlook; for of all the reformers he is apt to strike us today as the most medieval, the most unmodern, so little touched was he, in any essential respect, by the spirit of contemporary humanism. Between him and us, that is, there stands an intellectual barrier such as makes him appear remote in comparison with an Erasmus or a Montaigne, or even, in some ways, a Zwingli, and it is only with a real effort of the imagination that one can hope to surmount it. In fact, Luther's medievalism so conditions his thinking that in the opinion of a modern Catholic historian, Josef Lortz, it was not he but the great Dutch scholar who posed the true threat of 'dogmatic dissolution within the church'. For although Luther challenged the church it was on its own, not on alien, principles. Both sides in the momentous controversy would comprehend one another's meaning because fundamentally their presuppositions were the same. Now, however, it is only with some difficulty that even Christians, be they Protestant or Catholic, can grasp what exactly either the reformers or their opponents meant by what they said. Both Protestantism and—if only more recently—Catholicism have themselves changed greatly since the sixteenth century and much that was vital to the Reformation debate today seems distant and archaic.

Nevertheless, if we are to attempt to appreciate what moved a Luther as well as a Loyola we must make every endeavour to elucidate their ideas. Certainly in the case of the German reformer it is with the religious teacher and theological thinker that the modern student must come to grips if his historical significance is to be properly assessed. Other 'Luthers'—Marxist, Freudian—can be and have been trotted out and need not be summarily dismissed; but whatever the factors that combined to bring about revolutionary changes in sixteenth-century Europe, the dynamic of the Reform movement which Luther himself undoubtedly precipitated must be sought above all in his personal experience as a Christian believer. Indeed, but for the religious convictions that dominated his mind from early manhood until his death in 1546 at the age of sixty-three he would have no identity. Neither in theory or practice was he a political or social reformer, just as he was not in any modern sense a humanitarian or even a moralist. To understand what he accomplished, designedly or not, we must therefore see the man for what he preeminently was, a religious genius. As for unconscious psychological pressures, all men are affected by them, and what we loosely call temperament played no small part in shaping Luther's attitudes in particular. Those however who took up his cause were inspired by what he consciously believed and deliberately taught. Thus for all its strangeness to the mind of a secular age Luther's faith has proved itself of sufficient historical importance to claim our attention still. Moreover, what men in any age have thought about the profoundest issues of human life must, as such, always command respect.

Martin Luther was brought up in accordance with the ordinary Catholic teaching and piety of his day. At Magdeburg he attended a school run by the Brethren of the Common Life; then after three years at Eisenach he entered the university of Erfurt in 1501 with the purpose, encouraged by his father, of studying law. Erfurt at that time was the main centre of humanistic culture in Germany, but there is no evidence that he was in any way deeply influenced by it. He seems to have shown little intellectual curiosity and no aptitude for philosophy, even if some years later he was sent by his order, the Augustinian Eremites, which he had joined in 1505, to lecture on the subject at the newly founded university of Wittenberg. The truth is that, well-endowed though he was with humane good sense, he had no feeling for the spirit of the new age that was dawning. His choice of the religious life, whatever the circumstances that immediately prompted it, was natural to him and appropriate. The monastic house at Erfurt, strict in its observance of the order's rule, afforded him exactly the type of vocational environment for which he was suited by disposition

and conviction alike. His life there was uneventful and in itself entirely satisfying. His ordination to the priesthood, which took place on 2 May 1507, he
regarded with profound seriousness. Looking back on it many years afterwards
he recorded the powerful emotions which then seized him; while on the occasion of his first mass he was all but tongued-tied at the thought of the sudden
realization, at the moment of consecration, of the very presence of God. By the
words *Hic est Corpus meum* he was, he confessed, 'stupefied and terror-stricken.
I thought to myself, "With what tongue shall I address such Majesty, seeing that
all men ought to tremble at the presence of even an earthly prince?".' He felt
himself to be but dust and ashes, and full of sin.

None of the doctrines or practices of his religion did he at this time question; he was to all showing wholly without intellectual difficulties. He accepted
the current supernaturalism with the simplicity of a peasant and had no doubt
that the Catholic system was entirely adequate to meet the needs of the spiritual life. At least this was so until he became by degrees aware that in its actual
operation it was indeed *not* adequate, at all events for himself. But he discovered
this inadequacy only by putting the system to practical test. To those who took
it with something less than the absolute seriousness of his own attitude, or by
recognizing that between the precept and its fulfilment there is always, men
being what they are, some shortfall, that system was serviceable and effective.
The vicar-general of Luther's order in Saxony, Johann Staupitz, a thoughtful
and conscientious man, understood this and advised the over-scrupulous young
monk accordingly. The latter, nevertheless, was not satisfied—far from it. But his
theological revisionism—and theologically he was not especially well read—was
the consequence of his practical dissatisfaction; there was no speculative aim
behind it whatever.

It thus is no occasion for surprise that Luther never systematized his theological thinking. His interest was essentially in the needs and conditions of
the religious life itself. He was not even interested in the reform of ecclesiastical institutions simply as such. Changes, he realized, there would have to be,
consonant with the principles of his own teaching, of the truth of which he
had the firmest possible inner assurance. But in themselves they were largely
peripheral, and to give them detailed effect, like the proper schematization of
his own theology, was something he was content to leave to others.

Luther's Experience

For Luther the monk 'natural' man was a sinner in need of redemption. Furthermore, this sinfulness was deeply seated, the result of a condition described
only too aptly as fallen. Even in the beginning man, in the person of Adam,
had lapsed from his original state of righteousness and was now totally unable
to deliver himself from the moral depravity and spiritual corruption, which
were the consequences of his fall, without supernatural aid. Divine 'grace' was
a necessity therefore, and was dispensed by the church through a variety of
means, chief among which were the sacraments, seven in number, though the
most important were baptism, the eucharist and penance. Habitual or sanctify-
ing grace, according to the current teaching, was a supernatural quality which,

when added to, or infused into, the soul united it with Christ and rendered it acceptable to God by producing in it a new 'habit' (*habitus*) or disposition by which the recipient was enabled to perform virtuous acts. Such grace was *sufficient* in that it conveyed the power to obey God, but it was not automatically *efficacious* since its efficacy depended on its appropriation by the human will. A perpetual effort therefore was demanded for a man to acquire merit in the sight of God and so, in a true sense, earn the heavenly reward promised to the righteous. Further, entry into a religious order was held to be a kind of second baptism—St Thomas Aquinas himself had thus characterized it—offering an assured way of salvation to all who conscientiously pursued it. ('Keep this rule,' Luther was told at his profession, 'and I will promise you eternal life.') Detachment from a world essentially evil was deemed to be a most laudable thing, an anticipation of the bliss to come hereafter. This present life being merely probationary, self-denial, self-discipline and self-sacrifice, which the monastic vows of obedience, poverty and chastity served to achieve, were a challenge to all who sought to take religion seriously. One who in this way responded to the divine call with his whole heart could not fail to attain justification *coram Deo*.

The question, then, was whether a man could in fact lead a life of sufficient spiritual merit really to be certain of acceptability in the eyes of God. Luther (and his own testimony is not to be refuted) observed his monastic rule with unusual scrupulosity.

> I was a good monk [*he afterwards recalled*] and kept my order so strictly that I could claim that if ever a monk were able to reach heaven by monkish discipline I should have found my way there. All my fellows in the house, who knew me, would bear me out in this. For if it had continued much longer I would, what with vigils, prayers, readings and other such works, have done myself to death.

At first he was too much occupied to be unduly troubled, but with time came doubts. In spite of his diligence and conscientiousness, his repeated confessions and penances, he could not feel sure of success. 'The more I tried to remedy an uncertain, weak and afflicted conscience with the traditions of men, the more each day found it uncertain, weaker, the more troubled.' Those welltried austerities, fasts and vigils, were unavailing. Peace and tranquillity of mind eluded him, self-effort only increasing self-distrust. 'Who knows,' he would ask himself, 'whether such consolations are to be believed?' Too much, it seemed, was demanded of the mere human will, a condition which his nominalist training, with its emphasis on volition (*fac quod in se est*), did nothing to alleviate. The virtue of perseverance thus was undermined by scepticism. And behind all this was that fear of God's wrath and damnation by which he had been haunted since childhood and of which even 'the rustling of a dead leaf' was enough to remind him. For such assaults of conscience Luther used the word *Anfechtung*, 'temptation'. Later he wrote movingly of these awful experiences, in which it would come upon him that he was past redemption, with nowhere to turn for help. It was like a momentary glimpse of eternal punishment; momentary because, mercifully, the mood would not last. It is not of course difficult to see in this a state of mental anxiety verging on the pathological, but any attempt at a psychological analysis of Luther's condition at the time is likely in the nature of the case to be too speculative to be of serious use to the historian.....

Martin Luther: The Founder of Protestantism

Man and Society: The Two Kingdoms

The presence of sin in the world inevitably affects the structures of human society itself, and it is to the problem which this raises for Christian belief that Luther devotes some of his most fruitful thinking. Here on earth he distinguishes, following St Augustine, two 'kingdoms' or 'realms': that of God or Christ, and that of the world. The citizens of the first kingdom are the true believers in Christ, Christ's own subjects. The citizens of the second are those, the vast majority, who are not subject to him, and who thus, as Luther was wont to put it, are under the law. This distinction is registered in the difference between the church, where the gospel is operative, and the state, the organized society of men. But over each realm, the temporal as well as the spiritual, God exercises a final sovereignty. Were the whole world indeed, so Luther supposes, to consist of true and faithful Christians no civil government, 'no prince, king, lord, sword or law', would be needed. What would be the use of earthly rulers exerting coercive authority in a world made up of Christians having 'the Holy Spirit within their hearts, who instructs them to wrong no one, to love everyone, and willingly and cheerfully to suffer injustice and even death from everyone'? But as; on the contrary, the world consists very largely of unbelievers and sinners—for Luther is not persuaded that true believers are other than few—the civil power is necessary, enacting laws and wielding the sword in order to preserve the society of men from anarchy and satanic destruction. 'The law is given for the sake of the unrighteous that those who are not Christian may through the law be externally restrained from evil deeds. In this respect the state is the servant of God, performing what Luther characterizes as God's *oppus alienum,* his 'strange work' of forcible restraint and punishment; strange because at once needful yet alien to his nature and purposes. Thus the state may be called, thanks to the presence therein of sin, the 'Kingdom of God's left hand', whereas God's *opus proprium,* his 'proper work' declared in the gospel, has for its instrument the church, the 'Kingdom of his right hand'.

God's purposes in the world are ... realized through the natural 'orders': the family, men's differing vocations, the state itself. All these have their requisite function in human life and so their appropriate place in God's design, either to secure the continuance of his creation, as with the first two, or, as with the third, to prevent the devil from having his full way with it. Accordingly all three demand men's honour and respect. The idea of the 'natural law' (*lex naturae, lex naturalis*) Luther accepts as expressive of the will of God and therefore as a vehicle of his self-revelation; but he does not concede that it is so plainly written in the human heart that any one at all is in a position to act in obedience to it. 'Natural law and reason are a rare thing among the children of men', whereas 'natural idiots' are many. Luther, we may add, was no democrat, at any rate in the modern, egalitarian sense; of peasant stock himself, he had a shrewd understanding of, as well as a natural sympathy with, the common people, and he was not sentimental about their weaknesses and limitations. He feared what Erasmus called the 'tumult' no less than did that fastidious scholar himself, stressing non-resistance as a Christian duty. He was in no way therefore an apologist for rebellion, whatever the supposed justice of the cause. Only duly constituted authority had the right to use the sword, which was why, in principle, he denounced the Peasants' Revolt. But he insisted that princes had their obligations also, and needed to be reminded of them, especially as, more often than not, they were either fools or knaves.

But whatever the quality of secular rule, whether good or bad, the spheres of the two kingdoms should never be confused. In other words, the church must never become political, as had the papacy, just as the state should in no wise endeavour to impose the gospel by force of law. By overstepping its proper limits both alike could frustrate the will of God. Hence any attempt to bring about the Kingdom of Heaven by coercive means will only result in disaster. Nevertheless Luther's deep-rooted differences with radicals like Thomas Müntzer, for example, induced him more and more to press on external authority the obligation to maintain the teaching of sound doctrine as well as the liberty of true worship. Heresy accordingly was not to be tolerated: to propagate, for instance, the notion that Christ was not divine but a mere man, as certain anabaptists, so Luther believed, did do, he considered to be not simply heresy but sheer profanity and blasphemy, and to be punished accordingly. Moreover it would appear that, in the last resort, the actual determination of what constitutes heresy falls to the civil authority—an effective subjection of the church to the state, even in spiritual matters, such as Calvin could not for one moment have contemplated.

The influence of Luther's beliefs and ideas on the whole Protestant movement can hardly be overestimated. There were elements in it, no doubt, both doctrinal and ecclesiological, which did not stem from him and which, on certain matters, he vigorously opposed. The divergences in outlook between himself and the Swiss leaders were sometimes... sharply edged. Yet all but the most radical, perhaps, owed him much, and often far more than they were disposed to admit. Spiritually he was a true creator, the Reformation's most powerful personality and most fertile mind. When he died, prematurely aged, early in 1546, his disciple Melanchthon, the always-faithful 'Master Philipp', could only lament, 'Alas, gone is the horseman and the chariots of Israel!' For the Protestant cause had lost one who, as history already had shown, did more for it than any other human agent. But although Luther proved so great a force for change, giving rise to what was virtually a new religion in Christendom, his thought still stayed within the orbit of Catholic orthodoxy. Essentially, his viewpoint was medieval and he was little drawn to the insights and attitudes of the Renaissance. Thus his break with Erasmus resulted not simply from a theological difference, however significant: the two men were remote from one another, in outlook as in temperament, Luther's resting on the theocentricity of traditional belief, the humanist's on his sense of the inherent capacity of men to fashion their own destiny. The former's medievalism is apparent in his insistence on the objectivity, the sheer 'giveness', of revelation and grace, which is the real reason why the charge, so often brought against him by his critics, of individualism and subjectivism is misdirected. That Protestantism in some of its aspects was soon to manifest both is not in question. But Luther himself cannot rightly be accused of them, for what he strove to do was to make religion at once prophetic and personal, to teach men to see it as a relationship between God and humanity which the Almighty in his sovereign freedom himself determines but which is also to be gladly acknowledged and gratefully accepted by each and every man who recognizes himself to be a sinner. Hence Luther's consistent message was that the gospel of redemption which the scriptures so unambiguously proclaim must be met with the response of a living faith. But to say that he was interested only in individual salvation and the state of the believer's mind is refuted by his entire doctrine of the church, of the sacraments, and not least of the Christian life itself. For there is, again, no substantial truth in the further charge that Luther failed to draw out the ethical, and more particularly the social-ethical, implications of faith by inculcating a pietism that would effectually abandon the social order to secular authoritarianism. A distinction, in other words, has to be pressed between Luther's own teachings and the 'Lutheranism' subsequently moulded by historical circumstances, notably in Germany. Such later Lutheranism departed in important respects from Luther's spirit and characteristic positions. This is not to deny that the great reformer's work did lead to the establishment of new, 'Lutheran' churches and wrought large changes not only in theology but in the whole conception of the nature of the ecclesiastical institution and its role in society. Much of this, however, was more or less accidental, neither directly prompted by him nor of special concern to him.

Richard Marius

 **NO**

Martin Luther: The Christian Between God and Death

Preface

... My estimation of Luther's Reformation is much akin to Simon Schama's of the French Revolution or Richard Pipes's of the Bolshevik Revolution. They believe that these great upheavals were disasters for the peoples involved, and I believe that Luther represents a catastrophe in the history of Western civilization. This is not to say that the catastrophe was all his fault. All sides have a share of blame in the boiling hatreds and carnage that consumed Europe for well over a century after Luther died. But in my view, whatever good Luther did is not matched by the calamities that came because of him.

Our own bloody century has destroyed for the time being the easy vision of progress that prevailed in the West after the Enlightenment and continued through the nineteenth century. In that vision great historical events represented a forward march across time. Revolutions were part of progress, and although people got hurt in them, occasionally even beheaded or shot, they still marked a moral leap forward in a human crusade toward ever-expanding moral consciousness and virtue. It is impossible for a historian today to hold such a rosy view of the past. We know now that things can go terribly and catastrophically wrong and that all the good that comes from great events does not necessarily or even usually overbalance the evil. Some good came from the Reformation as Luther shaped it, but I remain convinced that our world would have been far better off had events taken a different course. ...

Epilogue

... At Augsburg in 1530 Catholics and Protestants in Germany under imperial oversight tried to resolve their differences. Philipp Melanchthon became the chief author of the Augsburg Confession as an expression of Lutheran beliefs in an effort to answer charges of heresy raised by Catholics. It was also an effort to compromise. The Confession strongly emphasized the divine institution of the secular order and so condemned insurrection and revolution. It did not mention justification by faith. Charles V and Catholic theologians rejected the Augsburg Confession. No serious chance for reuniting Western Christianity ever presented itself again.

It is a convenient place to leave Luther. He lived another twenty years, and it is a truism of scholarship that we need more work on the later Luther because we know best the dramatic story of his early life and his break with Rome. The darkly bound volumes of the *Weimarer Ausgabe,* standing in their solemn ranks in parts of university and clerical libraries frequented by few scholars, summon us to do our duty to the older man. But here I will beg off.

By 1526 the most creative part of his life was over, and his ceaseless battles with adversaries descended often into repetitive invective and vituperation that weary the soul. By his own account, his attacks of *tristitia* [sadness] increased. Luther was successful in that he lived to die a natural death, and the movement he began continued, offering spiritual renewal to many through the intervening centuries. Yet in a myriad of ways his movement failed, and the failure has about it the inevitability of tragedy. In a strict accounting, uncongenial to the religious spirit, we might argue that his movement produced as much spiritual woe as it did consolation. Although he never acknowledged failure, its evidence is scattered through his later works, and he became certain that only the return of Christ would accomplish the aims of his gospel. He felt himself to be in the last days, and he saw portents of the end. This conviction sustained him.

The hope for general reform and the optimism of his great treatises after the debate with Johann Eck dissolved into internecine Christian conflict in which atrocities on each side balance each other in volume of blood. Luther not only hoped to win over the Catholic Church through the scriptural rulings of a general council; he hoped to destroy the papal Antichrist. With the terrible sack of Rome in May 1527, the papacy seemed on the brink of extinction. But pope and emperor patched up a peace. The persecution of evangelicals in Catholic lands went on, and multitudes did not come spontaneously to Luther's standard. Exuberant popular enthusiasm for his doctrines faded. In the wake of the Peasants' Rebellion, Lutheranism at the Diet of Speyer became an affair of pastors, princes, and city governments while the people in Lutheran territories passed into religious indifference.

Evangelical pastors zealously interpreted Luther's doctrines to sparse congregations. Lutheran princes and city councils made sure that pastors hewed to orthodoxy, especially the doctrine of obedience to authority. Ironically enough, Lutheran pastors over the next couple of centuries resorted more and more to preaching vehement sermons about hell to frighten their subjects back to obedience to the church. Evidence abounds that attendance at sermons dropped off. As Hans-Christoph Rublack has shown in a brilliant essay, the consequence was only increased anticlericalism, encapsulated in the popular saying "In every parson you will find a little pope." Rublack concludes that the cultural differences between pastors and people were too much to overcome. With the sacraments removed from their central place, the common people—especially the peasants—were left with only the sermon to "negotiate" their relations with their pastors. For their part the pastors labored in vain to make congregations take seriously the doctrinal content of sermons or to live the moral lives that the sermons commanded. Congregations wanted consolation and help at the great rites of passage in life—birth, marriage, suffering, sickness, death—and the pastors wanted moral evidence that their sermons were effective. The consequence, Rublack maintains after exhaustive study, is that both sides were frustrated and alienated from each other. When the Enlightenment came, with its impersonal religiosity devoted to order and obedience, it found the way prepared by Lutheran churches. The ruling classes coldly professed their faith; the lower classes did not bother.

Such a division was already under way in Luther's life. He complained frequently and bitterly that congregations did not care enough about evangelical preachers to pay them a living wage. His emphasis on the priesthood of all believers and the importance of preaching led to a paradoxical result still with us. In a Catholic house of worship, the priest need not be present to bring into the sanctuary those who wish to worship and meditate. The Host reposes on the altar, the body of Christ, an object that may be venerated in silence by the pious refugee from the hurrying streets outside. Candles burn, sending into the holy gloom the wordless prayers of those who light their slender flames. Chapels with icons beckon the worshiper to quiet moments of reverence and meditation—all without the necessary presence of a clergyman. But in the evangelical church, the major reason for entry is the sermon, and if the minister is not present to preach, there is little reason for anybody else to be there. The occasional fugitive from a noisy world may steal into an evangelical church for prayer and mediation, but whereas today many Catholic churches in the large cities of the Western world are open through the week, most evangelical church buildings are locked up from Sunday to Sunday. The Anglicans, who never became fully Protestant, are often exceptions.

Attendance in evangelical churches depends considerably on whether the preacher can deliver an interesting and compelling discourse. A Catholic priest, administering the sacraments, need not be endowed with eloquence or even intelligence, and the sacraments at his hands will retain an emotional vitality for the participant because the power of the moment resides not in words conjured up by the priest for the occasion but in the familiarity of a sacred rite. Protestant ministers are called upon every week to hold the attention of a congregation by thinking of something new and different to say about very old and somewhat shopworn subjects.

In the final two decades of his life, Luther battled with the fissiparous tendencies of the evangelical movement. He continued to write and preach fiercely against the Anabaptists, though he had sympathy and respect for their bravery in the face of martyrdom. His most hated foes besides the papacy itself were the so-called sacramentarians, those who with [Andreas] Karlstadt and [Ulrich] Zwingli interpreted the Eucharist as a symbolic memorial and rejected the real presence of Christ in the elements. Luther's rhetoric against them was fierce and extreme. They were blasphemers pure and simple, he thought—an opinion he never changed. When his Swiss foes Oecolampadius and Zwingli tried to answer him with mild language, Luther responded with unmitigated rage and railing.

Philip of Hesse arranged a conference between Zwingli and Luther at his castle in Marburg in 1529 to try to patch up an evangelical peace. Luther came with Melanchthon and Justus Jonas and some lesser men. Zwingli came with Oecolampadius and Martin Bucer. Bucer would later help install the Reformation in England under young Edward VI. Arguments went on for days. The contestants agreed on some points of doctrine and were persuaded to put their names on a collection of articles, but they could not reach concord on the chief point of contention—the nature of the presence of Christ in the Mass. In later years Luther often recalled that in leaving Marburg Zwingli said, "Now God knows that I do not wish to be friends to anyone more than to those at Wittenberg." Luther was always proud of himself for refusing to shake Zwingli's hand. Two years later Zwingli died in battle, armed and fighting as a soldier, in a war against the Catholic cantons of Switzerland. Luther frequently said that he died as a murderer, reaping the punishment of God for his errors.

For the moment the most serious consequence of the division over the Eucharist was evangelical disunity before a growing Catholic military threat. The long-term consequences were perhaps more important—hatred, suspicion, and continued division among evangelicals.

Contemporaries—including both Catholics and sectarians—faulted Luther's doctrines for failing to create a lively sense of piety in congregations that heard Luther and others preach year after year. Martin Brecht has chronicled in gloomy detail continued troubles in Wittenberg. Luther was continually furious with his congregations for their stinginess and their immorality. On November 8, 1528, he preached a sermon that culminated in an angry outburst:

> What shall I do with you, people of Wittenberg! I shall not preach to you the kingdom of Christ, because you don't take it up. You are thieves, robbers, merciless. To you I must preach the law! You afflict the kingdom of Christ and ignore his preaching... You know that this week we will request an offering of money. I hear that no one will give anything to those who ask, but rather turn them ungratefully away. By the grace of God, you ingrates, who although you thirst so greedily for money, you do not give anything, you wound the ministers with evil words. Well, I hope you had a good year! I am frightened and do not know whether I will preach any more to you vulgar slobs, who cannot give four pennies a year out of a good heart. Know this, you Wittenbergers. You are altogether empty of good works, giving no salary to the ministers of the church to educate boys or to give shelter to the poor, always passing the buck to someone else... You have been freed from tyrants and papists. You ungrateful beasts are not worthy of this treasure of the gospel. If you don't do otherwise, repenting of your sins, I'm going to cease preaching to you, lest I cast pearls before swine or give holy things to dogs.

This does not sound like a sermon addressed to the true Christians who were the audience assumed for Luther's treatise of 1520 *On the Freedom of a Christian*. Sometimes he did go on strike for a while and refused to enter the pulpit—much to the consternation of his friends and his prince, who doubtless cherished Luther's continual preaching on obedience.

Beginning in 1526 "visitors" were sent out to look into the affairs of the parish churches around Saxony to see how both pastors and ministers were living, understanding, and teaching the gospel. By 1528 the findings were discouraging. Ignorance and religious indifference were everywhere. Around December Luther wrote to [member of his Augustinian order George] Spalatin a summary note about the situation. Pastors were trying to survive by farming less than two acres of land. The condition of the church was as miserable. The peasants were not learning anything, nor did they know anything. They did not pray, they did not do anything except abuse Christian liberty, neither confessing nor taking the Eucharist, as if in religion they had all become children. He blamed these faults on the neglect of the Catholic bishops before the gospel came.

Because the morals of his people seemed in precipitous decline, Luther preached more and more to emphasize the law. In the instructions to visitors published in 1528, he spoke of the difference between preaching to those who understood the gospel and preaching to those who did not. Souls are likely to be lost if the preacher spends too much time comforting the people and not enough on contrition for sin and fear of God's judgment. The sinfulness of all our works is too great for ordinary Christians to understand if they are the faith. In short, the people were to be told that if they did not do good works according to the moral law, God would punish them.

Now and then he preached against witchcraft. His fears of supernatural enemies seemed to grow with the years. At the end of a sermon in June 1529, he took a moment to advise his auditors to be cautious during the summer season. They should not take cold baths. Satan lurks in forests, groves, waters, and everywhere draws near to us that he may destroy us, for he does not sleep. Sometimes water sprites deceive so that they destroy us, as we have seen almost every year when even experienced swimmers drown in the Elbe. Always go swimming with someone, he said. Or bathe at home.

In August 1529, Luther concluded another sermon with an admonition against witches. Some sorcerers were stealing milk and harming people. They should stop, and he said the congregation would not wait to deal with such people. Later that month a short notice appeared at the end of a sermon saying that Luther had excommunicated "some" witches and sorcerers from the church....

How do we make an estimate of his life? Doubtless for many in his time and since, he opened the way to a religious experience of freedom, zest, and spontaneity capable of giving consolation and hope to those who share it. At a moment when serious penitential practice came clogged with definitions, elaborate rules, and the corrupt superstitions of the indulgence trade, Luther brought a simplicity that was a relief to many burdened souls. For those of deep introspection and harsh self-judgment, Luther delivered a saving paradox, that those in misery who recognize who and what they are have a sign of God's grace that lifts them with a power they know they cannot possess themselves. For those souls already in love with God, he provided a vocabulary of sovereignty that is still appealing.

But doubtless, too, he shut the doors on a Catholic experience that has retained an obvious power to hold both the simple and the sophisticated, the shallow and the profound, the ignorant and the educated in one enduring communion. This judgement is not to say that the Catholic Church of Luther's time was unworthy of his rebellion or that its evolution since the Council of Trent warrants idealization. But the fact remains that the sacramental experience of

Catholic worship maintains an impressive hold on its adherents. The sacraments have an existence independent of the pope and papal pronouncements.

With respect to the Jews Luther was part of a cultural stream that runs like an open sewer through our history, and he was worse than a legion of Catholics and Protestants who have spewed forth hatred upon a people more sinned against than sinning. Although the Jews for him were only one among many enemies he castigated with equal fervor, although he did not sink to the horrors of the Spanish Inquisition against Jews, and although he was certainly not to blame for Adolf Hitler, Luther's hatred of the Jews is a sad and dishonorable part of his legacy, and it is not a fringe issue. It lay at the center of his concept of religion. He saw in the Jews a continuing moral depravity he did not see in Catholics. He did not accuse papists of the crimes that he laid at the feet of Jews.

For Luther religion was primarily the means of conquering death, a collection of true doctrines that must be believed if the Christian was to be victorious over death, and in such a schema, tolerance had no place. The Jews who rejected his Jesus rejected also his own understanding of the meaning of life and death and the way we know God. I suspect that their patient endurance of suffering and death in their adhesion to their own faith, necessarily rejecting his, made him afraid, and so created in his mind a fantasy called "Jew" that was in part constructed of hated elements in his own soul. Those devoted to assuring themselves that they have found the only way of salvation from the grave are unlikely to be tolerant of contradiction by other religious views that threaten their only hope for life after death. Religious toleration in the West developed along with uncertainty about ultimate things.

Luther was responsible for much of that uncertainty. Confounded by competing absolutist claims in matters of faith, rulers and people alike eventually decided to live and let live in the interest of public order and tranquillity. Those who lived outwardly ethical lives were considered acceptable citizens. In another paradox, Luther's consistent belief that no one could tell if another was a true Christian, that we could not even be sure of the apostle Peter's salvation if we had him among us, could contribute to the notion that governments must finally judge by the outward appearance and, as Elizabeth I of England said, not make windows into men's souls.

Luther did not follow his own lead. Whatever their ethics, those who disagreed with him in matters of doctrine faced relentless vituperation, and if they lived in Wittenberg, they could be exiled. Eventually in countries where prosperity and cosmopolitan values reigned, religious conformity became too much to bear, its psychic expense too harsh. Consequently, a benefit that sprang from Luther's Reformation was freedom of both conscience and practice —including the freedom to reject religion in the public forum of ideas. Luther would have been appalled. Today Lutherans, Catholics, Jews, Unitarians, and other Protestant denominations follow their religious rites in the comforting familiarity of old forms that grant the peculiar consolations and comforts that lie beyond the justifications of logic and the details of dogma. Only professional theologians think much of dogma these days, and the most popular of these make doctrines symbolic rather than literal, inclusive rather than prohibitive. That tolerance came about finally from the horror of the religious wars that followed hard on Luther's career. In these merciless conflicts mutual hatred of competing parties was fueled by their different interpretations of what unprovable doctrines had to be believed if human beings were to have the assurance of conquering death. Catholics and Protestants slaughtered each other for the promise of eternal life.

A further irony is that Luther's preoccupation with scripture led to intense study of the sacred text, and under that study something of its sacredness dissolved. Under the higher criticism of scripture, developed largely by German Lutherans in the nineteenth century, Luther's own critical attitude toward some books of the Bible was expanded. Under the probing intellects of scholars such as Julius Wellhausen, any notion that scripture could be an infallible historical record fell to pieces except among those ignorant of this stream of thought or among those whose minds were shut to it or among those fundamentalists who can hold their own faith only within the carefully restricted boundaries of their own kind. This decay of biblical authority among the educated is one of Luther's legacies—shared with [Dutch theologian and humanist] Erasmus.

Worship in a spirit of meditation and contemplation goes on and enriches many hearts. Luther's words, selectively chosen, speak to many who, caught up in the hurly-burly of modern life and morality, seek a rhetoric of comfort and assurance. Yet we take it almost for granted that our worship may involve illusion, the kind of experience Erasmus described in the *Praise of Folly* when he told of the madman who sat alone in a theater day after day, laughing hugely at the comedy he saw acted in his imagination on the empty stage. When he was cured of his madness, he was distraught at the absence that had come into his life. Illusion or not, the experience of religion for most of us rises above dogma, even when we recite creeds and sing old hymns filled with doctrines few of us would profess literally. We have learned to live that way. To Luther we would have been blasphemers, just as he to us seems strangely remote and curious when we try to consider the whole man.

Above all, Luther was a human being, living in his unique moment of history—as all moments in history are unique. Making sense of him requires an effort not to decide whether he was right or wrong, good or bad, but rather to see what human quality in him tells us something about the human condition we all share in all the centuries. Despite remarkable consistency in Luther's voluminous labors, anyone laboring over his thoughts comes upon expressions unexpected and sometimes astonishing, sometimes vulgar and ugly, sometimes sublime. He was a man of highs and lows; he could be eloquent, generous, and compassionate in one moment and harsh, arrogant, unbending, gross, and savage in the next.

His exuberant complexities make him an enduring mystery. All writers and readers who consider him see him only in part. Sometimes he is as close to us as our hand that holds the pen seeking to sketch him; at other moments he swings away from us like the planet Pluto, a dark god with a stony heart sweeping the frozen reaches of outer space. He jovially remarked once of his doctors, who had ordered him not to take baths and to stay put when he was sick, "The doctors try to make me a fixed star. But I am planet." So he was—and is.

Luther was preoccupied with death, and still more with what came afterwards. Luther said that the souls of the dead sleep until the day of doom. A never-ending sleep was the ultimate horror, the ultimate sign of the wrath of God, and nothingness the ultimate terror.

Luther's temperament was his tragedy. He was an absolutist, demanding certainty in a dark and conflict-ridden world where nothing is finally sure and mystery abounds against a gloom that may ultimately be driven by fate, the impersonal chain of accident that takes us where we would not go because our destiny is to be the people we are, and so we have no choice but tragedy. Perhaps the ultimate wisdom that Luther taught us is the somewhat negative truth that every living soul of us must learn on his or her own how we should die.

What might have happened had Luther never been born? Erasmus might have been the harbinger of a benign kind of reform and piety that would have brought the Catholic Church along slowly into the tolerance and charity practiced by legions of Catholics today. But who can tell? Were Erasmus and the community of scholars like him influential enough to have brought such a result about? ... [M]y sympathies lie with Erasmus. But we know only what happened, not what might have been. Luther was struck down with an apparition of terror on a country road during a July thunderstorm, and he made a vow to ward off death. He demanded certainty about his meaning and destiny. He wanted to follow his own ideas about a religion of the heart so that he might protest the deceit and futility of a religious practice that was scarcely more than magic. In his view, the religious practices of the indulgence hawkers did justice neither to the true state of the human condition nor to the true nature of the all-powerful God who had to exist if we are to be raised from the dead. When he saw to his horror that these practices were sanctioned by the pope, supposedly the Vicar of Christ, he set out to destroy the papacy and, failing that, to expose it to shame and contempt so that the bishop of Rome would become contemptible to all the world. He believed that the word of God spoke unmistakably through scripture, that scripture was clear, and that true Christians would recognize on hearing it the divine revelation given centuries before in the incarnation of Christ. As a lesser desire, Luther hoped for the liberation of his "dear German people" from the oppressive yoke of Italian tyranny and their unity under the Christian government of an emperor dedicated to the gospel.

None of that happened.

Instead for more than a century after Luther's death, Europe was strewn with the slaughtered corpses of people who would have lived normal lives if Luther had never lived at all or if his friends had persuaded him to shake off the rash vow he made out of terror in a storm. Perhaps his influence would have been most benign had he died as a martyr shortly after he became a public figure, if he had been seized... and rushed to the stake. Then we could have been more free to idealize him. We would have had a more serene history, less hatred, less bloodshed, less massacre.

POSTSCRIPT

Did Martin Luther's Reforms Improve the Lives of European Christians?

For centuries after his death, Luther was either effusively praised or roundly condemned. Evangelicals extolled his reforms, whereas Catholics villified him for destroying the unity of Christianity. But passions have cooled, and an ecumenical spirit has taken the place of religious bickering. Thus, we are beginning to see more balanced accounts of Luther's life and work that credit him with bringing about needed reforms while acknowledging his personal and professional failings.

Roland Bainton's acclaimed biography *Here I Stand: A Life of Martin Luther* (Abingdon, 1950) is a good place to begin understanding this complex reformer. Bainton profiles Katherine von Bora and other women in *Women of the Reformation in Germany and Italy* (Augsburg Fortress Publishers, 1971). Jonathan W. Zophy's *A Short History of Renaissance and Reformation Europe: Dances Over Fire and Water,* 2nd ed. (Prentice Hall, 1998), covers cultural, economic, religious, political, and social developments and includes gender as a significant subject for historical analysis.

Other biographies include Heiko Oberman's *Luther: Man Between God and the Devil* (Yale University Press, 1989) and Eric Gritsch's *Martin—God's Court Jester: Luther in Retrospect* (Augsburg Fortress Publishers, 1983). The latter title reflects Luther's name for himself—the sometimes-mocked instrument of God's will on earth—and contains an excellent historiographic chapter called "God's Jester Before the Court of History." Perhaps the most respected work is Martin Brechts' three-volume biography *Martin Luther,* translated by James L. Schaaf (Fortress Press, 1985).

For background about the times that produced Luther and other reformers, Vivian Gren's *The European Reformation* (Sutton Publishing Limited, 1998) offers a helpful time line of dates and suggestions for further reading. Its opening chapter "The Medieval Background" sets the context for Luther, Zwingli, the English Reformation, and Calvin, which are discussed more extensively in later chapters. A massive collection of Luther's writings is available in the 55-volume *Luther's Works,* edited by Helmut Lehman and Jaroslav Pelikan (Concordia and Fortress Presses, 1955–1975).

The German political situation is discussed in Bob Scribner and Gerhard Benecke, eds., *The German Peasant War, 1525* (Humanities Press, 1991), which has an excellent collection of well-introduced primary source materials. Finally, the informative chapter "The Peasants' War" appears in Jonathan W. Zophy, ed., *The Holy Roman Empire: A Dictionary Handbook* (Greenwood Press, 1980).

ISSUE 9

Did Convents Expand Opportunities for European Women?

YES: Olwen Hufton, from *The Prospect Before Her: A History of Women in Western Europe* (Alfred A. Knopf, 1996)

NO: Elisja Schulte van Kessel, from "Virgins and Mothers Between Heaven and Earth," in Natalie Zemon Davis and Arlette Farge, eds., *A History of Women in the West, vol. 3: Renaissance and Enlightenment Paradoxes* (Belknap Press, 1993)

ISSUE SUMMARY

YES: Professor of history Olwen Hufton finds that, despite the harsh reforms instituted by the Council of Trent (beginning in 1563), convents remained a viable alternative for European women—a place where they could write, think, and live more independent lives than they could in the secular world.

NO: Professor of early modern cultural history Elisja Schulte van Kessel emphasizes the harshness of the Tridentine reforms, which took away the homey atmosphere of convents and restricted affectionate relationships between women, thus making convents a much less attractive alternative for European women.

Religious life has been an option for women since the earliest centuries of Christianity, when widows and unmarried women began living together in communities, uniting in common prayer and good works to benefit the sick and the poor. These communities were expanded and formalized during the seventh and eighth centuries as monastic life matured within the Christian church. Through the twelfth century dual monasteries of monks and nuns were often administered by abbesses or sometimes an abbot and abbess together, providing leadership opportunities for women as well as a space for learning and thinking not available to married women.

In some of these religious houses, a tradition of female scholarship developed. Until the twelfth century, most convents taught Latin, making their residents literate in both church and much secular literature. A woman who sought to expand her life beyond the traditional roles of wife and mother could

156

find in the convent freedom from domestic drudgery and forced obedience to a husband as well as a supportive community of women and a place to develop her mind and her administrative skills. A final benefit was a space free from negative attitudes toward women, especially denunciations of their innate inferiority, depravity, and responsibility for bringing sin into the world through Eve's disobedience.

For girls of gentle birth, a convent offered opportunities for spiritual fulfillment, an education, useful work, and the possibility of a profession or career that was not available in the secular world. Daily life was divided into periods of prayer, study, and labor, and nuns were typically allowed eight hours of sleep interrupted once for 2 a.m. chapel attendance at Matins and Lauds. They received three meals a day and expected to spend five hours at work (which might include digging, haymaking, embroidering, or manuscript copying) and recreation (which would certainly include reading and study). Convents also served as boarding houses for wealthy wives and widows as well as boarding schools for the children of the elite.

Convent life changed, however, with the reforms instituted by the Council of Trent (1545–1563), part of the Catholic Counter-Reformation. To consolidate power and exert discipline in the wake of the Protestant Reformation, the Church instituted a series of reforms. The most dramatic was the cloistering of nuns—restricting them to the convent and separating them from the life of the world "as if they were dead." Books remained available, but work in the world and, in some cases, even contact with families was discouraged or forbidden. Visits home, which had been permitted annually, were prohibited; and nuns were encouraged to have their most personal relationships with their confessors rather than other nuns. A dividing screen was placed between priest and penitent so that no eye contact would pass between them.

How much did these reforms restrict the expanded opportunities once available to European women who chose the convent over marriage? There was vigorous resistance to these reforms; some nuns committed suicide, while others chose semireligious status outside the control of the church. Concerning those who remained, scholarly opinion differs regarding whether the convent remained an attractive alternative.

A well-known Benedictine nun from Venice named Angela (or Arcangela) Tarabotti (1604–1652) wrote a parody of Dante's *Divine Comedy* with three sections titled: "Nun's Paradise," "Nun's Inferno," and "Purgatory of the Badly Married." Material for the last section came directly from victims of domestic abuse, who poured out their grievances to the nuns, no doubt believing the convent offered a better living situation than their own. Olwen Hufton points out that, in spite of criticisms detailed in the banned "Nun's Inferno," the convent could be a haven for those who chose it freely. And although Angela Tarabotti did not enter the convent freely, she never sought to leave. In her discussion of the same work, however, Elisja Schulte van Kessel explains that the rich convent spiritual tradition that many married women envied was drying up.

Olwen Hufton

Obedient to Thy Will

Religion, politicized and aggressive, gave the early modern period much of its dynamic, and caught up in the turbulence were the lives of ordinary people as well as of princes and clerics. For almost two centuries, the grip of religion tightened over the populace. Religious change and the fiery discussions which arose in sermon, print and tract found their way into the humblest parish as zealous missionaries and preachers sought to proselytize or churchmen struggled to maintain orthodoxy. Repressive forces were extended to weed out heresy. Reformation and Counter-Reformation touched the lives of individuals and communities on a scale never before achieved.

Indifference to change was possible; immunity to even a measure of change could be more difficult. With the Reformation and the Counter-Reformation, the writing of history extends to a consideration of the responses of the masses in a way reserved for peasant revolts in earlier periods. Not surprisingly, since women constituted half of any congregation and religion was a part of the warp and woof of their everyday lives and the system of values to which they subscribed, it is possible to discern a distinctive female presence in and response to many of the changes. Neither camp neglected to turn its attention to women, though both assumed that the real battle was for the minds of men and that women would then follow. The annals of the past assume a dynamic gender dimension. Women of all kinds, rich and poor, old and young, disciples of change or resolute adherents to old ways, appear, individually or in groups, to bear witness to personal or community concerns.

In some respects the goals of the two dominant orthodoxies, Catholic and Protestant, are remarkable for their similarity. Both stood for a clearly defined moral order based on chastity, fortitude and obedience to God's teaching as expressed in Scripture. If the Protestants posited a holy household, the Catholics worked to promote the model of the holy family. Both enjoined women to accept their subservient role but deplored passivity in the face of sin. Women had souls and were capable of sin and error. The Catholic faith urged upon women the courage to confess and so to speak out their faith. The Protestant confessions put the holy word, in the form of the Bible, into their hands. For both camps, the religious comportment of women was interpreted as a kind of marker. Women epitomized the ignorant and the superstitious, the sexually lax

From Olwen Hufton, *The Prospect Before Her: A History of Women in Western Europe* (Alfred A. Knopf, 1996). Copyright © 1996 by Olwen Hufton. Reprinted by permission of Alfred A. Knopf, a division of Random House, Inc. Notes omitted.

and the profane. The behaviour of women could then serve as a condemnation of, or as a recommendation for, a particular confession. Raving, undisciplined, wandering, chanting, immodest women who stepped out of the place laid down for them in the books of Genesis and Timothy were seen as evidence of the failure of that creed to conform to God's will. Religious reform involved both sexes, but it focused particularly on chastity and obedience—and who should be more chaste or more obedient than the female? They were, in short, to be brought into line. In a more positive light, both the Protestant and the Catholic reformers embraced the notion of good works and created a space for women in which they might perform them. Whatever the confession, the main enemy was seen as ignorance. For Protestants the way forward was the teaching of both sexes to know the word of God through the Bible. For Catholics knowledge expounded by the priest through catechitical instruction was at the heart of reform. However, as well as similarities in the goals there were differences, and those differences were variously expressed according to national, social and often class contexts.

The questions which have to be asked are, what differences did the changes and turmoil make in the lives of women as individuals or as groups? What were the choices which confronted women under changing circumstances? How did the Catholic and the Protestant experiences differ, and what were the consequences for women from the changes involved? Which women, and where were they touched the most profoundly? How did they react? Did they follow their husbands, or were they themselves in some instances the engineers of change? To what extent were they defenders or instigators of a fortress faith? What was the common ground between the protagonists? These necessary questions are daunting because they demand generalizations about a range of experiences which differed according to geographical location, social class and in many cases personal commitment and decisions. Indeed, there are few aspects of life which can be described without reference to the impact of the Reformation and of the Counter-Reformation.

❧

The immediate impact of the Council of Trent [ecumenical council of the Roman Catholic Church] on the lives of women in countries which continued to accept the authority of Rome was felt in the religious houses when they were placed on the agenda in 1563. For some women the regular religious life served as the only alternative to marriage. All towns and cities had a convent of some kind and the great ones could have a dozen or more. At the beginning of our period, when all countries were still attached to Rome, the incidence of such houses was highest in Italy, France, Germany, the Netherlands and Spain. Against the payment of a dowry far less than the sum needful to establish them in marriage, more than a third of the female children of the aristocracy and the patriciates entered, whether willingly or not, from the age of about fourteen on a way of life ostensibly dedicated to prayer and reflection. The nunnery attracted a lot of funding in these countries throughout the Renaissance.

The church insisted on enclosure for women. They were to be preserved separate from the world *tamquam vere mortua* (as if they were dead). Beyond learning—for there were several book-lined cells—such women seemed to have little to do and no social vocation. An attempt made in the thirteenth century to establish the Poor Clares, female Franciscans who might wander around the city begging their bread and that of the poor and dedicate themselves to caring for the unfortunate, had been modified by the reforms of Saint Colette, and by the beginning of the fifteenth century strict enclosure was the rule.

Whatever the letter of the law, however, the social realities of being an "enclosed" nun in early sixteenth-century Italy were very dependent upon the house and order chosen. These institutions were an integral part of family strategic planning for the children of the aristocracy, which may explain a rather perfunctory commitment in some houses to anything approaching strict discipline. Not only were many of the houses centres of learning for women, the cells "book-lined" and very comfortably furnished by the girl's family, but close family links were permitted. Entrance into a particular house could assume the aspect of a family reunion, and ties were far from severed with the family that remained in the world. Indeed, before Trent, in some houses annual holidays were permitted, when the nuns could go home for a few weeks. There was little restriction on family visits to the convent, and "family cells" were built and furnished for daughters which became on death the property of the convent, but usually passed to a relative or a spiritual daughter within the community. These institutions offered an alternative family structure which perhaps suited many of the women who entered.

The history of the nun has been written by reference to three stereotypes: the pious and holy; the reluctant victim of family strategy; and the "deviant" interested in lesbian or sado-masochistic behaviour. If all these types existed, ... the norm may well have been the moderately pious if not fervent aristocratic girl, convent-educated since the age of five, who joined other members of her family and thus eluded the terrors of childbed and the unknown in marriage. If in any way academically inclined, she could within the convent walls indulge this taste to the full. If musical, she could probably also practise her gifts. Bolognese convents in particular seem to have been noted for the high quality of the music they commissioned, which they sometimes performed publicly. Or the nuns themselves were composers, some of the first women to be so. There were sophisticated theatrical performances where the nuns dressed up to perform their parts. Many convents kept a chronicle (the earliest in Germany) to record important events in the life of the house, and some went further, permitting the nun who kept the record to name and describe not only incoming novices but visitors and events and the social life of the institution. The first writings by women of saints' lives and stories of holy women who were their foundresses, as well as spiritual reflections, came from these institutions.

Protestantism attacked the convent as unnatural and as a seat of unnatural activity. Luther in particular denied it a place in the godly society where God solemnized the first marriage and made the bearing of children every woman's path to salvation. However, chastity and the opportunity to live an institutional life of celibacy was maintained as a high ideal of the Catholic church. The convent must survive, but it must do so in purified form. The work of the Council of Trent therefore included an attempt to tighten up convent practices. Apart from the Poor Clares, whose standards were strict and whose cloister was a barrier to the outside world, enclosure was too loosely interpreted and must now be more rigorously respected. Public entertainments must cease, and there must also be, via the bishop and his officials, a closer scrutiny of this kind of activity within the convent. The coming and going of the nun into the outside world must be terminated and the grille rendered less permeable.

How successful was this attempt? Certainly the generality of women's houses found themselves more restricted in their contact with the outside world, and where the spirit of Trent was quickly put into effect, as at Bologna under the reforming hand of Paleotti, the response was strident.

> The nuns of the Monastery of Santi Naborre e Felice in Bologna... express to Your Holiness with all humility their miseries and misfortunes that, notwithstanding that most of them were shut up in this place by their relatives against their wills, for all that they have borne it with considerable patience, and during a time in which they have been so tormented with various statutes and orders that they no longer have the strength to endure it... Now most recently, besides having removed the organ from here, the doctor has been denied them, so that nobody except their father and mother can see and speak with them. Their old servants who were accustomed to serve them in the convent cannot speak to any nun... Wherefore we fear that, being deprived with such strictness and abandoned by everyone, we have only hell, in this world and the next.

Paleotti's successors were more tolerant of entertainments, provided enclosure was respected.

The history of any particular monastic or religious order needs separate consideration. The Carmelites, who felt the reforming hand of Saint Teresa of Avila in 1567, were persuaded to adopt a newly rigorous life involving considerable physical discomfort and mortification of the flesh and the promise of complete withdrawal from the world. Saint Teresa, who had been called upon by her confessor to resist her visions as the work of the Devil, became convinced of the rectitude of the way of life she planned as a means of securing the salvation of the women who entered. She met opposition from the women who were already in place and from the ecclesiastical hierarchy, who thought she was demanding too much and would deter potential donors to the institution. She drew some very fine lines. Excessive fasting and sleep deprivation could convert the pious nun into the false mystic. Whilst extolling deprivation, she insisted that it must be carefully controlled. She told this cautionary tale of a Cistercian:

> There was a nun... who by dint of fasting and discipline became so weak that every time she took communion or became inflamed with devotion, fell to the ground and lay there for eight or nine hours, and she and everyone else assumed it was rapture... The fame of her raptures was spreading through the town: I was dismayed to hear it, because the Lord wanted me to understand what it really was, and I was afraid the whole affair would turn out badly... I told her confessor that I understood what it was and that it

was a waste of time, not rapture but weakness. I told him to have her give
up fasting and discipline, and seek some distractions. She was obedient and
did as she was told. As soon as she gained strength she forgot completely
about raptures.

The Carmelites asked for little in dowries and hence drew in girls from a wide
social spectrum. In spite of the rigours of the life and its nominal seclusion, they
expanded considerably, and the expansion process itself profoundly modified
the lifestyle of the individual women. This was partly because the monarchy
in the person of Philip II saw this order as a tool of politics and encouraged it
to spread through France, the southern Netherlands and Germany, as well as in
Latin America. It may be that the order was regarded as intrinsically Spanish,
the product of a proven saintly mystic, and the impeccability of its rigorous
credentials was never called into question. To put a daughter in the Carmelites
was then a political statement, one of allegiance to a country and its cultural
creations. When the spiritual daughter of Saint Teresa, Ana de Jesús, found
herself at the head of a small group of nuns crossing France and establishing
themselves in half a dozen houses in the Netherlands, life was certainly not
enclosed. The sisters were on the road and hardly allowed to settle before they
had to move on and begin another foundation. Patronized heavily by the Regent
of the Netherlands, who went to the foundation not only for worship but to
converse with the mother of the house and to introduce aristocratic families
who might help in the expansion process, the group of founding nuns were
frequently denied the peace they sought. Although recruitment from the local
aristocracy was steady, the life as the institution settled itself was perhaps too
demanding in terms of fasting and penance to be an effective substitute for the
easier life of the established aristocratic house.

For many aristocratic institutions which managed to evade the over-
intrusive hand of a reforming bishop, life could continue much as before,
though with more respect given to the rules of enclosure. It is possible to
discern minor changes, such as the more rigorous separation of widows and virgins, a decline in the number of public entertainments and a reduction in the
number of servants; but on the whole, Reverend Mother or Abbess remained
largely untroubled by bishops in her internal management. Although holy
women outside the convent make frequent mention of the father confessor in
their writings, on this point the convent chronicles are for the most part silent.

What perhaps helped to ensure the largely unchanged nature of these
institutions was the need of aristocratic families for a place to settle their unmarried daughters. The same women from the same backgrounds lived essentially the same lives within their walls. A major problem of these houses in Spain
in the seventeenth century was the failure of families to pay the full amount of
the dowry. Many convents allowed payment to be made in instalments, but once
the woman had taken her full vows it could be impossible to send her away. Attempts at litigation could drag on for years. The recruitment to these houses
largely sustained itself until the late eighteenth century, though in France and
parts of Italy numbers had already fallen. In effect, and taken overall, the Tridentine reforms sustained for the next 130 years or so the numbers of women
in religion.

The volume of published work of many different kinds emanating from these institutions expanded very considerably as the Jesuits and mission priests encouraged the writing of lives of saints and holy women for distribution to the parishes they visited. However, there were more noteworthy compositions. For example, some remarkable historians are to be found in Italian convents in the seventeenth century. One such, Angelica Baitelli (1588–1650), a Benedictine of Brescia, first involved herself in a history of the founder of her convent, whose origins dated back to the eighth century, *Vita martirio e morte di S. Giulia Cartaginese Crocefissa.* This work transcended the purely hagiographic, drawing upon charters and histories of early Lombardy, and it was followed by *Annali historici dell'edificatione erettione e dotatione del Serenissimo Monasterio di S. Salvatore, e S. Giulia di Brescia.* It draws upon a massive archive of the convent, registers and charters, privileges and donations, benefactors who counted in their ranks emperors, princes and dukes who had given land, privileges and relics in exchange for prayers and intercessions by the nuns. She carefully transcribed, translated and analysed ancient Latin texts and drew on the collective memory of the community. The sisters themselves are traced over the centuries, and the prestige of the families from which they were drawn, and hence the significance of their political connections, is made apparent. Angelica was making a cogent statement on behalf of the entire community in troubled political times, when Brescia had passed under the tutelage of Venice. At the same time her brother Ludovico was engaged in a defence of the privileges of the Brescian nobility, which, unlike the work of his sister, was never published. Nevertheless, both were concerned with family business, a work of political affirmation of the aristocratic élites from which they came, and of their way of life.

Some nuns in these aristocratic institutions corresponded with the great and the famous to whom they were related and thus could promote the interests of other family members and exercise a degree of political influence. The papal nuncio in Venice was perfectly explicit on this subject, though Venice in the sixteenth and seventeenth centuries was remarkable for its politics and intellectual life and should not be taken to represent the rest of Italy.

A couple of decades after Angelica Baitelli, in the Benedictine convent of Sant'Anna in Castello, Venice, Arcangela Tarabotti (1604–52) was to write a series of tracts and letters which earn her a place among Europe's seventeenth-century literary feminists. A nun without vocation, in the sense that she was not imbued with a burning spiritual flame, she was nevertheless able to construct for herself a lifestyle which permitted her to think and write about the condition of women in the convent and women in their relationship to men. She was the author of six works published during her lifetime, though official permission for the most contentious of these was delayed almost until her death: the title, *Inferno monacale* (The convent as hell), explains why. Another of her works, *Semplicità ingannata* (Deceitful simplicity), published posthumously in 1654 under a pseudonym, was also very critical of the way in which the convent was used. On the other hand, *Paradiso monacale,* published in 1643, was a consideration of the terms under which life in the convent could be paradise. Her other works were: *Antisatira in riposta al "Lusso donnesco,"* which ran into two editions (1644 and 1646) and which defended women against the charge of greed and luxury in almost Veblenesque terms; *Che le donne siano della spetie degli huomini. Difesa delle donne* (Women the same species as men. A defence of women; 1651), a theological and philosophical disquisition on the minds and souls of women; *Lettere familiari e di complimento* (Familiar and complimentary letters; 1650) revealed the extent to which Tarabotti was a part of the Venetian literary world although living within an "enclosed" order.

She was endowed with a very powerful analytical mind but also one capable of descriptive power. The banned *Inferno monacale* begins with a swingeing indictment of the dowry system within aristocratic families, which determines the fate of all the children. She describes how the daughter elected for marriage is garbed and bejewelled and taught aristocratic manners—her skin feels silk—while those designed for the convent are deprived—their skin feels rough wool. Thus sacrificed to dynastic interests, she enters convent life under a cloak of hypocrisy. She must dissimulate, hide her feelings, suppress her true self. The church bears a large measure of blame. It is guilty of false teaching which hallows this hypocritical exercise.

The work is the more powerful if we turn to her *Paradiso monacale*. The convent was transformed into paradise for the woman who had a measure of spirituality. Above all, she must *want* to become a nun, the girl herself must make the choice. If Arcangela Tarabotti's work has a leitmotif, it is the denial of choice to women and the restriction of free will to the male sex. Her vocabulary is that of the Enlightenment, which has yet to take place. The convent is hell when free will is excluded.

Tarabotti is a far more cogent critic of the convent than Diderot. She allows for differences in temperament and sees nothing unnatural in women wanting to live together. Significantly, perhaps, though a "forced" nun, she herself never sought to leave. Although the convent clearly irked her, it provided her with the conditions to write and think. In the world outside she might not have had the opportunity for either. Perhaps she laboured in the knowledge that she had nowhere else to go. It is also perhaps significant that while Venice's most illustrious female poet was a courtesan, Veronica Franco, living on immoral earnings, her most illustrious female polemicist was a nun, living on her convent.

Elisja Schulte van Kessel

Virgins and Mothers Between Heaven and Earth

As winds of reform swept through the West, early modern reformers returned to the sources of Christianity, invoking Christ and his earliest disciples. They believed that they could recover Christ's message in its original intention by following the lead of the Church Fathers, precursors on the arduous path of orthodoxy. Their quest, obviously, was very different from ours. Of course, in the light of so many centuries of paternal authority, from Saint Paul to Leopold von Ranke, from Saint Augustine to Fernand Braudel, any attempt to achieve a feminist consciousness of these issues must seem forbiddingly daring....

Perfection and "Matronage"

The quest for perfection was the primary task of every believer. In reality, however, it was a duty imposed on women more than on men, and a girl's education placed greater emphasis on virtue than did a boy's. Moreover, women were scrutinized far more closely than men, because Eve, the prime instigator of evil, lurked in every member of her sex. Yet one sign suggested that women surpassed men in the virtue that was supposed to come before all others, namely, faith: women were more loyal to the church. When their enlightened husbands began to turn their backs on religion in the eighteenth century, women did not follow suit. Why not?

The Fidelity of Women

The answer usually given by historians runs like this: the church had always offered women more than the state did. Above all, it had offered a community of believers who shared the belief that God was the creator of every thing and every person. Hence all of life—seasonal change, good and bad harvests, birth, illness, education, marriage, death—became a shared experience. After the Reformation this sense of community was further reinforced: in Protestant churches and reformed Catholic parishes there was room for every believer.

From Elisja Schulte van Kessel, "Virgins and Mothers Between Heaven and Earth," in Natalie Zemon Davis and Arlette Farge, eds., *A History of Women in the West, vol. 3: Renaissance and Enlightenment Paradoxes* (Belknap Press, 1993). Copyright © 1993 by The President and Fellows of Harvard College. Reprinted by permission of The Belknap Press of Harvard University Press. Notes omitted.

This community placed a high priority on the quest for personal perfection. Even if women were excluded by the standards of intellectual and professional success that applied in the ordinary world, they could still pursue ethical ideals. For many women, it was the only area not determined by gender in which they could equal if not surpass the achievement of their male counterparts. As nondomestic skills were increasingly professionalized, the gulf between the moral aspirations of women and the professional ambitions of men widened. Virtue and piety were increasingly associated with the church's sphere, the world of ministers, monks, and women.

In the church personal virtue was always linked to the afterlife. For many men and women the hope of eternal salvation was the only light at the end of a long tunnel, the daily struggle to survive. Given the dependence of women, they, more than men, lived under the shadow of injustice and poverty. What is more, their primary function, procreation, increased their risk of premature death but at the same time gave them an intense feeling for the relation between life and the afterlife. Women were in contact with the kingdom of death: the children they brought into the world were bound to die sooner or later, and many were stillborn or nonviable. Last but not least, life after death offered equality between the sexes, which—in the view of most people, men and women alike—was something that could not be achieved on earth. Some of the more radical Protestant sects had offered at least the prospect of greater equality in life, but the few practical steps in this direction were soon thwarted by pressure to conform to prevailing norms.

The speculative remarks that follow remain to be corroborated by further research. Whatever motivated women's devotion to the church, it is simply a fact that daily religious practice occupied a far greater place in their lives than in the lives of men. Catholicism, which preserved its colorful ritual, lent itself to such daily communal experience more than Protestantism, which stressed individual devotion, the reading of scripture, and the private conscience. It would be interesting to learn more about how women experienced such activities as private prayer, Bible reading, participation in the Lord's Supper or Mass, receiving the sacraments, making pilgrimages, handling relics, and fasting. All these things were experienced in different ways by the many poor and the few rich, by the majority of rural women and the minority of urban ones, by the illiterate masses and the literate elite.

Leaving aside social and economic considerations, it remains unclear how religious experience influenced the choice—if one can call it choice—of confession. For obvious reasons, it was long believed that learned women were inclined to choose Protestantism, but we now know that this was not so. Women of letters were more apt to remain faithful to the Catholic church, as the philo-Protestant Marguerite d'Angoulême did (to cite only the most famous example). It is pointless, moreover, to try to discover whether Protestants or Catholics were more misogynist and more oppressive to women: even if we could answer the question, it would shed little light on the sensibilities of early modern women themselves. What we really want to know is how women experienced their faith, what they desired from it, and what they discovered in it.

Collaborators of the Clergy

One useful approach to this subject is a survey of early modern "matronage," acts of generosity and gift-giving by upper-class married women: the patronage of matrons, in other words. Such an approach complements the more common economic and sociocultural approaches by introducing anthropological and socioreligious perspectives, providing new insight into both the actual experience of women and the ambivalence of their position.

Charity and matronage were the only activities in which a wealthy woman could decently engage outside the home. Her motives were generally a complex mixture of the personal, the social, and the religious. The relations between benefactor and beneficiary were far more complex than those between a superior and an inferior. Until recently, historians tended to focus exclusively on the social and economic aspects of such relationships, overlooking the importance of the mutual dependence and affection typically found in them. Charity forged a bond between the rich and the poor, the strong and the weak, the healthy and the unhealthy—a bond rooted in a radical reading of the commandment "Love thy neighbor." Owing to the symbiosis between chivalry and *imitatio Christi*, courtly love and mendicancy, embodied by new apostles such as Francis of Assisi, it became an article of faith among Christians that Jesus was most likely to be found among the indigent. To help the needy was to love and to serve Christ. A woman's duty was thus transformed into an act of compassionate mercy: she now served not only her own family but Christ himself, whom every believer encountered in the guise of suffering neighbors clad in tattered rags. Thus *pietas* became *pietà*.

Wherever loving service to God became conflated with service to one's neighbor, the redemptive potential of suffering revealed itself. The poor rewarded generosity with prayers for the patron's salvation—and of course everyone knew that it was easier for a camel to pass through the eye of a needle than for a rich man to enter the kingdom of heaven. This reciprocity not only confirmed the hierarchy of earthly status but also demonstrated that from the standpoint of eternity it was merely provisional. The donor-recipient transaction took on a dual significance: it had an immediate, visible effect within the "order of creation," but it also produced an invisible yet incomparably greater effect within the "order of salvation." Both parties reaped benefits from their relationship, partly social and economic, partly political.

Women played a remarkable role on both sides. Those receiving charity were given preferential treatment, especially when protection of either their chastity or their fertility was involved. In Italy and elsewhere, dowry funds were established to promote prosperity by helping poor girls to marry; these funds survived well into the nineteenth century. Poor girls had no more choice than their wealthy benefactresses: they either married or became nuns. Any woman left without a husband in either this world or the next relinquished all hope of achieving a prestigious position in society. Only a small minority of women—courtesans and the semireligious—found ways to sustain themselves outside marriage, thereby escaping the prevailing value system: such women were either greatly venerated or deeply despised. Thus charity was mainly the work of married women, often widowed, aided by a very small number of the unmarried.

Family interests and the duty to procreate weighed heavily on the women of the elite. Charity work offered respectable reasons for evading certain family obligations. As the Catholic Counter-Reformation proceeded, the clergy increasingly asserted its control over charity. It was the very essence of the policy of church reform to impose a new discipline on pastoral work and charity. Because of their subordinate position in the family, wealthy women were only too pleased to collaborate with the church. As the clergy's authority waxed, that of husbands waned, thereby indirectly increasing the independence of wives.

These women played an important part in the reform policies of the clergy, which had every reason to want to sabotage the all-powerful kinship system. In fact, "the great obstacle to Tridentine uniformity was not individual backsliding or Protestant resistance but the internal articulations of a society in which kinship was a most important bond." In the prevailing kinship system women played a secondary role. A woman was expected to act in the interest of her husband's family, not her father's. Hence there was an ambiguity about the very idea of family, and acts of charity often were performed anonymously. Women were more likely than men to seek relief from family duties in works of piety and renunciation of the world. This should come as no surprise, because *pietà* and renunciation opened up far more opportunities, even in this world, than *pietas* generally did.

Middle-class women were much less involved in charity work than were wealthy women. There were also fewer of them in convents.

Perfection and Profession

Monasteries had always formed the backbone of universal Christianity. In the Catholic church they continued to expand, but in the Protestant church they were abolished. It has yet to be proved that the astonishing increase in the number of women entering convents toward the end of the Middle Ages was a phenomenon throughout Europe. Nor do we know with certainty that the subsequent desertion of the nunneries, which began before the Reformation in many places such as England, the northern Netherlands, and northern Italy, was a universal phenomenon. Such monographs as we have do not warrant general conclusions. A first step would be to map the locations of all European nunneries, and a project to do just that for the medieval period is already under way; it is to be hoped that the work will continue beyond the Middle Ages to explore more recent periods as well.

Nunneries

One issue that has received a great deal of attention is the relation between the number of women entering nunneries and the politics of marriage. In the early modern period, marked by violent wars not just on a local but on a continental scale, the "marriage market" was hit by a depression: the demand for women decreased, and so did the purchasing power of men. Economic uncertainty made marriage a risky business for the wealthy; there were no guarantees that hefty investments in dowries would ever pay off. Many women never married, and men tended to marry later in life, so that the number of widows (only the richest of whom would ever remarry) also rose. The Protestant policy of encouraging marriage did little to slow the resulting increase in the number of single women.

In Catholic countries nunneries continued to play an institutional role: they were a form of "social security," especially for wealthier urban women. A "marriage" with Christ required a much smaller dowry than an ordinary marriage. A man who sent his daughter to a nunnery also purchased a say in how the convent would be run, and if he had the influence to secure an administrative post for the girl he might also acquire an income. Most nunneries were safely located either inside or just outside city walls. They enjoyed tax exemptions and other privileges. In return, the nuns prayed every day for the salvation of their relatives and cities.

If the ecclesiastical authorities—a bishop, say—failed to impose discipline, powerful families were quick to intervene in spiritual matters, which were not always easy to distinguish from matters of pecuniary interest. The local elite profited not only economically but also spiritually: those who devoted their energies to worldly affairs could rest assured that others would occupy themselves with prayers for their salvation.

Nuns and citizens thus engaged in animated dialogue. Within the religious community, moreover, class distinctions were marked. Wealthy nuns tended especially to maintain ties to their families. How a nun lived depended on her social background. Those from wealthy families lived in comfortably furnished cells. They received inheritances from and made bequests to family members. A widow might share her living quarters with a daughter. The better-off nuns took meals privately in their rooms and kept their own hens and vegetable gardens. Their relatively luxurious circumstances were often the source of envy among poor members of the community.

Of course many convents, particularly those in the countryside, endured the harshest poverty. The greatest threat faced by nuns was not loss of chastity but impoverishment. Nunneries, moreover, were all too often victims of interminable power struggles between local and central governments and between lay and regular clergy; the consequences for their material and spiritual welfare were frequently disastrous.

Institutions of Perfection

The Council of Trent (1545–1563) initiated radical changes. Convents were increasingly exploited in the interests of central church policy and at the expense of local communities and families. The Tridentine reform institutionalized and professionalized the personal vocation of the nun, who felt called to perfect her virtue. Convents became nothing less than "institutions of perfection," sharply differentiated from secular institutions and claiming a monopoly on canonized sanctity.

Discipline was tightened so as to strengthen the sense of community. Family factions within the convents were broken up, with the effect of reducing the influence of families outside. Steps were also taken to root out libertine and heretical tendencies and to ensure that no dangerous influences leaked to the outside world. Much was said and written about overworldly convents, from which later historians inferred that "lust" and "laxity" were a major problem. In fact the opposite was true: the preachers were really afraid of excessively ardent devotion. Because the faithful of all ranks, from the most exalted to the humblest, frequently turned to consecrated women, and especially charismatics, in search of solace, care, or advice, the church felt a need to protect itself against these breeding grounds of local cults. Furthermore, many nuns, especially in rural areas but also in the towns, lived on alms. Church and civil authorities frowned on this practice and attempted to curb it and to isolate potentially dangerous elements. In fact many Tridentine regulations, especially those relating to the cloistering of consecrated women, were designed to achieve the same results as reforms undertaken by the secular authorities.

There was considerable opposition to cloistering, not only from nuns and their relatives but also from the clergy and urban communities. The clergy argued that many women lived in convents not out of devotion but because their families had sent them there. Even in the diocese of Milan, where Carlo Borromeo directed a zealous program of reform, older nunneries clung to their established ways. Newer convents were able to implement the Tridentine model more effectively, enforcing the new discipline from the start and above all adapting their facilities to the new way of thinking. Magical or sacred associations were no longer considered essential in the choice of a site. What mattered most was the distance from the bustle of the city and from monasteries. There had to be sufficient room to allow cloistered nuns a little air. High walls, heavy gates, innumerable locks, and iron bars left no doubt that Christ's brides had bidden the world a final farewell.

Cloistering radically changed the social connections of nuns, especially those of elite background. Previously, each nun had had her own circle of contacts and relationships; now the most important distinction was internal, between nuns and so-called lay sisters, or *conversae*. Lay sisters did the convent housework; they were not allowed to participate in canonical hours and had no role in administrative decisions concerning the institution. Most were country girls, illiterate and impecunious, but they still had to pay the convent a dowry, though a much smaller one than those brought by professed sisters. Whereas nunneries had once been comfortable, homey places, particularly in the wealthier nuns' quarters, reformed convents had a very different look. Nuns were required to sleep either alone or in dormitories; prohibiting two nuns from sharing a room put an end to the possibility of intimate or affectionate relationships. Not surprisingly, many felt emptiness, which one nun in Bologna expressed in these terms: "As for me, I wish things could be as they were before, that we could keep a niece with us or some other girl who was fond of us."

A nun's most personal relationships were with her confessor, who was chosen for her, and her spiritual director, whom she chose herself. There were obvious risks in such relationships. Unlike monks, nuns could not escape the influence of members of the opposite sex, chiefly male members of the same order to which they themselves belonged. Priests celebrated mass, administered the sacraments, and provided individual and collective spiritual guidance.

The emphasis on the inner life was in keeping with the late medieval tendency toward internalized spirituality, evident in female mysticism and Christian humanism. This inwardness found its fullest manifestation in the Devotio Moderna movement, as the unparalleled success of Thomas Hemerken van Kempen's *Imitatio Christi* attests. Individuals began to seek perfection through direct experience of God, the *summum* of human perfection, to be achieved through a combination of intellect, feeling, and imagination, developed through methodical spiritual exercise. Simplicity was the goal, but often the result was the opposite. An expert spiritual guide, a professional of the sort typical of the early modern period, became all but essential. The old textbooks were no longer good enough, and hundreds of new manuals examined every possible eventuality in exhaustive detail.

Confessors and spiritual directors needed consummate skill to deal with women. The very form of the confessional was modified: owing to the dangers inherent in hearing women's confessions, a dividing screen was placed between penitent and confessor in order to prevent eye contact. Confessors of consecrated women faced other dangers, for these women were thought to be more susceptible to erroneous ideas, immoderate passions, exaggerated scruples, and demonic passions of all sorts, including witchcraft, feigned mystical experiences, black magic, ascetic extravagance, and possession.

Yet the brides of Christ were considered lucky: they had made the right choice, it was felt, even though it was well known that few of them actually chose their condition. One of the changes instituted at Trent was to insist that women entering convents do so of their own free will. The council also raised the minimum age to sixteen. Yet men such as Galileo Galilei saw no way for their daughters to survive other than to commit them to a poor nunnery before they had reached that age. Some of the Tridentine reforms were intended to reduce poverty in the convents, but cloistering often made the situation worse rather than better. Why did nuns resist the Tridentine reforms so vigorously? The most convincing explanation is that they feared, with good reason, the loss of vital income from alms.

It is hard to gauge how widespread the resistance was, because all traces of it were later carefully covered up. In various places nuns quite simply ran away. When inspectors came to check on the application of the new rules, refractory sisters reportedly threw chairs at them, raising such a ruckus that the police had to be called in. Some Roman nuns saw no way out but suicide. Others preferred to take up illegal semireligious status, living at home or in small groups, often as tertiaries affiliated with an official order (generally the Franciscans). Some semireligious women, however, cultivated ties with the Jesuits, so that the label "Jesuitess" became synonymous with "semireligious" throughout Europe. At times the term carried a pejorative connotation, because some of the original "Jesuitesses" were wealthy women who provided substantial financial backing to the order, in return for which they received preferential treatment.

Nuns and Married Women

Were early modern convents really as dreadful as contemporary writers claimed? Yes and no. The negative image of convent life developed a life of its own over the years, aided by a pro-marriage ideology according to which the decline of convents was a sign of progress. The famous Venetian Benedictine Angela Tarabotti (died 1652) wrote a parody of Dante in three parts: the *Paradiso monacale* (Nun's Paradise, ms. 1643), the *Inferno monacale* (Nun's Inferno), and the *Purgatorio delle mal maritate* (Purgatory of the Badly Married). Material for the last came straight from victims of domestic abuse, for whom the convent parlor was the only place where they could speak freely. Perhaps it is no accident that of these three texts, only the *Purgatorio* remains lost. Be that as it may, in the late seventeenth century a Protestant woman in England published a proposal to create a semireligious community for women that offered further evidence of the almost unbearable conditions under which some married women suffered. The community, which was to require no religious oaths, was conceived as a "Monastery" to provide "Religious Retirement" (in the sense of decent accommodation) for unmarried women and to serve as a refuge for married ones.

Indeed, many women may have seen a vital need for communication between the world of the married and that of the religious. Shortly before the Council of Trent met, the "living saint" Angela Merici (died 1540) gave new impetus to the relationship between nuns and married women. Defying the spirit of the times, she preached unconditional, unlimited love of one's neighbor. Her followers lived in the world with families whose children they helped to educate. Angela herself made several pilgrimages, one all the way to the Holy Land. Though illiterate, she was supremely self-confident and convinced that her first obedience was to God. Ultimately she became a tertiary affiliated with the Franciscans, and it was only in the final years of her life that she decided to organize the Company of Saint Ursula, a community of women without oaths, habit, or rule. She was not canonized until the beginning of the nineteenth century, by which time memory of her living sainthood had faded, to be supplanted by the more reassuring image of her as the wise founder of a religious order, something she had never actually been.

The women's congregations of the nineteenth century are generally thought of as having descended from these early open communities, but this idea is misleading. The women who founded religious orders in the early modern period, many of them widows with several children—Ludovica Torelli, Jeanne de Lestonnac, Jeanne de Chantal, Luise de Marillac—exemplified a female spirituality with a rich past but little future.

POSTSCRIPT

Did Convents Expand Opportunities for European Women?

Images of convents as places that narrowed and restricted women's lives are undercut by our knowledge that for European gentlewomen they offered a respected alternative to marriage. The popular lectures of historian Eileen Power, long associated with the London School of Economics, did much to change perceptions about convent life. These lectures have been collected and posthumously edited by her husband M. M. Postan in *Medieval Women* (Cambridge University Press, 1997). Chapter 5 offers an intimate portrait of daily convent life, showing how convents, like other great estates, supported study and learning, provided professional training, and enabled those who lived and worked there to have productive lives.

Chapter 2 of Gerda Lerner's *The Creation of Feminist Consciousness* (Oxford University Press, 1994) addresses the educational disadvantaging of women and gives a strong historical summary of women's experiences in religious communities, including the dual communities of monks and nuns that were often headed by women. Lerner calls convents "privileged spaces" for women in which learning and an independent life were possible.

Margaret Wade Labarge's *A Small Sound of the Trumpet: Women in Medieval Life* (Beacon Press, 1988) studies the lives of women in feudal France, England, the Low Countries, and southern Germany from 1100 to 1500, with an emphasis on the hierarchical nature of feudal society, which was divided into those who fought and therefore ruled society, those who prayed and thereby linked the human with the divine, and those who labored. Chapter 5 situates convents in this schema, illustrating how they formally opened the option of prayer to women and counteracted negative stereotypes of women as inferior, sinful, and depraved.

Labarge's title comes from the work of Abbess Hildegard of Bingen, whose 800th anniversary has recently been celebrated. *The Journal of Hildegard of Bingen* by Barbara Lachman (1993) was inspired by the writings of Hildegard—visionary abbess, composer (compact discs of her music are widely available), healer, scholar, and advocate of women's full participation in the life of the spirit. Her visions may be explored in *Illuminations of Hildegard of Bingen* (1985), with an accompanying commentary by Matthew Fox. More about Hildegard and other women mystics, including Mechtilde of Magdeburg and Marguerite Porete, may be found in *Women Mystics in Medieval Europe* by Emilie Zum Brunn and Georgette Epiney-Burgard (1989).

On the Internet ...

African Timelines: History, Orature, Literature, and Film

Part III of this site, "African Slave Trade and European Imperialism," contains information and visuals relavant to the slave trade and European imperialism in Africa.

`http://www.cocc.edu/cagatucci/classes/hum211/`
`timelines/htimeline3.htm`

Scientific Revolution

This site explores the link between classical mathematics and science and the Scientific Revolution of the premodern world.

`http://metalab.unc.edu/expo/vatican.exhibit/`
`exhibit/d-mathematics/Mathematics.html`

The French Revolution Home Page

The French Revolution home page includes information about Louis XVI, the coming of the French Revolution, the role of women in the revolutionary process, essays on the Revolution covering a variety of subjects, as well as an annotated biliography.

`http://members.aol.com/agentmess/frenchrev/index.html`

Ireland's Potato Famine

This site provides an in-depth look at the origins of the potato blight, the famine that followed, and the famine's aftermath.

`http://www.geocities.com/Athens/Rhodes/6477/`
`potato.html`

The Premodern World

*T*his period marks the formation and maturation of the European state system—a new environment in which nation-states grew, competed, fought, expanded, and influenced the development not only of Europe but also of the world at large. The roots of modern Europe were established at this time.

- Was the West African Slave Trade a Precondition for the Rise of British Capitalism?

- Were the Witch-Hunts in Premodern Europe Misogynistic?

- Was the Scientific Revolution Revolutionary?

- Was the French Revolution Worth Its Human Costs?

- Did British Policy Decisions Cause the Mass Emigration and Land Reforms That Followed the Irish Potato Famine?

ISSUE 10

Was the West African Slave Trade a Precondition for the Rise of British Capitalism?

YES: William Darity, Jr., from "British Industry and the West Indies Plantations," in Joseph E. Inikori and Stanley L. Engerman, eds., *The Atlantic Slave Trade: Effects on Economies, Societies, and Peoples in Africa, the Americas, and Europe* (Duke University Press, 1994)

NO: James A. Rawley, from *The Transatlantic Slave Trade: A History* (W. W. Norton, 1981)

ISSUE SUMMARY

YES: Economics professor William Darity, Jr., argues that the profits derived from the West African slave trade and its concomitant economic ventures played a crucial role in the development of British capitalism.

NO: History professor James A. Rawley states that the economic effects of the West African slave trade on the development of British capitalism have been exaggerated due to the faulty use of data and statistics.

In the eighteenth century, England became the first European nation to initiate the economic process that marked the beginning of the Industrial Revolution. During that century Europeans also reached the high water mark of the transatlantic slave trade: 6 million Africans were torn from their homelands and brought to the New World to serve as chattel slaves. From time to time historians have debated whether or not these two movements were related, asking, "Did profits from the West African slave trade fuel England's Industrial Revolution?"

The transatlantic slave trade had its origins in the fifteenth century during what is commonly called the European Age of Exploration. Initiated by the Portuguese and the Spanish, who had a geographic and maritime advantage over their European rival states, the slave trade played a large role in the development of the Iberian colonies in the New World, providing plentiful and inexpensive labor for mines and plantations. But the Iberian monopoly did not last. Declining Spanish and Portuguese power and the concurrent rise of their European enemies—especially England—meant that by the eighteenth century England was the leading European nation involved in the West African slave trade.

The Englishmen who were personally involved in the slave trade—or witnessed its economic successes—spoke glowingly of its importance to the British economy, especially its role in the development of eighteenth-century British capitalism, which ultimately led to the Industrial Revolution. As years passed, the relationship between the slave trade and the Industrial Revolution seemed to be taken as a historical fact. For obvious reasons, the transatlantic slave trade was not a subject nineteenth-century historians wanted to deal with. In the twentieth century, however, changes in society in general and the historical profession in particular resulted in closer scrutiny. The opening salvo appeared in 1944 with the publication of *Capitalism and Slavery* (University of North Carolina Press, 1944) by West Indian politician/historian Eric Williams (1911–1981), who served as Trinidad and Tobago's prime minister from the islands' independence in 1962 until his death nearly 20 years later. His thesis was blunt and straightforward: the profits from the West African slave trade provided fuel for England's eighteenth-century Industrial Revolution. It had similar effects on other European nations who participated in it (especially France), but England reaped the most economic benefits from the exploitation of black African slave labor. A corollary thesis was that British interest in abolishing the slave trade did not come about until the nation began to lose its profit quotient. According to Williams, even abolition had a price tag attached.

Initial response to Williams' book was mixed, but he eventually received strong criticism. Many claimed that his misuse and misinterpretation of economic data gave an inaccurate picture of the slave trade's profitability. Williams continued to advance his cause, and in *From Columbus to Castro: The History of the Caribbean* (Random House, 1970) he restated his thesis. Despite continuing criticism, many readers agreed with historian David Brion Davis, who stated that "it is . . . it is more difficult . . . to get around the simple fact that no country thought of abolishing the slave trade until its economic value had considerably declined." This quote appeared in *The Transatlantic Slave Trade* (W. W. Norton, 1981) from which the No-side selection was taken.

In recent years, the "Williams thesis" controversy has continued, fueled by the interpretation of new historical data and enhanced by the availability of computers. Thus far, the results have been mixed, with William's work receiving support from a younger generation of economic historians. William Darity, Jr.'s selection represents this side of the ongoing debate, while James A. Rawley's selection exemplifies the critical approach.

British Industry and the West Indies Plantations

Is it not notorious to the whole World, that the Business of *Planting* in our *British Colonies*, as well as in the *French*, is carried on by the Labour of *Negroes*, imported thither from *Africa*? Are we not indebted to those valuable People, the *Africans* for our *Sugars, Tobaccoes, Rice, Rum*, and all other *Plantation Produce*? And the greater the Number of *Negroes* imported into our Colonies, from *Africa*, will not the Exportation of *British* Manufactures among the *Africans* be in Proportion, they being paid for in such Commodities only? The more likewise our Plantations abound in *Negroes*, will not more Land become cultivated, and both *better* and greater *Variety of Plantation Commodities* be produced? As those Trades are subservient to the Well Being and Prosperity of each other; so the more either flourishes or declines, the other must be necessarily affected; and the general Trade and Navigation of their *Mother Country*, will be proportionably benefited or injured. May we not therefore say, with equal Truth, as the *French* do in their before cited *Memorial*, that the general Navigation of *Great Britain* owes all its *Encrease and Splendor* to the Commerce of its *American* and *African Colonies*; and that it cannot be maintained and enlarged otherwise than from the constant Prosperity of both those branches, *whose Interests are mutual and inseparable?*

— Malachy Postlethwayt

The Atlantic slave trade remains oddly invisible in the commentaries of historians who have specialized in the sources and causes of British industrialization in the late eighteenth century. This curiosity contrasts sharply with the perspective of eighteenth-century strategists who, on the eve of the industrial revolution, placed great stock in both the trade and the colonial plantations as vital instruments for British economic progress. Specifically, Joshua Gee and Malachy Postlethwayt, once described by the imperial historian Charles Ryle Fay as Britain's major "spokesmen" for the eighteenth century, both placed the importation of African slaves into the Americas at the core of their visions of the requirements for national expansion. Fay also described both of them as "mercantilists hardening into a manufacturers' imperialism." For such a "manufacturers' imperialism" to be a success, both Gee and Postlethwayt saw the need for extensive British participation in the trade in Africans and in the maintenance and development of the West Indies.

However, for historians of the industrial revolution, British involvement in the Atlantic slave trade brings forth, at most, a proper and perfunctory moral abhorrence. It plays no part in the stories they weave about the origins of the industrial revolution. Not a single essay in the [Roderick] Floud and [Donald] McCloskey volume on British economic history since 1700 discusses the possibility of an important connection between Caribbean and/or North American slavery and the industrialization of England. Neither Nicholas Crafts nor Jeffrey Williamson nor Joel Mokyr gives even passing notice, in the special issue of *Explorations in Economic History* devoted to Britain's industrial revolution, to the potential relevance of Eric Williams's hypothesis that the development of British industrial capitalism bore intimate links to the Atlantic slave system. And in a slightly earlier collection of notable articles by the "new" economic historians on the industrial revolution, only Mokyr, the editor, offers a single sentence that refers to the Williams hypothesis.

In a discussion of the venerable puzzle of the initial sources of finance for British industry that later could have triggered a cumulative process of reinvestment of profits, Mokyr observes dismissively,

> While some curious mechanisms have been proposed to solve this problem such as the Williams . . . thesis, which attributed the "original accumulation" to profits generated in the slave trade, the difficulty seems a bit overstated, since in the early stages of the industrial revolution the fixed-cost requirements to set up a minimum-sized firm were modest and could be financed from profits accumulated at the artisan level.

Thus, the Williams hypothesis is reduced to the status of a "curious mechanism" advanced to handle an "overstated" problem.

The intellectual invisibility of the economic significance for British industry of the British trade in slaves is reinforced by the peculiar attitude of some economic historians over what constitutes true items of commerce. Apparently only nonhuman commodities merit consideration. We find the following strange passage in W. Arthur Lewis's Janeway lectures:

> At the end of the eighteenth century, trade between what are now the industrial countries and what is now the Third World was based on geography rather than on structure; indeed India was the leading exporter of fine cotton fabrics. The trade was also trivially small in volume. It consisted of sugar, a few spices, precious metals and luxury goods. It was then cloaked in much romance, and had caused much bloodshed, but it simply did not amount to much.

Similar sentiments were advanced by T. S. Ashton in his analysis of British industrialization over the period 1760–1830: "The overwhelming bulk of [British] import and export trade was with the Continent and, in particular, with the countries nearest to Britain. Compared with this the traffic with India, the West Indies, and North America was small, and that with Africa insignificant." So much for the more than 1.5 million African slaves transported from the African coast to the Americas by British slavers between 1761 and 1807 alone.

What accounts for the muteness of the economic historians of the industrial revolution on the slave trade and slavery in their analyses of British industrialization? Has there been a conspiracy of silence, or have they had a sound intellectual foundation for ignoring the Williams hypothesis? Or has it simply been a more innocent oversight among a group of scholars so passionately engaged in supporting or debunking one another's pet explanations for the rise of British industry that they have failed to consider explanations put forward by others outside their loop?

The polite explanation is, of course, that the historians of the industrial revolution have a valid reason for not mentioning arguments that assign a leading role in British industrial expansion to the foreign sector and, more specifically, to the slave trade and plantation slavery. The modern economic historians, ostensibly, have considered the case for the Williams hypothesis in careful, deliberate fashion and have simply found it wanting. For them, commerce with the colonial plantations and with the African coastal regions was no more than a handmaiden to the British process of industrialization, and a minor handmaiden at that—so minor that it can be ignored. The position... is blunt and by no means unrepresentative:

> Foreign trade expanded considerably faster than output throughout the Industrial Revolution. Between 1700 and 1800 the volume of foreign trade grew sixfold. Although the expansion was studded with leaps and bounds followed by sharp retreats, it was on the whole much faster than output and population growth. Perhaps this has led many historians to conclude that foreign markets were indispensable to British industrial growth. They were not.

Small Ratios?

The most prevalent justification for the foregoing attitude consistently appears to be Stanley Engerman's (1972) well-known "small ratios" argument. Engerman constructed what he viewed as overstated estimates of the profits earned from the slave trade by British capitalists. He then sought to demonstrate that slave trade profits, as a percentage of national income, investment, and commercial and industrial investment for Britain in several years during the eighteenth century, were too small to matter in an explanation of British industrialization. Note, first, that Engerman's intentionally overstated estimates are limited to profits from the British slave trade alone; they do not encompass the entire returns from the trade as well as the colonial plantation system in the British West Indies.... Second, in light of the more recent range of estimates of the profits from the slave trade, it is not clear that Engerman's numbers constitute a gross overstatement....

Third, it is not apparent that Engerman's percentages actually are small in a historical or relative sense, despite their apparent absolute smallness. In a critique of Engerman's argument, Barbara Solow makes exactly such a point:

> Focusing on 1770... we find that [Engerman's] overstated slave trade profits form one half of 1 percent of national income, nearly 8 percent of total investment, and 39 percent of commercial and industrial investment.
>
> These ratios are not small; they are enormous. The ratio of *total* corporate profits of domestic industries to GNP [gross national product] in the United States today (1980) amounts to 6 percent. The ratio of total corporate domestic profits to gross private domestic investment for that year amounts to over 40 percent. And the ratio of total corporate domestic profits to 1980 investment in domestic plant and equipment (non-residential fixed investment) runs at more than 55 percent....
>
> How can we be sure the ratio of slave trade profits to national income in 1770 is "small" at half a percent, when the ratio of total corporate profits to GNP today is only 6 percent? If slave trade profits were 8 percent of investment in Britain in 1770, is that "small" when today total corporate profits amount to 40 percent? No industry manages as much as 8 percent. Is the potential contribution of an industry whose profits can "only" amount to 39 percent of commercial and industrial investment to be ruled out because it is "small"?
>
> Naturally it is not my intention to make a serious comparison between 1770 and 1980, nor to claim that these figures make a case for Williams. Engerman never claims that they measure anything but an upper limit on what the slave trade could have contributed to British growth. On the evidence of his figures, the contribution *could have been* enormous....

Supernormal Profits?

The small ratios argument is the crux of the empirical basis for dismissing the proposition that the slave trade and the colonial plantation system were instrumental in British economic development. It is a weak basis. Another a priori argument that emerges with less frequency... is that the slave trade was a highly competitive industry where only "normal" profits could be earned. The inference then drawn is that in the absence of supernormal profits, the slave trade could not have played a key role in Britain's accumulation of wealth prior to or during the industrial revolution. But this is an insubstantial argument. As I have pointed out elsewhere, conclusions about the degree of competition in the slave trade industry provide no information about the volume of slave trade profits, slave trade profitability, or the specific channels into which slave trade profits subsequently flowed.

Ironically, [Patrick] O'Brien suggests that in the early stages of the slave trade, what he terms "superexploitative" profits were earned until additional entrants drove the profit rate in the slave trade into line with other sectors. This suggests that the slave trade, at least for a while, offered an investment outlet that propped up the general rate of profit. In fact, depending upon one's theory of the determination of the general profit rate, it is possible to argue that the slave trade led to a higher rate of profit than otherwise would have prevailed, thereby contributing a powerful stimulus to British industry. The important issue is the determination of the general profit rate and the mechanisms that led to equalization of profit rates across all activities. The monopoly versus nonmonopoly nature of slave trade profits is a false issue.

Theories of Growth, Trade, and Slavery

O'Brien does recognize correctly that a comprehensive assessment of the role of commerce with the periphery (or the role of the slave trade, for that matter) requires "historians [to] construct financial flow tables which reveal the sources of funds *actually* used to pay for the net and gross investment expenditures which occurred in Britain for a century after 1760." He then asserts that, unfortunately, construction of such flow tables "is not even a remote possibility" because of inadequate data.

But there are some clues to how such a flow table might look; they give a critical role to the slave trade. For example, two major British banks, Barclay's and Lloyds, developed rapidly from slave trade profits acquired during the mid-eighteenth century. Both later became important sources of credit for British industry. . . . Wilson Williams documented the extent to which the development of the port cities of Bristol and Liverpool was linked directly to the trade in Africans but, more provocatively, the extent to which the development of the manufacturing center of Manchester derived from that of Liverpool via credit relations and export activities. Manchester's businessmen, recognizing that the slave trade offered a major market for their products, erected a vast network of warehouses in Liverpool to store their goods for transport to Africa. Of special note was the Hibbert family, whose business activities included a 3,000-acre sugar plantation in Jamaica and a sugar commission enterprise in London as well as a cotton cloth manufactory in Manchester—an intrafamily triangle trade. . . .

Eric Williams itemized various routes taken by the capital accumulated by West Indian sugar planters and Liverpool slave traders to promote British industry: (1) A large number of eighteenth-century banks that developed in Liverpool and Manchester were established with funds generated by the triangle trade. These included the Heywood Bank, founded in Liverpool in 1773 and absorbed a century later by the Bank of Liverpool. Thomas Leyland's involvement in banking in the early nineteenth century followed his acquisition in the late eighteenth century of a fortune in the trade in Africans. The same was true of banking in Bristol, Glasgow, and London, the latter dominated by the aforementioned example of Barclay's. (2) Heavy industry received its stimulus as well. Williams highlights the examples of "capital accumulated from the West Indian trade [financing] James Watt and the steam engine" and ironmongers Antony Bacon and William Beckford, whose capital originated in the Africa trade and the West Indies. (3) The insurance industry also was nurtured by the triangle trade. In addition to Lloyds, the Phoenix and the Liverpool Underwriters' Association both possessed important West Indian planter connections. If a flow-of-finance matrix could be designed for Britain in the 1780s and 1790s, the point of origin of the flows often would have been the African trade.

This is indicative of an overarching scheme of expansion, of which the slave trade and plantations were a critical linchpin and a valuable direct source of funds. Ronald Bailey finds the answer to Mokyr's puzzle precisely at this point, suggesting that Eric Williams's solution is far from "peculiar": "Thus, for a source of capital sufficient to finance industrialization, and to support the expensive habits of the British ruling elites, we need look no further than the profits from the overseas trade to the Caribbean, of which the slave trade and related commerce was an indispensable prop." But what might be the precise nature of a scheme of British expansion that locates slave trading and plantation slavery at its core? A surprisingly wide variety of answers are available in various economic theories. The point in the discussion that follows is not to establish a single correct approach but to indicate a range of reasonable arguments compatible with a vital role for the slave trade and slavery in the analysis of British industrialization.

These potential answers must hinge on the inability of British growth strategists—or perhaps, more generally, European growth strategists—to develop an adequate labor force in the Americas and the Caribbean without resorting to enslavement of Africans. The native population was decimated by the European wars of conquest and exposure to new diseases. The natives also could flee inland. The "free" white laborers in a new and seemingly unsettled territory would be predisposed to acquire their own land, a point often made by the Marxists . . . , rather than work at another's behest for wages. To work instead as a wage laborer, the free laborer would have to have been paid relatively more, and the differential may have been prohibitive from the standpoint of profitability. Similarly, the expenses required to lure large numbers of free laborers to the Americas might have reduced perceived profitability relative to the use of slave labor.

Extensive proletarianization in the New World required slavery. British economic expansion required colonies. Therefore, British economy expansion required slavery in the colonies. . . .

In sum, there are several theories of growth and trade that give a prominent role to the African slave trade and slave plantations in British industrialization. Each is potentially rich and complex, and none can be dismissed or disproven by the small ratios argument. But what was the nature of the vision that served as the basis for actual British commercial policy in the eighteenth century? For one set of useful answers, we turn at last to Fay's two spokesmen for Britain in the eighteenth century, mercantilist writers Joshua Gee and Malachy Postlethwayt. What is especially notable is how many of their concerns about the importance of the slave trade and the West Indies plantations overlap with the various arguments advanced in this section of the essay.

Gee and Postlethwayt on British Trade and Navigation

The substance of Gee's views can be found in two documents that date from the 1720s: the monograph *The Trade and Navigation of Great Britain Considered* and an open letter addressed to a member of Parliament on pending legislation concerning naval stores. In the former work, first published in 1729, Gee explicitly described the African trade as "very profitable to the nation in general" because

> it carries no money out, and not only supplies our plantations with servants, but brings in a great deal of bullion for those that are sold to the Spanish West-Indies, besides gold dust, and other commodities, as redwood, teeth, Guinea grain, etc. some of which are re-exported. The supplying our Plantations with negroes is of that extraordinary advantage to us, that the planting sugar and tobacco, and carrying on trade could not be supported without them; which Plantations... are the great causes of the increase of the riches of the kingdom.

The nexus of economic progress for Gee was the triumvirate of "manufacturers, commerce and Plantations." Gee recognized, with respect to the latter, that the only source of riches for Spain and Portugal, aside from the wines and fruits they produced domestically for export, were their colonies. Their example demonstrated to Gee the importance of the plantation system as an outlet for manufactured exports. . . .

It is in Malachy Postlethwayt's ponderous writings that the most comprehensive statement of British mercantilist statecraft can be found. Economic growth and national power intertwined as the objectives Postlethwayt sought from British policy, with foreign trade at the fulcrum. For Postlethwayt, "the Balance of Trade... is in Fact the Balance of Power."

. . . Postlethwayt appears to be Joshua Gee in far more grandiose and expansive dress, with a crudely pragmatic bent. For instance, in the entry entitled "Africa" in his version of Savary de Brulon's *Universal Dictionary of Trade and Commerce*, Postlethwayt expresses some dismay over African slavery but concludes, "We must, however, at present take the state of the trade as it stands and men as they now are." After all, "this trade, in its present state, is of as great advantage as any we carry on."

The slave trade had numerous benefits in Postlethwayt's eyes. In a 1746 pamphlet, he argued that the provision of black labor for the colonies had distinct advantages over that of white labor. Specifically, the use of African slaves on the plantations would not depopulate Britain; colonies dependent on African slave labor for planting were unlikely to become independent; and such colonies would not become rival manufacturers (Postlethwayt 1968c). Furthermore, in the true spirit of humanitarianism, he suggested that such an arrangement was better for the Africans, who were better off being sold into slavery by warring African princes than being made into human sacrifices. The planters, Postlethwayt argued, would have an economic self-interest in treating their slaves "with great Levity and Humanity."

But it was the perceived contribution of black labor to British expansion, particularly of industry, that gave the African trade its decisive significance for Postlethwayt:

> The Trade to Africa is the Branch which renders our *American Colonies* and *Plantations* so advantageous to *Great-Britain*, that Traffic only affording our *Planters* a constant supply of *Negroe-Servants* for the Culture of their Lands

in the Produce of *Sugars, Tobacco, Rice, Rum, Cotton, Fustick, Pimento,* and all other our Plantation-Produce: so that the extensive Employment of our Shipping in, to and from *America,* the great Broad of Seamen consequent thereupon, and the daily Bread of the most considerable Part of our *British Manufacturers,* are owing primarily to the Labour of *Negroes....*

The *Negroe-Trade...* may be justly esteemed an inexhaustible Fund of Wealth and Naval Power to the Nation. And by the Overplus of *Negroes* above what have served our own Plantations, we have drawn likewise no inconsiderable Quantities of Treasure from the *Spaniards....*

...near Nine-tenths of those *Negroes* are paid for in *Africa* with *British Produce* and *Manufactures* only; and the Remaining with *East-India* Commodities. We send no Specie or Bullion to pay for the Products of *Africa,* but, 'tis certain, we bring from thence very large Quantities of *Gold;* and not only that but *Wax* and *Ivory....*

...the Trade to *Africa* may very truly be said to be as it were, all Profit to the Nation.

To run the desired trade surpluses with other European states would require continued development of the plantations. That, in turn, would require a prosperous African trade, since the colonies could not progress without a stable supply of slaves. Otherwise, Postlethwayt contended, the British colonies would sink into "Distress and Poverty."

For Postlethwayt, it was always what he perceived as Britain's national advantage that was at stake, not any individual's or group's private advantage (aside from, perhaps, that of the Royal African Company.) Postlethwayt mused about the terms of a future treaty of navigation and commerce with Spain, hoping for renewal of the Assiento that would sustain Britain's contract to supply slaves to the Spanish colonies. He noted that blacks transported from the African coast to New Spain by British vessels were bought with British manufactures. This would create employment in the shipping sector as well as employment for seamen. The Assiento, then, would make manufacturing exports to Africa larger than otherwise, giving Britain an edge in the competition with omnipresent France.

Postlethwayt's estimate of the annual British gain from slaves landed at Jamaica was £60,000. But even more striking was his estimate of an annual gain of £1,648,600 from British participation in the slave trade as a whole. Finally, consider the correspondence from Postlethwayt to the Duke of Newcastle, serving as secretary of state, which brings the mercantilist themes of trade and power together with great force. Reacting to the hostilities that took place in the 1750s and 1760s between England and France, Postlethwayt sought to maximize Britain's gains from the peace treaty. The treaty would have to alter interstate relations because the existing "System of Europe can never produce anything of a lasting Peace for Great Britain."...

No such formal alliance of Protestant Europe was ever made, but British mercantilism was sufficiently thorough and effective to make Britain the world's industrial leader by the start of the nineteenth century. Britain was the first to win in pursuit of the grand mercantilist scheme of commercial conquest, naval power, colonialism, slavery, and metropolitan industrialization. Nevertheless, historians of British industrialization have suppressed this story of the industrial revolution, consciously, subconsciously, or unconsciously. A blanket of scholarly silence, a cloak of historical invisibility, has been laid by these disputants over the causes of British industrialization and over the significance of the slave trade and the slave plantations. But it is not a golden silence, for it has served only to obscure the richer and brutal story of how the modern world took shape, "small" import and export ratios and nonmonopoly profits notwithstanding.

James A. Rawley

The Economics of the Slave Trade

Europe's impulse to conduct a trade in Africans enjoyed an ideological underpinning in the theory of mercantilism. However amorphous that body of doctrine may have been, certain familiar lineaments include: state intervention in the economy, securing national advantage in foreign relations, development of shipping and seapower, acquiring gold, a favorable balance of trade, supremacy of the metropolis over the colonies, drawing raw (especially tropical) materials from the colonies and venting manufactures in exchange, and keeping skilled artisans at home while supplying the colonies with low-priced unskilled labor.

The African slave trade was the very model of these notions. They were never put more perfectly than in 1745 by Malachy Postlethwayt, a member of the Court of Assistants of the Royal African Company and a London merchant, author of *The African Trade: The Great Pillar and Support of the British Plantation Trade in America*. State intervention was necessary, he wrote, to maintain the British presence in Africa. Looking to Britain's place in European affairs, he declared the colonies must "remain a perpetual Support to our *European* interest, by preserving to us a Superiority of Trade and Naval Power." He was clear about the source of shipping strength: "The general NAVIGATION of *Great Britain* owes all its *Encrease* and *Splendor* to the Commerce of its *American* and *African* Colonies."

Slave labor yielded tropical produce, consumed British manufactures, and provided a basis for continuing subordination of the colonies. "Are we not indebted to that valuable People, the *Africans*, for our *Sugars, Tobaccoes, Rice, Rum,* and all other *Plantation Produce?*" Postlethwayt asked. Continuing, he urged, "And the greater the Number of *Negroes* imported into our Colonies, from *Africa*, will not the Exportation of British Manufactures among the *Africans* be in Proportion?" Negro labor, maintaining a British sovereignty of economic interests, will keep the colonies in "due Subserviency." White labor should not be encouraged to emigrate, for it might turn the colonists to manufacturing in competition with the mother country.

"*The Negro-Trade,*" he exclaimed, "and the natural consequences resulting from it, may be justly esteemed an inexhaustible Fund of Wealth and Naval Power to this Nation." The slave trade, Postlethwayt asserted, is "the first principle and foundation of all the rest, the mainspring of the machine which sets every wheel in motion." When he had finished his tract, he had rung the changes of the mercantilist argument for the African slave trade....

A recurring argument in favor of the slave trade was the claim that it increased a nation's shipping; and one of the alarms sounded against abolition by England was that abolition would impair shipping, in Brook Watson's drastic prophecy, "annihilate our marine." Yet it is not clear that the slave trade was a stimulus to shipping. We have seen that French slave merchants tended to hire old ships, with an expectancy of only ten years of service. Similarly, Bristol merchants in the eighteenth century tended to employ small vessels, ranging in size from seventy-five to one-hundred-fifty tons, and not of much value in oceanic merchant shipping. If the Liverpool merchants did have large vessels built expressly for the trade and did readily copper sheath them, a study of the redeployment of the Liverpool slave fleet after abolition is arresting in the light of gloomy prophecies like Brook Watson's.

Liverpool did develop a slave fleet, specially built, young, and copper sheathed. Concentration conduced to ownership of substantial regular traders. In the waning years of the traffic, Liverpool had more than one-hundred vessels that regularly cleared for the African slave trade. What became of this fleet after abolition in 1807? Despite wartime interruption of trade, including the embargo imposed by the United States, 80 per cent of the former slave fleet was redeployed by the end of the year 1810. Many of the ships had new owners....

The slave trade... was a business fraught with more than normal risks, from slave mortality and insurrection, as well as from war, privateers, and pirates. The costs of conducting business were large, in procurement of cargo ships, payment of officers and crew, and in securing insurance. One other consideration remains to be examined, that of the pattern of trade, before we turn to the vexed question of the slave trade's profitability.

It was once axiomatic in English economic history that the structure of the slave trade was triangular. The historian T. S. Ashton described the trade in these words: "Cloth, firearms, hardware, and trinkets were sent to Africa and exchanged for slaves who were shipped to the West Indies to pay for the luxuries and raw material which constituted the final cargo in this disreputable, triangular trade."

The other extreme, that in the eighteenth century the triangular trade was "the exception rather than the rule," was the conclusion of J. E. Merritt. He argued that slave ships brought back little produce from the West Indies, and that a direct trade in sugar accounted for most of this article. The Privy Council in 1788 heard from the colonial assemblies and agents, "The ships bringing Negroes from Africa are not generally employed in transporting the Produce of the West India Islands." And a recent investigator of the Liverpool trade found, "of 110 ships' voyages... only 15 brought back produce to the venturers," from the West Indies or the American mainland. Slavers in fact often returned home in ballast, having found it uneconomical or impossible to secure a cargo. The mechanism of credit made it possible to accept bills of exchange in lieu of cargo; it also made it possible for English merchants to foster a direct trade.

A very considerable direct trade in tobacco and sugar, as we have seen, did exist. There were direct trade routes between Great Britain, on the one side, and Chesapeake Bay, the West Indies, and Africa, on the other. Side by side with this, nonetheless, went a triangular trade. Studies of the ports of Bristol, Nantes, Honfleur, and of the Dutch pattern disclose that slave ships regularly carried home cargoes bought with the proceeds of slave sales. Trade routes were a complex affair, and it would be imprudent to generalize that the structure was all one pattern or the other. The Portuguese trade in the South Atlantic was often a direct trade. The New England trade is a special subject we reserve for future consideration.

In the popular impression of the Atlantic slave trade few notions are more fixed than that the trade was immensely profitable. Both general writers and professional historians have long kept the notion alive. The myth of vast profitability may be traced back to an anonymous Liverpudlian of 1795, who called himself "an Eye Witness," and who calculated a profit of "upwards of thirty per cent," or £9 8s. 5d. per slave. Writing a century later, Gomer Williams, the widely quoted authority on the Liverpool slave trade, drastically raised this estimate, concluding that the profit on each slave, even when a ship returned to Liverpool without a West Indian cargo, was £26. Williams published figures from the account books of six voyages made between 1784 and 1805. One of these voyages, made by the *Lottery*, Captain Charles Kneal, transported 305 slaves to Jamaica in 1802, reaping a fabulous profit of £62 7s. 4d. per slave.

Other eyewitnesses of the last years of the trade, though generally ignored by historians, spoke with a greater measure of realism. The largest Bristol trader, James Jones, offset gain with risk. "It is a very uncertain and precarious Trade," he wrote to the president of the Board of Trade in 1788, "and if there is not a probable prospect of considerable Profit no Man of Property who hath any Knowledge of it would embark or continue in it." [William] Wilberforce observed about the trade: "It is a lottery, in which some men have made large fortunes, chiefly by being their own insurers, while others follow the example of a few lucky adventurers and lose money by it." Wilberforce had underscored the speculative character of the trade, and had particularized the cost of insurance to explain the difference between profit and loss. One of Liverpool's largest slave merchants, John Tarleton, recited many of the hazards in the trade, and judged that a one-hundred-ton vessel in 1788 "should produce to the Merchant by every Voyage... little more than 10 per Cent, upon the Capital employed; and a very moderate profit indeed when compared with the risks...."

The question of the profitability of the African slave trade is a mightily complex one, challenging the skills of economists and historians. Modern research has trimmed back the more extravagant growths of the profitability fable. Three approaches to the question have been fruitful. One is through the application of accounting techniques; another is through a sophisticated understanding of the economic organization of the trade; and the third is through consideration of the trade's relationship to economic change, especially to the Industrial Revolution.

Those classic examples of prodigal profits put forth by "an Eye Witness" and Gomer Williams have been sharply reduced by a closer look at the ship's accounts. Costs of the voyage of the *Lottery* had not been subtracted, and when this was done, profits per slave dropped from £62 7s. 4d. to £36 3s. 10d. For another of these ships not only had costs not been subtracted but also income from salvaging another vessel had been added to slaving profits. On still another ship it has been shown that a cargo of poor slaves was slow in selling, and profit averaged out at £5 9s. 6d. Failure to note that colonial currency did not exchange at par with sterling further skewed returns.

Distortion of slave trade profits has sprung in good part from oversimplication of accounting. The remainder after subtracting the cost of a slave in Africa from the price paid in America has often been taken as the profit, without reckoning overhead expenses. Profits from cargoes other than slaves, e.g., ivory, gum, and wood from Africa, sugar, tobacco, and cotton from America, have often been aggregated in profits from slaving. The trading transactions of many slaving voyages were intricate, requiring close attention to ledgers.

A more comprehensive and sophisticated understanding of the economic organization of the slave trade has altered evaluation of profits. At the African market a host of factors, to be later examined, affected profits. These factors included availability of slaves, length of time spent on the coast, costs of doing business with African traders, the complexities of currencies, and having the right assortment of trade goods.

Losses from the death of slaves, from privateering, piracy, shipboard revolt, and war could be severe. The captain of the *Grayhound* in 1723 reported to his owners after a seven weeks' voyage from Bonny to Barbados, "outt of 339 slaves I brought in hear butt 214 for the Like Mortality I think Never was known...." Capture by a privateer could result in a total loss, unless insurance protected owners. Depredations of pirates destroyed profits; a letter from Anamabo in 1766 graphically depicted the threat. "The Coast is very much infested with Pirates, and... one in particular, is a Schooner, copper sheathed, commanded by one Hide, has on board thirty-four Men, and is extremely well fitted with Swivels, and Small Arms. She has taken between 12 and 14 Shaloops, one of which belonged to Governor Brew, and had on board 1200 *l*. Sterling in Goods and 50 Ounces of Gold Dust...." Slave insurrections on shipboard—such as the one successfully staged by one-hundred-forty Negroes, who rose, killed the mate and most of the crew, and carried off the ship—"have occasioned a great Reducement in our Merchants Gains," a report of 1731 ran. Seamen who mutinied were at times a hazard to returns. War, among Europeans or Africans, intermittent throughout the slaving era, heavily influenced profits in diverse ways.

Price variations in African and American markets sharply altered profits. Two Jamaica factors in 1736 called to the attention of a South Sea Company officer the crucial nature of the cost of Negroes. "You will please to Observe how much Cheaper we buy Callabar and Angola Negroes, than these from the Gold Coast, on which Account we take as many from the former Countrys as possibly we can, in order to render the Negroes Account proffitable to the Company." On the western side of the Atlantic slave-ship captains on instructions from their owners searched for the best prices. Slave prices underwent fluctuations as well as regional differentiations. Moreover, prices of slaves rose and fell with demand in America, a phenomenon often connected with crop prices. Prospects of low prices for sugar, tobacco, rice, and indigo pushed down slave demand.

Lieutenant-Governor Alexander Spotswood of Virginia in 1712 reported that no Negroes had been imported there for at least two years, "nor like to be," he observed, "while the price of tobacco is so low, and the country so much in debt."

Operating costs consumed much of the proceeds. Charges for shipping, insurance, salaries, and commissions of ships' officers, wages of crewmen, the cost of maintaining an agent or factory in Africa, and the cost of selling slaves in America—all had to be deducted before profits could be counted. Added to these was the slowness of returns through bills of exchange, sometimes extending to thirty-six months by 1795; and if the merchant receiving bills wanted early payment he paid a discount to the person who advanced the money to him.

The reckless ascription of high profits to the trade springs in part from a simplistic comparison of prices paid for slaves in Africa and secured in America. Thus, the Privy Council Report on the Slave Trade disclosed that in the 1670s and 1680s average prices in Africa were about three pounds and in the West Indies about fifteen to seventeen pounds. In the eighteenth century prices rose, more sharply in proportion in Africa than in the West Indies, producing averages for the period 1763–88 of eight to twelve pounds and twenty-eight to thirty-five pounds respectively. These figures do not take into account the costs of doing business, including costs of goods, shipping, fees, commissions, insurance, crew, and losses by mortality.

Offsetting price data with costs causes a dramatic drop in profits. A study of the estimated profit per slave in the British trade to Jamaica, incorporating estimates of costs, shrank profits to a point where they "resemble those profits which could be earned upon alternative investments." For the years 1701–20 the estimated profit per slave was £8.46; for the succeeding score of years only £3.16; for 1741–60 £8.83; 1761–80 £2.22. Marked by much variation, and accompanied by a substantial element of risk as well as ease of entry by competitors when profits rose, these figures suggest that gains from the slave trade were "normal profits."

Clearly, the amount due in the balance of the slave traders' accounts has been exaggerated by many writers. The research done into the intricacies of the economics of the Atlantic slave trade raises doubts about great profitability. It will be remembered that the monopoly companies failed; although offsetting the failure of the Royal African Company was the burden placed upon it to maintain the British government's presence in Africa. Modern authorities stress the risk and complexity of the slaving enterprise. They conclude that, broadly viewed, the profit was not far different from that in other forms of business enterprise. A few individuals, as in any high-risk endeavor, may have made large profits. Liverpool merchants, specialists, and dealers in volume, may have been the most successful in realizing big returns.

A careful study of the profitability of the British slave trade from 1761 to 1810 led to the conclusion that profits stood just under 10 per cent of invested capital. A study of the great Liverpool merchant William Davenport, based on about seventy ventures from 1757 to 1785, reckoned his annual profits at 8 per cent.

The conclusion that profits in the slave trade were on average modest applies not only to the English trade but to the Dutch and French as well. Analysis of the accounts of 101 Dutch slaving voyages from 1733 to 1802 disclosed that only 59 returned a moderate profit, averaging only a little over 2 per cent. Examination of the slaving interest in the three major French ports from 1763 to 1792 suggested "an annual rate of return of no more than 6 per cent for the most successful family firms, and as little as 1 per cent for many other investors." This low return is all the more remarkable in view of the French bounty.

Analysis of the Nantes slave trade for the boom years 1783–92 found that net profits averaged 10 per cent, of which almost one-half sprang from government subsidies. The Danes, peripheral traders who were first among nations to abolish the slave trade, were in some part prompted to do so because they had found it unprofitable.

Arresting claims about the trade's relationship to economic change have been made, especially by Eric Williams in a book entitled *Capitalism and Slavery*. His argument appears in at least two forms. One is that the capital accumulation of Liverpool came from the slave trade, and this in turn "called the population of Lancashire into existence and stimulated the manufactures of Manchester." In this view the Liverpool slave trade nourished the heart of the Industrial Revolution in England. More broadly conceived in its second form the argument runs that "The triangular trade made an enormous contribution to Britain's industrial development. The profits from this trade fertilized the entire productive system of the country." Here it is the triangular trade, not the Liverpool slave trade alone, which fertilized the entire productive system of industrializing Britain, not Lancashire alone. A similar argument for the effect of the slave trade upon French industrialization had earlier been put forward, and Williams acknowledged his indebtedness to the previous interpretation.

It might appear that an Atlantic-wide economic system based upon the slave trade profited the international economy over a long period of time. British exports to Africa increased sevenfold between 1701 and 1786. A New World economy based upon slave labor arose and had its life for some three centuries in an immense area stretching from the Chesapeake through the Caribbean to the Rio de la Plata. Europeans drew profits from the slave trade, from the commodities produced, and from the services of shipping, financing, and insuring.

A direct relationship between the slave trade or the triangular trade and industrialization is difficult to demonstrate. Since the time when Eric Williams wrote his book in 1944, the estimated number of slaves transported in the trade has been drastically cut, reducing the probable size of profits. Secondly, it now seems accepted that the profits of slave merchants were on average moderate. Beyond all this, it has been estimated that of a number of periods studied, in only one, i.e., from 1761 to 1780, did profits from the slave trade rise to more than one-half of one per cent of Britain's national income. More commonly, they amounted to less than one-tenth of one per cent. As to English exports to Africa they were a small part of the whole, in 1766, for instance, they came to merely £497,000 in a total of £14,000,000. Finally, it has been suggested that

the component of slave trade profits in capital formation could only have been minor, in 1770, for example, only about eleven hundredths of one per cent of the entire nation's investments. Moreover, it is to be remembered that it is difficult to pinpoint the contribution of the slave trade to an individual's income, usually derived from several sources, as well as to pinpoint the individuals who invested slave trade earnings in industrial development. In summary, it would appear that claims about the trade's stimulus to the Industrial Revolution have been inflated.

Yet, among some historians nagging doubts about such revisionist views remain, and Eric Williams' generalizations still glitter. As he continued to study the question of whether England's sugar colonies drew wealth from the mother country or fed wealth to it, the eminent historian Richard Pares reversed himself between 1937 and 1960, concluding that much of the wealth of the West Indies "found a permanent home in Great Britain." This last assessment has been shared by the careful scholar Richard B. Sheridan, who wrote that "the West India colonies... became a vital part of the British economy in the eighteenth century." And writing in 1966, David Brion Davis, taking note that Williams had exaggerated the part of slavery and the slave trade in accumulating capital for industrialization, wryly continued, "it is more difficult, however, to get around the simple fact that no country thought of abolishing the slave trade until its economic value had considerably declined."

Recent scholarship has repelled the notion that the British abolished the trade because the West Indies were in decline, and maintenance of the trade conflicted with the emergence of a free-trade economy—that, in short, the trade was destroyed by developing industrial capitalism. Seymour Drescher has demonstrated, contrary to a long-accepted outlook, that the British slave system continued to expand until it was abolished. As a result of the wars of the French Revolution, Britain acquired fresh territory for expansion both of the slave system and of the slave trade. So far as free-trade dogma was concerned, the slave trade early went over to free trade, long before Great Britain began to dismantle protectionism in the second quarter of the nineteenth century. The increase of cotton cultivation after 1763 and the ease with which the growing and selling of cotton fitted into the slave trade system further show that the West Indies were not in decline in 1807. Drescher's view is that abolition was the product of new moral values rather than of a new economic order that found the slave trade an anachronism....

In summary, we can see that European economic theory warmly embraced the African slave trade, which was a natural partner. Practice shifted from monopoly to free trade to concentration in the hands of a few merchants—all with state sanction. The slave trade must be regarded as a business, not an adventure in kidnapping, piracy, or the sport of amateurs. To carry it on successfully required an immense breadth of knowledge and a degree of specialization.

As we have seen, many myths have developed about the business of slave trading—about the "typical" slave ship, the trade as a "nursery of seamen," the triangular trade, the trade's profitability, the existence of slavery among

Africans, European domination of African trade, and procurement of slaves by kidnapping and slave raids. In this [selection] it has been our task to explode some of these myths in order that we may possess a clearer view of the economics—European and African—of the traffic which put white men in possession of black slaves.

POSTSCRIPT

Was the West African Slave Trade a Precondition for the Rise of British Capitalism?

This issue offers a classic example of how the discovery of new sources of information (data) and the ability to use them (computer science) can influence historical research. Those who defend Eric Williams's work have made wide use of new sources of information and technology that makes them meaningful. A cross-disciplinary difference may also exist: many of Williams's supporters have a strong grounding in economics, while many of his critics (but not all) are traditional historians.

The issue begins with the question of the number of slaves imported, and Philip Curtin and Roger Anstey have made significant contributions in this field: Curtins's *The Atlantic Slave Trade: A Census* (University of Wisconsin Press, 1969) and Anstey's "The Volume and Profitability of the British Slave Trade, 1761–1807," in *Race and Slavery in the Western Hemisphere: Quantitative Studies,* edited by Stanley Engerman and Eugene Genovese (Princeton University Press, 1975). Their findings have been questioned by Joseph E. Inikori in "Measuring the Atlantic Slave Trade: An Assessment of Curtin and Anstey," *Journal of African History* (1976), pp. 197–223, who offers his own assessment of the data. In a subsequent issue (1976, pp. 596–627), Curtin and Anstey reply to Inikori's critique.

Although the relationship between the loss of the slave trade's profitability and the rise of British abolitionism is beyond the scope of this issue, it is nevertheless an important tangential question. David Eltis's *Economic Growth and the Ending of the Transatlantic Slave Trade* (Oxford University Press, 1987) and Seymour Dreschler's *Capitalism and Antislavery: British Mobilization in Comparative Perspective* (Oxford University Press, 1987) both take issue with Williams's attempts to connect these movements.

Books on the Atlantic slave trade are so numerous that listing a few would be unfair and exclusionary. But two edited series of essays may be useful avenues of pursuit: Barbara L. Solow and Stanley L. Engerman, eds., *British Capitalism and Caribbean Slavery: The Legacy of Eric Williams* (Cambridge University Press, 1987) and Joseph E. Inikori and Stanley L. Engerman, eds., *The Atlantic Slave Trade: Effects on Economies, Societies, and Peoples in Africa, the Americas, and Europe* (Duke University Press, 1994).

ISSUE 11

Were the Witch-Hunts in Premodern Europe Misogynistic?

YES: Anne Llewellyn Barstow, from *Witchcraze: A New History of the European Witch Hunts* (HarperCollins, 1994)

NO: Robin Briggs, from *Witches and Neighbors: The Social and Cultural Context of European Witchcraft* (Penguin Books, 1998)

ISSUE SUMMARY

YES: History professor Anne Llewellyn Barstow asserts that the European witch-hunt movement made women its primary victims and was used as an attempt to control their lives and behavior.

NO: History professor Robin Briggs states that although women were the European witch-hunts' main victims, gender was not the only determining factor in this sociocultural movement.

$\mathbf{V}$irgins and whores, goddesses and devils, mystics and conjurers—historically, women have been perceived as "troublesome creatures." Their very existence has often been considered a threat to human society, especially with regard to their sexuality. This has resulted in constant attempts on the part of the patriarchal system, which has so dominated the course of history, to control women's lives. Sometimes this system resulted in second-class status, shattered dreams, and crushed spirits for women; other times the treatment of women was downright hostile. The witch-hunt craze of early modern Europe was one such example.

Although belief in witches and witchcraft dates back to recorded history's earliest days, the persecution of those accused reached its apex in Europe's early modern period, especially the sixteenth and seventeenth centuries. In the northern, western, and central parts of the continent, witch trials became a frightening reality, as thousands were tried and many were executed for their evil doings and "pacts with the devil." Although exact figures are not known, a moderate estimate of 200,000 people tried with half of those executed has been offered by Anne Llewellyn Barstow. And certainly germane to this issue is the fact that 80 percent of both groups, those brought to trial and those executed, were women.

What factors caused such a wave of witch hysteria? First, the Protestant Reformation created a religious uncertainty, which gave the witch-hunts a *raison d'être*. Protestants and Catholics battled for the hearts, minds, and souls of Europe's populace, and religious wars became the order of the day. The witch crazes were a predictable outcome given this atmosphere. Furthermore, with the concomitant growth of national states in Europe and the resultant divine-right monarchs, orthodoxy of all sorts had to be enforced to keep the dynastic ship afloat. Those who deviated had to pay the price.

Social factors also entered into the witch-craze fray. Tensions between and amongst classes led to aberrant behavior usually geared toward keeping people of the lower classes down. The trials and resultant executions served as brutal reminders to women of the power of the status quo and the lengths to which those in power would go to maintain societal control.

Of course, one cannot escape the one constant of the multicentury witch-hunts: most of the victims were women. But was gender the only factor in determining the outcome of the witch-hunts? Were women singled out for prosecution solely on the basis of their sex? Or, were there other factors—political, economic, social, legal, or local—that influenced the witch-hunts? This question had been raised in the historical debates of previous generations, but interest was renewed in the 1960s, presumably due to the increased interest in women's studies. This interest includes the study of violence against women, which has reached epic proportions in the contemporary world. Were there signs of such actions against women in the past? Was the witch craze just one extreme example of violence against women?

A seminal article by Hugh Trevor-Roper entitled "The European Witch-craze of the Sixteenth and Seventeenth Centuries," *Encounter* (May/June 1967), later republished in *The European Witch-Craze of the Sixteenth and Seventeenth Centuries, and Other Essays* (Harper Torchbooks, 1969), got the historical ball rolling. Still, it was not until recent times that the idea of witchcraft as misogyny or hatred of women reached center stage. Since that time, it has been nearly impossible to remove the gender factor from any witchcraft studies.

The two selections represent the best in recent witchcraft scholarship. Barstow makes a persuasive case for gender as the key factor in determining witch-hunt outcomes. She sees this as part of a long struggle to "keep women down." Robin Briggs admits that the large preponderance of the witch-hunts' victims were women and that gender certainly was a factor in the genesis of the craze. But he favors the presence of socioeconomic, political, religious, and legal factors as better means to understanding the witch craze; after all, misogyny has been present since the beginning of time.

Why Women? Gender, Numbers, Class

Joan Peterson, a healer, "was searched again in a most unnatural and barbarous manner by four women" supplied by her accusers, who found "a teat of flesh in her secret parts more than other women usually had." After bribed witnesses testified against her, she was executed.

Searching an accused woman's body for the devil's teat was one of the chief proofs of witchcraft. Though the investigation was normally done by women (and not done gently, as Joan Peterson's case demonstrates), the sessions were often witnessed by male court officials. When the constable of Salisbury, New Hampshire, undressed Eunice Cole to be whipped for witchcraft, he saw "under one of her brests.... A blew thing like unto a teate hanging downeward about three quarters of an inch longe not very thick." Men standing by saw him "rip her shift down"; moving in closer, they affirmed that Eunice "violently scratched it away," implying that she tried to remove the evidence from her body. When women were appointed to examine her further, they found instead "a place in her leg which was proveable wher she Had bin sucktt by Imps."

This lewd scene can set the tone for much of what will be investigated in this [selection]. An analysis of violence such as this exposes the sexual terror and brutality at the heart of the witch hunts, a topic too little discussed. The American historian Lois Banner has observed that two of the cultural norms specific to patriarchal society—war and rape—have been little studied by feminist scholars, and a third, pornography, studied only by feminists and not enough by them. In matters pertaining to the abuse of bodies, especially women's bodies, we have been strangely silent. To her comment I would add that writers on witchcraft also, feminist or otherwise, have tended to avoid the specifics of what happened to the bodies of the victims and have not asked aloud what difference it made that most of them were female. That historians to date, following traditional interests in legal and intellectual history, have concentrated more on the judges and theoreticians of the witchcraft trials than on the witches may explain this omission. But one must ask if revulsion at the public exploration as well as the torture of female bodies may also have caused them to make that choice.

Having a female body was the factor most likely to render one vulnerable to being called a witch. The sexual connotations and the explicit sexual violence utilized in many of the trials make this fact clear. Just which women were targeted and under what circumstances reveals much about the status of women in early modern Europe....

Numbers...

This study of European society's persecutions of the people perceived to be witches will use the term in the sense that it was used at the time. Since long before the sixteenth century, people had believed that some persons had supernatural power, the ability to perform good or harmful magic (or both). A good witch, or cunning woman, as these magic workers were often called, might, for example, heal persons or animals by incantations or potions; she might just as readily kill with a curse or the evil eye. In either case, she possessed a power to be reckoned with. By the sixteenth century, many—especially among the elite—began to hold a new belief, namely, that such supernatural power came from the devil, who bestowed it chiefly on women in return for their absolute obedience to him.

Numbers are essential to this investigation. It is through an analysis of the percentage of women and men accused and of the percentage condemned that the gender bias of this persecution emerges. But first we must look at the overall size of the witchcraze. Contemporary accounts are of limited use....
[C]ontemporaries twisted the facts of a suspect's life, so they showed no more accuracy in estimating the number of witches: Henri Boguet, the French witch hunter active around 1600, claimed there were 1,800,000 witches in Europe. Because by "witch" Boguet meant persons dedicated to serving Satan, he therefore believed there was a terrifying and widespread conspiracy of witches against Christian society. Joseph Glanvill, holding out against the rising tide of skepticism in the 1670s, maintained that England was still home to thousands of witches, but the doubter Bishop Hutchinson concluded in 1718 that there had been only "above 140 [witches]" put to death in England since the Reformation.

Somewhere between these wildly differing claims we must find a sound compromise, but many modern commentators have not used caution either. Unless speculations are based on court records and other contemporary accounts and adjusted only by educated estimates, they are useless. This limitation, however, has not stopped some modern writers from claiming numbers ranging from two hundred thousand into the millions, and this not referring to witches in general but specifically to persons executed, thus implying a far larger pool of suspects among the population.

Working on the statistics of witchcraft is like working with quicksand. Because many of the records have been lost or are defective, in most areas we cannot even speculate about what the totals may have been. Of the surviving records, many have not yet been carefully analyzed, a problem especially for Polish accounts. Even the records that have been analyzed raise more questions than they answer, for many are lacking names (hence, gender), ages, and sentences; almost all are silent about class, occupation, and marital status. Worse still is the scattered evidence that many witch accusations and executions never made it into the records. How many persons were driven out of their villages or lynched by mobs, we have no idea. One may well then ask why the historian would attempt an essay on the statistics of witchcraft, and in fact many have eschewed it. Yet despite the hazards, it is well worthwhile to speculate.

One reason for the necessity to grapple with numbers is the unrealistic totals that have been circulated. The current trend among some feminist groups to claim three million, six million, or even ten million female victims is mistaken. A statistically based figure, though lower, still makes the same point: that this was an organized mass murder of women that cannot be dismissed by historians.

Among the feminist writers claiming millions of deaths is Andrea Dworkin. Working from the only estimates available in the early 1970s, Dworkin made the claim, "In Europe, women were persecuted as witches for nearly four hundred years, burned at the stake, perhaps as many as nine million of them...." The "nearly four hundred years" almost doubles the years of actual major persecution (1560–1760), and the "nine million of them" is off by about 8,900,000. Even further off the mark is the claim by certain German feminists that ten million women were killed. Faced with such exaggerations, the historian is forced to make an estimate based on the records, no matter how incomplete they may be.

An immediate corrective to these modern inaccuracies can be found in surveying the estimates made by contemporaries, which, although lacking a statistical base, are in the realm of the possible. Looking back over the recently ended holocaust, Voltaire claimed that one hundred thousand witches had been put to death. [Jean] Bodin believed that "many thousands" had died in France. Boguet wrote that there were "thousands and thousands of stakes" in Lorraine and that "there are witches by the thousand everywhere, multiplied upon the earth even as worms in a garden." Whatever one makes of these figures, one must note that they deal not in millions but in thousands.

An even more pressing reason for working on numbers, however, is the simple need to know how many persons shared this fate. Given the chaotic state of the records, the temptation to round off the numbers is strong. Yet I found myself carefully retaining each awkward figure, even though this added hours of work for each region I studied. As Joan Ringelheim, researcher of women in the Nazi holocaust, stated of her work, to drop numbers now is to kill these persons twice. Wanting to record every known victim, to ensure that the historical record finally acknowledges her death, I offer the most complete record available at this time....

Though one cannot add up estimates like these and expect any meaningful results, still, in order to settle on a reasonable total of victims, in contrast to figures such as ten million, it is imperative to reach a sum. The most careful totals made so far are those of Brian Levack, who estimates 110,000 accusations and 60,000 deaths. I believe that though his are reasonable figures, they are almost certainly too low.

There are two pressing arguments for raising Levack's estimate of 110,000 accusations. In addition to the fact that many cases were never recorded, and of those that were, many records have been lost or destroyed, many trial entries are for unknown numbers of victims. Furthermore, additional cases are steadily turning up. Especially in view of the rate at which we are learning of new victims, I believe that Levack's estimate should be doubled, bringing us to a figure of about two hundred thousand accused.

Death estimates are even harder to deal with. Many records do not list the verdict of the trial, a strange omission given the severity of the penalties for a verdict of guilty (death or banishment in most cases). Most records do not include those who died in prison, like Issobel Pain of Scotland, who "dyed the last winter through cold hunger and other inconveniences of the prison." The three women who survived Issobel complained in 1672 that they were kept "in a dark dungeon in a most miserable conditione being always at the point of starving... and are in such... miserie that it ware better for them to be dead than alyve."

Others, driven to despair by torture, or, like Didier Finance of Lorraine, by fear of being burned alive, killed themselves in prison. As an alleged witch and parricide, Didier faced being burned by red-hot tongs and incinerated alive at the stake. Many accused witches were murdered in prison: for example, when the wife of a cobbler in Constance was found strangled to death in her cell, her murder was blamed on a demon. Others died in prison from the torture inflicted on them, like two female witches accused of spreading the plague in the French Jura. A widow in Alsace, after being tortured, managed to struggle home, where she was found dead lying on her bed, her neck twisted, bruised, and disjointed.

To these deaths must be added lynchings and posse-style murders of alleged witches (three hundred killed in the Ardennes, for example) that because of their extralegal nature can only be estimated. Given all these factors, one must enlarge Levack's estimate of deaths. Claiming two hundred thousand accusations (a conservative estimate, I believe) and using a death rate of 50 percent of those arraigned, one reaches a figure of one hundred thousand dead —exactly what Voltaire estimated.

But the convicted were not the only ones harmed. Once accused of being witches, few women ever returned to a normal life. So great was the fear of witchcraft that suspicion and ill will followed them to their graves, even when they moved to other areas. Those who were let go often struggled with themselves over having been associated with the hated proceedings. An old Basque woman, Mariquita de Atauri, had, under pressure, named names. She confessed to her own witchcraft and was reconciled at Logroño, but she believed she was damned anyway because she had accused others who were innocent. When she tried to cross their names off the list of the accused and spoke to the inquisitor about her guilt, he called her a liar and a hussy and drove her away. In a desperate struggle with her conscience, Mariquita drowned herself.

Those whose lives were thus ruined must in some way be taken into account in the total number of victims; the number of accused, therefore, is as important to our story as the number executed. Yet estimates are the best that one can offer.

Gender

Almost everywhere more women than men were accused and killed. The figures show that in fact women were overwhelmingly victimized: on average, 80 percent of those accused and 85 percent of those killed were female. Some areas, however, hunted down women more ferociously than others. Among the accused in Essex, 92 percent were female, true also for the English Home Counties. The same percentage applied to the witch hunt in Namur County (in today's Belgium), and an even higher figure (95 percent) to the bishopric of Basel. I suggest that a restudy of the Essex materials, stressing women's declining economic roles and the increasingly patriarchal nature of England's society, will explain why 92 percent of those accused were women. As for Basel, the prominence there of hail-making accusations, a crime traditionally ascribed more often to women than men, may have contributed to the high number of female victims there but does not fully explain it.

What these numbers meant for women can be seen in the following facts. Not only were over 80 percent of the accused in some areas women, but even more frightening statistics emerge from local hunts: for example, all but two of the female inhabitants of Langendorf in the Rhineland were arrested. In twelfth-century Kiev, when periodic fears of witchcraft arose, all the old women of the area were seized and subjected to the ordeal by cold water (thrown, bound hand and foot, into the Dnieper). Christina Larner, the chronicler of Scottish witchcraft, observed that there were periods "when no mature woman in Fife or East Lothian can have felt free from the fear of accusation." Given these cases, we see that some notorious examples are not unbelievable: the two German villages left with only one female inhabitant apiece, and the Rhenish village where one person, most often female, out of every two families was put to death.

Though almost every area of Europe hunted women more than men, three countries reversed this ratio: in Finland, Estonia, and apparently Russia, the majority of accused witches were men.... Some other regions had relatively lower percentages of women. In the Swiss Pays de Vaud, for instance, the accused were "only" 58 percent female. The rate for men was high there because the Vaudois thought of witchcraft as heresy, and heretics were chiefly male. The Aragonese Inquisition (1600–1650) prosecuted the lowest percentage of women in any witch trials, 28 percent, but secular courts in Aragon restored the usual balance by accusing sixty-six women to only two men, raising the rate for women in Aragon to 58 percent.

The fact that overall about 20 percent of the accused were male is less an indication that men were associated with witchcraft than it appears. Most of these men were related to women already convicted of sorcery—as husbands, sons, or grandsons—and thus were not perceived as *originators* of witchcraft. Of the few who were not related, most had criminal records for other felonies, such as theft, highway robbery, murder, the theological crime of heresy, or sexual crimes such as rape, incest, fornication, adultery, or sodomy. For them, witchcraft was not the original charge but was added on to make the initial accusation more heinous. Witchcraft thus was perceived primarily as a female offense.

When brought into court on a sorcery charge, men were often let off with lighter sentences than women (hence the even smaller number executed, 15 percent, out of all persons put to death, whereas 20 percent of all accused were male). Laws favored men: for example, when the rulers of Flanders decreed no more death penalty for prepubescent witches, boys benefited more because they were seen as minors until twenty-one, whereas girls became adults at eighteen. Also, women, unable by law to give legal testimony, did not traditionally know how to use the courts, either for initial defense or for appeal. Therefore, appeals to the Parlement at Paris, which greatly moderated the force of the witchcraze in France, helped fewer women.

Legal bias led to a notorious French case in which a priest and his mistress were both accused: through money and the influence of friends, he was let go without punishment, whereas she was burned at the stake. In Lorraine, when Claudine Simonette and her son Antoine were imprisoned, she was convicted, but his fate was not mentioned in the record. When a gentleman hired Jeanette Neuve to poison his wife, she was burned at the stake, but there is no record that he received any punishment. Of the fifteen married couples convicted in England's Home Counties, more wives were executed than husbands. A combination of factors, including the greater value placed on men as workers in the increasingly wage-oriented economy and a greater fear of women as inherently evil, loaded the scales against women, even when the charges against them were identical to those against men.

The effect on the image of sixteenth-century women was dramatic: although women committed far fewer crimes than men, the chief criminal stereotype of the period, that of the witch, was female.

For all these reasons, the basic fact remains that throughout Europe during the period of major witch hunts (1560–1760), on average 80 percent of the accused and 85 percent of those executed were women. These lopsided figures are sufficiently telling when one thinks of them as individual burnings or hangings, especially considering that many of the victims were not guilty of this or any other crime. There is no need to inflate the numbers into millions; these statistics are sufficient to document an intentional mass murder of women. By documenting a persecution by gender, these numbers form the basis for this [selection]. To ignore them or acknowledge them and then put them aside is to deny the most persistent fact about the persecutions.

Class

[Reginald] Scot [an Englishman who was skeptical about witchcraft] describe[d] [witches] as "poore, sullen.... These go from house to house, and from doore to doore for a pot full of milk, yeast, drinke, pottage, or some such releefe; without the which they could hardlie live." In most areas of Europe the accused were very poor, and their accusers were better off than they. Even though most accusers were neighbors who also lived in poverty, still they possessed more goods than their victims. The witch in many cases was the poorest of the poor, dependent on her neighbors to stave off starvation. In the sixteenth century,... the poor were becoming poorer; more peasants were forced to beg or steal in order to survive. Old, single women, especially vulnerable in this economic crunch, came to be seen as nuisances. When they turned them down, people felt guilty, an uncomfortable state often exacerbated when the beggar cursed them for their refusal. Then when misfortune occurred, people turned on the beggars, a classic example of "blaming the victim."

Those who had a little—and the rising expectations that go with "a little" —took out their frustrations over crop failure and the high death rate of infants on those who were least able to fight back. They also used witch accusations to establish their social position. In northern France, for instance, accusers were often those villagers who could read and write, who may have identified with the new reforms of the Catholic Reformation and the central government and may have seen cooperation with the authorities as the way up in the world. They strengthened their power in the village by attacking the most vulnerable group. As John Webster remarked (in 1677) of women having a bodily mark that could be taken for the devil's mark, "few would go free, especially those that are of the poorer sort."

In some instances, wealthy women were attacked. Late in a witch hunt, after the pool of typical women victims had been depleted, bourgeois and even upper-class women and men might be accused. In some cases poor women sought revenge by naming well-to-do women. Powerful men sometimes attempted to destroy other successful men through their wives—some even used their own wives and daughters in order to effect this.

Temperament and Age

Scot's description furnishes some further clues as to just which women would be singled out for accusation: "They are doting, scolds, mad, divelish; ... so firme and steadfast in their opinions, as whosoever shall onelie have respect to the constancie of their words uttered, would easilie beleeve they were true indeed." In other words, uppity women—women given to speaking out, to a bold tongue and independent spirit, women who had what Scottish people called "smeddum": spirit, quarrelsomeness, a refusal to be put down. They talked back to their neighbors, their ministers, even to their judges and executioners.

Consider, for example, the case of a woman in the Spanish Netherlands known as the village curser. A poor but proud and outspoken woman, Marguerite Carlier, married with three children, voluntarily presented herself to be cleared of charges of killing animals. When she appealed to the privy council of the Hapsburg archduke, a number of well-off men from her village testified against her, revealing the real reason for their hatred of her—their fear that she had harmed them personally, that she was obsessed with causing them misery. But they had no proof, and under torture she confessed nothing; when released, she defended herself to one and all. Her defiance and open hostility made them fear her all the more, however, and she was banished, sent away from her family. After seven years in exile, she appealed again and was pardoned. Marguerite's case illustrates the price that an independent, outspoken woman might have to pay when she was up against the big men of the village, even when there was no proof against her. . . .

Still another way in which women were vulnerable to charges of sorcery was because of their age. Though the majority of alleged witches in New England were middle-aged, most European victims were older, over fifty. Older women were frequently notorious as scolds; those no longer beholden to father, husband, or children felt freer to express themselves and often said just what they thought. John Metcalf of Leeds, England, complained in court that Anne Dixon had cursed him, calling him, "Whoremaster, whoremonger and harlott and did sit her downe upon her knees and cursed and banned him, and his wife, and badd a vengeance light upon the wife of the said John Metcalf and upon that whoremaster and whoremonger harlott her husband... and prayed God that they might never thryve." The ability of early modern women to attack with words was fearsome. Curses like Anne Dixon's were the basis for many witchcraft accusations.

The typical scold and the typical witch were older females, and both were criminalized during the same period. Each had their own kind of power. By laying curses and giving "lip," old women used what power they had to make others fear them, give them "space," and maybe respect them. The fact that people feared their curse was proof that their words carried numinous power. This trait can be interpreted in two ways, as sheer bad nature or as a defensive strategy. John Demos believes that the "uppity" quality of middle-aged and older women in New England was the chief reason they "attracted" witch accusations. Seeing them as quarrelsome and intractable, especially in their relations with their husbands, and as offering unwanted advice to their neighbors, he explains their persecution by their behavior. He omits from discussion the way women were subordinated to men, especially to husbands, in Puritan New England, and thus does not include the observation that they might well turn to nagging to protect their space in their homes.

Another way of looking at this trait is as a sign of being independent-minded. Traditionally, peasant women in bad marriages had complained of how they were treated, but increasingly now when they did so they were branded as "traitors" to their husbands. The family, not only in New England but across Europe, was becoming more patriarchal in the sixteenth century, causing women's roles within the family to shrink. Outspoken wives were called shrews and suspected of witchcraft; when they spoke out against neighbors who had been unfair or ungenerous to them, they were hauled into court for being a nuisance and a witch.

Scolding done by a female was considered a crime and was punished in Britain by the scold's bridle, which locked the victim's head inside an iron cage that drove spikes through her tongue, and by the ducking stool, used for witches as well, by which they were ducked under water in stagnant ponds or cesspools. Sixteenth-century females, especially the older ones, *were* often scolds—and the punishment they received for scolding and witchcraft was so harsh that women kept a lower profile for several centuries afterward.

Another complaint against women, especially old women, was what was seen as their overassertive sexuality. Men fancied that old women still desired them and found the idea grotesque, hence Reginald Scot's saying that "to enforce a man, how proper so ever he be, to love an old hag, she giveth unto him to eate (among other meates) his owne doong." Likewise the Kent assize reported that Goodwife Swane "vehemently suspected by church authorities [as a witch]," boasted "that she can make a drink, which she saith if she give it to any young man that she liketh well of, he shall be in love with her."

One aspect of the witchcraze, undeniably, was an uneasiness with and hostility toward dependent older women. Witch charges may have been used to get rid of indigent elderly women, past childbearing and too enfeebled to do productive work. As Barbara Walker has put it, these women "could be called witches and destroyed, like domestic animals past their usefulness.... The old woman was an ideal scapegoat: too expendable to be missed, too weak to fight back, too poor to matter."

A final important lead from Scot, one seldom followed up on by historians of witchcraft, somewhat balanced out these female handicaps: these women were "so firme and steadfast in their opinions" that people listened to them. The alleged witch may have been sliding down into economic dependency, but she still had a certain authority, some standing in her community. As a healer, midwife, advice-giver, fortune-teller, spell-lifter, she was sought after; she could therefore boast "that she (as a goddes) hath brought such things to pass." People turned *to* witches as well as turned *on* them. Like female shamans in Korea today, they were both scorned *and* considered essential to the community, were both outcasts and authority figures. That their day as folk healers and cunning women was passing was part of the tragedy in which they were caught.

Men Against Women:
The Gendering of Witchcraft

Theories and Realities

Familial problems lead inevitably into the fascinating, difficult and higher controversial question of gender. The one thing everyone 'knows' about witches is that they were women. Although every serious historical account recognizes that large numbers of men were accused and executed on similar charges, this fact has never really penetrated to become part of the general knowledge on the subject. The *Malleus Maleficarum* is routinely quoted to establish that witch-hunters were woman-haters, and one can hardly deny that its principal author, the Dominican Henry Institoris (Heinrich Krämer), blamed witchcraft largely on unbridled feminine sexuality. It is not often recognized, however, just how far this was a peculiarly misogynistic text, many of whose assertions are very misleading as a guide to what happened in typical trials. Later writers were often content to repeat such material uncritically, while their statements about gender are usually both sketchy and inadequate. Pierre de Lancre stated that the Devil 'wins over more women than men, because they are naturally more imbecile. And we see that among those brought before the *parlements* on charges of witchcraft, there are ten times more women than men'. Jean Bodin went further still: 'When we read the books of those who have written about witches, it is to find fifty female witches, or even demoniacs, for every man.' He did concede that women often endured torture with more resolution than men, only to continue with the assertion 'that it is the power of bestial desire which has reduced women to extremities to indulge these appetites, or to avenge themselves... For the internal organs are seen to be larger in women than in men, whose desires are not so violent: by contrast, the heads of men are much larger, and in consequence they have more brains and prudence than women.' The identification of witches with women was already standard form, it would appear, in the decades when trials were at their height. The demonologists would have been shocked to find their confident assertions turned against them by modern writers who use the persecution as prime evidence for men's inhumanity to women, often seeming to assume that the sex ratio was not de Lancre's

90 per cent, or even Bodin's 98 per cent, but a stark 100 per cent. When this misconception has been coupled with vast exaggerations of the numbers executed it has proved all too tempting to create the image of an earlier holocaust, in which millions of women perished.

The best-informed recent estimates place the total number of executions for witchcraft in Europe somewhere between 40,000 and 50,000, figures which allow for a reasonable level of lost documentation. Men actually made up around 25 per cent of this total, although there were large variations from one area to another and between different types of trials. Bodin and de Lancre were simply wrong about the facts, before they proceeded to offer explanations which merely repeated the conventional wisdom of the day, and now appear remarkably feeble. Their inability to observe the reality around them is significant. It suggests that received opinions were blinding them to the obvious; in this they were actually typical of most traditional thinking, much more concerned with concept affirmation than with referential accuracy. What made their error so egregious was that their own country, France, was in fact a fascinating exception to the wider pattern, for over much of the country witchcraft seems to have had no obvious link with gender at all. Of nearly 1,300 witches whose cases went to the *parlement* of Paris on appeal, just over half were men. The appeal system may have been invoked more often by men in the years before it became automatic, yet there are many reasons to doubt that this has more than a modest effect on the figures. In around 500 known cases which did not reach the *parlement,* although there is a small majority of women, men still make up 42 per cent of the accused. Some local studies also show a predominance of men, as do the court decisions which de Lancre himself collected and printed in one of his works. There are variations within the *parlement's* jurisdiction (covering nearly half the country), for towards the east the proportion of women rises towards 70 per cent, which fits very well with the picture just across the border, and suggests that the figures are trustworthy, while the central and western regions had a clear majority of male witches. The great majority of the men accused were poor peasants and artisans, a fairly representative sample of the ordinary population.

Relatively high proportions of male witches were common elsewhere, as the overall statistics would lead us to expect. In south-west Germany, the figures were typically rising towards 25 per cent by the 1620s, while in another sample of well over a thousand cases from the Jura and the Alps the proportion of men was 22.5 per cent. For the modern French department of the Nord, then mostly in the Spanish Netherlands, men comprised 18 per cent of a much smaller group of 294. The Saarland and Lorraine correspond closely with eastern France, around 28 per cent of those tried being men; for a sample of 547 in the neighbouring duchy of Luxembourg it was 31 per cent. There are some extreme cases in peripheral regions of Europe, with men accounting for 90 per cent of the accused in Iceland, 60 per cent in Estonia and nearly 50 per cent in Finland. On the other hand, there are regions where 90 per cent or more of known witches were women; these include Hungary, Denmark and England. The fact that many recent writers on the subject have relied on English and north American evidence has probably encouraged an error of perspective here, with the overwhelming predominance of female suspects in these areas (also characterized by low rates of persecution) being assumed to be typical. Nor is it the case that the courts treated male suspects more favourably; the conviction rates are usually much the same for both sexes. These data create as many problems as they solve, not least because of the 'dark figure' familiar to criminologists. Formally accused witches were predominantly women, but was this also true of those suspected and never charged? Might men typically have found themselves better placed to stave off their accusers? How do we account for accusations being gender-biased, yet far from gender-specific? Is there any rational explanation for the massive variations between different regions? This last question is perhaps the most baffling of all, particularly in a case like the French one, where large differences are found within a single jurisdiction and there are no obvious cultural or social differences to invoke. Recent work on contemporary witchcraft beliefs in western France strongly suggests that the pattern has endured to the present day, without providing many clues to its rationale. It is possible that there may have been a particular tendency in these areas to see the cunning folk in very ambivalent terms, so that a high proportion of the men accused were 'good' witches reclassified as bad, but this only pushes the problem of explanation back another stage.

It remains true that most accused witches were women. Careful reading of the trial documents suggests that this was an accurate reflection of local opinion, in the sense that those tried were fairly typical of the wider group of suspects. Confessions include lists of those allegedly present at the sabbat, which obviously reflect local rumours about witchcraft, and some general statements about the attendance. Both of these usually (though not always) specify a majority of women, in line with the proportions found in the trials. Witchcraft was not a specifically feminine crime in the sense that infanticide and prostitution were, almost by definition; these offences, and domestic theft (the other crime often linked to women), were of course different in that there was something much more real to get a hold on. Infanticide and prostitution actually exemplify the double standard far better than witchcraft, since almost all those punished can fairly be depicted as the victims of male oppression, although this hardly exonerates them totally. Their seducers or clients, often from higher up the social scale, almost invariably escaped unscathed. A new punitive attitude towards these 'social' crimes, whose only direct victims were the new-born babies, was a striking feature of the sixteenth century; more women were probably executed for infanticide than for witchcraft. With very few exceptions they were denounced by other women, without whose participation the legislation would have remained a dead letter. The whole process is best seen not as the deliberate criminalization of women, but as part of a much broader drive to exercise greater moral and social control by labelling and punishing many kinds of deviant behaviour. This process was often deeply unfair and hypocritical, but patriarchy in this sense meant first and foremost the tyranny of the rich and powerful over the poor and weak. Social and gender hierarchies were naturally interlinked, so it comes as no surprise that harsher repressive policies had unfortunate consequences for women, as they did for vagrants, beggars and many others.

Historians who emphasize the social and psychological aspects of witch-craft beliefs are nevertheless bound to reject the idea that witchcraft persecution can be satisfactorily explained as the product of a great conglomerate of patriarchalism, absolutism and moral rigour. The point is not to deny all relevance to such factors, but rather to insist that witchcraft is much more than an elaborate delusion manufactured by outsiders, then misapplied to popular beliefs. It does rather seem that many interpretations imply, indeed require, such an underlying structure. At its crudest this can be seen in suggestions that clerics and judges diabolized feminine medical practice, or that women were the scapegoats for a variety of natural disasters. At a more respectable intellectual level, we have had attempts to show how a range of intellectual and symbolic devices (ranging from the equation of virtue with masculinity, through claims that women were biologically just incomplete men, to images of women as temptresses) were united by a persistent denigration of women. In its own terms there is much to be said for this view, provided we recognize the peculiar character and limited application of this kind of misogynistic language. What it cannot do is to provide a convincing explanation for persecutions which were largely initiated at village level, and whose motivation was quite clearly fear of witchcraft in the most direct sense. It is also very important not to confuse the rhetoric of justifications with the real motives for action. Another result of the tendency to see persecution as inspired from above is to give vastly exaggerated significance to the theories of the demonologists, attributing to them a causal role they simply did not possess. These approaches end up with the idea that witch-hunting was thinly disguised women-hunting, the diabolization of the feminine. In other words, here is the war between the sexes in a peculiarly violent form. Even if this were true, we would still have to account for change over time, since variables cannot be explained in terms of constants. The problem with these crude views goes deeper, for such generalized notions are too remote from the real world our ancestors inhabited. Gender did play a crucial role in witchcraft, but we will only understand this properly as part of the whole system, within which many other forces operated. What we need to explain is why women were particularly vulnerable to witchcraft accusations, not why witchcraft was used as an excuse to attack women. To achieve this, we must be constantly aware of gender as one of the crucial polarities within the vital frontier zone where beliefs and accusations interacted. Then we must tease out the ways in which it helped to structure the various operations which turned theory into action. In the process the information from the trials can tell us a great deal about gender, establishing a rewarding dialogue.

Counting heads is a useful way of shaking our ready assumptions, and of bringing a degree of rigour into the discussion. The figures can be broken down into numerous categories, to show distribution by age as well as gender, social and economic status, marital situation, childlessness and so forth. There has been no systematic work of this kind across Europe, and one would expect to find considerable variations by region. My own findings for Lorraine cannot therefore be regarded as a safer guide to general patterns, yet they do seem to conform to general impressions from several other regions. In this area of steady but very local persecution accused witches were on average much older and slightly poorer than their neighbours. Around half the women accused were widows, of whom a fair number appear to have had no surviving children. Some men seem to have been tainted by association with a suspected wife, but they were a minority; overall the masculine group formed a diverse cross-section of the peasant community. Although this evidence might seem to offer limited support to the stereotype of elderly women as witches, a more careful look at the material tells a different story. Age at the time of the trial is an artefact of the whole process by which reputations were built up. Since it took fifteen or twenty years for the typical witch to get to court, most were first suspected when still in the prime of life. There are signs that for women this transfer into the pool of suspects had a modest tendency to coincide with the menopause or the end of childbearing; while it would be rash to build too much on this flimsy basis, there may prove to be an important relationship here. This was an important watershed for everyone, physically, emotionally and socially, and, if the change of roles were not successfully accomplished, might prove an alienating experience. Those who missed out in some sense were likely to resent this, something their neighbours were all too likely to perceive. John Demos has suggested that midlife—roughly between the ages of forty and sixty—was the time when the exercise of power usually became central to personal experience. Wealth, prestige and responsibility all typically reached their highest point in these decades; while this was most obviously true for men, it was bound to affect women as well. Many themes could be related to this one; if illegitimate and misused power was a key meaning of witchcraft, then it is not surprising to find this age group notably suspect....

Psychology, Misogyny and Witchcraft Persecution

These cases also provide a particularly rich context for investigating witchcraft from a psychological standpoint. As Lyndal Roper [a professor at the University of London whose research interests include witchcraft and gender history] states, 'witchcraft confessions and accusations are not products of realism, and they cannot be analysed with the methods of historical realism'. She draws out how individuals borrowed the language and stereotypical images of witchcraft to express their own psychic conflicts, which centred on the earliest stages of the mother-child relationship.... [However,] we need to question why, as witchcraft has receded almost entirely into the sphere of fantasy in the modern world, it has come to be completely sex-specific. The witch is the bad mother, a being who subverts the basic duties of her sex by direct hostility to fertility and nurture. She also embodies the envy which originates in early mother-child relations. Again and again the details of cases can be assimilated to these underlying patterns; they are not 'caused' by them so much as structured through them. Every individual carries around a permanent legacy from the formative period of life that includes negative elements capable of being activated under stress. Such reactions are very likely to employ the processes known to psychoanalysts as splitting and projective identification, both of which first take shape in relation to the mother. Every individual's fundamental experience of love and hate is with a woman, in the mother-child relationship, or whatever surrogate takes its place. How far this creates a predisposition, perhaps independent of gender, to make women the target for murderous hostility, it is impossible to say with certainty. Nevertheless, the historical record suggests that both men and women found it easiest to fix these fantasies, and turn them into horrible reality, when they were attached to women. It is really crucial to understand that misogyny in this sense was not reserved to men alone, but could be just as intense among women. Behind it lay the position of mothers as primary objects who were felt to possess magically formidable qualities, and whose very intentionality (independent will) was perceived as dangerous.

Such analyses have severe limitations, above all because they are too general to offer useful explanations for change and local variations. We cannot suppose that child-rearing practices changed dramatically in ways which would even begin to account for the rise and fall of persecutions; no independent evidence suggests this, while only exceptional shifts would be likely to affect relations between mothers and babies significantly. Wet-nursing might seem to be a candidate here, but it simply does not correlate in any plausible way; it was characteristic of those urban and elite groups which seem to have been least involved in persecution. It is more helpful to think of numerous distinct factors meeting around a central void filled only by fantasy, a structure which related to the essential nature of witchcraft as a crime which never happened. Some people tried to practise it, although they were a minimal fraction among the accused; many more probably died of it, but in both cases the effects were only because of what people believed. The most enduring structures still persist in modern peasant societies, including some regions of Europe. They are to be found in parts of France, for example, as earlier variants of them doubtless were in Merovingian or pre-Roman Gaul. These include both social and psychological determinants, the elements which make all witchcraft beliefs fundamentally similar across great expanses of time and space. More ephemeral factors include the religious, legal and economic shifts which help to explain why persecution occurred when and where it did. It appears that certain combinations of the latter have been sufficiently powerful to deflect a normal tendency for witchcraft to be heavily—but not exclusively—attributed to women. We are unlikely to get much further on this last point until there has been a meticulous study of a region where men comprised the majority of the accused. A great deal might also be gained from a comparison between northern and southern Europe, with their strongly contrasted marriage systems. Mediterranean culture appears to have combined powerful witchcraft beliefs with very low rates of persecution, perhaps because older women were protected by their families, and enjoyed more power and esteem. This derived from a marriage pattern in which brides were much younger than their husbands, then commonly took over as effective heads of the household when they were widowed. Such women had to expect less power during their childbearing years, frequently dominated by mothers-in-law as well as husbands; it was only in mid-life that they acquired a new authority and status that was widely regarded as legitimate. By contrast, the theoretically more equal marriages of north-western Europe actually left older women at a grave disadvantage, unless they had the good fortune to find a caring, long-lived and forceful husband. Although it would be absurd to claim that one marriage system is more 'natural' than another, one of the most obvious biological differences between the sexes lies in the ages at which they cease to be fertile. The pattern of very late marriages for women, which was an essential condition for the closely-matched ages of spouses in the north-west, has long been regarded as an exception by historical demographers, and a puzzling one at that. It is at least possible that it may have made its own contribution to 'fixing' witchcraft accusations.

There are still reasons for linking witchcraft persecution to the assertion of patriarchal values, which can be seen as one aspect of a search for order in a period when many established patterns underwent severe disruption. Temporal coincidence does not establish causal relationships, however, and it is only by adopting a quite implausible picture of persecution imposed from above that patriarchalism can be made to carry direct blame. It is much more a case of underlying causes producing parallel effects, which were only mildly self-reinforcing. In a period when all tensions were being magnified by extremely harsh and painful social and economic pressures, those between the sexes were bound to be among them. The idea of the female sex as scapegoat misdescribes a situation of this kind, in which anxieties might be displaced into the area of gender. It is also dangerous to put too much weight on the kind of discourse employed by the demonologists. Their referential system was self-confirming, with the positive and negative polarities used for rhetorical purposes. As Stuart Clark has pointed out, they took the link between women and witchcraft as a given, rather than spending much time debating it. Even the overt misogyny of the *Malleus Maleficarum* really falls into this category. Within the confines of an agrarian society and early modern intellectual styles, it was virtually impossible for anyone to rethink gender relations, because everything was referred to ideal types. Polarized binary classification was the dominant style of early modern thought, so that demonologists had no choice but to associate women with evil and inferiority. For them gender took the form of polarity, rather than a range of overlapping possibilities, because this was how it was always conceptualized. This was such a powerful 'mind-set' that it could override empirical observation, as it often did in the medical theory of the time. At the popular level such views were expressed in the form of proverbial wisdom, later reinforced by chapbooks and almanacs. The result was an unfortunate mixture of fear and aggression towards women, whose passions were seen as a grave threat to husbands and society alike. Deficiency in capacity to reason supposedly left women unable to control the baser part of their nature, while their mysterious cycles were evidence for the way they were dominated by the womb. Eve had been responsible for original sin, and women's attraction for men led to corruption and death; women's inconstancy and self-love made them natural allies of the Devil, an eternal danger of betrayal for the men they lured on. The commonplace idea that women were more sexually voracious than men was just one expression of these attitudes, part of an association between women, original sin and sexual pollution.

Despite the pervasiveness of these grotesque misogynistic doctrines, it is not easy to find evidence that they functioned as a direct cause of action. They may indeed be evidence of a mixture of fear and ignorance which dominated gender relations, and whose roots are better sought in general psychological structures. Early modern Europe was a society in which women got a raw deal in many respects, but this did not often take the form of direct persecution; rather it operated through indirect pressures that frequently led to women accusing one another. It was of course inevitable that the courts which heard these charges would be male, but among the judges it was often those elite jurists most strongly linked to formal patriarchal theories who treated witches leniently. Ultimately witchcraft was a theory of power; it attributed secret and unnatural power to those who were formally powerless. In this way it allowed men to project their own aggression into women, notably those with whom they or their wives quarrelled. This tendency must have been strengthened because women typically responded with threats and curses, which then became part of the evidence for their malevolence. The evidence of the trials, however, suggests that quarrels between women followed much the same course as those between men and women, and often underlay subsequent direct accusations made by men as well as women. In this sense women too could use accusations as a vehicle to assert themselves and claim power against their enemies; seen in this light witchcraft did nothing to reinforce gender solidarities. The highly stressful circumstances experienced by early modern communities produced at least as much friction between those who were closest to one another as they did between those at opposite ends of the grids of wealth and gender. We do find peasant oligarchs accusing poor women, but only in a small minority of cases, compared to the significantly larger groups in which poor peasant households directed their suspicions against tiresome neighbours or persistent beggars.

It is all too easy to fall into anachronism when writing about witchcraft and gender. This is one reason why explanations should always be firmly bedded in the surrounding social realities. It should also warn us against the kind of knee-jerk reactions and facile assumptions which have too often resulted from failure to recognize the otherness of the past. We need to ask whether explanations that invoke gender as a motive could possibly apply in this period. It seems highly unlikely that any contemporary could have seen matters in this light. One must beware of false analogies between the past and the present. Gender is now an issue everyone has to confront, whereas at the time of witchcraft persecution it was a bundle of shared assumptions. Although there was a Renaissance debate about the status of women, it took place within strict limits, and hardly touched on the central questions as we might see them. In other words, modern views tend to be held consciously, whereas earlier ones were almost wholly unconscious. This did not necessarily make them less powerful, but it did mean that they were unlikely to motivate action directly. Gender differences are bound to remain a permanent and overt issue in our world, since the clock of consciousness cannot be put back. This also applies in reverse, however, and we must not project modern ideas and feelings back on to our ancestors, nor make them fight our battles. In the specific case of witchcraft we have a phenomenon which was permeated by gender, yet in much more subtle ways than any simple argument can convey. Hostility to women did play a crucial part at several levels; no general interpretation of the subject can or should obfuscate this basic truth. At the same time, this can only ever be part of a much more complex set of causes and connections. As so often, witchcraft tells us as much about the context from which it sprang—in this case gender relations—as that context helps us to understand witchcraft.

POSTSCRIPT

Were the Witch-Hunts in Premodern Europe Misogynistic?

V iolence against women, which is considered by many to be epidemic in this generation, has caused a reassessment of the history of violence against women. Domestic violence, spousal abuse, sexual assault, rape, and sexual harassment have occupied recent headlines and created an acute awareness of woman-as-victim issues. In seeking the roots of such violent behavior, a search for historical antecedents is a logical place to start. Renewed interest in the witch-hunt phenomenon has enlivened the interest in the subject of violence against women, a unique synthesis of two subjects with far-reaching results.

Despite a plethora of available information and data, we are no closer today to definitive answers to some of the major questions involving premodern Europe's witchcraft experiences. For example, were the witch-hunts a centralized movement initiated from society's "power elite," or did local variables play a more important role in their development and outcomes? If women's sexuality was a major force in the witch craze phenomenon, who introduced it into the public record, and why? If socioeconomic factors were important to the movement, why did it last through more than three centuries of societal change? And if women were viewed as "creatures of God," how could the executions of witches be accompanied by such violent tortures? Was there another lesson being taught here?

On the generation-long historiography of the European witch craze, Trevor-Roper's essay, mentioned in the introduction to this issue, is a good place to start. William Monter's *Witchcraft in France and Switzerland: The Borderlands* (Cornell University Press, 1969) and *Ritual, Myth, and Magic in Early Modern Europe* (Ohio University Press, 1984), along with his many articles, are important contributions to the study of witchcraft. It would be provocative and enlightening to read the two books on which the selections found in this issue are based.

Finally, an excellent primary sourcebook is Alan C. Kors and Edward Peters, eds., *Witchcraft in Europe, 1100–1700: A Documentary Issue* (University of Pennsylvania Press, 1995). See also Jonathan Barry, Marianne Hester, and Gareth Roberts, eds., *Witchcraft in Early Modern Europe: Studies in Culture and Belief* (Cambridge University Press, 1998), which contains many articles on the subject written by leading European scholars.

ISSUE 12

Was the Scientific Revolution Revolutionary?

YES: Herbert Butterfield, from *The Origins of Modern Science, 1300-1800,* rev. ed. (Free Press, 1965)

NO: Steven Shapin, from *The Scientific Revolution* (University of Chicago Press, 1996)

ISSUE SUMMARY

YES: Historian of ideas Herbert Butterfield argues that the late sixteenth and early seventeenth centuries witnessed a radical break with the past and the emergence of dramatically new ways of understanding both knowledge and the world—in short, a Scientific Revolution.

NO: Professor of sociology and historian of science Steven Shapin questions the idea of a Scientific Revolution, suggesting that there was no philosophical break with the past and rejecting the existence of a single event that might be called a Scientific Revolution.

When you open a world history or Western civilization textbook, you will likely find that it is conveniently divided into chapters and units with titles that mark the major turning points of history. One of those titles is likely to be "The Scientific Revolution." Known as *periodization,* this tendency of historians to interpretatively group events has recently been subjected to reappraisal. If "where you stand determines what you see," then the very act of labeling periods of history makes judgments about what is important and valuable. Traditional schemes of periodization, for instance, have taken the experiences of white men as the standard and ignored the often quite different lives of women and minorities. However, if only the concerns of the powerful provide the interpretation of historical significance, then much of history will be left out.

The assumption behind periodization is that there are moments when the path of history is rerouted, when a sharp break with the past leads to a new kind of experience or a new way of understanding the world. One of the questions historians must ask, therefore, is whether a particular event or series of events represents continuity with the past or discontinuity from it. Traditional periodization has seen the Scientific Revolution —a period in the late sixteenth and early seventeenth centuries in which the medieval Aristotelian model of scientific explanation was largely abandoned in favor of modern scientific methods —as a classic example of discontinuity, or as a sharp break with the medieval past and the ushering in of the modern world. Recently, however, historians have taken a fresh look at this period and wondered how scientific and how revolutionary it actually was.

A danger historians must also remain alert to is called *presentism*, the tendency to judge and interpret the past by the standards and concerns of the present. From the perspective of the late twentieth century, for example, we might be tempted to view the Industrial Revolution positively because it made it possible for backbreaking labor to be accomplished through the power of machines. People living through what we have come to call the Industrial Revolution, by contrast, might have focused on the negative consequences: the breakup of the family, as individuals left the home to do wage work, and the substitution of the factory for the productive unit in the home. The questions we must ask ourselves are these: Did the people living in the seventeenth century think that something revolutionary was going on? And how much of a break with the past did the scientific discoveries represent?

For Herbert Butterfield there is no question that a Scientific Revolution occurred, even if that fact did not become obvious to historians until the twentieth century. In the following selection, he contends that there is a discrete entity called science and that scientists such as Francis Bacon and philosophers such as René Descartes broke with medieval Christendom to create the modern world. A strong sense of discontinuity with the past leads Butterfield to rate the Scientific Revolution as one of the strongest turning points in the periodization of world history.

Steven Shapin, in response, begins with a bold statement: "There was no such thing as the Scientific Revolution." Reflecting a postmodern view of the world, Shapin questions whether or not it is even possible to speak about an "essence" of something called "science." Instead of a single, discrete entity, he sees a wide variety of ways of understanding, explaining, and controlling the natural world. If we list the characteristics of the so-called revolution, Shapin believes, we will find that the experimental method, mathematical approaches, and even mechanical conceptions of nature were both advocated and rejected by people who thought of themselves as scientists. Furthermore, Shapin sees continuity with the medieval past rather than a radical break from it.

Both historians agree that some people living at the time certainly thought of themselves as doing something revolutionary. The question seems to be whether or not most people, even most educated people, shared the beliefs of this tiny minority. Is it possible for the world to be transformed in a dramatic way at any single moment in time?

The Origins of Modern Science, 1300–1800

Bacon and Descartes

It is comparatively easy for people today to accommodate their minds to changes that may take place in upper regions of the different sciences—changes which from year to year may add further weight to the curriculum of the undergraduate student of the subject. It is not clear what the patriarchs of our generation would do, however, if we were faced with such a tearing-up of the roots of science that we had to wipe out as antiquated and useless the primary things said about the universe at the elementary school—if we had even to invert our attitudes, and deal, for example, with the whole question of local motion by picking up the opposite end of the stick. The early seventeenth century was more conscious than we ourselves (in our capacity as historians) of the revolutionary character of the moment that had now been reached. While everything was in the melting-pot—the older order undermined but the new scientific system unachieved—the conflict was bitterly exasperated. Men were actually calling for a revolution—not merely for an explanation of existing anomalies but for a new science and a new method. Programmes of the revolutionary movement were put forward, and it is clear that some men were highly conscious of the predicament in which the world now found itself. They seemed to be curiously lacking in discernment in one way, however, for they tended to believe that the scientific revolution could be carried out entirely in a single lifetime. It was a case of changing one lantern-slide of the universe for another, in their opinion—establishing a new system to take the place of Aristotle's. Gradually they found that it would need not merely one generation but perhaps two to complete the task. By the close of the seventeenth century they had come to see that they had opened the way to an indefinitely expanding future, and that the sciences were only in their cradle still.

Before the seventeenth century had opened, the general state of knowledge in regard to the physical universe had been conducive to the production of a number of speculative systems—these not founded upon scientific enquiry as a rule, but generally compounded out of ingredients taken from classical antiquity. Already in the sixteenth century, also, attention had been directed to the question of a general scientific method, and in the seventeenth century this problem of method came to be one of the grand preoccupations, not merely of the practising scientist, but, at a higher level, amongst the general thinkers and philosophers. The principal leaders in this seventeenth-century movement were Francis Bacon in the first quarter of the century, who glorified the inductive method and sought to reduce it to a set of regulations; and Descartes, whose work belongs chiefly to the second quarter of the century and who differed from Bacon not only in his glorification of mathematics as the queen of the sciences, but in the emphasis which he placed on a deductive and philosophical mode of reasoning, which he claimed to have screwed up to such a degree of tightness that it possessed all the discipline and certainty of mathematical reasoning. In the time of Newton and well into the eighteenth century, there was a grand controversy between an English school, which was popularly identified with the empirical method, and a French school, which glorified Descartes and came to be associated rather with the deductive method. In the middle of the eighteenth century, however, the French, with a charm that we must describe as Mediterranean, not only submitted to the English view of the matter, but in their famous *Encyclopédie* made even too ample a return, placing Bacon on a pedestal higher perhaps than any that had been given him before. It would appear that their excess of graciousness or charity brought some confusion into historical science at a later stage in the story.

Attacks on Aristotle had been increasingly common and sometimes exceedingly bitter in the sixteenth century. In 1543—a year which we have already seen to be so important in connection with Copernicus and Vesalius as well as the revival of Archimedes—Pierre Ramus produced his famous *Animadversions on Aristotle*. This work, which was known to Francis Bacon, and which attacked Aristotle without ever really understanding him, proposed an alternative method which was rather that of a humanist and professor of Belles Lettres —namely, studying nature through the best writers, and then applying deductive and syllogistic procedures to the result. In 1581 another writer, François Sanchez, produced a further attack on Aristotle, and more particularly on the modern followers of Aristotle—a work which provides a remarkable anticipation of Descartes. He said:

> I questioned the learned men of bygone centuries; then I consulted those who were my contemporaries... but none of their replies was satisfactory....
> So I turned in upon myself & put everything to doubt, as though I had never been told anything by anybody. I began to examine things myself in order to discover the true way of gaining knowledge—Hence the thesis which is the starting-point of my reflections: the more I think, the more I doubt.

He attacked the syllogistic reasoning of the prevalent Aristotelian school, because it turned men away from the study of reality and encouraged them to play a sophistical game of verbal subtlety. He promised to expound the true method of science, but in the fifty years of life that were left to him he never fulfilled the promise. One participant in the controversies over scientific method, Everard Digby, was teaching Logic in the University of Cambridge when Francis Bacon was there in his youth; and a German scholar has shown that at certain points Bacon appears to have followed the ideas of this man.

Bacon held that if Adam, owing to the Fall, had lost for the human race that domination over the created world which it had originally been designed to possess, still there was a subordinate command over nature, available if men worked sufficiently hard to secure it, though this had been thrown away by human folly. There had been only three short periods of genuine scientific progress throughout the whole course of human history, he said—one in Greek times, one in the Roman period, and the third which was being enjoyed in the seventeenth century. In each of the two ancient periods the era of scientific progress had been confined to two hundred years. The earlier Greek philosophers had set the course of enquiry on the right lines, but Plato and Aristotle had supervened, and they had come to prevail precisely because, being of light weight, they had managed to ride much farther down upon the stream of time. They had survived the storms of the Barbarian Invasions precisely because they had been shallow and buoyant, and Aristotle, in particular, had owed his remarkable sway in the world to the fact that, like the Ottoman sultans, he had pursued the policy of destroying all rivals. As for the scholastics of the middle ages, they had had "subtle and strong capacities, abundance of leisure, and but small variety of reading, their minds being shut up in a few authors"; and therefore they had "with infinite agitation of wit, spun out of a small quantity of matter those laborious webs of learning which are extant in their books." Bacon was impressed by the fact that scientific knowledge had made such extraordinarily little progress since the days of antiquity. He begins by saying that men ought to "throw aside all thought of philosophy, or at least to expect but little and poor fruit from it, until an approved and careful natural and Experimental History be prepared and constructed."

> For to what purpose are these brain-creations and idle display of power....
> All these invented systems of the universe, each according to his own fancy
> [are] like so many arguments of plays... every one philosophises out of the
> cells of his own imagination, as out of Plato's cave.

He uses the term "history" in the sense that we have in mind when we speak of natural history, and he regards it as comprising a collection of data, the fruits of enquiry.

He believed that many men had been led away by allowing their scientific work to become entangled in a search for final causes, which really belonged rather to philosophy, and which he said corrupted the sciences, except those relating to the intercourse of man with man. In education he thought that scholars were introduced too early to logic and rhetoric, which were the cream of the sciences since they arranged and methodised the subject-matter of all the others. To apply the juvenile mind to these before it had been confronted with the subject-matter of the other sciences was like painting and measuring the wind, he said—on the one hand it degraded logic into childish sophistry, on the other hand it had the effect of making the more concrete sciences superficial. In his reaction against the older ways of discussing science, Bacon carried the attack beyond the bounds of prudence on occasion—denying the value of syllogistic modes of reasoning in a way that the modern philosopher would disapprove of; though the general line of attack was understandable, and very useful in view of the situation of things at that time. Bacon wanted men to close in on nature and get to grips with her, bringing their minds to mix in its actual operations. "The secrets of nature," he said, "betray themselves more readily when tormented by art than when left to their own course." "It is best to consider matter, its conformation, and the changes of that conformation, its own action, and the law of this action in motion." He did not support a dead kind of empiricism; the empirics, he said, were like ants merely heaping up a collection of data. The natural philosophers still generally current in the world, however, were rather like spiders spinning their webs out of their own interior. He thought that the scientists ought to take up an intermediate position, like that of the bees, which extracted matter from the flowers and then re-fashioned it by their own efforts. Existing interpretations of nature, he said, were generally "founded on too narrow a basis of experiment." "In any case," he insisted, "the present method of experiment is blind and stupid"—men did it as though they were schoolboys engaged "as it were in sport." He talked of "desultory, ill-combined experiment." The alchemists, he said, had theoretical preconceptions which hindered them from either carrying out their experiments along useful lines or extracting anything important from their results. Men in general glanced too hastily at the result of an experiment, and then imagined that the rest could be done by sheer contemplation; or they would fly off into the skies with a hasty first impression and attempt to make this square with the vulgar notions already existing in their minds. Even Gilbert working on the magnet had no unity or order in his experiments—the only unity in his treatise lay in the fact that he had been ready to try out anything that there was to try out with a magnet.

Now it was Bacon's firm principle that if men wanted to achieve anything new in the world, it was of no use attempting to reach it on any ancient method —they must realise that new practices and policies would be necessary. He stressed above all the need for the direction of experiments—an end to the mere haphazard experimenting—and he insisted that something far more subtle and far-reaching could be achieved by the proper organisation of experiments. It is quite clear that he realised how science could be brought to a higher power altogether by being transported away from that ordinary world of common-sense phenomena in which so much of the discussion had hitherto been carried on. He insisted on the importance of the actual recording of experiments, a point which, as we have already seen, was now coming to be of some significance. He urged that experimenters in different fields should get together, because they would knock sparks off one another; and things done in one field would give hints to people working in another field. In this sense he anticipated the point of Professor Whitehead who shows how, precisely in this period, the knowledge of several different branches of science at once might have an enriching effect on each. Also, suggestions which are scattered in various parts of Bacon's work seem to have served as an inspiration to some of the men who founded the Royal Society....

Place of Scientific Revolution in History

... The changes which took place in the history of thought in this period, however, are not more remarkable than the changes in life and society. It has long been our tendency to push back the origins of both the industrial revolution and the so-called agrarian revolution of the eighteenth century, and though ... we can trace back the origin of anything as far as we like, it is towards the end of the seventeenth century that the changes are becoming palpable. The passion to extend the scientific method to every branch of thought was at least equalled by the passion to make science serve the cause of industry and agriculture, and it was accompanied by a sort of technological fervour. Francis Bacon had always laid stress on the immense utilitarian possibilities of science, the advantages beyond all dreams that would come from the control of nature; and it is difficult, even in the early history of the Royal Society, to separate the interest shown in the cause of pure scientific truth from the curiosity in respect of useful inventions on the one part, or the inclination to dabble in fables and freakishness on the other. It has become a debatable question how far the direction of scientific interest was itself affected by technical needs or preoccupations in regard to shipbuilding and other industries; but the Royal Society followed Galileo in concerning itself, for example, with the important question of the mode of discovering longitude at sea. Those who wish to trace the development of the steam-engine will find that it is a story which really begins to be vivid and lively in this period. Apart from such developments, the possibilities of scientific experiment were likely themselves to be limited until certain forms of production and technique had been elaborated in society generally. Indeed, the scientific, the industrial and the agrarian revolutions form such a system of complex and interrelated changes, that in the lack of a microscopic examination we have to heap them all together as aspects of a general movement, which by the last quarter of the seventeenth century was palpably altering the face of the earth. The hazard consists not in putting all these things together and rolling them into one great bundle of complex change, but in thinking that we know how to disentangle them—what we see is the total intricate network of changes, and it is difficult to say that any one of these was the simple result of the scientific revolution itself....

It is always easy for a later generation to think that its predecessor was foolish, and it may seem shocking to state that even after the first World War good historians could write the history of the nineteenth century with hardly a hint of the importance of Socialism, hardly a mention of Karl Marx—a fact which we should misinterpret unless we took it as a reminder of the kind of faults to which all of us are prone. Because we have a fuller knowledge of after-events, we today can see the nineteenth century differently; and it is not we who are under an optical illusion—reading the twentieth century back unfairly into the nineteenth—when we say that the student of the last hundred years is missing a decisive factor if he overlooks the rise of Socialism. A man of insight could have recognised the importance of the phenomenon long before the end of the nineteenth century. But we, who have seen the implications worked out in the events of our time, need no insight to recognise the importance of this whole aspect of the story.

Something similar to this is true when we of the year 1957 take our perspective of the scientific revolution—we are in a position to see its implications at the present day much more clearly than the men who flourished fifty or even twenty years before us. And, once again, it is not we who are under an optical illusion-reading the present back into the past—for the things that have been revealed in the 1950s merely bring out more vividly the vast importance of the turn which the world took three hundred years ago, in the days of the scientific revolution. We can see why our predecessors were less conscious of the significance of the seventeenth century—why they talked so much more of the Renaissance or the eighteenth-century Enlightenment, for example—because in this as in so many other cases we can now discern those surprising overlaps and time-lags which so often disguise the direction things are taking. Our Graeco-Roman roots and our Christian heritage were so profound—so central to all our thinking—that it has required centuries of pulls and pressures, and almost a conflict of civilisations in our very midst, to make it clear that the centre had long ago shifted. At one time the effects of the scientific revolution, and the changes contemporary with it, would be masked by the persistence of our classical traditions and education, which still decided so much of the character of the eighteenth century in England and in France, for example. At another time these effects would be concealed through that popular attachment to religion which so helped to form the character of even the nineteenth century in this country. The very strength of our conviction that ours was a Graeco-Roman civilisation—the very way in which we allowed the art-historians and the philologists to make us think that this thing which we call "the modern world" was the product of the Renaissance—the inelasticity of our historical concepts, in fact—helped to conceal the radical nature of the changes that had taken place and the colossal possibilities that lay in the seeds sown by the seventeenth century. The seventeenth century, indeed, did not merely bring a new factor into history, in the way we often assume—one that must just be added, so to speak, to the other permanent factors. The new factor immediately began to elbow the other ones away, pushing them from their central position. Indeed, it began immediately to seek control of the rest, as the apostles of the new movement had declared their intention of doing from the very start. The result was the emergence of a kind of Western civilisation which when transmitted to Japan operates on tradition there as it operates on tradition here—dissolving it and having eyes for nothing save a future of brave new worlds. It was a civilisation that could cut itself away from the Graeco-Roman heritage in general, away from Christianity itself—only too confident in its power to exist independent of anything of the kind. We know now that what was emerging towards the end of the seventeenth century was a civilisation exhilaratingly new perhaps, but strange as Nineveh and Babylon. That is why, since the rise of Christianity, there is no landmark in history that is worthy to be compared with this.

The Scientific Revolution

The Scientific Revolution: The History of a Term

There was no such thing as the Scientific Revolution, and this [selection is from] a book about it. Some time ago, when the academic world offered more certainty and more comforts, historians announced the real existence of a coherent, cataclysmic, and climactic event that fundamentally and irrevocably changed what people knew about the natural world and how they secured proper knowledge of that world. It was the moment at which the world was made modern, it was a Good Thing, and it happened sometime during the period from the late sixteenth to the early eighteenth century. In 1943 the French historian Alexandre Koyré celebrated the conceptual changes at the heart of the Scientific Revolution as "the most profound revolution achieved or suffered by the human mind" since Greek antiquity. It was a revolution so profound that human culture "for centuries did not grasp its bearing or meaning; which, even now, is often misvalued and misunderstood." A few years later the English historian Herbert Butterfield famously judged that the Scientific Revolution "outshines everything since the rise of Christianity and reduces the Renaissance and Reformation to the rank of mere episodes.... [It is] the real origin both of the modern world and of the modern mentality." It was, moreover, construed as a conceptual revolution, a fundamental reordering of our ways of *thinking* about the natural. In this respect, a story about the Scientific Revolution might be adequately told through an account of radical changes in the fundamental categories of thought. To Butterfield, the mental changes making up the Scientific Revolution were equivalent to "putting on a new pair of spectacles." And to A. Rupert Hall it was nothing less than "an *a priori* redefinition of the objects of philosophical and scientific inquiry."

This conception of the Scientific Revolution is now encrusted with tradition. Few historical episodes present themselves as more substantial or more self-evidently worthy of study. There is an established place for accounts of the Scientific Revolution in the Western liberal curriculum, and this [selection] is an attempt to fill that space economically and to invite further curiosity about the making of early modern science. Nevertheless, like many twentieth-century "traditions," that contained in the notion of the Scientific Revolution is not nearly as old as we might think. The phrase "the Scientific Revolution" was probably coined by Alexandre Koyré in 1939, and it first became a book title in A. Rupert Hall's *The Scientific Revolution* of 1954. Before that time there was no event to be studied in the liberal curriculum, nor any discrete object of historical inquiry, called the Scientific Revolution. Although many seventeenth-century practitioners expressed their intention of bringing about radical intellectual change, the people who are said to have made the revolution used no such term to refer to what they were doing.

From antiquity through the early modern period, a "revolution" invoked the idea of a periodically recurring cycle. In Copernicus's new astronomy of the mid-sixteenth century, for example, the planets completed their revolutions round the sun, while references to political revolutions gestured at the notion of ebbs and flows or cycles—fortune's wheel—in human affairs. The idea of revolution as a radical and irreversible reordering developed together with linear, unidirectional conceptions of time. In this newer conception revolution was not recurrence but its reverse, the bringing about of a new state of affairs that the world had never witnessed before and might never witness again. Not only this notion of revolution but also the beginnings of an idea of revolution in science date from the eighteenth-century writings of French Enlightenment philosophes who liked to portray themselves, and their disciplines, as radical subverters of ancien régime culture. (Some... seventeenth-century writers... saw themselves not as bringing about totally new states of affairs but as restoring or purifying old ones.) The notion of a revolution as epochal and irreversible change, it is possible, was first applied in a systematic way to events in science and only later to political events. In just this sense, the first revolutions may have been scientific, and the "American," "French," and "Russian Revolutions" are its progeny.

As our understanding of science in the seventeenth century has changed in recent years, so historians have become increasingly uneasy with the very idea of "the Scientific Revolution." Even the legitimacy of each word making up that phrase has been individually contested. Many historians are now no longer satisfied that there was any singular and discrete event, localized in time and space, that can be pointed to as "the" Scientific Revolution. Such historians now reject even the notion that there was any single coherent cultural entity called "science" in the seventeenth century to undergo revolutionary change. There was, rather, a diverse array of cultural practices aimed at understanding, explaining, and controlling the natural world, each with different characteristics and each experiencing different modes of change. We are now much more dubious of claims that there is anything like "a scientific method"—a coherent, universal, and efficacious set of procedures for making scientific knowledge—and still more skeptical of stories that locate its origin in the seventeenth century, from which time it has been unproblematically passed on to us. And many historians do not now accept that the changes wrought on scientific beliefs and practices during the seventeenth century were as "revolutionary" as has been widely portrayed. The continuity of seventeenth-century natural philosophy with its medieval past is now routinely asserted, while talk of "delayed" eighteenth- and nineteenth-century revolutions in chemistry and biology followed hard upon historians' identification of "the" original Scientific Revolution.

Why Write About the Scientific Revolution?

There are still other reasons for historians' present uneasiness with the category of the Scientific Revolution as it has been customarily construed. First, historians have in recent years become dissatisfied with the traditional manner of treating ideas as if they floated freely in conceptual space. Although previous accounts framed the Scientific Revolution in terms of autonomous ideas or disembodied mentalities, more recent versions have insisted on the importance of situating ideas in their wider cultural and social context. We now hear more than we used to about the relations between the scientific changes of the seventeenth century and changes in religious, political, and economic patterns. More fundamentally, some historians now wish to understand the concrete human *practices* by which ideas or concepts are made. What did people *do* when they made or confirmed an observation, proved a theorem, performed an experiment? An account of the Scientific Revolution as a history of free-floating concepts is a very different animal from a history of concept-making practices. Finally, historians have become much more interested in the "who" of the Scientific Revolution. What kinds of people wrought such changes? Did everyone believe as they did, or only a very few? And if only a very few took part in these changes, in what sense, if at all, can we speak of the Scientific Revolution as effecting massive changes in how "we" view the world, as the moment when modernity was made, for "us"? The cogency of such questions makes for problems in writing as unreflectively as we used to about the Scientific Revolution. Responding to them means that we need an account of changes in early modern science appropriate for our less confident, but perhaps more intellectually curious, times.

Yet despite these legitimate doubts and uncertainties there remains a sense in which it is possible to write about the Scientific Revolution unapologetically and in good faith. There are two major considerations to bear in mind here. The first is that many key figures in the late sixteenth and seventeenth centuries vigorously expressed *their* view that they were proposing some very new and very important changes in knowledge of natural reality and in the practices by which legitimate knowledge was to be secured, assessed, and communicated. They identified *themselves* as "moderns" set against "ancient" modes of thought and practice. Our sense of radical change afoot comes substantially from them (and those who were the object of their attacks), and is not simply the creation of mid-twentieth-century historians. So we can say that the seventeenth century witnessed some self-conscious and large-scale attempts to change belief, and ways of securing belief, about the natural world. And a book about the Scientific Revolution can legitimately tell a story about those attempts, whether or not they succeeded, whether or not they were contested in the local culture, whether or not they were wholly coherent.

But why do we tell *these* stories instead of others? If different sorts of seventeenth-century people believed different things about the world, how do we assemble our cast of characters and associated beliefs? Some "natural philosophers," for example, advocated rational theorizing, while others pushed a program of relatively atheoretical fact collecting and experimentation. Mathematical physics was, for example, a very different sort of practice from botany. There were importantly different versions of what it was to do astronomy and believe as an astronomer believed; the relations between the "proper sciences" of astronomy and chemistry and the "pseudosciences" of astrology and alchemy were intensely problematic; and even the category of "nature" as the object of inquiry was understood in radically different ways by different sorts of practitioners. This point cannot be stressed too strongly. The cultural practices subsumed in the category of the Scientific Revolution—however it has been construed—are not coextensive with early modern, or seventeenth-century, science. Historians differ about which practices were "central" to the Scientific Revolution, and participants themselves argued about which practices produced genuine knowledge and which had been fundamentally reformed.

More fundamentally for criteria of selection, it ought to be understood that "most people"—even most educated people—in the seventeenth century did not believe what expert scientific practitioners believed, and the sense in which "people's" thought about the world was revolutionized at that time is very limited. There should be no doubt whatever that one could write a convincing history of seventeenth-century thought about nature without even *mentioning* the Scientific Revolution as traditionally construed.

The very idea of the Scientific Revolution, therefore, is at least partly an expression of "our" interest in our ancestors, where "we" are late twentieth-century scientists and those for whom what they believe counts as truth about the natural world. And this interest provides the second legitimate justification for writing about the Scientific Revolution. Historians of science have now grown used to condemning "present-oriented" history, rightly saying that it often distorts our understanding of what the past was like in its own terms. Yet there is absolutely no reason we should not want to know how we got from there to here, who the ancestors were, and what the lineage is that connects us to the past. In this sense a story about the seventeenth-century Scientific Revolution can be an account of those changes that we think led on—never directly or simply, to be sure—to certain features of the present in which, for certain purposes, we happen to be interested. To do this would be an expression of just the same sort of legitimate historical interest displayed by Darwinian evolutionists telling stories about those branches of the tree of life that led to human beings—without assuming in any way that such stories are adequate accounts of what life was like hundreds of thousands of years ago. There is nothing at all wrong about telling such stories, though one must always be careful not to claim too much scope for them. Stories about the ancestors as ancestors are not likely to be sensitive accounts of how it was in the past: the lives and thoughts of Galileo, Descartes, or Boyle were hardly typical of seventeenth-century Italians, Frenchmen, or Englishmen, and telling stories about them geared solely to their ancestral role in formulating the currently accepted law of free fall, the optics of the rainbow, or the ideal gas law is not likely to capture very much about the meaning and significance of their own careers and projects in the seventeenth century.

The past is not transformed into the "modern world" at any single moment: we should never be surprised to find that seventeenth-century scientific practitioners often had about them as much of the ancient as the modern; their notions had to be successively transformed and redefined by generations of thinkers to become "ours." And finally, the people, the thoughts, and the practices we tell stories about as "ancestors," or as the beginnings of our lineage, always reflect some present-day interest. That we tell stories about Galileo, Boyle, Descartes, and Newton reflects something about our late twentieth-century scientific beliefs and what we value about those beliefs. For different purposes we could trace aspects of the modern world back to philosophers "vanquished" by Galileo, Boyle, Descartes, and Newton, and to views of nature and knowledge very different from those elaborated by our officially sanctioned scientific ancestors. For still other purposes we could make much of the fact that most seventeenth-century people had never heard of our scientific ancestors and probably entertained beliefs about the natural world very different from those of our chosen forebears. Indeed, the overwhelming majority of seventeenth-century people did not live in Europe, did not know that they lived in "the seventeenth century," and were not aware that a Scientific Revolution was happening. The half of the European population that was female was in a position to participate in scientific culture scarcely at all, as was that overwhelming majority—of men and women—who were illiterate or otherwise disqualified from entering the venues of formal learning.

Some Historiographical Issues

I mean this [selection] to be historiographically up to date—drawing on some of the most recent historical, sociological, and philosophical engagements with the Scientific Revolution. On the other hand, I do not mean to trouble readers with repeated references to methodological and conceptual debates among academics. This [selection] is not written for professional specialized scholars.... There is no reason to deny that this story about the Scientific Revolution represents a particular point of view, and that, although I help myself freely to the work of many distinguished scholars, its point of view is my own. Other specialists will doubtless disagree with my approach—some vehemently—and a large number of existing accounts do offer a quite different perspective on what is worth telling about the Scientific Revolution. The positions represented here on some recent historiographic issues can be briefly summarized:

1. I *take for granted* that science is a historically situated and social activity and that it is to be understood in relation to the *contexts* in which it occurs. Historians have long argued whether science relates to its historical and social contexts or whether it should be treated in isolation. I shall simply write about seventeenth-century science as if it were a collectively practiced, historically embedded phenomenon, inviting readers to see whether the account is plausible, coherent, and interesting.

2. For a long time, historians' debates over the propriety of a sociological and a historically "contextual" approach to science seemed to divide practitioners between those who drew attention to what were called "intellectual factors" —ideas, concepts, methods, evidence—and those who stressed "social factors"—forms of organization, political and economic influences on science, and social uses or consequences of science. That now seems to many historians, as it does to me, a rather silly demarcation, and I shall not waste readers' time here in reviewing why those disputes figured so largely in past approaches to the history of early modern science. If science is to be understood as historically situated and in its collective aspect (i.e., sociologically), then that understanding should encompass all aspects of science, its ideas and practices no less than its institutional forms and social uses. Anyone who wants to represent science sociologically cannot simply set aside the body of what the relevant practitioners *knew* and how they went about obtaining that knowledge. Rather, the task for the sociologically minded historian is to display the structure of knowledge making and knowledge holding *as social processes.*

3. A traditional construal of "social factors" (or what is sociological about science) has focused on considerations taken to be "external" to science proper —for example, the use of metaphors from the economy in the development of scientific knowledge or the ideological uses of science in justifying certain sorts of political arrangements. Much fine historical work has been done based on such a construal. However, the identification of what is sociological about science with what is external to science appears to me a curious and a limited way of going on. There is as much "society" inside the scientist's laboratory, and internal to the development of scientific knowledge, as there is "outside." And in fact the very distinction between the social and the political, on the one hand, and "scientific truth," on the other, is partly a cultural product of the period [I discuss]. What is commonsensically thought of as science in the late twentieth century is in some measure a product of the historical episodes we want to understand here. Far from matter-of-factly treating the distinction between the social and the scientific as a resource in telling a historical story, I mean to make it into a topic of inquiry. How and why did we come to think that such a distinction is a matter *of course?*

4. I do not consider that there is anything like an "essence" of seventeenth-century science or indeed of seventeenth-century reforms in science. Consequently there is no single coherent story that could possibly capture all the aspects of science or its changes in which we late twentieth-century moderns might happen to be interested. I can think of no feature of early modern science that has been traditionally identified as its revolutionary essence that did not have significantly variant contemporary forms or that was not subjected to contemporary criticism by practitioners who have also been accounted revolutionary "moderns." . . .

·◦·

The confrontation over Newton's optical work can stand as an emblem of the fragmented knowledge-making legacies of the seventeenth century. A theoretically cautious and experience-based conception of science was here juxtaposed to one that deployed mathematical as well as experimental tools to claim theoretical certainty. Diffidence was opposed to ambition, respect for the concrete particularities of nature to the quest for universally applicable idealizations, the modesty of the fact gatherer to the pride of the abstracted philosopher. Do you want to capture the essence of nature and command assent to representations of its regularities? Do you want to subject yourself to the discipline of describing, and perhaps generalizing about, the behavior of medium-sized objects actually existing in the world?

Both conceptions of science persist in the late twentieth century, and both can trace elements of their formation back to the seventeenth century. The one is not necessarily to be regarded as a failed version of the other, however much partisans may defend the virtues of their preferred practice and condemn the vices of another. These are, so to speak, different games that natural philosophers might wish to play, and decisions about which game is best are different in kind from decisions about what is a sensible move within a given game: an accurate pass from midfield to the winger in soccer is not a bad jump shot in basketball. In the seventeenth century natural philosophers were confronted with differing repertoires of practical and conceptual skills for achieving various philosophical goals and with choices about which ends they might work to achieve. The goal was always some conception of proper philosophical knowledge about the natural world, though descriptions of what that knowledge looked like and how it was to be secured varied greatly.

POSTSCRIPT

Was the Scientific Revolution Revolutionary?

The question of whether or not the Scientific Revolution was revolutionary is a philosophical as well as a historical one. At issue is how we understand key terms such as *science* and *revolution* as well as how we interpret what philosophers call "epistemology," or knowledge theory. Both historians agree that key people in the past understood that what they were doing represented a break with the past. Where they disagree is over how to evaluate the past in the context of what we know in the present. Butterfield assumes that we can all agree on the meaning of science, but Shapin questions his definition. In the 40 years between Butterfield's and Shapin's books, knowledge theory has changed. Taking apart texts to reveal their hidden meanings has led many to question whether or not it is possible to have a single, universal meaning for a term like *science*. What the word may have meant to people practicing it in the seventeenth century may be worlds away from what it means to people practicing it today. And those of us outside the scientific community in either period generally have even less idea what may be at stake.

Thomas Kuhn, whose widely read book *The Structure of Scientific Revolutions* (University of Chicago Press, 1962, 1970) has shed some light on this controversy, combines continuity with discontinuity. Revolutions, Kuhn contends, are occasional, dramatic breaks from periods of what he calls "normal science," when everyone in the scientific community operates from within an accepted paradigm. Revolutions occur when experiments repeatedly do not yield the expected results or when data do not conform to predicted outcomes. Scientists struggle to make the new material fit the old paradigm; those who challenge the paradigm are marginalized or forced to conform. When it becomes clear that the paradigm has broken down, a new paradigm is accepted. Then everything is explained in terms of the new paradigm. Students are educated in the new paradigm; textbooks are written to reflect it; and research takes it as its starting point. Has the world changed or only our way of explaining it to ourselves?

A selection from Kuhn's book is the concluding essay in Vern L. Bullough, ed., *The Scientific Revolution* (Holt, Rinehart & Winston, 1970). The opening essay is an excerpt from Andrew Dickson White's classic *A History of the Warfare of Science With Theology*, which was first published in 1896. A more modern collection of essays appears in *Reappraisals of the Scientific Revolution* edited by David C. Lindberg and Robert S. Westman (Cambridge University Press, 1990). In it, essays by philosophers of science and historians consider conceptions of science and the relationship between philosophy and science.

ISSUE 13

Was the French Revolution
Worth Its Human Costs?

YES: Peter Kropotkin, from *The Great French Revolution, 1789–1793*, trans. N. F. Dryhurst (Schocken Books, 1971)

NO: Simon Schama, from *Citizens: A Chronicle of the French Revolution* (Alfred A. Knopf, 1989)

ISSUE SUMMARY

YES: Peter Kropotkin (1842–1921), a Russian prince, revolutionary, and anarchist, argues that the French Revolution eradicated both serfdom and absolutism and paved the way for France's future democratic growth.

NO: History professor Simon Schama counters that not only did the French Revolution betray its own goals, but it produced few of the results that it promised.

Few historical eras have created the emotional responses and concomitant debates as has the French Revolution. Taking advantage of one of the largest bodies of historical data ever gathered, historians of the past two centuries have analyzed, synthesized, and evaluated every facet of this seminal event in the history of the Western world.

From this scholarship has come a myriad of important questions regarding the political, economic, social, religious, cultural, and intellectual aspects of the Revolution—questions involving causation, behavior, outcomes, and assessments. Each generation of historians has taken the work of its predecessors and used it to shape an understanding of the Revolution that emanates from the uncovering of new sources of information, the creation of new tools to assist in the process, and the development of new schools of thought that attempt to give a more contemporary, relevant slant to this important event. To list the major questions raised by this debate could well cover most of the pages in a work devoted to the subject.

But of all the questions that the French Revolution has raised, a double-edged one that is both elemental and significant is, What were its outcomes, and were they worth the price that was paid to achieve them?

The debate began before anyone knew what course the Revolution would take. In a 1790 treatise entitled *Reflections on the Revolution in France*, English statesman Edmund Burke (1729–1797) uncannily predicted the future course of the Revolution and its catastrophic consequences for both France and Europe. He also argued in favor of the slow, evolutionary style of change that was taking place in his own country, rather than the sudden, spasmodic one that was beginning to envelop France. Burke's message was simple: the revolution in France will be costly and counterproductive.

A year later, the French Revolution gained its first articulate defender, an English-born American citizen named Thomas Paine (1737–1809). In *Common Sense* (1776), a stirring call-to-arms for American colonists to throw off the yoke of English oppression, Paine acquired a reputation as a foe of tyrannical government and as a strong supporter of human freedom and equality. In Part 1 of his political pamphlet *The Rights of Man*, published in 1791, Paine argued that revolution was necessary to purge civilization of those elements that stood in the way of societal reform. According to Paine, no price was too high to pay for the realization of these cherished goals.

As generations passed, the basic question debated by Burke and Paine faded into the background as historians began to explore other fertile areas of historical research. There was either a general acceptance of the French Revolution's value in changing the course of human history or a quiet acquiescence in its outcomes, regardless of the consequences.

The following selection is by Peter Kropotkin, an early historical defender of the French Revolution. Obviously influenced by his radical, anarchistic background and his desire to see all people freed from the yoke of oppression, his view of the Revolution was somewhat simplistic and uncritical. Coming from a nineteenth-century environment, in which revolutions were common and seen by many as an inevitable part of political evolution, his opinions on the French Revolution are representative for his time—and for generations to come.

Of all the books written about the French Revolution in recent years, none have been as popular as Simon Schama's *Citizens: A Chronicle of the French Revolution*, which is excerpted in the second selection of this issue. Published in the midst of the Revolution's bicentennial celebration, the book aroused much controversy for many reasons; among them was his view that the French Revolution was not worth its human costs. Seeing violence as an endemic part of the revolutionary process, Schama states that the French Revolution produced few of the results that it had promised.

Peter Kropotkin

 **YES**

The Great French Revolution, 1789–1793

When one sees that terrible and powerful Convention wrecking itself in 1794–1795, that proud and strong Republic disappearing, and France, after the demoralising *régime* of the Directory, falling under the military yoke of a Bonaparte, one is impelled to ask: "What was the good of the Revolution if the nation had to fall back again under despotism?" In the course of the nineteenth century, this question has been constantly put, and the timid and conservative have worn it threadbare as an argument against revolutions in general.

... Those who have seen in the Revolution only a change in the Government, those who are ignorant of its economic as well as its educational work, those alone could put such a question.

The France we see during the last days of the eighteenth century, at the moment of the *coup d'état* on the 18th Brumaire, is not the France that existed before 1789. Would it have been possible for the old France, wretchedly poor and with a third of her population suffering yearly from dearth, to have maintained the Napoleonic Wars, coming so soon after the terrible wars of the Republic between 1792 and 1799, when all Europe was attacking her?

The fact is, that a new France had been constituted since 1792–1793. Scarcity still prevailed in many of the departments, and its full horrors were felt especially after the *coup d'état* of Thermidor, when the maximum price for all foodstuffs was abolished. There were still some departments which did not produce enough wheat to feed themselves, and as the war went on, and all means of transport were requisitioned for its supplies, there was scarcity in those departments. But everything tends to prove that France was even then producing much more of the necessaries of life of every kind than in 1789.

Never was there in France such energetic ploughing, Michelet tells us, as in 1792, when the peasant was ploughing the lands he had taken back from the lords, the convents, the churches, and was goading his oxen to the cry of *"Allons Prusse! Allons Autriche!"* Never had there been so much clearing of lands—even royalist writers admit this—as during those years of revolution. The first good harvest, in 1794, brought relief to two-thirds of France—at least in the villages, for all this time the towns were threatened with scarcity of food. Not that it was scarce in France as a whole, or that the *sans-culotte* municipalities neglected to take measures to feed those who could not find employment, but from the

From Peter Kropotkin, *The Great French Revolution, 1789–1793*, trans. N. F. Dryhurst (Schocken Books, 1971). Copyright © 1971 by Schocken Books.

fact that all beasts of burden not actually used in tillage were requisitioned to carry food and ammunition to the fourteen armies of the Republic. In those days there were no railways, and all but the main roads were in the state they are to this day in Russia—well-nigh impassable.

A new France was born during those four years of revolution. For the first time in centuries the peasant ate his fill, straightened his back and dared to speak out. Read the detailed reports concerning the return of Louis XVI. to Paris, when he was brought back a prisoner from Varennes, in June 1791, by the peasants, and say: "Could such a thing, such an interest in the public welfare, such a devotion to it, and such an independence of judgment and action have been possible before 1789?" A new nation had been born in the meantime, just as we see to-day a new nation coming into life in Russia and in Turkey.

It was owing to this new birth that France was able to maintain her wars under the Republic and Napoleon, and to carry the principles of the Great Revolution into Switzerland, Italy, Spain, Belgium, Holland, Germany, and even to the borders of Russia. And when, after all those wars, after having mentally followed the French armies as far as Egypt and Moscow, we expect to find France in 1815 reduced to an appalling misery and her lands laid waste, we find, instead, that even in its eastern portions and in the Jura, the country is much more prosperous than it was at the time when Pétion, pointing out to Louis XVI. the luxuriant banks of the Marne, asked him if there was anywhere in the world a kingdom more beautiful than the one the King had not wished to keep.

The self-contained energy was such in villages regenerated by the Revolution, that in a few years France became a country of well-to-do peasants, and her enemies soon discovered that in spite of all the blood she had shed and the losses she had sustained, France, in respect of her *productivity,* was the richest country in Europe. Her wealth, indeed, is not drawn from the Indies or from her foreign commerce: it comes from her own soil, from her love of the soil, from her own skill and industry. She is the richest country, because of the subdivision of her wealth, and she is still richer because of the possibilities she offers for the future.

Such was the effect of the Revolution. And if the casual observer sees in Napoleonic France only a love of glory, the historian realises that even the wars France waged at that period were undertaken to secure the fruits of the Revolution—to keep the lands that had been retaken from the lords, the priests and the rich, and the liberties that had been won from despotism and the Court. If France was willing in those years to bleed herself to death, merely to prevent the Germans, the English, and the Russians from forcing a Louis XVIII. upon her, it was because she did not want the return of the emigrant nobles to mean that the *ci-devants* would take back the lands which had been watered already with the peasant's sweat, and the liberties which had been sanctified with the patriots' blood. And France fought so well for twenty-three years, that when she was compelled at last to admit the Bourbons, it was she who imposed conditions on them. The Bourbons might reign, but the lands were to be kept by those who had taken them from the feudal lords, so that even during the White

Terror of the Bourbons they dared not touch those lands. The old *régime* could not be re-established.

This is what is gained by making a Revolution.

៚◉៚

There are other things to be pointed out. In the history of all nations a time comes when fundamental changes are bound to take place in the whole of the national life. Royal despotism and feudalism were dying in 1789; it was impossible to keep them alive; they had to go.

But then, two ways were opened out before France: reform or revolution.

At such times there is always a moment when reform is still possible; but if advantage has not been taken of that moment, if an obstinate resistance has been opposed to the requirements of the new life, up to the point when blood has flowed in the streets, as it flowed on July 14, 1789, then there must be a Revolution. And once the Revolution has begun, it must necessarily develop to its conclusions—that is to say, to the highest point it is capable of attaining— were it only temporarily, being given a certain condition of the public mind at this particular moment.

If we represent the slow progress of a period of evolution by a line drawn on paper, we shall see this line gradually though slowly rising. Then there comes a Revolution, and the line makes a sudden leap upwards. In England the line would be represented as rising to the Puritan Republic of Cromwell; in France it rises to the *Sans-culotte* Republic of 1793. However, at this height progress cannot be maintained; all the hostile forces league together against it, and the Republic goes down. Our line, after having reached that height, drops. Reaction follows. For the political life of France the line drops very low indeed, but by degrees it rises again, and when peace is restored in 1815 in France, and in 1688 in England—both countries are found to have attained a level much higher than they were on prior to their Revolutions.

After that, evolution is resumed: our line again begins to rise slowly: but, besides taking place on a very much higher level, the rising of the line will in nearly every case be also much more rapid than before the period of disturbance.

This is a law of human progress, and also a law of individual progress. The more recent history of France confirms this very law by showing how it was necessary to pass through the Commune to arrive at the Third Republic.

The work of the French Revolution is not confined merely to what it obtained and what was retained of it in France. It is to be found also in the principles bequeathed by it to the succeeding century—in the line of direction it marked out for the future.

A reform is always a compromise with the past, but the progress accomplished by revolution is always a promise of future progress. If the Great French Revolution was the summing up of a century's evolution, it also marked out in its turn the programme of evolution to be accomplished in the course of the nineteenth century.

It is a law in the world's history that the period of a hundred or a hundred and thirty years, more or less, which passes between two great revolutions, receives its character from the revolution in which this period began. The nations endeavour to realise in their institutions the inheritance bequeathed to them by the last revolution. All that this last could not yet put into practice, all the great thoughts which were thrown into circulation during the turmoil, and which the revolution either could not or did not know how to apply, all the attempts at sociological reconstruction, which were born during the revolution, will go to make up the substance of evolution during the epoch that follows the revolution, with the addition of those new ideas to which this evolution will give birth, when trying to put into practice the programme marked out by the last upheaval. Then, a new revolution will be brought about in some other nation, and this nation in its turn will set the problems for the following century. Such has hitherto been the trend of history.

Two great conquests, in fact, characterise the century which has passed since 1789–1793. Both owe their origin to the French Revolution, which had carried on the work of the English Revolution while enlarging and invigorating it with all the progress that had been made since the English middle classes beheaded their King and transferred his power to the Parliament. These two great triumphs are: the abolition of serfdom and the abolition of absolutism, by which personal liberties have been conferred upon the individual, undreamt of by the serf of the lord and the subject of the absolute king, while at the same time they have brought about the development of the middle classes and the capitalist *régime.*

These two achievements represent the principal work of the nineteenth century, begun in France in 1789 and slowly spread over Europe in the course of that century.

The work of enfranchisement, begun by the French peasants in 1789, was continued in Spain, Italy, Switzerland, Germany, and Austria by the armies of the *sans-culottes.* Unfortunately, this work hardly penetrated into Poland and did not reach Russia at all.

The abolition of serfdom in Europe would have been already completed in the first half of the nineteenth century if the French *bourgeoisie,* coming into power in 1794 over the dead bodies of Anarchists, Cordeliers, and Jacobins, had not checked the revolutionary impulse, restored monarchy, and handed over France to the imperial juggler, the first Napoleon. This ex-*sans-culotte,* now a general of the *sans-culottes,* speedily began to prop up aristocracy; but the impulsion had been given, the institution of serfdom had already received a mortal blow. It was abolished in Spain and Italy in spite of the temporary triumph of reaction. It was closely pressed in Germany after 1811, and disappeared in that country definitively in 1848. In 1861, Russia was compelled to emancipate her serfs, and the war of 1878 put an end to serfdom in the Balkan peninsula.

The cycle is now complete. The right of the lord over the person of the peasant no longer exists in Europe, even in those countries where the feudal dues have still to be redeemed.

This fact is not sufficiently appreciated by historians. Absorbed as they are in political questions, they do not perceive the importance of the abolition of serfdom, which is, however, the essential feature of the nineteenth century. The rivalries between nations and the wars resulting from them, the policies of the Great Powers which occupy so much of the historian's attention, have all sprung from that one great fact—the abolition of serfdom and the development of the wage-system which has taken its place.

The French peasant, in revolting a hundred and twenty years ago against the lord who made him beat the ponds lest croaking frogs should disturb his master's sleep, has thus freed the peasants of all Europe. In four years, by burning the documents which registered his subjection, by setting fire to the châteaux, and by executing the owners of them who refused to recognise his rights as a human being, the French peasant so stirred up all Europe that it is to-day altogether free from the degradation of serfdom.

On the other hand, the abolition of absolute power has also taken a little over a hundred years to make the tour of Europe. Attacked in England in 1648, and vanquished in France in 1789, royal authority based on divine right is no longer exercised save in Russia, but there, too, it is at its last gasp. Even the little Balkan States and Turkey have now their representative assemblies, and Russia is entering the same cycle.

In this respect the Revolution of 1789–1793 has also accomplished its work. Equality before the law and representative government have now their place in almost all the codes of Europe. In theory, at least, the law makes no distinctions between men, and every one has the right to participate, more or less, in the government.

                                            ◦

The absolute monarch—master of his subjects—and the lord—master of the soil and the peasants, by right of birth—have both disappeared. The middle classes now govern Europe.

But at the same time the Great Revolution has bequeathed to us some other principles of an infinitely higher import; the principles of communism. We have seen how all through the Great Revolution the communist idea kept coming to the front, and how after the fall of the Girondins numerous attempts and sometimes great attempts were make in this direction. Fourierism descends in a direct line from L'Ange on one side and from Chalier on the other. Babeuf is the direct descendant of ideas which stirred the masses to enthusiasm in 1793; he, Buonarotti, and Sylvain Maréchal have only systematised them a little or even merely put them into literary form. But the secret societies organized by Babeuf and Buonarotti were the origin of the *communistes matérialistes* secret societies through which Blanqui and Barbès conspired under the *bourgeois* monarchy of Louis-Philippe. Later on, in 1866, the International Working Men's Association appeared in the direct line of descent from these societies. As to "socialism" we know now that this term came into vogue to avoid the term "communism," which at one time was dangerous because the secret communist societies became societies for action, and were rigorously suppressed by the *bourgeoisie* then in power.

There is, therefore, a direct filiation from the *Enragés* of 1793 and the Babeuf conspiracy of 1795 to the International Working Men's Association of 1866–1878.

There is also a direct descent of ideas. Up till now, modern socialism has added absolutely nothing to the ideas which were circulating among the French people between 1789 and 1794 and which it was tried to put into practice in the Year II. of the Republic. Modern socialism has only systematised those ideas and found arguments in their favour, either by turning against the middle-class economists certain of their own definitions, or by generalising certain facts noticed in the development of industrial capitalism, in the course of the nineteenth century.

But I permit myself to maintain also that, however vague it may have been, however little support it endeavoured to draw from arguments dressed in a scientific garb, and however little use it made of the pseudo-scientific slang of the middle-class economists, the popular communism of the first two years of the Republic saw clearer, and went much deeper in its analyses, than modern socialism.

First of all, it was communism in the consumption of the necessaries of life—not in production only; it was the communalisation and the nationalisation of what economists know as consumption—to which the stern republicans of 1793 turned, above all, their attention, when they tried to establish their stores of grain and provisions in every commune, when they set on foot a gigantic inquiry to find and fix the true value of the objects of prime and secondary necessity, and when they inspired Robespierre to declare that *only the superfluity of food stuffs should become articles of commerce, and that what was necessary belonged to all.*

Born out of the pressing necessities of those troublous years, the communism of 1793, with its affirmation of the right of all to sustenance and to the land for its production, its denial of the right of any one to hold more land than he and his family could cultivate—that is, more than a farm of 120 acres—and its attempt to communalise all trade and industry—this communism went straighter to the heart of things than all the minimum programmes of our own time, and even all the maximum preambles of such programmes.

In any case, what we learn to-day from the study of the Great Revolution is, that it was the source of origin of all the present communist, anarchist, and socialist conceptions. We have but badly understood our common mother, but now we have found her again in the midst of the *sans-culottes,* and we see what we have to learn from her.

Humanity advances by stages and these stages have been marked for several hundred years by great revolutions. After the Netherlands came England with her revolution in 1648–1657, and then it was the turn of France. Each great revolution has in it, besides, something special and original. England and France both abolished royal absolutism. But in doing so England was chiefly interested in the personal rights of the individual, particularly in matters of religion, as well as the local rights of every parish and every community. As to France, she turned her chief attention to the land question, and in striking a mortal blow at the feudal system she struck also at the great fortunes, and sent forth into the world the idea of nationalising the soil, and of socialising commerce and the chief industries.

Which of the nations will take upon herself the terrible but glorious task of the next great revolution? One may have thought for a time that it would be Russia. But if she should push her revolution further than the mere limitation of the imperial power; if she touches the land question in a revolutionary spirit —how far will she go? Will she know how to avoid the mistake made by the French Assemblies, and will she socialise the land and give it only to those who want to cultivate it with their own hands? We know not: any answer to this question would belong to the domain of prophecy.

The one thing certain is, that whatsoever nation enters on the path of revolution in our own day, it will be heir to all our forefathers have done in France. The blood they shed was shed for humanity—the sufferings they endured were borne for the entire human race; their struggles, the ideas they gave to the world, the shock of those ideas, are all included in the heritage of mankind. All have borne fruit and will bear more, still finer, as we advance towards those wide horizons opening out before us, where, like some great beacon to point the way, flame the words—LIBERTY, EQUALITY, FRATERNITY.

NO

Simon Schama

Citizens: A Chronicle of
the French Revolution

Asked what he thought was the significance of the French Revolution, the Chinese Premier Zhou En-lai is reported to have answered, "It's too soon to tell." Two hundred years may still be too soon (or, possibly, too late) to tell.

Historians have been overconfident about the wisdom to be gained by distance, believing it somehow confers objectivity, one of those unattainable values in which they have placed so much faith. Perhaps there is something to be said for proximity. Lord Acton, who delivered the first, famous lectures on the French Revolution at Cambridge in the 1870s, was still able to hear firsthand, from a member of the Orléans dynasty, the man's recollection of "Dumouriez gibbering on the streets of London when hearing the news of Waterloo."

Suspicion that blind partisanship fatally damaged the great Romantic narratives of the first half of the nineteenth century dominated scholarly reaction during the second half. As historians institutionalized themselves into an academic profession, they came to believe conscientious research in the archives could confer dispassion: the prerequisite for winkling out the mysterious truths of cause and effect. The desired effect was to be scientific rather than poetic, impersonal rather than impassioned. And while, for some time, historical narratives remained preoccupied by the life cycle of the European nation-states—wars, treaties and dethronements—the magnetic pull of social science was such that "structures," both social and political, seemed to become the principal objects of inquiry.

In the case of the French Revolution this meant transferring attention away from the events and personalities that had dominated the epic chronicles of the 1830s and 1840s. De Tocqueville's luminous account, *The Old Regime and the Revolution,* the product of his own archival research, provided cool reason where before there had been the burning quarrels of partisanship. The Olympian quality of his insights reinforced (albeit from a liberal point of view) the Marxist-scientific claim that the significance of the Revolution was to be sought in some great change in the balance of social power. In both these views, the utterances of orators were little more than vaporous claptrap, unsuccessfully disguising their helplessness at the hands of impersonal historical forces. Likewise, the ebb and flow of events could only be made intelligible by being displayed to reveal the *essential,* primarily social, truths of the Revolution. At the core of those truths was an axiom, shared by liberals, socialists and for that matter nostalgic Christian royalists alike, that the Revolution had indeed been the crucible of modernity: the vessel in which all the characteristics of the modern social world, for good or ill, had been distilled.

By the same token, if the whole event was of this epochal significance, then the causes that generated it had necessarily to be of an equivalent magnitude. A phenomenon of such uncontrollable power that it apparently swept away an entire universe of traditional customs, mentalities and institutions could only have been produced by contradictions that lay embedded deep within the fabric of the "old regime." Accordingly, weighty volumes appeared, between the centennial of 1889 and the Second World War, documenting every aspect of those structural faults. Biographies of Danton and Mirabeau disappeared, at least from respectable scholarly presses, and were replaced by studies of price fluctuations in the grain market. At a later stage still, discrete social groups placed in articulated opposition to each other—the "bourgeoisie," "sans-culottes,"—were defined and anatomized and their dialectical dance routines were made the exclusive choreography of revolutionary politics.

In the fifty years since the sesquicentennial, there has been a serious loss of confidence in this approach. The drastic social changes imputed to the Revolution seem less clear-cut or actually not apparent at all. The "bourgeoisie" said in the classic Marxist accounts to have been the authors and beneficiaries of the event have become social zombies, the product of historiographical obsessions rather than historical realities. Other alterations in the modernization of French society and institutions seem to have been anticipated by the reform of the "old regime." Continuities seem as marked as discontinuities.

Nor does the Revolution seem any longer to conform to a grand historical design, preordained by inexorable forces of social change. Instead it seems a thing of contingencies and unforeseen consequences (not least the summoning of the Estates-General itself). An abundance of fine provincial studies has shown that instead of a single Revolution imposed by Paris on the rest of a homogeneous France, it was as often determined by local passions and interests. Along with the revival of place as a conditioner have come people. For as the imperatives of "structure" have weakened, those of individual agency, and especially of revolutionary utterance, have become correspondingly more important.

... I have pressed one of the essential elements in de Tocqueville's argument—his understanding of the destabilizing effects of modernization *before* the Revolution—further than his account allows it to go. Relieved of the revolutionary coinage "old regime," with its heavy semantic freight of obsolescence, it may be possible to see French culture and society in the reign of Louis XVI as troubled more by its addiction to change than by resistance to it. Conversely, it seems to me that much of the anger firing revolutionary violence arose from hostility towards that modernization, rather than from impatience with the speed of its progress.

... [I attempt] to confront directly the painful problem of revolutionary violence. Anxious lest they give way to sensationalism or be confused with counter-revolutionary prosecutors, historians have erred on the side of squeamishness in dealing with this issue. I have returned it to the center of the story since it seems to me that it was not merely an unfortunate by-product of politics, or the disagreeable instrument by which other more virtuous ends were accomplished or vicious ones were thwarted. In some depressingly unavoidable sense, violence *was* the Revolution itself. . . .

⋘⊚⋙

The tenth to the twelfth of March [1793] saw the first stage in the uprising, when spontaneously assembled crowds in villages and *bourgs* attacked the offices and houses of mayors, *juges de paix, procureurs* and dangerously isolated units of the National Guard. The riot at Machecoul was repeated, with less murderous consequences, in Saint-Florent-le-Veil, Sainte-Pazanne, Saint-Hilaire-de-Chaléons and Clisson. The leaders who emerged from this first wave of violence were often, like the gamekeeper and ex-soldier Stofflet, men who had long been identified in their locality with resistance to the revolutionary authorities. Once they had evicted their enemies and taken their weapons, the crowds coalesced with each other, forming processions towards larger towns and snowballing in size as they traveled along the roads.

At this stage, the riots in the Vendée seemed no different from similar antirecruitment riots taking place in many other parts of France from the Calvados in Normandy to the Côte d'Or in Burgundy and the Puy in the southern Massif Central. Some of the worst upheavals occurred north of the Loire in Brittany. But there the government had been so obsessed by the possibility of counter-revolutionary plots, it had in place sufficient force to take rapid and decisive action against the centers of resistance. The Vendée, in contrast, was dangerously depleted of troops. At Challans, for example, there were just two hundred Patriot Guards who had to face more than a thousand insurgents on the twelfth of March. By the time that reinforcements could be provided, the several riots had already fused into a general insurrection. Moreover, even of the fifty thousand republican soldiers who were eventually concentrated in the Vendée by the third week of March, only a tiny proportion—perhaps fewer than two thousand—were veterans of the "line"—the old royal army. The remainder were unseasoned volunteers, badly fed and equipped and, more critically for the situation they faced, extremely apprehensive about the rebels. None of the armies of France in the spring and summer of 1793 showed such propensity to take to panic and break ranks as the *bleus* of the Vendée. Perhaps they feared the fate of the republicans of Machecoul. As it was, many of them were dispersed in small units of fifty or some hundreds, numerous enough to provide a target for the infuriated rebels but not substantial enough to overawe them.

By the time that the Republic understood the gravity of the situation, the rebels had already taken many of the larger centers, in particular Cholet, Chemillé and Fontenay-le-Comte. On the fourteenth of March, Stofflet joined his forces with those attached to another gamekeeper, Tonnelet, and men following the wagoner-vendor Cathelineau. After failing to persuade the republican troops, commanded by the citizen-marquis de Beauveau, to lay down their arms, the rebels overwhelmed the *bleus* in a great barrage of fire, mortally wounding de Beauveau....

* * *

The second half of March brought a steady drumbeat of calamity to republican France. Within the same week, the Convention heard of the defeat at Neerwinden, a further military collapse near Louvain, Custine's abrupt retreat in the Rhineland and the Vendéan uprising. Report after report described Republican armies dissolving on contact with the enemy (especially in the Vendée); volunteers demoralized and disorderly, deserting or taking to their heels; the tricolor trampled in the mud. When Delacroix returned from the Belgian front, he brought with him a gloom as deep and as dark as the weeks before Valmy. French troops had fallen back on Valenciennes, but if that fortress fell, he warned, there was nothing between the Allied armies and Paris. To many deputies, and not just those of the Mountain, there could be only one explanation for this sorry trail of disasters: conspiracy. The commissioners with General Marcé's defeated army in the Vendée accused him of either "the most cowardly ineptness" or, worse, "the most cowardly treason." His son; his second-in-command, Verteuil; and another Verteuil presumed to be *his* son (but in fact a distant relative) were all arrested for being "in treasonable contact with the enemy."...

Faced with this military landslide, the Convention, with very few exceptions, acknowledged that it had to strengthen the powers of the state. Without an effective executive and a coherent chain of command, centrifugal forces would pull France apart. For the first time since the beginning of the Revolution, the legislature set about creating strong organs of central authority authorized to do the Republic's work without endless reference to the "sovereign body." On March 6 it dispatched eighty of its own members (known, from April on, as "representatives on mission") to the departments to ensure compliance with the central government's will. They were, in effect, a revolutionary version of the old royal *intendants,* traveling embodiments of sovereignty. Much of their work was meant to concern itself with judicial and punitive matters. On March 11 a special Revolutionary Tribunal was established in Paris to try suspects accused of counter-revolutionary activities. On March 20, with the rebellions in the Vendée and Brittany in mind, the Convention adopted Cambacérès' proposal giving military courts jurisdiction over anyone who had been employed in public positions (including clergy and nobles) and who was found with the white royalist cockade or fomenting rebellion. If guilty, they were to be shot within twenty-four hours. A day later, every commune in the country was equipped with committees of surveillance and all citizens were encouraged to denounce anyone they suspected of uncertain loyalties. Predictably, the law rapidly became a charter for countless petty dramas of revenge.

Finally, on April 6, it was decided to replace the Committee of General Defense, set up in January as a body of twenty-five to coordinate the work of the several committees of the Convention. In its place was to be a much tighter committee of just nine members, to be known as the Committee of Public Safety....

On October 10 Saint-Just came before the Convention to issue a report in the name of the Committee of Public Safety on the "troubles affecting the state." He took the righteously self-scrutinizing line of declaring that the people had only one enemy, namely the government itself, infected as it was with all sorts of spineless, corrupt and compromised creatures of the old regime. The remedy was unremitting austerity of purpose, implacable punishment for the backsliders and the hypocrites. The charter of the Terror—the Law of Suspects, enacted on September 17, which gave the Committee and its representatives sweeping powers of arrest and punishment over extraordinarily broad categories of people defined as harboring counter-revolutionary designs—should be applied with the utmost rigor. "Between the people and their enemies there can be nothing in common but the sword; we must govern by iron those who cannot be governed by justice; we must oppress the tyrant.... It is impossible for revolutionary laws to be executed unless the government itself is truly revolutionary."...

⚹

The Terror went into action with impressive bureaucratic efficiency. House searches, usually made at night, were extensive and unsparing. All citizens were required to attach to their front doors a notice indicating all residents who lived inside. Entertaining anyone not on that list, even for a single night, was a serious crime. Denunciations poured into the Commission. People were accused of defaming Chalier, of attacking the liberty tree, secreting priests or émigrés, making speculative fortunes and—one of the standard crimes of the year II— writing or uttering *"merde à la république."* From early December the guillotine went into action at a much greater tempo. As in Paris, pride was taken in its mechanical efficiency. On the eleventh of Nivôse, according to the scrupulous accounts kept, thirty-two heads were severed in twenty-five minutes; a week later, twelve heads in just five minutes.

For the most eager Terrorists, though, this was still a messy and inconvenient way of disposing of the political garbage. Citizens in the streets around the place des Terreaux, on the rue Lafont, for example, were complaining about the blood overflowing the drainage ditch that led from beneath the scaffold. A number of the condemned, then, were executed in mass shootings on the Plaine des Brotteaux—the field beside the Rhone where Montgolfier had made his ascent. Yet another ex-actor, Dorfeuille, presided over some of these *mitraillades,* in which as many as sixty prisoners were tied in a line by ropes and shot at with cannon. Those who were not killed outright by the fire were finished off with sabers, bayonets and rifles. On the fourth of December, Dorfeuille wrote to the President of the Convention that a hundred and thirteen inhabitants of "this new Sodom" had been executed on that single day and in those that followed he hoped another four to five hundred would "expiate their crimes with fire and shot."...

By the time that the killings in "Ville-Affranchie" had finished, one thousand nine hundred and five people had met their end....

⋅⟨◉⟩⋅

The violence did not stop, however, with the Terror. Richard Cobb has written eloquently of the waves of the Counter-Terror, especially brutal in the Midi and the Rhone Valley; of anarchic murder gangs picking off selected targets implicated in Jacobinism. Republican officials; army officers; members of departmental administrations; conspicuous militants of the popular societies; and, in the south, Protestant farmers and merchants—all became prey for the *sabreurs* of the year III. Corpses were dumped in front of cafés and inns in the Midi or thrown into the Rhone or Saône. In many areas, the Counter-Terrorists would gather together at an inn as if for a day's hunting, and go off in search of their quarry.

Considerable areas of the country—the Midi and Rhone Valley, Brittany and western Normandy—remained in a virtual state of civil war, though the violence now proceeded in a haphazard, hit-and-run fashion rather than by organized insurrection. The great engines of capitalist prosperity in late eighteenth-century France, the Atlantic and Mediterranean ports, had been broken by antifederalist repression and British naval blockade. When Samuel Romilly returned to Bordeaux during the peace of 1802, he was dismayed to find the docks silent and ghostly and grass growing tall between the flagstones of the quai des Chartrons. Marseille and Lyon only recovered as the Revolution receded and the reorientation of the Bonapartist state towards Italy offered new markets and trade routes....

What had the Revolution accomplished to balance these penalties? Its two great social alterations—the end of the seigneurial regime and the abolition of the guilds—both promised more than they delivered. Though many artisans were undoubtedly happy to be free of the hierarchy of the corporations that constrained their labor and reward, they were, if anything, even more nakedly exposed to the economic inequities that persisted between masters and journeymen. Likewise the abolition of feudalism was more in the way of a legal than a social change and merely completed the evolution from lords to landlords that had been well under way in the old regime. There is no question that peasants were thankful for the end of seigneurial exactions that had imposed a crushing burden of payments on static rural incomes. Equally certainly, they were determined at all costs to oppose their reimposition. But it is hard to say whether the mass of the rural population were measurably better off in 1799 than they had been in 1789. Though the redemption tariff for feudal dues had been abolished outright in 1793, landlords often compensated themselves by various rent strategies that deepened the indebtedness of share-cropping *métayers*. Moreover, the taxes demanded by the Republic—among them the single land tax, the *impot fôncier*—were certainly no lighter than those exacted by the King. Before long the Consulate and Empire would revert to indirect taxes on at least as onerous a scale as under the old regime. All that they were spared, fiscally, were extraordinary poll taxes, including the old *capitation* and the *vingtième*, but this relief was only a consequence of the ever-expanding military frontier. Taxes lifted from the shoulders of the French were now dropped on those of the Italians, Germans and Dutch. When that frontier suddenly retreated in 1814, back to the old limits of the hexagonal *patrie,* the French were stuck with the bill, which, just as in 1789, they adamantly refused to pay, thus sealing the Empire's fate.

Was the world of the village in 1799 so very different from what it had been ten years before? In particular regions of France where there had been heavy emigration and repression, rural life had indeed been emptied of noble dominance. But this obvious rupture disguises a continuity of some importance. It was exactly those sections of the population who had been gaining economically under the old regime that profited most from the sale of noble and church lands. Those sales were declared irreversible, so there was indeed a substantial transfer of wealth. But much of that transfer was *within* the landed classes—extending from well-to-do farmers up to "patriot" nobles who had managed to stay put and actually benefited from the confiscations. Fat cats got fatter.... There were, to be sure, many regions of France where the nobility as a group lost a considerable part of their fortune. But there were also others —in the west, the center and the south—where, as Jean Tulard has shown, lands that remained unsold could be recovered by families who returned in substantial numbers after 1796. Thus, while many of the leading figures in this history ended their lives on the guillotine, many others stayed put and reemerged as the leading notables of their department....

By contrast, the rural poor gained very little at all from the Revolution. Saint-Just's Ventôse laws remained a dead letter and it became harder than ever to pasture animals on common land or gather fuel from the open woods. In all these respects the Revolution was just an interlude in the inexorable modernization of property rights that had been well under way before 1789. No government—that of the Jacobins any more than that of the King—had really answered the cries for help that echoed through the rural *cahiers de doléances* in 1789....

Had the Revolution, at least, created state institutions which resolved the problems that brought down the monarchy? Here, too, as de Tocqueville emphasized, it is easier to discern continuities, especially of centralization, than any overwhelming change. In public finance, the creation of a paper currency came to be recognized as a catastrophe beside which the insolvencies of the old regime looked almost picayune. Eventually the Bonapartist Consultate (whose finances were administered overwhelmingly by surviving bureaucrats of the old regime) returned to a metallic system based on Calonne's important monetary reform of 1785 fixing the ratio of silver to gold. Fiscally, too, post-Jacobin France slid inexorably back to the former mixture of loans and indirect as well as direct taxes. The Republic and Empire did no better funding a large army and navy from these domestic sources than had the monarchy and depended crucially on institutionalized extortion from occupied countries to keep the military pump primed.

The Napoleonic prefects have always been recognized as the heirs of the royal *intendants* (and the revolutionary *représentants-en-mission*), brokering administration between central government priorities and the interest of the local notability. Without any question that notability had suffered a violent shock during the height of the Jacobin Terror, especially in the great provincial cities, where, after the federalist revolt, they were virtually exterminated. The constitution of the year III, however, with its reintroduction of tax qualifications for the electoral assemblies, returned authority to those who had, in many places, exercised it continuously between the mid-1780s and 1792. As we have seen, in some small towns, such as Calais, where adroit mayors paid lip service to passing regimes, there was unbroken continuity of office from 1789 through the Restoration.... For these men and countless others like them, the Revolution had been but a brutal though mercifully ephemeral interruption of their social and institutional power....

What killed the monarchy was its inability to create representative institutions through which the state could execute its program of reform. Had the Revolution done any better? On one level, the succession of elected legislatures, from the Estates-General to the National Convention, was one of the most impressive innovations of the Revolution. They took the intensive debate on the shape of governing institutions in France, which had been going on for at least half a century, into the arena of representation itself and articulated its principles with unparalleled eloquence. But for all their virtues as theaters of debate, none of the legislatures ever managed to solve the issue that had bedeviled the old regime: how to create a viable working partnership between the executive and the legislature? Once the Constituent had rejected Mounier and Mirabeau's "British" proposal of drawing ministers from the assembly, it regarded the executive not as the administration of the country, working in good faith, but as a fifth column bent on subverting national sovereignty. With this doomed beginning, the executive and legislative branches of the constitution of 1791 simply intensified the war with each other until their mutual destruction in 1792. The Terror effectively reversed matters by putting the Convention under the thrall of the committees, but still make it impossible to change governments except by violence.

The framers of the constitution of the year III (1795) obviously learned something from this unhappy experience. A two-chamber legislature was introduced, elected indirectly from colleges in which property was the criterion for membership. A governing council was in theory accountable to the legislature (as indeed the committees had been). In practice, however, the experiment remained darkened by the long shadow of the revolution itself, so that factions inevitably crystallized, not around specific issues of government but plans for the overthrow of the state, hatched either by royalists or neo-Jacobins. With the separate organs of the constitution in paralyzing conflict with each other, violence continued to determine the political direction of the state far more than did elections.

But the violence was, after the year III, no longer coming from the streets and *sections* but from the uniformed army. If one had to look for one indisputable story of transformation in the French Revolution, it would be the creation of the juridical entity of the citizen. But no sooner had this hypothetically free person been invented than his liberties were circumscribed by the police power of the state. This was always done in the name of republican patriotism, but the constraints were no less oppressive for that. Just as Maribeau —and the Robespierre of 1791—had feared, liberties were held hostage to the authority of the warrior state. Though this conclusion might be depressing, it should not really be all that surprising. The Revolution, after all, had begun as a response to a patriotism wounded by the humiliations of the Seven Years' War. It was Vergennes' decision to promote, at the same time, maritime imperialism and continental military power which generated the sense of fiscal panic that overcame the monarchy in its last days. A crucial element—perhaps, indeed, *the* crucial element—in the claim of the revolutionaries of 1789 was that they could better regenerate the *patrie* than could the appointees of the King. From the outset, then, the great continuing strand of militancy was patriotic. Militarized nationalism was not, in some accidental way, the unintended consequence of the French Revolution: it was its heart and soul. It was wholly logical that the multimillionaire inheritors of revolutionary power—the true "new class" of this period of French history—were not some *bourgeoisie conquérante* but *real* conquerors: the Napoleonic marshals, whose fortunes made even those of the surviving dynasts of the nobility look paltry by comparison.

For better or worse, the "modern men" who seemed poised to capture government under Louis XVI—engineers, noble industrialists, scientists, bureaucrats and generals—resumed their march to power once the irritations of revolutionary politics were brushed aside. "*La tragédie, maintenant, c'est la politique,*" claimed Napoleon, who, after the coup d'état that brought him to power in 1799, added his claim to that which had been made by so many optimistic governments before him, that "the Revolution is completed."

At other times, though, he was not so sure. For if he understood that one last achievement of the Revolution had been the creation of a military-technocratic state of immense power and emotional solidarity, he also realized that its *other* principal invention had been a political culture that perennially and directly challenged it. What occurred between 1789 and 1793 was an unprecedented explosion of politics—in speech, print, image and even music—that broke all the barriers that had traditionally circumscribed it. Initially, this had been the monarchy's own doing. For it was in the tens of thousands of little meetings convened to draft *cahiers* and elect deputies to the Estates-General that French men (and occasionally women) found their voice. In so doing, they became part of a process that tied the satisfaction of their immediate wants into the process of redefining sovereignty.

That was both the opportunity and the problem. Suddenly, subjects were told they had become Citizens; an aggregate of subjects held in place by injustice and intimidation had become a Nation. From this new thing, this Nation of Citizens, justice, freedom and plenty could be not only expected but required. By the same token, should it not materialize, only those who had spurned their citizenship, or who were by their birth or unrepentant beliefs incapable of exercising it, could be held responsible. Before the promise of 1789 could be realized, then, it was necessary to root out Uncitizens.

Thus began the cycle of violence which ended in the smoking obelisk and the forest of guillotines. However much the historian, in the year of celebration, may be tempted to see that violence as an unpleasant "aspect" of the Revolution which ought not to distract from its accomplishments, it would be jejune to do so. From the very beginning—from the summer of 1789—violence was the motor of the Revolution. The journalist Loustalot's knowing exploitation of the punitive murder and mutilation of Foulon and Bertier de Sauvigny conceded nothing in its calculated ferocity to the most extreme harangues of Marat and Hébert. *"Il faut du sang pour cimenter la révolution"* (There must be blood to cement revolution), said Mme Roland, who would herself perish by the logical application of her enthusiasm. While it would be grotesque to implicate the generation of 1789 in the kind of hideous atrocities perpetrated under the Terror, it would be equally naive not to recognize that the former made the latter possible. All the newspapers, the revolutionary festivals, the painted plates; the songs and street theater; the regiments of little boys waving their right arms in the air swearing patriotic oaths in piping voices—all these features of what historians have come to designate the "political culture of the Revolution"—were the products of the same morbid preoccupation with the just massacre and the heroic death.

Historians are also much given to distinguishing between "verbal" violence and the real thing. The assumption seems to be that such men as Javogues and Marat, who were given to screaming at people, calling for death, gloating at the spectacle of heads on pikes or processions of men with their hands tied behind their backs climbing the steps to the *rasoir national* were indulging only in brutal rhetoric. The screamers were not to be compared with such quiet bureaucrats of death as Fouquier-Tinville who did their jobs with stolid, silent efficiency. But the history of "Ville-Affranchie," of the Vendée-Vengé, or of the September massacres suggests in fact a direct connection between all that orchestrated or spontaneous screaming for blood and its copious shedding. It contributed greatly to the complete dehumanization of those who became victims. As "brigands" or the "Austrian whore" or "fanatics" they became nonentities in the Nation of Citizens and not only could but had to be eliminated if it was to survive. Humiliation and abuse, then, were not just Jacobin fun and games; they were the prologues to killing.

Why was the French Revolution like this? Why, from the beginning, was it powered by brutality? The question might seem to be circular since if, in fact, reform had been all that had been required, there would have been no Revolution in the first place. The question nonetheless remains important if we are ever to understand why successive generations of those who tried to stabilize its course—Mirabeau, Barnave, Danton—met with such failure. Was it just that French popular culture was already brutalized before the Revolution and responded to the spectacle of terrifying public punishments handed out by royal justice with its own forms of spontaneous sanguinary retribution? That all naive revolutionaries would do, would be to give the people the chance to exact such retribution and make it part of the regular conduct of politics? This may be part of the explanation, but even a cursory look beyond French borders, and especially over the Channel to Britain, makes it difficult to see France as uniquely damaged, either by a more dangerous distance between rich and poor or indeed by higher rates of crime and popular violence, than places which avoided violent revolution.

Popular revolutionary violence was not some sort of boiling subterranean lava that finally forced its way onto the surface of French politics and then proceeded to scald all those who stepped in its way. Perhaps it would be better to think of the revolutionary elite as rash geologists, themselves gouging open great holes in the crust of polite discourse and then feeding the angry matter through the pipes of their rhetoric out into the open. Volcanoes and steam holes do not seem inappropriate metaphors here, because contemporaries were themselves constantly invoking them. Many of those who were to sponsor or become caught up in violent change were fascinated by seismic violence, by the great primordial eruptions which geologists now said were not part of a single Creation, but which happened periodically in geological time. These events were, to borrow from Burke, both sublime and terrible. And it was perhaps Romanticism, with its addiction to the Absolute and the Ideal; its fondness for the vertiginous and the macabre; its concept of political energy, as, above all, electrical; its obsession with the heart; its preference for passion over reason, for virtue over peace, that supplied a crucial ingredient in the mentality of the revolutionary elite: its association of liberty with wildness. What began with Lafayette's infatuation with the hyena of the Gévaudan surely ended in the ceremonies of the pike-stuck heads.

There was another obsession which converged with this Romanticization of violence: the neoclassical fixation with the patriotic death. The annals of Rome (and occasionally the doomed battles of Athens and Sparta) were the mirrors into which revolutionaries constantly gazed in search of self-recognition. Their France would be Rome reborn, but purified by the benison of the feeling heart. It thus followed, surely, that for such a Nation to be born, many would necessarily die. And both the birth and death would be simultaneously beautiful.

POSTSCRIPT

Was the French Revolution Worth Its Human Costs?

In many ways, Schama's book was revolutionary and was considered so by his peers in the historical profession. Covering a subject that had been dominated by Marxists, Annalistes, and social historians, he returned to the domain of the historical narrative as his vehicle of expression, something that had lost favor with many of the French Revolution's leading scholars. Secondly, according to the preface from *Citizens*, Schama's focus was "an unfashionable 'top-down' rather than 'bottom-up' approach." Finally, although a scholar of impeccable credentials, he was considered an outsider in the field of French Revolution historiography because he had not "been a lifetime toiler in the vineyards of the Revolution," according to Alan Spitzer, in "Narrative's Problems: The Case of Simon Schama," *Journal of Modern History* (March 1993).

The most controversial feature of the French Revolution was the infamous Reign of Terror, and it is a subject that all toilers in the garden of the Revolution have to explain. The horrors of this century (some committed in the name of revolution) demand that the Terror gets the fullest treatment possible. Only then can the question of whether or not the Revolution was worth its human costs be answered. As always, the present and the search for relevance in the past will be the final arbiter. If Kropotkin's work speaks to the spirit of the nineteenth century's era of democratic revolutions, Schama's does the same to the dreams deferred and lives lost to that century's failed revolutions.

To list all of sources on the French Revolution is daunting. William Doyle, *The Oxford History of the French Revolution* (Oxford University Press, 1989) and Donald M. G. Sutherland, *France, 1789–1815: Revolution and Counter-Revolution* (Oxford University Press, 1986) are two scholarly, general accounts of the era. As always, much can be learned from Alexis de Tocqueville, whose *Old Regime and the French Revolution*, first published in the 1850s, could be a useful starting point for a study of French Revolutionary historiography. *The French Revolution and the Birth of Modernity* (University of California Press, 1990), edited by Ferenc Fehar, offers a series of essays about the past, present, and future of French Revolutionary historiography. Finally, the 1984 film *Danton*, which deals with the French Revolution and especially the Terror gone mad, is worth seeing.

ISSUE 14

Did British Policy Decisions Cause the Mass Emigration and Land Reforms That Followed the Irish Potato Famine?

YES: Christine Kinealy, from *This Great Calamity: The Irish Famine 1845–52* (Roberts Rinehart, 1995)

NO: Hasia R. Diner, from *Erin's Daughters In America: Irish Immigrant Women in the Nineteenth Century* (Johns Hopkins University Press, 1983)

ISSUE SUMMARY

YES: Christine Kinealy, fellow of the University of Liverpool, argues that the British government's response to the Irish potato famine was deliberately inadequate. The British government's "hidden agenda" of long-term economic, social, and agrarian reform was accelerated by the famine, and mass emigration was a consequence of these changes.

NO: Historian Hasia R. Diner documents large-scale emigration both before and after the Irish potato famine. Diner credits the Irish people with learning from their famine experiences that the reliance of the poor on the potato and the excessive subdivision of land within families were no longer in their own best interests.

$\mathbf{B}$eginning in 1845 a fungal disease repeatedly struck the potato crop of Ireland and was not eradicated until the early 1850s. The failure of the potato harvest in a country with a population of eight million people caused the death of approximately one million and the emigration of another million. On the eve of the famine, two-thirds of the population earned their living by working the land—for the most part land that they did not own. Still, Ireland was able to feed its own people and also to export food to feed two million Britons. During these years, Ireland was part of the United Kingdom, which also included England and Scotland.

Initially the British government responded to the failure of the Irish potato crop by purchasing and storing Indian corn from America, which it later sold to those who could afford to buy it. Unwilling to offer handouts, the British government provided subsidy only to those who entered the workhouses. As the crisis deepened, the government undertook public works projects, such as road and pier construction, to offer the poor a means to earn money. Ultimately it set up a network of soup kitchens.

By 1847, however, the British government transferred responsibility for Ireland's poor to Ireland itself, insisting that outside aid would be available only after local resources were exhausted or if it could be demonstrated that without outside aid people would die. As the blight continued, British aid was provided to the manufacturing districts in the north of England, which were undergoing an economic slump, but not to the Irish.

Prosperous counties in Ireland were less dependent on the potato crop and resented being held exclusively responsible for the financial bailout of the poorest of their neighbors. If Ireland is truly part of the United Kingdom, they argued, all of the United Kingdom should be equally responsible for alleviating the suffering of any of its members.

However, prevailing stereotypes frequently contrasted the "deserving" poor—industrious factory workers in England's manufacturing centers—with the "undeserving" poor—notably the Irish, who were believed to be lazy and without ambition. How much of a role did these prejudices, which appeared regularly in cartoons and print descriptions, play in the neglect that allowed a million people to die and forced another million to emigrate?

Laissez-faire (literally, to leave alone) economic principles, pioneered by British philosopher Adam Smith and others, contends that government should stay out of the regulation of the economy. Without outside manipulation, this theory suggests, the "hidden hand" of economic forces, such as supply and demand, will regulate the economy efficiently. The prevalence of this theory and others concerning the "undeserving" status of the Irish gave the British government solid justification for withholding economic aid to Ireland.

Christine Kinealy faults British government policies for exploiting the chaos of the famine in order to implement what she calls a "hidden agenda." Seeing the failure of the potato crop as a golden opportunity to force conversion of the Irish economy to a more commercial system of agriculture, the British government, Kinealy explains, was able to rid itself of "non-productive elements." These included landless laborers and apathetic landlords. The million Irish who emigrated, along with the million who died, improved the demographics and facilitated modernization of the Irish economy—but at a terrible cost.

Hasia R. Diner sees more continuity than discontinuity in emigration patterns. While the famine may have accelerated this process, the Irish had been moving to other parts of the British Empire and the United States in large numbers at least since the late eighteenth century. Calling the famine the "great convincer," Diner attributes changes in agricultural diversity, land inheritance patterns, and marriage practices to the Irish people themselves, acting on their own behalf as agents of historical change.

Christine Kinealy

 **YES**

This Great Calamity:
The Irish Famine 1845–52

The Famine that affected Ireland from 1845 to 1852 has become an integral part of folk legend. In the popular imagination, the Famine is associated with nationwide suffering, initially triggered by the potato blight, compounded by years of misrule and consolidated by the inadequate response of the British government and Irish landlords alike. The resultant large-scale emigration took the tragedy of the Famine beyond the shores of Ireland to an international stage. Recent scholarly studies of the Famine have attempted to move away from this traditional view. In doing so, a sanitised alternative has emerged that has endeavoured to remove the patina of blame from the authorities involved in providing relief, while minimising the suffering of those who were most directly affected by the loss of the potato crop.

Several specific issues need to be addressed in order to evaluate the varying responses of those in power. At a broad level there are three questions. First, what relief measures were implemented? Second, what were the determinants of the measures that were introduced? Third, and most significantly, how effective were they?

These questions are fundamental to an understanding of the Famine. There is still a widespread view that the Famine relief measures were inadequate. Much of the blame is laid at the door of the British government, and to a lesser degree, Irish landlords. Is this an unfair assessment, especially when seen in the context of the perceived role of government in the middle of the nineteenth century?

Early in the nineteenth century, Ireland was widely regarded as a poor country, dominated by a stagnant subsistence agriculture based substantially upon the ubiquitous potato. On the eve of the Famine, the Irish economy supported a population in excess of eight million people which was large by European standards and represented a sizeable portion of the United Kingdom population as a whole—the population of England and Wales at the same period was approximately sixteen million, and of Scotland, under three million. On the eve of the Famine, the economy of Ireland supported its own population and supplied food for a further two million mouths in Britain. Ireland, therefore, should have been a significant consideration in any social or economic policies that affected the United Kingdom as a whole.

The onset of the Famine was unexpected although partial crop failures and food shortages were not unusual. In 1845, therefore, the potato blight, regardless of the lack of understanding of either its origins or an antidote, was not regarded with undue alarm. Although approximately 50 per cent of the main subsistence crop failed in 1845–6, the consequence of the resultant shortages was not famine, nor did emigration or mortality increase substantially. The role played by the government, local landlords, clerics, and various relief officials was significant in achieving this outcome. The second, more widespread, blight of 1846 marked the real beginning of the Famine. Ominously, the impact of the shortages was apparent in the period immediately following the harvest. Inevitably also, the people undergoing a second year of shortages were far less resilient than they had been twelve months earlier. The government responded to this potentially more serious situation by reducing its involvement in the import of food into the country and by making relief more difficult to obtain.

The distress that followed the 1847 harvest was caused by a small crop and economic dislocation rather than the widespread appearance of blight. The government again changed its relief policy in an attempt to force local resources to support the starving poor within their district. The government professed a belief that this policy was necessary to ensure that a burden which it chose to regard as essentially local should not be forced upon the national finances. This policy underpinned the actions of the government for the remainder of the Famine. The relief of famine was regarded essentially as a local responsibility rather than a national one, let alone an imperial obligation. The special relationship between the constituent parts of the United Kingdom forged by the Act of Union appeared not to extend to periods of shortage and famine.

To what extent was a famine or other disaster inevitable when viewed within the context of the general, and some would say increasing, poverty of Ireland? This assumption of Irish poverty, which underpinned political prescription during the Famine, perhaps owed more to distantly derived dogmas than to the reality. For example, a number of recent studies have suggested that height is a reliable indicator of 'nutritional status' (that is, 'the balance of nutritional intake with growth, work, and the defeat of disease'). Surveys of nineteenth-century British military records indicate that Irish recruits were taller than recruits from the rest of the United Kingdom. This implies a sustained nutritional advantage within Ireland. Also, it is now widely accepted that Ireland's pre-Famine economy was more diverse, vibrant, dynamic and responsive to change than has traditionally been depicted. In contrast to this situation, recent quantitative studies of the British economy have reassessed the impact of industrialisation in the first half of the nineteenth century and concluded that, throughout this period, Britain's economic growth remained 'painfully slow'....

The slump of 1847 was a sharp reminder to the government of the problems on its own doorstep. During the autumn of 1847, news of Irish distress vied increasingly for column space in the English newspapers with stories of hardship, unemployment and bankruptcies in England, notably in Lancashire, the flagship of industrial Britain. Poverty and distress, therefore, were not confined to Ireland but were also evident in one of the wealthiest parts of the British Empire. The demands of the Irish poor were now in direct competition with the demands of the urban poor within Britain. An obvious comparison was drawn between the distress of the feckless Irish peasants and their irresponsible and greedy landlords, with the distress of the hard-working factory operatives and the enterprising entrepreneurs upon whom, it was believed, much of the success of the British Empire rested. Since the reign of Elizabeth I, Poor Law philosophy had drawn a distinction between the 'deserving' and the 'undeserving' poor. The English factory operatives, unemployed through no fault of their own, were regarded as deserving poor; it was apparent that the Irish peasants could be regarded with equal justification as falling into the latter category.

A hardening attitude to Irish distress was illustrated by the response to appeals for additional assistance as a third year of shortages became inevitable. An early indication of a resistant official response occurred in October 1847, when a group of Catholic bishops and archbishops appealed to the government for an increase in official aid. They were informed, in a widely published response, that such a request was unreasonable, particularly as it implied that:

> the means for this relief should be exacted by the government from classes all struggling with difficulties, and at a moment when in England trade and credit are disastrously low, with the immediate prospect of hundreds of thousands being thrown out of employment or being as destitute of the means of existence as the poorest peasant in Ireland.

An appeal for funds in the form of a second 'Queen's Letter' was also published in October 1847 and read out in all churches throughout England. It elicited more criticism than cash.

The government remained committed to the policy of forcing Ireland to depend on its own resources as far as possible, chiefly through the mechanism of the Poor Law. Within the domestic economy, however, the government did depart from its declared *laissez faire* policy and intervened to allow the terms of the 1844 Bank Charter Act to be relaxed in order to aid the industrial sector. By the end of 1847, the financial crisis in Britain was over and a period of prosperity was under way. The Great Exhibition of 1851 was a triumphant demonstration of Britain's international industrial and economic supremacy. In the same year, in a different part of the United Kingdom, the west of Ireland, a portion of the population was about to confront a seventh consecutive year of famine and shortages.

The contribution of outside charitable bodies was mostly confined to the early years of the Famine. By 1847, most of these sources had dried up or, as in the case of the Quakers, they had decided to use their remaining funds to concentrate on long-term improvements rather than immediate relief. Significantly, the Quakers' men on the ground who toured the west of Ireland in the winter of 1846-7 were critical both of absentee landlords and the policies pursued by the British government alike. The British Relief Association, which remained operative after 1847, allowed its funds to be allocated through the medium of the

Treasury. This was not without problems. Count Strzelecki, the Association's local agent, fought a hard battle with the Treasury to ensure that a successful scheme to feed schoolchildren was continued, regardless of the disapproval of [Charles] Trevelyan.

A fundamental policy position of government, enforced rigorously throughout the Famine, as noted earlier, was the determination to make local resources support local distress. The Irish landlords were singled out continually as a group that needed to be reminded of, and occasionally coerced into, undertaking their duties to the poor. Following the 1845 blight, however, the money contributed voluntarily by the landlords and other subscribers was the highest amount ever raised. Regardless of this achievement, the Irish contribution was represented as derisory and the landlords increasingly targeted as the object of public opprobrium. Irish landlords undoubtedly provided an easy and obvious scapegoat both as a cause of, and as contributors to, the Famine. This was a view taken both by their contemporaries and by some later historians....

To what extent, however, can any individual group, organisation or state body be blamed for the degree of suffering that resulted from successive years of potato blight? Would the outcome of the years of shortages and suffering have been different if the response of the authorities, various charitable organisations, and other key individuals to successive years of blight had been different?

There is no doubt that the part played by the government was pivotal within the whole relief endeavour. Was it, however, within the remit of the government—either ideologically or financially—to provide sufficient relief to keep suffering, emigration, and mortality to a minimum level? The policies of the government, and the way in which it perceived its role, are crucial to an understanding of the Famine years. The changing perceptions and strategies of the British government determined the type of relief provided and the methods and timing of its allocation. The role played by the Treasury, both in implementing the various relief policies and in advising the government, was critical. Charles Wood, the Chancellor of the Exchequer, together with his colleague, Charles Trevelyan, represented a school of economic orthodoxy which advocated both non-intervention and fiscal rectitude. A populist version of their views found a wider audience in the columns of *The Times* and the cartoons of *Punch*. It was also supported in the learned contributions to the *Edinburgh Review* and the fledgling *Economist*. In the wake of the financial and monetary crisis of 1847, the demand for retrenchment was also welcomed by a politically influential industrial middle class. The Treasury, in effect, became not only the guardian of the relief purse, but—mainly due to the energetic and prolonged involvement of Charles Trevelyan—was increasingly deferred to by members of the government as the oracle of all wisdom regarding Ireland. Although no one person can be blamed for the deficiencies of the relief policies, Trevelyan perhaps more than any other individual represented a system of response which increasingly was a mixture of minimal relief, punitive qualifying criteria, and social reform.

The Treasury's agenda for Irish relief went far beyond the mere allocation of government funds. Its imprint was evident throughout both the public and private sectors. Not only did it arbitrate on the crucial issue of who deserved to be given financial support and how much they should receive, but increasingly it attempted to control the day-to-day administration of relief. No other organisation played such a sustained role or showed such an obvious interest in the affairs of Ireland. The government, which was in the midst of a foreign crisis, an economic depression, and a year of revolutions and uprisings in Europe which extended both to Britain and Ireland, was no doubt glad to be able to allow the Treasury to shoulder such a large portion of the Irish relief burden. Also, despite evidence to the contrary, many officials, including even the well-informed Trevelyan, publicly declared the Famine to be over in 1848. The problems of Ireland, therefore, were necessarily a low priority to a government at the centre of a large and still expanding Empire. However, by allowing the Treasury to play such a pivotal role in the provision of relief, it was perhaps inevitable that the need to 'balance the books'—an excellent objective in Treasury terms—should at times overshadow the need to provide adequate relief. By using the Treasury in such a capacity, its role far exceeded that of guardian of the public purse and extended both to influencing public policy and, even more significantly, to final arbitrator in the provision of relief....

The Famine was a disaster of major proportions, even allowing for an inevitable statistical uncertainty on its estimated effect on mortality. Yet the Famine occurred in a country which, despite concurrent economic problems, was at the centre of a still-growing empire and was an integral part of the acknowledged workshop of the world. There can be no doubt that despite a short-term cyclical depression, the combined resources of the United Kingdom could either completely or much more substantially have removed the consequences of consecutive years of potato blight in Ireland. This remains true even if one accepts Trevelyan's proud assertion that no government had done more to support its poor than Britain had done during the Famine years. The statement implies that not only was enough done to help the suffering people in Ireland, but that it was accompanied by a generosity that patently is not borne out by the evidence. To have fed in excess of three million people in the summer of 1847 was a worthy and notable achievement. It also dispels the frequent assertion that the British government did not possess the administrative capability to feed such a large number of starving people. But if the measure of success is judged by the crudest yet most telling of all measures—that of mortality—the British government failed a large portion of the population in terms of humanitarian criteria.

In this context, Trevelyan's comment reveals the separateness of Ireland from the rest of the United Kingdom. His perception mocked the precepts of the Act of Union. It should not, however, be forgotten that the government and the Treasury had to provide a system of relief that would satisfy both parliamentary and public opinion. If measured by this criterion alone—accepting, however, the individual criticisms of the opposition party—the relief measures were undoubtedly regarded as successful, and to some, even over-generous.

The policies of the government increasingly specified criteria that disallowed external assistance until distress was considerable and evident. The leitmotif of relief provided by the central government throughout the course of the Famine was that assistance would be provided only when it—or, in fact, its agent, the Treasury—was satisfied that local resources were exhausted, or that if aid was not provided, the distressed people would die. By implementing a policy which insisted that local resources must be exhausted before an external agency would intervene, and pursuing this policy vigorously despite local advice to the contrary, the government made suffering an unavoidable consequence of the various relief systems which it introduced. The suffering was exacerbated by the frequent delays in the provision of relief even after it had been granted and by the small quantity of relief provided, which was also of low nutritional value. By treating the Famine as, in essence, a local problem requiring a local response, the government was, in fact, penalising those areas which had the fewest resources to meet the distress.

The government response to the Famine was cautious, measured and frequently parsimonious, both with regard to immediate need and in relation to the long-term welfare of that portion of the population whose livelihood had been wiped out by successive years of potato blight. Nor could the government pretend ignorance of the nature and extent of human tragedy that unfolded in Ireland following the appearance of blight. The Irish Executive and the Poor Law Commissioners sent regular, detailed reports of conditions within the localities and increasingly requested that even more extensive relief be provided. In addition, Trevelyan employed his own independent sources of information on local conditions, by-passing the existing official sources of the Lord Lieutenant. This information revealed the extent of deprivation caused by the Famine. It also showed the regional variations arising from the loss of the potato crop; and it exposed the inability of some areas to compensate for such losses from their own internal resources. There was no shortage of detailed and up-to-date information. What was crucial was the way in which the government used this information.

While it was evident that the government had to do something to help alleviate the suffering, the particular nature of the actual response, especially following 1846, suggests a more covert agenda and motivation. As the Famine progressed, it became apparent that the government was using its information not merely to help it formulate its relief policies but also as an opportunity to facilitate various long-desired changes within Ireland. These included population control and the consolidation of property through a variety of means, including emigration, the elimination of small holdings, and the sale of large but bankrupt estates. This was a pervasive and powerful 'hidden agenda'. The government measured the success of its relief policies by the changes which were brought about in Ireland rather than by the quality of relief provided *per se*. The public declaration of the Census Commissioners in the Report of the 1851 Census, which stated that Ireland had benefited from the changes brought about by the Famine, is a clear example of this....

The response of [Whig leader Lord John] Russell's government to the Famine combined opportunism, arrogance and cynicism, deployed in such a way as to facilitate the long-standing ambition to secure a reform of Ireland's economy. In the midst of dealing with a famine in Ireland, increasing reference was made to the need to restructure agriculture in Ireland from the top to the bottom. This had been the ambition of a succession of governments prior to

1845, but the Famine provided a real opportunity to bring about such a purpose both quickly and, most importantly, cheaply.

In the early decades of the nineteenth century, for example, state-sponsored emigration had been recommended by select committees, social theorists and government advisors alike, all of whom agreed that it would be beneficial to Ireland; but the government had refused to involve itself in the additional expenditure that an active pursuit of this policy would involve. The Famine, however, gave the impetus to emigration to flourish, without imposing an additional financial burden on the government. It, therefore, provided opportunities for change. The Whig administration, through legislation such as the Quarter-Acre Clause and the Encumbered Estates Acts, ensured that such opportunities were not wasted.

If the potato blight had been confined to 1845, its impact would have been insignificant and it would have been remembered only as one of the many intermittent subsistence crises which affected Ireland and all agricultural societies. Even though over half of the crop was lost through blight in 1845, the increase in excess mortality and emigration was insignificant. In 1845–6, as had so clearly been demonstrated in the subsistence crisis of 1782–4, if the political and social will existed, a subsistence crisis did not necessarily have to become a famine.

In the 1840s, the policy of the British government was shaped by a prevailing economic dogma, inspired by a particular interpretation of free market economics. The champions of this philosophy were Adam Smith and his successors such as Nassau Senior and Harriet Martineau. In the context of providing poor relief in Ireland, this influential philosophy decreed that ultimately such relief was damaging and that genuine improvements could be achieved only through self-help. In its more extreme form, the principles embodied in this dogma denied any government responsibility for the alleviation of distress. Proponents of such theories even managed to suggest that during periods of extraordinary distress it could be better for those affected not to have access to extraneous relief lest the self-righting mechanisms of the economic system—the allegedly ubiquitous yet truly imperceptible 'invisible hand'—became ensnared by unwarranted interference. The outcome of a slavish adherence to these self-adjusting mechanisms would inevitably be human suffering. Yet this appeared to be of little consequence to those who worshipped at the altar of *laissez faire*. Short-term suffering appeared to be a small price to be paid for long-term improvement, especially if the theoreticians did not have to participate directly in the experiment.

Despite the fashionable adherence to these theories at the time of the Famine, they were only one of the many influences upon political decision-making. It is clear that such theoretical dogma could be dismissed when prevailing pressures demanded: the intervention by the government in the autumn of 1847 to alleviate the impact of a slump in the manufacturing districts of England providing a concurrent example. The philosophy of non-interference was in practice employed selectively and pragmatically. Its content and application changed as the government considered necessary. Within the Whig government itself, there existed differences of opinion regarding the level of financial intervention in Ireland. Significantly, those who favoured a minimalist approach, spearheaded by the men at the Treasury, were in the ascendant. Nevertheless, during the crucial period in the provision of Famine relief, that is, after the complete devastation of the potato crop in 1846, there is no doubt that this economic theory had powerful public support and, more significantly, enjoyed a popular appeal among many of the ruling elite, particularly those most directly responsible for determining the extent and means of providing relief.

From the perspective of a political response to the Famine, the most substantial deviation from the purist theories of free market economics came about in Ireland itself. This deviation was motivated by the less than purist desire to seek a major reform of the Irish economy, especially in the 'potato economy' districts in the west. In these areas, the free market clearly had failed to deliver spontaneously the desired result, particularly in terms of larger, more efficient holdings, and the British government chose to use the Famine as a means of facilitating and imposing their own reforms. The Famine provided a unique opportunity to bring about long-term structural changes in Ireland's agrarian sector.

During the latter part of the Famine, notably following the transfer of relief to local responsibility through the mechanism of the Poor Law in the autumn of 1847, a 'hidden agenda' of reform is increasingly apparent. Much of this was covert. The government and its agents were not willing to admit openly that the suffering of many people in Ireland, and the consequent high levels of mortality and emigration, was being employed to achieve other purposes. The government was able to use the chaos caused by the Famine to facilitate a number of social and economic changes. In particular, it took the opportunity to bring about a more commercial system of farming within Ireland which no longer would offer refuge to a variety of non-productive elements—whether they were landless labourers or apathetic landlords. If, due to its ultimate aim, this policy could be judged as altruistic, its implementation, based on the prevailing view of the Irish, cannot be. Irish peasants, feckless and indolent as they were perceived to be, were judged less 'worthy' to receive relief than their counterparts in Britain. One consequence of this perception occurred in 1846 when Ireland was not allowed to receive imports of food until supplies had been delivered to Scotland first....

In conclusion, therefore, the response of the British government to the Famine was inadequate in terms of humanitarian criteria and, increasingly after 1847, systematically and deliberately so. The localised shortages that followed the blight of 1845 were adequately dealt with but, as the shortages became more widespread, the government retrenched. With the short-lived exception of the soup kitchens, access to relief—or even more importantly, access to food —became more restricted. That the response illustrated a view of Ireland and its people as distant and marginal is hard to deny. What, perhaps, is more surprising is that a group of officials and their non-elected advisors were able to dominate government policy to such a great extent. This relatively small group of people, taking advantage of a passive establishment, and public opinion which was opposed to further financial aid for Ireland, were able to manipulate a theory of free enterprise, thus allowing a massive social injustice to be perpetrated within a part of the United Kingdom. There was no shortage of resources to avoid the tragedy of a Famine. Within Ireland itself, there were substantial resources of food which, had the political will existed, could have been diverted, even as a short-term measure, to supply a starving people. Instead, the government pursued the objective of economic, social and agrarian reform as a long-term aim, although the price paid for this ultimately elusive goal was privation, disease, emigration, mortality and an enduring legacy of disenchantment.

Hasia R. Diner

Where They Came From

If poverty, persecution, and violence seem to have been eternal elements of Irish life, changes in the economic and social structure nonetheless did occur.... Historians love watersheds: dramatic incidents that set off one epoch from another; major upheavals that loom as signposts along the historic path. The Great Famine of the late 1840s has generally been considered the event in Irish history which sent shock waves throughout Irish society, whose reverberations could be felt around the world, in Boston, London, Toronto, Sydney, and Melbourne, and whose intensity lasted over a century. Nothing remained the same after the devastation of the Famine. The harrowing memory of the starvation, disease, and destruction that engulfed Ireland after the potato blights of 1845–49 altered all relationships; the footing between landlord and tenant changed, as did that between priest and parishioner. The ruler and the ruled shifted ground as they faced each other. Entire classes of people disappeared. The Famine signaled the demise of the Irish cottier class, that landless mass on the lowest stratum of the social structure.

Sheer numbers also confirm the brutal impact of the Famine. After the four years of continuous blight on the potato crop, the Irish staff of life, at least one million people had vanished. Some were felled by starvation, typhus, and dysentery. In the same year three million were reduced to charity. Others fled the Emerald Isle. The Famine's shadow seems to have left no one untouched. The memory of the starvation and what was considered the inaction of the British (some saw it as pure malice) would, over the course of the next century, become a major weapon of nationalist propaganda. Irish journalists, poets, novelists, and playwrights would constantly cull the maudlin scenes of those years for pathetic and gripping material. Father Theobald Matthew, who led Ireland's highly popular temperance movement in the 1870s, invoked such wrenching scenes in sermon after sermon:

> There, admist the chilling damp of a dismal hovel see yon famine-stricken fellow-creature; see him extended on his scanty bed of rotten straw; see his once manly frame, that labour had strengthened with vigour, shrunk to a skeleton; see his once ruddy complexion, the gift of temperance, changed by hunger and concomitant disease to a shallow ghastly hue. See him extend

his yellow withering arm for assistance; hear how he cries out in agony for food, for since yesterday he has not even moistened his lips!

Who could forget the vision of a strange and fearful sight like what we read of in beleaguered cities; its streets crowded with gaunt wanderers, sauntering to and from with hopeless air and hunger-struck look—a mob of starved, almost naked women around the poor-house clamoring for soup tickets.

People around the world gasped at the horrors of the Famine. Relief poured in. Generous Americans collected money to send food to Ireland's starving millions. American magazine readers were fed a constant diet of grim details about "a widow with two children who for a week had eaten nothing but cabbage.... Another woman with two children, and not far from being confined again, stated that during the last week they had existed upon two quarts of meal and two heads of cabbage... famine was written in the faces of this woman and her children."

Intimate relationships between men and women, husbands and wives, parents and children, brothers and sisters, were not exempted from this massive restructuring of life. The qualities of personal ties and social bonds were swept away by the Famine's blast. The 1851 Census of Ireland surveyed the ruin of the countryside and lamented that

> the closest ties of kinship were dissolved; the most ancient and long cher-
> ished usages of the people were disregarded; the once proverbial gaiety
> and lightheartedness of the peasant people seemed to have vanished com-
> pletely, and village merriment or marriage festival was no longer heard or
> seen throughout the regions desolated by the intensity and extent of the .
> Famine....

The watershed approach does have its pitfalls. Few of the changes that occurred after the cataclysm were totally unrelated to the nature of the earlier society. The great upheaval merely accentuated trends that had begun earlier and ac-celerated forces unleashed in more tranquil and stable times. For example, the great upsurge in religiosity that occurred in post-Famine Ireland, the devotional revolution with its tremendous growth in both the number and the power of the clergy, swept a society that was religiously oriented to begin with. Reli-gion had been a powerful political identity for a long time, and the priest, the *soggarth aroon*, had long held a cherished place in the hearts of the masses.

So, too, the trends in Irish demography—a constantly decreasing popu-lation with late and infrequent marriage and high rates of celibacy, a social environment of gender segregation and reluctant sexuality, the concomitant ethic of intense gender animosity—had roots that reached far back into Irish folk life and characterized some classes in the pre-Famine structure. Yet after the Famine these elements came to be synonymous with all of Irish culture and these trends became the norm of Irish behavior. Similarly, the Famine did not cause the massive emigrations. For one thing, the Famine of the late 1840s was not the first to ravage Ireland in modern times. In 1800, 1807, 1816, 1822, and 1839 massive crop failures and wide-ranging epidemics had shaken up the rural Irish. Immigration had in fact begun before the Famine and it continued well afterwards. At least seven hundred thousand people abandoned the thirty-two counties of Ireland between 1825 and 1844. As early as 1841 a half million Irish-born men and women had decided to settle permanently in England and Scotland, while in the same year over ten thousand new arrivals to the port of Boston listed Ireland as their birthplace. In the 1831–41 decade a half million Irish emigrated. Long after the Great Famine had become a memory and a closed chapter of Ireland's sorrowful history, twentieth-century Ireland continued to send its young men and women around the world, making people Ireland's chief export.

The legacy of the Famine as it shaped emigration to the United States, and particularly as it stimulated a massive female exodus, involved a demographic transition and an alteration in family relations much more subtle than millions of individuals merely fleeing their native land. Drawing upon older Irish traditions and social trends associated with the more stable classes in pre-Famine society, Ireland became a country that held out fewer and fewer attractions to women. By the last decades of the nineteenth century many young women had no reason to remain in the agricultural towns of Catholic Ireland. They had no realistic chances for marriage or employment. For Irish women to attain either, they had to turn their backs on the land of their birth.

Ireland became the Western world's most dramatic and stark example of a demographic pattern associated with the shift from traditional to modern societies. Ireland led the world by the 1870s as the nation with the latest age of marriage. Irish men and women decided more frequently than men and women elsewhere to eschew marriage and live out their lives in a single state. Ireland was, in fact, one of the only countries in Europe to enter the twentieth century unconcerned about overpopulation, because decades earlier it had achieved more than "zero population growth." This, however, had not always been the case. Before the Great Famine, more likely than not an Irish peasant or laborer married young. Until the decade of the Famine Irish population figures had risen with alarming rapidity. Ireland's mushrooming—perhaps, more appropriately, exploding—population had, in fact, provided Thomas Malthus with his gloomiest example of the improvidence of the poor and the inexorable cycle whereby population grew far out of proportion to resources.

A large and controversial body of demographic literature has attempted to explain how this happened. The issues in the analysis of Irish population trends are clouded by the difficulty of obtaining accurate statistics on just how many births and deaths occurred in any given year before 1864, when compulsory registration of nationwide vital statistics was enacted. The first official head count of any kind was made in 1821, and that of 1841 is considered the first that approached reliability. Generally, it is accepted by demographers and historians that the 1821 Census counted fewer people than actually existed, whereas the 1831 count overstated the number. Despite the technical problems of portraying

Irish demographic movement, scholars and commentators on the Irish scene have sought to come to terms with the ways in which the population changed and why. The impact of the Great Famine is central to this endeavor, and from it we can begin to discern the nature of women's lives in Irish society.

On the eve of the Famine, over eight million people inhabited Ireland. Fifty years later the same island had been home to fewer than three million. This tremendous growth occurred without any industrialization or increase in economic opportunities and without any influx of foreigners. In fact, this staggering proliferation occurred while emigration had already become an established part of life. Over four hundred thousand Irish-born men and women lived in Great Britain in 1841, whereas between 1780 and 1845 more than one million Irish had made their way to the United States and Canada. Thus, despite a continuous stream of Irish leaving Ireland in this same half century, the rate of population increase constituted a major demographic revolution.

One strand of analysis which attempts to explain Irish population dynamics focuses on diet—on the impact of the lowly potato on mortality and fertility trends. The potato culture, which gradually came to characterize all Ireland, triggered a constant and seemingly unending process by which the land was broken into smaller and smaller holdings. Widespread was "the general practice with farmers to divide their land into portions, which were given to their children as they got married. The last married frequently got his father's cabin along with his portion of the ground, and there the parents liked to stop feeling attached to the place where they spent their lives." The fleshy tuber could be grown anywhere, even on the most miniscule of plots, and contained just enough nutrients to sustain the life of the poor.

As the Irish had become potato-eaters by the end of the eighteenth century, they also had become early marriers. The poor, in particular, saw no reason not to marry spontaneously, that is, without protracted negotiations between families, and certainly without the aid of a matchmaker. Young men and women married when they wanted, and since they could always grow potatoes, a family of hungry mouths was not a burden. A priest from Mayo generalized to the Commission of Inquiry on the Irish Poor in 1836 that "small holders are induced to marry by feeling that their condition cannot be made worse, or rather, they know they can lose nothing, and they promise themselves some pleasure in the society of a wife." This testimony typified the statements that were offered by the clerics and laymen alike to the commission, to the Devon Commission, which met in 1841, and to other, similar bodies. One man in County Galway confessed in 1835, "if I had been a blanket to cover her, I would marry the woman I liked; and if I should get potatoes enough to put into my children's mouths, I would be as happy and content as any man." Similarly, very few Irish men and women did not marry. The nature of the economy and the social structure left very little room for the unattached adult. Within marriage, fertility was high. There was no incentive for, or seeming interest in, contraception of any kind as there was in France at the same time. Some scholars even argue that, by providing a cheap and easily cultivated source of nutrition, the potato improved the health of women and gradually led to heightened fertility.

Even before the Famine this pattern of early and improvident marriage characterized the depressed peasants—the cottiers and the poor laborers—much more than any other class. Townspeople, tradesmen, and farmers with more than a potato plot demonstrated greater reticence about marriage. For those with hope of economic stability and with aspirations for a more "middle-class" kind of existence improvident marriage could spell disaster. Marrying too young meant the expense of feeding and clothing a family too soon. Marrying too young was clearly associated with the reckless behavior of the poor, who inched closer and closer to doom as they subdivided and resubdivided their possessions.

A County Kilkenny observer noted that "those who are a grade above the cottier are more cautious as to marriage, and it is chiefly among small farmers that you will find bachelors." Similarly, in County Limerick one could have found "a greater proportionate number of unmarried men amongst the farmers and tradesmen than amongst the lowest classes of agricultural labourers." This same phenomenon could be plotted geographically. In the wealthier and more fertile East, which supported the cultivation of grains as well as potatoes, people generally married later than in the poverty-stricken West, which was home for the most destitute of laborers and cottiers. Thus, even in the early nineteenth-century, when Irish population grew rapidly, the growth was clustered in the bottom classes.

The late- and nonmarriers of "higher" social status in Irish society provided the link between the pre- and post-Famine eras of Irish history. They undermine the more dramatic interpretation that sees the Famine as the central and defining event in Ireland's development. It is in part because of these more prosperous farmers that the rapid population growth had actually begun to slacken by 1821, and the 1831 Census registered a marked increase in the number of nonmarried adults. What the Famine did accomplish was to dramatically universalize trends that were already in operation. This happened in a number of ways. In the first place, the Famine could claim grim responsibility for the almost total elimination of the cottier class. Second, the memory of the Famine impressed the British lawmakers enough in the succeeding decades to enact legislation that outlawed subdivision and other practices associated with pre-Famine agriculture, thus transforming most Irish men into holders of small, although viable, farms.

The Famine might also be seen as the great convincer. It demonstrated to all the folly of agrarian practices that defined a postage-stamp-size piece of land as enough just because it brought forth potatoes. Irish agriculture was going to have to become much more diversified, and though potatoes could remain a central dish on the Irish family's table, that same farm family would also have to produce a cash crop as well as butter, eggs, and other dairy products for markets. The Famine also demonstrated to Irish parents that no one prospered if they cut up their holdings into equal portions for all their sons. An inheritance came to be the entire holding or nothing. Similarly, the Famine also convinced Irish men and women that early marriage was reckless marriage; that nonmarriage was an option, too. As the Irish changed their marriage patterns, they basically adapted the behavior of the more economically stable elements in the society, convinced that the devastation and destruction of the late 1840s had in part been caused by irrational, carefree marriage and family practices that failed to treat conjugal life as a fundamentally economic enterprise.

Whereas before the Famine commentators on Irish life—Catholic clergymen, economists, and British officials alike—lamented the reckless marriage patterns that seemed to accompany the Irish descent into poverty and destitution, after the Famine concern mounted that the Irish in Ireland were increasingly uninterested in remaining at home, marrying, and reproducing themselves. In 1902 one writer mourned, "In saying all this we are fully alive to the sadness of seeing a grand old race disappear as it were, off the face of the earth." Richard J. Kelly in 1904 shared this pessimism with readers of the *New Ireland Review* and chided the experts. "Economists, so-called, read lessons to us on our over-population and improvident early marriages and, as they said, consequent wretchedness. But they can no longer, with any regard for truth say so now, with a smaller population, lower marriage and a lower birth rate than most countries in Europe." Descriptions of Irish life in the last decades of the century all stressed the gloom of decay, the moribund quiet of a society in decline, although perhaps a decline accompanied by increasing prosperity. A magistrate of County Meath saw his home as

> one of the most melancholy counties I know. This grass grown road, over which seemingly little, if any, traffic passes, is a type of solitude everywhere found. Tillage there is none; but in its stead one vast expanse of pasture land extends. Human habitations are rarer than the bare walls of roofless cottages. Where once a population dwelt, and as consequence, see how lonely and untrodden are these roads.

Census figures painfully recorded the dwindling of Irish numbers. In the fifty years between 1841 and 1891, Ireland lost 3,470,374 residents, plummeting from the pre-Famine population of 8,175,124 in 1841 to 4,704,750 in 1891. Constant migration picked off many of these Irish men and women, but migration could not alone be blamed. The decline in Irish population stemmed most fundamentally from a change in family life and a major demographic shift. There were, to be sure, bad harvests in the last half of the nineteenth century which took their toll, somewhat reminiscent of the Famine, but they lacked the bite of the 1840s devastation.

The bulk of the late-nineteenth-century population decline occurred in the rural areas, siphoning off the residents of farm regions much more rapidly than residents of towns. Ireland was becoming somewhat less overwhelmingly rural in the last half of the century. In 1841 only 17 percent of the population was urban; by 1891 over one-quarter of all the Irish could be found in cities like Dublin and Cork. Even the urban population of the country slumped, however, falling from over a million city dwellers in 1841 to eight hundred thousand in 1891. Only Dublin grew in that same time period, but that growth was hardly dramatic and clearly indicated the stagnation of Irish population and the absence of any industrial development or commercial rejuvenation to draw discontented farm people into the cities. Ireland had basically become a nogrowth nation. It had no urban-industrial attractions to stimulate a massive internal movement. It had in fact become a nation characterized by late and reluctant marriage as well as by a massive voluntary exodus.

In the early 1840s, before the Famine shocked and convinced the Irish out of impoverished, although perhaps comfortable, ways, the rate of marriage was 7.0–8.0 per thousand per year. It bore a close resemblance to the rate of marriage throughout Europe. From 1868, four years after compulsory registration of vital statistics, to 1870 the rate of marriage spiraled down to 5.1 per thousand and then fell to 4.0 in the years 1881–90. Clearly, in any given year or span of years during the second half of the century fewer Irish men and women were setting up families than in years past. Many were merely deferring, that is, they were marrying later than they might have in earlier periods. In 1864, for example, 18.1 percent of all women who married were under twenty-one. In 1911 only 5.3 percent entered marriage by that age. Similarly, in 1864 71.1 percent of all wives in a first marriage were under twenty-five; in 1911 only 51.1 percent were similarly situated. But Ireland also came to be the home of large numbers of men and women who just chose not to marry or who were unable to. In 1861, 11 percent of all men in Ireland sixty-five or over were permanent bachelors; in 1926 that figure had risen to 26 percent. Again using 1841, or the last pre-Famine census, as the point of contrast, the percentage of women age twenty-five or thirty-four who were single in Ireland went from 28 percent to 39 percent in 1851. It did not change in 1891. Although fewer Irish women continued to be unmarried as they approached old age, among women forty-five to fifty-four the number of singles also increased from 12 percent in 1841 to 17 percent in 1891. Figures for men were significantly higher in both age categories, in all years. No longer did Irish society live under the specter of the impetuous young rushing off emotionally to marry and set up homes.

Not surprisingly, this matrimonial trend occurred in tandem with yet another development that characterized post-Famine Irish society. Parents increasingly became reluctant to subdivide their land among heirs, and Ireland as a whole came to have fewer and fewer holdings. In 1841, for example, there were 691,000 holdings in all of Ireland, the largest percentage being the smallest holdings, one to five acres. In 1861, 568,000 estates were primarily of the five- to fifteen-acre size, whereas in 1891 the number of holdings declined to 469,000, most of them over thirty acres. Evictions certainly help account for this trend toward land accretion. The poorest could no longer hold onto their tiny plots, and consolidation in Ireland became the basic trend. The cottiers were gone and increasingly the middling Irish farmer had control of a reasonably viable piece of land, which was to be used for pasture-farming, not for tillage.

These middling Irish farmers either had survived the Famine themselves or their parents had witnessed the harrowing devastation, commonly attributed to the wrath of God, or to the heartlessness of the Saxon ruler, or, importantly, to the impetuous romanticism of the poor. The middling Irish farmers were *not* going to err again. They were not going to find themselves in the same position as had the Irish in the 1840s. To ensure their continuous survival without want and destitution they finally sought to shake off the yoke of British rule. To ensure their continued survival with a degree of material comfort and security they sought to establish families that enhanced their economic needs. Land and the economic security it brought became obsessions with the Irish. A folk proverb suggested, "Let any man go down to hell and open an Irish man's heart... the first thing writ across it was land."

Whereas there is no agreement in sight for the lively and sparring scholarly debate over the cause of the pre-Famine population growth, there is unanimity as to the nature of post-Famine marriage: what it was and why it developed into a more discriminate and rationalized institution. Marriages were based now on economic calculation with parents figuring and weighing the financial benefits and liabilities of their children's marital futures. Land would not be divided. An estate would pass intact and undisturbed from one generation to another. Therefore, only one member of the family's younger generation could hope to inherit the land. No systematic or established pattern developed which designated that single heir. Primogeniture was not the rule, nor was the younger son the immediately designated heir. Who inherited the land became the decision of father and mother and they made that decision as late in their lives as possible. Parents held onto control of their fields until well into old age. (Interestingly, Ireland had among Europe's most impressive statistics on longevity.) At the same time they tenaciously held onto control of their children's futures.

POSTSCRIPT

Did British Policy Decisions Cause the Mass Emigration and Land Reforms That Followed the Irish Potato Famine?

Ireland's leading economist, Cormac O'Grada, studies famine folklore, the limitations of medical science, the selection of who would emigrate (many through landlord-funded programs) and who would not, and even the role of the weather in intensifying the famine in *Black '47 and Beyond: The Great Irish Famine in History, Economy, and Memory* (Princeton University Press, 1999). This interdisciplinary work looks at stories and songs that suggest what it was like to live during famine times, explores the impact of famine-related diseases on the city of Dublin, and follows one group of emigrants to New York City's Sixth Ward. *Emigrants and Exiles: Ireland and the Irish Exodus to North America* (Oxford University Press, 1985) by Kerby A. Miller documents both pre- and post-famine exoduses and explores the traditional Irish Catholic worldview that led the Irish to regard themselves as involuntary "exiles."

The Great Irish Famine, edited by Cathal Poirteir and produced in association with Irish Television (Radio Telefis Eireann), has an especially interesting essay by Peter Gray on "Ideology and the Famine," which explores anti-Irish prejudice, the influence of economic theories on British policy, and the reality of political considerations. Two television series have explored this topic: *The Great Famine,* produced by Arts & Entertainment Television Networks (A&E) and *Ireland: A History,* produced by the British Broadcasting Company and Radio Telefis Eireann (BBC/RTE). Accompanying the latter is a well-illustrated book of the same title by Robert Kee (Sphere Books Ltd., 1982). A similar "you are there" feeling is available in *Famine Diary* (Irish Academic Press, 1999) by Brendan O'Cathaoir, author of *The Irish Times* column of the same name. It features longer, unabridged accounts from newspapers, official correspondence, and diaries.

The 150th anniversary of the beginning of the potato famine has sparked a scholarly reassessment of the traditional interpretation that focused on nationwide suffering, years of misrule, and inadequate responses from both the British government and Irish landlords. Revisionist interpretations have tended to minimize the degree of suffering and are reluctant to blame the authorities for the crisis. Works such as the YES selection by Kinealy are, in part, a response to what can be viewed as a "sanitized" version of the potato famine that trivializes the catastrophe and fails to acknowledge its causes.

On the Internet ...

Military History: World War I (1914–1918)

This site is dedicated to World War I, featuring links to many related subjects, including trench warfare, the Versailles Treaty, individual countries' participation, and lost poets of the war.

`http://wps.cfc.dnd.ca/links/milhist/wwi.html`

Russia on the Web

In addition to the many other links on this comoprehensive site, click on "History" for a variety of topics related to Russian history, including Mikhail Gorbachev's home page and Russian studies on the Internet, which lists sites related to Russian history and culture.

`http://www.valley.net/~transnat/`

World War II Commemoration

The World War II Commemoration site provides information on a number of subjects related to the war, including the story of the war, biographies and articles, air combat films, photographs, and World War II links to other Web sites. Also included is a 25-question test on World War II.

`http://gi.grolier.com/wwii`

PART 4

The Modern World

*I*nfluenced by the Industrial Revolution, imperialism, and the rise of the modern nation-state, the Western world gradually drifted into a war that affected most of the world's nations. This era marked the loss of Europe's innocence, paved the way for another major conflagration, and set the stage for the chaotic world in which we now find ourselves.

- Were Economic Factors Primarily Responsible for Nineteenth-Century British Imperialism?

- Were German Militarism and Diplomacy Responsible for World War I?

- Did the Bolshevik Revolution Improve the Lives of Soviet Women?

- Was World War II the Result of Hitler's Master Plan?

ISSUE 15

Were Economic Factors Primarily Responsible for Nineteenth-Century British Imperialism?

YES: Lance E. Davis and Robert A. Huttenback, from *Mammon and the Pursuit of Empire: The Economics of British Imperialism*, abridged ed. (Cambridge University Press, 1988)

NO: John M. MacKenzie, from *The Partition of Africa, 1880–1900: And European Imperialism in the Nineteenth Century* (Methuen & Co., 1983)

ISSUE SUMMARY

YES: Lance E. Davis and Robert A. Huttenback state that, although statistics prove that British imperialism was not a profitable venture, it was supported by an economic elite that was able to promote and derive profits from it.

NO: John M. MacKenzie argues that the motivation for British imperialism was multicausal and that most of the causes can be found in the general anxiety crisis permeating British society in the late nineteenth century.

From the earliest stages of history, civilizations have extended beyond their boundaries to conquer neighboring peoples. Historians use the term *empire* to describe this process of domination and what results from it. It is easy to chronicle human history as a series of eras in which one or more civilizations display dominance and maintain it until they are conquered by a more powerful force. With the development of nation-states in the early modern period, the nation replaced the civilization. But the process of conquest and dominance continued; perhaps there were more players in the game, but things didn't change very much.

The term *imperial* is used to characterize this empire building. Derived from the Latin *imperium* (command), it denotes the process by which a group of people extend their control over a larger area. For example, when the small

Roman republic extended its control over vast territories, it assumed the title *Imperium Romanum.*

The last half of the nineteenth century is considered to be imperialism's apex. During that era European nations (and ultimately the United States) began to extend their influence over the non-Western world. The results were swift and decisive; within a generation there were few areas in Asia and Africa that were free from European intrusion. The mad scramble for colonies had begun.

Why did Western nations begin this process of domination? Historians have offered many reasons, among them the development of global capitalism, nationalistic imperialism, religious missionary zeal, reflections and demands of popular culture, strategic protection for national interests, and new technology. Despite the fact that modern imperialism is little more than a century old, it has received much attention from historians due to its far-reaching consequences.

Because nineteenth-century imperialism accompanied the rapid rise and development of capitalism, historians first saw the two as symbiotic. The West expanded to procure raw materials, establish foreign markets for domestically produced goods, and provide additional sources for investment capital. In 1902, Englishman John A. Hobson was the first to state this viewpoint. Russian Vladimir Lenin took the argument one step further. Borrowing Karl Marx's idea that capitalism must expand to survive, Lenin saw imperialism as capitalism's last spasm before the Communist revolution would bring it to an end.

This economic interpretation of imperialism held sway for many years until newer examinations began to uncover other possibilities. The national rivalries that led to World War I caused some historians to see imperialism as an example of nationalism gone mad, with Western nations using the acquisition of colonies as manifestations of national pride. Other historians saw strategic territories as an excuse for the acquisition of overseas territories. Once some were acquired, others were needed to protect and defend them. Heaven forbid that a rival nation be in a position to endanger one's colonial possessions!

In recent years, historians have developed several new theses for the growth of nineteenth-century imperialism. Some point out the effect of the masses on its development, offering countless examples from popular culture as proof. Others show how the cultural images of non-Western peoples in Western literature and music (which are usually untrue and condescending) have created a "white man's burden" mentality that has both promoted and justified imperialism. Finally, there are those who stress the role of the military and diplomatic corps that led businesspeople, missionaries, and others down the primrose path of imperial conquest.

In the first selection, Lance E. Davis and Robert A. Huttenback investigate the profitability of nineteenth-century imperialism. They contend that, while on the whole the system did not pay for itself, an elite group did profit immeasurably and used its influence to promote it. Therefore, the authors propose an up-to-date use of economics as a factor in imperialist development. While not disagreeing with them, John M. MacKenzie finds all of the many causes of nineteenth-century imperialism rooted in a Europe strongly influenced by a crisis/anxiety mentality.

Lance E. Davis and
Robert A. Huttenback

Imperium Economicum: In Retrospect

M. K. Gandhi, an unlikely imperialist, once wrote, "Though Empires have gone and fallen, this Empire perhaps may be an exception." That opinion was based on the conviction that the British Empire was "not founded on material but on spiritual foundations." The future Mahatma was no more correct than the rhetoricians who saw the Empire as the expression of Britannia's divine mission. "Wherever her [Britain's] sovereignty has gone," one writer averred, "two blades of grass have grown where one grew before. Her flag wherever it has advanced has benefited the country over which it floats; and has carried with it civilization, the Christian religion, order, justice and prosperity." Other observers were not so certain. In response to Betsy Prig's comment, " ... ain't it lovely to see 'ow Britannia improved her position, since Benjy picked up the dropt threads of England's imperial tradition." Clio, less sure, in an 1878 issue of *Punch* replied: "Fine phrases and flatulent figures (sez she) are the charlatan's tools."

This book is essentially about the "flatulent figures" and the often eloquent message they carried. However difficult it may be to disentangle figures and messages, it is possible to measure one aspect of the Empire: its costs and its revenue. Even [Benjamin] Disraeli, the great avatar of Britain's conquering might, in a brief incarnation as Chancellor of the Exchequer, referred to "Those wretched colonies..." as "a mill stone around our neck." A few years later, Karl Marx, an observer of a different political stripe, filed a supportive brief in the *New York Daily Tribune* in which he wondered whether "this dominion [India] does not threaten to cost quite as much as it can ever to expected to come to."

For whatever reason, Empire to many Britons seemed not only politically desirable but hypnotically alluring. Disraeli, despite his earlier reservations, thundered: " ... no Minister in this country will do his duty who neglects the opportunity of reconstructing as much as possible of our colonial empire...." So potent was the message that the ordinarily archliberal [William] Gladstone was forced to dissemble and to protest: " ... Gentlemen, while we are opposed to imperialism we are devoted to empire." While he proclaimed that "nothing will induce me to submit to these colonial annexations," he nevertheless ordered the bombardment of Alexandria and the virtual annexation of Egypt. To conclude that Disraeli had suddenly discovered that Empire was costless is wrong. He merely felt that other considerations were of greater importance than cost effectiveness. Even in the Crystal Palace Speech, he admitted that: " ... It has been proved to us that we have lost money on our colonies. It has been shown with precise, with mathematical demonstration, that there never was a jewel in the Crown of England that was so costly as the possession of India." ...

No one can sanely argue that there were not British politicians dedicated to maintaining and expanding the Empire, nor that there were not business-men who recognized that such policies might redound to their profit. It may well have been that both groups increased in size after the mid-1880s as in-creasing political and economic competition from the continental powers and the United States exacerbated the rising protectionist sentiment both in the newly competitive nations and in the Dominions. [Joseph] Chamberlain, him-self, bought Canadian Pacific Railroad bonds and lost £50,000 in an ill-fated attempt to grow sisal in the Bahamas. Nevertheless, Lenin went too far when he concluded that, "leading British bourgeois politicians fully appreciated the con-nection between what might be called purely economic and the political–social roots of imperialism."

Few of the nineteenth-century proponents and critics of Empire thought that the enterprise was without expense. Adderley had railed against the colonies' refusal to pay their just share of expenses; and Marx doubted that the Empire would ever carry its own financial weight. Disraeli, even as he proposed further imperial expansions, acknowledged that the Empire was costly and that India was a particularly expensive undertaking. Chamberlain, although he looked at imperial expenditures as potentially profitable investments, admitted that they required money; and Hicks-Beach at the Treasury had threatened his resignation when presented with the estimated expenses of one of the Colonial Secretary's development schemes. For those, like Chamberlain, who argued that the Empire was good business for the British, imperial costs had still to be offset against private profits in any calculation of social gain: a point Marx had recognized as early as 1858. Even if the claim was only that the Empire was good for a few but not for the many, the question still remains: How much did it cost the many to enrich the few?

Both Marx and Adderley emphasized the major, but not the only, element in the British subsidy to the imperial investor. The former, in reference to In-dia, had pointed to "the military and naval expenses made by the people of England on Indian account," and the latter, speaking of a British colony, to the exemption "in purse and person from the cost of its own defense." Despite the widespread recognition of the absurdity of the situation—an appreciation that had already in 1861 led to the creation of a Parliamentary select committee—there is no evidence that circumstances were significantly better in 1914 than they had been in that earlier year. ...

The failure of a long succession of governments to distribute the defense burden between home and Empire in some more equitable fashion lay rooted in history, in the law, in the bureaucratic mire, and in the pressing nature of defense requirements. The colonies with responsible government argued that they did not have to contribute, the dependent Empire said that it could not afford to pay, and hence who but the British taxpayer was left to redress the balance?...

Nor was the peculiar inequity in the distribution of the burden a figment in the minds of British politicians. The expenditure figures suggest that, if anything, the magnitude of the problem was understated. On average, in the late nineteenth and early twentieth centuries, the cost of British defense was about two and a half times as great as that borne by the citizens of a typical developed country and almost twice that of the French and Germans. The denizens of the colonies with responsible government meanwhile assumed a fiscal responsibility only a quarter that of the resident of a foreign developed country; and in the dependent colonies, the impost was less than one-quarter of that demanded from inhabitants of underdeveloped nations....

Although defense was the largest single component in the total imperial subsidy, it was by no means the only one. De facto and de jure guarantees made it possible for Empire governments to borrow at rates much below those available to non-Empire nations. The gains were not spread evenly over the Empire but, given the actual level of borrowing, the differentials meant that the residents of the colonies with responsible government saved about 10 percent of their tax bill and those of the dependent Empire about one-half that amount.

The British government also provided regular administrative subsidies to the dependent colonies and a substantial additional amount of direct support on an irregular basis. At times, those latter awards were relatively small. (Newfoundland, for example, received a grant of £260 in 1906 to help offset the effects of a severe depression in the fishing industry.) At other times, however, they were not. The Gold Coast received more than £400,000 in 1900, and the Ugandan railroad cost the British taxpayer almost £9 million between 1896 and 1914.

The fact that the sun never set on the Empire may well have provided vicarious pleasure to many inhabitants of the home islands; however, the global dispersion of Dominions and colonies did present serious problems of administration and control. To help provide the links necessary to hold the Empire together, the government found it necessary to subsidize both telegraphs and steamship lines. The British, for example, paid a quarter of a million pounds to help finance a cable connection between Australia and Canada; and, even in the 1860s, Empire shipping subsidies were running over a million pounds a year.

Finally, the British government founded and underwrote the operations of the Crown Agents. This organization acted as the marketing agency for the sale of colonial securities and as the purchasing agent for colonial supplies. Acting as an effective monopolist in the market for colonial issues and as an monopsonist in the market for the supplies bought by those colonial governments, the Agents obtained very fortuitous marketing arrangements for bond issues and equally favorable prices for the goods and services destined for their colonial customers.

It is difficult to measure precisely the total cost to the British of the non-defense component of the imperial subsidy, but it appears unlikely to have been less than one-fifth of the defense subsidy and it may have been twice that. Although the actual amount of Empire investment is unknown, the best estimates indicate that it amounted on average to about £17–8 per capita in prices of 1913. As has been noted, the defense subsidy alone amounted to at least 10 shillings and 10 pence per year for every British man, woman, and child and it could have been as high as 12 shillings and 10 pence, more than 20 percent of national savings. The minimum figure suggests that private Empire returns would have to have been reduced by more than 3 percent to provide a true estimate of the social returns, even if the nondefense components of the subsidy were zero. At the other extreme, assuming the larger defense figure and a very generous £.20 for the nondefense component, the adjustment would be almost 5 percent. Even the lower charge is sufficient to reduce Empire returns below levels that could have been earned at home or in the foreign sector after the mid-1880s.

The British as a whole certainly did not benefit economically from the Empire. On the other hand, individual investors did. In the Empire itself, the level of benefits depended upon whom one asked and how one calculated. For the colonies of white settlement the answer is unambiguous: They paid for little and received a great deal. In the dependent Empire the white settlers, such as there were, almost certainly gained as well. As far as the indigenous population was concerned, while they received a market basket of government commodities at truly wholesale prices, there is no evidence to suggest that, had they been given a free choice, they would have bought the particular commodities offered, even at the bargain-basement rates.

It is clear that imperial exactions placed on the British taxpayer enabled the colonists and residents of the Dominions and the dependent Empire to pay fewer taxes and to devote a substantial proportion of the taxes they did pay to a variety of projects that did not include defense. The Empire was a political system, and it should have been possible to align the pattern of colonial expenditures so as to increase the level of support for business and to guarantee that the revenues required to command those resources were charged not to those businesses but to the taxpayers at large.

The potential for government subsidization is vast, and such subsidies can take as many forms as Joseph's coat had colors. Some, involving nothing but the manipulation of political decisions, are difficult to discover even at the time and probably impossible to uncover a century later. Many subsidies, however, involve government expenditures, and for those, the government budget provides a paper trail that can be followed. It is possible to measure the impact of government policy on expenditures on law and justice (costs incurred in part at least to maintain property rights and enforce contracts), public works (the real capital component of social overhead investment), science and human capital (the nontraditional component), and direct business support.

Whether it is the total package or its individual components that is analyzed, the pattern is the same. Great Britain spent somewhat more than other developed countries, but hardly more than that nation's advanced state of development would suggest. The same is not true for the colonies whether dependent or blessed with responsible government. On average the latter group of colonies spent at levels about twice those prevailing in Britain. The former spent at rates not much different from those at home; but that figure is remarkable given the fraction of a colony's total expenditures that were involved, the relative state of development of the colonies in question, and the amounts spent by countries in the underdeveloped world....

In general, the colonial Empire provides strong evidence for the belief that government was attuned to the interest of business and willing to divert resources to ends that the business community would have found profitable. That behavior is, however, not necessarily evidence that the British used the political process to distort the allocation of governmental resources. Expenditures that benefited business were greatest in the colonies with responsible government, where even the British government, let alone British businessmen, had almost no influence. They were next highest in the dependent colonies, where the British did have a very substantial voice in policy making but not a total monopoly. Moreover, within that set, expenditures tended to be larger in those colonies with some local participation in political decision making and smaller in those with little or no consultation. Finally, expenditures were lowest in India, where British influence was strongest and where there were no representative institutions at the national level.

Perhaps the explanation for this ordering lies not with the British but with the local business community. Those merchants and manufacturers may have been quite willing and able to bend the structure of government expenditures to their own benefit. If that is correct, except in India, where financial crisis and the threat of famine overrode all other considerations, they appear to have been successful. It cannot be denied, however, that the policies adopted, perhaps under local business pressure, served the interest of the British investor as well as his colonial cousin.

In the late nineteenth century the London capital market acted as a conduit for the greatest international movement of private capital in the history of the world. Nevertheless, most of the flow of funds that passed through the stock exchange was not destined for the Empire. Of the almost £5–billion total, less than 70 percent passed out of Britain and almost two-thirds of that amount went to Europe and other parts of the world not pledging fealty to the House of Hanover. The largest single recipient was the United States, but a not-insubstantial portion (more than a quarter) was directed to the underdeveloped but politically independent countries of South America. In fact these Latin countries received substantially more than all the funds destined for the dependent Empire. Although the Empire as a whole absorbed nearly a quarter of the total, two-thirds of that amount went to the colonies of white settlement; and those colonies were, at least in matters economic, not likely objects for British exploitation. They were colonies that, since the middle of the nineteenth century, had begun pursuing a strongly protectionist policy—one aimed explicitly at British manufacturers and traders.

If Britain itself absorbed 30 percent of the total, if the nations over which the British exercised no political control drew an additional 45, and if the colonies over which its control was, at best, limited took an additional 16: Less than £1 in 10 remained for all of India and for colonies such as St. Kitts, the Bahamas, the Falklands, the Gold Coast, Malta, and Hong Kong, which had few representative institutions. Certainly, the amount of finance that was directed to the dependent Empire was substantial enough (it averaged more than £8 million per year) to ensure that some Englishmen could have become rich, but it appears doubtful (unless the "exploitative" profit rate was higher than even Lenin dreamed) that the total was sufficient—even if there were no offsetting social costs—to make the "average" British subject substantially better off.

Perhaps profits were very high, or possibly the dependent Empire was good business for the few but not for the many. In either case, financial flows were not evenly distributed across the world or across the industrial map. Of the £415 million received by India and the colonies of the dependent Empire, Asia received 65 percent (India alone, 56) and Africa an additional 19 percent. In India that investment was largely associated with railroads and, to a lesser extent, government finance. In the dependent colonies the relative concentrations of British investment were in the agriculture and extractive industries, in finance (the financial, land, and development companies) and in government. Just how profitable were these investments?

Although the measure of "the" rate of return is only approximate, the general outlines confirm the individual industry comparisons. Questions of timing and level are still open, but it would take a massive reversal of the evidence to alter the general conclusions. If the standard is domestic earnings, it appears that in the years before 1885 Empire returns were substantially higher. While some of the observed differences may reflect the small size of the sample and the mix of firms included in the study, it would be very difficult to argue that colonial profits were any less than domestic, and they were almost certainly substantially higher. In the case of the returns on manufacturing and commercial investments, for example, Empire returns through 1880 were one and one-quarter of domestic—and that measure is the most favorable for the home economy. Over time, the advantage eroded, and for the last half of the period Empire returns were substantially below those available at home. There was, however, some recovery in Empire earnings after the turn of the century, and in the last decade before the War they may well have equaled domestic.

As Marx had predicted, profits were falling; however, they were declining more rapidly in the Empire than in the foreign sector and faster there than in the domestic. It is, of course, not the trend but the home–Empire differential that is important for the Hobson–Lenin argument [This argument, created by John A. Hobson and Vladmir Lenin, states that capitalism by nature must expand to survive. Imperialism is necessary to ensure this expansion.] In the same way that it is difficult to deny that the Empire was *relatively* very profitable in the earlier years, it is even more difficult to conclude that profits in the colonies were substantially above those at home in the later ones.

The explanation of the trends in relative returns can in large measure be traced to two phenomena. First, early entrants into new markets and regions had distinct advantages. To the extent that property rights were well defined and enforced they may have been able to acquire the potentially most profitable lands at bargain prices. Secondly, they frequently had an initial monopoly position that allowed them to exploit those new opportunities until, in [Joseph] Schumpeter's terms, the "herd like movement" of the imitative entrepreneurs undercut their profits. . . .

While some stockholders clearly benefited from the imperial connection, the evidence indicates that probably at no time, and certainly not after the 1870s, were Empire profits sufficient to underwrite *British* prosperity. However, for the shareholders in the agricultural and extractive and the public utility sectors (and perhaps others as well), where competition was blunted or enforced property rights pushed potential competitors onto inferior lands, the Empire was important, and it was profitable. One can readily conclude that there should have been some economic imperialists. How many and who they were is a different matter....

A separation of investors into businessmen and elites (peers, gentlemen, financiers, and the like) indicates that, place of residence aside, businessmen were less likely to invest in foreign securities than were their elite counterparts. Moreover, they were *far* less inclined to invest in Empire than foreign enterprise; and among all businessmen, only merchants displayed any significant willingness to invest beyond the seas. In the Empire the elites were most willing to invest in commercial banks; in financial, land, and development companies; in iron, coal, and steel firms; and in the public utilities. To the extent that they entrusted their resources to the Empire at all, businessmen tended to put their funds to work in the private sector—competitive and less in need of government charters or licenses—industries, in short, much less dependent on political control.

The geographic distribution of shareholder "tastes" indicates that there were two very different groups of investors: those who lived in London, and others, who made their homes in the provinces. A typical Londoner's portfolio was composed of about one-quarter domestic, one-third foreign, and two-fifths Empire shares. Outside the metropolis, the portfolio was more than one-half domestic and contained less than one-quarter each of foreign and Empire shares. Within London, those who gave the City as their address preferred Empire to domestic securities, but much preferred foreign to Empire. Beyond the Wall, however, London investors appeared largely indifferent between home and foreign issues, but displayed a very strong preference for Empire over both. The London connection was particularly well illustrated in the case of South African gold mines, and even [Cecil] Rhodes turned to metropolitan investors when he needed further capital.

Further exploration of the "two-England" hypothesis indicates that Empire investors in London were drawn from a different socioeconomic background than were the Empire investors who lived outside the capital. While London elites do not appear to have behaved substantially differently than their provincial counterparts, London businessmen acted very differently than their confreres residing elsewhere. London merchants, manufacturers, professionals, and managers all invested far less frequently in home and far more frequently in Empire activities. On average, London businessmen were only one-fifth as likely to invest in domestic securities as those businessmen who lived in places like Sheffield or Manchester, but they were half again as inclined to put their resources to work in the Empire.

Overall, Empire investors tended to be drawn from two groups: elites, wherever they lived, and businessmen (particularly, in terms of numbers, merchants) who resided in London. The attractiveness of the Empire seemed to decline almost exponentially the farther one traveled north from the City. In terms of the socioeconomic background of its participants, the British capital market was clearly two markets, and it is from one of those segments, the segment populated by elites and London businessmen, that the most strident Empire support could have been expected to come.

Finally, to the extent that the Empire investments were less profitable than home and foreign alternatives, it would have been expected that the elites, while continuing to rally political support for the Empire, would gradually have attempted to divest themselves of those securities and to reinvest their assets in other more viable enterprises. Although the data do not permit an exact test of this hypothesis, they do allow a less precise examination. If the firm sample is split at 1890 and the two parts compared, the ratio of elite to business investors is substantially lower in the second period. The decline, however, is not related to a rise in business holdings (in fact, they fell as well), but to an increase in the Other owners—including women, children, and retirees....

If the residents of the dependent Empire spent little on taxes, the British, as we have already seen, spent a great deal. Even the citizens of the colonies with responsible government, who chose to tax themselves more heavily than they might have, were largely freed of defense costs and thus able to devote the vast bulk of their resources to more directly productive ends. In the United Kingdom, however, the real tax level increased by about two-thirds over the half-century in question, and as a fraction of per capita national income it rose by about one-sixth. In England the tax structure historically had depended very heavily on consumption taxes, and it was certainly regressive. As the second half of the century wore on, however, regressivity declined as customs and excises were replaced by increases in the income and inheritance taxes. The latter sources together had produced only about one-quarter of the total when Disraeli first became prime minister but had risen to account for more than £2 in 5 by the election of 1911. Over the same period, consumption taxes had declined from more than three-fifths to less than one-half of all the imposts. Over Gladstone's protests, the income tax had "lost its terrifying character" and by the mid-1890s, again despite Gladstone's reservations, death duties had begun to bite.

Even with the very regressive tax structure of the 1860s, between three-fifths and two-thirds of British taxes were paid by the middle and upper classes. Given the increasing reliance on income and inheritance taxes, it seems reasonable to conclude that this proportion did not decline and may have risen as the century wore on. Of more direct interest, the fraction that fell on the middle class was probably close to two and a half times the amount paid by the upper class. It is hardly surprising that the Gladstonian Liberals opposed higher taxes while the upper classes found that, if the resources gained by tax increases could be used for "productive purposes," they would not only countenance but support such levies. The middle class bore far more than its share of the imperial subsidy and, as is so apparent in an enumeration of their investments, they did not share equally in its benefits. The profits of Empire accrued largely to the upper class.

When it came to the formulation and execution of official policy toward the Empire, the responsibility, of course, rested fundamentally with Parliament and particularly the House of Commons. It was a quintessentially patrician legislative body, dominated by the elite classes, business, and the professions. The members had attended the ancient universities and the major public schools and they were "club men" with a vengeance. It is this homogeneity that makes it difficult to explain individual political behavior. In general, on imperial issues Liberals deviated more from established party positions than Conservatives and university-educated Liberals were particularly anti-imperial. The safeness of a member's seat, his club memberships, his profession, his level of education, and the district from which he was elected seem to provide very little help in explaining his voting behavior. On the fundamental question of the degree to which economic self-interest affected a House member's voting behavior on imperial issues, no intimate connection appears to exist between the two, although further research may prove otherwise.

Parliament, much as any other democratic legislative body, was subject to considerable outside pressure. Individual companies, the chambers of commerce, the trade associations, and a fluctuating array of usually short-lived commercial coalitions all tried to influence the course of events. Although not usually successful in the foreign arena, in the colonies with responsible government, and in the dependent colonies, because of long-established British disinclination to interfere on behalf of private businessmen, they were more effective in the case of India—the cotton tariffs being a case in point. Tariffs in the self-governing colonies attracted considerable attention from the various pressure groups, but constitutional inhibitions and lack of Parliamentary sympathy precluded the implementation of the desired policy. Even in the dependent colonies, the Crown Agents actively sought foreign bids when they felt domestic ones were excessive.

Much, no doubt, remains to be said concerning the relationship between Empire and economics. But perhaps, when all is said and done, Cecil Rhodes came closest to summing the whole thing up when he said, not totally in jest, that imperialism was nothing more than philanthropy plus 5 percent! But philanthropy for whom? It appears that imperialism can best be viewed as a mechanism for transferring income from the middle to the upper classes. Because of the technology of the imperial machine, the process involved some transfer of those resources to the colonies; however, it is not obvious that either India or the dependent colonies would have chosen to accept that imperial subsidy had they been given the opportunity to object. The Elites and the colonies with responsible government were clear winners; the middle class, certainly, and the dependent Empire, probably, were losers. A strange kind of philanthropy—socialism for the rich, capitalism for the poor.

The Partition of Africa: 1880–1900

We have been witnesses of one of the most remarkable episodes in the history of the world.

So wrote Sir John Scott Keltie in the opening sentence of his book *The Partition of Africa*, published in 1893. Keltie and his contemporaries were enthralled by the statistics of that 'most remarkable episode'. More than 10 million square miles of African territory and over 100 million African people had fallen to European rule in the space of little more than a decade. The concluding acts of the Partition were yet to come in the late 1890s and in the years immediately preceding the first world war, but in Keltie's time the map of Africa was already beginning to look like its modern counterpart. In the middle of the century the European cartographer saw Africa as a continent of blank spaces where the principal physical features—rivers, lakes, mountains—were gradually being filled in by European exploration. In the late 1880s and early 1890s maps of Africa in school atlases were revised every year, for political boundaries and various colourings for the different empires were now the rage.

Since the publication of Keltie's book, writers and historians have conducted an energetic debate on the causes of the Partition of Africa, culminating in a veritable flood of books and articles in the last twenty years. This enduring interest is perhaps not surprising. The Scramble for Africa (as the Partition is sometimes more luridly known) was the most dramatic instance of the partition of the world by Europe and America in the late nineteenth century. It inaugurated a great revolution in the relationship between European and African peoples, and it sent out political, economic and social shock-waves, which continue to be felt in Africa to this day. Africans naturally find the Partition a distasteful event, yet they are prepared to defend the artificial boundaries established by it to the point of war if necessary. The modern challenge to Africa remains the struggle to consolidate and develop the national and economic units carved out by Europeans in the Partition period, and so knowledge of the Partition is fundamental to an understanding of contemporary Africa.

This [selection] is concerned, however, with one great problem. What were the causes of the Partition of Africa and why did it occur when it did? Why was

From John M. MacKenzie, *The Partition of Africa, 1880–1900: And European Imperialism in the Nineteenth Century* (Methuen & Company Ltd., 1983). Copyright © 1983 by John M. MacKenzie. Reprinted by permission of the author.

it that, after several centuries of nibbling at the edges of Africa, Europeans suddenly rushed in to establish direct military and political control over almost the entire continent? Why did European politicians who had traditionally resisted the extension of empire in Africa become caught up in a hectic demarcation of territory?...

Interpretation

... [T]he Partition was not a sudden and wholly unpremeditated affair. 'Creeping partition' had been going on in Africa for some time. The French had already conceived grand designs in the 1870s, and commercial pressures had been exerted on the British from the same period. Nevertheless, the speed with which the Partition was finally accomplished, after more than 300 years of European coastal activity, and the comprehensiveness of the land grab do suggest that this was a new and dramatic phase. Historians have elaborated and debated many different theories to explain the events of the 1880s and 1890s.

These interpretations have overlaid each other, and it is perhaps helpful to divide them into categories to bring some order to a very complex process of theorizing. It has become customary to divide explanations into metropolitan and peripheral, economic and non-economic. Metropolitan interpretations are those which seek to explain the Scramble in terms of developments in Europe, while peripheral ones look to events in Africa itself. The economic–non-economic categories cut across the metropolitan–peripheral ones, so that there are some metropolitan and some peripheral explanations which are also economic and some which are not.

Metropolitan

Capitalist imperialism

The first explanation offered for the Partition in the early years of this century saw the European grab for Africa as arising from an inherent problem in capitalism. To maintain their capacity for growth capitalist economies had repeatedly to find new outlets for investment. In the late nineteenth century, the capitalist economies entered upon a particularly difficult period. Rates of return on capital invested at home were falling, and so capitalists believed that surplus capital had to be exported. Further, this interpretation suggests that the power to dispose of capital was falling into fewer hands, particularly large banking interests. Those who disposed of such capital desired that it should be protected, and imperialism was therefore the policy of a small, highly influential capitalist group.

Certainly this was a period of considerable capital exports from Europe, and such exports played an important role in the development of Europe's relationship with the world as a whole, but this explanation seems to offer little help for the Partition of Africa. Significant amounts of capital were exported to South Africa, but Africa generally remained the continent receiving less investment than any other right up to the first world war. Moreover, the development of great capitalist combines and concentrated banking interests did not occur until after the Partition had been accomplished.

Markets

The second metropolitan explanation is also economic. This suggests that European capitalist economies had encountered not so much a crisis of excess capital as a crisis of excess competition and production. Germany and the United States were industrializing rapidly, and France and Italy were also attempting to produce their industrial response. The British experience showed that industrialism necessarily involved global specialization. The industrial state had to maintain itself through an exchange of foodstuffs and raw materials for industrial goods. No industrial state could be self-sufficient, and to survive it had to export. New industrial states had to find new markets or encroach on those of existing exporters. Colonies could offer assured markets, particularly if the European state's relationship with them was protected by tariffs which would keep competitors out.

In addition, the capitalist economies seemed to have moved into a period of depression between the 1870s and 1890s. There were downturns in trading activity in the decade preceding the Scramble and again in the 1880s and 1890s when the Scramble was at its height. These difficulties caused alarm to industrialists and merchants throughout Europe. Italy, Germany and France responded with new tariffs in 1878, 1879 and 1881 respectively, and that compounded alarm in Britain, where the Government was still wedded to free trade. It is true that protectionist policies did not come fully to fruition until the 1890s, but the anxiety was there at the earlier period. Some indication of the alarm in Britain can be secured from the Royal Commission appointed to enquire into the Depression of Trade and Industry in 1885–6. Chambers of Commerce and Trades Societies, representing both employers and labour, were circularized as to the reasons for the depression, and their suggestions for the measures that could be taken to alleviate it. Many commented on foreign competition and tariffs, and several urged the opening of new markets, for example in Africa, and the consolidation of trading relations with colonies.

Again this market explanation, though much used at the time as an argument that colonial expansion should be undertaken, is limited in the African case. Africa's population was small, and the opportunities for marketing industrial goods were slight. But hopes are invariably more potent than reality.

Raw materials

If markets are one end of the industrial chain, raw materials are the other. The early phase of the industrial revolution depended on iron and coal which were available in Europe, and on cotton which had to be supplied by the United States and later by India and Egypt. But by the late nineteenth century other raw materials were beginning to be important. Vegetable oils were used in the manufacture of soaps and industrial lubricants. The large firm of Lever Brothers on Merseyside built its power mainly on west African palm oil, and Liverpool was the port most closely connected with the west African trade. Rubber had become important for insulation of the new electrical and telegraph wires and for tyres. Until the rubber plantations were developed in Malaya at the beginning of this century, rubber was only collected in the wild in South America and in Africa. . . .

It was recognized too that the new industrial age would emphasize base metals like copper. Copper deposits were well known in Africa, for Africans had exploited them for hundreds of years, and in many places had used copper as a currency. If base metals were to become more important, gold retained the fascination it had held for Europeans for many centuries. All industrial states had placed their currencies on the gold standard in the nineteenth century in order to stabilize them, and were building up reserves of gold to underpin these currencies. Gold had therefore become, even more than before, a source of power and stability for the western economic system. Some of the older sources of gold were beginning to decline in significance, so no state could allow a vital source of gold like the Transvaal to fall into the hands of a protectionist rival.

There was, therefore, much discussion of Africa as a source of raw materials, and the continent was likely to be more significant as a supplier than as a market. But raw materials had been extracted from Africa for many years without the need for political controls. The mere existence of raw materials does not fully explain why Europe felt it necessary to partition the continent, although there can be no doubt that the pace was quickening, and the fears and hopes were intensifying at this period.

Statesmen's imperialism

This political and diplomatic explanation sees the Partition as part of European statesmen's power-play. Statesmen used overseas territories as bargaining counters in a global game of diplomacy, as a safety valve for European nationalist tensions. This idea has always been suggested most forcibly with reference to Bismarck, who has been seen by some as actually precipitating the Scramble in order to secure his diplomatic ends in Europe, namely the isolation of France. It is a view which is no longer fashionable, for it smacks too much of the influence of 'great men' upon history, and the forces at work in Africa were much too powerful and complex to be controlled or manipulated by single political figures. Even before Leopold and Bismarck took a hand, some form of Partition was gathering momentum.

However, the last acts of the Partition in north Africa do seem to have rather more diplomatic content. Britain had the most considerable economic interests in Morocco, but she allowed France to have a free run there. Even so France did not declare a protectorate over Morocco (partitioning it with Spain) until threatened by Germany in the Moroccan crises of 1905 and 1911.

Imperialism and nationalism

This is the argument that the Partition of Africa occurred as a by-product of the friction created by new aggressive nationalisms in Europe rubbing against old-established centralized states and imperial powers. Both Germany and Italy were newly united states in this period. Both had to satisfy strongly nationalist demands within them; both sought to use colonial policies to reconcile internal tensions. Italy was already dreaming of recreating the Roman empire in the

1870s and turned her attention to Tunis, the historic Carthage. Both Germany and Italy made grabs for territory in 1884 and 1885. Neither seemed to base its claim on strong existing commercial rights. In both countries there were powerful colonial propaganda groups at work looking to empire as a means whereby the new nation states could come of age. Moreover in Germany, with its liberal franchise, a colonial policy seemed to be a popular one. It has even been said that Bismarck staged his colonial advances on several fronts in 1884 as an electioneering stunt for the election that took place in Germany late that year.

If Germany and Italy represented the aggressive force of new nationalisms, Britain and France represented the defensiveness of the old. For France after all, the German empire had been proclaimed in the aftermath of the humiliation of the Franco-Prussian War of 1870–1, in which France lost Alsace-Lorraine. A forward French policy dated from the 1870s. Defeat forced France to look outwards. Colonies, it has been suggested, were a balm for French wounded pride. The British on the other hand had been accustomed to secure their commercial ends without competition from other powers. Sometimes they had been forced to annex territory in the mid-nineteenth century, but generally they had avoided it. The British had preferred to work through informal empire, and British politicians were reluctant to translate that into formal control unless some very important national interest demanded it. From 1880 the British were forced to do so repeatedly to protect their interests from the new aggressive nationalisms and the revived imperial vision of France.

Popular imperialism

It has also been argued that the new nationalisms were not just a matter for statesmen and colonial pressure groups; they also satisfied popular psychological needs. European peoples (and no state was immune from this) developed an aggressive xenophobia in order to define sharply their national identity and national ambition. In Britain this came to be known as jingoism, a term significantly coined from a music-hall song at the time of the Congress of Berlin of 1878, an international conference which had an important bearing on the Partition. Popular culture, as expressed in the theatre and popular songs, took on a strongly nationalist and patriotic tone, and this inevitably became bound up with at least the protection, if not the extension of empire. Indeed, it became a great age of propaganda. The expansion of education led to a considerable increase in literacy, and this was exploited by colonial pressure groups, the army, the navy and above all the missions.

The missions were very important in propagating imperial ideas. Mission societies, which had appeared in all denominations and in all European countries in the nineteenth century, became convinced of their divine mission to convert the world, to save other people from what they saw to be 'barbarism' and 'savagery'. To achieve this, they required both money and recruits, and they set about opening people's pockets and minds through every publicity technique available to them. Notable missionaries became heroes, and books by them or about them became best-sellers. These and other popular works propagated racial ideas which seemed at one and the same time both to explain and to justify European technical and military superiority in the world.

It has sometimes been objected that 'popular imperialism' was a result of the Partition and other imperial advances of the age, not a cause. But popular imperialism does seem to have its roots in the 1870s and imperial events did raise popular outcries.... Thus popular opinion certainly seems to have been significant by the 1890s when politicians were confirming the more tentative moves (the chartering of companies, for example) of the 1880s. These are all British examples, but 'jingoism' was just as evident in the rest of Europe.

Electoral behaviour is of course the best index of popular opinion. We have already seen that Bismarck may well have been responding to electoral pressures in 1884. In Britain, there can be no doubt that colonial discontents contributed to the fall of Gladstone in 1885, and when he formed his fourth ministry in 1892 the Liberal Party had developed a strongly imperialist complexion. His successor, Rosebery, was almost indistinguishable from any Conservative imperialist. Even the Labour movement had imperial elements within it: some Labour leaders accepted the idea that the possession of empire was important to the interests of the working classes, or that it was an inevitable obligation which had to be fulfilled in as ethical a manner as was possible. To attack the possession of colonies seemed to be unpatriotic, and therefore electorally dangerous.

Feudal atavism

Another social explanation is one that sees imperialism as the policy of the surviving feudal elements of European society, military castes which sought new employment and the continuation of their influence. In France, imperial attitudes were largely forged in the military establishments of Algeria. Both the German and Italian empires had a strongly military flavour, administrators being usually military men rather than civilians. Empire provided them with a source of power removed from domestic politics. Even in the British empire, where the principle of civilian rule was firmly established, the army found an opportunity for employment, and an excuse for growth. In all the empires, colonial revenues could be used to pay for a proportion of the army, a technique long used by the British in India.

Technology

Another explanation, at least for the timing of the Partition, is one which highlights the importance of technology. This suggests that railways, steamships, the telegraph, and medical advances were crucial to the Partition, which could not have been achieved without them....

Clearly, such technical advances did not create imperialism in Africa, but they did produce the vital conditions that rendered its extension more readily possible. Moreover, such technical achievements seemed to emphasize the cultural gap between Europe and Africa which was important in the popular thinking of the period.

Peripheral

Strategic and Egyptocentric

Perhaps the first and most influential peripheral explanation is that which relates the entire Partition to the crisis in Egypt and the two routes to India.... The British invaded Egypt in 1882. The French, having apparently lost their former influence in Egypt, now looked for compensation elsewhere and this provoked Anglo-French rivalries in west Africa.

The vital point about this interpretation is that the British went into Egypt not to protect the bondholders, but for strategic reasons, to protect the Suez Canal and the crucial route to India. Similarly, British interest in the Cape was strategic, to protect the Cape route to the East and the important Royal Navy base at Simon's Bay. The British could not permit any other power to achieve an interior preponderance which might threaten the Cape, and it was this that drew them into the interior. The Partition in east Africa was bound up with the strategic concern with the Nile. The British believed that their position in Egypt was only secure if they commanded the entire Nile system. To keep the French from the upper Nile they needed a convenient route from the east coast. It was this consideration that lay behind the retention of Uganda and the decision to build the east African railway. According to this view, the Partition of Africa is no more than a giant footnote to the British Indian empire. This interpretation had great influence for some time, but it can now be discounted. French advances were not necessarily related to Egypt. The complex interaction of peripheral and metropolitan forces, for example in south Africa, renders such a single-cause interpretation untenable....

The general crisis

Finally, there is an interpretation which we can perhaps describe as 'global'. It seems to combine aspects of several of the interpretations.... This suggests that there was a 'general crisis' in the relations between European and non-European peoples at this time, a general crisis induced by the European efforts to create a fully integrated world economy. Industrial Europe required a highly specialized world, in which some areas would produce food for its industrial proletariat, others would produce raw materials for the industrial process, and the entire world would constitute a market for industrial goods. But to achieve this Europe needed to recast the world in its own image, to create the same infrastructures and similar institutions that would permit resources to be exploited and trade to be conducted. By the end of the nineteenth century it was apparent that Europe required a greater degree of coercion to press forward this process, coercion that could only be effected by direct imperial rule. In some areas people were resisting the new dispensation, and in consequence new military and political techniques were required to supplement the purely economic relationship.

This explanation is attractive because it appears to subsume metropolitan and peripheral elements, social and military strains, the widening of the technological gap, and the heightened tensions of the period under one umbrella thesis associated with a particular stage of economic development in the world.

But there are some problems with it too. There were crises in some areas of the world, notably China, Siam, Persia and the Gulf, which did not lead to the imposition of direct political controls. But even more significantly from our point of view, there were large areas of Africa, on the face of it much less important economically than the Asian regions just mentioned, where no immediate crisis seemed to have occurred, and yet where political controls were established.

Conclusion

We must now attempt to draw from this complex set of explanations some answers to the question posed at the beginning of the [selection]. Why did the European powers cease their long-standing process of nibbling at Africa and suddenly seize huge chunks of the continent?

There are a number of theses that we can reject straightaway. It seems to have had little to do with the export of capital. The 'great man' explanation simply will not do, for statesmen were largely reacting to the growing pressures and a climate of opinion which they found difficult to oppose. Napoleon III may have had ambitions in the 1850s; Leopold II had personal pretensions by the 1870s; individual Germans like Nachtigal and Peters hoped that Germany would institute an imperial policy; Mackinnon, Goldie and Rhodes all developed, to varying degrees, a passionate interest in the extension of British rule. But none of these was able to achieve his ambitions until the necessary forces came together. Finally, the Egyptocentric and strategic thesis is no longer convincing except as a powerful expression of one motivation of one European country. French decisions to advance in west Africa were made ahead of the British invasion of Egypt. French and Italian rivalries in north Africa, for example over Tunisia, and new German ambitions cannot be related to it. And in southern Africa developments were much too complex to be linked solely to the route to India.

Other 'explanations' are not really explanations at all. Public opinion, technology and African initiatives cannot explain the Partition, but they can demonstrate that the convergence of forces was now such that a partition was more likely to take place. Indeed, one of the remarkable things about the 1870s and 1880s was that so many developments in the realm of ideas, in missionary activity, in propaganda, in the technical and military gap between Europe and the rest of the world did seem to converge. A set of background conditions made the partition much easier to accomplish.

Why then were the crucial decisions made against the background of these conditions? One thing does now seem to be clear, and that is that we cannot be satisfied with an explanation which is wholly European or solely peripheral. Very important lines of force were developed from the periphery, but the thinking of people in Europe was also vital. Despite the creeping imperialism of the British and the French in west Africa, or the creeping partition of southern Africa by Dutch and English settlers, wholesale extensions of territory were resisted for a time. Both Goldie and Mackinnon had their pleas for a recognition of their concessions and the provision of charters rejected at first. Yet a few years later they were accepted. This is not to say that they simply went into cold storage until statesmen decided to use them. It is to say that the tensions, anxieties and pressures had not yet reached the necessary pitch. If there was a convergence of background conditions, there also had to be a conjunction of economic, social and political tensions between metropolis and periphery.

The Scramble for Africa seems to have emerged from a combination of exaggerated hope and over-heated anxiety. The economic conditions of the day, the trough between the first industrial revolution of coal, cotton and iron, and the second of electricity, copper, steel; the appearance of new industrial states protecting themselves with tariffs; the decline in some commodity prices; and the heightened commercial competition everywhere produced all the alarms associated with the transition from one economic system to another. At the same time there were many publicists concerned to argue that Africa was a tropical treasure house, capable of producing plantation crops, base and precious metals, as well as other valuable commodities like rubber and ivory. Verney Lovett Cameron, who had been sent to find Livingstone, published just such an ecstatic account in his *Across Africa* in 1877. Many others wrote in similar vein. The growth in the palm oil trade, the buoyant prices of rubber and ivory, the discovery of diamonds and then of gold, all seemed to confirm this view. Africa could solve some of the problems of the age. A state which missed out on these opportunities might be imperilled in the future. These hopes and anxieties took some time to foment fully, but by the mid-1880s they were ready to blow the lid off the politicians' restraint. Politicians do not so much act as react to the forces round about them.

An influential generation was seized by this combination of exaggerated fear and overpowering ambition. Although it is difficult to see a small group of finance capitalists influencing governments to do their bidding, there was nevertheless a rather more extensive and powerful élite at work. In London, Paris and Berlin, commercial, shipping, geographical, intellectual and official figures did come together to press for imperial advance. Although politicians, particularly in Britain, liked to claim that no official actions were taken to further the interests of individual investors and economic concerns, in fact they were. The London élite was closely connected by ties of education, social life and marriage. Some officials in the Foreign and Colonial Offices developed close connections with the capitalist concerns and furthered their ends from a growing conviction of the need for British expansion. Ex-ministers joined the boards of companies, and colonial administrators were often rewarded with directorships of companies whose ends they had furthered when in office. This was not a conspiracy; it was merely the normal operations of such an élite group converted to a dominant idea.

There was, moreover, something irrational about the Partition—as reflected in the grandiose ambitions of figures like Leopold, Rhodes, Peters, even Mackinnon—which deeply disturbed the rational minds of politicians like Salisbury and Bismarck. In many respects the Scramble was not so much a reaction to events that had already taken place as to events it was feared might take place. It was less the result of a 'general crisis' than a symptom of the anxieties that a general crisis was on the way.

There was much that was chimerical about the Partition, and in many parts of Africa it produced disappointing results. South Africa remained the world's most important source of gold, yet by 1910 the British had abdicated political control there. Central Africa was to be one of the western world's most important sources of copper, but this was not fully exploited until the years before the second world war. In some places European coercion upon Africans to produce agricultural raw materials or to go out to work produced large-scale revolts. Railway lines often failed to pay, and administrations invariably required subsidies from the mother countries. Some of the resources of Africa, such as the oil of Nigeria, were scarcely even discovered during the imperial period.

In retrospect, Keltie's opening sentence takes on a new significance. Not only was the speed of Europe's grab for Africa a most remarkable episode, so was the speed of Europe's withdrawal. Many Africans were born before the Partition occurred, and were still alive when Europe departed in the early 1960s. By that time Africa had perhaps been recast in Europe's image, with recognizable national boundaries, an infrastructure of sorts, and relatively similar institutions. But was that what the original Scramblers really intended?

POSTSCRIPT

Were Economic Factors Primarily Responsible for Nineteenth-Century British Imperialism?

No historian who has researched nineteenth century British imperialism will discount any of the factors—economic, political, social, strategic, religious, cultural—that influenced its development. Rather, their work concentrates on discovering which ingredients were either more or less important than others. History seldom provides monocausal explanations for events and movements.

Works related to modern imperialism are numerous and significant. Two important studies of economic factors and imperialism are John A. Hobson's *Imperialism: A Study* (1902) and Vladimir Lenin's *Imperialism: The Highest Stage of Capitalism* (1916).

A seminal study is Ronald Robinson, John Gallagher, and Alice Denny's, *Africa and The Victorians: The Climax of Imperialism* (Doubleday, 1968), which argues that British imperialism's main impetus came from national security and sources of diplomatic rivalry. A work of ancillary value is Daniel R. Headrick's *Tools of Empire: Technology and European Imperialism* (Oxford University Press, 1981), which relates technology to the entire process of imperialism.

Exploring the relationship between culture and imperialism has been a hot topic, and the work in this field has been dominated by Edward Said. His *Culture and Imperialism* (Alfred A. Knopf, 1993) shows how nineteenth-century Western misperceptions of non-Westerners in cultural venues such as literature and grand opera played a role in imperialism's development. On a lighter side (culturally speaking), MacKenzie's edited volume *Imperialism and Popular Culture* (St. Martin's Press, 1989) relates the fascination of the masses with exotic people and places and sees it as a motivating factor in imperialism's maturation.

Because many of the world's contemporary problems can be traced to the effects of imperialism on indigenous peoples, it would be remiss not to include sources that deal with this subject. Eric Wolf's *Europe and the People Without History* (University of California Press, 1997) explores the topic as does David S. Landes's *The Wealth and Poverty of Nations: Why Some Are So Rich and Some So Poor* (W.W. Norton, 1998), which has provoked interesting responses from its reviewers.

ISSUE 16

Were German Militarism and Diplomacy Responsible for World War I?

YES: V. R. Berghahn, from *Imperial Germany, 1871–1914: Economy, Society, Culture, and Politics* (Berghahn Books, 1994)

NO: Samuel R. Williamson, Jr., from "The Origins of the War," in Hew Strachan, ed., *The Oxford Illustrated History of the First World War* (Oxford University Press, 1998)

ISSUE SUMMARY

YES: History professor V. R. Berghahn states that, although all of Europe's major powers played a part in the onset of World War I, recent evidence still indicates that Germany's role in the process was the main factor responsible for the conflict.

NO: History professor Samuel R. Williamson, Jr., argues that the factors and conditions that led to the First World War were a shared responsibility and that no one nation can be blamed for its genesis.

One could argue that the First World War was the twentieth century's most cataclysmic event. It was responsible for the destruction of four major empires (Turkish, Russian, Austrian, and German), was tied inexorably to the rise of fascism and communism, and caused more death and carnage than any event up to that time. It also created an age of anxiety and alienation that shook the foundations of the Western artistic, musical, philosophical, and literary worlds. No wonder it has attracted the attention of countless historians, who have scrutinized every aspect in search of lessons that can be derived from it.

The major historical questions to answer are why it occurred and who was responsible for it—a daunting task yet an important one if we are to learn any lessons from the mistakes of the past. Historians have identified four major long-range causes of the war: nationalism, militarism, imperialism, and the alliance system. But these causes only partly answer why in August 1914, after a Serbian nationalist assassinated Archduke Franz Ferdinand of Austria-Hungary, Europe divided into two armed camps—the Allied Governments (England, France, and Russia, and later, Italy) and the Central Powers (Germany,

Austria-Hungary, and the Ottoman Empire)—and engaged in a conflict that would involve most European countries and spread to the rest of the world.

Important as these factors are, they fail to include the human factor in the equation. To what extent were the aims and policies of the major powers, which were formulated by individuals acting on behalf of national states, responsible for the war? Is there enough culpability to go around? Or was one nation and its policymakers responsible for the onset of the Great War? Of course, the Treaty of Versailles, which brought an end to the war, answered the question of responsibility. In the now-famous Article 231, Germany and her allies were held accountable for the war and all concomitant damages since the war was imposed on the Allied and Associated Governments "by the aggression of Germany and her Allies." Little or no historical investigation went into making this decision; it was simply a case of winners dictating terms to losers.

The first to write of the war were the diplomats, politicians, and military leaders who tried to distance themselves from responsibility for what they allowed to happen and offered explanations for their actions suited to their country's needs and interests. Historian Sidney Bradshaw Fay was the first to offer an unbiased interpretation of the war's onset. In a monumental two-volume work, *Before Sarajevo: The Origins of the World War* and *After Sarajevo: The Origins of the World War* (The Macmillan Company, 1928), he stated that liability had to be shared by all involved parties. To find Germany and her allies solely responsible for it, "in view of the evidence now available, is historically unsound" (vol. 2, pp. 558).

Unfortunately, the influence of Fay's work was minimized by the effects of the worldwide economic depression and the fast-approaching Second World War. The historiography of the First World War was temporarily put on hold. It was reopened after 1945 with some surprising results.

In 1961 German historian Fritz Fischer's *Germany's Aims in the First World War* (W.W. Norton, 1967) ignited the debate. While believing that no nation involved in the war was blameless, Fischer found primary culpability in the expansionist, militarist policies of the German government. The book sparked a national controversy that later moved into the international arena. Thus, two works published more than 30 years apart established the framework of the debate.

Recent historical scholarship seems to balance both sides of the World War I historical pendulum. V. R. Berghahn, working within the framework of Germany's economy, society, culture, and politics from 1871 to 1914, holds Germany primarily responsible for the war. Samuel R. Williamson, Jr., sees the onset of World War I as a condition of joint responsibility.

The Crisis of July 1914 and Conclusions

In the afternoon of August 1, 1914, when the German ultimatum to Russia to revoke the Tsarist mobilization order of the previous day had expired, Wilhelm II telephoned [Chief of the General Staff Helmuth von] Moltke, [Reich Chancellor Theobald von] Bethmann Hollweg, [Admiral Alfred von] Tirpitz, and Prussian War Minister Erich von Falkenhayn to come without delay to the Imperial Palace to witness the Kaiser's signing of the German mobilization order that was to activate the Schlieffen Plan and the German invasion of Luxemburg, Belgium, and France. It was a decision that made a world war inevitable.

The meeting took place at 5 p.m. When the monarch had signed the fateful document, he shook Falkenhayn's hand and tears came to both men's eyes. However, the group had barely dispersed when it was unexpectedly recalled. According to the later report of the Prussian War Minister, "a strange telegram had just been received from Ambassador Lichnowsky" in London, announcing that he had been mandated by the British government "to ask whether we would pledge not to enter French territory if England guaranteed France's neutrality in our conflict with Russia." A bitter dispute apparently ensued between Bethmann Hollweg, who wanted to explore this offer, and Moltke, whose only concern by then was not to upset the meticulously prepared timetable for mobilization. The Chief of the General Staff lost the argument for the moment. The Kaiser ordered Foreign Secretary Gottlieb von Jagow to draft a reply to Lichnowsky, while Moltke telephoned the Army Command at Trier ordering the Sixteenth Division to stop its advance into Luxemburg. As Falkenhayn recorded the scene, Moltke was by now "a broken man" because to him the Kaiser's decision was yet another proof that the monarch "continued to hope for peace." Moltke was so distraught that Falkenhayn had to comfort him, while the latter did not believe for one moment "that the telegram [would] change anything about the horrendous drama that began at 5 p.m." Lichnowsky's reply arrived shortly before midnight, detailing the British condition that Belgium's border must remain untouched by the Germans. Knowing that German strategic planning made this impossible, Moltke now pressed Wilhelm II to order the occupation of Luxemburg as a first step to the German invasion of Belgium and France. This time he won; World War I had definitely begun.

After many years of dispute among historians about who was responsible for the outbreak of war in August 1914 in which German scholars either blamed the Triple Entente for what had happened or argued that all powers had simultaneously slithered into the abyss, the... Fischer controversy [a controversy involving historian Frite Fischer's theory of the origin of World War I] produced a result that is now widely accepted in the international community of experts on the immediate origins of the war—it was the men gathered at the Imperial Palace in Berlin who pushed Europe over the brink. These men during the week prior to August 1 had, together with the "hawks" in Vienna, deliberately exacerbated the crisis, although they were in the best position to de-escalate and defuse it. There is also a broad consensus that during that crucial week major conflicts occurred between the civilian leadership in Berlin around Bethmann Hollweg, who was still looking for diplomatic ways out of the impasse, and the military leadership around Moltke, who now pushed for a violent settling of accounts with the Triple Entente. In the end Bethmann lost, and his defeat opened the door to the issuing of the German mobilization order on August 1.

In pursuing this course, the German decision-makers knew that the earlier Russian mobilization order did not have the same significance as the German one. Thus the Reich Chancellor informed the Prussian War Ministry on July 30, that "although the Russian mobilization has been declared, her mobilization measures cannot be compared with those of the states of Western Europe." He added that St. Petersburg did not "intend to wage war, but has only been forced to take these measures because of Austria" and her mobilization. These insights did not prevent the German leadership from using the Russian moves for their purposes by creating a defensive mood in the German public without which the proposed mobilization of the German armed forces might well have come to grief. The population was in no mood to support an aggressive war. On the contrary, there had been peace demonstrations in various cities when, following the Austrian ultimatum to Serbia on 23 July, suspicions arose that Berlin and Vienna were preparing for a war on the Balkans. The Reich government responded to this threat by calling on several leaders on the right wing of the SPD [Social Democratic Party] executive and confidentially apprising them of Russia's allegedly aggressive intentions. Convinced of the entirely defensive nature of Germany's policy, the leaders of the working-class movement quickly reversed their line: the demonstrations stopped and the socialist press began to write about the Russian danger.

It is against the background of these domestic factors that a remark by Bethmann may be better understood. "I need," the Reich Chancellor is reported to have said to Albert Ballin, the Hamburg shipping magnate, "my declaration of war for reasons of internal politics." What he meant by this is further elucidated by other surviving comments. Thus Admiral von Müller, the Chief of the Naval Cabinet, noted in his diary as early as July 27 that "the tenor of our policy [is] to remain calm to allow Russia to put herself in the wrong, but then not to shrink from war if it [is] inevitable." On the same day, the Reich Chancellor told the Kaiser that "at all events Russia must ruthlessly be put in the wrong." Moltke explained the meaning of this statement to his Austro-Hungarian counterpart,

Franz Conrad von Hoetzendorff, on July 30: "War [must] not be declared on Russia, but [we must] wait for Russia to attack." And when a day later this turned out to be the sequence of events, Müller was full of praise. "The morning papers," he recorded in his diary on August 1, "reprint the speeches made by the Kaiser and the Reich Chancellor to an enthusiastic crowd in front of the Schloss and the Chancellor's palace. Brilliant mood. The government has succeeded very well in making us appear as the attacked."

While there is little doubt about the last days of peace and about who ended them, scholarly debate has continued over the motives of the Kaiser and his advisors. In order to clarify these, we have to move back in time to the beginning of July 1914. Fritz Fischer has argued in his *Griff nach der Weltmacht* and in *War of Illusions* that the Reich government seized the assassination of Archduke Ferdinand and his wife at Sarajevo on June 28 as the opportunity to bring about a major war. He asserted that Bethmann, in unison with the military leadership hoped to achieve by force the breakthrough to world power status which German diplomacy had failed to obtain by peaceful means in previous years. However, today most experts would accept another interpretation that was put forward by Konrad Jarausch and others and captured by a chapter heading in Jarausch's biography of Bethmann: "The Illusion of Limited War." In this interpretation, Berlin was originally motivated by more modest objectives than those inferred by Fischer. Worried by the volatile situation on the Balkans and anxious to stabilize the deteriorating position of the multinational Austro-Hungarian Empire (Germany's only reliable ally, then under the strong centrifugal pressure of Slav independence movements), Berlin pushed for a strategy of local war in order to help the Habsburgs in the southeast. Initially, Vienna was not even sure whether to exploit, in order to stabilize its position in power politics, the assassination crisis and the sympathies that the death of the heir to the throne had generated internationally. Emperor Franz Joseph and his civilian advisors wanted to wait for the outcome of a government investigation to see how far Serbia was behind the Sarajevo murders before deciding on a possible punitive move against Belgrade. Only the Chief of the General Staff Conrad advocated an immediate strike against the Serbs at this point. Uncertain of Berlin's response, Franz Joseph sent Count Alexander von Hoyos to see the German Kaiser, who then issued his notorious "blank check." With it the Reich government gave its unconditional support to whatever action Vienna would decide to take against Belgrade.

What did Wilhelm II and his advisors expect to be the consequences of such an action? Was it merely the pretext for starting a major war? Or did Berlin hope that the conflict between Austria-Hungary and Serbia would remain limited? The trouble with answering this question is that we do not possess a first-hand account of the Kaiser's "blank check" meeting with Hoyos and of the monarch's words and assumptions on that occasion. Jarausch and others have developed the view that Bethmann persuaded Wilhelm II and the German military to adopt a limited war strategy which later turned out to be illusory. They have based their argument to a considerable extent on the diaries of Kurt Riezler, Bethmann's private secretary, who was in close contact with his superior during the crucial July days. As he recorded on July 11, it was the Reich Chancellor's plan to obtain "a quick fait accompli" in the Balkans. Thereafter he proposed to make "friendly overtures toward the Entente Powers" in the hope that in this way "the shock" to the international system could be absorbed. Two days earlier Bethmann had expressed the view that "in case of warlike complications between Austria and Serbia, he and Jagow believed that it would be possible to localize the conflagration." But according to Riezler the Reich Chancellor also realized that "an action against Serbia [could] result in a world war." To this extent, his strategy was a "leap into the dark" which he nevertheless considered it as his "gravest duty" to take in light of the desperate situation of the two Central European monarchies.

A localization of the conflict since the risks of a major war seemed remote —this is how Bethmann Hollweg appears to have approached the post-Sarajevo situation. It was only in subsequent weeks, when Vienna took much longer than anticipated to mobilize against Serbia—and above all when it became clear that the other great powers and Russia in particular would not condone a humiliation of Belgrade—that the Reich Chancellor and his advisors became quite frantic and unsure of their ability to manage the unfolding conflict. In its panic, the German Foreign Ministry proposed all sorts of hopelessly unrealistic moves and otherwise tried to cling to its original design. Thus on 16 July, Bethmann wrote to Count Siegfried von Roedern that "in case of an Austro-Serbian conflict the main question is to isolate this dispute." On the following day the Saxon chargé d'affaires to Berlin was informed that "one expects a localization of the conflict since England is absolutely peaceable and France as well as Russia likewise do not feel inclined toward war." On 18 July, Jagow reiterated that "we wish to localize [a] potential conflict between Austria and Serbia." And another three days later the Reich Chancellor instructed his ambassadors in St. Petersburg, Paris, and London that "we urgently desire a localization of the conflict; any intervention by another power will, in view of the divergent alliance commitments, lead to incalculable consequences."

The problem with Bethmann's limited war concept was that by this time it had become more doubtful than ever that it could be sustained. Another problem is that Jarausch's main source, the Riezler diaries, have come under a cloud since the Berlin historian Bernd Sösemann discovered that, for the July days, they were written on different paper and attached to the diary as a loose-leaf collection. This has led Sösemann to believe that Riezler "reworked" his original notes after World War I. Without going into the details of these charges and the defense and explanations that Karl Dietrich Erdmann, the editor of the diaries, has provided, their doubtful authenticity would seem to preclude continued reliance on this source unless other documents from early July corroborate the localization hypothesis. This would seem to indicate at the same time that the strategy was not just discussed and adopted in the Bethmann Circle, but by the entire German leadership, including the Kaiser and the military. Several such sources have survived. Thus on July 5, the Kaiser's adjutant general, Count Hans von Plessen, entered in his diary that he had been ordered to come to the New Palace at Potsdam in the late afternoon of that day to be told about the Hoyos mission and Francis Joseph's letter to Wilhelm II. Falkenhayn, Bethmann, and the Chief of the Military Cabinet Moritz von Lyncker were also present. According to Plessen, the view predominated that "the sooner the Austrians move against Serbia the better and that the Russians—though Serbia's friends—would not come in. H.M.'s departure on his Norwegian cruise is supposed to go ahead undisturbed."

Falkenhayn's report about the same meeting to Moltke, who was on vacation, had a similar tone. Neither of the two letters which the Kaiser had received from Vienna, both of which painted "a very gloomy picture of the general situation of a Dual Monarchy as a result of Pan-Slav agitations," spoke "of the need for war"; "rather both expound 'energetic' political action such as conclusion of a treaty with Bulgaria, for which they would like to be certain of the support of the Germain Reich." Falkenhayn added that Bethmann "appears to have as little faith as I do that the Austrian government is really in earnest, even though the language is undeniably more resolute than in the past." Consequently he expected it to be "a long time before the treaty with Bulgaria is concluded." Moltke's "stay at Spa will therefore scarcely need to be curtailed," although Falkenhayn thought it "advisable to inform you of the gravity of the situation so that anything untoward which could, after all, occur at any time, should not find you wholly unprepared."

Another account of the "blank check" meeting on July 5 comes from Captain Albert Hopman of the Reich Navy Office. On the following day he reported to Tirpitz, who was vacationing in Switzerland, that Admiral Eduard von Capelle, Tirpitz's deputy, was "ordered this morning to go to the New Palace at Potsdam" where Wilhelm II briefed him on the previous day's events. Again the Kaiser said that he had backed Vienna in its demand "for the most far-reaching satisfaction" and, should this not be granted, for military action against Serbia. Hopman's report continued: "H.M. does not consider an intervention by Russia to back up Serbia likely, because the Tsar would not wish to support the regicides and because Russia is at the moment totally unprepared militarily and financially. The same applied to France, especially with respect to finance. H.M. did not mention Britain." Accordingly, he had "let Emperor Franz Joseph know that he could rely on him." The Kaiser believed "that the situation would clear up again after a week owing to Serbia's backing down, but he nevertheless considers it necessary to be prepared for a different outcome." With this in mind, Wilhelm II had "had a word yesterday with the Reich Chancellor, the Chief of the General Staff, the War Minister, and the Deputy Chief of the Admiralty Staff" although "measures which are likely to arouse political attention or to cause special expenditures are to be avoided for the time being." Hopman concluded by saying that "H.M., who, as Excellency von Capelle says, made a perfectly calm, determined impression on him, has left for Kiel this morning to go aboard his yacht for his Scandinavian cruise." That Moltke, clearly a key player in any German planning, had also correctly understood the message that he had received from Berlin and approved of the localization strategy is evidenced by his comment: "Austria must beat the Serbs and then make peace quickly, demanding an Austro-Serbian alliance as the sole condition. Just as Prussia did with Austria in 1866."

If, in the face of this evidence, we accept that Berlin adopted a limited war strategy at the beginning of July which turned out later on to have been badly miscalculated, the next question to be answered is: Why did the Kaiser and his advisors fall for "the illusion of limited war"? To understand this and the pressures on them to take action, we must consider the deep pessimism by which they had become affected and which also pervades the Riezler diaries.

In his account of the origins of World War I, James Joll, after a comprehensive survey of various interpretations, ultimately identified "the mood of 1914" as the crucial factor behind Europe's descent into catastrophe. Although he admits that this mood can "only be assessed approximately and impressionistically" and that it "differed from country to country or from class to class," he nevertheless comes to the conclusion that "at each level there was a willingness to risk or to accept war as a solution to a whole range of problems, political, social, international, to say nothing of war as apparently the only way of resisting a direct physical threat." In his view, it is therefore "in an investigation of the mentalities of the rulers of Europe and their subjects that the explanation of the causes of the war will ultimately lie." There is much substance in this perspective on the origins of the war, but it may require further sociological differentiation with regard to the supposedly pervasive pessimistic sense that a cataclysm was inevitable. As in other countries, there were also many groups in German society that were not affected by the gloomsters and, indeed, had hopes and expectations of a better future. They adhered to the view that things could be transformed and improved. After all, over the past two decades the country had seen a period of unprecedented growth and prosperity. German technology, science, and education, as well as the welfare and health care systems, were studied and copied in other parts of the world. There was a vibrant cultural life at all levels, and even large parts of the working-class movement, notwithstanding the hardships and inequalities to which it was exposed, shared a sense of achievement that spurred many of its members to do even better. As the urbanization, industrialization, and secularization of society unfolded, German society, according to the optimists, had become more diverse, modern, colorful, complex, and sophisticated.

However, these attitudes were not universally held. There were other groups that had meanwhile been overcome by a growing feeling that the *Kaiserreich* was on a slippery downhill slope. Some intellectuals, as we have seen, spoke of the fragmentation and disintegration of the well-ordered bourgeois world of the nineteenth century. Their artistic productions reflected a deep cultural pessimism, a mood that was distinctly postmodern. Some of them even went so far as to view war as the only way of the malaise into which modern civilization was said to have maneuvered itself. Only a "bath of steel," they believed, would produce the necessary and comprehensive rejuvenation. If these views had been those of no more than a few fringe groups, their diagnoses of decadence and decline would have remained of little significance. The point is that they were shared, albeit with different arguments, by influential elite groups who were active in the realm of politics. The latter may have had no more than an inkling of the artistic discourse that was pushing beyond modernism, but they, too, assumed that things were on the verge of collapse, especially in the sphere of politics. Here nothing seemed to be working anymore.

The sense of crisis in the final years was most tangible in the field of foreign policy. The monarch and his civilian and military advisors along with many others felt encircled by the Triple Entente. Over the years and certainly after the conclusion of the Franco-British Entente Cordiale in 1904 and the Anglo-Russian accord of 1907 they had convinced themselves that Britain, France, and Russia were bent on throttling the two Central Powers. While the Anglo-German naval arms race had gone into reverse due to Tirpitz's inability to sustain it financially, the military competition on land reached new heights in 1913 after the ratification of massive army bills in Germany, France, and Russia.

However, by then tensions on the European continent were fueled by more than political and military rivalries. [I]n the early 1890s Germany finally abandoned Bismarck's attempts to separate traditional diplomacy from commercial policy. Reich Chancellor Caprivi had aligned the two before Bülow expanded the use of trade as an instrument of German foreign policy following the Tsarist defeat in the Far East at the hands of the Japanese in 1904 and the subsequent revolution of 1905. By 1913 a dramatic change of fortunes had taken place. Russian agriculture had been hit hard by Bülow's protectionism after 1902, and now it looked as if St. Petersburg was about to turn the tables on Berlin. As the correspondent of *Kölnische Zeitung* reported from Russia on March 2, 1914, by the fall of 1917 the country's economic difficulties would be overcome, thanks in no small degree to further French loans. With Germany's commercial treaties coming up for renewal in 1916, the Tsar was expected to do to the Reich what Bülow had done to the Romanov Empire in earlier years. Accordingly an article published in April 1914 in Deutscher Aussenhandel warned that "it hardly requires any mention that in view of the high-grade political tension between the two countries any conflict in the field of commercial policy implies a serious test of peace."

What, in the eyes of Germany's leadership, made the specter of a Russo-German trade war around 1916 so terrifying was that this was also the time when the French and Russian rearmament programs would be completed. Not surprisingly, this realization added the powerful Army leadership to the ranks of German pessimists. Given the precarious strategic position of the two Central European monarchies, the thought that the Tsarist army was to reach its greatest strength in 1916 triggered bouts of depression, especially in Moltke, the Chief of the General Staff, and Conrad, his Austro-Hungarian counterpart. By March 1914 the latter's worries had become so great that he wondered aloud to the head of his Operations Department, Colonel Joseph Metzger, "if one should wait until France and Russia [are] prepared to invade us jointly or if it [is] more desirable to settle the inevitable conflict at an earlier date. Moreover, the Slav question [is] becoming more and more difficult and dangerous for us."

A few weeks later Conrad met with Moltke at Karlsbad, where they shared their general sense of despair and confirmed each other in the view that time was running out. Moltke added that "to wait any longer [means] a diminishing of our chances; [for] as far as manpower is concerned, one cannot enter into a competition with Russia." Back in Berlin, Moltke spoke to Jagow about his meeting at Karlsbad, with the latter recording that the Chief of the General Staff was "seriously worried" about "the prospects of the future." Russia would have "completed her armaments in two or three years time," and "the military superiority of our enemies would be so great then that he did not know how we might cope with them." Accordingly Moltke felt that "there was no alternative to waging a preventive war in order to defeat the enemy as long as we could still more or less pass the test." He left it to Jagow "to gear our policy to an early unleashing of war." That Russia had become something of an obsession not just for the generals, but also for the civilian leadership, can be gauged from a remark by Bethmann, as he cast his eyes across his estate northeast of Berlin. It would not be worth it, he is reported to have said, to plant trees there when in a few years' time the Russians would be coming anyway.

However serious Germany's international situation may have been, the Reich Chancellor and his colleagues were no less aware of the simultaneous difficulties on the domestic front. Surveying the state of the Prusso-German political system in early 1914, it was impossible to avoid the impression that it was out of joint. The Kaiser's prestige was rapidly evaporating.... The government was unable to forge lasting alliances and compromises with the parties of the Right and the center—the only political forces that a monarchical Reich Chancellor could contemplate as potential partners for the passage of legislation. Meanwhile the "revolutionary" Social Democrats were on the rise and had become the largest party in the Reichstag. The next statutory elections were to be held in 1916/17 and no one knew how large the leftist parties would then become. Faced with these problems and fearful of a repetition of the 1913 tax compromise between the parties of the center and the SPD, Bethmann had virtually given up governing. The state machinery was kept going by executive decrees that did not require legislative approval. At the same time the debt crisis continued. Worse, since 1910 there had been massive strike movements, first against the Prussian three-class voting system and later for better wages and working conditions. While the integration of minorities ran into growing trouble, reflecting problems of alienation among larger sections of the population who felt left behind and were now looking for convenient scapegoats, the working class became increasingly critical of the monarchy's incapacity to reform itself. Even parts of the women's movement had begun to refuse the place they had been assigned in the traditional order. So the situation appeared to be one of increasing polarization, and the major compromises that were needed to resolve accumulating problems at home and abroad were nowhere in sight. Even increased police repression and censorship was no longer viable.

Even if it is argued, with the benefit of hindsight, that all this did not in effect amount to a serious crisis, in the minds of many loyal monarchists and their leaders it certainly had begun to look like one. Perceptions are important here because they shaped the determination for future action and compelled those who held the levers of power to act "before it was too late." With the possibilities of compromise seemingly exhausted and the Kaiser and his advisors running out of options that were not checkmated by other political forces, there was merely one arena left in which they still had unrestricted freedom of action. It is also the arena where the broad structural picture that has been offered in previous chapters links up with the more finely textured analysis put forward in the present one. [T]he Reich Constitution gave the monarch and his advisors the exclusive right to decide whether the country would go to war or stay at peace. It was this prerogative that was now to be used in the expectation that a war would result in a restabilization of Germany's and Austria-Hungary's international and domestic situation. The question was, what kind of war would achieve this objective? From all we know and have said about the early response to the assassinations of Sarajevo, this was not the moment to unleash a world war with its incalculable risks. The conservatives in Berlin and Vienna were not that extremist. They expected that war would lead to a major breakthrough in the Balkans and would stabilize the Austria-Hungarian Empire against Serb nationalism. If Moltke's above-mentioned reference to Prussia's victory over Austria in 1866 is any guide, memories of that war may indeed have played a role in German calculations. After all, the Prusso-Austrian had been a limited war in Central Europe, and it had the added benefit of solving the stalemate in Prussian domestic politics, in the wake of the constitutional conflict. Bismarck's "splendid" victory not only produced, after a snap election, a conservative majority in the Prussian Diet that enabled him to overcome the legislative deadlock that had existed since 1862, but it also "proved" that such "shocks" to the international system could be absorbed without further crisis.

And so the Kaiser and his advisors encouraged Vienna to launch a limited war in the Balkans. Their expectations that the war would remain limited turned out to be completely wrong. The Kaiser and his entourage, who under the Reich Constitution at that brief moment held the fate of millions in their hands, were not prepared to beat a retreat and to avoid a world war. The consequences of that total war and the turmoil it caused in all spheres of life were enormous. The world had been turned upside down.

NO

Samuel R. Williamson, Jr.

The Origins of the War

Sarajevo

Košutnjak Park, Belgrade, mid-May 1914: Gavrilo Princip fires his revolver at an oak tree, training for his part in the plot. Those practice rounds were the first shots of what would become the First World War. Princip, a Bosnian Serb student, wanted to murder Archduke Franz Ferdinand, heir to the Habsburg throne, when the latter visited the Bosnian capital of Sarajevo. Princip had become involved with a Serbian terrorist group—the Black Hand. Directed by the head of Serbian military intelligence, Colonel Dragutin Dimitrijević (nicknamed Apis, 'the Bull'), the Black Hand advocated violence in the creation of a Greater Serbia. For Princip and Apis, this meant ending Austria-Hungary's rule over Bosnia-Hercegovina through any means possible.

Princip proved an apt pupil. If his co-conspirators flinched or failed on Sunday, 28 June 1914, he did not. Thanks to confusion in the archduke's entourage after an initial bomb attack, the young Bosnian Serb discovered the official touring car stopped within 6 feet of his location. Princip fired two quick shots. Within minutes the archduke and his wife Sophie were dead in Sarajevo.

Exactly one month later, on 28 July, Austria-Hungary declared war on Serbia. What began as the third Balkan war would, within a week, become the First World War. Why did the murders unleash first a local and then a wider war? What were the longer-term, the mid-range, and the tactical issues that brought Europe into conflict? What follows is a summary of current historical thinking about the July crisis, while also suggesting some different perspectives on the much studied origins of the First World War....

Vienna's Response to the Assassination

The Serbian terrorist plot had succeeded. But that very success also threatened [Serbian Prime Minister Nikolai] Pašić's civilian government. Already at odds with Apis and his Black Hand associates, Pašić now found himself compromised by his own earlier failure to investigate allegations about the secret society. In early June 1914, the minister had heard vague rumours of an assassination plot.

He even sought to make inquiries, only to have Apis stonewall him about details. Whether Belgrade actually sought to alert Vienna about the plot remains uncertain. In any event, once the murders occurred, the premier could not admit his prior knowledge nor allow any Austro-Hungarian action that might unravel the details of the conspiracy. Not only would any compromise threaten his political position, it could lead Apis and his army associates to attempt a coup or worse.

After 28 June Pašić tried, without much success, to moderate the Serbian press's glee over the archduke's death. He also sought to appear conciliatory and gracious towards Vienna. But he knew that the Habsburg authorities believed that Princip had ties to Belgrade. He only hoped that the Habsburg investigators could not make a direct, incontrovertible connection to Apis and others.

Pašić resolved early, moreover, that he would not allow any Habsburg infringement of Serbian sovereignty or any commission that would implicate him or the military authorities. If he made any concession, his political opponents would attack and he might expose himself and the other civilian ministers to unacceptable personal risks. Thus Serbia's policy throughout the July crisis would be apparently conciliatory, deftly evasive, and ultimately intractable. It did not require, as the inter-war historians believed, the Russian government to stiffen the Serbian position. Once confronted with the fact of Sarajevo, the Serbian leadership charted its own course, one which guaranteed a definitive confrontation with Vienna.

The deaths of Franz Ferdinand and Sophie stunned the Habsburg leadership. While there were only modest public shows of sympathy, limited by the court's calculation to play down the funeral, all of the senior leaders wanted some action against Belgrade. None doubted that Serbia bore responsibility for the attacks. The 84-year-old emperor, Franz Joseph, returned hurriedly to Vienna from his hunting lodge at Bad Ischl. Over the next six days to 4 July 1914, all of the Habsburg leaders met in pairs and threes to discuss the monarchy's reaction to the deaths and to assess the extensive political unrest in Bosnia-Hercegovina in the wake of the assassinations. Nor could the discussions ignore the earlier tensions of 1912 and 1913 when the monarchy had three times nearly gone to war with Serbia and/or Montenegro. Each time militant diplomacy had prevailed and each time Russia had accepted the outcome.

The most aggressive of the Habsburg leaders, indeed the single individual probably most responsible for the war in 1914, was General Franz Conrad von Hötzendorf, chief of the Austro-Hungarian general staff. In the previous crises he had called for war against Serbia more than fifty times. He constantly lamented that the monarchy had not attacked Serbia in 1908 when the odds would have been far better. In the July crisis Conrad would argue vehemently and repeatedly that the time for a final reckoning had come. His cries for war in 1912 and 1913 had been checked by Archduke Franz Ferdinand and the foreign minister, Leopold Berchtold. Now, with the archduke gone and Berchtold converted to a policy of action, all of the civilian leaders, except the Hungarian prime minister István Tisza, wanted to resolve the Serbian issue. To retain international credibility the monarchy had to show that there were limits beyond which the south Slav movement could not go without repercussions.

The Habsburg resolve intensified with reports from Sarajevo that indicated that the trail of conspiracy did indeed lead back to at least one minor Serbian official in Belgrade. While the evidence in 1914 never constituted a 'smoking gun', the officials correctly surmised that the Serbian government must have tolerated and possibly assisted in the planning of the deed. Given this evidence, the Habsburg leaders soon focused on three options: a severe diplomatic humiliation of Serbia; quick, decisive military action against Serbia; or a diplomatic ultimatum that, if rejected, would be followed by military action. Pressed by Conrad and the military leadership, by 3 July even Franz Joseph had agreed on the need for stern action, including the possibility of war. Only one leader resisted a military solution: István Tisza. Yet his consent was absolutely required for any military action. Tisza preferred the diplomatic option and wanted assurances of German support before the government made a final decision. His resistance to any quick military action effectively foreclosed that option, leaving either the diplomatic one or the diplomatic/military combination. Not surprisingly, those anxious for military action shifted to the latter alternative.

The Austro-Hungarian foreign minister, Berchtold, made the next move on 4 July, sending his belligerent subordinate Alexander Hoyos to Berlin to seek a pledge of German support. Armed with a personal letter from Franz Joseph to Wilhelm II and a long memorandum on the need for resolute action against Serbia, Hoyos got a cordial reception. The Germans fully understood Vienna's intentions: the Habsburg leadership wanted a military reckoning with Belgrade. The German leadership (for reasons to be explored later) agreed to the Habsburg request, fully realizing that it might mean a general war with Russia as Serbia's protector.

With assurances of German support, the leaders in Vienna met on 7 July to formulate their plan. General Conrad gave confident assessments of military success and the civilian ministers attempted to persuade Tisza to accept a belligerent approach. At the same time the preliminary diplomatic manoeuvres were planned. Finally on 13–14 July Hungarian Prime Minister Tisza accepted strong action and possible war with Serbia. He did so largely because of new fears that a possible Serbian-Romanian alignment would threaten Magyar overlordship of the 3 million Romanians living in Transylvania. Drafts of the ultimatum, meanwhile, were prepared in Vienna. Deception tactics to lull the rest of Europe were arranged and some military leaves were cancelled.

But there remained a major problem: when to deliver the ultimatum? The long-scheduled French state visit to Russia of President Raymond Poincaré and Premier René Viviani from 20 July to 23 July thoroughly complicated the delivery of the ultimatum. Berchtold, understandably, did not want to hand over the demands while the French leaders were still in St Petersburg. Yet to avoid that possibility meant a further delay until late afternoon, 23 July. At that point the forty-eight-hour ultimatum, with its demands that clearly could not be met, would be delivered in Belgrade.

Germany's decision of 5–6 July to assure full support to Vienna ranks among the most discussed issues in modern European history. A strong, belligerent German response came as no surprise. After all, Wilhelm II and Franz

Ferdinand had just visited each other, were close ideologically, and had since 1900 developed a strong personal friendship. Chancellor Theobald von Bethmann Hollweg, moreover, believed that Berlin must show Vienna that Germany supported its most loyal ally. Far more controversial is whether the civilian leaders in Berlin, pressured by the German military, viewed the Sarajevo murders as a 'heaven-sent' opportunity to launch a preventive war against Russia. This interpretation points to increasing German apprehension about a Russian military colossus, allegedly to achieve peak strength in 1917. And Russo-German military relations were in early 1914 certainly at their worst in decades. Nor did Kaiser Wilhelm II's military advisers urge any modicum of restraint on Vienna, unlike previous Balkans episodes. An increasingly competitive European military environment now spilled over into the July crisis.

However explained, the German leadership reached a rare degree of consensus: it would support Vienna in a showdown with Serbia. Thus the German kaiser and chancellor gave formal assurances (the so-called 'blank cheque') to Vienna. From that moment, Austria-Hungary proceeded to exploit this decision and to march toward war with Serbia. Berlin would find itself—for better or worse—at the mercy of its reliable ally as the next stages of the crisis unfolded.

The Austrian Ultimatum to Serbia

For two weeks and more Berlin waited, first for the Habsburg leadership to make its final decisions and then for their implementation. During this time the German kaiser sailed in the North Sea and the German military and naval high command, confident of their own arrangements, took leaves at various German spas. Bethmann Hollweg, meanwhile, fretted over the lengthy delays in Vienna. He also began to fear the consequences of the 'calculated risk' and his 'leap into the dark' for German foreign policy. But his moody retrospection brought no changes in his determination to back Vienna; he only wished the Habsburg monarchy would act soon and decisively.

By Monday 20 July, Europe buzzed with rumours of a pending Habsburg *démarche* in Belgrade. While the Irish Question continued to dominate British political concerns and the French public focused on the Caillaux murder trial, Vienna moved to act against Belgrade. Remarkably, no Triple Entente power directly challenged Berchtold before 23 July, and the foreign minister for his part remained inconspicuous. Then, as instructed, at 6 p.m. on 23 July Wladimir Giesl, the Habsburg minister in Belgrade, delivered the ultimatum to the Serbian foreign ministry. Sir Edward Grey, the British foreign secretary, would immediately brand it as 'the most formidable document ever addressed by one State to another that was independent'.

With its forty-eight-hour deadline, the ultimatum demanded a series of Serbian concessions and a commission to investigate the plot. Pašić, away from Belgrade on an election campaign tour, returned to draft the response. This reply conceded some points but was wholly unyielding on Vienna's key demand, which would have allowed the Austrians to discover Pašić's and his government's general complicity in the murders.

News of the Habsburg ultimatum struck Europe with as much force as the Sarajevo murders. If the public did not immediately recognize the dangers to the peace, the European diplomats (and their military and naval associates) did. The most significant, immediate, and dangerous response came not from the Germans, but from the Russians. Upon learning of the ultimatum, Foreign Minister Serge Sazonov declared war inevitable. His actions thereafter did much to ensure a general European war.

At a meeting of the Council of State on 24 July, even before the Serbians responded, Sazonov and others pressed for strong Russian support for Serbia. Fearful of losing Russian leadership of the pan-Slavic movement, he urged resolute behaviour. His senior military leaders backed this view, even though Russia's military reforms were still incomplete. The recently concluded French state visit had given the Russians new confidence that Paris would support Russia if war came.

At Sazonov's urgings, the Council agreed, with the tsar approving the next day, to initiate various military measures preparing for partial or full mobilization. The Council agreed further to partial mobilization as a possible deterrent to stop Austria-Hungary from attacking the Serbs. These Russian military measures were among the very first of the entire July crisis; their impact would be profound. The measures were not only extensive, they abutted German as well as Austrian territory. Not surprisingly, the Russian actions would be interpreted by German military intelligence as tantamount to some form of mobilization. No other actions in the crisis, beyond Vienna's resolute determination for war, were so provocative or disturbing as Russia's preliminary steps of enhanced border security and the recall of certain troops.

Elsewhere, Sir Edward Grey sought desperately to repeat his 1912 role as peacemaker in the Balkans. He failed. He could not get Vienna to extend the forty-eight-hour deadline. Thus at 6 p.m. on 25 July, Giesl glanced at the Serbian reply, deemed it insufficient, broke diplomatic relations, and left immediately for nearby Habsburg territory. The crisis had escalated to a new, more dangerous level.

Grey did not, however, desist in his efforts for peace. He now tried to initiate a set of four-power discussions to ease the mounting crisis. Yet he could never get St Petersburg or Berlin to accept the same proposal for some type of mediation or diplomatic discussions. A partial reason for his failure came from Berlin's two continuing assumptions: that Britain might ultimately stand aside and that Russia would eventually be deterred by Germany's strong, unequivocal support of Vienna.

Each of Grey's international efforts, ironically, alarmed Berchtold. He now became determined to press for a declaration of war, thus thwarting any intervention in the local conflict. In fact, the Habsburg foreign minister had trouble getting General Conrad's reluctant agreement to a declaration of war on Tuesday 28 July. This declaration, followed by some desultory gunfire between Serbian and Austro-Hungarian troops that night, would thoroughly inflame the situation. The Serbs naturally magnified the gunfire incident into a larger Austrian attack. This in turn meant that the Russians would use the casual shooting to justify still stronger support for Serbia and to initiate still more far-reaching military measures of their own.

By 28 July every European state had taken some military and/or naval precautions. The French recalled some frontier troops, the Germans did the same, and the Austro-Hungarians began their mobilization against the Serbs. In Britain, Winston Churchill, First Lord of the Admiralty, secured cabinet approval to keep the British fleet intact after it had completed manoeuvres. Then on the night of 29 July he ordered the naval vessels to proceed through the English Channel to their North Sea battle stations. It could be argued that thanks to Churchill Britain became the first power prepared to protect its vital interests in a European war.

Grey still searched for a solution. But his efforts were severely hampered by the continuing impact of the Irish Question and the deep divisions within the cabinet over any policy that appeared to align Britain too closely with France. Throughout the last week of July, Grey tried repeatedly to gain cabinet consent to threaten Germany with British intervention. The radicals in the cabinet refused. They wanted no British participation in a continental war.

Grey now turned his attention to the possible fate of Belgium and Britain's venerable treaty commitments to protect Belgian neutrality. As he did so, the German diplomats committed a massive blunder by attempting to win British neutrality with an assurance that Belgium and France would revert to the status quo ante after a war. Not only did Grey brusquely reject this crude bribery, he turned it back against Berlin. On 31 July, with cabinet approval, Grey asked Paris and Berlin to guarantee Belgium's status. France did so at once; the Germans did not. Grey had scored an important moral and tactical victory.

In St Petersburg, meanwhile, decisions were taken, rescinded, then taken again that assured that the peace would not be kept. By 28 July Sazonov had concluded that a partial mobilization against Austria-Hungary would never deter Vienna. Indeed his own generals argued that a partial step would complicate a general mobilization. Sazonov therefore got the generals' support for full mobilization. He then won the tsar's approval only to see Nicholas II hesitate after receiving a message from his cousin, Kaiser Wilhelm II. The co-called 'Willy-Nicky' telegrams came to nothing, however. On 30 July the tsar ordered general mobilization, with a clear recognition that Germany would probably respond and that a German attack would be aimed at Russia's French ally.

The Russian general mobilization resolved a number of problems for the German high command. First, it meant that no negotiations, including the proposal for an Austrian 'Halt in Belgrade', would come to anything. Second, it allowed Berlin to declare a 'defensive war' of protection against an aggressive Russia, a tactic that immeasurably aided Bethmann Hollweg's efforts to achieve domestic consensus. And, third, it meant that the chancellor could no longer resist General Helmuth von Moltke's demands for German mobilization and the implementation of German war plans. Alone of the great powers, mobilization for Germany equalled war; Bethmann Hollweg realized this. Yet once the German mobilization began, the chancellor lost effective control of the situation.

At 7 p.m. on Saturday, 1 August 1914, Germany declared war on Russia. The next day German forces invaded Luxembourg. Later that night Germany demanded that Belgium allow German troops to march through the neutral state on their way to France. The Belgian cabinet met and concluded that it would resist the German attack.

In France general mobilization began. But the French government, ever anxious to secure British intervention, kept French forces 6 miles away from the French border. In London Paul Cambon, the French ambassador, importuned the British government to uphold the unwritten moral and military obligations of the Anglo-French *entente*. Still, even on Saturday 1 August, the British cabinet refused to agree to any commitment to France. Then on Sunday 2 August, Grey finally won cabinet approval for two significant steps: Britain would protect France's northern coasts against any German naval attack and London would demand that Germany renounce any intention of attacking Belgium. Britain had edged closer to war.

On Monday 3 August, the British cabinet reviewed the outline of Grey's speech to parliament that afternoon. His peroration, remarkable for its candour and its disingenuousness about the secret Anglo-French military and naval arrangements, left no doubt that London would intervene to preserve the balance of power against Germany; that it would defend Belgium and France; and that it would go to war if Germany failed to stop the offensive in the west. This last demand, sent from London to Berlin on 4 August, would be rejected. At 11 p.m. (GMT) on 4 August 1914 Britain and Germany were at war.

With the declarations of war the focus shifted to the elaborate pre-arranged mobilization plans of the great powers. For the naval forces the issues were relatively straightforward: prepare for the great naval battle, impose or thwart a policy of naval blockade, protect your coast lines, and keep the shipping lanes open. For the continental armies, the stakes were far greater. If an army were defeated, the war might well be over. Committed to offensive strategies, dependent on the hope that any war would be short, and reliant on the implementation of their carefully developed plans, the general staffs believed they had prepared for almost every possible contingency.

In each country the war plans contained elaborate mobilization schedules which the generals wanted to put into action at the earliest possible moment. While mobilization raised the risks of war, in only two cases did it absolutely guarantee a generalized engagement: (1) if Russia mobilized, Germany would do so and move at once to attack Belgium and France; (2) if Germany mobilized without Russian provocation, the results were the same. Any full Russian mobilization would trigger a complete German response and, for Germany, mobilization meant war. Very few, if any, civilian leaders fully comprehended these fateful interconnections and even the military planners were uncertain about them.

The German war plans in 1914 were simple, dangerous, and exceptionally mechanical. To overcome the threat of being trapped in a two-front war between France and Russia, Germany would attack first in the west, violating Belgian neutrality in a massive sweeping movement that would envelop and then crush the French forces. Once the French were defeated, the Germans would redeploy their main forces against Russia and with Austro-Hungarian help conclude the war. The Russian war plans sought to provide immediate assistance to France and thereby disrupt the expected German attack in the west. The Russians would attack German troops in East Prussia, while other Russian forces moved southward into Galicia against the Habsburg armies. But to achieve their goals the Russians had to mobilize immediately, hence their escalatory decisions early in the crisis, with fateful consequences for the peace of Europe.

The Italians, it should be noted, took some preliminary measures in August 1914 but deferred general mobilization until later. Otherwise Rome took no further action to intervene. Rather the Italian government soon became involved in an elaborate bargaining game over its entry into the fray. Not until April 1915 would this last of the major pre-war allies enter into the fighting, not on the side of their former allies but in opposition with the Triple Entente.

The Process of Escalation

By 10 August 1914 Europe was at war. What had started as the third Balkan war had rapidly become the First World War. How can one assess responsibility for these events? Who caused it? What could have been done differently to have prevented it? Such questions have troubled generations of historians since 1914. There are no clear answers. But the following observations may put the questions into context. The alliance/*entente* system created linking mechanisms that allowed the control of a state's strategic destiny to pass into a broader arena, one which the individual government could manage but not always totally control. Most specifically, this meant that any Russo-German quarrel would see France involved because of the very nature of Germany's offensive war plans. Until 1914 the alliance/*entente* partners had disagreed just enough among themselves to conceal the true impact of the alliance arrangements.

The legacy of Germany's bombastic behaviour, so characteristic of much of German *Weltpolitik* and *Europolitik* after 1898, also meant that Berlin was thoroughly mistrusted. Its behaviour created a tone, indeed an edginess, that introduced fear into the international system, since only for Germany did mobilization equal war. Ironically, and not all historians agree, the German policy in 1914 may have been less provocative than earlier. But that summer Berlin paid the price for its earlier aggressiveness.

Serbia allowed a terrorist act to proceed, then sought to evade the consequences of its action. It would gain, after 1918, the most from the war with the creation of the Yugoslav state. Paradoxically, however, the very ethnic rivalries that brought Austria-Hungary to collapse would also plague the new state and its post-1945 successor.

Austria-Hungary feared the threat posed by the emergence of the south Slavs as a political force. But the Dual Monarchy could not reform itself sufficiently to blunt the challenge. With the death of the Archduke Franz Ferdinand, who had always favoured peace, the monarchy lost the one person who could check the ambitions of General Conrad and mute the fears of the civilians.

While harsh, Ottokar Czernin's epitaph has a certain truth to it: 'We were compelled to die; we could only choose the manner of our death and we have chosen the most terrible.'

Germany believed that it must support its Danubian ally. This in turn influenced Berlin's position towards Russia and France. Without German backing, Vienna would probably have hesitated to been more conciliatory toward Belgrade. But, anxious to support Vienna and possibly to detach Russia from the Triple Entente, Berlin would risk a continental war to achieve its short- and long-term objectives. Berlin and Vienna bear more responsibility for starting the crisis and then making it very hard to control.

Nevertheless, the Russians must also share some significant responsibility for the final outcome. St Petersburg's unwavering support of Serbia, its unwillingness to negotiate with Berlin and Vienna, and then its precipitate preparatory military measures escalated the crisis beyond control. Russia's general mobilization on 30 July guaranteed disaster.

Those Russian decisions would in turn confront the French with the full ramifications of their alliance with Russia. Despite French expectations, the alliance with Russia had in fact become less salvation for Paris and more assuredly doom. France became the victim in the Russo-German fight. Throughout the crisis French leaders could only hope to convince Russia to be careful and simultaneously work to ensure that Britain came to their assistance. Paris failed in the first requirement and succeeded in the second.

The decisions of August 1914 did not come easily for the British government. Grey could not rush the sharply divided cabinet. The decade-old *entente* ties to the French were vague and unwritten and had a history of deception and deviousness. Nor did the vicious political atmosphere created by Ireland help. Grey desperately hoped that the threat of British intervention would deter Germany; it did not. Could Grey have done more? Probably not, given the British political system and the precarious hold the Liberal Party had on power. Only a large standing British army would have deterred Germany, and that prospect, despite some recent assertions, simply did not exist.

In July 1914 one or two key decisions taken differently might well have seen the war averted. As it was, the July crisis became a model of escalation and inadvertent consequences. The expectation of a short war, the ideology of offensive warfare, and continuing faith in war as an instrument of policy: all would soon prove illusory and wishful. The cold, hard, unyielding reality of modern warfare soon replaced the romantic, dashing legends of the popular press. The élite decision-makers (monarchs, civilian ministers, admirals, and generals) had started the war; the larger public would die in it and, ultimately, finish it.

POSTSCRIPT

Were German Militarism and Diplomacy Responsible for World War I?

Recent events in the former Yugoslavia may have spurred interest in World War I—the first time that the Balkan powder keg exploded into the world's consciousness. Yugoslavia was created after that war, and some see its recent problems as a failure of the Versailles settlement.

Regardless of the truth of this assumption, it is certainly true that the last decade has seen the publication (and republication) of a number of important works on the Great War, including books by both authors in this issue: Berghahn's *Germany and the Approach of War in 1914* (St. Martin's Press, 1993) and Williamson's *Austria-Hungary and the Origins of the First World War* (St. Martin's Press, 1991). David G. Hermann's *The Arming of Europe and the Making of World War I* (Princeton University Press, 1996) concentrates on the size and strength of land armies and their role in the genesis of the war, a subject that has been neglected by historians who have emphasized naval buildup.

Many recent books on World War I have either been written by English historians or have concentrated on England's role in the war. Edward E. McCullough's *How the First World War Began: The Triple Entente and the Coming of the Great War of 1914–1918* (Black Rose Books, 1999) is a revisionist work that sees the creation of the Triple Entente as a prime force in the causes of the First World War. Comparing the condition of Germany today to England, France, and Russia, McCullough questions not only the folly of the war but notes its counterproductive results.

In *The Pity of War* (Basic Books, 1999), Scottish historian Niall Ferguson takes the revisionist viewpoint to a higher level. Arguing that the First World War was not inevitable, he asserts that the British declaration of war turned a continental conflict into a world war. He further argues that not only was Britain's participation in the war a colossal error, but it was counterproductive to the interests of the British nation and its people. He finds proof in the causes and results of World War II and the present condition of Great Britain.

Eminent English military historian John Keegan's *The First World War* (Alfred A. Knopf, 1999) may well prove to be one of the most widely read and influential volumes on the Great War. A general work written with skill, scholarship, and readability, it is strongly recommended. *World War I: A History* (Oxford University Press, 1998), edited by Hew Strachan, contains 23 chapters, each written by a different historian, that cover the war from origins to memory and everything in between. William Jannen's *The Lions of July: Prelude to War, 1914* (Presidio Press, 1997) is an extremely readable account of Europe's last month of peace as its statesmen and military men blundered into war.

ISSUE 17

Did the Bolshevik Revolution Improve the Lives of Soviet Women?

YES: Richard Stites, from *The Women's Liberation Movement in Russia: Feminism, Nihilism, and Bolshevism, 1860–1930* (Princeton University Press, 1978)

NO: Françoise Navailh, from "The Soviet Model," in Françoise Thébaud, ed., *A History of Women in the West, vol. 5: Toward a Cultural Identity in the Twentieth Century* (Belknap Press, 1994)

ISSUE SUMMARY

YES: History professor Richard Stites argues that in the early years of the Bolshevik Revolution, the Zhenotdel, or Women's Department, helped many working women take the first steps toward emancipation.

NO: Film historian Françoise Navailh contends that the Zhenotdel had limited political influence and could do little to improve the lives of Soviet women in the unstable period following the revolution.

Compared with life under the czars, life for women after the Bolshevik Revolution was characterized by greater variety and freedom. The Romanov dynasty had ruled Russia for 300 years, and the Orthodox Church had ruled for a much longer period. Both had reinforced a world of patriarchal authority, class structure, and patterns of deference. Although the revolution overthrew the power of both church and monarch, the new communist state had a power and authority of its own. Between 1917 and 1920 Soviet women received equal rights in education and marriage, including the choice to change or keep their own names and the opportunity to own property; the rights to vote and to hold public office; access to no-fault divorce, common-law marriage, and maternity benefits; workplace protection; and access to unrestricted abortion. They were the first women to gain these rights—ahead of women in France, England, and the United States—but the question is whether or not these legal rights translated into improvements in their day-to-day lives.

A feminist movement had developed in urban areas as early as the 1905 workers' revolution, and women joined men in leading strikes and protest demonstrations. By the time of the Bolshevik Revolution in 1917, however, the goals of the leadership were primarily economic, and feminism was dismissed as bourgeois or middle class. In a workers' revolution, women and men were to be equal. Housework and child care were to be provided collectively, and the family, like the monarchy, was to be replaced with something new. Women gained access to economic independence by becoming workers, which was supposed to provide them with the basis for equality within marriage.

The German philosopher Karl Marx had argued that the family reflects the economic system in society. Under capitalism, the bourgeois family exists to reproduce workers and consumers; it exploits women by unfairly burdening them with full responsibility for housework and child care. If similarly exploited workers—what Marx called the proletariat—overthrew the capitalist system that allowed factory owners to grow rich from their workers' labor, Marx believed that the family would undergo an equally dramatic transformation. In this scenario, no one would be "owned" by anyone else. Prostitution would disappear, and, as the state took responsibility for childrearing and education, women would be free to work and become economically self-sufficient. People would then be free to marry for love or sexual attraction rather than for economic considerations.

V. I. Lenin, who emerged as the leader and architect of the new order, was committed to women's rights. First and foremost, however, he was committed to a socialist revolution. When the struggle to make legal changes that would be felt in women's lives came into conflict with the goals of the revolution, there was no question in Lenin's mind about which would have to be sacrificed. In this early period, a fascinating group of women briefly held highly visible leadership positions and had the chance to put their ideas into practice, at least during the first decade. Alexandra Kollontai was one of the most articulate and effective leaders of the Zhenotdel, or Women's Department of the Communist Party, whose purpose between 1919 and 1930 was to educate and mobilize the women of the Soviet state to participate fully in the revolution.

In the following selections, Richard Stites focuses on the work of the Zhenotdel in reaching out to the Jewish, Christian, Muslim, and Buddhist women of the East whose lives in the Caucasus, Volga, and Central Asia were the most severely restricted. Raising the consciousness of these women in the face of brutal male opposition contributed significantly to women's liberation and the development of the socialist state, Stites concludes.

Françoise Navailh, in contrast, maintains that although Soviet women were granted unprecedented legal rights, almost without a struggle, the real task of Zhenotdel was to translate these rights into a new way of life. Navailh judges it to have failed in significantly improving the lives of Soviet women.

Richard Stites

Bolshevik Liberation

"Don't make an issue of my womanhood."

— Ninotchka (1939)
C. Brackett, B. Wilder, *and* W. Reisch

The Limits of Equality

"The future historian," said Kollontai after the Civil War, "will undoubtedly note that one of the characteristics of our revolution was that women workers and peasants played not—as in the French Revolution—a passive role, but an active important role." The following paragraphs may serve as a gloss on this remark. Though there was a good deal of spontaneous activity among the women of the Red side, Bolshevik women organizers—Kollontai foremost among them —did not leave much to chance. In a propaganda pamphlet of 1920 addressed to women, Kollontai directly invited working and peasant women to support the Red Front in every possible way including combat. Conscious of her own former anti-war propaganda, she was careful to point out the difference between the exploitative character of the Great War and the liberating and defensive nature of the present one, tying together the thesis of women's capacity to fight with the need to defend the equality that they had won in the Revolution. The Soviet publicist, V. Bystryansky, began his argument in *Revolution and Woman* (1920) with a reference to Fourier's statement about measuring a society's level of progress by examining the level of women's emancipation in that society, and made flattering comments about the military potential of women. Variations of these themes were the stock in trade of propagandists such as Krupskaya, Balabanova, and other Bolshevik women who held important propaganda posts during the Civil War.

What is striking about Russian women's participation in this War is the variety and novelty of the functions that they performed. As in the past, women carried out every conceivable support task on the home front, ranging from feeding and sanitary operations to building fortifications and digging trenches in beleaguered cities. As in World War I, women served in medical and combat capacities, but on a broader scale and in a much more organized context. Propaganda, psychological warfare, espionage, and police work

From Richard Stites, *The Women's Liberation Movement in Russia: Feminism, Nihilism, and Bolshevism, 1860–1930* (Princeton University Press, 1978). Copyright © 1978 by Princeton University Press. Reprinted by permission. Notes omitted.

—known previously to only a few exceptional women—now recruited large numbers of them. Women's participation was erratic and tentative during the first year of the War. In October 1919, the Zhenotdel gave greater definition to the functions of women and set up the machinery for large-scale and orderly recruitment. By the end of the war in 1920, conscription of young women for non-combatant service had begun, and high-ranking posts in Military Revolutionary Committees and Political Departments of the Red Army were occupied by women....

The role of women in the political life of the country in the generation following the Revolution may be seen in two fairly distinct stages. In the first, roughly 1917–1923, a small but visible group of women held responsible positions during and immediately after the Civil War. After 1923–1925, when there were no more prominent individual Bolshevik women even close to the seats of power, a second stage began. Women were then and for the future absent both from positions of power and prestige and largely from public prominence; but at the same time, the lowest strata of women had begun to stir and to participate in a limited but real way in the political process, such as it was. And a modest number of women were permanently lodged in the middle range of political and administrative authority. The "major" women Bolsheviks as a group were clearly less eminent than the men on any reasonable list of leading Bolsheviks. There are, however, a few who, in terms of political work, public image, or both, may be set off from other Bolshevik women: Stasova, Armand, Balabanova, Kollontai, and Krupskaya, all born between 1869 and 1878, and all possessing revolutionary credentials dating from the turn of the century or earlier (though only Krupskaya and Stasova could claim to be Old Bolsheviks).

Elena Stasova was at the very center of events in 1917, serving as the functioning Secretary of the Party during and immediately after the Revolution. Her reputation as storehouse of the Party's traditions had made her the logical candidate for the job. When the government moved to Moscow, however, Stasova remained behind; Lenin had found a more effective administrator in Yakov Sverdlov who had a talent for making policy as well. When Sverdlov died in 1919, Stasova resumed her work in the Secretariat under the tripartite management of Krestinsky, Preobrazhensky, and Serebryakov. But in 1920, when the staff was reorganized, Stasova resigned and requested a chancery position in one of the higher Party organizations. Krestinsky suggested instead that she go to work in Zhenotdel—a suggestion that Stasova immediately declined. Having worked at the center of political life, she perhaps resented being shunted off to what might have seemed mere auxiliary work. Stasova eventually found a congenial assignment as leader of the International Red Aid (MOPR)—a Comintern version of the old political Red Cross. From 1920 onward, she had no impact on the Soviet political scene. Here is a clear case of a woman who, in spite of certain administrative talents, was by her own admission always hazy on matters of theory and thus ultimately unsuited for top leadership in a Party which was still composed largely of intellectuals.

Inessa Armand died of cholera in 1920. She had been second only to Kollontai in energy and range of political work. In addition to founding and directing Zhenotdel, Inessa held important posts in the highest Party, Soviet, and economic agencies of Moscow Province; and she helped shape the international communist movement by organizing foreigners of Bolshevik sympathies into the Club of the Third International. Her political prominence was clearly enhanced by her exceptionally close relationship with Lenin (and Krupskaya). The notion, however, that Inessa had been Lenin's mistress—though gaining acceptance among a number of Western students—has no relevance to the question of her political importance, and the evidence is flimsy and unconvincing.

Angelica Balabanova (Balabanoff)... was an almost archetypical radical Russian woman. Brought up amid the luxury of a large Ukrainian manor house, she had felt the stirrings of revolutionary consciousness early, perceiving, as she says, the "difference between those who could *give* and those who had to *receive.*" "My ardent desire," she recalled, "was to escape my conventional and egoistic milieu in order to devote myself fully to a cause from which I could live and die. This was not self-abnegation, but a wish to live a life which would make me *useful* to the suffering masses." The route of her "escape" took her to Brussels and then to Italy where she became a key figure in the socialist movement, acting for a time as Mussolini's secretary. After 1917, she came back to Russia and served in a number of posts including Foreign Minister of the Ukraine and Secretary of the Comintern. But her ardent service to the Bolshevik regime did not prevent her from repudiating it when it failed to meet her expectations. "The deformation of the October Revolution," she wrote, "progressed at the same rate at which the individual replaced the masses. This substitution, which was made at the outset in good faith, was bound to degenerate in time." In 1921, she resigned her positions and left Soviet Russia forever.

Kollontai was by far the most active and versatile of the Bolshevik women of this era. A member of the tiny Central Committee at the time of the overthrow, she was soon appointed Commissar of Public Welfare. During her brief tenure as Commissar, Kollontai betrayed some administrative vacillation. At first she was reluctant to use force in dealing with left-over recalcitrant civil servants of the tsarist days. Lenin chided her by asking if she thought a revolution could be made with white gloves. But when she took some rather strong public measures against the Orthodox Church, he warned her to exercise tact when dealing with religious sensibilities. But it was her marriage to the younger revolutionary sailor, Pavel Dybenko,... that undercut the confidence that the Party leaders had briefly shown in her. Her association with him and his reckless and erratic behavior brought no credit upon her political reputation. "I will not vouch for the reliability or the endurance" said Lenin a few years later "of women whose love affair is intertwined with politics." Not that her revolutionary career was over by any means. She served as Commissar for Propaganda in the Ukraine, toured the front with Dybenko on an agit-train, and headed Zhenotdel.

Kollontai's exit from Soviet politics came in 1922, in connection with her role in the dissenting Workers' Opposition Group whose leader, Shlyapnikov, was her former lover. Kollontai herself drafted the program and distributed it to Party members in 1921. It was as much a product of her longstanding faith in the creative powers of the proletariat, first enunciated in *Social Bases,* as it was a tract for the times. Against the increasing centralism, authoritarianism, and bureaucratism which had overtaken the Party during the Civil War, she proposed "the collective, creative effort of the workers themselves." Her most suggestive theme was that collective, interpersonal relations among the producers generated great productivity, and that this productivity was diminished by the alienating presence of authoritarian officials—"the bosses and the bureaucrats." Kollontai's form of syndicalism, shared by many in the Russian labor movement, was seen by Lenin and others as a menace to unity and discipline in the Party. Lenin displayed his fury at the fateful Tenth Party Congress; when Kollontai persisted in her efforts to disseminate her ideas, she was removed from her posts and sent off to Norway on a minor diplomatic mission. She was eventually promoted to Soviet ambassador to Sweden; but her career as a Bolshevik political figure was over.

As Lenin's wife, Krupskaya had been a key organizational figure of the early Bolshevik movement in emigration because of her network of correspondence with agents in Russia. But after Lenin and Krupskaya arrived in revolutionary Russia, Stasova, not she, was appointed to head up the Secretariat of the Party in the Kseshinskya Palace. Krupskaya's main work and her abiding concern both before and after Lenin's death was propaganda and education. By her own admission, high politics held little interest for her, and she was almost reprimanded by the Central Committee for failing to attend Party meetings regularly. On the other hand, she was certainly a good deal more than "first lady of the great Russian state" (Zetkin's pious phrase). Her pedagogical and journalistic activities contributed much to the training and liberation of women. After her well-known clash with Stalin during Lenin's illness, she did emerge as a potential rallying point for oppositional elements; but by 1925, this was all over, and she had come to realize that she was far from being a political match for the wily Stalin....

Zhenotdel

Whenever a revolution has been preceded by a long established underground movement, the structure of that movement—just as much as its leadership and its ideology—super-imposes itself on the political life of the new society. This is why Bolshevik Russia became a land of committees, commissions, congresses, and cells. Before 1917, the Bolshevik Party had been a congeries of local committees directed from the center by a small group that communicated with its branches by means of a newspaper (for general ideas) and peripatetic agents (for specific instructions); feedback to the center came through correspondence and rare congresses and conferences. After 1917, the Bolsheviks used these devices (now amplified by railroad, telegraphy, and wireless) of political organization and communication for social mobilization of the country in the same way that they had used them to destroy its former regimes. The "novel" methods of social communication all had their counterparts in the history of the revolutionary underground. The techniques of Zhenotdel—the post-revolutionary organ responsible for women's liberation in Soviet Russia—were no exception. They were summarized long before Zhenotdel came into existence in a list of instructions given by Klavdiya Nikolaeva to women workers in May 1917: Organize Social Democratic groups in your factory; appoint a liaison to *Rabotnitsa;* arrange meetings. It was all there—organization, filtering down of leaders, responsibility to the center (an editorial board), communication back to the rank and file through liaison and newspaper, and processing the instructions at local meetings. And it had been there, in embryo, for a generation.

But would the machinery be used? And to what end? That the "proletarian women's movement" would continue after the Revolution was a tacit assumption of its leaders and was inherent in the revolutionary movement itself. Kollontai, in 1921, spoke in retrospect of the hostility to the regime nourished by the vast majority of women and of their fears that it would uproot the family, decree the "heartless" separation of children from parents, and destroy the church. In 1918, she was already aware of the danger of disillusionment among the masses of women and of the need for long-range and patient work among them. Lenin, though he had little time to voice his opinion on the matter in the first years of Soviet power, was in full agreement with Kollontai, Inessa, and the others on the need for active liberation of Russian women—in life as well as in law. Thus the formal, legislative program of emancipation (the only one usually noted by historians) had to be given meaning in a social revolution from below. This is the true historical context of the Zhenotdel....

During the Civil War, Inessa used the Zhenotdel to mobilize women in support of the Red Army and the new regime. Propaganda teams, like the ones headed by Krupskaya and Kollontai, threaded their way on agit-trains and boats through the Red areas, stopping at remote villages to regale the population with poster art, song-and-dance groups, and speeches. The popular "Natasha" (K. I. Samoilova), known affectionately among Russian women as "our own mother," sailed up and down the Volga with a plea for support and a promise of liberation which she proclaimed from the decks of the *Red Star.* She died of cholera during one of her cruises. At the local level, "volunteer Saturdays" (*subbotniki*) and "days of wounded Red Army Men" were launched to recruit previously inactive women in jobs like sewing underwear, bathing soldiers, and bandaging wounds. Recruiting work grew very slowly; and the Party sometimes tended to use Zhenotdel workers exclusively in such endeavors as food distribution, child and orphan care, and the struggle against illiteracy and superstition —areas of activity that, in the context, were really the Soviet equivalents of *Küche, Kinder,* and *Kirche.* Inessa Armand drove herself to exhaustion working fourteen to sixteen hours a day. By a stroke of fate, she was ordered by the Party to the Caucasus for a rest. There, in the fall of 1920, she took cholera and died.

Kollontai was chosen to succeed her. If she had been bypassed in 1918, it was probably only because of the Party's, especially Lenin's, greater confidence in Armand's reliability and obedience. Kollontai and Inessa had helped forge the women's movement, separately before the Revolution and together after it; and they shared the same philosophy of women's liberation. Kollontai held no brief for a "feminist" movement separate from or outside the Party; she even hoped to dissolve some of the purely "female" features of Zhenotdel work (such as the "women's pages" in Party newspapers). But she was equally firm in resisting any suggestions of liquidating the Zhenotdel itself. Passivity and lack of consciousness were the hallmarks of Russian women. She told Emma Goldman (who refused her invitation to work in Zhenotdel) that women "were ignorant of the simplest principles of life, physical and otherwise, ignorant of their own functions as mothers and citizens." It was imperative, then, to raise the consciousness of these women and to deal with specifically woman-related problems, such as maternity care, in their own special way. This, she said, was not feminism.

Kollontai was right. It was not feminism, at least as the word was then understood. The feminist movement in Western Europe and America, from 1848 to 1920, had ultimately settled on the vote as the capstone of emancipation. After acquiring it, no feminist movement in the West, until recent years, made many further steps toward realizing economic or sexual liberation; even less did it engage in any mass movement for the liberation of women of the working class or minorities. Bolshevik "feminism" reversed the social timetable of Western feminism. For the latter, political emancipation was the goal; for the former, it was only the beginning.

During her manifold assignments of the Civil War period, Kollontai had always (except during a serious illness) kept in touch with Zhenotdel activities. After her appointment, she led Zhenotdel with the abundant optimism, energy, and talent which she had displayed in other realms of revolutionary work. Her two year tenure as its leader (1920–1922) also happened to be a period of deep emotional and political tribulation for her. Kollontai's most important practical accomplishment was to turn Zhenotdel's energy away from wartime auxiliary work (the War ended in 1920) toward the subtler tasks of psychological and social demobilization. More spectacular and in the long run just as important was initiating the liberation of the so-called women of the East—the Muslim, Christian, Jewish, and Buddhist women of the non-western borderlands of Caucasia, the Volga, and Central Asia who were subjected to codes of sexual behavior unknown in the rest of Russia. The most severe of these was the Muslim *şeriat* that in practice gave women no status and no purpose other than as pleasure-giver, servant, housekeeper, and childbearer. Their isolation and untouchability was symbolized by "the veil" in all its varieties, the most severe of which was the *paranja*, a heavy horsehair garment that hung from the nose to the floor. Aside from serious organizational work among these women, Kollontai also brought some of them to Moscow for congresses where the exotic guests would tear off their face coverings before a startled audience. Criticized by some for excessive theatricality, Kollontai told Louise Bryant that "all pioneering work is theatrical." It was not the last time that an article of women's clothing would be seen as an enslaving, sexist fetish; and the doffing of the veil became the favorite gesture of baptism into free womanhood in the Soviet East....

Provincial Zhenotdels were assigned only eight full-time people in the organizational setup. Since five of them sat in the center, this meant only one instructor or *zhenorg* for every three districts of a province. Furthermore, [Bette] Stavrakis' study indicates that Zhenotdel, like most analogous Party organizations, suffered from personnel deficiency, shortage of funds, jurisdictional overlap, and superficiality at the grass roots level. The areas of greatest resistance to its efforts were the villages and the non-Slavic borderlands. The Ukrainian organizer, Kiselëva, walked miles from *raikom* headquarters to the little village of Sripal to gather the women into a reading cabin in order to organize them. The menfolk surrounded the cabin and shouted, "We'll beat you up if you touch our wives." In Chigirin district, three Zhenotdel workers were killed in one year by "bandits." At the beginning of collectivization, women organizers in the Ukraine had to dispel the rumors which said that in the new kolkhozes the young women would be "shared" by the men and the old ones boiled down for soap. Everywhere, men (invariably called "kulaks" in the literature) fought efforts of the Zhenotdel to organize and politicize their wives.

Of vastly greater difficulty was Zhenotdel work among "eastern" women. Kollontai's congresses were only the beginning. These women could barely hint, and only after patient prying, at the kind of life they had had under the traditional order. "We were silent slaves," said one. "We had to hide in our rooms and cringe before our husbands, who were our lords." Another recalled: "Our fathers sold us at the age of ten, even younger. Our husband would beat us with a stick and whip us when he felt like it. If he wanted to freeze us, we froze. Our daughters, a joy to us and a help around the house, he sold just as we had been sold." These words were spoken to Clara Zetkin who inspected the Zhenotdel operations in the Caucasus during her recuperation there in the early 1920's. Lacking in native Bolshevik cadres, Zhenotdel sent out Russian revolutionaries and educators to take up the work. Typical of these was Nadezhda Kolesnikova, veteran propagandist and wife of one of the fabled Twenty-Six Commissars. Another was Olga Chulkova, a librarian-teacher and Bestuzhev graduate, who worked from her Zhenotdel base in Sukhumi to organize the women of Abkhaziya. Teams were sent out into the mountain villages and women who had never left their native settlements before were brought down to Sukhumi. Some were shuttled off to Moscow to study; the rest went back to the mountains to organize day nurseries.

As Bette Stavrakis has observed, the lack of native Bolsheviks, the difficulties of language, the size of the territory, the prevalence of illiteracy, the varieties of religion, the tenuous communist control of some areas, and, most important, the ferocious hostility of the males, led the Zhenotdel leaders to adopt methods in accordance with the local situation. These included secret visits, rendezvous in bath-houses, and small groups or *artels* in the initial stages, and the "women's clubs"—social covers for political consciousness raising. In Batumi, the woman's club used male speakers at first until the first shrouded woman stood up and tore off her veil; in Baku it had thousands of members and became the school, church, and social center for women, replacing the gossipy bazaar. Zhenotdel workers appeared in places where a city person had never been seen before; in Central Asia they wandered over the steppe in makeshift transport, stopping at camp, *aul,* and oasis to lecture with the magic lantern (as the Sunday School teachers of Petersburg had done in the 1890's) or to show a motion picture featuring a Muslim heroine who refused to marry the old man who had bought her.

Men reacted to all this with savage violence. Women coming out of the club at Baku were assaulted by men with wild dogs and boiling water. A twenty-year-old Muslim girl who flaunted her liberation by appearing in a swimsuit was sliced to pieces by her father and brothers because they could not endure the social indignity. An eighteen-year-old Uzbek woman activist was mutilated and thrown into a well. Central Asia witnessed three hundred such murders during one quarter of 1929 alone. The Presidium of the Soviet Central Executive Committee, after consulting with the Zhenotdel, decided to classify such crimes as "counter-revolutionary offences." Yet, in spite of the danger, hundreds of native women volunteered as translators and assistants and eventually worked their way into administrative Zhenotdel positions. And each May Day or International Women's Day, thousands of women would assemble in the market places of "eastern" Soviet lands and defiantly tear off their chadras, paranjas, and veils. If it had accomplished nothing else, Zhenotdel would deserve a place in social history for having brought this about.

The variety of enterprises engaged in by the Zhenotdel was enormous: child and orphan care, school service and inspection, food distribution, housing supervision, preventive medicine and public health, anti-prostitution campaigns, war work, education, legislation, placement, family service, and mass propaganda for every campaign that the Party decided to undertake. Some of this resembled the kind of activity which traditional feminists had busied themselves with. But, as an arm of the Party, Zhenotdel had better resources to help it unlock the energies of the most backward and remote communities of Russia's women. In doing this, Zhenotdel served not only the cause of women's liberation but also the regime as a whole by helping to create new reserves of skilled and politically conscious labor....

A final word about Zhenotdel. There can be little doubt that it made an enormous impact on Soviet society, particularly in the cities. Its frequent mention in Soviet literature attests to its prominent place in everyday consciousness. Fictional treatment of Zhenotdel varied. Sometimes it was used merely as a backdrop; often it was a cause of domestic friction or an object of ridicule —and just as often as a problem-solver and proper haven for the newly conscious Soviet woman, but always a symbol of newness on the social landscape. The images were never far from the reality; Zhenotdel was an engine of mobilization in an environment of extreme social backwardness. Organizational and communication skills enabled it to go beyond the specific social task—the "small deed" of the nineteenth-century intelligentsia—toward the larger goal of mass socialization. As an arm of the Party, it lacked the independence and perhaps some of the imaginative initiative of prewar feminism; but, in spite of weaknesses noted above, the Zhenotdel surpassed the feminists in power and prestige. Zhenotdel represented a combination of class and sexual struggle and thus was a working out not only of Marxist notions about the female half of the labor movement, not only of the revolutionary Populist tradition of the "common cause," but also, in some ways, of the much more feminist belief, given expression by Lenin in 1919 that "the emancipation of working women is a matter for the working women themselves." The successes registered by Zhenotdel in raising the consciousness of poor and backward women were proof enough that there was something more to female emancipation than winning the suffrage. But its abolition in 1930 was also proof that without political equality, the "common cause" for which women had fought for three generations would always be defined by men.

The Soviet Model

The Russian Empire that preceded the Soviet Union was an autocracy. Although serfdom was not abolished until 1861 and the first elections were not held until 1906, the opposition quickly grew radical, and the "woman question" was incorporated into a broad revolutionary program. From the beginning large numbers of women joined the revolutionary movement, accounting for between 15 and 20 percent of the active membership of the revolutionary parties. In urban areas an independent feminist movement was especially active between 1905 and 1908. It concentrated its efforts chiefly on obtaining the right to vote, but in vain. On the eve of World War I Russian society consisted of a very small cultivated and westernized elite, a bourgeoisie still in embryo, and a backward peasantry that made up the remaining 80 percent of the population. People belonging to these different strata of society generally kept to themselves and knew little of other groups. This ignorance would prove a major impediment later on.

World War I broke out on August 1, 1914. Between 1914 and 1917 more than ten million men were mobilized, mostly peasants. Conditions in the countryside, already wretched, grew even worse. Many women were pressed into farm work, so many that women ultimately accounted for 72 percent of the rural workforce. They also replaced men in industrial jobs: the proportion of women in the workforce rose from 33 percent in 1914 to nearly 50 percent in 1917. From 1915 on, women found employment in new branches of industry and joined the government bureaucracy in large numbers. Their wages were lower than men's, however, at a time when prices were soaring. After 1916, the effort to keep food flowing to the cities and to the troops collapsed. The war, always unpopular, seemed hopeless, with no end in sight. For more than a year the country had been afflicted with bread riots and hunger strikes in which women played leading roles. Tension mounted. The regime began to crumble. The honor of initiating the revolution fell to women.

On February 23, 1917 (according to the Julian calendar, or March 8, according to our calendar), working women took their children out into the streets of Petrograd and staged a demonstration. Since the socialists had been unable to agree on a theme for the demonstration, the women improvised, calling for peace and bread. On the following day their ranks were swelled by an influx of male demonstrators, and the scope of the turmoil grew rapidly. On March 2 the czar abdicated. A provisional government was formed, and on July 20 it granted women the rights to vote and hold office (rights not granted in England until 1918 and the United States until 1920). Feminists, having achieved their goal, disappeared as an autonomous force. Liberal women lost control of events. When the Winter Palace was seized by the Bolsheviks on the night of October 25–26, it was defended by a women's contingent composed of intellectuals along with women of the bourgeoisie, aristocracy, and working class. The revolution now erupted into a bloody civil war whose outcome hung for a long time in the balance.

A Decade of Contradiction

Though surrounded by Whites, forces of the Allied powers, and nationalists, the Bolsheviks sallied forth from Moscow and Petrograd (later Leningrad) to regain control of nearly all of the territory that had constituted the old Russian Empire. They lost no time adopting a host of new laws concerning women. A decree of December 19, 1917, stipulated that in case of mutual consent divorce was to be granted automatically by the courts or the Registry offices (ZAGS); the principle according to which one party must be assigned blame was abolished, and the divorce decree no longer had to be publicized. Russia was the first country in the world to adopt such a liberal divorce policy. A decree of December 20, 1917, abolished religious marriage and standardized and simplified the civil marriage procedure. All children, legitimate or not, enjoyed the same legal rights. These two measures were extended by the Family Code of December 16, 1918–the most liberal in Europe at the time. The ZAGS became the chief agency for dealing with family matters. A man could no longer force his wife to accept his name, residence, or nationality. Husband and wife enjoyed absolute equality even with respect to the children. Maternity leave and workplace protection were guaranteed. The Family Code adopted a narrow definition of the family: direct ancestors and descendants together with brothers and sisters. A spouse enjoyed the same status as kin and collaterals, with no special privileges or prerogatives. The new family proved less stable than the old. Bonds between individuals were loosened: inheritance was outlawed in April 1918 (and only partially restored in 1923). Unrestricted abortion was legalized on November 20, 1920.

The Code of November 19, 1926, confirmed these earlier changes and took yet another step, abolishing all differences between marriages legally recorded by the ZAGS and *de facto* (common-law) marriages. Divorce could henceforth be obtained on the written request of either party: "postcard divorce" was now legal. Love was freer, but mutual obligations were more onerous owing to new alimony and child support requirements. The new Family Code was intended to liberate men, women, and children from the coercive regulations of another era. The past was to be completely effaced. People were urged to change their family names in March 1918 and their first names in 1924: suggestions for new names included Marlen (short for Marxism-Leninism), Engelsine, and Octobrine. Though intended to be an instrument of liberation, the code was also an instrument of coercion that could be used to strike at conservative segments of the society, particularly peasants and Muslims. In fact, the Communist Party, composed of a handful of urban intellectuals, deliberately ignored the views of those whom it sped along the road to a better tomorrow. Although lawmakers occasionally reversed themselves, their actions were always guided by two principles: to destroy czarism and build socialism....

Kollontai: A Reluctant Feminist

Alexandra Kollontai (1872–1952) was a pivotal figure in debates on women and the family during the first Soviet decade. She epitomizes all the contradictions of the period. Her biography is typical of her generation. Aristocratic by birth, she enjoyed a luxury-filled, dreamy childhood. After marrying at age nineteen to escape her family and milieu, she left her husband at age twenty-six and went to school in Zurich, then a Mecca for Russian intellectuals, where she became involved in politics, took increasingly radical positions, and eventually became a professional revolutionary. Her record was brilliant: as the first woman elected to the Central Committee in 1917, she voted in favor of the October insurrection. She then became the first woman to serve in the government, as people's commissar for health, and took an active part in drafting the Family Code of 1918. As an active member of the Workers' Opposition in 1920–1921, she sought to limit the vast powers of the Communist Party. In 1922 she became the first woman ambassador in the world. Her diplomatic career abroad kept her away from Moscow until 1945, yet her name is inseparable from the controversies of the 1920s, whose passions she fueled with countless articles, pamphlets, and brochures that were widely criticized, distorted, and even caricatured. She also wrote a number of theoretical tomes (*The Social Bases of the Woman Question*, 1909; *The Family and the Communist State*, 1918; *The New Morality and the Working Class*, 1918), as well as six works of fiction, all published in 1923. Although certain aspects of her work now seem dated, much of it remains remarkably up to date.

Kollontai proposed a synthesis of Marxism with a feminism she never avowed (and in fact always combated). Marxism, combined with a touch of Fourierist utopianism, would facilitate the realization of feminist goals. Like Marx and Engels, Kollontai believed that the bourgeois family had fallen apart and that revolution would lead to the regeneration of family life. She also drew extensively on the work of Bebel, particularly his idea that oppression tends to create unity among women. But she tried to go beyond these general arguments. Aware that the revolution was merely a starting point, she argued that to change the essence of marriage required changing people's attitudes and behavior. Therein lay her originality. She stressed the reifying tendency of the masculine will and noted the alienation of women who prefer any kind of marriage to solitude and are thus driven to wager everything on love. So Kollontai taught that love could be a kind of sport: if tender erotic friendship were based on mutual respect, jealousy and the possessive instinct might be eliminated. The "new woman," one of her recurrent subjects, was energetic and self-assertive. She let men know what she wanted; she refused to be dependent either materially or emotionally; she rebelled against socioeconomic obstacles, hypocritical morals, and "amorous captivity." Autonomous and active, she was free to explore "serial monogamy." In "Make Room for Wingèd Eros," an article published in 1923, Kollontai analyzed love's many facets: friendship, passion, maternal affection, spiritual affinity, habit, and so on. "Wingless Eros," or purely physical attraction, was to make room for "wingèd Eros," wherein physical gratification was combined with a sense of collective duty, that indispensable attribute in the era of transition to socialism. Finally, once socialist society had been established, there would be room for "Eros transfigured," or marriage based on healthy, free, and natural sexual attraction. To allow couples to develop, "kitchens must be separated from homes": in other words, society must build cafeterias, day-care centers, and dispensaries in order to relieve women of certain of their traditional responsibilities. Last but not least, motherhood was cast in a new light: it was "no longer a private affair but a social duty." Women must have children for the sake of the community. Kollontai considered abortion to be a temporary evil, to be tolerated only until the consciousness of working women had been raised to the point where it was no longer necessary. She denounced the refusal to bear children as petty-bourgeois selfishness. Nevertheless, she did not advocate the collectivization of child-rearing: parents should decide whether children were to be raised in a nursery school or at home.

As a spiritual value, however, love in general—and sex—should take precedence over the maternal instinct: "The workers' state needs a new type of relation between the sexes. A mother's narrow, exclusive love for her own child must broaden to embrace all the children of the great proletarian family. In the place of indissoluble marriage, based on the servitude of women, we look forward to the birth of free matrimony, an institution made strong by the mutual love and respect of two members of the brotherhood of Labor, equals in rights as well as obligations. In place of the individualistic, egoistic family will arise the great universal family of working people, in which everyone, men and women alike, will be first and foremost brothers and comrades." Kollontai called upon women to defend, propagate, and internalize the idea that they had value as human beings in their own right.

To be sure, Kollontai's argument was framed in terms of classical Marxism, to which the economy is primary, but she also insisted on the qualitative aspect of interpersonal relations: men and women should be attentive to each other's needs and playful toward one another. Ethics mattered to her as much as politics. Well before Wilhelm Reich, she was among the first to link sexuality with class struggle: "Why is it that we are so unforgivably indifferent to one of the essential tasks of the working class? How are we to explain the hypocritical relegation of the sexual problem to the realm of 'family affairs' not requiring collective effort? As if sexual relations and the morals governing them have not been a constant factor in social struggle throughout history."

Few people shared Kollontai's ideas in the Soviet Union of the 1920s. Her comrades looked upon her ideas as frivolous and ill-timed. Her views presupposed a yet-to-be-achieved social and economic infrastructure, and they came in for vehement criticism in a 1923 article by the Bolshevik P. Vinogradskaya, who had worked with Kollontai on the Women's Department of the Central Committee Secretariat *(Zhenotdel)* in 1920. Vinogradskaya attacked her opponent for confusing priorities, neglecting the class struggle, and encouraging sexual anarchy in an irresponsible way, since disorder in private life could lead to counterrevolutionary agitation. The task of the moment was to protect wives and children and to champion the cause of women without attacking men. Marx and Engels had already said everything there was to be said on the question, and it was pointless to indulge in "George-Sandism."

Lenin, for his part, related everything to the economy and opted in favor of monogamous marriage, egalitarian, earnest, and devoted to the cause, like his own tranquil union with Nadezhda Krupskaya. When Ines Armand saw poetry in free love, Lenin responded that what she mistook for poetry was nothing but bourgeois immorality. He borrowed his ideal from Nikolai Chernysbevski's austere novel *What Is to Be Done?* (1863), which, as he said, "bowled him over." Indeed, he thought so highly of the book that he used its title for his own theoretical work of 1902. His conversations with Clara Zetkin, which took place in 1920 but were not published until 1925, after Lenin's death, accurately reflected his rejection of lack of discipline in love and sexual matters. Lenin saw such lack of discipline as a sign of decadence and a danger to young people's health, hence to the revolution itself. He attacked the "anti-Marxist" theory according to which "in Communist society the satisfaction of sexual desires is as simple and soothing as drinking a glass of water." Lenin had nobody particular in mind. He was not attacking Kollontai, for his remarks preceded the polemic of 1923, but later Kollontai's adversaries used his wrath against her: "Of course thirst must be satisfied! But would a normal man, under normal conditions, prostrate himself in the street to drink from a filthy puddle? Or even from a glass previously soiled by dozens of other lips?" Here, purity is restored as an absolute value, and the underlying idea is that having more than one sexual partner is in itself immoral. Lenin's credo was a negative one: "No to the monk, no to the Don Juan, and no to that supposed happy medium, the German philistine." To be sure, he denounced the slavery of housework: "Woman is stifled, strangled, stupefied, and humiliated by the trivial occupations of domestic life, which chain her to the kitchen and nursery and sap her strength for work that is as unproductive, difficult, and exhausting as one can imagine." But he said nothing about the new family.

For orthodox Marxists, children did not figure in the conjugal scheme. They were to be taken care of either by certain designated women or by all the women of the community collectively—at the outset the choice is not clear. Fathers certainly play no role in the new system of child-rearing. The community supports, envelops, permeates, and transcends the reduced couple, in which man and woman are strict equals. The woman, like her husband, is a worker; traditional femininity is disparaged as a product of old bourgeois social relations. Equality in fact means identity of the sexes. The new industrious humanity consists of male and female twins, identical insofar as both are workers. "Economically and politically, which also means physiologically, the modern proletarian woman can and must become more and more like the modern proletarian man," wrote Marxist psychoneurologist Aaron Zalkind in 1924. Sexual relations, we are told, will not be a matter of great importance for such indistinguishable twins. One can interpret this claim in two ways. If sex is merely a physiological need, then the number of partners is unimportant: this is the attitude of the youth Zhenya in Kollontai's short story, "Three Generations of Love." The other interpretation leads to Leninist asceticism. In either case love must be restrained; it is a disruptive force. All of this was merely speculative, however. During the 1920s the private sphere remained intact, and various norms of sexual behavior coexisted.

A New Russia

In order to enforce the law, achieve economic equality, bring uniformity to a very disparate country, and accelerate the integration of women into the society, the Party in 1919 created the Zhenotdel, or Women's Department of the Central Committee Secretariat, with equivalents at every echelon of the hierarchy. Five women in succession led this Department during its existence, among them Ines Armand in 1919–20 and Alexandra Kollontai from 1920 to 1922. The Zhenotdel offered advice and assistance, settled labor and domestic conflicts, proposed laws and suggested amendments to Central Committee edicts, joined in actions such as the campaigns to eradicate illiteracy and abolish prostitution, coordinated the work of various agencies, oversaw the application of quotas that favored women in hiring and admission to soviets, dealt with problems of supply, housing, and sanitation, and inspected schools and orphanages. In addition to the Zhenotdel there was also a system of female delegates: women workers and peasants elected by their colleagues to participate in year-long training and indoctrination courses, after which they spent two months working with the soviets or the courts before returning to work. This system trained women to become "Soviet citizens." More than ten million of them signed up during the 1920s. Dasha, the heroine of Fedor Gladkov's novel *Cement* (1925), is a perfect example of the liberated woman. A militant delegate, she so completely threw off her old bonds that she sacrificed her marriage, her home, and even her little daughter, who died in an orphanage. There is no doubt that the Zhenotdel, together with the delegate system, had an impact on the consciousness of women. Its political influence remained negligible, however, and all too often it served only to convey the wishes of the hierarchy to the rank and file. In 1923 it was accused of "feminist deviationism," a fatal sin....

Freedom and Disorder

... In one sense, women were granted all they could have hoped for right at the outset, without a struggle. But the most difficult part of the task remained: they had to learn how to make use of their newly won rights to forge a new way of life. But given the sociohistorical context and the gaps in the codes of 1918 and 1926, new freedoms gave rise to unintended consequences.

Two signs of the times were marital instability and a widespread reluctance to have children. The number of abortions rose, the birthrate declined precipitously, and newborn babies were frequently abandoned. Orphanages, overwhelmed by new admissions, became veritable charnel houses. Infanticide and wife-murder increased. In effect, women and children were the first victims of the new order. The condition of women clearly became more dire, especially in the cities. Men abandoned their families, leaving their wives without resources. The availability of divorce merely on application by either party led to cynical abuses. The government allowed common-law marriages in order to protect women from seduction and abandonment (and also to protect any children that might result from fleeting affairs); men were required to provide for the women they left behind, and thus to assume a burden that the government itself was unable to bear. But women had to prove that an affair had taken place, and the law failed to specify what constituted proof. The courts improvised. Lengthy and often fruitless paternity suits poisoned relations between the sexes and became a recurrent theme of contemporary fiction. The laws governing alimony were just as vague, and the courts were obliged to fix amounts on a case-by-case basis. Often it was set at one-third or one-fourth of the man's monthly wage, which sometimes created insurmountable difficulties. How was a man to survive if ten rubles were deducted from his wage of forty rubles? How was he to support a child born out of wedlock when he already had four "legitimate" children to take care of? Few men earned enough to cover alimony, and many refused to pay up. Rulings of the court went unenforced in more than half the cases.

There were practical problems as well. Allocation of housing was a state monopoly, and waiting lists were extremely long. Divorced couples were therefore obliged in some cases to go on living together. Abram Room's film *Bed and Sofa* (1927) is a marvelous depiction of conditions under the NEP [New Economic Policy]. It offers a new perspective on the eternal triangle, portraying a husband, wife, and lover forced to share a single room. After the seduction, moreover, the two men take a nonchalant attitude toward the situation and join in a macho alliance against the woman, the wife of one and mistress of the other.

Many women who wanted children were nevertheless forced to seek abortions because of the scarcity of housing, low wages, short supplies, and/or lack of a man. In a survey conducted in Moscow in 1927, 71 percent of women seeking abortions cited "living conditions" as the reason and 22 percent mentioned unstable love lives." Only 6 percent rejected motherhood on principle.

Although intellectuals and quasi-intellectuals in the cities went on leading bohemian lives, some segments of the population resisted any change in traditional mores. In 1928, 77.8 percent of the population still consisted of peasants, compared with only 17.6 percent blue- and white-collar workers. The Code of 1926 triggered a huge controversy that illustrates the continuing influence of the peasantry. Since accurate news was hard to come by despite innumerable published articles, brochures, and meetings, peasants were liable to be affected by unsubstantiated rumors, and many were convinced that the new code was going to make the sharing of women compulsory. The most controversial provision of the law concerned the treatment of de facto marriage as completely equivalent to lawful matrimony. The Agrarian Code of 1922 reinforced the communal organization of the village, or *mir*, and retained the undivided family property, or *dvor*. If a couple sharing in the *dvor* divorced and payment "of alimony led to division of the property, the farm might cease to be viable. Wary after years of ceaseless combat (1914–1921), the peasantry, fearful of novelty, drew back and clung to its traditional values.

It was an ambiguous image of woman that emerged from all the articles, brochures, pamphlets, investigations, speeches, novels, and films of the day: sometimes she was portrayed as a member of the vanguard of the working class, wearing an earnest look, work clothes, and a red scarf; at other times she was the backward peasant with her white kerchief pulled down over her eyes; or the mannish girl of the Komsomol (Young Communists), shockingly liberated in her ways; or the pert, flirtatious typist. Woman simultaneously embodied the past and the future. Conviction vied with confusion in the minds of the masses. Novels of the late 1920s are filled with restless, confused, unhappy heroines. Urban immorality and rural conservatism were matters of concern to both rulers and ruled. Women wanted stability, men declined responsibility, and the Party wanted to keep its program on course. By 1926 it was clear that, like it or not, the family would survive. Certain sectors of light industry were sacrificed in the name of economic progress. Home and children once again became the concern of women. The woman question was held to have been resolved once and for all, and in 1929 the Zhenotdel was abolished....

A Contestable and Contested Model

By 1923 the die was cast. Although there was progress at the grass roots, there was stalemate at the top. The masses were enlisted in the struggle, but the once competent, combative, and cultivated elite was supplanted by squadrons of colorless yes-men. Strong personalities such as Alexandra Kollontai were removed or liquidated.

In the end Kollontai's fears were justified. Without a redefinition of sex roles economic emancipation proved to be a trap, for women were obliged to conform to a male model without being relieved of their burden as women. It may be that a comparable danger exists in any developing industrial society. A century of European evolution was compressed into two decades in the Soviet Union: the sexual revolution of the 1920s broke down the old family unit, while the Stalinist reaction of the 1930s reshaped the family in order to impose breakneck industrialization on a backward peasant society. The gap between the idealistic slogans and everyday reality was enormous.

The one-party state was not solely responsible for these developments, however. As in other countries, the role of women was ambiguous. Whether responding by instinct to ensure their own survival and that of their children or acting out of alienation, women accepted and internalized the rules of the Soviet game to a greater extent than men—and much to men's annoyance. Sober, long-suffering, conscientious, and disciplined, woman was one of the pillars of the regime: she did the washing, stood in line to buy food, cooked meals, took care of the children, worked in factories and offices and on collective farms, and did whatever she had to do. But to what end? Equality only added to her burden.

POSTSCRIPT

Did the Bolshevik Revolution Improve the Lives of Soviet Women?

It is one of history's ironies that, with the stroke of a pen, Soviet women were granted all the legal and political rights that women in Britain and the United States were struggling to achieve. Having won the rights to vote and hold public office, Soviet women struggled to translate those paper rights into improved lives for themselves and their children. It has been a conviction of Western feminism that legal and political equality pave the way for full emancipation of women. The Soviet case raises interesting questions about the confusion that arises when there are conflicting revolutions. Real political power belongs to those who can ensure that the goals of their revolution receive first priority. It was the socialist revolution, not women's emancipation, that the party leadership worked to achieve.

Popular accounts of the Russian Revolution may be found in John Reed's *Ten Days That Shook the World* (Penguin, 1977) and Louise Bryant's *Mirrors of Moscow* (Hyperion Press, 1973). The story of Reed and Bryant, two Americans who find themselves eyewitnesses to the Bolshevik Revolution, is captured in the film *Reds*. Another film covering the same period is *Doctor Zhivago*, which is based on the book of the same title by Boris Pasternak (1958). For Lenin's views on women, one of the best sources is his book *The Emancipation of Women* (International Publishers, 1972). *The Unknown Lenin: From the Secret Archives* edited by the eminent Russian historian Richard Pipes (Yale University Press, 1996) dips into the secret archives and brands Lenin a ruthless and manipulative leader. Robert McNeal's *Bride of the Revolution* (University of Michigan Press, 1972) focuses on the fascinating marriage and revolutionary relationship between Lenin and Bolshevik propagandist Nadezha Krupskaya. And Sheila Fitzpatrick, in *The Russian Revolution* (Oxford University Press, 1982), surveys the critical 1917–1932 period with special emphasis on the work of Zhenotdel. For essays on the lives of women during this period, students may want to see *Women in Soviet Society* edited by Gail Lapidus (University of California Press, 1978) and *Women in Russia* edited by D. Atkinson, A. Dallin, and G. Lapidus (Stanford University Press, 1977), which grew out of a 1975 conference that was held at Stanford University entitled "Women in Russia." The fascinating character Alexandra Kollontai, who died at 80, may be explored through her own writings in *Selected Writings* (W. W. Norton, 1972), *Red Love* (Hyperion Press, 1990), and *Love of Worker Bees* (Academy of Chicago Press, 1978). Books about Kollontai include *Bolshevik Feminist* by Barbara Clements (Indiana University Press, 1979).

ISSUE 18

Was World War II the Result of Hitler's Master Plan?

YES: Andreas Hillgruber, from *Germany and the Two World Wars,* trans. William C. Kirby (Harvard University Press, 1981)

NO: Ian Kershaw, from *The Nazi Dictatorship: Problems and Perspectives of Interpretation,* 3rd ed. (Edward Arnold, 1993)

ISSUE SUMMARY

YES: German scholar and history professor Andreas Hillgruber states that Hitler systematically pursued his foreign policy goals once he came to power in Germany and that World War II was the inevitable result.

NO: Ian Kershaw, a professor of history at the University of Sheffield, argues that Hitler was responsible for the execution of German foreign policy that led to World War II but was not free from forces both within and outside Germany that influenced his decisions.

Adolf Hitler and World War II have become inseparable in the minds of most people; any discussion of one ultimately leads to the other. Due to the diabolical nature of Hitler's actions and the resulting horrors, historical analyses of the war were slow to surface after the war. World War II was simply viewed as Hitler's war, and all responsibility for it began and ended with him.

This all changed in 1961 with the publication of A. J. P. Taylor's *The Origins of the Second World War* (Atheneum, 1985). Taylor extended the scope of World War II beyond Hitler and found British and French actions culpable. Furthermore, he stated that Hitler was more of an opportunist than an idealogue and that war was the result of misconceptions and blunders on both sides. His work was both praised for its openmindedness and condemned for its perceived apologetic attitude toward Hitler. Regardless of its mixed reception, it opened the origins of the war and Hitler's role to historical scrutiny.

Nowhere was this move more welcome than in Germany, where scholars and citizens had been forced to live with the Hitler legacy. Scholars began investigating the Nazi era and Hitler's role in it more openly, letting the chips fall where they would. In the 1980s this developed into a national debate known as the *Historikerstreit* (historical quarrel or debate), and the result was a flood of new works raising several interesting and provocative questions. Were Hitler and Nazism an aberration, or did they reflect a tradition well established in German history? Can Hitler be held solely responsible for the war and its horrors, or were others culpable as well? Was Hitler master of the Third Reich or a fragmented reflection of it?

German historians were not the only ones to participate in this process. They were joined by historians from other countries, many of them British. Scholars such as Ian Kershaw, Tim Mason, and others began to reevaluate the origins of the war and the concomitant responsibility for it. Eventually, most of this scholarship was divided into two schools of thought: the intentionalists, who believed that the Third Reich and all that resulted from it emanated from Hitler's will; and the functionalists or structuralists, who saw Hitler as a product of the environment he helped to create and could not ignore when it was time to make major policy decisions. The intentionalists are represented by the scholarship of Ebhard Jackel, Klaus Hildebrand, and Andreas Hillgruber; the functionalists by Tim Mason, Hans Mommsen, and Martin Broszat.

According to the intentionalists, despite international and national pressures on Hitler after his accession to power in 1933, the course of events that led to World War II was primarily planned and implemented by him. Surely there were times when things didn't work out according to his master plan. But in the words of eminent diplomatic historian Donald Cameron Watt in *How War Came: The Immediate Origins of the Second World War, 1938–1939* (Pantheon Books, 1989, p. 619), "Always one returns to Hitler: Hitler exultant, Hitler vehement, Hitler indolent, Hitler playing the great commander... threatening, cajoling, and appealing to German destiny."

The structuralist response is more complex. Some, such as Mason, emphasize how socioeconomic pressures within 1930s German society influenced Hitler's decision-making process. Others, such as Mommsen, highlight the decentralized leadership system preferred by Hitler as a reason for the seemingly unplanned nature of his regime. Still others emphasize the lack of a coherent plan in much of the Third Reich, seeing Hitler an opportunist rather than a master planner.

Here we have chosen Hillgruber to represent the intentionalist side of the question, arguing that World War II was part of Hitler's grand scheme. Ian Kershaw offers a clear statement of the structuralist side of the debate in a work that synthesizes the two schools.

Andreas Hillgruber

 **YES**

Germany and the Two World Wars

Hitler's Program

Hitler's conception of his future foreign policy developed in many stages between 1919 and 1928 before solidifying into a firm program, to which he then single-mindedly adhered until his suicide in the Reich Chancellery on April 30, 1945. What was at once decisive and totally novel in the formation of his program—and this must be stressed—was the complete permeation of originally crude Machiavellian objectives by the most radical variety of anti-Semitism. Although he drew on the theory of the worldwide Jewish conspiracy as propagated in the "Protocols of the Elders of Zion," widely distributed by White Russian immigrants in *völkisch* circles in Germany in 1919–1920, there were, in Hitler's case, crucial psychological factors. The wide-ranging political aims of Hitler's foreign policy were subordinated to a central goal: the eradication of the Jewish "archenemy."

The full scope and thrust of the foreign policy which Hitler had already set as his life's mission in the 1920s became clear only some time after the Second World War with the enrichment of our source materials, especially through the publication of Hitler's early speeches and his "Second Book" of 1928. This documentation made it possible to place the programmatic utterances of *Mein Kampf,* which previously had appeared fragmentary and unrelated to the actual practice of the Third Reich (at least in the years of peace) in the context of their origin and elaboration. In time it became clear how systematically Hitler had pursued his aims after the mid-1920s without, however, forfeiting any of his tactical flexibility. It emerged that the sentence printed in bold-face letters in *Mein Kampf,* "Germany will either be a world power or there will be no Germany," was, quite literally, the crux of Hitler's program.

In brief, his aim was this. After gaining power in Germany and consolidating his rule in Central Europe, he would lead the Reich to a position of world power in two main stages. First, he would set up a continental empire that would control all Europe with a solid economic and strategic power base in vast stretches of Eastern Europe. Then, by adding a colonial realm in Africa and by building a strong Atlantic-based navy, he would make Germany one of the four remaining world powers (after forcing out France and Russia), beside the British

Empire, the Japanese sphere in East Asia, and (most important to Hitler's mind) the United States. He anticipated for the generation after his death a decisive struggle between the two leading world powers, Germany and America, for a sort of world dominion. For this violent confrontation in the future, a battle of continents, he wanted to create in his own time the necessary geopolitical basis (the "sphere of control") for the anticipated "Germanic Empire of the German Nation." Failing this, as Hitler saw the alternative, Germany would inevitably be condemned to insignificance in world politics.

In his "Second Book," Hitler rated American strength extremely high, albeit assuming that it would reach its apogee only around 1980. He therefore saw the unification of all Europe under his rule as imperative, and an alliance between this super-Germany and the British Empire as desirable in order to challenge America later. By contrast, he held Russian power in extraordinarily low esteem. He believed that a Germany shaped by racial principles need not fear a potential Russian world power, as they should fear the racially "high-grade" Americans. "These people," he wrote of the Russians at a crucial juncture in his "Second Book,"

> live in a state structure whose value, judged traditionally, would have to be even higher than that of the United States. Despite this, however, it would never occur to anybody to fear Russian world hegemony for this reason. No such inner value is attached to the number of Russian people that this number could endanger the freedom of the world. At least never [like the United States] in the sense of an economic and political mastery of other parts of the globe, but at most in the sense of an inundation by disease bacilli which at the moment have their breeding ground in Russia.

The conquest of European Russia, the cornerstone of the continental European phase of his program, was thus for Hitler inextricably linked with the extermination of these "bacilli," the Jews. In his conception they had gained dominance over Russia with the Bolshevik Revolution. Russia thereby became the center from which a global danger radiated, particularly threatening to the Aryan race and its German core. To Hitler, Bolshevism meant the consummate rule of Jewry, while democracy—as it had developed in Western Europe and Weimer Germany—represented a preliminary stage of Bolshevism, since the Jews had there won a leading, if not yet a dominant influence. This racist component of Hitler's thought was so closely interwoven with the central political element of his program, the conquest of European Russia, that Russia's defeat and the extermination of the Jews were—in theory as later in practice—inseparable for him. To the aim of expansion per se, however, Hitler gave not racial but political, strategic, economic, and demographic underpinnings.

By what method was he to reach this goal, so fantastic from the standpoint of 1928, but brought so close to realization in the turbulent years from the beginning of 1938 to the end of 1941? To understand Hitler's method one must assume that in the development of his schemes, as later in their execution, he had already come to terms, in a complex manner, with the real and prewar Vienna period and postwar Munich years, the war provided the politician (and later commander-in-chief) Hitler with his formative experiences. It made him recognize the impossibility of a German victory in a war where Germany was pitted against both the continental power, Russia, and the British Empire, let alone the two Anglo-Saxon sea powers. His memory was alive with the hopelessness of Germany's predicament surrounded by enemies in a Central European bastion—even one somewhat expanded by larger perimeters in east and west—in a world war in which the superior economic and armaments potential of the hostile coalition would ultimately tell. While holding firmly to Ludendorff's expansive principles of the latter phase of the First World War, Hitler linked these to considerations of power politics and geopolitical perspectives and drew his own unique conclusions.

In following a systematic foreign policy whose final prize was to be reached in several stages, the immediate objectives had always to be limited to a single direction of expansion. The net gain of these intermediate goals (seen in both military-economic and strategic terms, with an eye to the great war expected in the future) was to bring Germany into such a favorable situation that a repetition of the Reich's predicament in the First World War would be forever excluded. The basic hypothesis of the politically and ideologically decisive phase of this program, Germany's "break out" to the east, was that Germany would defer colonial and overseas ambitions in return for British recognition of German hegemony over continental Europe (including European Russia), with the United States standing aside. With his typical equation of political with territorial interests in all great power politics (which he understood in terms of "spheres of influence"), Hitler was incapable of foreseeing any conflict with British and American interests in this phase of his program for expansion. "England does not want Germany to be a world power; but France wants no power that is named Germany," he had maintained in *Mein Kampf.* "Today, however"—that is, the period of the Weimar Republic in the mid-1920s—"we are not fighting for a world power position." Thus, for this period of struggle "for the survival of the Fatherland" (as also for the following period of German expansion on the continent) he deemed an alliance with Great Britain possible and desirable. Furthermore—and this is crucial to an understanding of Hitler's practice of foreign policy from 1933 to 1941—the alliance was to take the form of a "grand solution" involving German dominance over the whole of continental Europe.

Hitler's ultimate aspiration in power politics, however, went well beyond this. To his mind, the achievement of German rule over continental Europe would itself provide the basis for a German position of world power. This position would then, in a new phase of imperialist expansion—with a view toward an ultimate war with America—be built by a strong German navy and a large colonial empire in Africa. If possible, this would be accomplished with England's acquiescence and at the expense of France, which was to be defeated before the conquest of the East.

The preliminary stage of the program, the winning of a broader base in Central Europe, was to be reached by gradual expansion of German territory and initially by peaceful means. Here the slogan "struggle against Versailles" and the exploitation of pan-German agitation in German Austria and the Habsburg successor-states provided the best opportunities to conceal the real, far

more extensive aims. When these means had been exhausted, further partial objectives would be won through localized wars, using a qualitatively superior army against one enemy at a time. In addition to the political gains, Germany's meager military-economic base would thus be broadened to such an extent that the German-ruled sphere could withstand a new world war even with a comprehensive economic blockade by the sea powers. But until that time Germany's position would be vulnerable and a great, long war was to be avoided at all costs.

Only when all of these steps had been taken would Germany no longer need fear the quantitative arms and economic superiority of the established world powers, including American potential. Germany's military-economic and geographical base area, an armaments program geared to superior quality, not quantity, and Hitler's conception of "lightning war" (*Blitzkrieg*) were all closely related central components of his method. If despite such obviously difficult preconditions all the premises proved valid, Hitler believed that he would succeed in creating an autarkic, blockade-proof, and defensible sphere that would grant Germany real autonomy (and not just formal sovereignty) for all time. In short, he would create a German world power to stand beside the other world powers.

In comparison with the German war goals developed during the First World War, Hitler's aims were radically simplified; moreover, the racial-ideological conclusions drawn in his program, which were directed to a complete transformation of Europe along racial principles, represented something entirely different. True, purely in terms of power politics and territory, the war goals of the latter part of the war were not so different from Nazi expansionist aims. But to Hitler, the prerequisite for the establishment and maintenance of German rule over Europe was the physical extermination of the Russian ruling stratum and its putative basis, the millions of Eastern European Jews. In National Socialist ideology, this prerequisite was grounded in the mythical link between Bolshevist rule and Jewry. It was to be following by the destruction of all Jews in the rest of continental Europe, subjugated, directly or indirectly, to German control. The diverse territories of the former Russian state were not merely, like the rest of continental Europe, to be brought into close dependence on Germany, but reduced to the level of colonies, to be exploited economically and settled by members of the ruling race. Colonialism, which in the imperialist era had been limited to overseas regions and suggestions of which had marked Germany's eastern policy in 1918 (and to a lesser extent the later Allied intervention in the Soviet Union), was now fully transferred to Europe.

These enormous schemes, and particularly their connection with racist ideology, were, to be sure, the program of a single individual. But in the case of such prominent provisions as the revision of the Versailles Treaty and the creation of a "Greater Germany," they overlapped with the aims of the old German leadership and the fantasies of a large part of the German public that had never assimilated the loss of the war. To this one must add, however, that the essence of Hitler's program "violated all traditions of German foreign policy and foresook all established standards and concepts to such a radical degree that it . . . did not penetrate the consciousness of the German public," despite its continual proclamation in his speeches from 1926 to 1930.

The experiences of the First World War had proved the impossibility of a German victory over a coalition of other great powers that, according to elementary rules of power politics, was almost certain to be formed in response to a German "break-out" to the east or west. Thus, only in an uncommonly narrow ideological perspective was it imaginable to achieve the ultimate objective of Hitler's program by taking on isolated enemies one by one and exploiting current and sometimes serious differences among the other European powers. This was unlikely to occur without the planned "duels" in the form of "lightning wars" provoking premature counter-actions on the part of other states and thus endangering an undesired, unwinnable general war.

Hitler's utterly unrealistic image of Russia can only be called mythical. It was devoid of any comprehension of the actual foundations of the Soviet system. He matched it with a one-sided idealized conception of England, in which only certain elements of British reality—the colonial and maritime traditions—were included. That component of British policy most important in respect to his program—Britain's interest in the continental European balance of power—was ignored. Any German foreign policy based upon such misconceptions was likely to fail fast unless uncommonly favorable conditions in international relations provided a lengthy period for illusory successes. This was precisely the case in the 1930s as, in contrast to the period before 1914, deep antagonisms between Britain and Russia granted Germany a relatively large space for maneuver.

Hitler's Foreign Policy and the Alignment of the Powers, 1933–1939

... While the other powers were uncertain in their attitudes toward the Third Reich, and despite several risks (the sudden withdrawal from the League [of Nations] on October 14, 1933, and the subversive activity of Austrian Nazis), Hitler was able, through unscrupulous and shifting tactics, to overcome the diplomatic isolation that threatened three times: in the autumn of 1933; in the summer of 1934, after the abortive Nazi coup in Vienna; and in the spring of 1935, following the declaration of German military sovereignty. With the conclusion of the Anglo-German Naval Agreement of July 18, 1935, he finally won greater freedom of action in foreign policy. His room for maneuver abroad was considerably broadened thereafter by Italy's Abyssinian war of October 1935 to the summer of 1936 and by the outbreak of the Spanish Civil War in July 1936. The sanctions imposed against Italy by the League of Nations pushed Mussolini into Hitler's arms, while the course of the Spanish Civil War showed that England still perceived her conflict with the Soviet Union, which intervened in Spain, to be of greater consequence than her tensions with the German and Italian "Axis powers" also militarily engaged in Spain. France, however, no longer possessed the strength to realize her own divergent objectives. With the acceptance of Hitler's occupation of the demilitarized zone of the Rhineland on March 7, 1936, France was essentially reduced to following England's lead in foreign policy....

The year 1936 saw the transition from domestic German reconstruction to the actualization of Hitler's foreign program. Noteworthy in this process was how the floodlights of propaganda were directed at certain distant goals, while the immediate objectives remained in the dark. Before Hitler actually entered upon the first phase of his policy of open expansion in continental Europe, German propaganda already forecast the phase of winning world power. On March 7, 1936, Hitler, for the first time as Reich Chancellor, officially demanded the return of Germany's former African colonies. From then on, this was a recurrent theme in his speeches. Yet he drew back when the British government sought to start concrete colonial negotiations in 1937–1938; the hour for the African land-grab was supposed to strike only after continental hegemony had been won. On March 16, 1939, a day after the occupation of Prague and the creation of the Protectorate of Bohemia and Moravia, Goebbels' instructions to the press hinted vaguely at the long-range aim: "Use of the term 'Greater German World Empire' is undesirable. The term 'World Empire' is reserved for later eventualities." Such a dominion, Himmler told S.S. group leaders on November 8, 1938, would be "the greatest empire that man ever established and the world ever saw."

The most important measure anticipating this last stage of Hitlerian foreign policy, taken on January 27, 1939, was the decision to build a powerful German high seas fleet. By 1944–1946, 10 capital ships, 3 battle cruisers, 8 heavy cruisers, 44 light cruisers, 4 aircraft carriers, 68 destroyers, 90 torpedo boats, and 249 submarines were to be built. With this decision, Hitler broke the 1935 Anglo-German Naval Agreement even before denouncing it officially on April 28, 1939, following England's March 31 guarantee of Polish independence. The decision to build a fleet over a long period had a political implication that Hitler acknowledged to the naval commander-in-chief, Admiral Erich Raeder: until the fleet was completed around 1945, risk of war with Britain had to be avoided at all costs.

The naval construction fit in with the planned sequence of Hitler's program as it had meanwhile been roughly fixed. In his secret memorandum of August 1936 on the Four Year Plan, Hitler reckoned that peaceful means for German expansion would be exhausted by 1940 at the latest. He therefore demanded that in four years' time "the German army be ready for action" and "the German economy capable of waging war." But these pronouncements should not be understood as Hitler's intention to unleash a general war in Europe in 1940. (The main stage of the continental European phase of his program, the conquest of European Russia, was planned for 1943–1945.) Rather, the military and economic measures taken in 1936 were designed to enable Hitler to exert "political pressure up to the threat of war" and pursue an "audacious policy of risk" in accomplishing the intermediate aims of the years 1938–1939. Consequently, a significant, if steadily diminishing, discrepancy always existed between German readiness for war as described in propaganda and the real level of armament achieved. On the basis of the general economic mobilization begun with the Four Year Plan of 1936, which represented a stage between a peacetime and a "total war" economy, Hitler meant to wage distinct, separately timed "lightning wars" against one enemy at a time without bringing on a world war. . . .

The phase of open expansion began in 1938–1939. Austria was incorporated into the Reich on March 13, 1938, followed by the Sudentenland after the Munich pact of September 29; the remainder of Czechoslovakia was dismantled on March 15, 1939. From the beginning of this phase, Hitler's basic problem was whether England would accept his step-by-step conquest of the entire continent or, from a certain point on, would intervene to oppose the unfolding of his program. Beginning in late 1937, warnings and misgivings about England's position came from a variety of sources. Some issued from those conservative forces of the German upper stratum (chiefly leading military figures) who, despite criticism of certain aspects of Nazi policy, had promoted Germany's resurgence under Hitler. These leaders supported a foreign policy of moderate territorial revisions in Europe that seemed to coincide with Hitler's aims, at least as represented in his public speeches after 1933. Their opposition was awakened when Hitler (with only a hint at the ultimate goals) revealed his program of expansion to the commanders of the armed forces and Foreign Minister Konstantin von Neurath on November 5, 1937. . . .

Under the influence of [his chief foreign policy adviser Jaachim von] Ribbentrop, whom he made foreign minister on February 4, 1938, Hitler's political attitude toward Britain grew ambivalent. Although he never truly embraced Ribbentrop's foreign policy—it was, after all, the very opposite of his own—after mid-1938 Hitler no longer excluded the possibility of a conflict with England in an early phase of his program. Still, he continued to aspire to his "grand solution" of global Anglo-German compromise and to consider English neutrality attainable during the phase of German continental expansion. On Hitler's orders, the navy and air force began to plan in mid-1938 for a potential war with England, a contingency previously ignored. As, however, German rearmament had been geared solely to continental Europe, the military could only conclude that the technical prerequisites for victory over England would be lacking for several years.

At the end of March 1939, following the establishment of the Protectorate of Bohemia and Moravia and the inclusion of Slovakia as a satellite in the German sphere, Hitler realized that he had exhausted his potential for peaceful expansion, particularly since his attempt to include Poland as a junior partner in the German-led continental bloc for the later drive to the East had now completely failed. Britain's guarantee of Polish independence on March 31, 1939, made this perfectly clear. With often divergent aims in mind, Hitler and Ribbentrop then turned all their efforts to the political isolation of Poland, now designated an enemy, and to her defeat in the localized war that was being prepared for September 1939. . . .

Hitler, Stalin, and The British Government: August 1939

Even as the tactical shift toward an arrangement with the Soviet Union was in full swing, Hitler gave expression to the constancy of his aims in a conversation of August 11, 1939, with Carl J. Burckhardt, the High Commissioner of the League of Nations in the free city of Danzig: "Everything that I undertake is directed against Russia; if the West is too stupid and too blind to understand this, then I will be forced to reach an understanding with the Russians, smash the West, and then turn all my concentrated strength against the Soviet Union. I need the Ukraine, so that no one can starve us out again as in the last war." Poland, which Hitler had resolved since the spring to remove as an independent power, was no longer even an issue. By "smashing the West," Hitler meant the defeat of France and the elimination of all British influence on the continent; both aims were to be accomplished during the period of détente with Stalin, before the German march to the East. Hitler's argument that Germany had to rule a blockage-proof area hinted at the more distant future: the expected confrontation with the sea powers following the winning of the Ukraine.

The continuity of Hitler's far-reaching strategy is also visible in his hint of a "generous offer" to England of August 25, 1939, an offer to come in the period after Poland's fall. Apart from the tactical motive of having England stand aside during the Polish campaign, the initiative showed Hitler's continued desire for a "grand solution" whereby England would let Germany control the continent in return for a German guarantee of the British Empire. His rejection of the British proposals for compromise transmitted through [Helmuth] Wohlthat and [Hermann] Göring must be seen in the light of this announcement of his own "generosity" toward England.

On August 25, two days after the conclusion of the German-Soviet Nonaggression Pact, which Hitler expected to have a powerful effect on England, he told the British ambassador, Sir Neville Henderson, that after the Polish question had been resolved, he would "approach England once more with a large and comprehensive offer." He was "ready to conclude agreements with England which... would not only guarantee the existence of the British Empire in all circumstances as far as Germany is concerned, but would also if necessary assure the British Empire of German assistance regardless of where such assistance should be necessary...."

Forced after September 3, 1939, to deal with the Western coalition, Hitler found himself hard pressed at an early stage of his program, not the least because the build-up of the German forces, particularly the navy, was by no means completed. He could escape his predicament only by rapid and risky military action. Far more than before, he now had to relate each step of his program to the political and strategic strengths of his present and potential enemies (above all the United States) if he were not to fall into ever greater difficulties.

Hitler's broad program of future expansion by stages had excluded any and all contingency planning for a European war against the Western powers before that war in fact broke out. Indeed, apart from the plan for the Polish campaign, there existed no general staff guidelines for future operations. Even in the summer of 1939, Hitler expressly ordered that the German High Command give no consideration to overall strategy in the event of war with the West. Rejecting the possibility that the situation of September 3 would result from his attack on Poland, Hitler had simply not given it the attention it required.

Only in one particular did Hitler gain from the European war having been ignited by the conflict with Poland. The German-Polish borders, as drawn by the Versailles Treaty of 1919 and the division of Upper Silesia in 1921, were felt to be intolerable by all political forces in Germany and indeed by the German people as a whole during the period of the Weimar Republic. There was a general demand for the revision of these frontiers, especially the return of Danzig and the elimination of the corridor separating East Prussia from the rest of the Reich. Hitler's 1934 pact with Poland was among the least acclaimed of his foreign policy successes in Germany. When he sought the "small solution" of revised boundaries with Poland, however, he gained the broadest consensus, and not just within his party. Even those leading military figures of the old conservative elite who had planned a coup against Hitler in the autumn of 1938, when the Sudeten crisis threatened to ignite a European war, saw his demands against Poland as justified. In addition, conservative diplomats and army leaders mistook the Hitler-Stalin pact for a renewal of Bismarck's Russian policy; from their historical standpoint, too, the defeat of the Polish state formed at Germany's and Russia's expense in 1919–1920, and the reestablishment of a German-Russian border in Poland, seemed desirable. Warsaw's strict refusal to negotiate revisions with Hitler was not understood in Germany. "We believe we will make quick work of the Poles, and, in truth, we are delighted at the prospect. That business *must* be cleared up." So wrote General Eduard Wagner, staff chief to the Army Quartermaster-General, to his wife on August 31, 1939. Wagner was anything but an uncritical supporter of Hitler; he was, on the contrary, one of the leaders of the officers' *fronde.*

With his tactic of making seemingly liberal offers to Poland, Hitler sought to arouse the impression that he was striving for "reasonable" border revisions so that the public would blame Polish intransigence for the war. The result was an enormous propaganda success within Germany and, to a certain degree, even abroad in the West—in France, for example, under the slogan, *"Mourir pour Danzig?"* Resonances of such a short-sighted view of the war's origins may be discerned today in the so-called revisionist historiography of David L. Hoggan, A. J. P. Taylor, and their German imitators in radical right circles. On August 29, however, Hitler had already decided the sequence of events of the next few days, in case a Polish negotiator should yet appear in Berlin. Army Chief of Staff General Franz Halder noted tersely and unequivocally in his diary: "August 30, Poles in Berlin. August 31, collapse of negotiations. September 1, use of force."

Yet the campaign against Poland that began on September 1 was a mere preliminary. In no sense was it *the* war that Hitler sought as the crucial stage in the realization of his program. To his mind, the European war that came on September 3 was as incomprehensible as it was contrary to his aims. The interests of France and England, he thought, were unaffected by the "clearing up" of a regional problem. Instead, they intervened to stop him.

Hitler's responsibility for the war would be quite insufficiently revealed by focusing exclusively on his role in unleashing the European war in August and September 1939. His decision for a second war, totally different in character, must be brought into the picture. This war began with the attack on the Soviet Union on June 22, 1941. Only then did the Second World War truly begin.

Nazi Foreign Policy: Hitler's 'Programme' or 'Expansion Without Object'?

Several important aspects of German foreign policy in the Third Reich are still unresolved issues of scholarly debate. In this sphere too, however, interpretations—especially among West German scholars—have come to be divided in recent years around the polarized concepts of 'intention' and 'structure', which we have encountered in other contexts. Research in the GDR [German Democratic Republic] before the revolution of 1989-90 showed no interest in this division of interpretation, and proceeded on the basis of predictably different premises, concentrating on documenting and analysing the expansionist aims of Germany's industrial giants—a task which was accomplished with no small degree of success. Nevertheless, with all recognition of the imperialist aspirations of German capitalism, explanations which limit the role of Hitler and other leading Nazis to little more than that of executants of big business aims have never carried much conviction among western scholars. Conventional orthodoxy in the West, resting in good measure upon West German scholarship, has ... tended to turn such explanations in their heads in advocating an uncompromising 'primacy of politics' in the Third Reich. And whatever the nuances of interpretations, Hitler's own steerage of the course of German aggression in accordance with the 'programme' he had outlined (for those with eyes to see) in *Mein Kampf* and the *Second Book* is generally and strongly emphasized. Parallel to explanations of the Holocaust, outright primacy is accorded to Hitler's ideological goals in shaping a consistent foreign policy whose broad outlines and objectives were 'programmed' long in advance.

Such an interpretation has in recent years been subjected to challenge by historians seeking to apply a 'structuralist' approach to foreign policy as to other aspects of Nazi rule—even if the 'structuralist' argument appears in this area to be on its least firm ground. Exponents of a 'structuralist' approach reject the notion of a foreign policy which has clear contours unfolding in line with a Hitlerian ideological 'programme' in favour of an emphasis upon expansion whose format and aims were unclear and unspecific, and which took shape in no small measure as a result of the uncontrollable dynamism and radicalizing momentum of the Nazi movement and governmental system. In this gradual and somewhat confused process of development—as in the 'Jewish Question'—terms such as *'Lebensraum'* served for long as propaganda slogans and 'ideological metaphors' before appearing as attainable and concrete goals. Again, the *function* of Hitler's foreign-policy image and ideological fixations rather than his direct personal intervention and initiative is stressed. And rather than picturing Hitler as a man of unshakeable will and crystal-clear vision, moulding events to his liking in accordance with his ideological aims, he is portrayed as 'a man of improvization, of experiment, and the spur-of-the-moment bright idea'. Any 'logic' or inner 'rationality' of the course of German foreign policy gains its appearance, it is argued, only teleologically—by looking at the end results and interpreting these in the light of Hitler's apparently prophetic statements of the 1920s....

Serious attempts to challenge this dominant orthodoxy which emphasizes the autonomy of Hitler's programmatic aims in determining foreign policy have come from a number of different directions. They might conveniently be fitted into three interlocking categories:

(i) Rejection of any notion of a 'programme' or 'plan in stages', denial of concrete and specific long-range foreign policy aims, and portrayal of Hitler as a man of spontaneous response to circumstances—not far removed from the image of the 'unprincipled opportunist'—with a central concern in propaganda exploitation and the protection of his own prestige.

(ii) The claim that Hitler was not a 'free agent' in determining foreign policy, but was subjected to pressures from significant élite groups (*Wehrmacht* leadership, industry etc.), from a variety of agencies involved in making foreign policy, from the demands of the Party faithful for action consonant with his wild promises and propaganda statements (with the corresponding need to act to maintain his Führer image), from the international constellation of forces, and from mounting economic crisis.

(iii) The view that foreign policy has to be seen as a form of 'social imperialism' an outward conveyance of domestic problems, a release from or compensation for internal discontent with the function of preserving the domestic order.

The most radical 'structuralist' approach, that of Hans Mommsen, returns in part, in its emphasis on Hitler's improvised, spontaneous responses to developments which he did little directly to shape, to the early view of the German Dictator as little more than a gifted opportunist. In Mommsen's view, 'it is questionable, too whether National Socialist foreign policy can be considered as an unchanging pursuit of established priorities. Hitler's foreign policy aims, purely dynamic in nature, knew no bounds: Joseph Schumpeter's reference to "expansion without object" is entirely justified. For this very reason, to interpret their implementation as in any way consistent or logical is highly problematic... In reality, the regime's foreign policy ambitions were many and varied, without clear aims, and only linked by the ultimate goal: hindsight alone gives them some air of consistency'—a danger implicit in such concepts as 'programme' or 'stage-by-stage plan'. According to Mommsen, Hitler's behaviour in foreign as in domestic and anti-Jewish policy was shaped largely—apart, that is, from the demands of the international situation—by considerations of prestige and propaganda. Seen in this light, then, Nazi foreign policy was 'in its form domestic policy projected outwards, which was able to conceal (*überspielen*) the increasing loss of reality only by maintaining political dynamism through incessant action. As such it became ever more distant from the chance of political stabilization'.

A not dissimilar interpretation was advanced by Martin Broszat, who also saw little evidence of a design or plan behind Hitler's foreign policy. Rather, the pursuit of *Lebensraum* in the East—parallel to the case of anti-semitism—has, he argued, to be regarded as reflecting Hitler's fanatical adherence to the need to sustain the dynamic momentum he had helped unleash. In foreign policy this meant above all breaking all shackles of restraint, formal bonds, pacts or alliances, and the attainment of complete freedom of action, unrestricted by international law or treaty, in German power-political considerations. The image of unlimited land in the East, according with traditional mythology of German colonization, with utopian ideals of economic autarky, re-agrarianization, and the creation of a master-race, meant that *Lebensraum* (matching as it did also expansionist aims of the First World War) was perfectly placed to serve as a metaphor and touchstone for German power-politics in which, as in the 'Jewish Question' and by equally circuitous route, the distant symbolic vision gradually emerged as imminent and attainable reality. The absence of any clear thinking by Hitler before 1939 on the position of Poland, despite the fact that its geographical situation ought to have made it a central component of any concrete notions of an attack on the Soviet Union, is seen by Broszat as one example of the nebulous, unspecific, and essentially 'utopian' nature of Hitler's foreign policy goals. He reached the conclusion, therefore, that 'the aim of winning *Lebensraum* in the east had until 1939 largely the function of an ideological metaphor, a symbol to account for ever new foreign political activity'. Ultimately, for Broszat, the plebiscitary social dynamic of the 'Movement', which in the sphere of foreign policy pushed Hitler and the regime inexorably in the direction of turning the *Lebensraum* metaphor into reality, was, in its demand for ceaseless action, the only guarantee of any form of integration and diversion of 'the antagonist forces' in the Third Reich. As a consequence, it was bound to veer further and further from rational control, and to end in 'self-destructive madness'. And though Hitler remains indispensable to the explanation of developments, he ought not to be envisaged as an autonomous personality, whose arbitrary whim and ideological fixations operated independently of the social motivation and political pressures of his mass following.

Tim Mason's interpretation, ... can be regarded as a third variant of 'structural' approaches to Nazi foreign policy. In Mason's view, the domestic-economic crisis of the later 1930s greatly restricted Hitler's room for manoeuvre in foreign affairs and war preparation, and an inability to come to terms with the growing economic crisis forced him back on the one area where he could take 'clear, world-historical decisions': foreign policy. More recently, Mason again argued that the later 1930s bore more the hallmarks of confusion than of a programmatic line of development in Hitler's foreign policy. Mason's own emphasis on the 'legacy of 1918' and the compulsion this brought to bear on German foreign as well as domestic policy meant that for him—as in somewhat different ways for Mommsen and Broszat—Nazi foreign policy and the war it-self could be seen under the rubric of the 'primacy of domestic politics', as a barbarous variant of social imperialism. . . .

Evaluation

There seems little disagreement among historians that Hitler did personally take the 'big' decisions in foreign policy after 1933. Even the most forceful 'structuralist' analyses accept that Hitler's 'leadership monopoly' was far more in evidence in the foreign-policy decision-making process than in the realm of domestic policy. There is less agreement, however, about the extent to which Hitler stamped a peculiarly personal mark on the development of German for-eign affairs and whether 1933 can be seen to indicate a break in German foreign policy deriving from Hitler's own ideological pre-possessions and 'programme'. The question of the continuity or discontinuity of German foreign policy after 1933 lies, therefore, at the centre of the first part of our enquiry.

Whatever the differences in interpretation, there has been a general readi-ness since the publication of Fritz Fischer's work in the early 1960s to accept that Germany's expansionist aims form one of the continuous threads linking the Bismarckian and especially the Wilhelmine era with the Third Reich. The clamour for massive expansion and subjection of much of central and eastern Europe, as well as overseas territories, to German dominance was by the early years of the twentieth century not confined to a few extremists, but featured in the aspirations and propaganda of heavily supported and influential pressure groups. It was reflected during the war itself in the aims of the German High Command—aims which can certainly be seen as a bridge to Nazi *Lebensraum* policy. Defeat and the loss of territory in the Versailles settlement kept alive expansionist demands on the Right, and encouraged revisionist intentions and claims, which seemed legitimate to the majority of Germans. The popular suc-cess of Hitler in the foreign policy arena after 1933 was based squarely upon this continuity of a consensus about the need for German expansion which ex-tended from the power élite to extensive sections of society (with the general exception of the bulk of the now outcast and outlawed adherents of the left-wing parties). This is the context in which the role of Hitler in the formulation of German foreign policy after 1933 has to be assessed.

The most significant steps in German foreign policy during the first year of Nazi rule were the withdrawal from the League of Nations in October 1933, and the reversals in relations with Russia and Poland which had taken place by the beginning of 1934. Obviously, these developments were not unconnected with each other. Together they represented a break with past policy which con-ceivably could have taken place under a different Reich Chancellor—say Papen or Schleicher—but which, at the same time, in the manner, timing, and speed it came about owed not a little to Hitler's own direction and initiatives.

In the decision to leave the Geneva disarmament conference and the League of Nations, not much more than the timing was Hitler's. The with-drawal was inevitable given the generally accepted commitment to rearmament (which would have been high on the agenda of any nationalist—revisionist government in Germany at that time), and Hitler acted in almost total concert with leading diplomats, the army leadership, and the other dominant revisionist forces in the country.

In the case of Poland, Hitler played a greater role personally—initially in the teeth of the traditional foreign ministry line, against revisionists instincts, and against the wishes of Party activists in Danzig—in steering a new course of *rapprochement*. While Foreign Minister von Neurath, representing the traditional approach, argued at a Cabinet meeting in April 1933 that 'an understanding with Poland is neither possible nor desirable', Hitler was prepared to explore the possibilities of a new relationship with Poland, especially following initial feelers put out by the Polish government in April. The withdrawal from the League of Nations made a *rapprochement* more urgently desirable from the point of view of both sides. Again it was a Polish initiative, in November 1933, which accelerated negotiations. Agreement to end the long-standing trade war with Poland—a move which satisfied many leading German industrialists—was followed by a decision, taking up an original suggestion of Hitler himself, to embody the new relationship in a non-aggression treaty, which came to be signed on 26 January 1934. The Polish minister in Berlin wrote to his superiors in December that 'as if by orders from the top, a change of front toward us is taking place all along the line'. While Hitler was by no means isolated in his new policy on Poland, and while he was able to exploit an obvious desire on Poland's part for a *rapprochement,* the indications are that he personally played a dominant role in developments and that he was not thinking *purely* opportunistically but had long-term possibilities in mind. In a mixture of admiration and scepticism, the German ambassador in Bern, von Weiszäcker; wrote shortly afterwards that 'no parliamentary minister between 1920 and 1933 could have gone so far'.

The mirror image of the changing relations with Poland in 1933 were those with the Soviet Union. After the maintenance during the first few months of Nazi rule of the mutually advantageous reasonably good relations which had existed since the treaties of Rapallo (1922) and Berlin (1926)—despite some deterioration even before 1933 and the anti-communist propaganda barrage which followed the Nazi takeover—Hitler did nothing to discourage a new basis of 'natural antagonism' towards the Soviet Union from the summer of 1933 onwards. This development, naturally conducive ideologically to Hitler and matching the expectations of his mass following, took place against the wishes both of the German foreign ministry and—despite growing fears and suspicions—of Soviet diplomats, too. When, however, suggestions came from the German foreign ministry in September 1933 for a renewed *rapprochement* with the Soviet Union, Hitler himself rejected it out of hand, stating categorically that 'a restoration of the German-Russian relationship would be impossible'. In like fashion, and now supported by the opportunistic foreign minister von Neurath, he personally rejected new overtures by the Soviet Union in March 1934—a move which prompted the resignation of the German ambassador to the Soviet Union. In this case, too, Hitler had not acted autonomously, in isolation from the pressures within the Nazi Party and the ranks of its Nationalist partners for a strong anti-Russian line. But he had certainly been more than a cypher or a pure opportunist in shaping the major shift in German alignment, here as in relations with Poland.

More than any other sphere of foreign policy, Hitler's hand was visible in shaping the new approach towards Britain. As is well known, this was also the area of the most unmitigated failure of German foreign policy during the 1930s. The first major (and successful) initiative led to the bilateral naval treaty with Britain concluded in 1935. Hitler's personal role was decisive both in the formation of the idea for the treaty, and in its execution. Von Neurath thought the idea 'dilettante' and correspondingly found himself excluded from all negotiations and not even in receipt of the minutes. Hitler's insistence also carried the day on the nature of German demands, which were lower than those desired by the German navy. In the light of criticism to be heard in the foreign ministry and in the navy, signs of growing coolness towards the idea in Britain, and the absence of any notable influence from economic interest groups, an armaments lobby, or the *Wehrmacht*, Hitler's own part—and to a lesser extent that of Ribbentrop—was the critical factor. Hitler himself, of course, attached great importance to the treaty as a step on the way towards the British alliance he was so keen to establish.

The remilitarization of the Rhineland—and with it the breaking of the provisions of Versailles and Locarno—was again an issue which would have been on the agenda of any revisionist German government. The question was already under abstract discussion between the army and foreign ministry by late 1934, and before that Hitler had played with the idea of introducing a demand for the abolition of the demilitarized zone into the disarmament negotiations that year. The issue was revived by the foreign ministry following the ratification of the French-Soviet pact in May 1935, and Hitler mentioned it as a future German demand to the English and French ambassadors towards the end of the year. A solution through negotiation was by no means without prospect of success, and corresponded to the traditional revisionist expectations of Germany's conservative élites. Hitler's main contribution in this case was timing—he claimed he had been originally thinking in terms of a reoccupation in early 1937—and a decision for the theatrical coup of immediate military reoccupation rather than a lengthier and less dramatic process of negotiation. The opportunist exploitation of the diplomatic upheaval—which Hitler feared would be shortlived—arising from Mussolini's Abyssinian adventure was coupled with internal considerations: the need to lift popular morale, revitalize the sinking élan of the Party, and to reconsolidate the support for the regime which various indicators suggested had seriously waned by early 1936. Though a surprisingly large body of diplomatic and military 'advisers', along with leading Nazis, shared the secret planning for the reoccupation, the decision was Hitler's alone, and was taken after much worried deliberation and again in the face of coolness from the foreign ministry and nervousness on the part of the military. Jose Dülffer's conclusion, that 'Hitler was the actual driving force' in the affair, seems undeniable.

In the case of Austria, which along with Czechoslovakia had an intrinsic economic and military-strategic significance according with Nazi ideological expansionist ideas, early Nazi policy of supporting the undermining of the State from within was shown to be a disastrous failure, and was promptly ended, following the assassination of the Austrian Chancellor Dollfuss in July 1934. The Austrian question thereafter took a subordinate place to the improvement of relations with Italy in foreign-policy thinking until the latter part of 1937. In the actual *Anschluss* crisis which unfolded in March 1938, it was Göring rather than Hitler who pushed the pace along—probably because of his interest in seizing Austrian economic assets and avoiding the flight of capital which a prolonged crisis would have provoked. Before the events of February and March 1938, the indications are that Hitler was thinking in terms of subordination rather than the outright annexation of Austria. In fact, he appears to have taken the decision for annexation only *after* the military invasion had occurred—characteristically, under the impact of the delirious reception he had encountered in his home town of Linz. While this points to Hitler's spontaneous, *reactive* decisions even in vitally important matters, and though the chain of developments in the crisis weeks again shows his opportunistic and *ad hoc* exploitation of favourable circumstances, it would be insufficient to leave it at that. The evidence suggests that Göring and Wilhelm Keppler, whom Hitler had placed in charge of Party affairs in Austria in 1937, both believed that Hitler was determined to move on the Austrian question in spring or summer 1938. Goebbels' diary entries also record Hitler speaking about imposing a solution by force 'sometime' on a number of occasions in August and September 1937, and of course Austria formed an important part of Hitler's thinking in November 1937, according to the notes which Colonel Hossbach made of the meeting with top military leaders. In this case too, therefore, Hitler had played a prominent personal role in determining the contours for action, even if his part in the actual events —which could not have been exactly planned or foreseen—was opportunistic, even impulsive.

The remaining events of 1938 and 1939 are sufficiently well known to be summarized briefly. The Sudeten crisis of summer 1938 again illustrates Hitler's direct influence on the course of events. Although traditional power politics and military-strategic considerations would have made the neutralization of Czechoslovakia a high priority for any revisionist government of Germany, it was Hitler's personal determination that he would 'smash Czechoslovakia by military action'—thereby embarking on a high-risk policy in which everything indicates he was not bluffing—that, because of the speed and danger rather than the intrinsic nature of the enterprise, seriously alienated sections of the regime's conservative support, not least in the army. Only the concessions made to Hitler at the Munich Conference deflected him from what can justifiably be regarded as *his* policy to wage war *then* against Czechoslovakia. As is well known, it was Hitler—learning the lessons of Munich—who rejected any alternative to war in 1939, whereas Göring, the second man in the Reich, attempted belatedly to defer any outbreak of hostilities.

Our first set of questions about Hitler's influence on the making of decisions in foreign policy has met with a fairly clear response—and one which would be further bolstered if we were to continue the survey to embrace foreign, strategic, and military affairs during the war years. Whereas in domestic matters Hitler only sporadically intervened in decision-making, and in anti-Jewish policy, which was ideologically highly conducive to him, felt unwilling for prestige reasons to become openly involved, he showed no reluctance to unfold new initiatives or to take vital decisions in the field of foreign policy. In some important areas, as we have seen, he not only set the tone for policy, but pushed through a new or an unorthodox line despite suspicion and objections, particularly of the foreign ministry. There is no sign of any foreign-policy initiative from any of the numerous agencies with an interest in foreign affairs which could not be reconciled with—let alone flatly opposed—Hitler's own thinking and intentions. Evidence of a 'weak dictator' is, therefore, difficult to come by in Hitler's actions in the foreign-policy arena.

Any 'weakness' would have to be located in the presumption that Hitler was the captive of forces limiting his ability to take decisions. Certainly there were forces at work, both within and outside Germany, conditioning the framework of Hitler's actions, which, naturally, did not take place in a vacuum as a free expression of autonomous will. The pressures of foreign-policy revisionism and rearmament, for instance, which would have preoccupied any German government in the 1930s and demanded adjustments to the international order, developed in the years after 1933 a momentum which substantially restricted Germany's options and ran increasingly out of control. The arms race and diplomatic upheaval which Germany had instigated, gradually imposed, therefore, their own laws on the situation, reflected in Hitler's growing feeling and expression that time was running against Germany. Built into Germany's accelerated armaments production were additional economic pressures for German action, confirming the prognosis that war would have to come about sooner rather than later. The nature of his 'charismatic' authority and the need not to disappoint the expectations aroused in his mass following also constrained Hitler's potential scope for action. Finally, of course, and most self-evidently of all, the relative strength and actions of other powers, and strategic-diplomatic considerations imposed their own restrictions on Hitler's manoeuvrability—though these restrictions diminished sharply in the immediate pre-war years.

Hitler's foreign policy was, therefore, in no way independent of 'structural determinants' of different kinds. These, however, pushed him if anything still faster on the path he was in any case determined to tread. When all due consideration is given to the actions—and grave mistakes—of other governments in the diplomatic turmoil of the 1930s, the crucial and pivotal role of Germany as the active catalyst in the upheaval is undeniable. Many of the developments which took place were in certain respects likely if not inevitable as the unfinished business of the First World War and the post-war settlement. The continuities in German foreign policy after 1933 are manifest, and formed part of the basis of the far-reaching identity of interest—certainly until 1937–8—of the conservative élites with the Nazi leadership, rooted in the pursuit of a traditional German power policy aimed at attaining hegemony in central Europe. At the same time, important strands of discontinuity and an unquestionable new dynamism were also unmistakable hallmarks of German foreign policy after 1933 —such that one can speak with justification of a 'diplomatic revolution' in Europe by 1936. Hitler's own decisions and actions, as we have seen, were central to this development. . . .

Our survey of differing interpretations of Hitler's contribution to shaping domestic, anti-Jewish, and foreign policy in the Third Reich is now completed. In each case, we have argued, Hitler's 'intentions' *and* impersonal 'structures' are both indispensable components of any interpretation of the course of German politics in the Nazi State. And there is no mathematical formula for deciding what weighting to attach to each factor. We have seen that Hitler shaped initiatives and personally took the major decisions in foreign policy, though this was less frequently the case in domestic affairs or even in anti-Jewish policy. In domestic matters his uneven intervention was usually prompted by varied and often conflicting requests for his authorisation for legislative or executive action; in the 'Jewish Question' his main contribution, consisted of setting the distant target, shaping the climate, and sanctioning the actions of others; in foreign policy he *both* symbolized the 'great cause' which motivated others *and* played a central role personally in the course of aggression. Hitler's ideological aims were one important factor in deciding the contours of German foreign policy. But they fused for the most part in the formulation of policy so inseparably with strategic power-political considerations, and frequently, too, with economic interest that it is usually impossible to distinguish them analytically. And alongside Hitler's personality, the *function* of his Führer role was also vital to the framing of foreign policy and determining the road to war in its legitimation of the struggle towards the ends it was presumed he wanted. It legitimized the self-interest of an army leadership only too willing to profit from unlimited rearmament, over-ready to engage in expansionist plans, and hopeful of a central role for itself in the State. It legitimized the ambitions of a foreign office only too anxious to prepare the ground diplomatically for upturning the European order, and the various 'amateur' agencies dabbling in foreign affairs with even more aggressive intentions. It also legitimized the greed and ruthlessness of industrialists only too eager to offer plans for the economic plunder of much of Europe. Finally, it provided the touchstone for the wildest chauvinist and imperialist clamour from the mass of the Party faithful for the restoration of Germany's might and glory. Each of these elements—from the élites and from the masses—bound in turn Hitler and the Nazi leadership to the course of action, gathering in pace and escalating in danger, which they had been partly instrumental in creating. The complex radicalization, also in the sphere of foreign policy, which turned Hitler's ideological dreams into living nightmares for millions can, thus, only inadequately be explained by heavy concentration on Hitler's intentions divorced from the conditions and forces—inside and outside Germany—which structured the implementation of those intentions.

POSTSCRIPT

Was World War II the Result of Hitler's Master Plan?

At first glance this debate may seem to be germane only to historians. But it is an important issue with wide ramifications, and many questions may have significance for the future. In *From Weimar to Auschwitz* (Princeton University Press, 1991), Hans Mommsen states: "The fact that Germany—a civilized and highly developed industrial society—rampaged violently out of control has political implications for us today, and it would be wrong to hide these behind a facade that isolates Hitler as the sole and root cause of it all. How Hitler could succeed in securing various degrees of support from considerable sections of the German population must be explained in this context." If Mommsen is correct, can Third Reich experiences be reproduced elsewhere without the a "madman" to make them happen?

The parameters of this debate have also entered into the world of Holocaust historiography, where scholars have developed their own intentionalist/structuralist debate. To them the major question is, "To what extent was Hitler personally responsible for the organization and implementation of the final solution?" Once again, the significance of the answer is inestimable. If the Holocaust cannot be laid solely on Hitler's doorstep, what can we anticipate about the horrors of the future? Perhaps recent events in Kosovo can give us insights into this question.

There are so many books about Hitler, the Nazi era, World War II, and all that resulted from it that any attempt to list sources is daunting. Although the following list speaks directly to the issue's question, many important works must still be omitted. For the intentionalist side, see Klaus Hildebrand's *The Third Reich* (George Allen & Unwin, 1984), Eberhard Jackel's *Hitler In History* (University Press of New England, 1984), and Geoffrey Stoakes's *Hitler and the Quest for World Domination* (St. Martin's Press, 1986). For structuralist arguments see Mommsen's *From Weimar to Auschwitz* (Princeton University Press, 1991), Martin Broszat's *The Hitler State: The Foundation and Development of the Internal Structure of the Third Reich* (Longman, 1981), and Jane Caplan, ed., *Nazism, Fascism and the Working Class: Essays by Tim Mason* (Cambridge University Press, 1995).

Kershaw's *Hitler, 1889-1936: Hubris* (W. W. Norton, 1998) offers a fresh look at the twentieth-century's most written-about man. A second volume of the biography is expected, and it may shed new light on the subject of this issue.

On the Internet ...

Center for Strategic and International Studies

The Center for Strategic and International Studies is a public policy institution dedicated to analysis and policy impact. This site includes links for international news updates.

http://www.csis.org

The World Lecture Hall/History

At this Web site you can locate professors' lectures on many history topics by clicking on subjects such as Europe in the twentieth century, history of Western civilization, Renaissance creativity, as well as many others.

http://www.utexas.edu/world/lecture/his/

European Monetary Unit: The Legal Framework

This site explains the need for the monetary union of Europe and surveys the legal implications of the merger.

http://www.1999.cliffordchance.com/library/publications/
emu_legal/index.html

Feminism and Women's Resources

The Feminism and Women's Resources page contains a fairly comprehensive listing of many of the Internet's feminism, women's studies, and women-related sources.

http://www3.50megs.com/jmansfield/feminism/

PART 5

The Contemporary World

*T*he last half of the twentieth century has been dominated by the cold war and all its manifestations. Few nations and peoples have escaped its influence. Since the disintegration of the Soviet Empire, however, 50 years of rancor have come to an end. This section covers some of the major events influenced by the cold war and ends with an important question concerning the future of Western civilization in our fast-changing world.

- Was Stalin Responsible for the Cold War?

- Were Ethnic Leaders Responsible for the Disintegration of Yugoslavia?

- Will the European Monetary Union Increase the Potential for Transatlantic Conflict?

- Should Contemporary Feminism Ally Itself With Individualism?

- Is Western Civilization in a State of Decline?

Was Stalin Responsible for the Cold War?

YES: John Lewis Gaddis, from *We Now Know: Rethinking Cold War History* (Clarendon Press, 1997)

NO: Martin J. Sherwin, from "The Atomic Bomb and the Origins of the Cold War," in Melvyn P. Leffler and David S. Painter, eds., *Origins of the Cold War: An International History* (Routledge, 1994)

ISSUE SUMMARY

YES: Historian John Lewis Gaddis states that after more than a half a century of cold war scholarship, Joseph Stalin still deserves most of the responsibility for the onset of the cold war.

NO: Historian Martin J. Sherwin counters that the origins of the cold war can be found in the World War II diplomacy involving the use of the atomic bomb, and he places much of the blame for the cold war on the shoulders of Franklin D. Roosevelt, Harry S. Truman, and Winston Churchill.

I t is hard to imagine that the cold war is over when it played such a pivotal role in world affairs for five decades. But the disintegration of the Soviet Empire has ushered in a new era in strategic diplomacy. What shape this new international relations era will take has yet to be determined, but it is unlikely that it will influence our lives in the same manner as the cold war. It is now the job of historians to compose a reassessment of the cold war, which would cover causes, effects, and responsibility.

The historiography of the cold war seemed to begin simultaneously with the onset of tensions between the free and communist worlds. In addressing the question of responsibility, the debate among historians seemed to center around two distinct groups of scholars. The first group, commonly referred to as the orthodox or traditional school, held the Soviet Union responsible for the cold war. Because some of the school's proponents were themselves participants in the events of the era, it was easy for them to see Soviet culpability in the broken promises and duplicitous actions highlighting the early cold war years. And as the Soviet Empire cast its menacing shadow over Eastern Europe, it became increasingly apparent that Joseph Stalin in particular could not be trusted. Also, the volatile nature of the postwar world—especially the vulnerability of the newly emerging nations of the postimperialist era—created a tempting morsel for the "Russian Bear." A new policy, "containment," was created to control the voracious Soviet appetite. It would last for almost half a century and would lead to many crises, wars, and conflicts, which marked the cold war.

A new school of thought was created to counteract the influence of the traditionalists. Members of this school of thought became known as the revisionists, and they began to view the cold war from an entirely different perspective. From this would come a new set of assumptions, including: (1) the postwar weakness of the Soviet Union, which prevented the Soviets from being the threat to world peace that many felt they were; (2) the obsession of free-world leaders in viewing any world problem as being Soviet-created; (3) the view that, after a careful examination of World War II diplomacy, many of the actions of the Western Allies, including the use of the atomic bomb, induced Soviet leaders to feel threatened and to react accordingly. Thus, much of the responsibility for the cold war, according to the revisionists, must be laid at the feet of the West and its leaders.

Subsequently, much of cold war historiography was dominated by this traditionalist/revisionist dichotomy. And as the historical profession became more influenced by a conflict-oriented mode rather than a consensus-centered one, the revisionists began to gain momentum in the crisis-laden 1960s and 1970s. The Vietnam War helped to trigger this response, as many began to see the mistakes of the cold war being played out again and again. There were no longer any "sacred cows" of the traditionalist variety.

The sudden decline of world communism seemed to usher in an aura of cold war justification. After all, in the eyes of many, the West had won; the enemy had been vanquished, and the end of the struggle seemed to have a ring of vindication to it. But the scars of the past were too deep, and the critical examination of cold war politics continued.

New sources of information, especially those from the formerly secret Soviet archives, were opened up in order to assist historians in their search for answers. Not so surprisingly, the results derived from these sources were not uniform. John Lewis Gaddis named this recent reexamination the "New Cold War." Having been involved in cold war historiography for most of its existence, he drew the conclusion that the Soviet Union and Stalin in particular bear most of the responsibility for the cold war.

Historians such as Gar Alperovitz, Gabriel Kolko, Martin J. Sherwin, and others continued to push the revisionist agenda, and Sherwin represents their viewpoint in his selection.

John Lewis Gaddis

 **YES**

We Now Know:
Rethinking Cold War History

[Joseph] Stalin appears to have relished his role, along with [Franklin D.] Roosevelt and [Winston] Churchill, as one of the wartime Big Three. Such evidence as has surfaced from Soviet archives suggests that he received reassuring reports about Washington's intentions: "Roosevelt is more friendly to us than any other prominent American," Ambassador Litvinov commented in June 1943, "and it is quite obvious that he wishes to cooperate with us." Whoever was in the White House, Litvinov's successor Andrei Gromyko predicted a year later, the Soviet Union and the United States would "manage to find common issues for the solution of... problems emerging in the future and of interest to both countries." Even if Stalin's long-range thinking about security did clash with that of his Anglo-American allies, common military purposes provided the strongest possible inducements to smooth over such differences. It is worth asking why this *practice* of wartime cooperation did not become a *habit* that would extend into the postwar era.

The principal reason, it now appears, was Stalin's insistence on equating security with territory. Western diplomats had been surprised, upon arriving in Moscow soon after the German attack in the summer of 1941, to find the Soviet leader already demanding a postwar settlement that would retain what his pact with Hitler had yielded: the Baltic states, together with portions of Finland, Poland, and Romania. Stalin showed no sense of shame or even embarrassment about this, no awareness that the *methods* by which he had obtained these concessions could conceivably render them illegitimate in the eyes of anyone else. When it came to territorial aspirations, he made no distinction between adversaries and allies: what one had provided the other was expected to endorse....

On the surface, this strategy succeeded. After strong initial objections, Roosevelt and Churchill did eventually acknowledge the Soviet Union's right to the expanded borders it claimed; they also made it clear that they would not oppose the installation of "friendly" governments in adjoining states. This meant accepting a Soviet sphere of influence from the Baltic to the Adriatic, a concession not easily reconciled with the Atlantic Charter. But the authors of that document saw no feasible way to avoid that outcome: military necessity required continued Soviet cooperation against the Germans. Nor were they themselves prepared to relinquish spheres of influence in Western Europe and the Mediterranean, the Middle East, Latin America, and East Asia. Self-determination was a sufficiently malleable concept that each of the Big Three could have endorsed, without sleepless nights, what the Soviet government had said about the Atlantic Charter: "practical application of these principles will necessarily adapt itself to the circumstances, needs, and historic peculiarities of particular countries."

That, though, was precisely the problem. For unlike Stalin, Roosevelt and Churchill would have to defend their decisions before domestic constituencies. The *manner* in which Soviet influence expanded was therefore, for them, of no small significance. Stalin showed little understanding of this. Having no experience himself with democratic procedures, he dismissed requests that he respect democratic proprieties. "[S]ome propaganda work should be done," he advised Roosevelt at the Tehran conference after the president had hinted that the American public would welcome a plebiscite in the Baltic States. "It is all nonsense!" Stalin complained to [Soviet Foreign Minister V. M.] Molotov. "[Roosevelt] is their military leader and commander in chief. Who would dare object to him?" When at Yalta F.D.R. stressed the need for the first Polish election to be as pure as "Caesar's wife," Stalin responded with a joke: "They said that about her, but in fact she had her sins." Molotov warned his boss, on that occasion, that the Americans' insistence on free elections elsewhere in Eastern Europe was "going too far." "Don't worry," he recalls Stalin as replying, "work it out. We can deal with it in our own way later. The point is the correlation of forces."

The Soviet leader was, in one sense, right. Military strength would determine what happened in that part of the world, not the enunciation of lofty principles. But unilateral methods carried long-term costs Stalin did not foresee: the most significant of these was to ruin whatever prospects existed for a Soviet sphere of influence the East Europeans themselves might have accepted. This possibility was not as far-fetched as it would later seem. . . . [Stalin] would, after all, approve such a compromise as the basis for a permanent settlement with Finland. He would initially allow free elections in Hungary, Czechoslovakia, and the Soviet occupation zone in Germany. He may even have *anticipated an enthusiastic response* as he took over Eastern Europe. "He was, I think, surprised and hurt," [W. Averell] Harriman [one of Roosevelt's closest advisors] recalled, "when the Red Army was not welcomed in all the neighboring countries as an army of liberation." "We still had our hopes," [Nikita] Khrushchev remembered, that "after the catastrophe of World War II, Europe too might become Soviet. Everyone would take the path from capitalism to socialism." It could be that there was another form of romanticism at work here, quite apart from Stalin's affinity for fellow authoritarians: that he was unrealistic enough to expect ideological solidarity and gratitude for liberation to override old fears of Russian expansionism as well as remaining manifestations of nationalism among the Soviet Union's neighbors, perhaps as easily as he himself had overridden the latter—or so it then appeared—within the multinational empire that was the Soviet Union itself.

If the Red Army could have been welcomed in Poland and the rest of the countries it liberated with the same enthusiasm American, British, and Free French forces encountered when they landed in Italy and France in 1943 and 1944, then some kind of Czech–Finnish compromise might have been feasible. Whatever Stalin's expectations, though, this did not happen. That non-event, in turn, removed any possibility of a division of Europe all members of the Grand Alliance could have endorsed. It ensured that an American sphere of influence would arise there largely by consent, but that its Soviet counterpart could sustain itself only by coercion. The resulting asymmetry would account, more than anything else, for the origins, escalation, and ultimate outcome of the Cold War.

⋅⟨◉⟩⋅

... It has long been clear that, in addition to having had an authoritarian vision, Stalin also had an imperial one, which he proceeded to implement in at least as single-minded a way [as the American]. No comparably influential builder of empire came close to wielding power for so long, or with such striking results, on the Western side.

It was, of course, a matter of some awkwardness that Stalin came out of a revolutionary movement that had vowed to smash, not just tsarist imperialism, but all forms of imperialism throughout the world. The Soviet leader constructed his own logic, though, and throughout his career he devoted a surprising amount of attention to showing how a revolution and an empire might coexist....

Stalin's fusion of Marxist internationalism with tsarist imperialism could only reinforce his tendency, in place well before World War II, to equate the advance of world revolution with the expanding influence of the Soviet state. He applied that linkage quite impartially: a major benefit of the 1939 pact with Hitler had been that it regained territories lost as a result of the Bolshevik Revolution and the World War I settlement. But Stalin's conflation of imperialism with ideology also explains the importance he attached, following the German attack in 1941, to having his new Anglo-American allies confirm these arrangements. He had similar goals in East Asia when he insisted on bringing the Soviet Union back to the position Russia had occupied in Manchuria prior to the Russo-Japanese War: this he finally achieved at the 1945 Yalta Conference in return for promising to enter the war against Japan. "My task as minister of foreign affairs was to expand the borders of our Fatherland," Molotov recalled proudly many years later. "And it seems that Stalin and I coped with this task quite well." ...

⋅⟨◉⟩⋅

From the West's standpoint, the critical question was how far Moscow's influence would extend *beyond* whatever Soviet frontiers turned out to be at the end of the war. Stalin had suggested to Milovan Djilas that the Soviet Union would impose its own social system as far as its armies could reach, but he was also very cautious. Keenly aware of the military power the United States and its allies had accumulated, Stalin was determined to do nothing that might involve the USSR in another devastating war until it had recovered sufficiently to be certain of winning it. "I do not wish to begin the Third World War over the Trieste question," he explained to disappointed Yugoslavs, whom he ordered to evacuate that territory in June 1945. Five years later, he would justify his decision not to intervene in the Korean War on the grounds that "the Second World War ended not long ago, and we are not ready for the Third World War." Just how far the expansion of Soviet influence would proceed depended, therefore, upon a careful balancing of opportunities against risks. . . .

Who or what was it, though, that set the limits? Did Stalin have a fixed list of countries he thought it necessary to dominate? Was he prepared to stop in the face of resistance within those countries to "squeezing out the capitalist order"? Or would expansion cease only when confronted with opposition from the remaining capitalist states, so that further advances risked war at a time when the Soviet Union was ill-prepared for it?

Stalin had been very precise about where he wanted Soviet boundaries changed; he was much less so on how far Moscow's sphere of influence was to extend. He insisted on having "friendly" countries around the periphery of the USSR, but he failed to specify how many would have to meet this standard. He called during the war for dismembering Germany, but by the end of it was denying that he had ever done so: that country would be temporarily divided, he told leading German communists in June 1945, and they themselves would eventually bring about its reunification. He never gave up on the idea of an eventual world revolution, but he expected this to result—as his comments to the Germans suggested—from an expansion of influence emanating from the Soviet Union itself. "[F]or the Kremlin," a well-placed spymaster recalled, "the mission of communism was primarily to consolidate the might of the Soviet state. Only military strength and domination of the countries on our borders could ensure us a superpower role."

But Stalin provided no indication—surely because he himself did not know —of how rapidly, or under what circumstances, this process would take place. He was certainly prepared to stop in the face of resistance from the West: at no point was he willing to challenge the Americans or even the British where they made their interests clear. . . . He quickly backed down when confronted with Anglo-American objections to his ambitions in Iran in the spring of 1946, as he did later that year after demanding Soviet bases in the Turkish Straits. This pattern of advance followed by retreat had shown up in the purges of the 1930s, which Stalin halted when the external threat from Germany became too great to ignore, and it would reappear with the Berlin Blockade and the Korean War, both situations in which the Soviet Union would show great caution after provoking an unexpectedly strong American response.

What all of this suggests, though, is not that Stalin had limited ambitions, only that he had no timetable for achieving them. Molotov retrospectively confirmed this: "Our ideology stands for offensive operations when possible, and if not, we wait." Given this combination of appetite with aversion to risk, one cannot help but wonder what would have happened had the West tried containment earlier. To the extent that it bears partial responsibility for the coming of the Cold War, the historian Vojtech Mastny has argued, that responsibility lies in its failure to do just that....

Stalin's policy, then, was one of imperial expansion and consolidation differing from that of earlier empires only in the determination with which he pursued it, in the instruments of coercion with which he maintained it, and in the ostensibly anti-imperial justifications he put forward in support of it. It is a testimony to his skill, if not to his morality, that he was able to achieve so many of his imperial ambitions at a time when the tides of history were running against the idea of imperial domination—as colonial offices in London, Paris, Lisbon, and The Hague were finding out—and when his own country was recovering from one of the most brutal invasions in recorded history. The fact that Stalin was able to *expand* his empire when others were contracting and while the Soviet Union was as weak as it was requires explanation. Why did opposition to this process, within and outside Europe, take so long to develop?

One reason was that the colossal sacrifices the Soviet Union had made during the war against the Axis had, in effect, "purified" its reputation: the USSR and its leader had "earned" the right to throw their weight around, or so it seemed. Western governments found it difficult to switch quickly from viewing the Soviet Union as a glorious wartime ally to portraying it as a new and dangerous adversary. President Harry S. Truman and his future Secretary of State Dean Acheson—neither of them sympathetic in the slightest to communism—nontheless tended to give the Soviet Union the benefit of the doubt well into the early postwar era....

Resistance to Stalin's imperialism also developed slowly because Marxism-Leninism at the time had such widespread appeal. It is difficult now to recapture the admiration revolutionaries outside the Soviet Union felt for that country before they came to know it well.... Because the Bolsheviks themselves had overcome one empire and had made a career of condemning others, it would take decades for people who were struggling to overthrow British, French, Dutch, or Portuguese colonialism to see that there could also be such a thing as Soviet imperialism. European communists—notably the Yugoslavs—saw this much earlier, but even to most of them it had not been apparent at the end of the war.

Still another explanation for the initial lack of resistance to Soviet expansionism was the fact that its repressive character did not become immediately apparent to all who were subjected to it....

One has the impression that Stalin and the Eastern Europeans got to know one another only gradually. The Kremlin leader was slow to recognize that Soviet authority would not be welcomed everywhere beyond Soviet borders; but as he did come to see this he became all the more determined to impose it everywhere. The Eastern Europeans were slow to recognize how confining incorporation within a Soviet sphere was going to be; but as they did come to see this they became all the more determined to resist it, even if only by withholding, in a passive but sullen manner, the consent any regime needs to establish itself by means other than coercion. Stalin's efforts to consolidate his empire therefore made it at once more repressive and less secure. Meanwhile, an alternative vision of postwar Europe was emerging from the other great empire that established itself in the wake of World War II, that of the United States, and this too gave Stalin grounds for concern. . . .

<hr/>

What is there new to say about the old question of responsibility for the Cold War? Who actually started it? Could it have been averted? Here I think the "new" history is bringing us back to an old answer: that *as long as Stalin was running the Soviet Union a cold war was unavoidable.*

History is always the product of determined *and* contingent events: it is up to historians to find the proper balance between them. The Cold War could hardly have happened if there had not been a United States and a Soviet Union, if both had not emerged victorious from World War II, if they had not had conflicting visions of how to organize the postwar world. But these long-term trends did not in themselves *ensure* such a contest, because there is always room for the unexpected to undo what might appear to be inevitable. *Nothing* is ever completely predetermined, as real triceratops and other dinosaurs discovered 65 million years ago when the most recent large asteroid or comet or whatever it was hit the earth and wiped them out.

Individuals, not asteroids, more often personify contingency in history. Who can specify in advance—or unravel afterwards—the particular intersection of genetics, environment, and culture that makes each person unique? Who can foresee what weird conjunctions of design and circumstance may cause a very few individuals to rise so high as to shape great events, and so come to the attention of historians? Such people may set their sights on getting to the top, but an assassin, or a bacillus, or even a carelessly driven taxicab can always be lurking along the way. How entire countries fall into the hands of malevolent geniuses like Hitler and Stalin remains as unfathomable in the "new" Cold War history as in the "old."

Once leaders like these do gain power, however, certain things become highly probable. It is only to be expected that in an authoritarian state the chief authoritarian's personality will weigh much more heavily than those of democratic leaders, who have to share power. And whether because of social alienation, technological innovation, or economic desperation, the first half of the twentieth century was particularly susceptible to great authoritarians and all that resulted from their ascendancy. It is hardly possible to imagine Nazi Germany or the world war it caused without Hitler. I find it increasingly difficult, given what we know now, to imagine the Soviet Union or the Cold War without Stalin.

For the more we learn, the less sense it makes to distinguish Stalin's foreign policies from his domestic practices or even his personal behavior. Scientists have shown the natural world to be filled with examples of what they call "self-similarity across scale": patterns that persist whether one views them microscopically, macroscopically, or anywhere in between. Stalin was like that: he functioned in much the same manner whether operating within the international system, within his alliances, within his country, within his party, within his personal entourage, or even within his family. The Soviet leader waged cold wars on all of these fronts. The Cold War *we* came to know was only one of many from *his* point of view.

Nor did Stalin's influence diminish as quickly as that of most dictators after their deaths. He built a *system* sufficiently durable to survive not only his own demise but his successors' fitful and half-hearted efforts at "de-Stalinization." They were themselves its creatures, and they continued to work within it because they knew no other method of governing. Not until [Mikhail] Gorbachev was a Soviet leader fully prepared to dismantle Stalin's structural legacy. It tells us a lot that as it disappeared, so too did the Cold War and ultimately the Soviet Union itself.

This argument by no means absolves the United States and its allies of a considerable responsibility for how the Cold War was fought—hardly a surprising conclusion since they in fact won it. Nor is it to deny the feckless stupidity with which the Americans fell into peripheral conflicts like Vietnam, or their exorbitant expenditures on unusable weaponry: these certainly caused the Cold War to cost much more in money and lives than it otherwise might have. Nor is it to claim moral superiority for western statesmen. None was as bad as Stalin —or Mao—but the Cold War left no leader uncorrupted: the wielding of great power, even in the best of times, rarely does.

It is the case, though, that if one applies the always useful test of counterfactual history—drop a key variable and speculate as to what difference this might have made—Stalin's centrality to the origins of the Cold War becomes quite clear. For all of their importance, one could have removed Roosevelt, Churchill, Truman, Bevin, Marshall, or Acheson, and a cold war would still have probably followed the world war. If one could have eliminated Stalin, alternative paths become quite conceivable. For with the possible exception of Mao, no twentieth-century leader imprinted himself upon his country as thoroughly and with such lasting effect as Stalin did. And given his personal propensity for cold wars—a tendency firmly rooted long before he had even heard of Harry Truman—once Stalin wound up at the top in Moscow and once it was clear his state would survive the war, then it looks equally clear that there was going to be a Cold War whatever the west did. Who then was responsible? The answer, I think, is authoritarianism in general, and Stalin in particular.

NO

Martin J. Sherwin

The Atomic Bomb and the
Origins of the Cold War

During the Second World War the atomic bomb was seen and valued as a potential rather than an actual instrument of policy. Responsible officials believed that its impact on diplomacy had to await its development and, perhaps, even a demonstration of its power. As Henry L. Stimson, the Secretary of War, observed in his memoirs: "The bomb as a merely probable weapon had seemed a weak reed on which to rely, but the bomb as a colossal reality was very different." That policymakers considered this difference before Hiroshima has been well documented, but whether they based wartime diplomatic policies upon an anticipated successful demonstration of the bomb's power remains a source of controversy. Two questions delineate the issues in this debate. First, did the development of the atomic bomb affect the way American policymakers conducted diplomacy with the Soviet Union? Second, did diplomatic considerations related to the Soviet Union influence the decision to use the atomic bomb against Japan?

These important questions relating the atomic bomb to American diplomacy, and ultimately to the origins of the Cold War, have been addressed almost exclusively to the formulation of policy during the early months of the Truman administration. As a result, two anterior questions of equal importance, questions with implications for those already posed, have been overlooked. Did diplomatic considerations related to Soviet postwar behavior influence the formulation of [Franklin D.] Roosevelt's atomic energy policies? What effect did the atomic legacy Truman inherited have on the diplomatic and atomic energy policies of his administration?

Although Roosevelt left no definitive statement assigning a postwar role to the atomic bomb, his expectations for its potential diplomatic value can be recalled from the existing record. An analysis of the policies he chose from among the alternatives he faced suggests that the potential diplomatic value of the bomb began to shape his atomic energy policies as early as 1943. He may have been cautious about counting on the bomb as a reality during the war, but he nevertheless consistently chose policy alternatives that would promote the postwar diplomatic potential of the bomb if the predictions of scientists

From Martin J. Sherwin, "The Atomic Bomb and the Origins of the Cold War," in Melvyn P. Leffler and David S. Painter, eds., *Origins of the Cold War: An International History* (Routledge, 1994). Copyright © 1994 by Martin J. Sherwin. Originally published in *American Historical Review*, no. 78 (October 1973). Reprinted and abridged by permission of the author. Notes omitted.

proved true. These policies were based on the assumption that the bomb could be used effectively to secure postwar diplomatic aims; and this assumption was carried over from the Roosevelt to the Truman administration.

Despite general agreement that the bomb would be an extraordinarily important diplomatic factor after the war, those closely associated with its development did not agree on how to use it most effectively as an instrument of diplomacy. Convinced that wartime atomic energy policies would have postwar diplomatic consequences, several scientists advised Roosevelt to adopt policies aimed at achieving a postwar international control system. [Winston] Churchill, on the other hand, urged the President to maintain the Anglo-American atomic monopoly as a diplomatic counter against the postwar ambitions of other nations—particularly against the Soviet Union. Roosevelt fashioned his atomic energy policies from the choices he made between these conflicting recommendations. In 1943 he rejected the counsel of his science advisers and began to consider the diplomatic component of atomic energy policy in consultation with Churchill alone. This decisionmaking procedure and Roosevelt's untimely death have left his motives ambiguous. Nevertheless it is clear that he pursued policies consistent with Churchill's monopolistic, anti-Soviet views.

The findings of this [selection] thus raise serious questions concerning generalizations historians have commonly made about Roosevelt's diplomacy: that it was consistent with his public reputation for cooperation and conciliation; that he was naive with respect to postwar Soviet behavior; that, like [Woodrow] Wilson, he believed in collective security as an effective guarantor of national safety; and that he made every possible effort to ensure that the Soviet Union and its allies would continue to function as postwar partners. Although this [selection] does not dispute the view that Roosevelt desired amicable postwar relations with the Soviet Union, or even that he worked hard to achieve them, it does suggest that historians have exaggerated his confidence in (and perhaps his commitment to) such an outcome. His most secret and among his most important long-range decisions—those responsible for prescribing a diplomatic role for the atomic bomb—reflected his lack of confidence. Finally, in light of this [selection's] conclusions, the widely held assumption that Truman's attitude toward the atomic bomb was substantially different from Roosevelt's must also be revised.

Like the grand alliance itself, the Anglo-American atomic energy partnership was forged by the war and its exigencies. The threat of a German atomic bomb precipitated a hasty marriage of convenience between British research and American resources. When scientists in Britain proposed a theory that explained how an atomic bomb might quickly be built, policymakers had to assume that German scientists were building one. "If such an explosive were made," Vannevar Bush, the director of the Office of Scientific Research and Development, told Roosevelt in July 1941, "it would be thousands of times more powerful than existing explosives, and its use might be determining." Roosevelt assumed nothing less. Even before the atomic energy project was fully organized he assigned it the highest priority.

The high stakes at issue during the war did not prevent officials in Great Britain or the United States from considering the postwar implications of their atomic energy decisions. As early as 1941, during the debate over whether to join the United States in an atomic energy partnership, members of the British government's atomic energy committee argued that the matter "was so important for the future that work should proceed in Britain." Weighing the obvious difficulties of proceeding alone against the possible advantages of working with the United States, Sir John Anderson, then Lord President of the Council and the minister responsible for atomic energy research, advocated the partnership. As he explained to Churchill, by working closely with the Americans British scientists would be able "to take up the work again [after the war], not where we left off, but where the combined effort had by then brought it."

As early as October 1942 Roosevelt's science advisers exhibited a similar concern with the potential postwar value of atomic energy. After conducting a full-scale review of the atomic energy project, James B. Conant, the president of Harvard University and Bush's deputy, recommended discontinuing the Anglo-American partnership "as far as development and manufacture is concerned." What prompted Conant's recommendations, however, was his suspicion—soon to be shared by other senior atomic energy administrators—that the British were rather more concerned with information for postwar industrial purposes than for wartime use. What right did the British have to the fruits of American labor? "We were doing nine-tenths of the work," Stimson told Roosevelt in October. Early in January 1943 the British were officially informed that the rules governing the Anglo-American atomic energy partnership had been altered on "orders from the top."

By approving the policy of "restricted interchange" Roosevelt undermined a major incentive for British cooperation. It is not surprising, therefore, that Churchill took up the matter directly with the President and with Harry Hopkins, "Roosevelt's own, personal Foreign Office."

Conant and Bush understood the implications of Churchill's intervention and sought to counter its effect. Information on manufacturing an atomic bomb, Conant noted, was a "military secret which is in a totally different class from anything the world has ever seen if the potentialities of this project are realised." Though British and American atomic energy policies might coincide during the war, Conant and Bush expected them to conflict afterward.

The controversy over the policy of "restricted interchange" of atomic energy information shifted attention to postwar diplomatic considerations. The central issue was clearly drawn. The atomic energy policy of the United States was related to the very fabric of Anglo-American postwar relations and, as Churchill would insist, to postwar relations between each of them and the Soviet Union. The specter of Soviet postwar military power played a major role in shaping the Prime Minister's attitude toward atomic energy policies in 1943.

Churchill could cite numerous reasons for this determination to acquire an independent atomic arsenal after the war, but Great Britain's postwar military-diplomatic position with respect to the Soviet Union invariably led the list. When Bush and Stimson visited London in July, Churchill told them quite frankly that he was "vitally interested in the possession of all [atomic energy] information because this will be necessary for Britain's independence in the future as well as for success during the war." Nor was Churchill evasive about his reasoning: "It would never do to have Germany or Russia win the race for something which might be used for international blackmail," he stated bluntly and then pointed out that "Russia might be in a position to accomplish this result unless we worked together." Convinced that the British attitude toward the bomb would undermine any possibility of postwar cooperation with the Soviet Union, Bush and Conant vigorously continued to oppose any revival of the Anglo-American atomic energy partnership.

On July 20, however, Roosevelt chose to accept a recommendation from Hopkins to restore full partnership, and he ordered Bush to "renew, in an inclusive manner, the full exchange of information with the British." At the Quebec Conference, the President and the Prime Minister agreed that the British would share the atomic bomb. The Quebec Agreement revived the principle of an Anglo-American atomic energy partnership, albeit the British were reinstated as junior rather than equal partners.

The debate that preceded the Quebec Agreement is noteworthy for another reason; it led to a new relationship between Roosevelt and his atomic energy advisers. After August 1943 the President did not consult with them about the diplomatic aspects of atomic energy policy. Though he responded politely when they offered their views, he acted decisively only in consultation with Churchill. Bush and Conant appear to have lost a large measure of their influence because they had used it to oppose Churchill's position. What they did not suspect was the extent to which the President had come to share the Prime Minister's view.

Roosevelt was perfectly comfortable with the concept Churchill advocated —that military power was a prerequisite to successful postwar diplomacy. As early as August 1941, during the Atlantic Conference, Roosevelt had rejected the idea that an "effective international organization" could be relied upon to keep the peace: an Anglo-American international police force would be far more effective, he told Churchill. By the spring of 1942 the concept had broadened: the two "policemen" became four, and the idea was added that every other nation would be totally disarmed. "The Four Policemen" would have "to build up a reservoir of force so powerful that no aggressor would dare to challenge it," Roosevelt told Author Sweetser, an ardent internationalist. Violators first would be quarantined, and, if they persisted in their disruptive activities, bombed at the rate of a city a day until they agreed to behave. A year later, at the Tehran Conference, Roosevelt again discussed his idea, this time with Stalin. As Robert A. Divine has noted: "Roosevelt's concept of big power domination remained the central idea in his approach to international organization throughout World War II."

Precisely how Roosevelt expected to integrate the atomic bomb into his plans for keeping the peace in the postwar world is not clear. However, against the background of his atomic energy policy decisions of 1943 and his peacekeeping concepts, his actions in 1944 suggest that he intended to take full advantage of the bomb's potential as a postwar instrument of Anglo-American diplomacy. If Roosevelt thought the bomb could be used to create a more peaceful world order, he seems to have considered the threat of its power more effective than any opportunities it offered for international cooperation. If Roosevelt was less worried than Churchill about Soviet postwar ambitions, he was no less determined than the Prime Minister to avoid any commitments to the Soviets for the international control of atomic energy. There could still be four policemen, but only two of them would have the bomb.

The atomic energy policies Roosevelt pursued during the remainder of his life reinforce this interpretation of his ideas for the postwar period. The following three questions offer a useful framework for analyzing his intentions. Did Roosevelt make any additional agreements with Churchill that would further support the view that he intended to maintain an Anglo-American monopoly after the war? Did Roosevelt demonstrate any interest in the international control of atomic energy? Was Roosevelt aware that an effort to maintain an Anglo-American monopoly of the atomic bomb might lead to a postwar atomic arms race with the Soviet Union?

The alternatives placed before Roosevelt posed a difficult dilemma. On the one hand, he could continue to exclude the Soviet government from any official information about the development of the bomb, a policy that would probably strengthen America's postwar military-diplomatic position. But such a policy would also encourage Soviet mistrust of Anglo-American intentions and was bound to make postwar cooperation more difficult. On the other hand, Roosevelt could use the atomic bomb project as an instrument of cooperation by informing Stalin of the American government's intention of cooperating in the development of a plan for the international control of atomic weapons, an objective that might never be achieved.

Either choice involved serious risks. Roosevelt had to balance the diplomatic advantages of being well ahead of the Soviet Union in atomic energy production after the war against the advantages of initiating wartime negotiations for postwar cooperation. The issue here, it must be emphasized, is not whether international control was likely to be successful, but rather whether Roosevelt demonstrated any serious interest in laying the groundwork for such a policy.

Roosevelt knew at this time, moreover, that the Soviets were finding out on their own about the development of the atomic bomb. Security personnel had reported an active Communist cell in the Radiation Laboratory at the University of California. Their reports indicated that at least one scientist at Berkeley was selling information to Russian agents. "They [Soviet agents] are already getting information about vital secrets and sending them to Russia," Stimson told the President on September 9, 1943. If Roosevelt was indeed worried to death about the effect the atomic bomb could have on Soviet-American postwar relations, he took no action to remove the potential danger, nor did he make any effort to explore the possibility of encouraging Soviet postwar cooperation on this problem.

Had Roosevelt avoided all postwar atomic energy commitments, his lack of support for international control could have been interpreted as an attempt to reserve his opinion on the best course to follow. But he had made commitments in 1943 supporting Churchill's monopolistic, anti-Soviet position, and he continued to make others in 1944. On June 13, for example, Roosevelt and Churchill signed an Agreement and Declaration of Trust, specifying that the United States and Great Britain would cooperate in seeking to control available supplies of uranium and thorium ore both during and after the war. This commitment, taken against the background of Roosevelt's peacekeeping ideas and his other commitments, suggests that the President's attitude toward the international control of atomic energy was similar to the Prime Minister's.

Churchill rejected the assumption that international control of atomic energy could be used as a cornerstone for constructing a peaceful world order. An atomic monopoly would be a significant diplomatic advantage in postwar diplomacy, and Churchill did not believe that anything useful could be gained by surrendering this advantage. The argument that a new weapon created a unique opportunity to refashion international affairs ignored every lesson Churchill read into history. "You can be quite sure," he would write in a memorandum less than a year later, "that any power that gets hold of the secret will try to make the article and this touches the existence of human society. This matter is out of all relation to anything else that exists in the world, and I could not think of participating in any disclosure to third or fourth parties at the present time."

When Roosevelt and Churchill met at Hyde Park in September 1944 following the second wartime conference at Quebec, they signed an *aide-mémoire* on atomic energy. The agreement bears the markings of Churchill's attitude toward the atomic bomb. It contained an explicit rejection of any wartime efforts toward international control: "The suggestion that the world should be informed regarding tube alloys [the atomic bomb], with a view to an international agreement regarding its control and use, is not accepted. The matter should continue to be regarded as of the utmost secrecy." The *aide-mémoire* then revealed the full extent of Roosevelt's agreement with Churchill's point of view. "Full collaboration between the United States and the British Government in developing tube alloys for military and commercial purposes," it noted, "should continue after the defeat of Japan unless and until terminated by joint agreement." Finally the *aide-mémoire* offers some insight into Roosevelt's intentions for the military use of the weapon in the war: "When a bomb is finally available, it might perhaps, after mature consideration, be used against the Japanese, who should be warned that this bombardment will be repeated until they surrender."

Within the context of the complex problem of the origins of the Cold War the Hyde Park meeting is far more important than historians of the war generally have recognized. Overshadowed by the Second Quebec Conference on one side and by the drama of Yalta on the other, its significance often has been overlooked. But the agreements reached in September 1944 reflect a set of attitudes, aims, and assumptions that guided the relationship between the atomic bomb and American diplomacy during the Roosevelt administration and, through the transfer of its atomic legacy, during the Truman administration as well. Two alternatives had been recognized long before Roosevelt and Churchill met in 1944 at Hyde Park: the bomb could have been used to initiate a diplomatic effort to work out a system for its international control, or it could remain isolated during the war from any cooperative initiatives and held in reserve should cooperation fail. Roosevelt consistently favored the latter alternative. An insight into his reasoning is found in a memorandum Bush wrote following a conversation with Roosevelt several days after the Hyde Park meeting: "The President evidently thought he could join with Churchill in bringing about a US-UK postwar agreement on this subject [the atomic bomb] by which it would be held closely and presumably to control the peace of the world." By 1944 Roosevelt's earlier musings about the Four Policemen had faded into the background. But the idea behind it, the concept of controlling the peace of the world by amassing overwhelming military power, appears to have remained a prominent feature of his postwar plans.

⋆⟨◉⟩⋆

Harry S. Truman inherited a set of military and diplomatic atomic energy policies that included partially formulated intentions, several commitments to Churchill, and the assumption that the bomb would be a legitimate weapon to be used against Japan. But no policy was definitely settled. According to the Quebec Agreement the President had the option of deciding the future of the commercial aspects of the atomic energy partnership according to his own estimate of what was fair. Although the policy of "utmost secrecy" had been confirmed at Hyde Park the previous September, Roosevelt had not informed his atomic energy advisers about the *aide-mémoire* he and Churchill signed. Although the assumption that the bomb would be used in the war was shared by those privy to its development, assumptions formulated early in the war were not necessarily valid at its conclusion. Yet Truman was bound to the past by his own uncertain position and by the prestige of his predecessor. Since Roosevelt had refused to open negotiations with the Soviet government for the international control of atomic energy, and since he had never expressed any objection to the wartime use of the bomb, it would have required considerable political courage and confidence for Truman to alter those policies. Moreover it would have required the encouragement of his advisers, for under the circumstances the most serious constraint of the new President's choices was his dependence upon advice. So Truman's atomic legacy, while it included several options, did not necessarily entail complete freedom to choose from among all the possible alternatives.

"I think it is very important that I should have a talk with you as soon as possible on a highly secret matter," Stimson wrote to Truman on April 24. It has "such a bearing on our present foreign relations and has such an important effect upon all my thinking in this field that I think you ought to know about it without further delay." Stimson had been preparing to brief Truman on the atomic bomb for almost ten days, but in the preceding twenty-four hours he had been seized by a sense of urgency. Relations with the Soviet Union had declined precipitously. The State Department had been urging Truman to get tough with the Russians. He had. Twenty-four hours earlier the President met with the Soviet Foreign Minister, V. M. Molotov, and "with rather brutal frankness" accused his government of breaking the Yalta Agreement. Molotov was furious. "I have never been talked to like that in my life," he told the President before leaving.

With a memorandum on the "political aspects of the S-1 [atomic bomb's] performance" in hand, Stimson went to the White House on April 25. The document he carried was the distillation of numerous decisions already taken, each one the product of attitudes that developed along with the new weapon. The Secretary of War himself was not entirely aware of how various forces had shaped these decisions: the recommendations of Bush and Conant, the policies Roosevelt had followed, the uncertainties inherent in the wartime alliance, the oppressive concern for secrecy, and his own inclination to consider long-range implications. It was a curious document. Though its language revealed Stimson's sensitivity to the historic significance of the atomic bomb, he did not question the wisdom of using it against Japan. Nor did he suggest any concrete steps for developing a postwar policy. His objective was to inform Truman of the salient problems: the possibility of an atomic arms race, the danger of atomic war, and the necessity for international control if the United Nations Organization was to work. "If the problem of the proper use of this weapon can be solved," he wrote, "we would have the opportunity to bring the world into a pattern in which the peace of the world and our civilizations can be saved." To cope with this difficult challenge Stimson suggested the "establishment of a select committee" to consider the postwar problems inherent in the development of the bomb.

What emerges from a careful reading of Stimson's diary, his memorandum of April 25 to Truman, a summary by [Major General Leslie R.] Groves of the meeting, and Truman's recollections is an argument for overall caution in American diplomatic relations with the Soviet Union: it was an argument against any showdown. Since the atomic bomb was potentially the most dangerous issue facing the postwar world and since the most desirable resolution of the problem was some form of international control, Soviet cooperation had to be secured. It was imprudent, Stimson suggested, to pursue a policy that would preclude the possibility of international cooperation on atomic energy matters after the war ended. Truman's overall impression of Stimson's argument was that the Secretary of War was "at least as much concerned with the role of the atomic bomb in the shaping of history as in its capacity to shorten the war." These were indeed Stimson's dual concerns on April 25, and he could see no conflict between them.

Despite the profound consequences Stimson attributed to the development of the new weapon, he had not suggested that Truman reconsider its use against Japan. Nor had he thought to mention the possibility that chances of securing Soviet postwar cooperation might be diminished if Stalin did not receive a commitment to international control prior to an attack. Until the bomb's "actual certainty [was] fixed," Stimson considered any prior approach to Stalin as premature. As the uncertainties of impending peace became more apparent and worrisome, Stimson, Truman, and the Secretary of State-designate, James F. Byrnes, began to think of the bomb as something of a diplomatic panacea for their postwar problems. Byrnes had told Truman in April that the bomb "might well put us in a position to dictate our own terms at the end of the war." By

June, Truman and Stimson were discussing "further *quid pro quos* which should be established in consideration for our taking them [the Soviet Union] into [atomic energy] partnership." Assuming that the bomb's impact on diplomacy would be immediate and extraordinary, they agreed on no less than "the settlement of the Polish, Rumanian, Yugoslavian, and Manchurian problems." But they also concluded that no revelation would be made "to Russia or anyone else until the first bomb had been successfully laid on Japan."

Was an implicit warning to Moscow, then, the principal reason for deciding to use the atomic bomb against Japan? In light of the ambiguity of the available evidence the question defies an unequivocal answer. What can be said with certainty is that Truman, Stimson, Byrnes, and several others involved in the decision consciously considered two effects of a combat demonstration of the bomb's power: first, the impact of the atomic attack on Japan's leaders, who might be persuaded thereby to end the war; and second, the impact of that attack on the Soviet Union's leaders, who might then prove to be more cooperative. But if the assumption that the bomb might bring the war to a rapid conclusion was the principal motive for using the atomic bomb, the expectation that its use would also inhibit Soviet diplomatic ambitions clearly discouraged any inclination to question that assumption.

Thus by the end of the war the most influential and widely accepted attitude toward the bomb was a logical extension of how the weapon was seen and valued earlier—as a potential instrument of diplomacy. Caught between the remnants of war and the uncertainties of peace, policymakers were trapped by the logic of their own unquestioned assumptions. By the summer of 1945 not only the conclusion of the war but the organization of an acceptable peace seemed to depend upon the success of the atomic attacks against Japan. When news of the successful atomic test of July 16 reached the President at the Potsdam Conference, he was visibly elated. Stimson noted that Truman "was tremendously pepped up by it and spoke to me of it again and again when I saw him. He said it gave him an entirely new feeling of confidence." The day after receiving the complete report of the test Truman altered his negotiating style. According to Churchill the President "got to the meeting after having read this report [and] he was a changed man. He told the Russians just where they got on and off and generally bossed the whole meeting." After the plenary session on July 24 Truman "casually mentioned to Stalin" that the United States had "a new weapon of unusual destructive force." In less than three weeks the new weapon's destructive potential was demonstrated to the world. Upon learning of the raid against Hiroshima Truman exclaimed: "This is the greatest thing in history."

As Stimson had expected, as a colossal reality the bomb was very different. But had American diplomacy been altered by it? Those who conducted diplomacy became more confident, more certain that through the accomplishments of American science, technology, and industry the "new world" could be made into one better than the old. But just how the atomic bomb would be used to help accomplish this ideal remained unclear. Three months and one day after Hiroshima was bombed Bush wrote that the whole matter of international relations on atomic energy "is in a thoroughly chaotic condition." The wartime relationship between atomic energy policy and diplomacy had been based upon the simple assumption that the Soviet government would surrender important geographical, political, and ideological objectives in exchange for the neutralization of the new weapon. As a result of policies based on this assumption American diplomacy and prestige suffered grievously: an opportunity to gauge the Soviet Union's response during the war to the international control of atomic energy was missed, and an atomic energy policy for dealing with the Soviet government after the war was ignored. Instead of promoting American postwar aims, wartime atomic energy policies made them more difficult to achieve. As a group of scientists at the University of Chicago's atomic energy laboratory presciently warned the government in June 1945: "It may be difficult to persuade the world that a nation which was capable of secretly preparing and suddenly releasing a weapon as indiscriminate as the [German] rocket bomb and a million times more destructive, is to be trusted in its proclaimed desire of having such weapons abolished by international agreement." This reasoning, however, flowed from alternative assumptions formulated during the closing months of the war by scientists far removed from the wartime policymaking process. Hiroshima and Nagasaki, the culmination of that process, became the symbols of a new American barbarism, reinforcing charges, with dramatic circumstantial evidence, that the policies of the United States contributed to the origins of the Cold War.

POSTSCRIPT

Was Stalin Responsible for the Cold War?

Time, place, perspective—all play a role in historical assessment, and any analysis of responsibility for the cold war must consider these factors. The cold war's first chroniclers were participants in postwar global politics, and their views were shaped by their personal experiences. Time provided distance, and the events of the coming decades nurtured a movement toward radical politics, which some have referred to as the "New Left." This paved the way for revisionist interpretations of the cold war's origins.

The use of the atomic bombs against Japan in 1945 created a cloud over cold war historiography. What course might the post–World War II era have followed if the West had sought different means to end the war? Many feel that the use of atomic weapons and the start of the cold war are inextricably connected.

Useful sources on cold war historiography begin with the authors of the two selections. Gaddis's career as a cold war scholar can be traced from his *The United States and the Origins of the War, 1941-1947* (Columbia University Press, 1972) to *We Now Know: Rethinking Cold War History* (Routledge, 1997). Sherwin has extended the scholarship of his original *American Historical Review* article, "The Atomic Bomb and the Origins of the Cold War: U.S. Atomic Energy Policy and Diplomacy 1941-1945" (October 1973) in *A World Destroyed: The Atomic Bomb and the Grand Alliance* (Alfred A. Knopf, 1975).

Other significant works written in the traditionalist vein include Louis Halle, *The Cold War as History* (Harper & Row, 1967); Herbert Feis, *From Trust to Terror: The Onset of the Cold War, 1945-1950* (W. W. Norton, 1970); and Norman Graebner, *Cold War Diplomacy: American Foreign Policy 1945-1960* (Princeton University Press, 1962). Important revisionist works on the origins of the cold war include Gar Alperovitz, *Atomic Diplomacy: Hiroshima and Potsdam* (Penguin Books, 1985) and *The Decision to Use the Bomb and the Architecture of an American Myth* (Alfred A. Knopf, 1995). The many works of George F. Kennan, considered to be containment's prime mover, provide invaluable assistance to the study of this issue, as do the works of Russian diplomats Vyacheslav Molotov and Andrei Gromyko, both of whom were "present at the creation." Two recent cold war anthologies are David Reynolds, ed., *The Origins of the Cold War in Europe: International Perspectives* (Yale University Press, 1994) and Allan Hunter, ed., *Rethinking the Cold War* (Temple University Press, 1998).

ISSUE 20

Were Ethnic Leaders Responsible for the Disintegration of Yugoslavia?

YES: Warren Zimmermann, from *Origins of a Catastrophe* (Times Books, 1996)

NO: Steven Majstorovic, from "Ancient Hatreds or Elite Manipulation? Memory and Politics in the Former Yugoslavia," *World Affairs* (Spring 1997)

ISSUE SUMMARY

YES: Career diplomat Warren Zimmermann, the United States' last ambassador to Yugoslavia, argues that the republic's ethnic leaders, especially Slobodan Milosovic, bear primary responsibility for the nation's demise.

NO: Political science professor Steven Majstorovic contends that while manipulation by elite ethnic leaders played a role in the disintegration of Yugoslavia, the fragile ethnic divisions within the country also played an important role in the country's demise.

I t is not often that the world witnesses the death of a country, but that is precisely what many say we witnessed in the 1990s with the passing of Yugoslavia. Since World War II, the creation of nations has been a common occurrence. However, what was dramatic about the situation in Yugoslavia is that we witnessed the country's disintegration on television. The nature of Balkan history has long been complicated and confusing.

The Balkans were once referred to as Europe's "powder keg." The area's history began when it was settled by the southern branch of the Slavic family tree a millennium ago. During Europe's medieval period, Serbs, Croats, and Bosnians established Balkan kingdoms, which were soon overrun and conquered by the forces of the Ottoman Empire, which maintained control over part of the area for almost 500 years. These kingdoms were eventually joined by the Austrian Hapsburgs, as the Balkans became a battleground between two rival empires, one Muslim, the other Christian. The ethnic groups were forced to make the best of an untenable situation and wait for better days.

The next major change in Balkan history would begin in 1914 with the outbreak of World War I, which began with the assassination of the heir to the Austrian Hapsburg empire by a Serbian nationalist. At the war's conclusion, the victorious Allies decided that the solution to the Balkan question was a federal republic comprising the disparate ethnic groups, many of whom had been there for 1,000 years. Thus, Serbs, Croats, Slovenes, Bosnians, Herzegovinians, Montenegrins, Muslims, Macedonians, and Albanians were asked to live together in the new nation of Yugoslavia.

The nation's initial period of establishment was brief, as World War II brought Nazi occupation to Yugoslavia. Complicating things further was the fact that while most "Yugoslavs" fought against the German occupation (Josip Broz, soon to be known as Tito, would emerge as the leader of the "Partisans"), others (Croats and Bosnian-Herzegovinians) actually collaborated with the Nazis, resulting in atrocities on both sides. The main victims of this era would be the Serbs, many of whom were massacred by the Croat Ustase puppet state. This massacre was not forgotten by the Serbs.

After the war, Yugoslavia once again became a federal republic, with separate states established in Slovenia, Croatia, Bosnia-Herzegovina, Serbia, Montenegro, and Macedonia. Tito was given the difficult job of keeping the country together, something which he was able to do until his death. He was the only European communist leader to escape Stalin's influence, and he managed to create in Yugoslavia a nonaligned communist state with a market-oriented economy. It was only after Tito's death that the republic began to disintegrate, partially caused by horrendous economic conditions. By the 1980s, Yugoslavia was a troubled area; in 1995 it had virtually disintegrated.

The problems that brought about Yugoslavia's disintegration are many. The ancient ethnic rivalries and conflicts were extremely difficult to overcome. Complicating matters were the religious differences, with Eastern Orthodoxy, Roman Catholicism, and Islam claiming the allegiance of the area's peoples. And of course there is the history—who did what to whom and when did they do it—which has influenced the myths and realities of the Balkan landscape.

Contemporary leaders of the former Yugoslavia—former communists—now represent neither ideology nor country but ethnic constituencies. To what extent are these leaders personally responsible for Yugoslavia's demise? Or, was the country eventually doomed to failure by ethno-religious-historical forces beyond control? With ethnic groups skewed within the former Yugoslavian-federated states, was the war in Bosnia-Herzegovina that occurred in the 1990s inevitable, as Croats, Serbs, Bosnian Serbs, Bosnian Croats, and Bosnian Muslims began attempts to improve their lot in Bosnia? A treaty signed in 1995 produced a tenuous peace, as the current Serbian attempt to take control of the independent province of Kosovo attests.

The answers to many questions about Yugoslavia's demise may be found in the selections by Warren Zimmermann and Steven Majstorovic. Zimmermann holds the former Yugoslavia's ethnic leaders primarily responsible for the country's disintegration. Majstorovic accepts that "elite manipulation" played a role in Yugoslavia's demise, but he states that the "ancient hatreds" that have become embedded in the Balkan psyches are difficult to ignore as factors.

Warren Zimmermann

 **YES**

Origins of a Catastrophe

Preface

This is a story with villains—villains guilty of destroying the multiethnic state of Yugoslavia, of provoking three wars, and of throwing some twenty million people into a distress unknown since the Second World War. How could this tragedy have happened to a country that by most standards was more prosperous and more open than any other in Eastern Europe? My thesis is that the Yugoslav catastrophe was not mainly the result of ancient ethnic or religious hostilities, nor of the collapse of communism at the end of the cold war, nor even of the failures of the Western countries. Those factors undeniably made things worse. But Yugoslavia's death and the violence that followed resulted from the conscious actions of nationalist leaders who coopted, intimidated, circumvented, or eliminated all opposition to their demagogic designs. Yugoslavia was destroyed from the top down.

This [selection] is primarily about those destroyers. As American ambassador between 1989 and 1992, I saw them frequently and came to know them well. Speaking with me before their faces had become familiar to Western television viewers, they hadn't yet learned the full panoply of defenses against questions from foreigners. They described their plans, sometimes honestly, sometimes deceitfully, but always passionately and with a cynical disregard for playing by any set of rules. This record of their words and actions provides evidence for a coroner's report on the death of Yugoslavia....

The prime agent of Yugoslavia's destruction was Slobodan Milošević, president of Serbia. Milošević claimed to defend Yugoslavia even as he spun plans to turn it into a Serb-dominated dictatorship. His initial objective was to establish Serbian rule over the whole country. When Slovenia and Croatia blocked this aim by deciding to secede, the Serbian leader fell back on an alternative strategy. He would bring all of Yugoslavia's Serbs, who lived in five of its six republics, under the authority of Serbia, that is, of himself.

Milošević initiated this strategy in Croatia, using the Yugoslav army to seal off Serbian areas from the reach of Croatian authority. His plan in Bosnia was even bolder—to establish by force a Serbian state on two-thirds of the territory of a republic in which Serbs weren't even a plurality, much less a majority.

In league with Radovan Karadžić, the Bosnian Serb leader with whom he later broke, Milošević was responsible for the deaths of tens of thousands of Bosnians and for the creation of the largest refugee population in Europe since the Second World War.

Franjo Tudjman, elected president of Croatia in 1990, also played a leading role in the destruction of Yugoslavia. A fanatic Croatian nationalist, Tudjman hated Yugoslavia and its multiethnic values. He wanted a Croatian state for Croatians, and he was unwilling to guarantee equal rights to the 12 percent of Croatia's citizens who were Serbs. Tudjman's arrogance in declaring independence without adequate provisions for minority rights gave Milošević and the Yugoslav army a pretext for their war of aggression in Croatia in 1991. And Tudjman's greed in seeking to annex Croatian areas of Bosnia prolonged the war and increased the casualties in that ill-starred republic.

Slovenian nationalism was different from the Serbian or Croatian sort. With a nearly homogeneous population and a location in the westernmost part of Yugoslavia, Slovenia was more democratically inclined and more economically developed than any other republic in Yugoslavia. The Slovenes wanted to be free of the poverty and intrigue of the rest of Yugoslavia. They particularly detested Milošević, charging him with making Yugoslavia uninhabitable for non-Serbs. Under the presidency of Milan Kučan—a conflicted figure buffeted toward secession by the winds of Slovenian politics—Slovenia unilaterally declared its independence on June 25, 1991. The predictable result, irresponsibly disregarded by Kučan and the other Slovene leaders, was to bring war closer to Croatia and Bosnia....

Decline...

A law graduate of Belgrade University, Milošević began his career as a communist apparatchik with an authoritarian personality already noticed by schoolmates. He was too young and too junior to have been close to [Josip Broz] Tito, but he was old enough (thirty-eight when Tito died) to have prospered in the Titoist system. I never saw in him the personal animus against Tito that many other Serbs felt. In fact, on my first visit to his office I noticed a large painting of Tito behind his desk; significantly, he took it down in 1991, the year Yugoslavia fell apart.

As he cultivated a nationalist persona, Milošević dropped the external aspects of his communist formation. He purged himself of the wooden language that makes communists the world over such hapless communicators. He dropped all references to communism. And he renamed the League of Communists of Serbia the Serbian Socialist Party.

In two ways, however, Milošević failed to break the ties. The first was his continued reliance on communist techniques of control over his party, the Serbian police, the media, and the economic sector. The second was his highly visible wife, Mirjana Marković, a Belgrade University professor and frequent author of turgid Leninist essays in glossy Serbian magazines. Marković flaunted her communism; in fact, she cofounded a communist party in 1990. She was thought to have the influence of a Lady Macbeth over her husband, particularly with regard to his frequent abrupt dismissals of hitherto trusted subordinates. Liberal Serbs described her variously as flaky, crafty, amoral, or vicious.

Whatever his real views of Tito, Milošević was nevertheless the vessel for the Serbian claim that Tito had denied Serbs the role to which destiny had entitled them. The charge may have been partly true, but it was certainly exaggerated. Serbs were a major element of Tito's partisan army during World War II, including its first two elite units, and played a prominent role in the Yugoslav army and police afterward. At his death, however, Tito left Yugoslavia so decentralized that no ethnic group—and certainly not the Serbs—could possibly dominate it. Given Serbian messianism, it became inevitable that a Serbian nationalist would rise up to redress the imagined wrongs dealt his nation. It was a tragedy for Serbia, its neighbors, and Europe as a whole that this nationalist turned out to be Slobodan Milošević....

Milošević deploys his arguments with force and apparent conviction. They're always internally consistent, even when based on fallacies or delusions. "You see, Mr. Zimmermann," he would say, "only we Serbs really believe in Yugoslavia. We're not trying to secede like the Croats and Slovenes, we're not tied to a foreign country like the Albanians in Kosovo, and we're not trying to create an Islamic state like the Muslims in Bosnia. They all fought against you in World War II. We were your allies." ...

In my view, Milošević is an opportunist rather than an ideologue, a man driven by power rather than nationalism. In the late 1980s he was a communist official in search of a legitimation less disreputable than communism, an alternative philosophy to help him consolidate his hold on Serbia, and a myth that would excite and energize Serbs behind him. He calculated that the way to achieve and maintain power in Serbia was to seize the nationalist pot that Serbian intellectuals were brewing and bring it to a boil.

I don't see Milošević as the same kind of ethnic exclusivist as Croatia's President Franjo Tudjman, who dislikes Serbs, or Bosnian Serb politician Radovan Karadžić, who hates everybody who isn't a Serb. Milošević felt no discomfort in bragging to me, no matter how fraudulently, about Serbia as a multiethnic paradise. Nor, I'm sure, did it disturb his conscience to move ruthlessly against Serbian nationalists like Karadžić when they got in his way. He has made a compact with nationalism as a way to bring him power. He can't break the compact without causing political damage to himself, but it has a utilitarian rather than an emotional value for him.

I can't recall ever seeing a cooler politician under pressure than Slobodan Milošević. In March 1991 he lunched with me and six other Western ambassadors. The meeting came during one of the most explosive crises of his political career. The week before, he had weathered the largest street demonstration ever mounted against his rule, had lost a bid to overthrow the leaderships of Slovenia and Croatia, and was in the process of trying to destroy the presidency of Yugoslavia.

He had come to our lunch from a four-hour meeting with hostile Belgrade University students. Yet he looked and acted as if nothing gave him greater pleasure than to sit down for a long conversation with us. He addressed all our questions with equanimity, asserting with good humor that the Kosovo Albanians were the most pampered minority in Europe, that street demonstrations (which had brought him to power) were wrong, and that Serbia had the freest media and the freest election system in Yugoslavia.

As I pondered the surreal quality of Milošević's remarks, I couldn't help admiring his imperturbability. I went back to the embassy and wrote a facetious cable saying that I had finally penetrated the mystery of the man. There were really two Milošević's. Milošević One was hard-line, authoritarian, belligerent, bent on chaos, and wedded to the use of force to create a Greater Serbia. Personally, he was apoplectic, he hated Westerners, and he spoke in Serbian. Milošević Two was polite, affable, cooperative, and always looking for reasonable solutions to Yugoslavia's problems. He was calm, he liked to reminisce about his banking days in New York, and he spoke good English.

I did note that Milošević One and Milošević Two had several traits in common: they disliked Albanians, they were strong in the defense of Serbian interests, and they seemed to believe that the world was ganging up against Serbia. Milošević Two, I wrote, would often be summoned to repair the horrendous damage caused to Serbia's reputation by Milošević One, who would be sent back to the locker room. There his handlers would salve his wounds and get him ready for the next round. The one sure thing, I concluded, was that Milošević One would always be back.

The strategy of this schizoid figure was based on the fact that Serbs were spread among five of Yugoslavia's six republics. Slovenia was the only exception. At the foundation of Yugoslavia after World War I, Serbia's chief interest was that all these Serbs live in a single state. Before Tito, Serbia had dominated that state. Now, after Tito, Milošević wanted to restore that dominance. His chief obstacle in the late 1980s was Slovenia, ironically the only republic without large numbers of Serbs. The Slovenes were the first to challenge the unity of Yugoslavia.

Milošević, no supporter of Yugoslav unity except as a vehicle for Serbian influence, wrapped himself in the mantle of unity as he sharpened his duel with the Slovenes. His concept of unity was Serbian nationalism buttressed by communist methods of control. It tolerated neither democracy nor power-sharing with other national groups. Because it was unacceptable to all Yugoslavs who wanted real unity or real democracy, or both, it was bound to be divisive. In fact, Milošević's pursuit of a narrow Serbian agenda made him the major wrecker of Yugoslavia. . . .

Departures

On May 12, 1992, the State Department announced that I was being recalled to Washington in protest against the Serbian aggression in Bosnia. . . .

The days before our departure and the weeks after gave us time for introspection about a country where we had lived six years and that had affected us deeply. How was it possible that such attractive people, on whom the gods of nature and fortune had smiled, could have plowed their way straight to hell? Shortly before we left Belgrade, I tried to answer that question in a cable entitled

"Who Killed Yugoslavia?" It was intended as an analysis of the fatal elements in Yugoslavia's distant and recent past, laced with some nostalgia for what had been lost. I used as a framework the old English folk song "Who Killed Cock Robin?" a tale of murder complete with witnesses, grave-diggers, and mourners, but nobody to save the victim or bring him back to life....

With the perspective of years, of the Bosnian war, and of many gross misrepresentations of Yugoslavia's collapse, it's important to eliminate some of the reasons often cited. First, Yugoslavia was not destroyed by ancient Balkan hatreds. This doesn't mean that the Balkans don't seethe with violence. The First World War was touched off by the assassination in Sarajevo of an Austrian archduke by a Bosnian Serb; the Second was for Yugoslavia not only a liberation war but a civil war with over half a million Yugoslav deaths.

But is Yugoslavia so unique? Europe, taken as a whole, has endured two civil wars in this century, involving sixty million deaths, including the genocidal annihilation of six million European Jews. Placid England suffered in the fifteenth century the Wars of the Roses, which moved Charles Dickens to remark: "When men continually fight against their own countrymen, they are always observed to be more unnaturally cruel and filled with rage than they are against any other enemy." The English lived through an even bloodier period in the seventeenth century: a king was executed and many of the people of Ireland massacred by Cromwell's forces. France had its wars of religion in the sixteenth century and its blood-drenched revolution in the eighteenth. Nor has the United States been immune from domestic conflict. More Americans died in our civil war than in any foreign war we have ever fought.

Balkan genes aren't abnormally savage. Bosnia enjoyed long periods of tranquility as a multiethnic community. Serbs and Croats, the most antagonistic of adversaries today, had never fought each other before the twentieth century. The millennium they spent as neighbors was marked more by mutual indifference than by mutual hostility. Serbs, though demonized by many as incorrigibly xenophobic, don't fit that stereotype. Milovan Djilas's son Aleksa, author of a brilliant history of nationalism in Yugoslavia, points out that, with all the manipulative tools at Milošević's disposal, it still took him four years to arouse the Serbian population and that, even then, thousands of Serbs fled the country to avoid fighting in Croatia.

The Yugoslav wars can't be explained by theories of inevitable ethnic hatreds, even when such explanations conveniently excuse outsiders from the responsibilities of intervening. There was plenty of racial and historical tinder available in Yugoslavia. But the conflagrations didn't break out through spontaneous combustion. Pyromaniacs were required.

Second, religion wasn't at the heart of Yugoslavia's demise. The Yugoslav wars were primarily ethnic, not religious, wars. The major proponents of destructive nationalism weren't driven by religious faith. Franjo Tudjman had been a communist most of his life; he converted to Catholicism when he turned to nationalist activities. Milošević, a lifelong communist, never, as far as I know, entered a Serbian Orthodox church except for blatant political purposes. I recall a visit he made for electoral reasons to a Serbian monastery on Mt. Athos in northern Greece. Not even the official photographs could disguise the disconcerted and uncomfortable look on his face. Even Bosnia was largely a secular society; a 1985 survey found that only 17 percent of its people considered themselves believers.

None of this absolves the Serbian and Croatian churches. There were many religious people in Yugoslavia, particularly among rural folk. The Serbian Orthodox Church and the Catholic Church in Croatia were willing accomplices of the political leaders in coopting their parishioners for racist designs. These two churches were national churches, in effect arms of their respective states when it came to ethnic matters. They played a disgraceful role by exacerbating racial tensions when they could have urged their faithful toward Christian healing.

With regard to Bosnia, both the Serbian and Croatian regimes felt the need to impute fanatic religiosity to the Muslims in order to satanize them. But the portrayal was false. The Bosnia I knew was probably the most secular Muslim society in the world. The growing number of Muslim adherents today is a consequence of the war, not one of its root causes.

Third, Yugoslavia was not a victim of communism or even of its demise. Yugoslavs didn't live under the Soviet yoke, unlike their neighbors in the Warsaw Pact, for whom communism was an alien and evil implant. Gorbachev's withdrawal from Eastern Europe liberated whole countries but had little direct effect on Yugoslavia, whose communism, whatever its defects, was homegrown. In Eastern Europe the fault line was between communism and Western-style democracy; in Yugoslavia it was between ethnic groups. Tito's relative liberalism within the European communist world coopted many people for the Yugoslav party who would have been Western-oriented dissidents in Czechoslovakia or Poland.

In Yugoslavia the dissidents were for the most part nationalists, not liberals, and they marched to domestic drummers beating out racist, not Western, themes. Communists in Yugoslavia wore black hats or white hats, depending on whether they were nationalists or not. The most rabid nationalists, like Milošević or Tudjman, were or had been communists. So had many antinationalist, democratic figures, like Drnovšek, Gligorov, Tupurkovski, and many courageous journalists and human rights activists. In most of Eastern Europe, the word "communist" explained a good deal about a person; in Yugoslavia it explained next to nothing.

Fourth, Yugoslavia wasn't destroyed by foreign intervention or the lack of it. General Kadijević, in his paranoid account of the end of Yugoslavia, blames the United States, Germany, and the European Community, acting in collusion with traitors in Slovenia, Croatia, and Kosovo. Foreign countries did make serious mistakes in Yugoslavia, but they didn't destroy it. The failure to do more to support Prime Minister Marković, the lack of a forceful Western reaction to the shelling of Dubrovnik, and the European Community's premature decision to recognize the independence of Yugoslavia's republics were all mistakes, but not fatal ones. Whatever inducements or penalties the West might have devised, they wouldn't have been enough to suppress the nationalistic rage that was overwhelming the country. The war in Bosnia was another matter; there the West could have saved the situation and didn't. But the murder of Yugoslavia was a crime of domestic violence.

The victim itself had congenital defects. Yugoslavia was a state, but not a nation. Few felt much loyalty to Yugoslavia itself. Tito sought to encourage fealty by guaranteeing ethnic autonomy rather than by trying to create an ethnic melting pot. Political energy was directed more toward gaining a better position in Yugoslavia for one's ethnic group than toward preserving the viability of the state. Nobody wanted to be a member of a minority; nobody expected minorities automatically to be protected. Vladimir Gligorov, son of the wise president of Macedonia and a perceptive scholar, captured this feeling when he asked ironically, "Why should I be a minority in your state when you can be a minority in mine?"

These character traits damaged, but didn't doom, Yugoslavia. The country didn't commit suicide. As the court of history pursues its investigation of the death of Yugoslavia, I can imagine the following indictments: Slovenia for selfishness toward its fellow Yugoslavs; Tudjman's Croatia for insensitivity toward its Serbian population and greed toward its Bosnian neighbors; the Yugoslav army for ideological rigidity and arrogance, culminating in war crimes; Radovan Karadžić for attacking the principle of tolerance in Yugoslavia's most ethnically mixed republic; and—most of all—Slobodan Milošević for devising and pursuing a strategy that led directly to the breakup of the country and to the deaths of over a hundred thousand of its citizens. Nationalism was the arrow that killed Yugoslavia. Milošević was the principal bowman.

The Serbian leader made Yugoslavia intolerable for anybody who wasn't a Serb. He is hated among Albanians, Slovenes, Croats, Muslims, Macedonians, and Hungarians. And he has brought his own people into poverty and despair. The potentially prosperous and influential Serbia on which he expatiated in our last meeting in April 1992 is now an economic and civil shambles. Much of its youth and middle class—the foundation of democratic construction—has fled to the west. Milošević's dream of "all Serbs in one state" is a nightmare today; Serbs are now scattered among four states—"Yugoslavia" (Serbia and Montenegro), Bosnia, Croatia, and Macedonia. In seeking to dominate Yugoslavia, Milošević destroyed it. In seeking to tear out the pieces where Serbs lived, he wrecked, for a generation or more, the future of all Serbs.

Ancient Hatreds or Elite Manipulation? Memory and Politics in the Former Yugoslavia

Any optimism generated by the Dayton peace accords in late 1995 was substantially eroded by events during the spring and summer of 1996. These events marked a protracted and tragic endgame in the former Yugoslavia. The flight from Sarajevo by Bosnian Serbs in February and March 1996 was the first indication of things to come. During the summer, refugees who tried to return to their former homes were harassed and attacked by paramilitary gangs. The early focus was on the behavior of the Bosnian Serbs, but now it is apparent that a policy of ethnic apartheid is being pursued by all sides in Bosnia....

The complexity of the Yugoslav conflict illustrates that the genesis of the war and the issues of ethnonational identity that fed the flames of conflict are far from being understood in any way that reflects some set of shared perspectives among scholars and pundits. For example, the exodus from Sarajevo by the Serbs in February and March 1996 seems to defy logic and rationality. One analytic perspective contends that the war is a product of "ancient hatreds" rooted in primordial identity and consequently any national group that falls under the political control of another is in mortal danger. The experience of some Serbs who left Sarajevo certainly reinforces this contention, as they ran a gauntlet of hostile Bosnian Muslims, supposedly bent on revenge. An opposing perspective views the war as the product of elite manipulation and fear-mongering by ethnic entrepreneurs who fanned the flames of hatred for their own purposes and who manipulated ethnonational identity issues that are themselves just a product of an "invented tradition." Analysts who adhere to the second perspective suggested that Serbs should take hold of their senses, accept the guarantees of the Bosnian-Croat Federation, ignore their leader's warnings, and stay in Sarajevo. Despite assurances, however, the Serbs who stayed in Sarajevo have been continually threatened. Bosnian Prime Minister Hasan Muratovic promised that the violence against Serbs in Sarajevo would be stopped. But unfortunately, most of the Serbs in Sarajevo now want to leave, including many who were loyal to the Bosnian government during the war.

From Steven Majstorovic, "Ancient Hatreds or Elite Manipulation? Memory and Politics in the Former Yugoslavia," *World Affairs*, vol. 159, no. 4 (Spring 1997). Copyright © 1997 by The American Peace Society. Reprinted by permission of *World Affairs*. Notes omitted.

Clearly, the Yugoslav conflict is an almost ideal laboratory for addressing some of the central questions that scholars of nationalism and ethnicity pose. Those who espouse a primordialist conception of national identity have ample evidence to support their position, while the constructionists also have abundant data that support their contention that national identity is essentially an artificial and modern phenomenon that is often at the mercy of ambitious leaders who manipulate and instrumentalize ethnonational identity.

This [selection] argues that prevailing analyses of ethnic conflict in the former Yugoslavia that focus either on a notion of ancient, primordial hatreds rooted in centuries-old identities, or on the premise that ethnic identity in the Balkans is a modern social construction that has been instrumentalized by political elites, miss the essential nature of the ongoing struggle. Historical memory constrains the options that leaders exercise in conflict creation and in peacemaking. Ethnic identity in the former Yugoslavia, however, has also been and will continue [to] be somewhat flexible and politically adaptive but only within a framework that does not threaten the constraints imposed by myth and memory. The constraints on masses and elites imposed by historical experience are particularly applicable for the Serbs, somewhat less so for the Croats, and even less so for the Bosnian Muslims. The Balkan conflict has both premodern, primordial characteristics and modern, constructed/instrumentalized elements in which ancient antagonisms (sometimes hatreds) and modern politics have both contributed appreciably to the tragedy, and an overemphasis on either perspective misrepresents the nature of ethnic conflict and politics in the former Yugoslavia. . . .

Memory and Myth in Serbian, Croatian, and Bosnian Muslim Ethnonational Identity

When the term "Balkan politics" is conjured up, a mental picture that many people might have is one of incessant conflict, ethnic tinderboxes, and terrorist plots. This stereotypical view of Balkan politics is not wholly inaccurate. The Balkans have historically been a crossroads for conquest and occupation. The area that is now Yugoslavia was settled by the migration of Slavic tribes during the sixth century. Those tribes were independent until the beginning of the twelfth century, when the Croatians yielded to Hungarian political dominance, and until the beginning of the fifteenth century when the Serbians were defeated by the Ottoman Turks. External rule from Austria, Hungary, Italy, or Turkey lasted until the beginning of the twentieth century, although in a series of revolts the Serbs had formed an independent state by the middle of the nineteenth century.

In addition to being distinguished from each other by self-defined differences in tribal custom and culture, the South Slavs were further differentiated by the split in the Christian church. As a consequence, the Croats and Slovenes identified with Roman Catholicism, while the Serbs were under the jurisdiction of Byzantium and had formed by the thirteenth century an independent Serbian Orthodox Church. This division between East and West was reinforced when the Eastern Orthodox Serbs fell under Turkish rule, while the Croats and Slovenes answered to Rome and Hungary, and eventually to the Austro-Hungarian Empire. Thus, when the South Slavs were brought into a common state in 1918, the stage for ethnonational conflict had been set by a thousand years of history.

Serbian identity can best be understood as a combination of three historical experiences: the memory of the Battle of Kosovo in 1389 and the subsequent five hundred years of servitude and resistance against the Ottoman Turks; the successful revolts against the Turks early in the nineteenth century that culminated in an independent Serbian state by the middle of the century; and the role of the Serbs as allies of the West in two World Wars.

By the fourteenth century, the Serbs under Tsar Dusan had grown into a medieval empire that spanned the Balkans from the Adriatic to Western Bulgaria and to most of Albania and some areas in northern Greece. After his death in 1355, centralized power started to ebb, and various Serb nobles started to unravel the system set up by Dusan. In 1371, however, Prince Lazar came to power and a temporary recentralization of control was established. This short period ended at Kosovo Polje (The Field of Blackbirds) on 28 June 1389.

The battle between the Serb forces of Prince Lazar and the Ottoman Turks was at the time perceived as either a pyrrhic victory for the Turks or indecisive. The Serbian state survived for another seventy years before finally succumbing to Ottoman rule. However, the cataclysmic nature of a battle in which Prince Lazar and his son were beheaded, the Turkish Sultan Murad disemboweled by the Serbian knight Milos Obilic, and in which there were horrific losses on both sides (over 100,000 deaths in an eight-to-ten-hour battle) created a myth-making apparatus that has shaped Serbian consciousness to this day.

The battle decimated the Serb nobility and cost the Ottomans dearly. Almost immediately, Serbian poets, priests, and peasants started to propagate the notion of Christian martyrdom by the Serbian people, Prince Lazar, and Milos Oblic. The primordialization of the event had all the elements of a passion play played out in real life. Interestingly enough, the perspective of the Ottoman Turks only reinforces the Serbian myths:

> Yet this Ottoman view in some ways mirrors traditional Serbian views. Both the Ottoman and Serbian accounts emphasize the battle's cataclysmic nature. Both traditions have martyrdom as a theme.

Added to this vision shared between the Serbs and the Turks, the battle itself is routinely listed in historical surveys as one of the most important events in history. The result of all this valorization is an identity marker that is so rooted in real historical events that it is almost impossible for Serbs to escape its ubiquitous presence in Serbian identity.

Also a part of the Kosovo myth is the tale of migration by Serbs from Kosovo, the failed attempts to migrate back over a period of centuries, and the final triumphant return to Kosovo in 1912. Taken together, these events, which were kept alive by the Serbian Orthodox church in the liturgy and by traveling troubadours who annually embellished the story in an ever-growing epic poem ("The Kosovo Cycle"), suggest that even the horrible events in Bosnia may have been less destructive than the potential for catastrophe in the Serbian province of Kosovo that is today 90 percent Albanian.

The memory of an independent state that was relinquished to form the Kingdom of South Slavs is also a critical part of Serb identity. The theme of successful revolt and emancipation dominates the mythicizing of the Balkan Wars. Finally, the Serbian role in World War I and World War II completes the picture. Serbs suffered enormous losses in both wars and continually stress their part in the Allied victories, comparing their role to Croat, Bosnian Muslim, and Albanian collaboration. In particular, the role of General Draza Mihailovich and the Chetnik resistance in World War II is highlighted, as archival evidence has suggested a reassessment of [Josip Broz] Tito and the role of the partisans.

Surprisingly, Serbs do not consider the genocidal policies of the Croatian Ustasha state and their Bosnian Muslim allies during World War II as an important element of Serbian identity. Instead, the events are often used as a way to stereotype all Croatians and Muslims by both Serb masses and elites. In particular, the Ustasha- and Muslim-led genocide of Serbs in Croatia and Bosnia in World War II has been the key to understanding Bosnian Serb and Croatian Serb propaganda and military mobilization strategies against Croats and Muslims in the contemporary period. Both Rodovan Karadzic and Ratko Mladic, the Bosnian Serb military leader, have used the events of World War II to successfully demonize Croats and Muslims in the eyes of the Serbs.

Croatian identity also has a memory of a medieval kingdom, but one that peacefully gave up its sovereignty to the Hungarian crown in 1102. The project of identity primordialization by the Croats has been to present events since 1102 as evidence for the continuity of a Croatian state in waiting. The keys to this continuity are peasant uprisings, a succession of Croatian kings, advances in Croatian culture and learning that depict Croatia as a part of a Western European culture that is distinct from the Serbs, and the unbroken reality of Croatian national consciousness that goes back to the seventh century. What is often ignored by Serbs is that it was the efforts of Croat intellectuals and church leaders in the nineteenth century that first broached the idea of a single South Slav state.

Croatian identity is also tied to the Catholic church and its role in resisting Serbian dominance in the interwar period. The issue of Serbian dominance is hotly debated between Serbs and Croats. While Croats refer to Serbian dominance, Serbs refer to Croat obstructionism. The debate has no resolution, but by 1938 Croatia did win considerable autonomy from Belgrade and was, effectively, a state within a state.

Another part of the Croatian primordialization project is to address the events of World War II by minimizing the Ustasha aspect and emphasizing the role of the Croats in the partisan resistance led by Tito. This interpretation, however, is also open for debate between Croats and Serbs, since most sources that address Tito's partisan movement make it clear that an overwhelming majority of the partisans were Serbs, and that many Croatians did not join until Tito, a Croat, offered a pardon at the end of 1943 to anyone who joined the partisans, although Tito's action did alienate many Serb partisans. It should also be noted that many Serb renegade units participated in revenge massacres against

Croatian and Muslim civilians toward the end of World War II. These killings numbered in the thousands and are remembered by Croats and Muslims who insist that the slaughter was mutual and that the world has tended to ignore Croatian and Muslim victims of World War II.

Croatian identity is also reinforced by the failure of the Croatian Republic to separate from Yugoslavia during what is called the Croatian Crises or Croatian Spring of 1968–72. The crises started out as an attempt to liberalize the economic and political system. But the movement was eventually taken over by nationalist elements who pushed for Croatian independence. An alarmed Tito brutally ended the movement and purged the Croatian party of liberals. He then did the same thing to the Serbian party to effect some semblance of ethnic symmetry. Unfortunately, many of the liberals who were purged in both the Serbian and Croatian Communist parties were the type of leaders who might have been effective in heading off the level of conflict in the Yugoslav conflict of 1991–95. But it is from the experience of 1968–72 that many Croatians today stereotype Serbs as conservative Communists while Croats see themselves as liberal democrats in the Western tradition. It was also during the period of the Croatian Crises that Franjo Tudjman became a staunch nationalist who started to write revisionist tracts about what he labeled the myth of the number of Serbian deaths in World War II.

The next element in the continual primordialization of Croatian identity will become the successful secession from Yugoslavia in 1991, Croatian suffering at the hands of the Serbs, and the German-led recognition by the world community. Pronouncements from Zagreb seem to support this view, although it is still too early for any complete evaluation.

Until the Bosnian war and the siege of Sarajevo began in 1992, Bosnian Muslim identity was essentially a tug of war between Serbian, Croatian, and Bosnian Muslim interpretations of history. The Serb perspective is that the Muslims are Islamicized Slavs who were mostly Serbs. The Croat view is that these same Slavs were Catholic Croats. Some Bosnian Muslims, however, claim that they are descended from the Bogomils, who were a heretic Manechean sect. Moreover, many Muslim intellectuals during the nineteenth century started to claim that the Bogomils were really Turks from Anatolia and that the "only thing Slavic about the Bosnian Muslims is their language, which they absorbed from the indigenous population." There are also perspectives that contend that the Bogomils were much more than a sect and that contemporary Bosnian Serbs are not really Serbs but an offshoot of the Vlachs, a sheep-herding people related to the Rumanians.

Muslim ethnic identity got a boost in 1971 when they were officially declared a nationality by the Tito regime. He thought that this declaration might end the warring claims for Muslim identity by the Serbs and Croats. Tito's rationale was that the creation of Bosnia-Hercegovina as a republic at the end of World War II had outlived its usefulness as a buffer between the Croats and the Serbs and that some other policy was necessary.

There are many recent works that present the history of Bosnia as generally one of interethnic harmony and cooperation. But it is [Robert J.] Donia and [John V. A.] Fine's thorough research that, despite their contentions, highlights very ancient roots of the conflict in Bosnia. They present a rich chronology of Bosnian life from antiquity to the present tragedy. Their most important contribution is the thorough and impressive debunking of the incessant claims of Croatian and Serbian chauvinists. Serb nationalists produce evidence that most Bosnian Muslims are Orthodox Serbs who were forcibly converted to Islam by the Ottoman Turks, while Croat nationalists argue that Bosnian Muslims are by blood the "truest" and "purest" of Catholic Croats who were led astray by the Turks.

The conversion to Islam in Bosnia was characterized by a very complex process. Bosnian Muslims were once Slavic Christians who were neither Serbs nor Croats but had a distinct Bosnian identity and belonged to a Bosnian church that ostensibly bowed toward Rome, a fact that Croats seize upon to make their claims. But the rites of this church closely followed the Eastern Orthodox model, which Serbs contend establishes Serbian identity. But what is most evident is that the Bosnian church was never well established, there were few priests, and the Bosnian Slavic peasants maintained only a tenuous tie to Christianity. Thus, with the Ottoman penetration into Bosnia in the fifteenth century, these peasants began a gradual conversion to Islam in a pragmatic decisionmaking process that took between one and two centuries. Moreover, the contention by some modern Bosnian Muslim scholars that Muslim identity was never Christian but instead sprang from the Bogomils, a sect that rejected Christianity and its rituals, is also refuted by evidence that the Bogomils in Bosnia were very few in number and were never influential in the development of Bosnian history.

Eventually, Muslims adapted to the erosion of Ottoman hegemony, the nineteenth century influence of the Austro-Hungarian empire, the Balkan Wars and World War I, the first Yugoslavia in which Serbs predominated, World War II, the Tito period in which the Muslims finally gained official status as a nation in Bosnia, and the final degeneration into civil war. During this period, the Muslims often exhibited a predilection for compromise and pragmatism, especially after the fall of the Ottoman empire, as the Muslims formed political parties and interest groups whose purpose was to tread the narrow balance point between blatant Croat and Serb attempts to capture their loyalty. Throughout the period, the tolerant, cooperative, and multicultural nature of Bosnian society is stressed by Bosnian Muslim nationalists. But a closer examination reveals that Bosnian society was somewhat less tolerant and harmonious than some would contend.

The constructionist and instrumentalist perspectives suggest that Croat and Serb ethnic consciousness did not exist in Bosnia prior to the nineteenth century and that the often mentioned notion that the current war is based on "ancient hatreds" is false. But history presents a more complex picture. It is clear that the development of medieval Bosnia did not occur in isolation and was closely connected to events in Serbia and Croatia. Also, the Ottoman millet system identified ethnic groups by religion instead of ethnicity. Consequently, it is often mistakenly assumed that since the Turks used a non-ethnic marker to identify Croats and Serbs, a pre-nineteenth-century Croat and Bosnian ethnicity did not exist. But Serbian settlers started moving into Bosnia by the early fifteenth century to escape Ottoman expansion into Kosovo, the Serbian heartland. After some initial migration of Croats out of Bosnia, the Franciscan order successfully helped to maintain a Croat presence in the area of western Bosnia known as Hercegovina. Furthermore, the Austrians offered Serbs land to act as a military buffer against the Turks, and by the seventeenth century Serbs occupied the Krajina in Croatia and adjacent areas in Bosnia. Croat and Serb consciousness was well established and was not simply a construction of nineteenth-century nationalism.

In the social system built by the Ottomans, the Muslim converts were landowners and freeholders, and the overwhelming majority of peasants, who were taxed heavily and lived as second-class citizens, were Serbs, along with a number of Croats. The peasants, especially the Serbs, who lived in this Jim Crow system chafed at the inequities and started to revolt by the nineteenth century. Of particular interest to a contemporary understanding of ethnic frictions is that, as the Ottoman empire eroded and was forced to make concessions to subject populations, it was in Bosnia where the local Muslim landlords were the most reactionary and hostile to any changes that threatened their paramountcy.

If the above-recounted issues are not evidence of "ancient hatreds," then at least there was fertile ground in Bosnia for ancient antagonisms. When it came to manipulating public opinion, Milosevic in Serbia and Tudjman in Croatia are often cited as architects of the war in Bosnia. However, Bosnian President Alija Izetbegovic should not be left off the hook. His role in the war, his rather radical political views, and his reneging on the Lisbon Agreement of 1992 that would have maintained a multiethnic Bosnia need to be examined closely. Still, it is clear from the evidence that despite the protestations of extremist Serbs and Croats, the reality of a Muslim national identity is undeniable. The notion of a Bosnia in multiethnic harmony before the current struggle is an insupportable myth that could be maintained only by a centralized Communist system. When Tito died and the system collapsed, history started to catch up rather quickly.

It should be apparent that at this point Muslim identity is still in the process of primordialization. The sieges of Sarajevo and Mostar and the killing fields of Srebrenica will be the building blocks as Kosovo was for the Serbs. Instead of historical records and oral history, the Bosnian Muslims will have access to videotapes, and Benedict Anderson's notion of the printing press as a vehicle for the imaging of identity has evolved to NPR and PBS. The Bosnian Muslims are quickly moving from being Yugoslavs to Bosnian Muslims, and women wearing veils have started to appear in villages and even on the streets of Sarajevo. Moreover, the flirtation with Islamic forces from the Middle East, particularly Iran, has been recently documented.

In contrast to Muslim identity, Serbian identity is rooted in a centuries-old primordialization project. Despite Milosevic's manipulation of the Serbian media and elections, the force of elite manipulation in an instrumentalist fashion is not as significant as one would think for Serbian identity today because Milosevic, or any democratic alternative to him, would be constrained by history from stepping too far outside the successful Kosovo-inspired primordialization of identity. There are even arguments that in the case of the Serbs it is the elites who have been shaped by the memories and the myths of the masses.

The Serbs, more than the Croats or Muslims, are shackled by their view of history and may not be able to escape what they see as an apocalyptic destiny, a destiny that unfortunately combines national paranoia with a sense of a messianic mission to defend Christianity from the mounting forces of Islam.

The Croatian model represents an ethnic identity that is still in the process of primordialization, which is committed to reinforce the notion of a thousand-year history. This project is augmented by a heavy dose of instrumentalism as President Tudjman and his supporters on the Right try to hold onto the power and privileges that they enjoyed during the Communist era. An example of this effort is the release of the new Croatian currency during May 1994. The new currency is called the "Kuna" and refers to a forest marten. The only memory of this currency dates back to the Ustasha regime, and Jews and Serbs in Croatia have protested in vain. Croatian historians, some quite reluctantly, have scrambled to discover or perhaps imagine instances where marten skins have been used in trade within Croatia during the past thousand years. Some isolated instances have been discovered and so the process of primordialization continues.

Moreover, the Croats, as they did during the 1960s, have recently declared that Croat is a separate language from Serbian and have introduced numerous words that go back to Slavic anachronisms from the past. Differences in dialect between Serbian, Croatian, and Bosnian are probably less pronounced, according to most linguists, than between American and British English. But the process of identity differentiation through language policy is in high gear. In reaction, the Serbs and the Bosnian Muslims have also jumped on the bandwagon, and perhaps in five hundred years there will be three different languages created from the current Serbo-Croation.

The Muslims are in some sense the most free to pursue their own vision of an ethnic identity. Without a Kosovo or a thousand-year state to guide them, they are in a Big Bang period of imagining their place in the world. The process of primordialization occurs under the watchful eye of the world, and the instrumental policies of the government in Sarajevo are profoundly tied to this process. Primordialist, constructivist, and instrumentalist categories have collapsed upon each other in Sarajevo, and the Bosnian Muslims have the luxury of picking and choosing, although there is growing evidence that their role as absolute victim is starting to come under question as more recent evidence has started to point toward a more symmetrical structure of suffering in the current conflict. Choices for the Croats are more limited but still possible.

The Serbs are fanatically committed to a mythic identity that may not allow choices, even if they desire them. Moreover, the Serbs have already started to mythicize the expulsion of 250,000 civilians from the Krajina region of Croatia, an expulsion that the United States refrained from labeling "ethnic cleansing." The Serbs have also started to focus on the slaughter of Serbs in the Srebrenica area before the Bosnian Serb army atrocities of July 1995 as new fodder for their continued vision of martyrdom. If the Serbs cannot break out of a primordialization process that has exhausted itself, then the outlook for the Balkans is very bleak indeed, and the post-Dayton events of 1996 may be the harbinger of tragedy when the NATO forces leave Bosnia.

The complexity of the ethnic conflict in the former Yugoslavia has illustrated the difficulty of mono-causal analyses. Despite the penchant in postmodern analysis for stressing the decentered person who can change identities like clothing, ethnonational identity often predisposes people to dispense with rational decisionmaking and instead embrace a policy of radical ethnic altruism in which lives are sacrificed. And although the examination of elite behavior is part and parcel of the methodology of social scientists, this methodology falls short when historically rooted conflicts are examined. In the dark street of available data, it is elite behavior that is lit by the lamp at the end of the street. But it is the rest of the street in which the richness and cultural thickness of memory, myth, and shared experience lurks in shadows. The data in these shadows are often difficult to measure empirically. We must, however, seriously consider their validity lest we ignore them at great cost to future peacemaking and conflict resolution.

POSTSCRIPT

Were Ethnic Leaders Responsible for the Disintegration of Yugoslavia?

The biggest loss caused by the disintegration of Yugoslavia is to the country's people. They are the ones who have been driven from their homes, placed in "detention centers," beaten, humiliated, raped, and brutally murdered in frighteningly high numbers. The actual number of the displaced, humiliated, tortured, and dead is hard to come by, given the fluid and anarchic nature of the Yugoslavian battleground. Most chilling has been the use of the term *ethnic cleansing* to describe the "Balkan killing fields," conjuring up memories of the Nazi Holocaust. In support of such indictments, charges of genocide and "crimes against humanity" have been leveled against many former Yugoslavs, both participants in the crimes and the leaders who may have ordered or permitted them. Thus far, only some of the former have been brought to trial. Whether the latter will ever be tried remains to be seen.

It is in Bosnia-Herzegovina where many agree the suffering has been the greatest, most of it caused by forces outside the province whose actions were supposed to support their ethnic "cousins" living there. And what was the end result of all this suffering?

After years of neglect by the outside world, it is ironic that it took the disintegration of Yugoslavia to bring the country adequate attention. Many books on the subject have been written recently, and some writers have attempted to look at this crisis through the eyes of its victims, such as Roger Cohen in *Hearts Grow Brutal: Sagas of Sarajevo* (Random House, 1998). Laura Silber and Allan Little's *Yugoslavia: Death of a Nation* (Penguin Books, 1997) gives a blow-by-blow account of Yugoslavia's disintegration. It is a concise, chronological account of the last 10 years of the country's existence. Some works have examined the genocide factor; a useful anthology on this subject is Thomas Cushman and Stjepan Mestrovic, eds., *This Time We Knew: Western Responses to Genocide in Bosnia* (New York University Press, 1998). For those who need some historical background on Yugoslavia's past, see John R. Lampe's *Yugoslavia As History: Twice There Was a Country* (Cambridge University Press, 1996).

A final source recommendation is from noted writer Michael Ignatieff, who has written a small volume entitled *The Warrior's Code: Ethnic War and the Modern Conscience* (Henry Holt, 1997). The entire book is thought-provoking and well presented, but of particular value to the study of the disintegration of Yugoslavia is the chapter entitled "The Narcissism of Minor Difference," in which he attempts to take a Freudian view on the subject of human motivation and behavior as it existed in this former country.

ISSUE 21

Will the European Monetary Union Increase the Potential for Transatlantic Conflict?

YES: Martin Feldstein, from "EMU and International Conflict," *Foreign Affairs* (November/December, 1997)

NO: Werner Weidenfeld, from "The Euro and the New Face of the European Union," *The Washington Quarterly* (Winter 1999)

ISSUE SUMMARY

YES: Harvard economics professor Martin Feldstein states that the real rationale for the European Monetary Union is political rather than economic. He predicts that a united Europe, free of threats from the Soviet Union, may seek alliances and pursue policies contrary to the interests of the United States.

NO: Werner Weidenfeld, director of the Munich Center for Applied Policy Research, sees the European Union as a vehicle for restructuring the transatlantic relationship between Europe and the United States. If they develop a partnership between equals, they will be positioned for international crisis management and other global challenges.

Starting in January 1999, 11 European states (Austria, Belgium, Finland, France, Germany, Ireland, Italy, Luxembourg, the Netherlands, Portugal, and Spain) began using a common European currency called the euro in electronic transactions. By 2002 the euro will also replace coin and paper currencies in these nations. What impact will this European Monetary Union (EMU) have on world politics? A united Europe, with a population of 300 million and an economy equal in size to that of the United States, will become another superpower, capable of safeguarding Europe's interests politically and militarily in a worldwide balance of power. The most intriguing question is whether an economically and politically united Europe will find its own interests diverging from or converging with those of the United States.

The European Union had a modest beginning as the European Coal and Steel Community in 1952. The so-called Common Market countries of Belgium, France, Italy, Luxembourg, the Netherlands, and West Germany signed the Treaty of Rome in 1958, forming the European Economic Community, and new members have gradually been added (Austria, Britain, Denmark, Finland, Greece, Ireland, Portugal, Spain, and Sweden), bringing the present total to 15 member nations. In 1992 a Treaty of European Union was signed at Maastricht in the Netherlands, with the goal of creating a more comprehensive economic and political union through (1) a common European citizenship, (2) a single European currency (the euro), and (3) a central European bank.

Displaced persons from the prison and concentration camps of World War II (guestworkers) who helped rebuild postwar Europe as well as the subjects of former colonies arriving in Europe as citizens have changed population mixes during the past 50 years. Since 1968 workers have been free to seek the best opportunities available within the Common Market; and a 12-year-old scholarship program (Socrates-Erasmus) has permitted European university students to study in other countries within the Union for up to a year tuition-free. Faces of European political leaders are widely seen on the news and even in television ad campaigns throughout Europe. Over the past 20 years, a number of European business schools have started offering American-style MBA programs and teaching an American approach to business. What will this economic and cultural amalgamation mean as Europe begins to see itself as a single political entity?

Is it possible to imagine a Europe in which moving from one country to another or living in one country and working in another would be as routine as living in New Jersey and working in New York? Will a common currency and increasingly common economic and political interests forge a European supernation that does not need the military power of the United States to resolve its internal conflicts and does not want either American culture or American pressure to marginalize rogue nations such as Libya, Iran, and Iraq? Will the world order since the breakup of the Soviet Union be one of increased transatlantic tension or enhanced transatlantic cooperation?

Martin Feldstein predicts that a European federal state will assume military responsibility for its own security and that this is likely to lead to increased conflicts over foreign policy and international trade issues. Positioned as a counterweight to the United States in world affairs, a united Europe can no longer be counted on to automatically ally with the United States in its relations with third world or nonaligned countries. Moreover, a legacy of history and resurgent national pride might lead Europeans to pursue courses of action contrary to the interests of the United States.

Werner Weidenfeld is more optimistic. With Europe and the United States as the only reliable guarantors of stability in the world today, the need for a restructured transatlantic partnership between equals is greater than ever. Faced with similar challenges regarding reform of social security and education as well as common issues of environmental management, crime, and migration, Europe and the United States must find a way to share solutions and assume joint responsibility on the world stage.

Martin Feldstein

 **YES**

EMU and International Conflict

Monnet Was Mistaken

To most Americans, European economic and monetary union seems like an obscure financial undertaking of no relevance to the United States. That perception is far from correct. If EMU [European Monetary Union] does come into existence, as now seems increasingly likely, it will change the political character of Europe in ways that could lead to conflicts in Europe and confrontations with the United States.

The immediate effects of EMU would be to replace the individual national currencies of the participating countries in 2002 with a single currency, the euro, and to shift responsibility for monetary policy from the national central banks to a new European Central Bank (ECB). But the more fundamental long-term effect of adopting a single currency would be the creation of a political union, a European federal state with responsibility for a Europe-wide foreign and security policy as well as for what are now domestic economic and social policies. While the individual governments and key political figures differ in their reasons for wanting a political union, there is no doubt that the real rationale for EMU is political and not economic. Indeed, the adverse economic effects of a single currency on unemployment and inflation would outweigh any gains from facilitating trade and capital flows among the EMU members.

The 1992 Maastricht Treaty that created the EMU calls explicitly for the evolution to a future political union. But even without that specific treaty language, the shift to a single currency would be a dramatic and irreversible step toward that goal. There is no sizable country anywhere in the world that does not have its own currency. A national currency is both a symbol of sovereignty and the key to the pursuit of an independent monetary and budget policy. The tentative decision of the 15 European Union (EU) member states (with the exceptions of Denmark and the United Kingdom), embodied in the Maastricht Treaty, to abandon their national currencies for the euro is therefore a decision of fundamental political significance.

For many Europeans, reaching back to Jean Monnet [French economist and proponent of European unity] and his contemporaries immediately after World War II, a political union of European nations is conceived of as a way of reducing the risk of another intra-European war among the individual nation-states. But the attempt to manage a monetary union and the subsequent development of a political union are more likely to have the opposite effect. Instead of increasing intra-European harmony and global peace, the shift to EMU and the political integration that would follow it would be more likely to lead to increased conflicts within Europe and between Europe and the United States.

What are the reasons for such conflicts? In the beginning there would be important disagreements among the EMU member countries about the goals and methods of monetary policy. These would be exacerbated whenever the business cycle raised unemployment in a particular country or group of countries. These economic disagreements could contribute to a more general distrust among the European nations. As the political union developed, new conflicts would reflect incompatible expectations about the sharing of power and substantive disagreements over domestic and international policies. Since not all European nations would be part of the monetary and political union, there would be conflicts between the members and nonmembers within Europe, including the states of Eastern Europe and the former Soviet Union.

Conflicts would also develop between the European political union and non-European nations, including the United States, over issues of foreign policy and international trade. While disagreements among the European countries might weaken any European consensus on foreign affairs, the dominant countries of the EU would be able to determine the foreign and military policies for the European community as a whole. A political union of the scale and affluence of Europe and the ability to project military power would be a formidable force in global politics.

Although 50 years of European peace since the end of World War II may augur well for the future, it must be remembered that there were also more than 50 years of peace between the Congress of Vienna and the Franco-Prussian War. Moreover, contrary to the hopes and assumptions of Monnet and other advocates of European integration, the devastating American Civil War shows that a formal political union is no guarantee against an intra-European war. Although it is impossible to know for certain whether these conflicts would lead to war, it is too real a possibility to ignore in weighing the potential effects of EMU and the European political integration that would follow.

The Politics and Economics of Monetary Policy

The most direct link between EMU and intra-European conflicts would be disagreement about the goals and methods of monetary policy. The Maastricht Treaty established the ECB and transfers all responsibility for monetary policy after the start of EMU from individual national central banks to the ECB. The ECB alone would control the supply of euros and set the short-term euro interest rate.

Maastricht makes price stability the primary objective of European monetary policy, paralleling the charter of Germany's Bundesbank. The treaty also provides that the ECB would be independent of all political control by the member states and by European-level political institutions. (Although the treaty states that the ECB will report to the European Parliament, this was intended to follow the Bundesbank tradition of an information report rather than any political oversight.) These conditions are very much what Germany wants for the ECB and for monetary policy. Because of its historical experience, the German public is hypersensitive on inflation and fears any monetary arrangement that does not give primacy to price stability and insulate monetary policy from political influence.

But German opinion differs sharply from the opinions about monetary policy in France and other European countries. The notion of a politically independent central bank is contrary to European traditions. Until recently, when Maastricht required all prospective EMU countries to give their central banks independence, most of the central banks of Europe reported to their ministries of finance, and the finance ministers were at least partially responsible for setting interest rates.

The French have been particularly vocal in calling for political control over monetary policy. In a televised speech just before the 1992 French referendum on the Maastricht Treaty, then-President François Mitterrand assured the French public that, contrary to the explicit language of the treaty, European monetary policy would not be under the direction of European central bankers but would be subject to political oversight that, by implication, would be less concerned with inflation and more concerned with unemployment. Mitterrand's statement was a political forecast; France recognizes that the institutions of the EMU would evolve, and continually presses for some form of political body to exert control over the ECB. It has already made considerable progress toward that end.

The December 1996 meeting of the EU Council of Ministers in Dublin emphasized that growth as well as price stability would be an explicit goal of future EMU monetary policy. It also established a new ministerial-level "stability council" described as a "complement" or a "counterweight" to the ECB. Although this body falls short of one that could exercise political control over the ECB, it marked a first French success in establishing that monetary policy should be subject to some counterweight and that growth (that is, short-run macroeconomic expansion) as well as price stability should be a goal of EMU policy. At the European summit in Amsterdam in June 1997, the newly elected French government of Lionel Jospin made further progress. The summit added an employment chapter to the Maastricht Treaty, emphasizing that employment is a parallel goal to price stability. More important, statements by politicians at the Amsterdam summit appear to have redefined the role of the political authorities in making exchange rate policy and, therefore, in managing monetary policy.

More specifically, the Maastricht Treaty divided responsibility for exchange rate policy between the ECB and the EU Economics and Finance Council, which consists of cabinet ministers of member governments, in an ambiguous way. The drafters of that part of the treaty (the German participants in particular) intended to limit ECOFIN's [European Council of Economics and Finance Ministers] role to fundamental aspects of the exchange rate system and to leave to the ECB policies that cause short-run changes in the value of the euro. For example, a decision to fix the exchange rate between the euro and the Japanese yen permanently would be a decision for ECOFIN. In contrast, raising or lowering euro interest rates to increase or decrease the exchange value of the euro would be left to the ECB. Although this distinction was the German view, the French expected that ECOFIN would eventually get to give orders about short-run variations in the desired level of the euro exchange rate. The formal rules remain ambiguous, but the government leaders at the Amsterdam summit appear to have accepted a shift of responsibility for short-run exchange rate policy to ECOFIN. Since discretionary changes in nominal exchange rates can be achieved only by changes in monetary policy, this shift would establish a much more fundamental role for ECOFIN, a political body, in the making of monetary policy.

One further recent development relating to the independence of the ECB is noteworthy. Members of the key monetary policy committee of the European Parliament have called for a role for the parliament in supervising the ECB, including its interest rate policies. They have specifically pointed to congressional oversight of the U.S. Federal Reserve as a possible model for such supervision. Although this arrangement may strike a reasonable balance between independence and accountability, parliamentary oversight would clearly be a major shift from the complete independence called for in the Maastricht Treaty, and consequently an area for contention.

At present, individual European governments (especially in France and Germany) are suppressing their disagreement about the control of monetary policy to minimize the risk of political disapproval of EMU in their respective countries. But if EMU proceeds, the independence of the ECB and the goals of monetary policy will become a source of serious conflict among member countries.

Inflation Versus Unemployment

The issue of who controls monetary policy is closely related to the question of the proper goal of monetary policy. In recent years, because of the Maastricht Treaty's requirements for entering EMU, most countries have resisted the temptation to use monetary policy to reduce unemployment and have followed the Bundesbank in keeping inflation rates below three percent. But once the disciplining example of the Bundesbank is eliminated and monetary policy is made by an ECB in which all member countries vote equally, there is a strong risk that the prevailing sentiment will be for higher inflation. Over the past 12 months, international financial markets have anticipated that outcome by depressing the value of the deutsche mark, the French franc, and the other European currencies that move with them by 25 percent relative to the dollar and the yen.

If the German public sees the inflation rate rise under EMU, it will become increasingly antagonistic toward the EMU arrangement and toward the countries that vote for inflationary monetary policy. Moreover, since an inflationary monetary policy would lower unemployment only temporarily (while leaving the inflation rate permanently higher), the persistence of high unemployment would lead to political pressure for recurring rounds of expansionary monetary policy, causing continuing dissatisfaction among the anti-inflationary countries.

Countries that are more concerned about unemployment than inflation might nevertheless be critical of the ECB for not pursuing an even more aggressive expansionary policy. Although countries have been properly reluctant to attempt such policies in recent years, they can regard their decisions not to do so as decisions they made themselves. But with a single currency, such governments would suffer the frustration of not being able to decide for themselves and of being forced to accept the common monetary policy created by the ECB.

This general conflict about the governance and character of monetary policy would be exacerbated whenever a country experienced a decline in exports or other type of decline in aggregate demand that led to a cyclical increase in unemployment. The shift to a single currency would mean that the fall in demand in a country could not be offset, as it could be with an individual national currency, by an automatic decline in the exchange value of the currency (making its exports more competitive) and a decline in its interest rates (increasing domestic interest-sensitive spending by households and businesses) or by using its own monetary policy to shift interest rates and exchange rates. The ECB would have to make monetary policy with a view to the conditions in all of Europe, not just a particular country or region. The result would be a conflict between the country with rising unemployment and the rest of the EU.

Taxes and Transfers

Without the automatic countercyclical response of financial markets and the ability to use monetary policy to offset a decline in demand, European governments would want to use tax cuts and increases in government outlays to stimulate demand and reverse cyclical increases in unemployment. But the "stability pact" that was adopted under pressure from Germany tells governments that they cannot run fiscal deficits above three percent of GDP [gross domestic product] after the start of EMU. This restriction creates an important source of tension between countries with cyclical unemployment increases and the other members of the monetary union. The decision at the 1997 Amsterdam summit to weaken the application of financial penalties for violating this deficit ceiling would undoubtedly encourage more violations and, therefore, more quarrels about "irresponsible" fiscal policies.

Since national monetary and fiscal policies would be precluded, the most likely outcome of the shift to a single monetary policy would be the growth of substantial transfers from the EU to countries that experience cyclical increases in unemployment. Financing those transfers would require a significant increase in tax revenues collected by the EU.

The debates about how large such transfers should be and how the taxes to finance them should be collected would exacerbate the more general disagreement that will inevitably arise as the union seeks to restrict the level and structure of the taxes that individual countries may levy. The European Commission is already trying to get countries to move toward more coordination of their domestic tax policies on the grounds that existing differences in tax rates and rules create competitive advantages for some countries. The shift to a single currency would increase the pressure for tax harmonization. As general responsibility for economic policy shifts from national capitals to the European Commission, the European tradition of focusing taxing authority at a single level would be likely to lead to a shift of the exclusive taxing power from the national to the European level. The EU will therefore be disregarding national preferences about redistribution, the size of government, and the structure of taxes. While the pressures for such coordination might be overwhelming once a single currency has been adopted, the loss of national control over taxes and transfers would be another serious source of irritation within the EU.

Long-Term Unemployment

As the decisions shift away from national governments, it will become harder to reach agreement on policy changes to deal with the high unemployment due to excessive regulation and social welfare payments. The shift of policy decisions from national governments to the European level would eliminate the ability to learn from the experiences of individual countries that try different policies and to benefit from the competitive pressures to adopt national policies that succeed. Moreover, the changes in labor market rules and social benefits that have been proposed by certain national governments are now being opposed not only by labor unions within the individual countries but also by other European governments that fear the resulting gains in competitiveness. Thus we hear of opposition to "social dumping" when an inefficient enterprise is closed and witness the imposition of a Europe-wide limit on the number of hours that employees can work. A politically more unified Europe would make it easier to enforce policies that prevent changes in national labor laws or national transfer payments that would reduce structural unemployment and increase national competitiveness.

If EU legislation succeeds in preventing member countries from competing with each other, they will collectively become less able to compete with the rest of the world. The result would undoubtedly be pressure for increased EU trade barriers, justified by reference to differences in social policy between Europe and other countries. European imposition of such protectionist policies would undermine the entire global trading system and create serious conflicts with the United States and other trading partners.

Incompatible Expectations

As the monetary union evolves into a more general political union, conflicts would arise from incompatible expectations about the sharing of power. France sees EMU and the resulting political union as a way of becoming a comanager of Europe and an equal of Germany, which has nearly 50 percent more people. In the economic sphere, the current domination of European monetary policy by the Bundesbank would be replaced by that of the ECB, in which France and

Germany would sit and vote as equals. As the French contemplate the eventual membership of the economic and political union, they may also hope that their natural Mediterranean allies, Italy and Spain, will give France a decisive influence on European policies. And the skillful international French civil servants might come to dominate the administration of the European government.

Germany's expectations and aspirations are more difficult to interpret. Some German leaders no doubt believe, as Chancellor Helmut Kohl frequently says, that joining a political union improves the prospects for peace by "containing a potentially dangerous Germany within Europe." Other Germans are no doubt less self-sacrificing and simply disagree with the French assessment of the consequences of greater economic and political integration. They see Germany as the natural leader within the EU because of its economic weight, military capability, and central location in an EU that will soon include Poland, the Czech Republic, and Hungary. As Kohl has said, not without ambiguity, "Germany is our fatherland, but Europe is our future."

What is clear is that a French aspiration for equality and a German expectation of hegemony are not consistent. Both visions drive their countrymen to support the pursuit of EMU, and both would lead to disagreements and conflicts when they could not be fulfilled.

The aspirations of the smaller countries to have a seat at the table may be frustrated. As the EU expands from 15 current members to include at least 6 more countries of Eastern Europe, the role that smaller countries will be allowed to play will become more and more limited. Current EU voting rules will give way to weighted voting arrangements in which the larger countries have a predominant share of the votes. This change will frustrate countries that recognize that they have sacrificed the ability to control their own domestic policies and their own foreign relations without having received in exchange an effective say in Europe's policies.

This loss of sovereignty would affect not just monetary and tax policies but a wide range of current domestic policies that will gradually come under the jurisdiction of the European Commission or European Parliament. Rule-making by the European Commission reached a crescendo in 1994 with edicts about such things as the quality of beer and the permissible shape of imported bananas. A fear that complaints about bureaucratic meddling could jeopardize approval of the Maastricht Treaty in national referendums led to a reduction in rule-making by the Brussels bureaucracy and a rhetorical emphasis on Maastricht's principle of "subsidiarity," which asserts that activities will be assigned to whatever level of government is most appropriate—European, national, or local. There is, however, little reason to believe that this vague principle will do much to restrain the substitution of Brussels rules or Strasbourg legislation for what are now domestic policies. Even the Tenth Amendment to the U.S. Constitution, which reserves to the states (or to the people) any powers not delegated to the national government, has not prevented the shift of power to the national government over an enormous range of local issues, such as speed limits on local roads and the age at which individuals may consume alcohol.

A European Military and Foreign Policy

The collapse of the Soviet Union has changed the basis for European foreign policy and military collaboration. Although the United States and the countries of Western Europe have had an extremely close alliance since the end of World War II and continue to coordinate military efforts within the NATO structure, many Europeans in positions of responsibility see their economic interests and foreign policy goals differing from those of the United States with respect to many parts of the world, including Eastern Europe, the Middle East, Africa, and even Latin America. The French and German governments also want to develop an independent military capability that can operate without U.S. participation or consent.

Although the European nations could now more readily pursue an independent foreign policy and military strategy, they are clearly hampered in doing so effectively by the decentralized political structure of Europe. Chancellor Konrad Adenauer summarized the situation in stark terms for French Foreign Minister Christian Pineau on the day in 1956 when England and France gave in to American pressure to abandon their attack on the Suez Canal: "France and England will never be powers comparable to the United States and the Soviet Union. Nor Germany, either. There remains to them only one way of playing a decisive role in the world; that is to unite to make Europe. England is not ripe for it but the affair of Suez will help to prepare her spirits for it. We have no time to waste: Europe will be your revenge." That was a year before the Treaty of Rome launched the Common Market.

The creation of a political union based on the EMU with explicit authority to develop a common foreign and defense policy would accelerate the development of an independent European military structure capable of projecting force outside Western Europe. Steps in that direction are already occurring in anticipation of the stronger political union that will follow the start of EMU. In March 1997, on the 40th anniversary of the Treaty of Rome, France and Germany announced their desire to see a merger of the EU with the existing European military alliance, the Western European Union, so as to strengthen the military coordination of European nations outside the NATO framework. An explicit agreement was reached with the United States that will allow the European members of NATO to use European NATO forces and equipment under European control without U.S. participation.

The attempt to forge a common military and foreign policy for Europe would be an additional source of conflict among the member nations (as well as with those outside the group). European countries differ in their national ambitions and in their attitudes about projecting force and influencing foreign affairs. An attempt to require countries like Portugal and Ireland to participate in an unwanted war in the Middle East or Eastern Europe could create powerful conflicts among the European nations.

The Risk of War

There is no doubt that a Europe of nearly 300 million people with an economy approximately equal in size to that of the United States could create a formidable military force. Whether that would be good or bad in the long run for world peace cannot be foretold with any certainty. A politically unified Europe with an independent military and foreign policy would accelerate the reduction of the U.S. military presence in Europe, weaken the role of NATO, and, to that extent, make Europe more vulnerable to attack. The weakening of America's current global hegemony would undoubtedly complicate international military relationships more generally.

Although Russia is now focusing on industrial restructuring, it remains a major nuclear power. Relations between Russia and Western Europe are important but unpredictable. Might a stronger Russia at some time in the future try to regain control over the currently independent Ukraine? Would a stronger, unified EU seek to discourage such action by force? Could that lead to war between Russia and the EU? How would a strong and unified Europe relate to other nations in the vicinity, including those of North Africa and the Middle East, and the Muslim states of the former Soviet Union, which are important or potential sources of energy for Western Europe?

War within Europe itself would be abhorrent but not impossible. The conflicts over economic policies and interference with national sovereignty could reinforce long-standing animosities based on history, nationality, and religion. Germany's assertion that it needs to be contained in a larger European political entity is itself a warning. Would such a structure contain Germany, or tempt it to exercise hegemonic leadership?

A critical feature of the EU in general and EMU in particular is that there is no legitimate way for a member to withdraw. This is a marriage made in heaven that must last forever. But if countries discover that the shift to a single currency is hurting their economies and that the new political arrangements also are not to their liking, some of them will want to leave. The majority may not look kindly on secession, either out of economic self-interest or a more general concern about the stability of the entire union. The American experience with the secession of the South may contain some lessons about the danger of a treaty or constitution that has no exits.

Implications for the United States

If, as seems most likely, EMU does occur and does lead to a political union with an independent military and foreign policy, the United States must rethink its own foreign policy with respect to Europe. First, the United States would have an opportunity to play a new, useful role within Europe, helping to balance national pressures and prevent the inevitable conflicts from developing into more serious confrontations. The United States should therefore emphasize that it wants its relations with the individual nations of Europe to remain as strong as they are today and should not allow Brussels to intervene between Washington and the national capitals of Europe.

Second, the United States must be aware that an economically and politically unified Europe would seek a different relationship with the United States. French officials in particular have been outspoken in emphasizing that a primary reason for a European monetary and political union is as a counterweight to the influence of the United States, both within European and in international affairs more generally. For the French, American influence is an old issue that frustrated de Gaulle and recurs in attacks on American "cultural imperialism" and U.S. attempts to influence Europe's policies toward countries like Libya, Iraq, and Iran. Such issues would become more widespread in a powerful, independent Europe.

Finally, the United States must recognize that it would no longer be able to count on Europe as an ally in all its relations with third countries. It was safe to assume such support when conflict with the Soviet Union dominated international relations and Europe's interest in containing the Soviet Union coincided with America's. But the global configuration of relations is now more complex. And the Europeans, guided by a combination of economic self-interest, historical traditions, and national pride, may seek alliances and pursue policies that are contrary to the interests of the United States. Although this divergence may tend to happen in any case because of the apparent end of the Soviet threat, the creation of a monetary union that led to a strong political union would accelerate it. If EMU occurs and leads to such a political union in Europe, the world will be a very different and not necessarily safer place.

 **NO**

The Euro and the New Face of the European Union

Future generations of historians will consider the introduction of the euro an historic turning point. The boldest integration project of the European Union (EU) to date, it will change the map of Europe as fundamentally as the end of World War II and the demise of the communist bloc. But not until some time has passed will the curious fabric of the debate over the introduction of the single European currency become truly transparent. Pronouncements both for and against the euro, doubts and fears, speculation and insinuations obscure rather than illuminate a complicated issue. The filibustering over the stability criteria was always strangely superficial and has hardly created confidence. Anyone noticing this quickly realizes that the euro enterprise has not been based on truthfulness.

Among euro supporters, for example, even those with doubts about the timetable of the Maastricht Treaty, had to publicly profess their commitment to it if they were not to risk panicking the financial markets. Even those who did not believe that the stability criteria could be strictly observed had to laud them if budgetary discipline was not to erode. Even those who invested a great deal of effort into considering how to restructure budgets and reinterpret expenditure items had to strongly condemn any form of "creative accounting" to meet the stability criteria. Even those who knew that the stability criteria were relatively arbitrary and say very little about the future stability of the currency had to revere them as European icons, because the central players would otherwise have suffered a loss in credibility.

Euro opponents engaged in the same tactics. Even those who were aware of the German mark's integration into international structures and its dependency on global economic and monetary trends had to hail it as a paragon of stability in favorable contrast to the euro. Even those who doubted the mark's long-term stability had to hide their doubts to make their attack on the idea of the euro more effective.

The debate on the euro was therefore marked by rationality rather than truthfulness. Every comment on the euro was not simply a statement of fact, but a form of speculation about the new reality. Merely hinting that the euro would eventually be introduced "in accordance with provisions in the Maastricht Treaty," for example, was regarded as a step away from the stability criteria, because the treaty left considerable leeway for their interpretation. Indeed, the sage intention of the signatories of the Maastricht Treaty was to develop a culture of monetary stability rather than to follow preestablished criteria to the letter by use of creative budget statistics. Any financial expert worth his or her salt would have known these elementary facts but had to be careful of the chain reaction that might be set off by reference to "the introduction of the euro as provided for in the treaty." Thus the perceived move away from the stability criteria gave rise to doubts about the euro's credibility before it had even got off the ground.

Every remark about the euro therefore had an effect on several levels—it was not merely a comment on the issue itself but also provided a focus for speculative conjectures and helped create a new reality. Rarely has the phenomenon that sociologists call the "reciprocity of perspectives"—what does the other think I am thinking that the other thinks I think—been as tangible as in this case. Any remark had to take into account the possible chain of escalating reactions. That is why the euro debate has seemed so sterile and ritualized: Every new term, every new nuance on the part of decisionmakers could have uncontrollable consequences. The creators of the euro therefore found themselves maneuvering on very difficult territory between multiple reflections of facts and ambiguous descriptions of reality.

The Euro as the Key to a New European Solidarity

But even the ritualized debate cannot explain the seriousness, breadth, and depth of Europeans' concern about the introduction of the euro. Suddenly, a new kind of interest in Europe has developed. After the age of visionary ideas and pancontinental dreams, after the era of those of little faith, after the celebrations marking the end of continental division, greater personal involvement in the European reality can now be observed. The times in which Europe sparked off solemn rhetoric are long gone—as are the years when European developments served primarily as a reason for bureaucracy bashing and egoism over national contributions. More essential matters are now at stake. What is the secret of the euro that is so much on the minds of Europeans?

Evidently Europeans sense that the introduction of the euro concerns much more than the financial details—the question of identity is of greater urgency now than it has ever been. At all times Europeans have had various sources of identity, both positive and negative: the great cultural conflicts, empires, and dynasties; religious and philosophical hegemonies; and finally, major power struggles, such as the East-West conflict, that divided the continent. With the end of this conflict the last important tool for interpreting the political and cultural map of Europe has disappeared. Hitherto Europe was held together by the need for the political classes to forge links between their societies and by external threats; these ties are growing weaker now that the threat is gone. There are noticeable symptoms of renationalization, and national interests allow for only minimal steps forward on the European project, as the 1997 Amsterdam Treaty makes abundantly clear.

Since then we have found ourselves in a kind of a limbo without a clearly defined mission. How should we organize our lives together? What does a left or right standpoint mean? Why should we integrate nation-states into a European framework if there is no longer a serious threat? Without future-oriented options the old modes of perception will return. Old thinking about the balance of power is experiencing a renaissance; the major European powers are again deciding matters among themselves. Old dividing lines such as those between Habsburgs and Ottomans, between Catholicism and Orthodoxy, have reemerged. Nationalist and ethnic tensions are erupting into violent conflicts involving minorities. All of this is gnawing at and wearing out a Europe that finally has an opportunity to grow together in freedom.

This does not, however, mean that a return to earlier disasters is unavoidable, if we succeed in giving Europe a plausible form and a tangible identity. Identities develop from various sources: from experiences of being a stranger, from threats to one's very existence, and from positive experiences of solidarity. At a time when serious threats no longer provide a basic rationale for a united Europe, we are left with a peaceful link: the new currency. This currency is both a symbolic tie and a day-to-day, concrete link that in the future can make the interdependence of Europeans tangible. The vacuum that emerged with the end of the menacing East-West conflict will be filled by the magnetic field of the euro. The struggles surrounding the euro will become the core of Europe's common cause; the currency will be the key to our identity. Many people will define Europe as the area in which the single currency is in circulation, and conditions in this area will become an integral part of citizens' assessment of their own situation. Crises in distant EU regions will be felt more directly and urgently; events in all parts of the common currency area will influence the stability of the area and its currency as a whole. Buffers provided by information filters at the national level will disappear—Europe will move closer together, to both the approval and disapproval of its citizens.

From the outset European integration has always been about more than merely maximizing the benefits for its member states. The EU combines economic prosperity and political stability with structures aimed at reconciling interests in a productive manner. Linking these elements also adds a further dimension to integration: integration means sharing a common destiny. From joint control of coal and steel—industries formerly essential to the war effort —to the Common Market, the development of cooperation in foreign policy, and the creation of a single currency, Europeans are increasingly uniting their economic and political needs, interests, objectives, and thus their future.

The concept of European solidarity, which today is embedded in many facets of the EU's policies and institutions, forms part of the basic idea of a shared destiny. It is to be found in the EU's political sphere—above all in the structural funds, the cohesion fund, the agricultural sector, and a host of back-up policies governing everything from vocational training to the promotion of small languages. It is to be found in the financing of the community on the basis of the economic performance of its members. And it is to be found in the institutional balance between the community and state and the balance between large, medium-size, and small member states in the EU's institutions.

This concept of solidarity-based Europe will be faced with difficult tasks in the years ahead. Increased competition in the global economy has restricted the scope for distribution in Europe, too. The social security network of the classic welfare state is stretched to the breaking point, and the old solidarity models are already being called into question at the national level. Countries are keener than ever before to ensure that they are the net beneficiaries of European integration. Nevertheless, the expansion of the prosperous Western European community cannot be postponed: the accession of the reforming states of Central and Eastern Europe is an historic mandate that the EU cannot reject. In all areas, from a common agricultural policy to the distribution of power in the EU institutions, this mandate will sorely test European solidarity. What can the single currency contribute to the future viability and enhancement of European solidarity?

New Currency—and a New Urgency to Modernize

... Monetary union will generate an accompanying need for legitimization on the part of the other time-honored union institutions: the European Parliament, the European Commission, and, above all, the European Council. Their democratic legitimization rests, at best, on shaky ground—this is true even of the Parliament, which is directly elected but invariably with a low voter turnout. They therefore must justify their powerful intervention in the affairs of citizens by their efficiency and the tangible benefits they produce for the common good. Questions about the efficiency of European institutions in economic, employment, or social policy will become louder as the public grows accustomed to regarding economic issues and the single monetary policy from a European perspective. The fact that the European treaties and the consensus of the member states have granted only limited powers in these areas has little influence on public expectations—a fact vividly illustrated by the community's impotence in the Yugoslav conflict.

If the EU wants to avoid losing its legitimacy in the eyes of its citizens, then, it will need more effective powers in the field of economic policy, powers beyond its current authority to monitor the budgets of member states. Leaving sovereignty over economic issues in the hands of the nation-states may be reassuring for citizens as long as the quantum leap toward the single currency has not yet been visibly completed. Once it has taken place, however, and the inefficiencies of competing national economic policies are evident, the public will quickly become frustrated with the again seeming inactivity of the EU—all the more so if the EU wants to tackle the task of leading the European community to success after the enlargement eastward.

The euro should be viewed as a great historic project—by both supporters and opponents. Those who regard this project as a mundane enterprise, who merely juggle figures or even distort them, have failed to recognize the true consequences of the decision. Opponents of the euro must understand that the failure of the single currency will not bring back the supposed idyll of the nation-state. Supporters must make it clear that the introduction of the single currency will bring about a radical transformation in Europe: The euro will create a genuinely European community without external threats, and it will force large-scale financial transfers Europe-wide, thus triggering off newly intense conflicts. They should be fully aware of this now rather than discovering it later with alarm when the euro has come in through the back door. Opponents must openly admit what the consequences of the failure of this historic project could be—namely, that Europeans could turn their backs on further integration and revert to fighting among themselves without a binding consensus or any clear rules. Europe has no comparable alternative should this project fail.

This is the key point. The old and new Europes are vying for ascendancy —but this has not been openly discussed. Europe must begin to discuss these opposing concepts out in the open.

Europe's Response to Globalization

The euro will alter Europe's image not only insofar as it is the motor of internal modernization. The EU must also redefine its role in world politics once it has completed the transformation to monetary union. It will have new opportunities as well as new responsibilities when the euro assumes its position beside the dollar in the global financial system.

The economic performance of the enlarged EU will exceed that of the United States. Already today the EU produces 31 percent of worldwide output and handles more than 20 percent of world trade. Europe's global role will be enhanced by the euro as a world-power factor. Alongside the dollar the European currency will become a major world reserve currency, a trading currency, and an international investment currency—the European response to globalization. The current small-scale national currency areas seem like impotent dwarfs in the face of the immense flows of capital that circulate daily in the world. The vast euro area will force Europe to think globally: the continent will become a key region in the world currency market. A new bipolar world currency system dominated by Europe and the United States will replace the old hegemony of the dollar.

One result will be that the euro will exert enormous pressure on Europe to live up to its new role as a world power. Whether Europeans can summon the required will and solidarity remains to be seen. Global thinking will have to be redefined in the wake of the eastward enlargement of the EU. Three factors mitigate against the EU's development of a global orientation:

- The conflicts on distribution inherent in the enlargement policy will direct attention to internal issues, European policy will be dominated by EU internal policy.
- Differences in interests and efficiency will increase. The new members will only partly share old members' experiences of taking action and dealing with conflicts (for example, in Bosnia); the new members have shown little willingness to relinquish sovereignty. After integration they could endeavor to compensate for their loss of power

over economic and domestic policies by insisting on preserving their sovereignty in foreign policy.

- The ambition to act on the global stage will be shared by only a minority of states.

Several competing factors foster global orientation: The expanded power base of a larger EU; its vicinity to the former superpower Russia in the East; its growing economic interests in the Asian arena; the global economic and political impact of the euro; and, last but not least, the readiness of some new members such as Poland to take action and make a considerable commitment to peacekeeping operations over the last few years. A European global role would have three immediate objectives: to widen the area of political stability around the union, to maintain the EU's key role in maintaining order in the region, and to safeguard Europe's interests at a global level. In addition, a European world policy should develop strategic partnerships with other major international players. In the surrounding area such a policy would involve major states such as Russia, Ukraine, and Turkey; in the Middle East it would mean safeguarding the security and integrity of Israel and supporting Palestinian independence; and in Asia it would give strategic priority to Japan and China.

If the euro transforms Europe into a world power, then the transatlantic relationship will also have to be restructured. The challenge lies not only in overcoming the deficiencies in Europe's global policies but also in redefining the transatlantic partnership as a whole. The security link between Europe and the United States will continue to exist, but without the presence and mentality of a defense organization always on standby to repulse a large-scale attack. The political community across the Atlantic will continue to exist but it will lack the challenge of competition with an antagonistic value system and a special sensitivity to the development of transatlantic relations. Europe and the United States still share values and a Western identity but lack a definition of what they have in common and of their specific contribution to the new issues in international politics. On the other hand, no political ideology challenges the supremacy of pluralist democracy worldwide, and the existing fundamentalist movements in the Islamic world, the ethno-ideologies and movements with charismatic leaders, are not of an antagonistic nature, nor do they possess the power to threaten the West militarily. The West's stabilizing policy now has an opportunity to actively shape conditions instead of merely reacting by repelling threats.

Western states are more involved in international cooperation and supranational integration than other players in world politics. However, within European societies this policy is not consolidating and being accepted at the same rate. Politicians are reacting to the globalization of challenges with regional integration, the phases of which have to be justified on a national level. Problems, decisions, and legitimization must be made to coincide.

A new order of international politics, new norms aimed at ensuring peace and at reconciling interests, and a new conflict-prevention strategy cannot emerge from ad hoc coalitions. Such coalitions can be thwarted at any time by calculated aggression if they are not supported and credibly protected by visibly cohesive communities of nations. Europe and the United States are the only reliable guarantors of stability in the world today; their readiness and ability to impose order will be needed in the future, especially in regions and spheres that lie beyond the current structures of transatlantic cooperation. Many necessary solutions are feasible only if the burden is shared, a high degree of political coordination is developed, and an adequately dense communications network is built.

The advent of the euro will considerably increase the need for consultation and coordination in the transatlantic relationship. With the introduction of the single currency Europe will, at least in economic terms, move into the newly structured league of world powers. At the same time, the transatlantic partners will become more interdependent. Awareness of internal economic developments will increase on both sides. This will have at least two consequences for the transatlantic relationship.

- First, monetary policy. The United States will observe Europe closely to see whether the euro is being deliberately manipulated for the benefit of European interests and to the detriment of its own. If Europe and the United States use the external value of their currencies to increase their own competitiveness, the transatlantic community will face new conflicts. This is a potential source of mistrust that, if not tackled, could slowly poison relations.
- Second, there is the question of global responsibility. The United States will ask itself to what extent a monetary power such as Europe must also assume responsibility for global security, and the issue of burdensharing will become more pressing with the introduction of the euro. A gap will open between the demands on Europe and the staying power of European foreign policy. Further tensions can then be expected if Europe's effectiveness and power increase internationally but its preferences and actions are not in harmony with Washington's interests.

The start of monetary union will mean more joint responsibility for the transatlantic partners, including responsibility for developing a reliable set of rules for the world economy. While a tried and tested system of rules and arbitration for world trade exists in the form of the World Trade Organization, there is no comparable framework for the global financial markets. The fact that capital circulates globally within a matter of minutes presents not only opportunities but also risks, as has been vividly illustrated by the Asian crisis. The United States realized even more readily than the EU that the impact of such financial slumps can no longer be limited regionally. They have a detrimental effect on the global economy and quickly reach dimensions no longer controlled with the traditional international instruments for fighting balance of payments crises, in particular those available to the International Monetary Fund. The United States and Europe, the two largest global players in the world's financial markets, are therefore faced with an important task: they must join forces and work to create a global framework for recognizing and combating crises such as the one in Asia even before they develop. Furthermore, the growing funding difficulties of the International Monetary Fund show that new methods that can be financed over the long term are needed to control the debt crises that have already emerged.

Restructuring Transatlantic Relations

In the light of this array of tasks, it would seem that the increasing institutionalization of transatlantic communications is unavoidable as the need for consultations and coordination between Europe and America grows. Several proposals for this have already been put forward.

A transatlantic process of mutual learning.   Now that the common threat presented by the Soviet Union has evaporated, societal relations between Europe and America offer a special chance to place Atlantic integration on a long-term, stable basis. The internal challenges facing European and American societies have determined their common agenda during the last few years. It is obvious that there is a need for common action in cross-border problems affecting both regions in equal measure—for example, crime and migration. However, Europe and the United States are also faced with common challenges in the reform of social security systems and education. Frequently, the approach of each side to these problems is very different, which means that conditions for establishing a transatlantic process of mutual learning are ideal. Only through a systematic exchange of experiences can the potential for innovation on both sides of the Atlantic be put to maximum use. A transatlantic process of mutual learning could do this by providing a structural framework for the currently rather random contacts at the social level.

European-American political cooperation.   At the level of political cooperation our task is to create a framework for relations that can act as a catalyst rather than an obstacle to greater integration. Such new political structures can no longer be based on the rationale of defense against a common enemy. International crisis management and global challenges are the issues in which the partners have a prime interest in cooperating. The approach to rogue states such as Iraq, Iran, or Libya, international environmental policy, and, after the introduction of the euro, monetary policy all clearly illustrate the need for close coordination. The establishment of a process of European-American political cooperation along the lines of European political cooperation could give our joint endeavors a future-oriented structure. Even a minimal institutional framework—for example, a secretariat—could guarantee continuity and effectiveness. It could provide a modern forum for mastering the issues that the international community now takes to the transatlantic partners and for which an appropriate organizational form is lacking.

A new transatlantic market.   Nowhere is the degree of transatlantic interdependence and the potential for future cooperation more apparent than in economic relations. Economically Europe and the United States are the most closely integrated regions in the world. New regulatory mechanisms are required if the full potential of transatlantic economic relations is to be realized in the context of growth and crises in East and Southeast Asia and trade and monetary competition. The development of a new transatlantic market is overdue. Although most bilateral trade is no longer subject to restrictions, there are important exceptions and nontariff trade barriers. A joint liberalization initiative on the part of Americans and Europeans could help in the development of the World Trade Organization, in the creation of a common strategy for dealing with the consequences of opening up markets, in the preparation of international standards, and in the coordination of the economic policies of Europe and the United States. Such an initiative would be a stepping stone to a transatlantic internal market in which goods, capital, services, and persons circulate freely. It could also defuse conflicts in trade and monetary policy.

Until we have a new transatlantic market, a process of European-American political cooperation, and a transatlantic process of mutual learning, European-American relations will not acquire the substance and vitality they urgently need to master the challenges of the twenty-first century. In the light of the risks involved, the completion of European integration could be delayed or even hindered if the transatlantic partnership is not intensified. The United States needs Europe as a world power that, despite its cultural, historical, and political diversity, is in a position to safeguard its interests and pool its resources. However, Europe's importance to the United States cannot lie in seconding U.S. global policies. The distribution of burdens and responsibility, a partnership between equals, is the prerequisite of a future alliance.

The dynamic process of economic and monetary union offers us an opportunity to revitalize transatlantic structures of cooperation. If we boldly seize this chance, the introduction of the euro could stimulate a new era in relations between Europe and the United States. Entry into the third stage of EMU marks the last important milestone of European integration in this century. Which road the EU chooses to take from here will determine its destiny, both internally and externally, for decades to come. If the EU wants to continue its success story, the states of Europe must keep to the path of cooperation—both with one another and with their partners across the Atlantic.

POSTSCRIPT

Will the European Monetary Union Increase the Potential for Transatlantic Conflict?

Agood place to begin unraveling the complicated process that has led to the European Monetary Union is Michael Maclay's *The European Union* (Sutton Publishing, 1998). This 100-page book begins with a timeline of important dates and a map of member states, includes dates of their joining the Union, and ends with a glossary of terms and abbreviations and an annotated bibliography. In between are six clearly written chapters that follow the development of the European Union from 1945 to the present.

Weidenfeld, author of the NO selection, is coeditor with Wolfgang Wessels of *Europe from A to Z* (European Commission, 1997), a mini-encyclopedia of events translated from the German. For a useful guide to the treaties that have created the present Union, see Alexander Noble's *From Rome to Maastricht: Essential Guide to the European Union* (Warner Books, 1996).

Britain's decision to opt out of the common currency is explained in Michael Charlton's *The Price of Victory* (Parkwest Publications, 1985). Using radio interviews with leading politicians and officials from the postwar years, Charlton examines British ambivalence. Widening the scope, Brian Brivati and Harriet Jones have edited *From Reconstruction to Integration* (Leicester University Press, 1993), a collection of analytical and historical essays.

Analysis of the current situation is best studied through journals. University of Chicago professor Stephen M. Walt explains why Europe and America are drifting apart in "The Ties That Fray," *The National Interest* (Winter 1998/1999). C. Fred Bergsten, director of the Institute for International Economics, sees a looming clash between the euro and the dollar in "America and Europe: Clash of the Titans," *Foreign Affairs* (March/April 1999). And Timothy Garton Ash, fellow of St. Anthony's College, Oxford, argues in "Europe's Endangered Liberal Order," *Foreign Affairs* (March/April 1998), that the appropriate strategic goal of European policy should be consolidating the new model of liberal order achieved in much of Western and Southern Europe rather than an idealistic and perhaps unachievable vision of unity.

ISSUE 22

Should Contemporary Feminism Ally Itself With Individualism?

YES: Françoise Thébaud, from "Explorations of Gender," in Françoise Thébaud, ed., *A History of Women in the West, vol. 5: Toward a Cultural Identity in the Twentieth Century* (The Belknap Press, 1994)

NO: Elizabeth Fox-Genovese, from *Feminism Without Illusions: A Critique of Individualism* (The University of North Carolina Press, 1991)

ISSUE SUMMARY

YES: A lecturer in women's history at the Université Lumière Lyon, Françoise Thébaud states that the pursuit of individualism and the acquisition of full citizenship rights have permitted women to escape from the confines of the family and achieve independence in the modern world.

NO: Elizabeth Fox-Genovese, Emory University professor of history and director of women's studies, argues that individualism, which refuses to place any limits on the tyranny of the individual will, is a dead end for feminists, who must insist that the rights of individuals derive from society and not from their innate nature.

The term *feminism* originated in France during the early nineteenth century, when women and men denounced the failure of the French Revolution to free women from their traditional roles and stereotypes. During this first wave of feminism, gender was already understood to be a constructed rather than a natural category—that is, women's apparent inferiority was blamed on lack of opportunity and outright oppression, not on inherent deficits. At the turn of the twentieth century, ideas about gender equality had spread throughout Europe, and a vocabulary of emancipation for women had made its way into countries adjacent to France under the banner of feminism. Eventually, organized feminist movements developed across Western Europe and spread to South America, Asia, and the Middle East.

Feminism is usually defined as the theory that women should have political, economic, and social rights equal to those of men. This language, however, is a source of controversy for some modern feminists. There are two broad foundations for feminist theory: one based on individualism and emphasizing self-realization through the acquisition of personal legal rights and protections (the Anglo-American tradition), the other emphasizing the complementary relationship between women and men and pointing to women's distinct natures and unique contributions to society (the Western European tradition). The first mode of argument, known as individualist feminism, focuses on natural rights and insists on the basic equality between women and men. The second mode of argument, known as relational feminism, situates women firmly within the family and the community and highlights ways in which women differ from men and can therefore make distinct contributions to society.

Although these traditions have been associated respectively with Americans and Europeans, contemporary feminists on both sides of the Atlantic are debating which approach is more likely to result in better lives for women. The two selections considered in this issue actually reverse traditional positions, with the European writer supporting individualism and the American scholar mistrusting it. Neither author stresses the differences between women and men, and both seek equality for women.

Feminism has its roots in the European Enlightenment, which emphasized rationalism and saw in it the key to understanding the world and improving it. The rhetoric of natural rights, justice, and freedom, first articulated during the American and French Revolutions, is based on individualism. Even the poor and marginalized could make justice claims founded on their natural rights as individuals. The question this issue raises is whether contemporary feminists are better off continuing to press for change using these traditional claims or whether the return to a family- and community-based theory of rights has greater potential for liberation.

Françoise Thébaud, in her survey of European feminism during the twentieth century, finds individualism to be a natural ally of feminism and the basis from which many equality and justice claims have been successfully argued. The same rhetoric that launched political revolutions and challenged slavery has, in Thébaud's judgment, also served women well. Without it, they would have lacked a compelling argument for changing the status quo and bringing themselves into the modern world as full citizens. Elizabeth Fox-Genovese is deeply distrustful of individualism because, in practice, it often results in the unrestrained excesses that lead to exploitation. She asserts that feminists make a crucial error in assuming that the historical oppression of women within the family means that women can only be liberated apart from family and community. For Fox-Genovese, the only freedom worthy of the name (or even historically possible) is both "socially obligated and personally responsible." Without this social and communal grounding, women will be freed from one set of constraints but vulnerable to the even greater threat of unrestrained individualism.

Françoise Thébaud  **YES**

Explorations of Gender

Observing women whose lives have spanned this century, one is struck by their tragedy and greatness. Buffeted by war, revolution, and dictatorship, they also witnessed a major upheaval in relations between the sexes. Have we now reached an "end" of women's history, the culmination of years of steady, ineluctable progress toward emancipation? Not at all. If the geopolitical twentieth century that was born in the maelstrom of the First World War and the Russian Revolution is now definitively over, the notion of an "end of history" following the triumph of liberalism after the collapse of the Eastern bloc did not survive the assault of events in Europe and elsewhere. What might an end of history mean for women, anyway? A twilight of male domination and the dawn of a new society? A new era in which sexual division would all but disappear? Or a world in which men and women could maintain their distinctive identities yet enjoy equal rights and opportunities? Contemporary feminists are still arguing over these issues. Although their goal is to establish women as subjects of history, constant tension arises between the need to construct a feminine identity and the further need to demolish the category "woman" altogether. Separatism no longer seems a viable option; some form of coexistence with men on terms yet to be defined appears to be increasingly desirable. What does a woman want? What do women want? Readers of this [selection]—gendered actors in a history that is still unfolding—will find not answers to these questions (for it is not the place of scholars to give such answers) but rather food for thought.

Readers may be surprised that [this selection] contains no chronological narrative of women's liberation. That women's lives no longer resemble the lives of their mothers is a fact so obvious that it hardly needs to be stated. There is no denying all that women have achieved: the right to vote, a dramatic reduction of risk in childbearing, contraception, new opportunities in the workplace. But just what is an "achievement"? A social construct—just the kind of icon that stands in urgent need of deconstruction. What did the women's movement achieve? Who opposed and who supported specific changes? And what were the issues and consequences—symbolic as well as real? These are questions that need to be asked. And remember, too, that no achievement is definitive: the strength of the present-day anti-abortion movement and the spread of AIDS stand as reminders of this important truth. Women's history grew out of the

From Françoise Thébaud, "Explorations of Gender," in Françoise Thébaud, ed., *A History of Women in the West, vol. 5: Toward a Cultural Identity in the Twentieth Century* (Belknap Press, 1994). Copyright © 1994 by The President and Fellows of Harvard College. Reprinted by permission of The Belknap Press of Harvard University Press. Notes omitted.

women's movement, but those militant beginnings must not mislead us into thinking that the story we have to tell is essentially one of progress. It is actually a good deal more complex.

The image of the twentieth century as a time of progress for women, in stark contrast to the Victorian era, is based on a series of clichés. One forgets the massacres and world wars and remembers only the flapper of the Roaring Twenties, the liberated woman set free by "the pill," or the superwoman of the 1980s, that creature of feminism and consumer society, capable of juggling career, children, and lovers without missing a beat. In fact, the stereotypes of the flapper and the liberated female were more often invoked to denounce the collapse of the sex barrier and the double standard than to applaud the victories of the women's movement. And the superwoman image, which Betty Friedan criticized in *The Second Stage* (1981), is at the very least ambiguous: few women can live up to such an ideal, and the tensions arising out of the contradictory demands it imposes are swept under the rug. Indeed, Rose-Marie Lagrave has argued that the social function of the superwoman ideal is to conceal growing inequality between the sexes.

Like the critique of the movement's achievements, these stereotypes are nevertheless interesting for the questions they raise about what events are significant for the history of women, and how they fit or jar the masculine chronology of standard history. It must also be emphasized that the history of women is unthinkable without a history of representations, that is, a decoding of images and discourses shaped by the male imagination and masculine social norms. The twentieth century—the century of psychology and images—has demonstrated, among other things, that Western culture has developed few positive ways of representing women. Although Freud complicated the whole business of sex and sexual identity, philosophy and social science went right on reflecting the sexism of society at large: women were seen as filling a special role in service of men and the family. Decked out in the trappings of modernity, approved by science, publicized in film, newspapers, magazines, and advertising, the model of the housewife and mother was triumphantly democratized. Governments—and not just dictatorial ones—made population growth a matter of official concern. Child-rearing became a medical specialty. Psychologists issued normative pronouncements about mother-child relations. All these factors created new pressures for women to stay at home. Sexuality was now regarded as a legitimate source of pleasure and the sexuality of women was recognized, but marriage was held to be the proper place for its expression, and women worried about failing to live up to new ideals of beauty symbolized by impossibly slender film stars, models, and beauty queens. Meanwhile, a new image of the modern woman took hold: she was a professional homemaker, at once queen of the household and shrewd consumer. Advertisements sold images along with merchandise. The new woman might seem flashier than the old, but at bottom not much had changed, as advertising simultaneously turned women themselves into sexual objects, desirable commodities. Pervasive, intrusive pornographic images were promulgated in magazines and video tapes. Meanwhile, however, growing numbers of women began to speak out and seize control of their own visual identities. Emphasizing the political importance of representation, they tried to break down old stereotypes and to suggest a variety of ways in which women might fulfill themselves. At no time in history has the image of women changed as rapidly as it has in recent years. We will attempt to measure, date, and comprehend that change.

This [selection] is not simply a narrative of women's liberation or a history of representations.... [W]e conceive our task in ... ambitious terms, informed by twenty years of work in women's history. This is not the place to explore the far-reaching debates on what the subject of that history ought to be. Let me simply give a quick overview of the common approach to our subject that transcends differences among individual contributors and leads, we hope, to a new interpretation of the twentieth century.

History was for a long time the history of men, presented as typical of the human race. More recently, numerous works (thousands have been written about the twentieth century alone) have shown that women, too, have a history; indeed, that they have been full participants in the history of humankind. But to study women in isolation from men, as if in a vacuum, is a theoretical dead-end and a possible source of historical misunderstandings. What we propose, rather, is a gendered approach. Relations between men and women are an important dimension of history. These relations are not a natural fact but a social construct, and they are constantly being redefined. This redefinition is at once an effect and a cause of the social dynamic. Hence relations between the sexes are a useful category of analysis, on a par with other categories more familiar to historians, such as relations between classes, races, nations, and generations. Like any new way of looking at the past, this change of perspective yields new knowledge. It may even lead to rewriting history in such a way as to take account of a wider range of human experience than earlier approaches allowed for. For example, a gendered approach to Nazi racism leads to the conclusion that Hitler's policy toward women was not pronatalist and based on a cult of motherhood but rather antinatalist and based on a cult of virility and mass extermination of inferior people, in which women were the preferred and easiest targets. Wherever relevant, contributors have tried to relate gender and class, gender and nationality, gender and age, gender and religion: gender turns out to be a differentiating factor within groups too often treated as homogeneous.

Readers should therefore ask themselves not about women's achievements but about the evolution of the "gender system," by which I mean the set of gendered social roles together with the system of ideas and representations that culturally define masculine and feminine and thus shape sexual identity. Changes in the condition of women must be seen in relation to changes in the condition of men. If, for example, on one end of the scale the feminization of certain trades perpetuates a disparity between men and women, on the other end modern methods of birth control do not merely allow women to avoid unwanted pregnancies but to take control by themselves of the reproductive cycle. The development of new contraceptives must therefore be seen in relation to simultaneous changes in the law, changes that ended women's subservience to men in the domestic sphere. Readers should also ask themselves what it was that gave meaning and value to the respective activities of men and women. What are the functions and consequences of the gender symbolism promoted in one way or another by governments, individuals, and groups? Such symbolism is most commonly used to establish hierarchies and represent relations of power and tends to impede change rather than accelerate it. Although war in general and World War I in particular have often been described as liberating for women, armed conflict (whose psychological and social aftereffects generally persist long after the cessation of hostilities) is in fact profoundly conservative because it encourages, even within the feminist frame, thinking of gender issues in terms of dichotomy. Or consider politics: when all men received the right to vote, the term "universal suffrage" was misleadingly applied to a situation that still excluded women. More than that, politics is still a male preserve: only a handful of elected officials are women even where women voters are in the majority. Women tend to be relegated to certain designated areas of government, preserving the age-old division between the male world of politics and the female world of social concerns. Female officials are often seen as intruders by their male colleagues and as marginal even by one another. Yet women in government deserve credit for what they have accomplished. For instance, the Russian revolutionary Alexandra Kollontai, the Spanish anarchist Federica Montseny, and the French politician Simone Veil, all three ministers of health, worked to legalize abortion in their respective countries.

This history of women therefore has a subtext: that men, too, are gendered individuals. Readers should be aware of how the story told here modifies and contributes to our picture of history in general. Obviously it has something to add to social history. But it also leads to revision of the conventional periodization of cultural history and, more surprisingly perhaps, of political history, which remains one of the most influential ways of looking at the past. Our approach leads, for example, to a new interpretation of paternalistic wartime policies for the protection of women. It leads to reflection on the nature of fascism and Nazism, which, among other things, intended to quell gender conflict in the interest of more efficient exploitation. It reveals distinctive features of the Vichy and the "Catholic nationalist" Franco regimes. It leads to a reconsideration of the origins and workings of the welfare state, which took early feminist demands for public recognition of the social utility of motherhood and reinterpreted them in a paternalistic sense. It also helps us to understand the uniqueness of Quebec, whose history is interpreted here in feminist-nationalist terms. And it sheds new light on the reasons for the failure of Soviet-style communism, which imposed a voluntaristic, economistic model even in the sphere of gender relations. Alexandra Kollontai, who did not believe in the self-generated "withering away" of the bourgeois family and dreamed of a new working-class morality, was criticized for "George-Sandism." But since she preached her doctrine in a poor agricultural nation under siege, where civil society in general and women in particular were subject to constant interference from the central authorities, she was most likely ahead of her time.

The history of feminism and women's movements is of course an integral part of Western political history. Much work remains to be done in this area. The period 1920–1960, long regarded as a fallow patch between two "waves" of feminism, is just now being explored for the first time, yet understanding it is essential to understanding the century as a whole. How did the movement for women's rights, steeped as it was in nineteenth-century rationalism and liberalism, cope with the challenges of mass politics, communism, nationalism, and Freudianism? What was the relation between this earlier movement and the women's liberation movement that grew out of the New Left, the anticolonial movement, and the sexual liberation of the 1960s? In attempting to understand all this, it is best to be wary of pejorative labels such as "bourgeois feminism" and to question whether there really was a hard-and-fast distinction between egalitarian feminism and the "feminism of difference." The question of gender can lead to a renewal of political thought, because it forces one to recognize that equality requires the acceptance and inclusion of difference. Women's history can also enrich general history by examining itself and history in general as a cognitive process. By analyzing the gendered categories that structure our culturally determined notions of sexual difference, we learn to look at sources in new ways and to revise our methodologies appropriately. Although women's history is sometimes criticized for being a "discourse on discourse," such an approach is a necessity, not a fad or a device for avoiding hard work.

Other fields of knowledge have also been influenced, along with history, by contemporary feminist thought: philosophy, law, sociology, political science, and literary criticism have also played a role in the preparation of this [work]. A one-sided approach can no longer be mistaken for universal. Feminist critique questions the ideological assumptions that may lie hidden in even the most learned studies or the most comprehensive statistics. This is particularly true of labor studies and statistics. It is invariably assumed that women are responsible for child care and housework, as if work outside the home were a natural right for men and an anomaly for women. Contemporary political economists, like their nineteenth-century predecessors, try to justify the sexual division of labor by arguing that it is grounded in nature.

❧◉☙

But what about the twentieth century? It has been, of course, the bloodiest century in the history of humankind, a century of total war, whose victims, civilian as well as military, number in the tens of million, and a century of genocide, which has shown women no special mercy and indeed exterminated Jewish and Gypsy women purposefully to prevent the birth of a new generation. Women have had to suffer, too, for their political choices. Repression, harsh for all its victims, was sometimes aimed particularly at women, whose heads were shaved, whose bodies were violated. And totalitarian regimes frequently resorted to the terrifying idea of family guilt. In memory of all the victims of totalitarian regimes, let me mention here the names of two extraordinary women who became friends while interned at Ravensbrück: the Czech journalist Milena Jesenká, Kafka's friend and translator and an ardent enemy of oppression in all its forms, and the German communist Margarete Buber-Neumann, who not only told the world about the camps of Stalin and Hitler but also kept alive the memory of her friend, who died in 1944.

Yet this century has also been one in which women at last—and long after men—entered the modern world. Modern technology brought women as well as men the boon of better health and longer lifespans. Infant mortality has been dramatically reduced. Women have obtained the finest educations available. The growth of cities and the proliferation of consumer goods have changed the way we live. Less of life is given over to toil and pain, and on balance this must be counted as progress, even granting the failures and inequalities of consumer society. For women this has meant changes in the nature of housework and child-rearing. Since less time needs to be devoted to these activities, more is left over for participation in social life. But for women modern life means something else as well. Long trapped in the web of that natural community, the family, women failed to reap the benefits of the dynamic expansion of individual rights initiated by the French Revolution. Hence for them modernity has meant the achievement of individuality and full citizenship status and the conquest of economic, legal, and symbolic independence vis-à-vis fathers and husbands. A once powerful vise-like grip has thus been loosened, as any number of monographic studies have shown.

When did this revolution in gender relations begin, and how are we to explain it? It appears to have been the cause of a crisis of masculine identity, signs of which are numerous though difficult to grasp. The end of the Second World War, which ushered in a lasting period of democracy and economic growth in the West, is not the crucial date in this history (although it did bring women in France the right to vote). For the second time in this century, the end of a world war signaled a return of women to the private sphere. Since the children of the next generation were declared to be the key to national reconstruction, women were told that it was their civic duty to return home, just as it had been their duty a few years earlier to join the workforce. Indeed, in several countries the wartime generation turned out to be the least active professionally and the most prolific in terms of childbearing. This generation of women had little taste for politics in the usual sense: the 1950s saw the apotheosis of the housewife, whose ideological conditioning by the media—to say nothing of psychoanalysis—Betty Friedan denounced in *The Feminine Mystique* (1963), history's best-selling book about women, a fundamental text on feminism along with Virginia Woolf's *A Room of One's Own* (1929) and Simone de Beauvoir's *The Second Sex* (1949). In the case of France, the Vichy regime broke politically with the republican past but continued the family policies of previous governments: from the 1920s to the 1960s French women were expected to serve as mothers while their husbands worked for a living. Few democrats questioned the totalitarian potential in such policies, just as few advocates of the separation of church and state questioned the influence of religion on this government's meddling in the nation's bedrooms.

More space might have been devoted to advocates of birth control such as Margaret Sanger in the United States or Madeleine Pelletier and Jeanne and Eugène Humbert in France. And we might have said more about the proponents of family planning and single-woman motherhood, many of whom were also active in the international movement for sexual reform of the 1920s and 1930s. We might have tried to gauge the place of religion in the lives of women: the issue is important but vast. Gender difference is one of the cornerstones of the Catholic Church, which seems to have been more conservative than most on the issue: witness its refusal to countenance contraception in any form, to permit priests to marry, and to ordain women. This intransigence gave rise to generations of Catholic militants, reformers who helped to bring about change in the Church and in the condition of women. Even so, there has been an unmistakable decline in religious practice in France.

But it was not until the middle of the 1960s, more than fifty years after the first hopes of the Belle Epoque, that gender relations began to change in most Western countries. It is not easy to say what factors were most responsible. Peace, prosperity, and scientific discoveries certainly helped, and I must at least mention the name of Gregory Pinkus, the inventor of the contraceptive pill. But the student unrest of 1968 was also important: the student movement is a field that remains open for future scholars to explore from a gender-conscious point of view. And, above all, there is the women's movement, which fervently denounced "patriarchy" and all its icons. Change has been greatest, it seems, in the private sphere: the idea that husband and wife are equal partners in marriage, and that the man is not "head of the household," is one that influenced first American and British law and, later, continental legal systems as well. The law now admits a variety of family types and female roles. More liberal attitudes toward contraception and abortion have enabled women to reclaim possession of their bodies and sexuality. Women can now determine when they wish to have children, and governments have been forced to abandon the most coercive family policies. When feminists insisted on a woman's right to determine when and if she would have children, they were in fact giving voice to a wish to privatize a reproductive function that, for better or for worse, had throughout the century been seen as a public duty. In a more fundamental sense, they were seeking to redefine the relation of women to childbearing. Few contemporary feminists have followed their predecessors on this controversial issue. Liberation, it seems, is more easily attained through self-fulfillment in the workplace and private pressure on husbands to share in parental responsibilities, than through seeking to gain state recognition and assistance for motherhood as a social function.

Change is best measured, however, not by opposing public and private but by noting how the two spheres interact. There is no single cause, no primary factor, in producing social change. Rather, we must look at the interaction of causes and effects. As more and more women entered the labor market and participated in cultural and political activities, private law also evolved. The diminished burden of housework itself encouraged women to participate more fully in the public sphere. Although social legislation and tax codes continued to embody the marital inequalities of the past, discouraging many women from working, the advent of the welfare sate afforded women greater independence. It not only offered protection but also created new jobs and lightened the burden of family care. Women sought schooling and work in record numbers, and although the educational system favored boys and many jobs were reserved for men, the effects of these changes were nevertheless considerable. Autocracy in marriage disappeared, along with the traditional housewife. And women increasingly tended to vote for the left, contradicting their reputation for political conservatism. In France, in fact, younger women of the present generation are more likely than their male counterparts to vote for left-wing candidates. Perhaps, too, there has been a democratization of family life, although that is more difficult to measure. The culture of love may have evolved, and men and women may have come to see each other in a new light. In all these changes, especially the conquest of political and symbolic autonomy (the ability to say "we women"), the feminism—or, rather, feminisms—of the 1960s and 1970s played a key role by establishing womanhood as a fundamental political category and by organizing themselves as a group capable of deconstructing and reconstructing its meaning. In using the past tense here, I mean to imply only that the pace of change has been rapid, not that the process is complete. I do not claim that women have won a victory, nor am I suggesting that there has been a return to more "normal" gender relations following the alleged "excesses" of the feminist era. The apparent decline of feminism (which has led some commentators to speak of a "postfeminist era") is as much a transformation as a loss: history continues, constantly shaking things up in ways that are unpredictable yet wholly implicit in the past.

Elizabeth Fox-Genovese

 **NO**

Feminism Without Illusions

Introduction

Feminism enjoys a poor to middling press these days, among many women as well as men. One of my undergraduates at Emory University captured this unease in a paper she wrote for a Women's Studies course. When she had begun the course, feminism to her "meant the denial of femininity and womanhood. It suggested lesbianism. It led to 'bra burnings,' men-hating, and an almost irritating aggressiveness." She has not been alone in her associations. To many women, feminism even betokens the destruction of family values and the defiance of divine and natural order. In the time-honored tradition of blaming the victims of injustice and those who protested against it for the consequences of injustice itself, some women and too many men find it easy to blame feminism for some of the most disturbing aspects of modern life: divorce, latch-key children, teenage alcoholism, domestic violence, the sexual abuse of children. From that indictment only a few short steps are required to arrive at an indictment of feminism for the collapse of academic standards and the decline of Western civilization. Many young women simply consider feminism outmoded—a relic of former times that no longer constructively affects their lives.

Feminists reply that only our vigilance protects and improves women's hard-won and still-precarious place in work and politics. Yet even those who call themselves feminists frequently disagree about the meaning and implications of feminism. For some, feminism articulates women's rights as individuals and as women, women's needs as parents, and women's opportunities as workers. Others insist upon the radical implications of women's experience for society as a whole, arguing that women speak "in a different voice" than men; have different "ways of knowing" than men; would, if given power, order the world more humanely than men. Some hold that justice can obliterate, or radically minimize, the differences between women and men. Others hold that those differences are fundamental and that our ideals of justice should be rewritten to take account of women's experience. Still others dismiss the very idea of difference as the product of invidious and hierarchical dichotomies that should be replaced by an appreciation of diversity.

The differences over the meaning of feminism reflect the larger confusion of our times. Less the cause of the unsettling changes in our world than their symptom, feminism embodies a variety of dissatisfactions with things-as-they-are and a variety of visions about how they could be improved. Above all, feminism represents different attempts to come to terms with women's changing position in American society, particularly the economy. Since the beginning of the twentieth century, women have steadily increased their participation in the labor force, most dramatically, married women with children, and most ominously, single mothers. American women are working outside the home in many cases by preference but in many cases because they have to—because they and frequently their families depend upon their doing so.

This century has also witnessed a steady increase in divorce, and analysts now project a divorce rate of 50 percent for all new marriages. And with the increase in the number of divorces has come the collapse of alimony and the erosion of child support. The most dramatic change in the lives of young women—although many have no wish to recognize it—is that marriage is not a viable career. Under favorable circumstances it remains a rewarding personal relation, but it no longer serves as a surrogate career. Today, no law, no father, no brother can force a man to support a woman, and the law is not successfully forcing him to support even their children properly.

Although the substance of feminism constitutes a response to harsh social and economic realities, much of its rhetoric and that of its opposition has focused on problems of sexuality and identity, rather than on problems of livelihood. Sexual freedom, sexual preference, abortion, figure prominently in public consciousness of the implications of feminism. Men and women understandably worry about radical transformations of our sense of what it means to be a man or woman. Accordingly, many men and some women intuitively respond to any talk of women's rights as if it portended the direst consequences. At the extreme, there are women who apparently oppose abortion out of a deep sense that sexual freedom for any woman exacerbates the pervasive threats to the security of married women; others more vaguely plead that if women would only be women, everything would return to normal. If women would only assume their ordained roles as the bearers and rearers of children and helpmeets to men, men would have to support them. There is no point in arguing with those who desperately cling to such illusions, for economic realities foreclose the return to that "normality" for most women.

The student who wrote of her initial distaste for feminism devoted the remainder of her paper to a discussion of what each of the books in her Women's Studies course had taught her about women's situations and possibilities. "Today," she concluded, "as I turn in my last paper, I consider myself a feminist. Maybe not an *active* feminist, but a definite proponent of feminism." The course, she avowed, had offered her a rare educational experience. "Although I am always academically challenged by my classes at Emory, rarely have I ever been personally challenged. Not only has my definition and attitude towards feminism matured and changed from what I have learned and studied about women in this course, but my own personal self has been affected; I have been challenged to think and reflect on my past, present, and future life as a woman.

I have not just learned about women this semester, but I have also grown as a woman."

I shall not pretend that I was not pleased by her conversion, although I do not regard the teaching of Women's Studies as an excuse for proselytizing and do not require that my students espouse any particular ideology. Not all students who study the subject seriously become feminists, but few, if any, male or female, find it possible to dismiss feminism as intellectually unworthy of respect. And that, rather than an alleged and perhaps sometimes actual abuse of the classroom, may be the reason so many anti-feminists condemn Women's Studies courses out of hand and confuse, or pretend to confuse, Women's Studies with feminist ideological indoctrination.

The question remains: What do we want for our daughters, our students, the young women for whom we feel responsible? As the director of a Women's Studies program, I live with that question. As one who sees herself as temperamentally and culturally conservative, I harbor no consuming desire to turn the world upside down and by no means subscribe to all that is advanced in the name of feminism. But I am convinced that (1) the changes of which feminism is a symptom will not be reversed; (2) feminism is having a broad and profound impact on our society and our ways of thinking; (3) young women must be trained to support themselves, preferably by work that draws upon their talents and enhances their self-respect.

ᴇⓞ

The impact of feminism on American cultural and intellectual life has been extraordinary, notwithstanding abiding resistance to it. But we have now reached a point at which what we make of feminism, and, above all, how we convince the majority of American women of its relevance to their lives, is everything. Many feminists have, since the late sixties, fought, with a measure of success, for a transformation of human consciousness and culture as well as social practice. A many-pronged attack on what is frequently called "the patriarchy" has resulted in sharp challenges to religious, educational, and cultural traditions and, yet more portentously, to our inherited ways of thinking, including our conception of justice.

The gains made by women in the academic world alone would have been unimaginable a scant fifteen years ago. Today, Women's Studies programs abound on college and university campuses. Conferences and sessions at professional meetings in such disciplines as English, Modern Languages, History, Religious Studies, Sociology, and even Political Science and Philosophy feature programs in which sessions on some aspect of women, gender, or feminist theory are steadily displacing traditional topics. Each of these disciplines now boasts at least one professional journal devoted exclusively to women, gender, and feminist theory, and interdisciplinary journals are addressing these issues as well. Most "mainstream" journals are devoting increasing amounts of space to Women's Studies and explicitly feminist scholarship.

The heated debate over the canon, which is now being waged in books and on campuses and is being covered by the national press, directly testifies to the impact of feminist concerns. To be sure, these debates also reflect a concern with exposing students to the writings and experiences of working-class, nonwhite, and non-Western male authors, but feminist scholarship is now spearheading the challenge and is offering the most sustained theoretical program. For if feminist scholarship argues that women have been excluded from the canon, it does not rest its case with rectifying that exclusion. It insists that women have been—and remain—fundamentally alienated from a culture that casts them as objects and with which they cannot identify.

Feminism has, in this respect, emerged as the cutting edge of postmodernist (a fancy word for contemporary) anxieties about the status of knowledge, certainty, subjectivity, the self. For feminism is increasingly challenging received notions about the fundamental structures of human knowledge. In particular, some influential feminists are rejecting all of our assumptions about knowledge on the grounds that they represent an oppressive and outmoded "binary thinking"—a way of thinking that rests on the delineation of difference as the foundation of all knowledge and therefore promotes hierarchy, notably the hierarchy that places men over women. Rather than thinking with reference to dichotomies—white/black, male/female, self/object—we must, according to this version of feminist theory, learn to think with reference to pluralism and indeterminacy.

These complex debates cannot be ascribed solely to the influence of feminism, but feminism is emerging as a magnetic pole within them, for it potentially cuts across all boundaries of class, race, and nationality to confront the fundamental identity of the thinking subject. Although not all feminists focus on these debates or even accept their implications, the combined impact of various feminist projects has begun to erode our confidence in the culture we have inherited. Religious Studies provides an especially striking example. Christian feminist ethicists and theologians are formulating a searching critique of the Christian tradition. Insisting above all on women's right to become ministers, they are also wrestling with women's relation to a faith that represents God and the Savior as male. How, they ask, can women be expected to find a positive image of themselves in a faith that historically has excluded them from leadership and relegated them to secondary status?

If many applaud feminism for its contribution to the erosion of confidence in our inherited culture, others have been retreating into a rigid adherence to the time-honored status quo. Neither position will serve. Our inherited culture and values contain much that many feminists, including myself, cherish, as have innumerable women before us. Yet, we cannot hope to prepare young women to deal confidently with the world if we offer them a vision of themselves as dependent upon men for everything from material support to physical protection to a sense of their identities.

Another undergraduate student in Women's Studies wrote her final paper about the education that she had received at Emory. A joint major in English and Spanish, on the eve of graduation, she treated the paper as her private commencement address and assessed the place of women in the liberal education she had received. Never, she insisted, had she viewed that education as restrictive, but her Women's Studies class did open her eyes to "the limitations of my male dominated education." For until she read an article on the canon for that class she "would not have viewed the canon as a political statement."

From this perspective, she reviewed the syllabi for all of the courses in English and Spanish that she had taken during her undergraduate career to determine how many women authors had been included. (It is a measure of the value she attached to those courses that she had kept the syllabi.) Out of a total of 128 authors, her ten English courses had included sixteen women. She believed it predictable that her courses in Chaucer and Shakespeare included only male authors—she did not comment on whether any feminist critics had been read—and also noted that the numbers of women authors had recently begun to increase in all courses. She was not complaining about, certainly not berating, her professors, whom she obviously very much admired, but she did hope that things might be different in the future. "If inspiration can take the form of a charge or revelation," she wrote in conclusion, "then my evaluations and this paper will have succeeded in creating a personal impact for me. While the insights that I have gained and the advances of any one woman do not make up for the countless and often unjustified exclusion of women and minorities from the canon today, it lessens the probability that such a reality will mark the canon of the future."

The feminisms of the eighties are raising a myriad of questions unlikely to yield easy answers, but one thing remains clear. We have a responsibility to train young women, as seriously as we try to train young men, to take their place in a complex world. I do not believe that we could—or should—entirely rewrite our history and our culture, even if we must significantly revise them, and even if we must acknowledge that they have been dominated by men. Now, perhaps more than ever, we need history, not myth. But, as many of our talented women students have the wit to agree, to accept the past does not bind us to a perpetuation of its wrongs. Our world is changing and so must our visions. Young women are entitled to an education that empowers them to make choices and accept responsibility—to realize their talents and to recognize their accountability.

❧❦❧

This [work] has grown from my preoccupations as a woman, a teacher, and an intellectual who came of age just as the modern women's movement was coming into being. Betty Friedan's *The Feminine Mystique* appeared the year that I graduated from college. Like many others, I did not immediately grasp its full implications for myself or for our society. My adult personal and professional lives have unfolded in tandem with contemporary feminism, to which I have been committed despite firm opposition to some of its tendencies that I regard as irrational, irresponsible, and dangerous. As a proud feminist, I confess to intense irritation over once more having to defend the term and explain its premises to a new generation. So much for irritation. Feminists cannot avoid the challenge, and I intend this [selection] as a contribution to the defense and explication of feminism or, rather, of a feminism.

The Supreme Court's recent *Webster* decision, which limited women's access to abortion and raised the possibility that *Roe v. Wade* might yet be reversed, is engaging the imagination of young women, who fear the implications for themselves, although that engagement does not guarantee their adherence to a broader feminist program, much less their concern with the problems of women of other classes and races. The fight for women's "right" to choice in the matter of abortion is being misguidedly waged in the name of women's absolute right to their own bodies and, ironically, on the grounds of reproduction as a private matter. It qualifies as ironical since so much feminist energy has been devoted to an insistence that familial relations are not private matters, that "the personal is political," and that women cannot, in justice, be excluded from the public business of society. But the fight over abortion is being waged more in the name of women's sexuality than in the name of their reproductive capacities. That confusion alone indicates the extent to which feminism has absorbed aspects of individualism, which, to be coherent, it must resolutely oppose.

[My work] offers a critique of feminism's complicity in and acceptance of individualism—or rather of its contemporary atomized version that replaces the early and glorious recognition of the claims of the individual against the state with the celebration of egotism and the denial or indefensible reduction of the just claims of the community. Throughout, I am using "individualism" to mean the systematic theory of politics, society, economics, and epistemology that emerged following the Renaissance, that was consolidated in the great English, American, French, and Haitian revolutions of the seventeenth and eighteenth centuries, and that has found its purest logical outcome in the laissez-faire doctrines of neoclassical economics and libertarian political theory. The political triumph of individualism has led to its hegemony as *the* theory of human nature and rights, according to which, rights, including political sovereignty, are grounded in the individual and can only be infringed upon by the state in extraordinary circumstances.

That hegemony has proved so powerful that most of us intuitively associate individualism with the defense of individual freedom, our highest value. Here I am arguing that individualism actually perverts the idea of the socially obligated and personally responsible freedom that constitutes the only freedom worthy of the name or indeed historically possible. Theoretically, individualism does not contain the possibility of establishing necessary limits on the will of the individual, on what Nietzsche called the "will to power." The problem lies at the heart of every modern discussion of democracy since Rousseau: What can be the relation between the will of the individual and the will of the majority? Theorists of individualism have not, in fact, arrived at a better definition of the social good than the individualistic notion that what more people want must be accepted as better. In practice, modern individualistic societies have significantly curtailed individual right in the name of the public good, but they have done so apologetically, defensively, not on the grounds of the prior rights of the collectivity. (To be sure, socialist societies have proclaimed the priority of society in a way that has stifled the just claims of the individual, but that deeply disquieting problem ... is today being recast by events with unpredictable consequences.) Western societies, in any case, have, as some conservative and feminist critics are beginning to argue, failed to develop a notion of individual right as the product of collective life rather than its justification.

The defense of individual freedom has properly prompted the most generous aspects of our national tradition, which includes the abolition of slavery and the growing recognition of women's rights. But we have had difficulty in separating the defense of individual freedom from the basic premise of individualism, namely that rights derive from the individual's innate being. The origins of the confusion lie in the theory of the social contract, dear to seventeenth- and eighteenth-century political theorists according to which individual right derives from nature and, accordingly, precedes any form of social organization. The political institutions built on this theory did not, initially, expose the radicalism of the concept, if only because they did not acknowledge all people as individuals. Excluding propertyless men, slaves, and women from political participation, they perpetuated the illusion that individualism and collective life could coexist. But, as the dispossessed increasingly insisted that collective life depended upon the denial of their individuality, the last bastions began to fall and to expose individualism's growing inability to curtail any exercise of the individual will. No wonder, then, that free marketeers, who today call themselves conservatives as the result of a massive misunderstanding, probably choke when confronted with what they have wrought.

In our own time individualism, fueled by the capitalist market, threatens to swing the balance between the individual and society—the balance between personal freedom and social order—wholly to the side of the individual. In this process feminism has played an ambiguous and sometimes destructive role. The implementation of women's rights has whittled away at the remaining bastions of corporatism and community—notably the family—even as women, released to the dubious mercies of the public sphere, require new forms of protection from the state. The issues defy easy solutions but do suggest that we have reached a period in our history at which we can no longer deceive ourselves that individualism suffices to define our collective purposes as a people and a nation.

৵⊙৵

[My work] does not offer a political program. It explores some ways of imagining the claims of society—the collectivity—as prior to the rights of the individual, some ways of imagining and protecting the rights of the individual as social, not private, rights. I have attempted to identify aspects of our current political difficulties and to relate them to the history of the Western tradition in general and the American in particular. [I] offer thoughts upon the relation between feminism and political life [as well as] feminism and intellectual life, notably the academic canon, which has emerged as the center of a heated debate.

These questions suggest the need for a reformed political practice but fall short of suggesting its content. In general, I believe that our political system does have the flexibility to meet the needs of women with justice but that for it to do so, we must rethink our basic assumptions about the relation between the individual and the collectivity and especially rethink our assumptions about the "freedom" of the market in a society as complex and interdependent as our own. Many of the most pressing feminist issues are, in truth, broadly social issues—for example, it seems extraordinary that we (or our legislators) are unwilling to recognize that in our time the "right to life" of our Declaration of Independence might not include comprehensive national medical insurance. The arguments against such insurance turn primarily upon expense—the rights of property—not upon the principles of democracy or upon our sense of collective decency and self-respect. At issue, in short, is how we interpret our political tradition and identify its most fundamental and admirable aspects.

   ... [T]he claims of feminism require the maximum clarity because feminism will shape our future as people—and whether it does so for good or ill entails a heavy responsibility.

   At a number of points my arguments may seem to constitute opposition to what I in fact support—for example, the necessity for granting women the power to choose to have an abortion under socially determined conditions. I have proceeded on the conviction that honest readers will have no trouble in grasping the essentials of the argument—that one may accept that limited right to choice and yet emphatically deny that women have, or that a man has, an absolute right to the disposition of her or his body. For if we fight for a worthy goal on the basis of unworthy premises that could open the floodgates to undesirable and even vile consequences, we shall go down to a well-deserved defeat or, worse, have to assume responsibility for the destruction of the healthiest, as well as the unhealthiest, elements in civilized life. The greatest problems of our time arise from the need to get our premises as well as our priorities straight.

POSTSCRIPT

Should Contemporary Feminism Ally Itself With Individualism?

In 1792 Mary Wollstonecraft published *Vindication of the Rights of Women* simultaneously in London and New York. She argued in the tradition of individualist feminism for women's inherent rationality and fundamental equality with men; any differences between the genders were due to the unequal treatment and restricted opportunities women encountered from birth. Seventy-seven years later, in 1869, John Stuart Mill wrote *The Subjection of Women* in which he agreed with Wollstonecraft that the characters of both women and men are shaped by the society in which they live. In the tradition of relational feminism, Mill argues that women and men in general excel at different things and these female differences are very much needed by society. Together Wollstonecraft and Mill represent what has been called the first wave of feminism, a largely nineteenth-century phenomenon.

Feminism was reborn in the Western world in the 1960s (some say with the publication of Betty Friedan's *The Feminine Mystique* [Dell Publishing, 1963]), when modern feminists challenged restrictive laws and oppressive traditions both within and outside the family. A key insight of this second wave of feminism was that "the personal is the political." In other words, individual problems have their roots in larger political and social realities and cannot be solved apart from changing those institutions that structure the lives of all people. Second-wave feminists (including Nancy Cott, Joan Kelly, Gerda Lerner, and Joan W. Scott) explored gender as an explanatory principle and as a category of analysis to help them understand how gender assumptions shape the lives of women and men as well as how gender interacts with other categories, such as race and class, to shape human experience and the way we record it as history.

Largely a middle-class movement, twentieth-century feminism purported to speak for all women. Its proponents were shocked when third-wave feminists of the 1980s and 1990s insisted that race, social class, sexual orientation, age, and a host of other variables were as important as gender in shaping women's experiences. The key insight of third-wave feminism is that there is no single, essentialist category of woman, to which all women belong. Instead, there are multiple and varied feminisms, all of which reflect valid aspects of women's experiences. Insight into third-wave feminism may be found in Josephine Donovan's *Feminist Theory: The Intellectual Traditions of American Feminism* (Continuum, 1995) and its varieties are well explored in *Modern Feminisms: Political, Literary, Cultural,* edited by Maggie Humm (Colorado University Press, 1992).

Structuralists and poststructuralists (including Jacques Lacan), deconstructionists (such as Michel Foucault), and object-relations theorists (Nancy

Chodorow and Carol Gilligan) have further complicated the claims and understandings of third-wave feminism. Lacan and Foncault ask, "What role do the deep-meaning structures of language and the subtexts of everything we read and hear play in shaping human identity?" Chodorow asks, "Is there a unique women's culture?" Gilligan asks, "Do women and men have different moral senses? And if they do are they inherent or learned?" In the postmodern world, nothing is as simple as it might appear.

ISSUE 23

Is Western Civilization in a State of Decline?

YES: Samuel P. Huntington, from *The Clash of Civilizations and the Remaking of World Order* (Simon & Schuster, 1996)

NO: Francis Fukuyama, from *The End of History and the Last Man* (Free Press, 1992)

ISSUE SUMMARY

YES: Samuel P. Huntington, a professor of the science of government, maintains that due to internal weaknesses and threats from potential rivals organized along civilizational lines, the West is in danger of losing its status as the world's preeminent power base in the twenty-first century.

NO: Francis Fukuyama, a former deputy director with the U.S. State Department, argues that with the end of the cold war and the absence of alternatives to liberal democracy, the West is in a position to maintain and expand its role as the world's primary power base.

For over 50 years the cold war occupied the attention of most of the world's nations. Beginning in the last years of World War II—when it became obvious that the two major powers to emerge from the war, the United States (and its Western allies) and the Soviet Union, had different plans for the future of the postwar world—the cold war turned into an ideological conflict between two dominant superpowers, each of which attempted to export its influence in search of the upper hand in this power struggle. The possession of nuclear arsenals by both the United States and the Soviet Union raised the stakes to the potential of total war and annihilation. It made for a very uneasy, unsettling half century.

The cold war also produced its own language—Iron Curtain, containment, nuclear proliferation, massive retaliation, flexible response, regional alliances— as well as a long list of interesting personalities, all of whom lent their names to this colorful yet dangerous era. It also threatened to involve all of the world's nations, whether they wished it or not. With world dominance the prize, both sides sought to obtain the most favorable situation in which to push their different agendas. Sometimes the cold war developed into armed conflict, endangering the delicate balance-of-power politics that it had created.

Suddenly, the cold war was over. With the crumbling of the Soviet Empire and the disintegration of the Soviet Union into a number of separate republics, the West was faced with a novel situation: there was no major power to threaten hegemony or well-being. A collective sigh of relief emanated from the West's citizens and leaders.

What does all this mean to today's world? What will conditions and circumstances be like in the post-cold war era? Will the world be in any less danger? Are there any potential enemies who can replace the Soviet Union and create a new cold war, or worse? And, most important, what will be the position of the West in world affairs in the new millennium?

Diplomatic historians and foreign policy experts seem to be divided with regard to the state of the West today and its ability and willingness to shoulder the responsibilities of world leadership. They also differ in their analysis of the twenty-first century's new world order. Who will be the new major players in the world arena, and what effect will they have on the body politic? Will the twenty-first century be a more peaceful one than the twentieth?

In the selection that follows, Samuel P. Huntington argues that in the future, civilizations (with core states) rather than nations will be the twenty-first century's power brokers. He lists nine such civilizations that he predicts may play a role in the future world order: Japanese, Buddhist, Orthodox (Russia), Hindu (India), Sinic (Chinese), Islamic, African, Latin American, and Western. If the West is to compete with its civilizational rivals in the future, says Huntington, it will have to unify and develop the strength and will to maintain its status as the world's leading power base. If it fails to do so, the decline of the West will become a reality.

On the other hand, argues Francis Fukuyama in the second selection, with the defeat of enemies on both the political Left and Right, the West's liberal democracy is in an enviable position to provide the only viable alternative for the nations of the world in their search for a just and profitable life for their citizens. If the West succeeds in spreading its systems throughout the world, Fukuyama asserts, it will be able to extend its power status well into the twenty-first century.

Samuel P. Huntington

The Fading of the West:
Power, Culture, and Indigenization

Western Power: Dominance and Decline

Two pictures exist of the power of the West in relation to other civilizations. The first is of overwhelming, triumphant, almost total Western dominance. The disintegration of the Soviet Union removed the only serious challenger to the West and as a result the world is and will be shaped by the goals, priorities, and interests of the principal Western nations, with perhaps an occasional assist from Japan. As the one remaining superpower, the United States together with Britain and France make the crucial decisions on political and security issues; the United States together with Germany and Japan make the crucial decisions on economic issues. The West is the only civilization which has substantial interests in every other civilization or region and has the ability to affect the politics, economics, and security of every other civilization or region. Societies from other civilizations usually need Western help to achieve their goals and protect their interests. Western nations, as one author summarized it:

- Own and operate the international banking system
- Control all hard currencies
- Are the world's principal customer
- Provide the majority of the world's finished goods
- Dominate international capital markets
- Exert considerable moral leadership within many societies
- Are capable of massive military intervention
- Control the sea lanes
- Conduct most advanced technical research and development
- Control leading edge technical education
- Dominate access to space
- Dominate the aerospace industry
- Dominate international communications
- Dominate the high-tech weapons industry

The second picture of the West is very different. It is of a civilization in decline, its share of world political, economic, and military power going down relative to that of other civilizations. The West's victory in the Cold War has produced not triumph but exhaustion. The West is increasingly concerned with its internal problems and needs, as it confronts slow economic growth, stagnating populations, unemployment, huge government deficits, a declining work ethic, low savings rates, and in many countries including the United States social disintegration, drugs, and crime. Economic power is rapidly shifting to East Asia, and military power and political influence are starting to follow. India is on the verge of economic takeoff and the Islamic world is increasingly hostile toward the West. The willingness of other societies to accept the West's dictates or abide its sermons is rapidly evaporating, and so are the West's self-confidence and will to dominate. The late 1980s witnessed much debate about the declinist thesis concerning the United States. In the mid-1990s, a balanced analysis came to a somewhat similar conclusion:

> [I]n many important respects, its [the United States'] relative power will decline at an accelerating pace. In terms of its raw economic capabilities, the position of the United States in relation to Japan and eventually China is likely to erode still further. In the military realm, the balance of effective capabilities between the United States and a number of growing regional powers (including, perhaps, Iran, India, and China) will shift from the center toward the periphery. Some of America's structural power will flow to other nations; some (and some of its soft power as well) will find its way into the hands of nonstate actors like multinational corporations.

Which of these two contrasting pictures of the place of the West in the world describes reality? The answer, of course, is: they both do. The West is overwhelmingly dominant now and will remain number one in terms of power and influence well into the twenty-first century. Gradual, inexorable, and fundamental changes, however, are also occurring in the balances of power among civilizations, and the power of the West relative to that of other civilizations will continue to decline. As the West's primacy erodes, much of its power will simply evaporate and the rest will be diffused on a regional basis among the several major civilizations and their core states. The most significant increases in power are accruing and will accrue to Asian civilizations, with China gradually emerging as the society most likely to challenge the West for global influence. These shifts in power among civilizations are leading and will lead to the revival and increased cultural assertiveness of non-Western societies and to their increasing rejection of Western culture.

The decline of the West has three major characteristics.

First, it is a slow process. The rise of Western power took four hundred years. Its recession could take as long. In the 1980s the distinguished British scholar Hedley Bull argued that "European or Western dominance of the universal international society may be said to have reached its apogee about the year 1900." Spengler's first volume appeared in 1918 and the "decline of the West" has been a central theme in twentieth-century history. The process itself has stretched out through most of the century. Conceivably, however, it could accelerate. Economic growth and other increases in a country's capabilities often proceed along an S curve: a slow start then rapid acceleration followed by reduced rates of expansion and leveling off. The decline of countries may also occur along a reverse S curve, as it did with the Soviet Union: moderate at first then rapidly accelerating before bottoming out. The decline of the West is still in the slow first phase, but at some point it might speed up dramatically.

Second, decline does not proceed in a straight line. It is highly irregular with pauses, reversals, and reassertions of Western power following manifestations of Western weakness. The open democratic societies of the West have great capacities for renewal. In addition, unlike many civilizations, the West has had two major centers of power. The decline which Bull saw starting about 1900 was essentially the decline of the European component of Western civilization. From 1910 to 1945 Europe was divided against itself and preoccupied with its internal economic, social, and political problems. In the 1940s, however, the American phase of Western domination began, and in 1945 the United States briefly dominated the world to an extent almost comparable to the combined Allied Powers in 1918. Postwar decolonization further reduced European influence but not that of the United States, which substituted a new transnational imperialism for the traditional territorial empire. During the Cold War, however, American military power was matched by that of the Soviets and American economic power declined relative to that of Japan. Yet periodic efforts at military and economic renewal did occur. In 1991, indeed, another distinguished British scholar, Barry Buzan, argued that "The deeper reality is that the centre is now more dominant, and the periphery more subordinate, than at any time since decolonization began." The accuracy of that perception, however, fades as the military victory that gave rise to it also fades into history.

Third, power is the ability of one person or group to change the behavior of another person or group. Behavior may be changed through inducement, coercion, or exhortation, which require the power-wielder to have economic, military, institutional, demographic, political, technological, social, or other resources. The power of a state or group is hence normally estimated by measuring the resources it has at its disposal against those of the other states or groups it is trying to influence. The West's share of most, but not all, of the important power resources peaked early in the twentieth century and then began to decline relative to those of other civilizations.

Territory and Population. In 1490 Western societies controlled most of the European peninsula outside the Balkans or perhaps 1.5 million square miles out of a global land area (apart from Antarctica) of 52.5 million square miles. At the peak of its territorial expansion in 1920, the West directly ruled about 25.5 million square miles or close to half the earth's earth. By 1993 this territorial control had been cut in half to about 12.7 million square miles. The West was back to its original European core plus its spacious settler-populated lands in North America, Australia, and New Zealand. The territory of independent Islamic societies, in contrast, rose from 1.8 million square miles in 1920 to over 11 million square miles in 1993. Similar changes occurred in the control of population. In 1900 Westerners composed roughly 30 percent of the world's population and Western governments ruled almost 45 percent of that population then and 48 percent in 1920. In 1993, except for a few small imperial remnants like Hong Kong, Western governments ruled no one but Westerners. Westerners amounted to slightly over 13 percent of humanity and are due to drop to about 11 percent early in the next century and to 10 percent by 2025. In terms of total population, in 1993 the West ranked fourth behind Sinic, Islamic, and Hindu civilizations.

Quantitatively Westerners thus constitute a steadily decreasing minority of the world's population. Qualitatively the balance between the West and other populations is also changing. Non-Western peoples are becoming healthier, more urban, more literate, better educated. By the early 1990s infant mortality rates in Latin America, Africa, the Middle East, South Asia, East Asia, and Southeast Asia were one-third to one-half what they had been thirty years earlier. Life expectancy in these regions had increased significantly, with gains varying from eleven years in Africa to twenty-three years in East Asia. In the early 1960s in most of the Third World less than one-third of the adult population was literate. In the early 1990s, in very few countries apart from Africa was less than one-half the population literate. About fifty percent of Indians and 75 percent of Chinese could read and write. Literacy rates in developing countries in 1970 averaged 41 percent of those in developed countries; in 1992 they averaged 71 percent. By the early 1990s in every region except Africa virtually the entire age group was enrolled in primary education. Most significantly, in the early 1960s in Asia, Latin America, the Middle East, and Africa less than one-third of the appropriate age group was enrolled in secondary education; by the early 1990s one-half of the age-group was enrolled except in Africa. In 1960 urban residents made up less than one-quarter of the population of the less developed world. Between 1960 and 1992, however, the urban percentage of the population rose from 49 percent to 73 percent in Latin America, 34 percent to 55 percent in Arab countries, 14 percent to 29 percent in Africa, 18 percent to 27 percent in China, and 19 percent to 26 percent in India.

These shifts in literacy, education, and urbanization created socially mobilized populations with enhanced capabilities and higher expectations who could be activated for political purposes in ways in which illiterate peasants could not. Socially mobilized societies are more powerful societies. In 1953, when less than 15 percent of Iranians were literate and less than 17 percent urban, Kermit Roosevelt and a few CIA operatives rather easily suppressed an insurgency and restored the Shah to his throne. In 1979, when 50 percent of Iranians were literate and 47 percent lived in cities, no amount of U.S. military power could have kept the Shah on his throne. A significant gap still separates Chinese, Indians, Arabs, and Africans from Westerners, Japanese, and Russians. Yet the gap is narrowing rapidly. At the same time, a different gap is opening. The average ages of Westerners, Japanese, and Russians are increasingly steadily, and the larger proportion of the population that no longer works imposes a mounting burden on those still productively employed. Other civilizations are burdened by large numbers of children, but children are future workers and soldiers.

Economic Product.   The Western share of the global economics product also may have peaked in the 1920s and has clearly been declining since World War II. In 1750 China accounted for almost one-third, India for almost one-quarter, and the West for less than a fifth of the world's manufacturing output. By 1830 the West had pulled slightly ahead of China. In the following decades, as Paul Bairoch points out, the industrialization of the West led to the deindustrialization of the rest of the world. In 1913 the manufacturing output of non-Western countries was roughly two-thirds what it had been in 1800. Beginning in the mid-nineteenth century the Western share rose dramatically, peaking in 1928 at 84.2 percent of world manufacturing output. Thereafter the West's share declined as its rate of growth remained modest and as less industrialized countries expanded their output rapidly after World War II. By 1980 the West accounted for 57.8 percent of global manufacturing output, roughly the share it had 120 years earlier in the 1860s.

Reliable data on gross economic product are not available for the pre-World War II period. In 1950, however, the West accounted for roughly 64 percent of the gross world product; by the 1980s this proportion had dropped to 49 percent. By 2013, according to one estimate, the West will account for only 30% of the world product. In 1991, according to another estimate, four of the world's seven largest economies belonged to non-Western nations: Japan (in second place), China (third), Russia (sixth), and India (seventh). In 1992 the United States had the largest economy in the world, and the top ten economies included those of five Western countries plus the leading states of five other civilizations: China, Japan, India, Russia, and Brazil. In 2020 plausible projections indicate that the top five economies will be in five different civilizations, and the top ten economies will include only three Western countries. This relative decline of the West is, of course, in large part a function of the rapid rise of East Asia.

Gross figures on economic output partially obscure the West's qualitative advantage. The West and Japan almost totally dominate advanced technology industries. Technologies are being disseminated, however, and if the West wishes to maintain its superiority it will do what it can to minimize that dissemination. Thanks to the interconnected world which the West has created, however, slowing the diffusion of technology to other civilizations is increasingly difficult. It is made all the more so in the absence of a single, overpowering, agreed-upon threat such as existed during the Cold War and gave measures of technology control some modest effectiveness.

It appears probable that for most of history China had the world's largest economy. The diffusion of technology and the economic development of non-Western societies in the second half of the twentieth century are now producing a return to the historical pattern. This will be a slow process, but by the middle of the twenty-first century, if not before, the distribution of economic product and manufacturing output among the leading civilizations is likely to resemble that of 1800. The two-hundred-year Western "blip" on the world economy will be over.

Military Capability. Military power has four dimensions: quantitative—the numbers of men, weapons, equipment, and resources; technological—the effectiveness and sophistication of weapons and equipment; organizational—the coherence, discipline, training, and morale of the troops and the effectiveness of command and control relationships; and societal—the ability and willingness of the society to apply military force effectively. In the 1920s the West was far ahead of everyone else in all these dimensions. In the years since, the military power of the West has declined relative to that of other civilizations, a decline reflected in the shifting balance in military personnel, one measure, although clearly not the most important one, of military capability. Modernization and economic development generate the resources and desire for states to develop their military capabilities, and few states fail to do so. In the 1930s Japan and the Soviet Union created very powerful military forces, as they demonstrated in World War II. During the Cold War the Soviet Union had one of the world's two most powerful military forces. Currently the West monopolizes the ability to deploy substantial conventional military forces anywhere in the world. Whether it will continue to maintain that capability is uncertain. It seems reasonably certain, however, that no non-Western state or group of states will create a comparable capability during the coming decades.

Overall, the years after the Cold War have been dominated by five major trends in the evolution of global military capabilities.

First, the armed forces of the Soviet Union ceased to exist shortly after the Soviet Union ceased to exist. Apart from Russia, only Ukraine inherited significant military capabilities. Russian forces were greatly reduced in size and were withdrawn from Central Europe and the Baltic states. The Warsaw Pact ended. The goal of challenging the U.S. Navy was abandoned. Military equipment was either disposed of or allowed to deteriorate and become nonoperational. Budget allocations for defense were drastically reduced. Demoralization pervaded the ranks of both officers and men. At the same time the Russian military were redefining their missions and doctrine and restructuring themselves for their new roles in protecting Russians and dealing with regional conflicts in the near abroad.

Second, the precipitous reduction in Russian military capabilities stimulated a slower but significant decline in Western military spending, forces, and capabilities. Under the plans of the Bush and Clinton administrations, U.S. military spending was due to drop by 35 percent from $342.3 billion (1994 dollars) in 1990 to $222.3 in 1998. The force structure that year would be half to two-thirds what it was at the end of the Cold War. Total military personnel would go down from 2.1 million to 1.4 million. Many major weapons programs have been and are being canceled. Between 1985 and 1995 annual purchases of major weapons went down from 29 to 6 ships, 943 to 127 aircraft, 720 to 0 tanks, and 48 to 18 strategic missiles. Beginning in the late 1980s, Britain, Germany, and, to a lesser degree, France went through similar reductions in defense spending and military capabilities. In the mid-1990s, the German armed forces were scheduled to decline from 370,000 to 340,000 and probably to 320,000; the French army was to drop from its strength of 290,000 in 1990 to 225,000 in 1997. British military personnel went down from 377,100 in 1985 to 274,800 in 1993. Continental members of NATO also shortened terms of conscripted service and debated the possible abandonment of conscription.

Third, the trends in East Asia differed significantly from those in Russia and the West. Increased military spending and force improvements were the order of the day; China was the pacesetter. Stimulated by both their increasing economic wealth and the Chinese buildup, other East Asian nations are modernizing and expanding their military forces. Japan has continued to improve its highly sophisticated military capability. Taiwan, South Korea, Thailand, Malaysia, Singapore, and Indonesia all are spending more on their military and purchasing planes, tanks, and ships from Russia, the United States, Britain, France, Germany, and other countries. While NATO defense expenditures declined by roughly 10 percent between 1985 and 1993 (from $539.6 billion to $485.0 billion) (constant 1993 dollars), expenditures in East Asia rose by 50 percent from $89.8 billion to $134.8 billion during the same period.

Fourth, military capabilities including weapons of mass destruction are diffusing broadly across the world. As countries develop economically, they generate the capacity to produce weapons. Between the 1960s and 1980s, for instance, the number of Third World countries producing fighter aircraft increased from one to eight, tanks from one to six, helicopters from one to six, and tactical missiles from none to seven. The 1990s have seen a major trend toward the globalization of the defense industry, which is likely further to erode Western military advantages. Many non-Western societies either have nuclear weapons (Russia, China, Israel, India, Pakistan, and possibly North Korea) or have been making strenuous efforts to acquire them (Iran, Iraq, Libya, and possibly Algeria) or are placing themselves in a position quickly to acquire them if they see the need to do so (Japan).

Finally, all those developments make regionalization the central trend in military strategy and power in the post-Cold War world. Regionalization provides the rationale for the reductions in Russian and Western military forces and for increases in the military forces of other states. Russia no longer has a global military capability but is focusing its strategy and forces on the near abroad. China has reoriented its strategy and forces to emphasize local power projection and the defense of Chinese interests in East Asia. European countries are similarly redirecting their forces, through both NATO and the Western European Union, to deal with instability on the periphery of Western Europe. The United States has explicitly shifted its military planning from deterring and fighting the Soviet Union on a global basis to preparing to deal simultaneously with regional contingencies in the Persian Gulf and Northeast Asia. The United States, however, is not likely to have the military capability to meet these goals. To defeat Iraq, the United States deployed in the Persian Gulf 75 percent of its active tactical aircraft, 42 percent of its modern battle tanks, 46 percent of its aircraft carriers, 37 percent of its army personnel, and 46 percent of its marine personnel. With significantly reduced forces in the future, the United States will be hard put to carry out one intervention, much less two, against substantial regional powers outside the Western Hemisphere. Military security throughout the world increasingly depends not on the global distribution of power and the actions of superpowers but on the distribution of power within each region of the world and the actions of the core states of civilizations.

In sum, overall the West will remain the most powerful civilization well into the early decades of the twenty-first century. Beyond then it will probably continue to have a substantial lead in scientific talent, research and development capabilities, and civilian and military technological innovation. Control over the other power resources, however, is becoming increasingly dispersed— among the core states and leading countries of non-Western civilizations. The West's control of these resources peaked in the 1920s and has since been declining irregularly but significantly. In the 2020s, a hundred years after that peak, the West will probably control about 24 percent of the world's territory (down from a peak of 49 percent), 10 percent of the total world population (down from 48 percent) and perhaps 15–20 percent of the socially mobilized population, about 30 percent of the world's economic product (down from a peak of probably 70 percent), perhaps 25 percent of manufacturing output (down from a peak of 84 percent), and less than 10 percent of global military manpower (down from 45 percent).

In 1919 Woodrow Wilson, Lloyd George, and Georges Clemenceau together virtually controlled the world. Sitting in Paris, they determined what countries would exist and which would not, what new countries would be created, what their boundaries would be and who would rule them, and how the Middle East and other parts of the world would be divided up among the victorious powers. They also decided on military intervention in Russia and economic concessions to be extracted from China. A hundred years later, no small group of statesmen will be able to exercise comparable power; to the extent that any group does it will not consist of three Westerners but leaders of the core states of the world's seven or eight major civilizations. The successors to Reagan, Thatcher, Mitterrand, and Kohl will be rivaled by those of Deng Xiaoping, Nakasone, Indira Gandhi, Yeltsin, Khomeini, and Suharto. The age of Western dominance will be over. . . .

At various times before the nineteenth century, Byzantines, Arabs, Chinese, Ottomans, Moguls, and Russians were highly confident of their strength and achievements compared to those of the West. At these times they also were contemptuous of the cultural inferiority, institutional backwardness, corruption, and decadence of the West. As the success of the West fades relatively, such attitudes reappear. People feel "they don't have to take it anymore." Iran is an extreme case, but, as one observer noted, "Western values are rejected in different ways, but no less firmly, in Malaysia, Indonesia, Singapore, China, and Japan." We are witnessing "the end of the progressive era" dominated by Western ideologies and are moving into an era in which multiple and diverse civilizations will interact, compete, coexist, and accommodate each other.

The Worldwide Liberal Revolution

The distant origins of the present [selection] lie in an article entitled "The End of History?" which I wrote for the journal *The National Interest* in the summer of 1989. In it, I argued that a remarkable consensus concerning the legitimacy of liberal democracy as a system of government had emerged throughout the world over the past few years, as it conquered rival ideologies like hereditary monarchy, fascism, and most recently communism. More than that, however, I argued that liberal democracy may constitute the "end point of mankind's ideological evolution" and the "final form of human government," and as such constituted the "end of history." That is, while earlier forms of government were characterized by grave defects and irrationalities that led to their eventual collapse, liberal democracy was arguably free from such fundamental internal contradictions. This was not to say that today's stable democracies, like the United States, France, or Switzerland, were not without injustice or serious social problems. But these problems were ones of incomplete implementation of the twin principles of liberty and equality on which modern democracy is founded, rather than of flaws in the principles themselves. While present-day countries might fail to achieve stable liberal democracy, and others might lapse back into other, more primitive forms of rule like theocracy or military dictatorship, the *ideal* of liberal democracy could not be improved on.

The original article excited an extraordinary amount of commentary and controversy, first in the United States, and then in a series of countries as different as England, France, Italy, the Soviet Union, Brazil, South Africa, Japan, and South Korea. Criticism took every conceivable form, some of it based on simple misunderstanding of my original intent, and others penetrating more perceptively to the core of my argument. Many people were confused in the first instance by my use of the word "history." Understanding history in a conventional sense as the occurrence of events, people pointed to the fall of the Berlin Wall, the Chinese communist crackdown in Tiananmen Square, and the Iraqi invasion of Kuwait as evidence that "history was continuing," and that I was *ipso facto* proven wrong.

And yet what I suggested had come to an end was not the occurrence of events, even large and grave events, but History; that is, history understood as a single, coherent, evolutionary process, when taking into account the experience of all peoples in all times. This understanding of History was most closely associated with the great German philosopher G. W. F. Hegel. It was made part of our daily intellectual atmosphere by Karl Marx, who borrowed this concept of History from Hegel, and is implicit in our use of words like "primitive" or "advanced," "traditional" or "modern," when referring to different types of human societies. For both of these thinkers, there was a coherent development of human societies from simple tribal ones based on slavery and subsistence agriculture, through various theocracies, monarchies, and feudal aristocracies, up through modern liberal democracy and technologically driven capitalism. This evolutionary process was neither random nor unintelligible, even if it did not proceed in a straight line, and even if it was possible to question whether man was happier or better off as a result of historical "progress."

Both Hegel and Marx believed that the evolution of human societies was not open-ended, but would end when mankind had achieved a form of society that satisfied its deepest and most fundamental longings. Both thinkers thus posited an "end of history": for Hegel this was the liberal state, while for Marx it was a communist society. This did not mean that the natural cycle of birth, life, and death would end, that important events would no longer happen, or that newspapers reporting them would cease to be published. It meant, rather, that there would be no further progress in the development of underlying principles and institutions, because all of the really big questions had been settled....

We stand at the gates of an important epoch, a time of ferment, when spirit moves forward in a leap, transcends its previous shape and takes on a new one. All the mass of previous representations, concepts, and bonds linking our world together are dissolving and collapsing like a dream picture. A new phase of the spirit is preparing itself. Philosophy especially has to welcome its appearance and acknowledge it, while others, who oppose it impotently, cling to the past.

— G. W. F. Hegel, in a lecture on September 18, 1806

On both the communist Left and the authoritarian Right there has been a bankruptcy of serious ideas capable of sustaining the internal political cohesion of strong governments, whether based on "monolithic" parties, military juntas, or personalistic dictatorships. The absence of legitimate authority has meant that when an authoritarian government met with failure in some area of policy, there was no higher principle to which the regime could appeal. Some have compared legitimacy to a kind of cash reserve. All governments, democratic and authoritarian, have their ups and downs; but only legitimate governments have this reserve to draw on in times of crisis.

The weakness of authoritarian states of the Right lay in their failure to control civil society. Coming to power with a certain mandate to restore order or to impose "economic discipline," many found themselves no more successful than their democratic predecessors in stimulating steady economic growth or in creating a sense of social order. And those that were successful were hoisted on their own petard. For the societies on top of which they sat began to outgrow them as they became better educated, more prosperous, and middle class. As memory of the specific emergency that had justified strong government faded, those societies became less and less ready to tolerate military rule.

Totalitarian governments of the Left sought to avoid these problems by subordinating the whole of civil society to their control, including what their citizens were allowed to think. But such a system in its pure form could be maintained only through a terror that threatened the system's own rulers. Once that terror was relaxed, a long process of degeneration set in, during which the state lost control of certain key aspects of civil society. Most important was its loss of control over the belief system. And since the socialist formula for economic growth was defective, the state could not prevent its citizens from taking note of this fact and drawing their own conclusions.

Moreover, few totalitarian regimes could replicate themselves through one or more succession crises. In the absence of commonly accepted rules of succession, it would always be a temptation for some ambitious contender for power to throw the whole system into question by calls for fundamental reform in the struggle against his rivals. The reform card is a powerful trump because dissatisfaction with Stalinist systems is high everywhere. Thus Khrushchev used anti-Stalinism against Beria and Malenkov, Gorbachev used it against his Brezhnev-era competitors, and Zhao Ziyang used it against the hardline Li Peng. The question of whether the individuals or groups contending for power were real democrats was in a sense irrelevant, since the succession process tended to undermine the old regime's credibility by exposing its inevitable abuses. New social and political forces, more sincerely committed to liberal ideas, were unleashed and soon escaped the control of those who planned the first limited reforms.

The weakness of strong states has meant that many former authoritarianisms have now given way to democracy, while the former post-totalitarian states have become simple authoritarianisms, if not democracies. The Soviet Union has devolved power to its constituent republics, and while China continues to be a dictatorship, the regime has lost control of significant parts of society. Neither country possesses any longer the ideological coherence once given them by Marxism-Leninism: the conservatives opposed to reform in the Soviet Union are as likely to place an Orthodox icon on their wall as a picture of Lenin. The would-be makers of the August 1991 coup resembled a Latin American military junta, with army officers and police officials playing a major role.

In addition to the crisis of political authoritarianism, there has been a quieter but no less significant revolution going on in the field of economics. The development that was both manifestation and cause of this revolution was the phenomenal economic growth of East Asia since World War II. This success story was not limited to early modernizers like Japan, but eventually came to include virtually all countries in Asia willing to adopt market principles and integrate themselves fully into the global, capitalist economic system. Their performance suggested that poor countries without resources other than their own hardworking populations could take advantage of the openness of the international economic system and create unimagined amounts of new wealth, rapidly closing the gap with the more established capitalist powers of Europe and North America.

The East Asian economic miracle was carefully observed around the world, nowhere more than in the communist bloc. Communism's terminal crisis began in some sense when the Chinese leadership recognized that they were being left behind by the rest of capitalist Asia, and saw that socialist central planning had condemned China to backwardness and poverty. The ensuing Chinese liberalizing reforms led to a doubling of grain production in five years and provided a new demonstration of the power of market principles. The Asian lesson was later absorbed by economists in the Soviet Union, who knew the terrible waste and inefficiency that central planning had brought about in their own country. The Eastern Europeans had less need to be taught; they understood better than other communists that their failure to reach the living standards of their fellow Europeans in the West was due to the socialist system imposed on them after the war by the Soviets.

But students of the East Asian economic miracle were not restricted to the communist bloc. A remarkable transformation has taken place in the economic thinking of Latin Americans as well. In the 1950s, when the Argentine economist Raul Prebisch headed the United Nations Economic Committee for Latin America, it was fashionable to attribute the underdevelopment not only of Latin America but of the Third World more generally to the global capitalist system. It was argued that early developers in Europe and America had in effect structured the world economy in their favor and condemned those who came later to dependent positions as providers of raw materials. By the early 1990s, that understanding had changed entirely: President Carlos Salinas de Gortari in Mexico, President Carlos Menem in Argentina, and President Fernando Collor de Mello in Brazil, all sought to implement far-reaching programs of economic liberalization after coming to power, accepting the need for market competition and openness to the world economy. Chile put liberal economic principles into practice earlier in the 1980s under Pinochet, with the result that its economy was the healthiest of any in the Southern Cone as it emerged from dictatorship under the leadership of President Patricio Alwyn. These new, democratically elected leaders started from the premise that underdevelopment was not due to the inherent inequities of capitalism, but rather to the insufficient degree of capitalism that had been practiced in their countries in the past. Privatization and free trade have become the new watchwords in place of nationalization and import substitution. The Marxist orthodoxy of Latin American intellectuals has come under increasing challenge from writers like Hernando de Soto, Mario Vargas Llosa, and Carlos Rangel, who have begun to find a significant audience for liberal, market-oriented economic ideas.

As mankind approaches the end of the millennium, the twin crises of authoritarianism and socialist central planning have left only one competitor standing in the ring as an ideology of potentially universal validity: liberal democracy, the doctrine of individual freedom and popular sovereignty. Two hundred years after they first animated the French and American revolutions, the principles of liberty and equality have proven not just durable but resurgent.

Liberalism and democracy, while closely related, are separate concepts. Political liberalism can be defined simply as a rule of law that recognizes certain individual rights or freedoms from government control. While there can be a wide variety of definitions of fundamental rights, we will use the one contained in Lord Bryce's classic work on democracy, which limits them to three: civil rights, "the exemption from control of the citizen in respect of his person and property"; religious rights, "exemption from control in the expression of religious opinions and the practice of worship"; and what he calls political rights, "exemption from control in matters which do not so plainly affect the welfare of the whole community as to render control necessary," including the fundamental right of press freedom. It has been a common practice for socialist countries to press for the recognition of various second- and third-generation economic rights, such as the right to employment, housing, or health care. The problem with such an expanded list is that the achievement of these rights is not clearly compatible with other rights like those of property or free economic exchange. In our definition we will stick to Bryce's shorter and more traditional list of rights, which is compatible with those contained in the American Bill of Rights.

Democracy, on the other hand, is the right held universally by all citizens to have a share of political power, that is, the right of all citizens to vote and participate in politics. The right to participate in political power can be thought of as yet another liberal right—indeed, the most important one—and it is for this reason that liberalism has been closely associated historically with democracy.

In judging which countries are democratic, we will use a strictly formal definition of democracy. A country is democratic if it grants its people the right to choose their own government through periodic, secret-ballot, multi-party elections, on the basis of universal and equal adult suffrage. It is true that formal democracy alone does not always guarantee equal participation and rights. Democratic procedures can be manipulated by elites, and do not always accurately reflect the will or true self-interests of the people. But once we move away from a formal definition, we open up the possibility of infinite abuse of the democratic principle. In this century, the greatest enemies of democracy have attacked "formal" democracy in the name of "substantive" democracy. This was the justification used by Lenin and the Bolshevik party to close down the Russian Constituent Assembly and proclaim a party dictatorship, which was to achieve substantive democracy "in the name of the people." Formal democracy, on the other hand, provides real institutional safeguards against dictatorship, and is much more likely to produce "substantive" democracy in the end.

While liberalism and democracy usually go together, they can be separated in theory. It is possible for a country to be liberal without being particularly democratic, as was eighteenth-century Britain. A broad list of rights, including the franchise, was fully protected for a narrow social elite, but denied to others. It is also possible for a country to be democratic without being liberal, that is, without protecting the rights of individuals and minorities. A good example of this is the contemporary Islamic Republic of Iran, which has held regular elections that were reasonably fair by Third World standards, making the country more democratic than it was in the time of the Shah. Islamic Iran, however, is not a liberal state; there are no guarantees of free speech, assembly, and, above all, of religion. The most elementary rights of Iranian citizens are not protected by the rule of law, a situation that is worse for Iran's ethnic and religious minorities.

In its economic manifestation, liberalism is the recognition of the right of free economic activity and economic exchange based on private property and markets. Since the term "capitalism" has acquired so many pejorative connotations over the years, it has recently become a fashion to speak of "free-market economics" instead; both are acceptable alternative terms for economic liberalism. It is evident that there are many possible interpretations of this rather broad definition of economic liberalism, ranging from the United States of Ronald Reagan and the Britain of Margaret Thatcher to the social democracies of Scandinavia and the relatively statist regimes in Mexico and India. All contemporary capitalist states have large public sectors, while most socialist states have permitted a degree of private economic activity. There has been considerable controversy over the point at which the public sector becomes large enough to disqualify a state as liberal. Rather than try to set a precise percentage, it is probably more useful to look at what attitude the state takes *in principle* to the legitimacy of private property and enterprise. Those that protect such economic rights we will consider liberal; those that are opposed or base themselves on other principles (such as "economic justice") will not qualify.

The present crisis of authoritarianism has not necessarily led to the emergence of liberal democratic regimes, nor are all the new democracies which have emerged secure. The newly democratic countries of Eastern Europe face wrenching transformations of their economies, while the new democracies in Latin America are hobbled by a terrible legacy of prior economic mismanagement. Many of the fast developers in East Asia, while economically liberal, have not accepted the challenge of political liberalization. The liberal revolution has left certain areas like the Middle East relatively untouched. It is altogether possible to imagine states like Peru or the Philippines relapsing into some kind of dictatorship under the weight of the crushing problems they face.

But the fact that there will be setbacks and disappointments in the process of democratization, or that not every market economy will prosper, should not distract us from the larger pattern that is emerging in world history. The apparent number of choices that countries face in determining how they will organize themselves politically and economically has been *diminishing* over time. Of the different types of regimes that have emerged in the course of human history, from monarchies and aristocracies, to religious theocracies, to the fascist and communist dictatorships of this century, the only form of government that has survived intact to the end of the twentieth century has been liberal democracy.

What is emerging victorious, in other words, is not so much liberal practice, as the liberal *idea*. That is to say, for a very large part of the world, there is now no ideology with pretensions to universality that is in a position to challenge liberal democracy, and no universal principle of legitimacy other than the sovereignty of the people. Monarchism in its various forms had been largely defeated by the beginning of this century. Fascism and communism, liberal democracy's main competitors up till now, have both discredited themselves. If the Soviet Union (or its successor states) fails to democratize, if Peru or the Philippines relapse into some form of authoritarianism, democracy will most likely have yielded to a colonel or bureaucrat who claims to speak in the name of the Russian, Peruvian, or Philippine people alone. Even non-democrats will have to speak the language of democracy in order to justify their deviation from the single universal standard.

It is true that Islam constitutes a systematic and coherent ideology, just like liberalism and communism, with its own code of morality and doctrine of political and social justice. The appeal of Islam is potentially universal, reaching out to all men as men, and not just to members of a particular ethnic or national group. And Islam has indeed defeated liberal democracy in many parts of the Islamic world, posing a grave threat to liberal practices even in countries where it has not achieved political power directly. The end of the Cold War in Europe was followed immediately by a challenge to the West from Iraq, in which Islam was arguably a factor.

Despite the power demonstrated by Islam in its current revival, however, it remains the case that this religion has virtually no appeal outside those areas that were culturally Islamic to begin with. The days of Islam's cultural conquests, it would seem, are over: it can win back lapsed adherents, but has no resonance for young people in Berlin, Tokyo, or Moscow. And while nearly a billion people are culturally Islamic—one-fifth of the world's population—they cannot challenge liberal democracy on its own territory on the level of ideas. Indeed, the Islamic world would seem more vulnerable to liberal ideas in the long run than the reverse, since such liberalism has attracted numerous and powerful Muslim adherents over the past century and a half. Part of the reason for the current, fundamentalist revival is the strength of the perceived threat from liberal, Western values to traditional Islamic societies.

We who live in stable, long-standing liberal democracies face an unusual situation. In our grandparents' time, many reasonable people could foresee a radiant socialist future in which private property and capitalism had been abolished, and in which politics itself was somehow overcome. Today, by contrast, we have trouble imagining a world that is radically better than our own, or a future that is not essentially democratic and capitalist. Within that framework, of course, many things could be improved: we could house the homeless, guarantee opportunity for minorities and women, improve competitiveness, and create new jobs. We can also imagine future worlds that are significantly worse than what we know now, in which national, racial, or religious intolerance makes a comeback, or in which we are overwhelmed by war or environmental collapse. But we cannot picture to ourselves a world that is *essentially* different from the present one, and at the same time better. Other, less reflective ages also thought of themselves as the best, but we arrive at this conclusion exhausted, as it were, from the pursuit of alternatives we felt *had* to be better than liberal democracy.

The fact that this is so, and the breadth of the current worldwide liberal revolution, invites us to raise the following question: Are we simply witnessing a momentary upturn in the fortunes of liberal democracy, or is there some longer-term pattern of development at work that will eventually lead all countries in the direction of liberal democracy?

It is possible, after all, that the present trend toward democracy is a cyclical phenomenon. One need only look back to the late 1960s and early 70s, when the United States was undergoing a crisis of self-confidence brought on by its involvement in the Vietnam War and the Watergate scandal. The West as a whole was thrown into economic crisis as a result of the OPEC oil embargo; most of Latin America's democracies were overthrown in a series of military coups; and un- or anti-democratic regimes seemed to be prospering around the world, from the Soviet Union, Cuba, and Vietnam to Saudi Arabia, Iran, and South Africa. What reason, then, do we have to expect that the situation of the 1970s will not recur, or worse yet, that the 1930s, with its clash of virulent anti-democratic ideologies, can not return?

Can it not be argued, moreover, that the current crisis of authoritarianism is a fluke, a rare convergence of political planets that will not recur for the next hundred years? For careful study of the different transitions away from authoritarianism in the 1970s and 80s will yield a plethora of lessons concerning the accidental nature of these events. The more one knows about a particular country, the more one is aware of the "maelstrom of external contingency" that differentiated that country from its neighbors, and the seemingly fortuitous circumstances that led to a democratic outcome. Things could have worked out very differently: the Portuguese Communist party could have emerged victorious in 1975, or the Spanish transition might not have resulted in democracy had King Juan Carlos not played so skillful and moderating a role. Liberal ideas have no force independent of the human actors who put them into effect, and if Andropov or Chernenko had lived longer, or if Gorbachev himself had a different personality, the course of events in the Soviet Union and Eastern Europe between 1985 and 1991 would have been quite different. Following the current fashion in the social sciences, one is tempted to say that unpredictable political factors like leadership and public opinion dominate the democratization process and ensure that every case will be unique both in process and outcome.

But it is precisely if we look not just at the past fifteen years, but at the *whole scope of history*, that liberal democracy begins to occupy a special kind of place. While there have been cycles in the worldwide fortunes of democracy, there has also been a pronounced secular trend in a democratic direction.... [T]he growth of democracy has not been continuous or unidirectional; Latin America had fewer democracies in 1975 than it did in 1955, and the world as a whole was less democratic in 1940 than it was in 1919. Periods of democratic upsurge are interrupted by radical discontinuities and setbacks, such as those represented by nazism and Stalinism. On the other hand, all of these reverses tended to be themselves reversed eventually, leading over time to an impressive overall growth in the number of democracies around the world. The percentage of the world's population living under democratic government would grow dramatically, moreover, should the Soviet Union or China democratize in the next generation, in whole or in part. Indeed, the growth of liberal democracy, together with its companion, economic liberalism, has been the most remarkable macropolitical phenomenon of the last four hundred years.

It is true that democracies have been relatively rare in human history, so rare that before 1776 there was not a single one in existence anywhere in the world. (The democracy of Periclean Athens does not qualify, because it did not systematically protect individual rights.) Counted in the number of years they have existed, factory production and automobiles and cities with multiple millions of inhabitants have been equally rare, while practices like slavery, hereditary monarchies, and dynastic marriages have persisted for enormous periods of time. What is significant, however, is not the frequency or length of occurrence, but the trend: in the developed world, we would as little expect to see the disappearance of cities or cars in the near future as we would the re-emergence of slavery.

It is against this background that the remarkable worldwide character of the current liberal revolution takes on special significance. For it constitutes further evidence that there is a fundamental process at work that dictates a common evolutionary pattern for *all* human societies—in short, something like a Universal History of mankind in the direction of liberal democracy. The existence of peaks and troughs in this development is undeniable. But to cite the failure of liberal democracy in any given country, or even in an entire region of the world, as evidence of democracy's overall weakness, reveals a striking narrowness of view. Cycles and discontinuities in themselves are not incompatible with a history that is directional and universal, just as the existence of business cycles does not negate the possibility of long-term economic growth.

Just as impressive as the growth in the number of democracies is the fact that democratic government has broken out of its original beachhead in Western Europe and North America, and has made significant inroads in other parts of the world that do not share the political, religious, and cultural traditions of those areas. The argument was once made that there was a distinct Iberian tradition that was "authoritarian, patrimonial, Catholic, stratified, corporate and semi-feudal to the core." To hold Spain, Portugal, or the countries of Latin America to the standards of the liberal democracy of Western Europe or the United States was to be guilty of "ethnocentrism." Yet those universal standards of rights were those to which people in the Iberian tradition held *themselves,* and since the mid-1970s Spain and Portugal have graduated to the ranks of stable democracies, tied ever more tightly to an economically integrating Europe. These same standards have had meaning for peoples in Latin America, Eastern Europe, Asia, and many other parts of the world as well. The success of democracy in a wide variety of places and among many different peoples would suggest that the principles of liberty and equality on which they are based are not accidents or the results of ethnocentric prejudice, but are in fact discoveries about the nature of man as man, whose truth does not diminish but grows more evident as one's point of view becomes more cosmopolitan.

The question of whether there is such a thing as a Universal History of mankind that takes into account the experiences of all times and all peoples is not new; it is in fact a very old one which recent events compel us to raise anew. From the beginning, the most serious and systematic attempts to write Universal Histories saw the central issue in history as the development of Freedom. History was not a blind concatenation of events, but a meaningful whole in which human ideas concerning the nature of a just political and social order developed and played themselves out. And if we are now at a point where we cannot imagine a world substantially different from our own, in which there is no apparent or obvious way in which the future will represent a fundamental improvement over our current order, then we must also take into consideration the possibility that History itself might be at an end.

POSTSCRIPT

Is Western Civilization in a State of Decline?

Both Huntington and Fukuyama agree that the West is the main power in the world today and will continue to be well into this century. They disagree, however, over what the long-term future will bring. Huntington believes that the United States must solve its internal problems (multicultural conflicts, economic stagnation, social decay, and a decline in morality and moral values) and then reinvigorate the Atlantic Community to present a united front against the other civilizations. Convincing Latin America to join would bring added strength.

Fukuyama offers a concise analysis of his thesis in his article "The End of History," *The National Interest* (Summer 1989). Critiques of this article appeared in subsequent 1989 issues of *The National Interest*, and Fukuyama's rebuttal appeared in the Winter issue. We have likely not seen the last word on this debate. The optimism that Fukuyama expressed in his 1989 article is tempered somewhat in his later book *The End of History and the Last Man* (Free Press, 1992), from which his selection was excerpted. Despite this, he still sees the West's liberal-capitalist democracy as the only road to a fair and just world.

The book from which Huntington's selection was excerpted, *The Clash of Civilizations and the Remaking of World Order* (Simon & Schuster, 1996), is a must-read for anyone interested in the world's future. Huntington repeats the need for Western unity in "The West and the World," *Foreign Affairs* (November/December 1996). Criticism of Huntington's work can be found in the September/October 1993 issue of *Foreign Affairs*; his rebuttal is contained in the publication's November/December 1993 issue.

Needless to say, Huntington and Fukuyama are not the first to speculate about the future of the West. Earlier in the twentieth century, Oswald Spengler's *Decline of the West* (Alfred A. Knopf, 1926–1928) explored the inevitability of the West's decline, with its place of power being taken by a Eurasian nation. A comparison of Spengler's conclusions with those of Fukuyama and Huntington would be a fruitful endeavor.

Contributors to This Volume

EDITORS

JOSEPH R. MITCHELL is a history instructor at Howard Community College in Columbia, Maryland. He also teaches for the Evergreen Society, a branch of the Johns Hopkins University's Continuing Studies Program. He received an M.A. in history from Loyola College in Maryland and an M.A. in African American History from Morgan State University, also in Maryland.

HELEN BUSS MITCHELL is a professor of philosophy and director of the women's studies program at Howard Community College in Columbia, Maryland. She is the author of *Roots of Wisdom: Speaking the Language of Philosophy* and *Roots of World Wisdom: A Multicultural Reader*. Both books were published by Wadsworth Publishing Company and are now in their second editions. She has also created, written, and hosted a philosophy telecourse, *For the Love of Wisdom*, which has been distributed throughout the country by PBS. She has earned numerous degrees, including a Ph.D. in women's history from the University of Maryland.

STAFF

Theodore Knight   List Manager
David Brackley   Senior Developmental Editor
Juliana Poggio   Developmental Editor
Rose Gleich   Administrative Assistant
Brenda S. Filley   Production Manager
Juliana Arbo   Typesetting Supervisor
Diane Barker   Proofreader
Lara Johnson   Design/Advertising Coordinator
Richard Tietjen   Publishing Systems Manager
Larry Killian   Copier Coordinator

AUTHORS

KAREN ARMSTRONG teaches at the Leo Baeck College for the Study of Judaism and the Training of Rabbis and Teachers in London, England. An honorary member of the Association of Muslim Social Sciences, her published works include *Beginning the World* (St. Martin's Press, 1983) and *Holy War* (Macmillan, 1988).

ANNE LLEWELLYN BARSTOW is professor of history, retired, at the State University of New York at Old Westbury, New York. She is the author of *Joan of Arc: Heretic, Mystic, Shaman* (Edwin Mellen Press, 1986).

MARY R. BEARD (1876–1958), the founder of the World Center for Women Archives, was a leading suffragist and participant in the labor movement. She coauthored with her husband Charles many works in American history, and she is the author of *A Short History of the American Labor Movement* (Greenwood Press, 1924).

V. R. BERGHAHN is John P. Birkelund Professor of European History at Brown University. He is the author of 15 books, including *Imperial Germany, 1871–1914* (Berghahn Books, 1994).

JOHN BOSWELL (1947–1994) was A. Whitney Griswold Professor of History at Yale University. He is the author of *The Kindness of Strangers: The Abandonment of Children in Western Europe from Late Antiquity to the Renaissance* (Pantheon Books, 1988).

ROBIN BRIGGS is a senior research fellow of All Souls College and a university lecturer in modern history.

HERBERT BUTTERFIELD taught for many years at Cambridge University. He is the author of several works, including *The Englishman and His History* (Archon Books, 1970) and *Herbert Butterfield on History* (Garland, 1985).

AVERIL CAMERON is a professor of late antique and Byzantine studies at King's College of the University of London.

WILLIAM DARITY, JR. is a professor of economics at the University of North Carolina at Chapel Hill. He is the author of numerous articles on the profitability of the slave trade.

LANCE E. DAVIS is a member of the faculty at the California Institute of Technology. He is coauthor, with Robert Gallman and Karin Gleiter, of *In Pursuit of Leviathan: Technology, Institutions, Productivity, and Profits in American Whaling, 1816–1906* (University of Chicago Press, 1997).

HASIA R. DINER is professor of history at New York University. Her research interests include American Jewish history, immigration-ethnic history, and women's history.

MARTIN FELDSTEIN is a professor of economics at Harvard University and president of the National Bureau of Economic Research.

RONALD C. FINUCANE is professor of history at Oakland University in Rochester, Michigan. He is the author of *Soldiers of the Faith: Crusaders and Moslems at War* (St. Martin's Press, 1984).

ELIZABETH FOX-GENOVISE is Eleanor Raoul Professor of Humanities and director of women's studies at Emory University. She is the author of the award-winning *Within the Plantation Household: Black and White Women of the Old South* (University of North Carolina Press, 1988).

FRANCIS FUKUYAMA is Omer L. and Nancy Hirst Professor of Public Policy and director of the international commerce and policy program at George Mason University. His most recent book is *The Great Disruption: Human Nature and the Reconstitution of Social Order* (Free Press, 1998).

JOHN LEWIS GADDIS is Robert Lovett Professor of History at Yale University. He has contributed extensively to cold war historiography and has authored at least six major works on the subject.

N. G. L. HAMMOND is professor emeritus of Greek at Bristol University in England and an honorary fellow of Clare College at Cambridge University. He is the author of *Alexander the Great: King, Commander, and Statesman* (Noyes Press, 1981).

ANDREAS HILLGRUBER (1925–1989) held a university chair in Germany and was the author of more than 50 books, most of them dealing with Hitler and the Nazi era.

OLWEN HUFTON is a professor of history at the European Institute in Florence, Italy. She was the architect and first head of the woman's studies program at Harvard and is the author of many books, including *The Poor of Eighteenth-Century France* (Oxford University Press, 1974) and *Women and the Limits of Citizenship in the French Revolution* (University of Toronto Press, 1981).

SAMUEL P. HUNTINGTON is Albert J. Weatherhead III University Professor at Harvard University, where he is also director of the John M. Olin Institute for Strategic Studies. He is the author of *Political Order in Changing Societies* (Yale University Press, 1968).

ROBERT A. HUTTENBACK was a professor of history at the University of California, Santa Barbara, where he was chancellor from 1977 to 1986.

DONALD KAGAN is Bass Professor of History, Classics, and Western Civilization at Yale University. Among his many publications is the highly acclaimed *On the Origins of War* (Doubleday, 1995).

JOAN KELLY-GADOL (1928–1982) was a Renaissance scholar and theorist in women's history. Her works include *Leon Battista Alberti: Universal Man of the Early Renaissance* (University of Chicago Press, 1969).

CHRISTINE KINEALY, formerly the assistant director of the Ulster Historical Foundation in Belfast, is now a fellow of the University of Liverpool lecturing on Irish and British history.

IAN KERSHAW is a professor and department head at the University of Sheffield in England. He is the author of *The Hitler Myth: Image and Reality in the Third Reich* (Oxford University Press, 1987) and *Hitler, 1889–1936: Hubris* (W. W. Norton, 1998). A second volume of the Hitler biography is expected in the near future.

PETER KROPOTKIN (1842–1921) was a Russian revolutionary who wrote his autobiography *Memoirs of a Revolutionist* in 1899.

JOHN M. MacKENZIE is a professor of imperial history and dean of humanitites at Lancaster University in England. He is the editor of *Imperialism and Popular Culture* (Manchester University Press, 1986).

STEVEN MAJSTOROVIC is an assistant professor of political science at Duquesne University in Pittsburgh, Pennsylvania.

RICHARD MARIUS is professor emeritus at Harvard University. He is the author of *Thomas More: A Biography* (Harvard University Press, 1984).

HANS EBERHARD MAYER is professor of medieval and modern history at the University of Kiel, Germany.

FRANÇOISE NAVAILH is a Russian film historian at the University of Paris. She teaches Russian language and is a specialist in Russian cinema.

ORLANDO PATTERSON is a professor of sociology at Harvard University. His published works include *Slavery and Social Death* (Harvard University Press, 1982).

JAMES A RAWLEY is a professor of history at the University of Nebraska. His publications include *Race and Politics* (Lippincott, 1969).

BERNARD M. G. REARDON was, until his retirement, reader and head of the Department of Religious Studies at the University of Newcastle upon Tyne in England.

PHILIP LYNDON REYNOLDS is director of the Aquinas Center of Theology at Emory University. He is the author of *Marriage in the Western Church: The Christianization of Marriage During the Patristic and Early Medieval Periods* (Brill Academic Publishers, 1994).

E. E. RICE is senior research fellow at Wolfson College at Oxford and lecturer in classical archaeology at Herford College at Oxford. She is a specialist in military history, topography, and the social history of the Greek world in the Hellenistic period.

SIMON SCHAMA is a professor of art and art history at Columbia University. He is the author of *The Embarrassement of Riches: An Interpretation of Dutch Culture During the Golden Age* (Alfred A. Knopf, 1987) and *Landscape and Memory* (Alfred A. Knopf, 1995).

STEVEN SHAPIN is a professor of sociology at the University of California at San Diego. He has written extensively on the social history of science and the sociology of scientific knowledge. He is the author of *Leviathan and the Air-Pump: Hobbes, Boyle, and the Experimental Life* (Princeton University Press, 1985).

MARTIN J. SHERWIN is Walter S. Dickson Professor of History at Tufts University and the director of the University's Nuclear Age History and Humanities Center. He is the author of *A World Destroyed: The Atomic Bomb and the Grand Alliance* (Random House, 1977).

RICHARD STITES is a professor of history at Georgetown University. He is the author of *Revolutionary Dreams* (Oxford University Press, 1989) and *Russian Popular Culture* (Cambridge University Press, 1992).

FRANÇOISE THÉBAUD is a lecturer at the Université Lumière in Lyon, France, and is a specialist in the history of women in the twentieth century. She has written extensively on this subject in collected volumes and periodicals.

KAREN JO TORJESEN is the Margo L. Goldsmith Chair of Women's Studies and Religion at Claremont Graduate School in California. She is also an associate of the Institute for Antiquity and Christianity.

ELISJA SCHULTE VAN KESSEL is a professor of early modern cultural history at the Netherlands Institute in Rome. She is the author of *Men and Women in Spiritual Culture, XVI–XVII Centuries* (The Hague and Rome, 1986).

WERNER WEIDENFELD is director of the Center for Applied Policy Research at Ludwig Maximilians University in Munich, Germany.

DEREK WILLIAMS has a longstanding interest in the Roman borderlands and is the author of *The Reach of Rome* (Saint Martin's Press, 1997).

SAMUEL R. WILLIAMSON, JR. is professor of history and vice-chancellor of the University of the South. He is the author of *Austria-Hungary and the Origins of the First World War* (Saint Martin's Press, 1991).

WARREN ZIMMERMANN served as the last United States ambassador to Yugoslavia and is retired from the Foreign Service. Currently, he is a professor of international diplomacy at Columbia University.

Index

Africa, economic factors as responsible for
British imperialism and, 286, 289–298
*African Trade: The Great Pillar and Support of
the British Plantation Trade in America*
(Postlethwayt), 187
ageism, witch-hunts and, 204–206
Alamans, 74
Alexander the Great, controversy over the
reputation of, 24–38
Alexander II, 107, 108
Alfonso VI, king of Spain, 114–115
Ammian, 76–77
Ancient Economy, The (Finley), 67
Andrews, Anthony, 9
Animadversions on Aristotle (Ramus), 221
Apis, 311–312
archons, of Athens, 12, 13
Areopagus, of Athens, 12
Aristotle, 15, 221–222
Armand, Inessa, 325, 326, 328, 337, 338
Armstrong, Karen, on Christianity as liberating
women, 51–58
Ashton, T. S., 179–180, 188
Athens, slavery as essential for freedom and,
4–19
atomic bomb, as responsible for the cold war,
375–384
Augsburg Confession, 146–147
Austria, 358–359
Austria-Hungary, World War I and, 311–319

Bacon, Francis, 221, 222–223, 224
Baitelli, Angelica, 163
Balabanova, Angelica, 325, 326
banks, slave trade as a precondition for British
capitalism and, 182
Banner, Lois, 198
Barbarians, collapse of the Roman Empire and,
67, 68, 70–78
Barstow, Anne Llewellyn, on the witch-hunts in
premodern Europe as misogynistic,
198–206
Basil I, 84–86
Battle of Kosovo, 397
Beard, Mary R., on women and men benefiting
equally from the Renaissance, 122–127
Berchtold, Leopold, 312, 313, 315
Berghahn, V. R., on German militarism and
diplomacy as responsible for World War I,
302–310
Bethmann Hollweg, Theobald von, 302,
303–305, 314, 316

birth control, women's movement and,
432–433, 435–436
Black Hand, 311–312
"blank check" meeting, between Germany and
Austria-Hungary, 304, 306, 314
Boccaccio, 125–126
Bodin, Jean, 207–208
Boguet, Henri, 199, 200
Bosnia, ethnic leaders as responsible for the
disintegration of, 388–403
Boswell, John on the existence of same-sex
unions in the early Middle Ages, 82–88
Briggs, Robin, on the witch-hunts in premodern
Europe as misogynistic, 207–215
Broszat, Martin, 355
Bundesbank, 409–410
Burckhardt, Jacob, 125
Bush, Vannevar, 376, 377–378, 382, 383–384
Butterfield, Herbert, on the Scientific Revolution
as revolutionary, 220–225, 226
Byrnes, James F., 382–383

Cameron, Averil, on the collapse of the Roman
Empire as being due to its own weight,
62–69
Capitalism and Slavery (Williams), 192
capitalism, the slave trade as a precondition for
the rise of, in Great Britain, 178–194
Carmelites, 161–162
Castiglione, Baldassare, 131–132, 133
Catholic Church: of Croatia, 393; and convents
as expanding opportunity for women,
158–172; gender differences and, 436; in
Roman Empire, 63, 66
Chamberlain, Joseph, 281
charity, convents and, 167–168
Chiavello, Livia, 123
China, 454, 456
Christianity: as liberating women, 42–58;
Crusades as motivated by religious
factions and, 102–117; controversy over
whether Martin Luther's reform improved
lives within, 138–153
Churchill, Winston, 368–369, 376, 377–378,
379–381
Cité des Dames (de Pisan), 127
citizenship, Athens and, 7–8, 12
class, witch-hunts and social, 203–204
Cleisthenes, 9, 10
cold war, controversy over Stalin as responsible
for, 368–384
Colonna, Vittoria, 127

Committee of Public Safety, in France, 246–247
communism, 460–461
Conant, James B., 377, 378, 382
confessors, nuns and, 170–171
Conrad von Hötzendorf, Franz, 312, 313, 315, 318–319
Constantine, 63
convents, as expanding opportunities for women, 158–172
Council of Clermont, 102
Council of 500, of Athens, 14, 15
Council of Trent, 159, 169, 171, 172
courtly love, medieval, 130–131
Croatia, 388, 389, 392, 393, 398, 402
Crusades, as motivated by religious factors, 102–117
crusading indulgence, 104–105, 107
Czechoslovakia, 359

Darity, William Jr., on the West African slave trade as a precondition for the rise of British capitalism, 178–186
Davis, Lance E., on economic factors as primarily responsible for nineteenth-century British imperialism, 280–288
De Casibus Virorum Illustrium (Boccaccio), 125
De Claris Mulieribus (Boccaccio), 125–126
de Feltre, Vittorino, 123, 124–125
de la Mirandola, Pico, 123
de Lancre, Pierre, 207–208
de Pisan, Christine, 127
democracy: decline of Western civilization and the spread of liberal, 458–467; slavery as essential for, 4–19
Demos, John, 211
Descartes, René, 221
Devotio Moderna movement, 171
Die Kultur der Renaissance (Burckhardt), 125
Diner, Hasia R., on whether British policy decisions caused the mass emigration and land reforms that followed the Irish potato famine, 267–274
Disraeli, Benjamin, 280–281
Drescher, Seymour, 193
Dworkin, Andrea, 200
Dybenko, Pavel, 326

ECOFIN (European Council of Economics and Finance Ministers), 410–411
EMU. See European Monetary Union
Engerman, Stanley, 180–181
Essay on the Character, Manners, and Genius of Women in Different Ages (Thomas and Russell), 126
European Central Bank (ECB), European Monetary Union as potentially increasing transatlantic conflict and, 408, 409–411, 412, 413–414
European Commission, 412–413, 414

European Council of Economic and Finance Ministers (ECOFIN), 410–411
European Monetary Union (EMU), as potentially increasing transatlantic conflict, 408–426
euthyna, 15

Falkenhayn, Erich von, 302, 306
Fatamids, 110
Fay, Charles Ryle, 178–179
Feldstein, Martin, on the European Monetary Union as increasing the potential for transatlantic conflict, 408–417
Feminine Mystique, The (Friedan), 442
feminism, as allying itself with individualism, 430–445
Fidele, Cassandra, 123
Finance, Didier, 201
Finley, M. I., 10–11, 67
Finucane, Ronald C., on the Crusades as motivated primarily by religious factors, 110–117
First Epistle to Timothy, 51–52
Fischer, Frite, 303, 304
Fox-Genovese, Elizabeth, on whether contemporary feminism should ally itself with individualism, 438–445
France, 127, 317, 410, 413–414; controversy over the French Revolution and, 236–253
Franks, 68, 76
Franz Josef, emporer of Austria-Hungary, 312, 313
freedom, controversy over slavery as essential for, 4–19
French Revolution, as being worth its human cost, 236–253
Friedan, Betty, 431, 442
Fukuyama, Francis, on whether Western civilization is in a state of decline, 458–467

Gaddis, John Lewis, on Stalin as responsible for the cold war, 368–374
Gandhi, M. K., 280
Gee, Joshua, 178–179, 183–184
Germany, 292–293, 409–410, 411–412, 413–414; as responsible for World War I, 302–319; World War II as the result of Hitler's master plan and, 344–361
Glanvill, Joseph, 199
Gonzaga, Cecelia, 123
Gonzaga, Gian Francesco, II, 124–125
Gonzaga, Paola, 124–125
Gospel of Mary, 44, 48–49
Great Britain, influence of, on emigration and reform in Ireland, 258–274; economic factors as responsible for imperialism and, 280–298; slave trade as a precondition for the growth of capitalism in, 178–194

Greece: Alexander the Great and, 24–25, 26–27; slavery as essential for freedom, 4–19

Grey, Edward, 315, 316, 319

Gryson, Roger, 44–45

Guiscard, Roger, 115

Haines, Keith, 117

Hammond, N. G. L., on whether Alexander the Great merits his exalted historical reputation, 24–29

Hegel, G. W. F., 459

Hemerken van Kempen, Thomas, 171

Hillgruber, Andreas, on World War II as the result of Hitler's master plan, 344–352

Hitler, Adolph, World War II as the result of the master plan of, 344–361

Hobson, John A., 285

homosexuality, existence of same-sex unions in the early Middle Ages and, 82–96

Hufton, Olwen, on convents as expanding opportunities for European women, 158–164

Huns, 76, 77

Huntingdon, Samuel P., on whether Western civilization is in a state of decline, 450–457

Huttenback, Robert A., on economic factors as primarily responsible for nineteenth-century British imperialism, 280–288

Ibn Kammūna, 117

IMF (International Monetary Fund), 424–425

Imitatio Christi (Hemerken van Kempen), 171

imperialism, economic factors as responsible for British, 280–298

indulgences, 104–108

Industrial Revolution, slave trade as a precondition for British capitalism and, 178–194

Inferno monacale (Tarabotti), 163, 164, 172

International Monetary Fund (IMF), 424–425

Ireland, influence of Great Britain on emigration and reform in, 258–274

Isabella, queen of Spain, 127

Islam, Crusades as motivated by religious factions and, 110–117

Italy, 292–293, 318; equality during the Renaissance and, 122–127, 128, 132–133

Jews, attitude of Martin Luther toward, 151

Joanna, 46

Jospin, Lionel, 410

Justinian, 83

Kagan, Donald, on slavery as essential to the development of Athenian democracy, 12–19

Keegan, John, 37–38

Kelly-Gadol, Joan, on women and men benefiting equally from the Renaissance, 128–133

Keltie, John Scott, 289

Kershaw, Ian, on World War II as the result of Hitler's master plan, 353–361

Khrushchev, Nikita, 369

Kinealy, Christine, on whether British policy decisions caused the mass emigration and land reforms that followed the Irish potato famine, 258–266

Kollontai, Alexandra, 324, 326–327, 328–329, 335–337, 433

Kosovo, 397–398

Kropotkin, Peter, on whether the French Revolution was worth its human costs, 236–242

Larner, Christina, 202

Lenin, Vladmir, 285, 327, 337

Levack, Brian, 200–201

Lewis, W. Arthur, 179

liberal democracy, decline of Western civilization and the spread of, 458–467

Livre des trois Vertus, Le (de Pisan), 127

love, medieval, 130–131

Luther, Martin, 100; controversy over whether the reforms of, improved lives of Christians, 138–153

Maastricht Treaty, 408, 409

MacKenzie, John M., on economic factors as primarily responsible for nineteenth-century British imperialism, 289–298

Majstorovic, Steven, on ethnic leaders as responsible for the disintegration of Yugoslavia, 395–403

"Make Room for Winged Eros" (Kollontai), 336

Malleus Maleficarum, 207, 213

Marcomannic War, 71–72

Marcus Aurelius, 72

Marković, Mirjana, 389–390

marriage, existence of same-sex unions in early Middle Ages and gay, 82–96

Marius, Richard, on whether Martin Luther's reforms improved the lives of European Christians, 146–153

Marx, Karl, 280, 281, 285, 459

Mary Magdalene, 42, 44, 47–49

Mask of Command, The (Keegan), 37–38

Mason, Tim, 355

matronage, 165–168

Matthew, Theobald, 267–268

Mayer, Hans Eberhard, on the Crusades as motivated primarily by religious factors, 102–109

Mein Kampf (Hitler), 344, 346, 353

Melanchthon, Philipp, 146–147, 148–149

Melania, 64

Michael II, 85–86

military capability, decline of Western civilization and, 455–457

Milosević, Slobodan, 388–394

Ministry of Women in the Early Church, The (Gryson), 44–45

Mitterrand, François, 410

Mokyr, Joel, 179

Molotov, V. M., 369, 381–382

Moltke, Helmuth von, 302, 306, 308–309, 316

Molza, Tarquinia, 123

Mommsen, Hans, 354–355

Monnet, Jean, 408–409

Morata, Olympia, 123–124, 125

nationalism, imperialism and, 292–293

natural law, Martin Luther on, 143–144

Navailh, Françoise, on the Bolshevik Revolution as improving the lives of Soviet women, 333–340

Nogarola, Ginevra, 123

Nogarola, Isotta, 123

O'Brien, Patrick, 181–182

Old Regime and the Revolution, The (de Tocqueville), 243

Oliver, James H., 6

On the Veiling of Virgins (Tertullian), 53

Ostrogoths, 68, 73, 76, 77

Ottoman Turks, 397

Paradiso monacle (Tarabotti), 163, 164, 172

Partition of Africa, The (Keltie), 289

Pasić, Nikolai, 311–312, 314

Patterson, Orlando, on slavery as essential to the development of Athenian democracy, 4–11

Peisistratids, 6, 7

Pericles, 11, 12, 13, 16, 17, 18–19

Petronius Probus, 64

pilgrimage, 104, 107

Plato, 16, 17, 18

Pohlenz, Max, 8, 9

Poland, 352, 357

popular courts, of Athens, 13, 15, 17

population, decline of Western civilization and, 452–453

Postlethwayt, Malachy, 178–179, 184–185, 187–188

Purgatorio delle mal maritate (Tarabotti), 172

Quadans, 75

Quebec Agreement, 378

Raaflaub, Kurt, 8, 9

Ramus, Pierre, 221

raw materials, economic factors as responsible for British imperialism and, 291–292, 297

Rawley, James A., on the West African slave trade as a precondition for the rise of British capitalism, 187–194

Reardon, Bernard, M. G., on whether Martin Luther's reforms improved the lives of European Christians, 138–145

Reformation, controversy over whether Martin Luther's reforms improved the lives of Christians, 138–153

Renaissance, controversy over women and men benefiting equally from, 122–133

Reynolds, Philip Lyndon, on the existence of same-sex unions in the early Middle Ages, 89–96

Rice, E. E., on whether Alexander the Great merits his exalted historical reputation, 30–38

Roman Empire, controversy over the collapse of, 62–78

Roosevelt, Franklin D., 368–369, 375–376, 377, 378–381

Rublack, Hans-Christoph, 147–148

Russia, 318, 319, 357; Bolshevik Revolution as improving the lives of women in, 324–340

same-sex unions, existence of, in early Middle Ages, 82–96

Samoilova, K. I., 328

Sanchez, François, 221–222

Schama, Simon, on whether the French Revolution was worth its human costs, 243–253

Schulte van Kessel, Elisja, on convents as expanding opportunities for European women, 165–172

Scientific Revolution, as revolutionary, 220–232

"Second Book" (Hitler), 344, 345, 353

Seljuk Turks, 110–111, 113

Semplicità ingannata (Tarabotti), 163

Serbia, 311–312, 314, 315–316; ethnic leaders as responsible for the disintegration of Yugoslavia and, 388–403

Serbian Orthodox Church, 393, 396–397

sexuality, 129; of women, and Christianity, 43–44, 52–57; women's movement and, 431–432

Shapin, Steven, on the Scientific Revolution as revolutionary, 226–232

Sherwin, Martin J., on Stalin as responsible for the cold war, 375–384 shipping industry, importance of the slave trade to, 188

slavery: as essential for freedom, 4–19; trade in, as a precondition for British capitalism, 178–194; wealth in the Roman Empire and, 64–66

Slovenia, 388, 389

"small ratios" argument, on slave trade, 180–181

Solon, 6, 8

Solow, Barbara, 181

spiritual directors, nuns and, 170–171

St. Aubin of Angers, 114

St. Augustine, 57

St. Bacchus, 82

St. Jerome, 54–57, 77

St. Paul, 47

St. Paula, 54

St. Peter, 47–48

St. Serge, 82

St. Teresa of Avila, 161–162

St. Theodore of Sykeon, 83

St. Thomas Aquinas, 58, 105

Stalin, Joseph, as responsible for the cold war, 368–384

Stasova, Elena, 325

Stavrakis, Bette, 330

Stimson, Henry L., 375, 377–378, 381, 382–383

Stites, Richard, on the Bolshevik Revolution as improving the lives of Soviet women, 324–332

structuralist approach, to history, on World War II as the result of Hitler's master plan, 353–361

Tarabotti, Arcangela, 163–164, 172

taxes: economic factors as responsible for British imperialism and, 287; European Monetary Union and, 412–413

temperament, witch-hunts and, 204–206

Tertullian, 52–54

Thébaud, Françoise, on whether contemporary feminism should ally itself with individualism, 430–437

Theodosius II, 62

Tocqueville, Alexis de, 243, 244, 249

Torjesen, Karen Jo, on Christianity as liberating women, 42–50

Trade and Navigation of Great Britain Considered (Gee), 183–184

Treasury of Merits, 105, 106

Truman, Harry S., 380, 381, 382–383

Trudjman, Franjo, 389, 399

United States, European Monetary Union as potentially increasing transatlantic conflict and, 416–417, 422–426

Urban II, Pope, 102, 114

Vandals, 73, 76, 77

Verronese, Guarino, 123

Visigoths, 68, 73, 76

wealth, in the Roman Empire, 63–64

weapons of mass destruction, proliferation of, and the decline of Western civilization, 456

Weidenfeld, Werner, on the European Monetary Union as increasing the potential for transatlantic conflict, 418–426

Whitehead, David, 8

Wilhelm II, kaiser of Germany, 302, 304, 306, 309, 310, 313–314, 316

Williams, Derek, on the collapse of the Roman Empire as being due to its own weight, 70–78

Williams, Eric, 179, 180, 182, 183, 192–193

Williams, Gomer, 184–190

Williamson, Samuel R., on German militarism and diplomacy as responsible for World War I, 311–319

Williams, Wilson, 182

witches: misogyny in hunts of, in premodern Europe, 198–215; Martin Luther and, 150

women: as benefiting equally from the Renaissance, 122–133; Christianity as liberating, 42–58; convents as expanding opportunities for, 158–172; feminism allying itself with individualism and, 430–445; misogyny in witch-hunts in premodern Europe and, 198–215; Russian Revolution as improving the lives of, 324–340

Women's Department of the Central Committee Secretariat, 327–332, 338

World War I, Germany as responsible for, 302–319

World War II, as the result of Hitler's master plan, 344–361

Yugoslavia, ethnic leaders as responsible for the disintegration of, 388–403

Zhenotdel, 327–332, 338

Zimmermann, Warren, on ethnic leaders as responsible for disintegration of Yugoslavia, 388–394

Zwingli, Ulrich, 148–149